Revenue Law—
principles and practice

Revenue Law—principles and practice

Second edition

Chris Whitehouse
BA, BCL, Barrister

Elizabeth Stuart-Buttle
LLB, Solicitor

London
Butterworths
1984

England	Butterworth & Co (Publishers) Ltd, 88 Kingsway, London WC2B 6AB
Australia	Butterworths Pty Ltd, Sydney, Melbourne, Brisbane, Adelaide, Perth, Canberra and Hobart
Canada	Butterworth & Co (Canada) Ltd, Toronto and Vancouver
New Zealand	Butterworths of New Zealand Ltd, Wellington and Auckland
Singapore	Butterworth & Co (Asia) Pte Ltd, Singapore
South Africa	Butterworth Publishers (Pty) Ltd, Durban and Pretoria
USA	Butterworth Legal Publishers, St Paul, Minnesota, Seattle, Washington, Boston, Massachusetts, Austin, Texas and D and S Publishers, Clearwater, Florida

© Butterworth & Co (Publishers) Ltd 1984

ISBN 0 406 00529 X

Typeset by Cotswold Typesetting Ltd, Gloucester
Printed by Billings Bookplan, Worcester

Preface

In the twelve months since the first edition of this book was published major changes have occurred in revenue law and practice. The Finance Act 1984 is inordinately long and complex and in the sphere of business taxation has effected important changes. A major result of those changes has been to improve the position of the incorporated business as against the sole trader or partnership. Indeed, it has been argued with some conviction, that the Chancellor forgot that business activity is very often unincorporated.

So far as case law is concerned the year has seen the House of Lords' decision in *Furniss v Dawson* [1984] STC 153. Although the precise ambit of the speeches remains to be worked out there is little doubt that the decision represents a most significant development in judicial attitudes to taxation matters.

We have incorporated comments on these developments in this new edition and, as stated in the preface to the first edition, 'we have tried to explain the principles and practical application of the tax system in simple language and have followed our belief that revenue law can be made more comprehensible and human by the use of numerous examples. No advantage is gained from a mere recitation or paraphrase of statutory material. However, the course that we have adopted, necessarily, in places, involves the expression of opinions on provisions whose obscurity may yet try the intellects of the House of Lords'.

Once again we must thank Butterworths and especially the taxbooks department, for their kindness and patience. Despite assistance from colleagues and friends errors and omissions will inevitably remain and for those the responsibility is ours. The law is as stated as at 31 July 1984.

C.J.W.
E.S-B.
College of Law
Chancery Lane

Acknowledgment
The cartoons in this book are reproduced by kind permission of *Punch* and *The Daily Telegraph*. The cartoon on the cover is adapted from an original which appeared in *The Sunday Times*.

Contents

Table of statutes

Capital Transfer Tax Act 1984—destination table

The Capital Transfer Tax Act 1984 comes into effect on 1 January 1985. All statutory references to CTT in the text are to the old Acts. The destination table below gives only those derivations which are relevant to this text. The left hand column lists the statutory references to CTT which are cited in the text, while the corresponding references from CTTA 1984 are given in the right hand column.

Finance Act 1975	CTTA 1984
s 19 (1)	s 1
20	ss 2 (1), 3 (1)–(3), 10 (1)–(3), 55 (2), 66 (5), 67 (3), 68 (4)
(2)	s 3 (1)
(3)	s 3 (2)
(4)	ss 10 (1)–(3), 55 (2)
(5)	ss 2 (1), 66 (5), 67 (3), 68 (4)
(7)	ss 3 (3), 10 (3)
22	s 54 (1)–(4). Sch 6 para 2
(4)	Sch 6 para 2
(9)	s 54 (4)
23 (1)	s 5 (1)
(3)	s 55 (1)
24 (2)	s 6 (1)
(3)	s 48 (1)
25	ss 199, 200, 201 (1), (2), (5), (6), 205
(3)	s 201 (1), (2)
(8)	s 203 (1)
26	ss 199 (3), 200 (2), 202 (4), 206, 209 (1)
27	s 204
28 (1A)	s 211 (3)
(2)	s 213
28 (6)	s 214 (1)
37 (3)	s 7 (3), Sch 1
38 (1)	s 160
39	ss 94 (1), 98 (1), 202 (1)–(3)
(1)	s 94 (1)
(5)	s 98 (1)
40	s 262
42	s 263
43 (2)	s 266 (1)
44	s 268
45	s 267
46	s 11
47 (1A)	s 144
(4)	s 93
51 (1)	ss 5 (4), 47, 164, 174 (2), 178 (1), 190 (1), 272
(4)	s 270
Sch 4 para 5	s 219
13 (4)	s 227 (4)
(6)	ss 227 (3), (5), (6), 228 (1), (3)
17 (1)	s 230 (1)
20 (1)	s 237 (1)
23 (2)	s 240 (2)
(3)	s 240 (3)
25 (2)	s 239 (2)
30	s 247

Table of cases

References and abbreviations

All statutory references are given in the text.
The standard abbreviations used are as follows:

ACT	Advance corporation tax
CGT	Capital gains tax
CGTA 1979	Capital Gains Tax Act 1979
CTT	Capital transfer tax
DLT	Development land tax
DLTA 1976	Development Land Tax Act 1976
ESC	Extra statutory concession
FA (year)	Finance Act (year)
FII	Franked investment income
FYA	First year allowance
IA	Initial allowance
IRC	Inland Revenue Commissioners
LPA 1925	Law of Property Act 1925
LS Gaz	Law Society Gazette
MIRAS	Mortgage Interest Relief at Source
MCT	Mainstream corporation tax
PAYE	Pay As You Earn
PR	Personal representative
PYB	Preceding year basis
SA 1891	Stamp Act 1891
SAYE	Save As You Earn
SI	Statutory Instrument
SP	Statement of Practice
TA 1970	Income and Corporation Taxes 1970
TMA 1970	Taxes Management Act 1970
VAT	Value added tax
WDA	Writing down allowance

Any other abbreviations in the text are defined there.

PART A   PRINCIPLES

Section 1   Introduction

Chapters

1 UK taxation—structure and philosophy

I   The UK tax picture
II Features of the system
III Conclusions

> '*Singleton J*—Your appeal must be dismissed. I will pass you back your documents. If I might add a word to you, it is that I hope you will not trouble your head further with tax matters, because you seem to have spent a lot of time in going through these various Acts, and if you go on spending your time on Finance Acts, and the like, it will drive you silly.
> *Mrs Briggenshaw*—I will appeal to the higher court.
> *Singleton J*—I cannot stop you, if I would. The advice which I gave you was for your own good, I thought. That is all.' (*Briggenshaw v Crabb* (1948) 30 TC 331).

I THE UK TAX PICTURE

1 Taxes in general

Taxes imposed in the UK may be classified in various ways. A tripartite division might be adopted into taxes on income, on capital and on expenditure. Alternatively, and arguably more satisfactorily, the classification might be into direct and indirect taxes. This book is concerned only with the following direct taxes:

    income tax (Chapters 3–13)
    capital gains tax (CGT) (Chapters 14–20)
    capital transfer tax (CTT) (Chapters 21–27)
    corporation tax (Chapter 28)
    development land tax (DLT) (Chapter 30)
    stamp duty and capital duty (Chapter 31)

It, therefore, omits indirect taxes such as VAT, car tax and customs and excise duties, as well as such direct taxes as petroleum revenue tax and the general rate. In principle, the distinction between direct and indirect taxes is that a direct tax is borne by the taxpayer and is not passed on to any other person, whereas an indirect tax is passed on by the payer so that the burden of the tax is ultimately borne by another, eg VAT which although paid by the businessman, is passed on to the customer.

2 What is a tax?

The basic features of a tax may be simply stated. First, it is a compulsory levy. Secondly, it should be imposed by government or, in the case of rates, by a local authority. Finally, the money raised should be used either for public purposes or, if the purpose of the tax is not to raise money, it should encourage social justice within the community (CGT, for instance, was specifically intended to have that effect). So to describe the main features of a tax is not, however, to define the concept. Taxes shade off into criminal fines and into levies imposed for other purposes; water rates, for instance, are probably not taxes since they are paid to the water authority and are not used for general public purposes. So far as the distinction between fines and taxes is concerned the line is often blurred. H L A Hart in the *Concept of Law* (Oxford, 1975) commented that:

> 'Taxes may be imposed not for revenue purposes but to discourage the activities taxed, though the law gives no express indications that these are to be abandoned as it does when it "makes them criminal". Conversely the fines payable for some criminal offence may, because of the depreciation of money, become so small that they are cheerfully paid. They are then perhaps felt to be "mere taxes", and "offences" are frequent, precisely because in these circumstances the sense is lost that the rule is, like the bulk of the criminal law, meant to be taken seriously as a standard of behaviour'.

3 The purpose of taxation

The primary object of taxation is, and always has been, to raise money for government expenditure. The twentieth century has witnessed increasing expenditure on social welfare whilst the use of taxation both as an economic regulator and for the promotion of the public good (or to discourage certain forms of conduct) may also be discerned in the legislation of this century. Thus, alterations to the rate of VAT can affect the level of economic life in the community as much as adjustments to the money supply and credit regulation. The various tax incentives afforded for gifts to charities may be seen as the promotion of public good and altruism; whilst the duties levied on tobacco and alcohol may be seen as bordering on moral control.

Finally, there is the vexed question of who should pay the bill? Apportioning the burden of taxation fairly amongst the community can turn into the more radical contention that tax should operate as a method for effecting a redistribution of wealth or even the confiscation of wealth above a certain level. One striking feature of the statistics of direct taxation is that the vast proportion of the total yield is from income tax with CTT producing about 1% p a; CGT 1.43% p a; and DLT 0.09% p a. Further, within income tax, the bulk of the money is raised by the taxation of employees and office holders (some 76% of the income tax total and 60% of the total revenue raised by direct taxation).

Traditionally, the Conservative party has favoured indirect taxation and the provision of incentives to business and to the higher rate taxpayer. The Labour party has inclined towards direct taxation and to increased social welfare. There is little statistical evidence to suggest that taxation is or has been used as an engine to achieve a dramatic shift in the ownership of wealth.

II FEATURES OF THE SYSTEM

1 Legislation

Fiscal legislation is complex and detailed. In part this is inevitable since, above all, tax legislation should be certain: persons should know whether they are or are not subject to tax or duty on a particular transaction or sum of money. It has always been held to be a cardinal principle that in a taxation matter the burden lies upon the Crown to show that tax is chargeable in the particular case. In a famous passage, Rowlatt J in *Cape Brandy Syndicate v IRC* (1921) expressed this rule as follows:

> '. . . It is urged . . . that in a taxing Act clear words are necessary in order to tax the subject. Too wide and fanciful a construction is often sought to be given to that

maxim, which does not mean that words are to be unduly restricted against the Crown, or that there is to be any discrimination against the Crown in those Acts. It simply means that in a taxing Act one has to look merely at what is clearly said. There is no room for any intendment. There is no equity about a tax. There is no presumption as to a tax. Nothing is to be read in, nothing is to be implied. One can only look fairly at the language used . . .'

It follows that where the meaning of the statute is clearly expressed, the court will not consider any contrary intention or belief of Parliament or, indeed, any contrary indication by the Revenue. Recent illustrations of provisions being used against the expressed wishes of their authors include *Page v Lowther* (1983) in which an anti-avoidance section (TA 1970 s 488) appears to have been used as a charging provision (see Chapter 8) and *Leedale v Lewis* (1982) where a provision that was intended to give relief was held not to do so (see Chapter 20).

Much of the complexity of recent legislation has been prompted by the growth of the tax avoidance industry. Whilst tax evasion is unlawful, the avoidance of tax is both lawful, and, on a relatively minor scale, widely practised. The growth of larger scale schemes, often devoid of all commercial reality, has inevitably prompted legislation. Hence, the Finance Bill of 1960 was the most technical in the history of income tax with its wide ranging provisions aimed at bond washing and dividend stripping (see Chapter 32). Avoidance schemes have also affected judicial interpretation of the tax statutes with certain judges apparently being prepared to look beyond the words to the underlying purpose and beyond the form of the transaction to its substance. Nowhere is this approach more obvious than in the House of Lords' judgments in *Furniss v Dawson* (1984). Apart from illustrating that in certain circumstances it is the substance of the transaction which determines whether or not tax is chargeable, the case also shows an acceptance by the House of Lords that the courts can and should bolster up taxing statutes with judge-made law. Lord Scarman stated that:

'I am aware, and the legal profession (and others) must understand, that the law in this area is in an early stage of development. Speeches in your Lordships' House and judgments in the appellate courts are concerned more to chart a way forward between principles accepted and not to be rejected, than to attempt anything so ambitious as to determine finally the limit beyond which the safe channel of acceptable tax avoidance shelves into the dangerous shallows of unacceptable tax evasion. The law will develop from case to case. Lord Wilberforce in *Ramsay's* case referred to "the emerging principle" of the law. What has been established is that the determination of what does, and what does not constitute unacceptable tax evasion is a subject suited to development by judicial process. Difficult though the task may be for judges, it is one which is beyond the power of the blunt instrument of legislation.'

His approach marks a radical departure from established tradition and contrasts strikingly with the views of Rowlatt J quoted above. Quite apart from doubts about its constitutional legality, it should be noticed that the views of the Law Lords on the approach to be adopted to avoidance schemes are at odds with those expressed by puisne judges and by members of the Court of Appeal (compare for instance the judgments of Vinelott J and the Court of Appeal in *Furniss v Dawson*). The decision leaves the efficacy of many tax-saving devices open to doubt (Lord Scarman appears to distinguish between acceptable and unacceptable tax avoidance) and the law in a state of uncertainty. One consequence of the emergence of judge-made anti-avoidance rules is that legislation like FA 1975 s 44 (the CTT associated operations provisions) may no longer be necessary.

2 **Practice**

Given the volume of legislation, it is not surprising that some provisions may impose hardship and cause unforeseen results in individual cases. As a result the Revenue operate a system of extra-statutory concessions (ESC) and publish Statements of Practice (SP). The current ESC are set out in the booklet IRI (1980) and comprise in all some 122 concessions, the effect of which is that tax is not charged despite the case falling within the provisions of a taxing statute. Take for instance the ESC that permits miners to enjoy free coal or, alternatively, an allowance in lieu (ESC A6). The coal or cash allowance would undoubtedly be charged as emoluments under the rules of Schedule E were it not for the concession. The fairness of concessions is perhaps open to question as is their constitutional legality. In a pungent judgment Walton J expressed the objection to ESC as follows:

> 'I, in company with many other judges before me, am totally unable to understand upon what basis the Inland Revenue Commissioners are entitled to make extra-statutory concessions. To take a very simple example (since example is clearly called for), upon what basis have the commissioners taken it upon themselves to provide that income tax is not to be charged upon a miner's free coal and allowances in lieu thereof? That this should be the law is doubtless quite correct: I am not arguing the merits, or even suggesting that some other result, as a matter of equity, should be reached. But this, surely, ought to be a matter for Parliament, and not the commissioners. If this kind of concession can be made, where does it stop: and why are some groups favoured against others? . . .
> . . . This is not a simple matter of tax law. What is happening is that, in effect, despite the words of Maitland, commenting on the Bill of Rights, "This is the last of the dispensing power", the Crown is now claiming just such a power . . .' (*Vestey (No 2) v IRC* (1979)).

SPs set out the view that the Revenue take of a particular provision and should be treated with caution since they may not accurately state the law. There is an argument against inviting the Revenue to express views upon the meaning to be given to particular provisions since in cases where they indicate that tax is chargeable, it places professional advisers in a difficult position. Do they advise their clients that the Revenue are wrong and that the House of Lords are bound to accept the taxpayer's arguments or do they advise prudence in the face of the risk of protracted and expensive litigation?

III CONCLUSIONS

Tax is often seen as an ephemeral area: as a part of law devoid of principle and subject to the whims of politicians. In part this view is true; the annual (sometimes biannual) Finance Act often effects considerable changes. The underlying principles do, however, remain and it is usually only the surface landscape that is altered. The bedrock of income tax, for instance, can be traced back to 1803, whilst although CTT is of more recent origin, it is based upon a relatively simple conceptual structure. In understanding tax law the principle must be to ignore the form in favour of the substance. Given that the whole edifice is man-made and is designed to achieve practical ends, it should also follow that it is fully comprehensible. There is nothing here of the divine and, in the last resort, one should follow the approach of Lord Reid in the House of Lords in *Fleming v Associated Newspapers Ltd* (1972):

> 'On reading it my first impression was that it is obscure to the point of unintelligibility and that impression has been confirmed by the able and prolonged

arguments which were submitted to us . . . I have suggested what may be a possible meaning, but if I am wrong about that I would not shrink from holding that the subsection is so obscure that no meaning can be given to it. I would rather do that than seek by twisting and contorting the words to give to the subsection an improbable meaning. Draftsmen as well as Homer can nod, and Parliament is so accustomed to obscure drafting in Finance Bills that no one may have noticed the defects in this subsection.'

2 Administrative machinery

I GENERAL STRUCTURE

The government departments responsible for administering UK taxes are the Inland Revenue and Customs and Excise. All the taxes that are dealt with in this book, namely, income tax, corporation tax, CGT, CTT, DLT and stamp duty, are under the 'care and control' of the Inland Revenue, which is headed by a small number of higher civil servants known as the Commissioners of Inland Revenue ('the Board'). The commissioners answer to the Treasury and, therefore, to the Chancellor of the Exchequer.

The country is divided into tax districts headed in each case by an inspector of taxes who, first assesses the taxpayer's tax liability; the tax that is due is then collected by a collector of taxes. Both the inspectors and collectors of taxes are full-time civil servants appointed by the Revenue.

Any appeal by a taxpayer against an assessment is first heard by the General or the Special Commissioners. Both bodies are appointed by the Lord Chancellor (TMA 1970 ss 2, 4). The General Commissioners are part-time unpaid laymen appointed locally for a district, like lay magistrates and are assisted by a clerk who is usually a solicitor (TMA 1970 s 3). The Special Commissioners, who are 'overseen' by a Presiding Special Commissioner chosen by the Lord Chancellor, must be barristers, advocates or solicitors of at least seven years' standing (TMA 1970 s 4). To some extent the taxpayer can appeal to whichever of the two bodies he prefers. However, changes introduced by FA 1984 are aimed at ensuring that complicated appeals involving technical questions of law should be heard by the Special Commissioners with the more routine appeals coming before the General Commissioners.

In practice, the different taxes are not all administered together. Income tax, corporation tax and CGT are administered from the Revenue's head office in the Strand (although delegated to districts) under TMA 1970. CTT is administered on a daily basis by the Capital Taxes Office in London, Edinburgh and Belfast (FA 1975) and DLT by the Development Land Tax Office in Middlesborough (DLTA 1976). Stamp duty, which requires little administration, is under the supervision of the Controller of Stamps (Stamp Duties Management Act 1891). This chapter considers the administration of income tax, corporation tax and CGT; the procedures for CTT and DLT which are similar, and for stamp duty, are dealt with in the appropriate chapters on those taxes.

II   RETURNS, INFORMATION AND ASSESSMENTS

1 **Returns**

Every person (including a company) liable to tax in a tax year should inform the Revenue of this fact by the end of the following tax year (TMA 1970 ss 7, 10, 23). Failure to do so can give rise to a fine.

In practice, the Revenue send out tax returns requiring the taxpayer to give details of income or capital gains for the tax year and inviting him to claim any personal allowances (TMA 1970 ss 8, 11, 12). In the case of a partnership, the precedent partner is responsible for returning details of the partnership's profits and gains (TMA 1970 s 9). If no return is made, the Revenue can impose sanctions such as withholding personal allowances and levying penalties (TMA 1970 ss 93, 98).

2 **Information**

The Revenue can obtain information about a person's income from sources other than the taxpayer, eg from an employer the names of employees and details of payments to them (TMA 1970 s 15); from traders (and certain others) details of payments made for services to persons other than their employees, eg commissions and 'backhanders' (TMA 1970 s 16); from banks names of customers to whom they have paid interest (at present it is paid gross) on a deposit account exceeding £15 in the tax year (TMA 1970 s 17); from persons paying interest gross (eg the Director of National Savings) the names of recipients of the interest and the amounts paid (TMA 1970 s 18); finally, from lessees and other occupiers of land details of rent and other payments made for the use of the land (TMA 1970 s 19).

Considerable powers exist in TMA 1970 s 20 (as extended by FA 1976 Sch 6) for the Revenue to demand and obtain information from taxpayers who have failed to make a return, or whose return is believed to be incorrect. Further, the inspector can require the taxpayer on penalty of a fine (TMA 1970 s 98) to produce specified documents which are in his possession or under his authority and which may be relevant to his tax liability. With the Board's authority and the consent of a commissioner this requirement can be imposed on the taxpayer's spouse, child, business associate or adviser.

Similarly, a 'tax accountant' (see TMA 1970 s 20A) who has been convicted of an offence or been subject to a penalty for making or assisting in making an incorrect tax return, can be required with the consent of a circuit judge or, in certain circumstances, the Board's authority, to produce any documents in his possession or under his authority regarding the tax affairs of any client past or present.

Apart from these provisions, an inspector may request a circuit judge for a warrant to enter private premises (if necessary by force) to search for and remove anything which he 'reasonably' believes to be evidence of a tax fraud (other than the privileged documents of a barrister or a solicitor; TMA 1970 s 20C). This power is extremely wide. No particular offence need be specified in the warrant other than 'tax fraud' (for a discussion of this power see *IRC v Rossminster Ltd* (1980)). Further, the occupier of the premises has no right to be informed of the precise grounds for which the warrant was issued. However, he is entitled to a list of the items removed and must be allowed reasonable access to them whilst they are in the possession of the Revenue.

One informal method available to the Revenue to compel the production of information in the absence of a return, or where a return is suspect, is to make a 'best of judgment' assessment on the basis of an estimate, often exaggerated, of the taxpayer's true liability. The taxpayer, if he appeals, can be compelled to produce all relevant documents on pain of losing that appeal.

3 Assessments

Assessments are usually made by inspectors, but sometimes by the Board (TMA 1970 s 29(1)). An assessment is the process from inspecting returns (should there be any) to determining the amount due from the taxpayer. However, where the taxpayer has not submitted a return or the inspector is not satisfied with the information produced, he may make an estimated ('best of judgment') assessment as a means of extracting correct or more complete information at an appeal (see above).

Where tax is deducted at source assessments are unnecessary if the Revenue collects the correct amount of tax. In fact, under the PAYE machinery of Schedule E, they receive the tax by automatic deduction from the employee's current year emoluments on the basis of the facts known to them in the previous year. Accordingly, only if the facts change (eg if the employee acquires another source of income) need an assessment be made and an appropriate adjustment made to the tax bill (TA 1970 s 205).

By contrast, direct assessments under Schedule D Cases I and II and for corporation tax are extremely important and are usually made on the basis that the Revenue and the taxpayer have already agreed the relevant accounts.

The assessment of the taxpayer's liability is conclusive unless he appeals against it (below) or makes an agreement with the Revenue pending appeal. However, the making of an assessment does not preclude the Revenue from revising their own calculation if they 'discover' some grounds for an additional assessment. This 'discovery' need not be of new facts; it can be simply a discovery that the wrong conclusion was drawn from the same facts (*Cenlon Finance Co Ltd v Ellwood* (1962)) or that they had made an arithmetical error (*Vickerman v PRs of Mason decd* (1984)).

The normal time limit within which to raise or revise an assessment is six years from the end of the tax year to which it relates (TMA 1970 s 34), although this is extended in cases of fraud, wilful default or neglect (post). Thus, in the tax year 1984–85 an assessment cannot normally be made for any year earlier than 1978–79.

III APPEALS

1 Structure of appeals

At the first level, an appeal is heard either by a panel of General Commissioners or by a single Special Commissioner unless the Presiding Special Commissioner directs otherwise (TMA 1970 s 45). From the decision of the commissioners, either the taxpayer or the inspector may appeal on a point of law to the High Court although certain appeals from decisions of the Special Commissioners may be referred direct to the Court of Appeal (TMA 1970 ss 56, 56A). For the taxpayer to appeal he must formally require the commissioners to state a case, ie to prepare a summary of their findings and the reasons for their decision. The difficult borderline between points of law and questions of fact and the role of the appellate courts was discussed by Lord Radcliffe in *Edwards v Bairstow & Harrison* [1956] AC 14 at 35,

> 'I think that the true position of the court in all these cases can be shortly stated. If a party to a hearing before commissioners expresses dissatisfaction with their

determination as being erroneous in point of law, it is for them to state a case and in the body of it to set out the facts that they have found as well as their determination. I do not think that inferences drawn from other facts are incapable of being themselves findings of fact, although there is value in the distinction between primary facts and inferences drawn from them. When the case comes before the court, it is its duty to examine the determination having regard to its knowledge of the relevant law. If the case contains anything *ex facie* which is bad law and which bears upon the determination, it is, obviously, erroneous in point of law. But, without any such misconception appearing *ex facie*, it may be that the facts found are such that no person acting judicially and properly instructed as to the relevant law could have come to the determination under appeal. In those circumstances, too, the court must intervene. It has no option but to assume that there has been some misconception of the law and that this has been responsible for the determination. So there, too, there has been error in point of law. I do not think that it much matters whether this state of affairs is described as one in which there is no evidence to support the determination or as one in which the evidence is inconsistent with and contradictory of the determination or as one in which the true and only reasonable conclusion contradicts the determination. Rightly understood each phrase propounds the same test.'

It follows that a decision of the commissioners will not be reversed simply because an appeal court would have come to a different conclusion on the particular facts. The Schedule E case of *Glantre Engineering Ltd v Goodhand* (1983) illustrates the importance of the commissioners' finding of fact. Once they had concluded that the payment in question was an emolument (a finding of fact), the taxpayer was left with the burden of showing that such a finding was inconsistent with the only reasonable conclusion to be drawn from the evidence.

Unless the appeal is referred directly to the Court of Appeal under s 56A (above) there is a right of appeal from the High Court to the Court of Appeal and, with leave, to the House of Lords. Alternatively, use may be made of the 'leapfrog' procedure under the Administration of Justice Act 1969 to appeal directly to the House of Lords.

2   Procedure before the commissioners

In general, the taxpayer can appeal to either of the General or Special Commissioners although the latter will not hear 'delay' cases: ie those which lack the information necessary to settle the appeal. In certain other cases, eg from an assessment by the Board, the taxpayer has no choice and the appeal must be to the Special Commissioners. Where the appeal involves difficult questions of law the taxpayer often chooses the Special Commissioners. In back duty cases, he may be better off with the General Commissioners whose business experience and local knowledge may help him.

The taxpayer must make his appeal within 30 days after his notice of assessment (TMA 1970 s 31) and in Schedule D cases, he must specify the grounds of appeal.

Where the taxpayer elects for the Special Commissioners, this election may be disregarded at any time before the determination of the appeal by agreement between the parties or, failing agreement, by a non-appealable direction of the General Commissioners given after hearing the parties (TMA 1970 s 31(5A)).

Once started, an appeal cannot be withdrawn except by the agreement in writing of the inspector (TMA 1970 s 54 and see *Beach v Willesden General Comrs* (1982)). However, an appeal which is started before the General Commissioners may, on agreement with the Special Commissioners, be transferred to them (TMA 1970 s 44(3A). The general principles of court procedures apply to the hearing at which the Crown is usually represented by the inspector and the taxpayer may appear in person or be represented by a barrister, solicitor or accountant.

The commissioners can call before them and examine on oath any person other than the taxpayer himself. However, there are no written pleadings, costs are not awarded, and legal aid is not available. Under FA 1984 the Lord Chancellor may make procedural rules including providing for appeals which have been heard in the absence of the taxpayer to be reheard in certain circumstances. It is envisaged that the rules will provide for attendance at hearings by members of the Council on Tribunals unless the taxpayer objects; and may also permit the publication of Special Commissioners' decisions.

The onus of proof is generally on the taxpayer to disprove an assessment, but, if the Crown alleges fraud, wilful default or neglect, it must prove it.

3 Postponement of tax pending appeal

Where a taxpayer disagrees with an assessment, he must inform the inspector within 30 days of his intention to appeal and within the same period of the amount of tax he considers excessive. If he fails to do so the whole amount becomes payable as if there were no appeal (TMA 1970 s 55). This provision prevents a taxpayer from postponing his payment of tax by instituting an appeal which he then abandons before the hearing. If the taxpayer and inspector are unable to agree on the amount of tax which is at issue on the appeal, the commissioners decide the matter. Only the amount of tax which it is agreed or decided to depend on the outcome of the appeal is postponed until the appeal is heard. The balance is payable within 30 days of the agreement or the commissioners' decision. On determination of the appeal any tax that was overpaid is repaid with interest (below).

On a further appeal to the High Court, the amount of tax as determined by the commissioners remains payable. If the court's decision results in an increased tax liability, this additional tax becomes due in accordance with a revised notice of assessment issued after the hearing.

4 Interest on overdue tax (TMA 1970 s 86)

Where tax is overdue, interest is charged (currently at 8% pa) from the due date. Where, however, tax has been postponed pending appeal, interest runs from the later of the date when tax is payable, ignoring the appeal, and the earlier of the date specified in the table in TMA 1970 s 86(4) which is generally six months after the date when the tax is normally due, and the date when the tax is due and payable as a result of the appeal.

The taxpayer should be further dissuaded from a frivolous appeal by FA 1982 s 69 which provides that where assessments after 30 July 1982 result in additional tax becoming due, interest shall be charged on that sum as if it were postponed tax contained in the original notice of assessment (ie as above).

5 Repayment supplement

The Revenue must repay overpaid tax (eg where the taxpayer's appeal succeeds) together with interest in certain (limited) circumstances and provided that the overpaid tax exceeds £25. Interest is only payable in respect of the period from the end of the tax year following the one for which the tax was paid to the end of the tax month (the 5th day of the month) when the repayment was ordered. Where the tax was itself paid more than 12 months after the relevant tax year, interest runs only from the end of the tax year in which it was paid (F (No 2) A 1975 s 47).

EXAMPLE 1

A taxpayer's appeal in respect of tax paid in 1984–85 is heard on 8 May 1986 and is successful. He will be entitled to interest on a repayment of tax for the period from 6 April 1986 to 5 June 1986.

6   Procedural changes for certain income tax appeals

The majority of income tax appeals are the result of 'best of judgment' assessments raised simply because of the taxpayer's delay in returning his income, particularly his business profits ('delay appeals'). In an attempt to reduce the large number of delay appeals and the consequently huge administrative costs, the Revenue (aided by FA 1982 s 69 above) introduced a procedural approach for income tax appeals (excluding Schedule E) against assessments made after August 1982 where the payment of tax on account under TMA 1970 s 55 is thought to be reasonable, the source of the income is continuing, and the tax charged is £10,000 or less. The appeals will not be listed for a hearing until two years' accounts are outstanding whereupon all the 'two year appeals' will be listed at the same time after the June following the second year instead of being individually listed after the June following the relevant tax year.

IV   COLLECTION OF TAX

Once an assessment becomes final the collectors of taxes have wide powers to collect the tax. If the taxpayer fails to pay they can levy distress (TMA 1970 ss 61, 62) or, if he is an employee, arrange for the tax to be deducted at source under PAYE. Alternatively, the tax charged can be recovered in the Magistrates Court, in the County Court or in the High Court depending on the sum involved (TMA 1970 ss 65–67).

The bankruptcy of the taxpayer is no bar to the Revenue pursuing the debt and in a bankruptcy they are preferential creditors.

V   BACK DUTY

A back duty case arises when the Revenue discover that a taxpayer has evaded tax, usually by not disclosing his true income, or by supplying inaccurate or incomplete information, or by claiming reliefs and allowances to which he is not entitled. They often discover this from 'tip-offs' that they receive about the taxpayer, or by a 'confession' from the taxpayer himself. On discovering a back duty case the Revenue can commence criminal proceedings, and/or make assessments for the lost tax plus interest and/or claim penalties. What the Revenue choose to do in any case depends largely on the degree of co-operation of the taxpayer. Criminal proceedings are rarely taken (the odds are roughly one in fifteen hundred); and the Revenue generally prefer to reach some settlement with the taxpayer. However, the Revenue's wide discretion in this area is aided by a rule of evidence (TMA 1970 s 105) which applies to all court proceedings whereby the Revenue can tell the taxpayer that they may accept a pecuniary settlement and that they are influenced by a full confession. Despite these inducements, statements made by the taxpayer are admissible in evidence, and any settlement creates a contractual debt for which the Revenue can sue (for a discussion of when arrangements with a taxpayer will estop the Revenue from claiming tax see *R v IRC, ex parte Preston* (1983)).

Small back duty cases are dealt with by local inspectors who have the power to agree settlements. In larger cases the approval of the head office is required before any settlement can be reached.

When arriving at a settlement, the factors that the Revenue consider include the amount of tax lost, interest payable, penalties available, the co-operation of the taxpayer and, most importantly, the need for uniformity in cases of a similar nature.

1 Criminal proceedings

Prosecutions can be brought against the taxpayer under the Perjury Act 1911; for forgery; for conspiracy to defraud; or under the Theft Act 1968 for obtaining a pecuniary advantage by deception or false accounting. Company officers can be made liable for such offences if committed by the company.

2 Assessments for lost tax plus interest

The six year time limit for assessments under TMA 1970 s 34 does not apply where tax has been lost through fraud, wilful default, or neglect by the taxpayer. These terms bear their common law meaning and whether tax has been lost as a result of any of them is decided objectively. Fraud or wilful default by an agent of the taxpayer, eg by his accountant, is imputed to the taxpayer (*Clixby v Pountney* (1968)).

The legislation distinguishes between fraud or wilful default on the one hand and, on the other, neglect. If fraud or wilful default is established, an assessment can be made without time limit, back to 1936–37 (TMA 1970 s 36) but for an assessment outside the six year limit the inspector must obtain the permission of the General or Special Commissioners. Where neglect is established, the Revenue can make retrospective assessments for more than six years (the

"*I didn't think you people could re-open a case after a five year period.*"

'normal years') but subject to certain limitations in TMA 1970 s 37:

Stage 1 If there has been an assessment for fraud, wilful default or neglect in one of the normal years, the Revenue may within one tax year of the determination of that assessment make a back duty assessment for any year which is not more than six years before that normal year ('the earlier years').
Stage 2 Where there has been a back duty assessment in an earlier year for fraud, wilful default or neglect, the Revenue may (on satisfying the General or Special Commissioners that there are grounds for suspecting neglect in a still earlier year) make an assessment for a further six years before the year of the existing back duty assessment, provided that they do so within one tax year of that in which the assessment is determined.

EXAMPLE 2

In October 1983, the Revenue make an assessment on A for 1979–80 ('normal year') proving loss of tax through fraud (or wilful default or neglect). As a result they can assess A for loss through neglect for any year from 1973–74 onwards ('earlier years') provided that they do so before 5 April 1985 *(Stage 1)*.

Assuming that that assessment is determined in January 1985 they may raise a further assessment for loss due to neglect in any of the years from 1967–68 onwards provided that they do so by 5 April 1986 *(Stage 2)*.

If a partnership is guilty of neglect, the rules operate slightly differently (TMA 1970 s 38). Basically, a partner who was assessed for a normal year because of fraud, wilful default or neglect in the partnership, can be assessed for an earlier year for neglect, whether his or another partner's. However, if he was not included in the normal year assessment (eg because he was no longer a partner), he cannot be assessed for neglect in an earlier year even though he was a partner then and the neglect was his. His share of the profits is excluded from assessment.

Notice that in the case of neglect the same time limits apply to assessments for past years for CGT and corporation tax, except that in the latter case the rules operate by reference to the company's accounting period.

For a back duty assessment to be made on a deceased taxpayer's PRs it must be made within three tax years of the year of death for fraud, wilful default or neglect by the deceased in any of the six years up to and including the year of his death (TMA 1970 s 40). Thus, if the deceased dies in the tax year 1982–83, the Revenue have until 5 April 1986 in which to assess his PRs for loss of tax because of his fraud, wilful default or neglect in the years from 1977–78 to 1982–83.

Interest in back duty cases is charged (currently at 8% pa) from the date when the tax should have been paid.

3 **Penalties**   (TMA 1970 ss 93–107)

An inspector can take penalty proceedings without the Board's leave for a simple failure by the taxpayer to make returns (TMA 1970 s 93 or s 98). More relevant, however, in back duty cases is TMA 1970 s 95 which provides, in the case of negligence, for a penalty of £50 plus the tax underpaid and, in the case of fraud, £50 plus twice the tax underpaid. The penalty is, of course, on top of the tax itself and interest. These proceedings (which are not criminal proceedings) require the Board's leave and the penalties are fixed by the commissioners, or, occasionally, in the High Court. In practice, penalties may be agreed between the parties.

In addition to claiming penalties against the offending taxpayer, the Revenue can impose a penalty of up to £500 on anyone (eg an accountant) who knowingly assists in preparing an incorrect return or account (TMA 1970 s 99).

The time limit for commencing penalty proceedings is generally six years from the date when the offence was committed, except that penalties levied for fraud or wilful default (but not neglect) can be taken at any time within three years of the final determination of the tax (TMA 1970 s 103(1) and (2)). The time period is also extended when an assessment is made within six years of the offence to allow for penalties to be levied within three years of the final determination of that assessment. The bankruptcy of the taxpayer does not preclude the Revenue from claiming maximum penalties (see *Re Hurren, ex parte the Trustee v IRC* (1982)).

EXAMPLE 3

(1) Tax was underpaid because of the taxpayer's fraud in 1971–72. If the assessment only becomes final in May 1985, the Revenue have until May 1988 to raise penalties, even though the offence was committed more than six years from the date of the assessment.

(2) An assessment is made in June 1985 for back duty caused by the taxpayer's neglect in 1971–72 and 1982–83. Although the Revenue can recover the tax lost in both those periods (TMA 1970 s 37), they can only raise penalties for the offence in 1982–83. The offence in 1971–72 is outside the six year time limit.

VI REFORM OF THE ENFORCEMENT POWERS ENJOYED BY REVENUE DEPARTMENTS: THE KEITH REPORT

A committee under the chairmanship of Lord Keith of Kinkel was set up in 1980 to carry out an extensive review of the enforcement powers enjoyed by the revenue departments which affect both the individual rights of the citizen and the ability of the Revenue to apply and enforce the law.

The committee published three substantial volumes in 1983 running collectively to 1056 pages (Cmnd 8822 and 9120) and dealing with all the direct taxes. The Report contains a mine of detailed information and recommendations. It will require a technical bill of some length to deal with all the proposals and the fullest public debate to ensure that the balance between individual freedom and fiscal enforcement has been correctly drawn.

Section 2 Income tax

Chapters

3 General principles

'... No one has ever been able to define income in terms sufficiently concrete to be of value for taxation purposes ... where it has to be ascertained whether a gain is to be classified as an income gain or a capital gain, the determination of that question must depend in large measure upon the particular facts of the particular case.' (Abbott J in *Oxford Motors Ltd v Minister of National Revenue* (1959) 18 DLR (2d) 712.)

I HISTORY

Income tax is sometimes referred to as the 'tax which beat Napoleon'. Such claims amount to a gross exaggeration although it is true that the tax was first introduced in 1799 by Pitt the Younger as a wartime measure. Pitt's tax was not wholly innovatory; there had always been a tradition of direct taxation even if that taxation had been applied spasmodically. The origins of income tax may be seen in the land tax and in the Triple Assessment of 1798.

Early yields were disappointing; estimates predicted a yield of £10m in the first year, but under £6m was actually raised. Although the tax was repealed when peace with France was concluded in 1802, it was reintroduced by Addington when hostilities recommenced in the following year. Addington included two basic changes which have survived more or less intact: first, a requirement that returns should be of income from particular sources and not just a lump sum; and secondly, provisions for deduction of tax at source.

The final cessation of hostilities in 1816 led to the repeal of the tax with the resulting financial deficit being made good by increased yields from customs and excise. Income tax was brought back, this time for good, by Peel in 1842. It was not revived because of its own inherent merits, but as a way to simplify and reduce the tariff; as a first step towards the repeal of the Corn Laws in 1846.

By the end of the century, the tax, although an accepted part of the fiscal landscape, raised less than either customs or excise. The twentieth century with the extraordinary demands of war and welfare transformed the picture. By the end of the 1914–18 war, the income tax yield was some £585m as compared with the pre-war figure of £34m and the complexity of the modern tax had been established with earned income relief, supertax, a range of personal allowances, and a primitive system of capital allowances. The process was accelerated by the Second World War with the yield rising from £371m in 1938 to £1,426m in 1945. PAYE was improved in 1943 and the tax avoidance industry maintained a steady growth.

Today, the flood of income tax legislation shows little sign of diminution; the statutory material was consolidated in 1952, again in 1970, and such is the output of Parliament that a further consolidation bill is in preparation and should be laid before Parliament in 1987 or 1988.

II   STATUTORY BASIS OF THE TAX

1   The statutes and case law

The authority for imposing taxation is Act of Parliament and in the case of income tax, the statutory basis is TA 1970 as amended by later Finance Acts. TMA 1970 deals with the administration of the tax. The system of capital allowances (see Chapter 7) was consolidated by the Capital Allowances Act 1968, but later changes have left that area in a state of some chaos. The meaning of the statute is primarily a question for a judiciary which ranges from commissioners to House of Lords. Many concepts are not defined by statute (eg what is a trade? what is an income receipt/expense?), many provisions are obscure, and it is the role of the judiciary to resolve such difficulties and of case law to fill the gaps. It may even be the job of the courts to create judge-made law to deal with sophisticated avoidance schemes (see *Furniss v Dawson* (1984)).

2   Years and rates

The tax needs annual renewal by Parliament. The annual Finance Act normally receives the Royal Assent in late July or early August. By virtue of the Provisional Collection of Taxes Act 1968, however, the budget resolutions (such as the rates of tax) are given limited statutory force until the passage of the Act.

The income tax year runs from 6 April to the following 5 April and is termed the 'year of assessment' or simply the 'tax year'. It is referred to by reference to both the calendar years that it straddles—hence, the year of assessment beginning on 6 April 1984 is referred to as the tax year 1984–85. The curious starting date for the year (6 April) is explicable, as is so much of income tax, on historical grounds. Originally, the fiscal year was linked to Lady Day (25 March), but with the adoption of the calendar reforms of Pope Gregory XIII in the eighteenth century, a jump of 11 days was necessary.

III   THE SCHEDULES

1   The source doctrine

Income tax is levied according to the source of the income and the six Schedules (see p 21) exhaustively list the various sources. Each Schedule has its own rules for determining the amount of income and the available deductions (if any). Schedule A, for instance, taxes income from land. The charge is on rents and other receipts which arise as a result of the ownership of land (or of an interest therein) but the landlord may deduct expenses such as repairs and rates on the property. In arriving at the income of a taxpayer it is, therefore, necessary to discover what sources of income he possesses and then, by applying the rules of the relevant Schedules, to calculate the income arising under each. It follows that tax is only charged so long as a taxpayer possesses the source of the income. Once a trade (taxed under Schedule D Case I) has ceased, for instance, a subsequent sale of trading stock will not be subject to income tax under Case I because the source of the income (the trade) has ended. (Notice that avoidance schemes based upon a cessation of business are largely frustrated by rules taxing post-cessation receipts: see p 75.)

2 **The mutually exclusive rule**

The Schedules are mutually exclusive with the result that the Revenue cannot assess income to tax under any Schedule other than the one to which that income is properly attributable (*Fry v Salisbury House Estate Ltd* (1930)). The same principle applies to the taxpayer who may not deduct expenses attributable to a different Schedule nor opt to have his income taxed under a different Schedule (*Mitchell and Edon v Ross* (1962)). So far as Schedule D is concerned there is some authority for the view that the Revenue can choose between the different Cases in the rare situations when an overlap between them exists (*Liverpool and London and Globe Insurance Co v Bennett* (1913)).

EXAMPLE 1

(1) Roger lets several properties to university students and works full time in the management of the properties. Tax must be charged under Schedule A (which applies to rent and other receipts from land), not under Schedule D Case I, because except for furnished holiday lettings there cannot be a trade of letting properties (see *Griffiths v Jackson* (1983) discussed in Chapter 8).

(2) A firm of solicitors acted as secretaries for a number of companies. The profits from the profession of solicitors are assessed under Schedule D Case II; remuneration from the office of company secretary is, however, charged under Schedule E (*IRC v Brander and Cruickshank* (1971) see Chapter 5).

3 **What is income?**

Income is not defined in the legislation. Furthermore, any definition is a matter for acute debate by both economists and philosophers. How, therefore, does the tax operate if the subject matter of the tax (income) is not defined? The answer is that it means all the sums calculated under the six Schedules. Hence, a sum of money falling under one of the Schedules is subject to tax (and is, therefore, 'income' for these purposes), whilst a sum which escapes the six Schedules is untaxed (and may, therefore, be termed 'capital'). This approach results in 'income' and 'capital' being given artificial meanings; certain capital sums (notably premiums under Schedule A and golden handshakes and restrictive covenant payments under Schedule E) are deemed to be income for the purposes of the tax. It is likewise odd to refer to certain sums excluded from charge (such as student grants and Christmas presents) as 'capital'.

EXAMPLE 2

Augustus gives his grandson John £100 every Christmas. Despite the regular nature of the payment it is not income in John's hands because it does not fall within any of the Schedules. Were he to covenant the sum each year, however, it would become income because it is an annual payment falling within Schedule D Case III. (Note: just because the sum is income it does not follow that Augustus is worse off. There may be tax advantages from payments by deed of covenant; see Chapter 10).

Although the lack of a definition of income does not generally cause problems, difficulties do arise when the Schedule prescribes that only income receipts are subject to tax or only income expenses can be deducted (as under Schedules A and D Cases I and II where the tax is levied on the profits that

The Schedules

Schedule	Source	Basis of assessment
A	Rents and other receipts from land in UK	Rents receivable less outgoings of the current year of assessment
B	Occupation of certain woodlands in UK	One-third of the gross annual value for the current year of assessment
C	Public revenue	Income of the current year of assessment
D Case I	Profits of a trade in UK	Usually, the income of the preceding accounting year (Cases I and II) or preceding tax year (Cases III, IV and V)
Case II	Profits of a profession or vocation in UK	
Case III	Interest, annuities and other annual payments	
Case IV	Securities out of the UK not charged under Sch C	
Case V	Possessions out of the UK not charged under Sch C (but excluding foreign employment)	
Case VI	Annual profits or gains not falling under Cases I–V and not charged by virtue of any other Schedule; and certain income directed to be so charged	Income of the current year of assessment or, at the Revenue's option, average income of any period not exceeding one year
E Cases I, II and III	Offices, employments and pensions (both 'home' and foreign). Also, chargeable benefits under the social security legislation	Income of the current year of assessment
F	Dividends and certain other distributions by companies	Income of the current year of assessment

remain after income deductions have been taken from income receipts). The meaning of 'income' has accordingly been debated all too frequently before the courts and the various tests that have been suggested for resolving the problem are considered in Chapter 6.

EXAMPLE 3

Sid and Sad are employees of Said Ltd. Sid is sacked and paid compensation of £10,000, whereas Sad retires and receives £10,000 in return for entering into a restrictive covenant not to compete with Said Ltd for the rest of his life.

(1) *The payment to Sid* is an income expense of the company and is, therefore, deductible from its profits (*Mitchell v B W Noble Ltd* (1927)). It is taxable in Sid's hands as income in accordance with the rules of TA 1970 s 187. Hence, it will escape any charge because the first £25,000 of any golden handshake payment is tax free.

(2) *The payment to Sad* is a capital payment by the company (*APC v Kerr* (1946)), but may be subject to income tax at the higher rates in Sad's hands (TA 1970 s 34).

A lack of symmetry in the treatment of the payment so far as payer and payee are concerned is apparent from *Example 3,* whilst it is not perhaps immediately obvious why the first payment is an income expense of Said Ltd, but the second is capital.

4 Computation—charges, allowances and rates

I   INTRODUCTION: STAGES OF THE INCOME TAX CALCULATION

Only income as defined by the six Schedules is subject to income tax. The tax is levied at graduated rates from the 30% basic rate to a top rate of 60%. It may be collected either by direct assessment, or by deduction at source. The following steps are involved in calculating the taxpayer's income and in working out his tax bill for the year:

Step 1   Calculate the individual's 'statutory income', ie the income which is taxable under the rules of the various Schedules and Cases.

Step 2   Calculate the taxpayer's charges on income, ie certain payments which the taxpayer is bound to make, such as certain interest payments.

Step 3   Deduct charges on income from statutory income to obtain 'total income' (TA 1970 s 528).

Step 4   Deduct personal reliefs from total income to obtain 'taxable income'.

Step 5   Calculate income tax at basic and higher rates on the taxable income.

Step 6   From the total tax calculated in *Step 5* deduct any income tax which has been deducted at source.

Step 7   Calculate basic rate tax on any charges on income from which the individual has deducted tax when making the payment.

The result of *Step 6* plus *Step 7* is the final amount of tax payable.

Since all these steps involve terms requiring explanation, this chapter will continue by considering in detail the various stages in the income tax calculation.

II   STATUTORY INCOME *(Step 1)*

1   General

Statutory income consists of the taxpayer's income from all sources calculated according to the rules of the particular Schedule or Case under which it arises and after deducting expenses appropriate to the particular Schedule or Case.

Since the income tax year runs from 6 April to 5 April following, the income tax assessment (the 'basis of assessment') should logically be on the statutory income of an individual for that period (ie on a current year basis). This is so for income arising under all the Schedules except for Schedule D, which operates according to a preceding year basis. Hence, the taxable profits of a trade assessable under Schedule D Case I are deemed to be the profits of the accounts which ended in the previous tax year (the preceding year basis).

EXAMPLE 1

Mack, a trader, (Schedule D Case I) makes up his accounts to 30 June 1983 showing receipts of £12,000. Certain deductions may be made (for instance, £2,000 paid by Mack in salaries to employees). As a result, Mack will include £10,000 of Schedule D Case I income in his statutory income for the year of assessment 1984–85.

2   Income received after deduction of tax

Most income is received and enters the statutory income calculation gross: ie without having suffered any tax. The tax on that income is collected by direct assessment. For certain types of income, however, tax is deducted at source. In such cases, the payer of the income is obliged to act as a tax collector by deducting from the payment an amount of tax (usually at basic rate) and handing it to the Revenue. If the recipient is not liable to income tax, he will obtain a repayment from the Revenue of the tax deducted. If, however, he is liable to higher rate tax, a further assessment will be necessary.

Accordingly, any sum received after deduction of tax, must be grossed up to discover the original sum from which the tax was deducted. The resulting (gross) figure must be entered in the recipient taxpayer's calculation of statutory income to discover his tax liability. The tax that has already been paid on this income is credited against his tax bill.

EXAMPLE 2

Austin (with other statutory income of £10,000) receives a dividend (Schedule F) of £700 from which basic rate (30%) tax has already been deducted and handed to the Revenue by the paying company. Austin must include the 'grossed-up' amount of the dividend in his statutory income calculation for the year to work out whether the tax deducted is correct.

To gross up multiply the dividend received by $\dfrac{100}{100-R}$ where R is the rate at which tax was deducted ie

$$700 \times \frac{100}{100-30} = 700 \times \frac{100}{70}$$

= £1,000 (gross dividend—therefore tax paid is £300)

Austin's statutory income is

Other sources	£10,000
Schedule F	£ 1,000
Statutory income	£11,000

When the tax due on this income is calculated, Austin can deduct the £300 tax deducted at source by the company. If his liability to tax is for less than £300, he can reclaim from the Revenue the amount for which he is not liable.

The main examples of income received after deduction of tax at source are:
(1) Dividends and other distributions from companies, assessable under Schedule F (received after deduction of basic rate tax).
(2) Trust income received by a beneficiary after deduction (normally) of basic rate tax.
(3) Emoluments assessable under Schedule E from which tax (at the appropriate rate) is deducted under the PAYE system.
(4) Annuities and other annual payments, assessed under Schedule D Case III, from which basic rate tax is deducted, eg maintenance payments.
(5) Building society interest is treated as received after deduction of basic rate tax and must be grossed up accordingly. The societies pay tax at a special composite rate (TA 1970 s 343), so that although the recipient is not liable to tax at basic rate, he cannot usually obtain a refund from the Revenue if he is not a basic rate taxpayer. This investment will, therefore, be unattractive for an investor who is not liable to basic rate tax. This composite rate is to be extended after 5 April 1985 to interest payments by banks and certain other institutions when the payments are to UK residents (FA 1984 s 27).

3 **Aggregation of spouses' income** (TA 1970 s 37)

Generally, the income of a married woman living with her husband is treated as his income for all tax purposes (see Chapter 35). It is the only case where the income of different persons is aggregated; minor children, for instance, are taxed independently of their parents. Accordingly, a married man must include his wife's income in his calculation of statutory income. An election for separate assessment (see TA 1970 s 38) does not affect the total tax bill, but merely apportions that bill between the couple so that the wife is responsible for her share of the total tax.

Spouses can elect for separate taxation of wife's earnings (FA 1971 s 23), but this only affects her earned income. Her unearned income continues to be aggregated with her husband's.

4 **Earned and investment income**

With the abolition as from 1984–85 of the surcharge of 15% on investment income above a certain limit, the distinction between earned and investment income is only relevant in a few instances, eg the spouse election.

Under TA 1970 s 530 'earned income' falls into two categories:
(a) All income chargeable under Schedule E which is derived from an office or employment (see Chapter 5).
(b) 'any income which is charged under Schedule A, Schedule B or Schedule D and is *immediately derived* by the individual from the carrying on or exercise by him of his trade, profession or vocation, either as an individual or, in the case of a partnership, as a partner personally acting therein.

The borderline between earned and unearned income is not always easy to draw. The phrase 'immediately derived' has been strictly construed by the courts (see, for instance, *Northend v White, Leonard and Corbin Greener* (1975) and *Bucks v Bowers* (1970)).

Generally, income under Schedules B and D Cases I and II is earned income, whereas that assessable under Schedule A (rent), Schedule D Case III (such as interest and trust income), Schedule D Case IV (foreign securities, such as dividends), Schedule F (dividends from UK companies), Schedule C (such as interest on government stock), and Schedule D Case VI will be investment income. Note, however, that rent from 'holiday lettings' is specifically treated as earned income (FA 1984 s 50 at p 136).

EXAMPLE 3

Winnie owns a honey shop and is chargeable for 1984–85 on £10,000 profit. He also receives rent of £300 from letting a garage. Mrs Winnie has a part-time job in a fur shop from which she earned £2,000 in 1984–85

Calculation of statutory income for 1984–85:

	Investment £		Earned £
Profits from shop (Schedule D Case I)			10,000
Wife's salary (Schedule E)			2,000
Rent (Schedule A)	300		
Statutory income	£300	+	£12,000

Winnie's statutory income for the year is £12,300 from which various deductions will be made before tax is chargeable.

III   CHARGES ON INCOME *(Step 2)*

1   General

Charges on income are described in TMA 1970 s 8(8) as 'amounts which fall to be deducted in computing total income'. Thus, they are deductible from the individual's statutory income and technically may be deducted from investment income first. The 'amounts which fall to be deducted' are not defined, but consist of certain transfers of income which the taxpayer is obliged to make. The theory is that such income ceases to be that of the payer and becomes the income of the payee so that the payer should not be taxed on it. Charges are, therefore, deducted before personal reliefs because the latter cannot be deducted from income which is not the taxpayer's.

EXAMPLE 4

In 1984–85 Viola has statutory income from her employment (Schedule E) and from trading (Schedule D Case I) amounting to £16,400 from which she may deduct her charges on income for 1984–85 of £1,000 to leave her with total income of £15,400.

There are three charges on income: annuities and other annual payments; small maintenance payments; and certain interest payments.

2   Annual payments

The meaning of an annual payment is discussed in Chapter 10. They are treated for tax purposes as part of the income of the person (the payee) to whom they are paid. Typical examples are:
(a) payments under a deed of covenant to an individual for a period of seven years or more, or to a charity for four or more years, and

(b) annuities, certain royalties and maintenance payments (except small maintenance payments—see below).

Although annual payments constitute a charge on the payer's income and, accordingly, are free of tax in his hands, the payer is used as an agent to collect basic rate tax on the amount paid (see TA 1970 ss 3, 52, 53). The annual payment is, therefore, added back to the payer's income for this purpose. To recompense himself, he is allowed to deduct and retain from the payment a sum equal to tax at basic rate on that payment.

EXAMPLE 5

Viola has statutory income of £16,400 (see *Example 4*). She is under a legal obligation to pay her ex-husband, Michael, maintenance of £1,000 pa (an annual payment). Under TA 1970 s 52 Viola may deduct from the gross payment of £1,000 a sum equivalent to basic rate tax on that figure (ie £300). She, therefore, pays £700 and retains £300.

The income on which she is subject to tax (before deducting personal reliefs) is:

	£
Statutory income	16,400
Less: charge on income (gross)	1,000
Total income	£15,400

From this Viola may deduct her personal allowance and she will be taxed on the balance. In addition, however, she must pay tax at 30% on the maintenance payment.

Notice that Michael receives the sum of £700 after deduction of basic rate tax at source. When calculating his income tax liability he must, therefore, include the gross payment of £1,000 in his statutory income and is given a tax credit for the £300 deducted by Viola.

3   Small maintenance payments (TA 1970 s 65)

Small maintenance payments are payable under a court order and are for amounts below certain specified limits (see generally Chapter 36). As with annual payments, small maintenance payments become the income of the payee and constitute a charge on the payer's income. However, they differ from annual payments in that they are paid gross (without deduction of tax), so that they are not added back to the payer's income for basic rate tax.

EXAMPLE 6

Taking the facts of *Example 5* except that £84 per month is ordered by the court to be paid to Michael. This is a small maintenance payment and Viola, therefore, pays Michael £84 (gross) with no deduction of tax and is taxed on her remaining income. Michael receives £84 (gross) with no tax credit.

4   Certain interest payments

An individual obtains income tax relief for certain interest payments by deducting them from his statutory income as a charge. Certain other interest payments are deductible in computing income from a particular source only (eg, interest payments made for the purposes of a trade are deductible in computing the profits of that trade under Schedule D Case I). Most interest payments receive no tax relief at all. The ordinary bank overdraft, credit card interest, and hire purchase interest payments, to take three typical instances, receive no tax relief.

The rules governing the deductibility of interest are complex (the provisions are mainly in FA 1972 s 75 and Sch 9 and in FA 1974 Sch 1). The interest must be payable on a loan made for one of the eight qualifying purposes dealt with below. Further, it must be either annual interest chargeable as the payee's income under Schedule D Case III, or must be payable in the UK on a loan from a bank, or from a person bona fide carrying on business as a member of a UK Stock Exchange or as a UK discount house. As a general rule, interest that is eligible for tax relief is paid gross and is deductible from the payer's statutory income as a charge. For exceptional cases where basic rate income tax must be deducted at source by the payer of the interest see p 153.

Loans to acquire an interest in a close company (FA 1974 Sch 1 paras 9–10)   An individual may obtain income tax relief for the interest paid on a loan to acquire ordinary share capital in close trading companies (which must satisfy the requirements in FA 1972 Sch 16 para 3A(2)), and on a loan raised to lend money to such a company so long as it is used wholly and exclusively for the business of the company (or of an associated company which is likewise a qualifying close company). To qualify for relief, the borrower has to show either that he is a shareholder and works for the greater part of his time in the management or conduct of the company or that he controls more than 5% of the ordinary share capital (in the latter case the borrower need not work for the company). To the extent that he recovers any capital from the company during that time (eg by repayment of ordinary share capital), he is treated as having repaid the loan and the amount of interest available for relief is reduced accordingly.

EXAMPLE 7

Gatty Ltd is the family trading company of the Gatty family. Sam Freebie, a full-time working director owning no shares in the company, borrows £5,000 from his bank to subscribe for ordinary shares. He will own a 4% shareholding and tax relief is available on the interest he pays. If, however, Jack Floor, the caretaker of the company's factory, were to subscribe for a similar number of shares no relief will be available because he is not concerned in the management or conduct of the company.

Loan to acquire an interest in a partnership (FA 1974 Sch 1 paras 11–12)   Interest relief is available to an individual on a loan used to purchase a share in a partnership or to contribute capital or make a loan to the partnership, if it is used wholly and exclusively for the business purposes of the partnership. Relief is only available if, from the application of the loan to the payment of interest, the individual has been a member of the partnership (otherwise than as a limited partner) and has not recovered any capital from the partnership.

Loan to acquire an interest in a co-operative (FA 1974 Sch I paras 10A, 10B)   Relief is available for interest payments made on a loan to acquire an interest in a co-operative, or to be used wholly and exclusively for the business of that body or a subsidiary. A co-operative is defined as a common ownership enterprise or a co-operative enterprise within the meaning of the Industrial Common Ownership Act 1976 s 2. Relief is only available if the individual shows that from the application of the loan to the payment of the interest he has worked for the greater part of his time as an employee in that co-operative or in a subsidiary thereof.

Loan to invest in an employee-controlled company (FA 1974 Sch I paras 10C and 10D)   Relief is available for interest payments on a loan taken out by an individual to acquire ordinary shares in an employee-controlled company (which must be a UK resident unquoted trading company). An employee-controlled company is one where full-time employees or their spouses own more than 50% of the ordinary share capital and voting power of the company. When an employee and his spouse together own more than 10% of the issued share capital, the excess is treated as not being owned by a full-time employee (except that where husband and wife are both full-time employees the 10% limit applies separately to each). Other conditions for relief are that the shares must be acquired within 12 months of the company becoming employee-controlled and that the taxpayer or his spouse must be full-time employees of the company from the time when the loan is applied to the date when interest is paid.

Loan to purchase plant or machinery (FA 1972 Sch 9 paras 10–15)   Where a partner or a Schedule E employee, borrows money to purchase machinery or plant for which capital allowances are available, he can claim interest relief on that loan for up to three years after the end of the tax year when the debt was incurred. (Note that for a sole trader interest on such loans is a deductible business expense.)

Loan to pay capital transfer tax (FA 1974 Sch 1 paras 17–21)   PRs are eligible for interest relief on a loan used by them to pay CTT attributable to personal property situated in the UK to which the deceased was beneficially entitled and which has vested in them (see further Chapter 12).

Loan to purchase a life annuity (FA 1974 Sch 1 para 24)   Interest relief is available on a loan not exceeding £30,000 to a person aged 65 or over to purchase an annuity on his life provided that the annuity is secured on land in the UK (or Republic of Ireland) in which he has an interest and uses as his only or main residence at the time when the interest is paid (see below).

5   Loans for the purchase or improvement of land and the MIRAS scheme (FA 1972 s 75, Sch 9; FA 1974 s 19 and Sch 1; FA 1982 s 26 and Sch 7)

a) *Conditions for relief*

Interest is eligible for tax relief if it is paid on a loan by the owner of an estate or interest in land in the UK or the Republic of Ireland for the purpose of acquiring or improving or developing the land for use as his only or main residence. Spouses are treated as one person for this relief. Land includes a large caravan or houseboat. Improvement is not defined, but involves expenditure of a capital nature rather than repairs or maintenance. The following conditions must be satisfied for a borrower to qualify:

Ownership   The interest payments must be made by the person owning the interest in the land and not, eg by his rich mother-in-law. If the borrower dies, his PRs may claim the relief against estate income if the deceased could have claimed it, so long as the property is used as the residence of his widow or dependent children.

Qualifying purpose   The loan must be used for the 'qualifying purpose' (viz the acquisition or improvement of land) either when it is obtained or within a reasonable time thereafter.

EXAMPLE 8

Fred takes out a loan of £5,000 in October to build an extension/conservatory. However, the work cannot be started until the spring and in the meantime Fred invests the money in shares. The interest on this loan will not be eligible for tax relief. Fred should, therefore, repay the loan out of the sale proceeds of the shares and take out a new loan to be used for the conservatory.

Only or main residence   The land must be used as the only or main residence of the borrower, a dependent relative or a former or separated spouse (for the definitions of 'dependent relative' and 'separated' spouse see FA 1974 Sch 1 para 4(4)). Relief is not restricted by the number of houses that the borrower owns, provided, in each case, that the loans are for a qualifying purpose and that the houses are inhabited as their only or main residence by one of the permitted categories of person (contrast the CGT exemption p 230). However, it is effectively limited by the total amount of the loans that will attract the relief (see p 31).

EXAMPLE 9

Mr Quiverfull owns ten houses. He lives in one with his present wife. The other nine are inhabited by various dependent relatives and former spouses of Mr Quiverfull, all living rent free, He instals central heating in all ten houses for which he takes out ten separate loans, one on each house of £3,000. He can obtain interest relief on aggregate loans of £30,000.

Whether land is used as a person's 'only or main residence' is a question of fact and degree and, if the borrower has more than one residence, he cannot choose which is to be treated for income tax purposes as the main residence (compare the CGT and DLT exemptions; pp 230 and 437). The amount of time spent in the residence is only one of the facts to be taken into account. In *Frost v Feltham* (1981) the taxpayer was the tenant and licensee of a public house in Essex which he was required by the terms of his employment to occupy. He bought a house in Wales with the aid of a mortgage on which he successfully claimed interest relief even though he only visited the house irregularly.

In practice, the Revenue take the view that the accommodation should be furnished and more or less in a state of readiness for permanent occupation if relief is to be available. Temporary absences of up to one year are ignored. So too is an absence of up to four years caused by the borrower having to move elsewhere in the UK or abroad because of his job. In practice, he can string together several four year periods provided that he returns for a period of three months between each.

Where the taxpayer is required by his employment to live in job-related accommodation, he can claim relief for interest paid on another property after 6 April 1977, even though it is not his main residence, provided that at the time of the payment it is used by the borrower as a residence (for instance at weekends); or that he intends to use it in due course as his only or main residence (for instance after the job ends)—FA 1974 Sch 1 para 4A. The accommodation is job-related if it fulfills the conditions laid down in FA 1977 s 33 (see p 54). This relaxation of the residence rule for job-related accommodation has been extended (by FA 1984 s 25) to the self-employed taxpayer or his spouse who is bound, under a contract made at arm's length, to carry on his business on the land of another and to occupy property provided by that person except where the accommodation is provided by a company in which he or his spouse has a material interest or by his or his spouse's firm.

£30,000 limit Relief is available only to an individual for interest on a qualifying loan of up to £30,000. Insofar as the loan exceeds £30,000 the interest on the excess is disallowed. If the borrower has more than one qualifying loan, they are aggregated for the purpose of the £30,000 limit and interest on earlier loans is relieved before interest on later ones. ('Top ups' involving a higher rate of interest should be signed first, therefore, although, if it is part of a single contract to purchase, the Revenue would treat them as both made on the same day.)

EXAMPLE 10

If in *Example 9* Mr Quiverfull had taken out ten loans of £4,000 each, totalling £40,000, interest relief would be limited to loans of £30,000, relief being given in the order in which the loans were obtained.

In the case of bridging loans, to which FA 1974 Sch 1 para 6 applies, each residence is treated separately for determining the £30,000 ceiling (see b) below).

Finally, FA 1972 Sch 9 para 8 prevents relief in the case of artificial transactions; in particular, where the vendor and purchaser are husband and wife, or where the loan to improve the property is from a connected person and exceeds the value of that work.

b) *Exceptions where relief is given despite non-occupation of the property*

In the cases considered below interest relief is available despite the fact that the property is not used as the only or main residence when the loan is acquired.

First, when the property becomes the main residence within 12 months after the loan (FA 1974 Sch 1 para 4(1)(a)). This caters for property that requires substantial improvement before it can be occupied.

Secondly, where the taxpayer has obtained bridging finance, he will continue to receive interest relief on the loan on his old property for 12 months after acquiring a 'new loan' on the new property which he occupies as his main residence, provided that the new loan is acquired for a qualifying purpose and that he intends to sell the old property (FA 1974 Sch 1, para 6; FA 1984 s 22). The 12 month period may, by concession, be extended if the taxpayer can show that he has been unable to sell the old property. In this situation, the loans are not aggregated and as from 1984–85 each loan is considered separately in applying the £30,000 ceiling. The relief for delay in occupying a new house and for bridging finance will often be useful when a couple get married.

EXAMPLE 11

In the following cases Hugh and Wilma (H and W) are newly-weds. Assume that the loans referred to are for a qualifying purpose and do not (individually) exceed £30,000.

Case A   H pays interest on loan 1 on a house which before marriage was his main residence. After marriage, it becomes the matrimonial home. H continues to receive interest relief.

Case B   As in *Case A* above, except that H and W take out a new loan, loan 2, to purchase a house which becomes the matrimonial home. H continues to receive interest relief on loan 1 (as well as on loan 2) for 12 months from obtaining loan 2 so long as he intends to sell his original house.

Case C   H and W both have loans (1 and 2) on houses acquired before their marriage. They take out another loan, loan 3, on a house which becomes the matrimonial home. By concession they will continue to receive interest relief on loans 1 and 2 (as well as on loan 3) for 12 months from taking out loan 3.

Case D   As in *Case C* above except that H and W do not acquire a new house, but occupy W's existing house as the matrimonial home. FA 1974 Sch 1 para 6 cannot apply to this situation because H and W have not taken out a 'new' loan. However by ESC A38 they continue to receive relief on loans 1 and 2 provided that the property which is not the matrimonial home is sold within 12 months of H ceasing to live there.

Case E   As in *Case C* above except that H and W occupy another property as their matrimonial home without taking out a new loan. H and W lose interest relief on loans 1 and 2 once they cease to occupy those properties. Neither para 6, the concession, nor ESC A38 apply to these facts.

c)   *Method of obtaining tax relief—the MIRAS scheme*

Tax relief for interest payments is given by way of charge on income, so that the payment is free of tax in the payer's hands and reduces his statutory income for the purposes of higher rate tax. However, when the interest payments fall within FA 1982 s 26, Sch 7 and supplementary regulations, tax relief at basic rate is given to the payer by deduction at source under MIRAS (Mortgage Interest Relief At Source). The main reasons for the introduction of the scheme (from 6 April 1983) were first, that a large proportion of borrowers are only basic rate taxpayers and so only require relief at this rate; and, secondly, there are obvious administrative savings in placing the burden of running the scheme on the lender. Tax relief at higher rates is given as a charge on income (see below).

MIRAS will cover the majority of mortgage interest payments because it applies whenever:
(a) a 'qualifying borrower' (basically all individuals);
(b) makes a payment of relevant loan interest, which is defined as interest paid in the UK after 5 April 1983 on a loan not exceeding £30,000 and made for a qualifying purpose; and
(c) the payment is to a 'qualifying lender'. This term covers all bodies who normally make such loans (eg building societies and local authorities).

If the loan exceeds £30,000, MIRAS may apply to so much of it as is within the limit if the lender gives notice to the Revenue that he is prepared to accept the deduction in respect of all loans above £30,000 made by him (FA 1982 Sch 7 para 5).

Although it is clear how the Revenue operate the scheme in practice, it should be noted that the legislation contains a number of inconsistencies and in particular that certain subsections cannot easily be reconciled with each other (see FA 1982 s 26(1) and ss 26(4), (5)).

The practical application of the MIRAS scheme can be illustrated by the

MIRAS, MIRAS, ON THE WALL...

following three cases. The first is where the payer is a basic rate taxpayer who will receive all his tax relief within the scheme. The second is where the taxpayer is liable for higher rate tax, but is otherwise within the scheme. The third is where the taxpayer, whether liable to basic or higher rate tax, is outside the scheme (eg because his loan exceeds £30,000).

Case A—basic rate taxpayer   Basic rate tax on the interest payments is collected from the taxpayer along with his other income tax. Hence, his income is not reduced by the interest payments. To compensate the payer, he is entitled to deduct from the interest payment a sum equivalent to basic rate tax on the gross figure.

EXAMPLE 12

Sebastian, who has taxable income of £13,400, pays £200 relevant loan interest to the Dodgy Building Society each month. He satisfies his obligation to the building society by paying them each month:

	£
Gross payment	200
Less sum equivalent to basic rate tax	60
Payment to building society	£140

The building society recover the amount deducted by Sebastian (ie £60) from the Revenue (s 26(7)). Sebastian's income tax liability for the year is 30% of his taxable income of £13,400 ie £4,020. Because Sebastian has deducted the equivalent of basic rate tax from his payments over the year (£720), the interest payments are effectively free of tax in his hands.

Case B—higher rate taxpayer   The higher rate taxpayer gets relief from basic rate tax by deduction at source. He obtains relief from higher rate tax by an adjustment to his tax bill (as happened in all cases before 6 April 1983). For higher rate tax purposes, the interest remains a charge on income.

EXAMPLE 13

As in *Example 12* except that Sebastian's statutory income is £17,800. He pays relevant loan interest of £140 per month (£200–£60) to the Dodgy Building Society. His income tax calculation is as follows (ignoring personal reliefs):

	£
Statutory income	17,800
Less interest payments (gross)	2,400
	£15,400

Tax on £15,400 at 30% = £4,620
tax at 30% (basic rate) on £2,400 = £   720
Tax due   £5,340

Case C—taxpayer outside MIRAS   Where the taxpayer is outside the scheme the interest payments are paid gross and are deductible as charges from the taxpayer's income for all tax purposes.

EXAMPLE 14

As in *Example 13*, except that Sebastian's payments are not within MIRAS because his loan exceeds £30,000. Accordingly, he pays £200 to the Dodgy Building Society each month. His income tax calculation is (ignoring personal reliefs):

	£
Statutory income	17,800
Less interest payment (gross)	2,400
	£15,400

Tax on £15,400 at 30% = £4,620

The operation of **MIRAS** does not increase the cost of mortgages since, instead of tax relief, the borrower obtains a reduction in the interest payments made. However, there is a timing difference, in that the payer will pay less to his lender each month, thereby increasing his cash flow. (For the particular advantages on matrimonial breakdown see Chapter 36). **MIRAS** is positively advantageous to the taxpayer in the (unlikely) circumstances where his personal allowances exceed his income left after deducting the interest payments. Before the introduction of **MIRAS** the result would have been a loss of personal allowances, but now unused allowances can effectively be set against the interest payments on which the taxpayer is subject to basic rate income tax (see FA 1982 s 26(5), which was designed to compensate for the abolition of the mortgage option scheme).

EXAMPLE 15

Bertrand, a single man, has income for 1984–85 of £3,000 and pays relevant loan interest of £3,000 for the year. Therefore, he pays the lender £2,100 and retains £900 (being equivalent to basic rate tax). His income tax for 1984–85 is basic rate tax (s 26(4)) on £3,000 = £900.

But he has unused allowances of £2,005 so that by s 26(5):

	£
Sum assessed under s 26(4)	3,000
Less unused allowance	2,005
Sum taxed	£995
Tax at 30%	£298.50

This may be contrasted with the position of Bertrand in 1982–83 (ie before the introduction of MIRAS) when, assuming the same figures, he would have paid no income tax since his interest payments (£3,000) would have been deducted from his income (£3,000). His personal reliefs for the year would have been wasted. Although £298.50 was paid in tax under MIRAS, in 1982–83 Bertrand would have made gross payments to the lender of £3,000 instead of £2,100 under MIRAS. As a result, Bertrand is better off under the MIRAS scheme by £601.50 (£900 – £298.50). Note that when a taxpayer is away from the UK but still qualifies for interest relief he may benefit if the MIRAS scheme applies since, if he has no UK income, interest relief will otherwise be lost.

IV TOTAL INCOME *(Step 3)*

Charges are deducted from income before any other deductions and the resultant sum is 'total income'. Insofar as charges exceed statutory income, the unabsorbed charge receives no tax relief and cannot be carried forward to a future year. After charges, the individual deducts personal reliefs from total income to arrive at his taxable income. However, there are certain other deductions which may be available, in which case, they will be deducted before personal reliefs. Notice that it is the total income figure before further deductions are made that is used to calculate (where applicable) the age allowance, the dependent relative relief and (where available) the $\frac{1}{6}$th for life assurance premium relief (see p 44).

1 **Loss relief** (TA 1970 s 168; FA 1978 s 30)

Sometimes losses arising under a particular Schedule are only deductible in computing profits from the same source. Such losses, therefore, affect the calculation of the individual's statutory income by reducing income from that source.

EXAMPLE 16

Anita receives a salary as a lecturer (Schedule E) of £12,000 pa. She also owns a house in Chelsea which she rents to nurses from the Chelsea Hospital. In 1984–85 her allowable expenses on the property under Schedule A exceeded her Schedule A rental income by £1,000. Her statutory income for 1984–85 is:

	£
Schedule E	12,000
Schedule A (loss £1,000)	NIL
Statutory income	£12,000

Anita cannot deduct her £1,000 Schedule A loss from income from any other source. All she can do is carry the loss forward to a subsequent year and deduct it from Schedule A profits of that year. Thus, if in 1985–86 her rental income exceeds her allowable expenses under Schedule A by £2,000, Anita's statutory income is:

	£	£
Schedule E		12,000
Schedule A: profit	2,000	
Less 1984–85 loss	1,000	
		1,000
Statutory income		£13,000

Where the individual makes a loss in his trade, profession or vocation, however, he may choose to deduct that loss from his total income before deducting personal reliefs (see TA 1970 s 168; FA 1978 s 30 and Chapter 7). The danger with claiming this loss relief is that it may so reduce total income that personal allowances are unused.

EXAMPLE 17

Andrew is a barrister (Schedule D Case II) and a part-time lecturer (Schedule E) with a salary for 1984–85 of £12,000 pa. He pays maintenance to his ex-wife Michele of £2,000 pa. In 1984–85 he makes a loss in his first year at the bar of £5,000 which he chooses under TA 1970 s 168 to deduct from his total income. His income tax calculation (in part) for 1984–85 is as follows:

	£
Schedule E	12,000
Schedule D (loss £5,000)	NIL
Statutory income	12,000
Less charge on income	2,000
Total income	10,000
Less loss (TA 1970 s 168)	5,000
	£5,000

Andrew has £5,000 income from which he can deduct his personal reliefs.

2   The business expansion scheme (FA 1983 s 26 and Sch 5 as amended)

The scheme seeks to encourage investment in the ordinary share capital of private trading companies. Investment may be by direct subscription or through an approved fund.

Subject to the conditions below being satisfied, a 'qualifying individual' can claim a deduction from his total income for the amount invested in 'eligible shares' in a 'qualifying company'. The maximum sum for which relief may be claimed each year is £40,000 and the minimum investment in any one company £500 (there is no prescribed minimum when the investment is through an approved fund, but in practice all funds set their own minimum investment which is usually greater than £500!). The scheme operates for four tax years from April 1983 to April 1987.

EXAMPLE 18

Croesus is subject to income tax at a maximum rate of 60%. He invests £40,000 under the scheme in 1984–85.

	£
Total investment	40,000
Less income tax relief at 60%	24,000
Net cost of shares	£16,000

The following conditions have to be satisfied for the relief to operate:

Investment by a qualifying individual   The relief is only available to an individual (not, therefore, to a trustee or company) who is resident and ordinarily resident in the UK throughout the tax year when the shares are issued and who is not connected with the company in either the two years preceding the issue (or from the date of incorporation, if later) or within the five years after the issue.

Broadly, an individual is connected with the company if he, or an associate of his, is an employee or paid director of the company; or if he and his associates possess more than 30% of the capital (including loan capital) or voting power in the company. For these purposes an associate excludes brothers and sisters, but otherwise has the close company meaning (see p 402) whilst a director is not debarred from the relief if the only payments that he receives from the company are for travelling and other tax-deductible expenses. It follows that the obvious investors in small companies (working directors, employees and their relations) do not qualify and that the relief will not be available in management or employee buy-outs.

Investment in a qualifying company   Two conditions must be satisfied by the company. First, it must have been incorporated in the UK and be UK-resident at the time of the share issue and for three years thereafter; all its share capital must be fully paid up; its shares must not be quoted on The Stock Exchange or dealt in on the Unlisted Securities Market; it must not be a subsidiary of, or be controlled by, any other company; and any subsidiaries that it has must be wholly owned. Secondly, the company must exist for the purpose of trading 'wholly or mainly' in the UK (see SP 7/83) or exist to hold shares in subsidiaries which carry on qualifying trades. Certain trades do not qualify eg dealing in land, shares and commodities; leasing and letting assets; banking, insurance and other financial services; and, as from 14 March 1984, farming as defined in TA 1970 s 526 (FA 1984 s 37).

Subscription for eligible shares   Relief is only given for investment in new ordinary shares. The shares may carry different voting rights but otherwise they must not have any advantage over other shares, either in respect of dividends, a right to company's assets on a winding up or a present or future right to be redeemed.

If the conditions relating to the company cease to be satisfied within three years of the investment being made, the relief is withdrawn. It is also wholly or partly withdrawn if the individual receives value from the company (in the form, inter alia, of a redemption of his shares, a loan or the provision of a benefit) or disposes of his shares within five years of their purchase. Withdrawal of relief involves reopening the income tax assessment for the year in which relief was given. In addition to the revised assessment, interest may be charged on the extra tax payable.

Claims for relief can be made when the qualifying trade has been carried on for at least four months and must be made within two years of that date or, if later, two years from the end of the year of assessment in which the shares were issued. Further, the company must begin trading within two years of the share issue. A claim is made on a Revenue form completed by the company and on which it certifies that it has complied with the necessary conditions.

On a disposal of shares acquired under the scheme, normal CGT rules generally apply, so that the full acquisition cost will be deducted from the sale proceeds. If the disposal is for less than the taxpayer's acquisition cost and other expenses, there will normally be no allowable loss because the acquisition cost must first be reduced by so much of the business expansion relief as is necessary to reduce the loss to zero (FA 1983 Sch 5 para 16 (I)).

EXAMPLE 19

(1) Assume in *Example 18* that Croesus sold the shares (purchased for £40,000 in 1984–85) for £70,000 some six years later. His gain for CGT purposes would be £30,000 (ignoring indexation and other incidental expenses) so that after deducting his annual exemption (currently £5,600) the tax would be £7,320 (30% × £24,400). His profit on investment would be:

	£	£
Sale proceeds		70,000
Less total investment after tax relief		
(£40,000 – £24,000)	16,000	
CGT	7,320	
		23,320
		£46,680

$$\text{Return on capital} = \frac{£46,680}{£16,000} \times 100 = 292\%$$

(2) If Croesus were to sell the shares for £30,000, his acquisition cost (£40,000) must be reduced by £10,000 of the relief given (£24,000) so as to produce neither gain nor loss on disposal. If the shares become valueless, eg on the company becoming insolvent, Croesus would have an allowable loss of £16,000 (£40,000 less relief of £24,000). That loss may be eligible for income tax relief under FA 1980 s 37 (the 'venture capital scheme', see p 120).

V   PERSONAL RELIEFS (TA 1970 s 5) *(Step 4)*

1   General

Individuals resident in the UK can deduct personal reliefs from their total income. The availability of the reliefs depends not on the type of income involved, but on the taxpayer's personal circumstances. He must claim his reliefs each year by completing the section headed 'Allowances' in the income tax return. If personal allowances exceed the total income of the taxpayer, the surplus is unused and cannot be carried forward for use in future years. The position of a taxpayer who makes interest payments falling within the MIRAS scheme and who has surplus allowances has already been discussed at p 34.

A summary of the personal reliefs available for 1984–85 is set out below. It should be noted that since 1982–83, certain reliefs (marked with an asterisk) are linked to increases in the Retail Prices Index between December preceding the year of assessment and the previous December.

* Personal allowance: married (MMA)   £3,155
                      single (SPA)   £2,005
* Wife's earned income relief (WEIR)   £2,005

*	Additional personal allowance (APA)	£1,150
*	Age allowance: married	£3,955
	single	£2,490
	Widow's bereavement allowance	£1,150
	Dependent relative allowance	£100/145
	Children's services relief	£55
	Housekeeper allowance	£100
	Blind persons allowance	£100

A limited category of non-UK residents (as set out in TA 1970 s 27) may claim a proportion of the personal reliefs in respect of their UK income (see p 187).

2 The reliefs

Personal allowance (TA 1970 s 8(1)) The single person's allowance (for 1984–85 £2,005) is available to all individuals including minor children. A married couple who are living together will be taxed by aggregating their incomes and treating the total as that of the man. Instead of two single allowances he is given a married man's allowance (£3,155). Special rules operate in the year of marriage, on separation, and when an election for the separate taxation of the wife's earnings is in force; these matters are discussed in Chapter 35. The availability of one allowance in cases where the taxpayer has two wives was accepted by the Revenue in *Nabi v Heaton* (1983).

Wife's earned income allowance (TA 1970 s 8(2)) If a wife is working and so long as the couple have not elected for the separate taxation of her earnings a further allowance (the wife's earned income allowance) is available, equal to the lesser of the single person's allowance and the amount of her earnings for the tax year.

The allowance cannot be used against the wife's unearned income nor against any of her husband's income and is not available in the year of marriage.

EXAMPLE 20

Hulk and Violet have been married for many years. In 1984–85 Hulk has earned income of £20,000 and Violet has earned income of £1,000 and unearned of £12,000. Hulk is taxed as follows:

		£
Hulk		20,000
Violet		13,000
Total income		33,000
Less: personal reliefs:		
married man's allowance	£3,155	
wife's earnings allowance (restricted)	£1,000	
		£4,155
Taxable income		£28,845

Additional personal allowance (TA 1970 s 14) This is also known as the single parent family allowance, which as the name suggests is intended to alleviate the financial position of the 'one-parent' family. It is £1,150 for 1984–85 (the difference between the single and the married allowance) and is given to a taxpayer who is not entitled to the married allowance (because single, widowed, divorced or separated), but who has a 'qualifying child' living with him for the whole or part of the year of assessment. A qualifying child is one who is:

(a) born in that tax year; or

(b) under the age of 16 at the start of the tax year; or

(c) over 16, but attending a full-time educational course or undergoing vocational training with an employer for at least two years;

and who is:

(a) the taxpayer's own natural legitimate or legitimated issue (including stepchild and adopted child under 18 at the date of adoption); or

(b) any other child born in, or under 18 at the beginning of the year and maintained at the taxpayer's expense for the whole or part of the year (legal custody is not required).

Only one allowance is available to any one taxpayer, regardless of the number of qualifying children that he may have. When more than one person is entitled to the allowance (for instance, because they each maintain the child for a part of the year) the one allowance is apportioned between them, but not more than £1,150 can be received in total.

The allowance is not available to spouses, even if they are separately taxed. However, a claimant need not be living alone to receive the allowance provided that the above conditions are fulfilled. Thus, cohabitees, who have produced more than one offspring, can each claim the full allowance in respect of one child, provided that they can convince the Revenue that they are each separately responsible for the maintenance of one child.

A married man entitled to the married man's allowance may claim the additional personal allowance if his wife was totally incapacitated mentally or physically throughout the tax year and there are qualifying children. There is no equivalent increase in allowances where the husband is similarly incapacitated. A widow or widower who receives this allowance cannot claim the housekeeper allowance (see p 41).

Age allowance (TA s 8(1A)(1B))   Where the taxpayer is 65 or older at any time during the year of assessment, he receives a higher personal allowance of £2,490 for 1984–85. If he is married and living with, or wholly and voluntarily maintaining, a wife, he receives a higher married allowance of £3,955 for 1984–85. This higher allowance only applies to those whose total income does not exceed £8,100. If the income exceeds £8,100 in the year, the allowance is reduced by two-thirds of the excess, but not so as to deprive the taxpayer of the normal personal allowances. This higher allowance is not available to spouses who have elected for separate taxation of the wife's earnings.

EXAMPLE 21

William and Mary are an elderly married couple both over 65 with a total income (earned) of £8,700. Their taxable income is:

	£
Total income	8,700
Less age allowance (restricted)	
(£3,955 – (2/3rds × £600 (excess over £8,100))	3,555
Taxable income	£5,145

Widow's bereavement allowance (TA 1970 s 15A)   Where a married man dies in a year of assessment for which he was entitled to the married allowance (or would have been, but for an election for the separate taxation of wife's earnings), his widow is entitled to an allowance in addition to her single allowance both in the year of his death (against her income accruing from death) and in the following year provided she has not remarried before then. This allowance is the difference between the married man's and single person's allowance; for 1984–85 it is £1,150. Widows with dependent children are also entitled to the single parent allowance (see p 39).

Dependent relative allowance (TA 1970 s 16)   Where a taxpayer voluntarily maintains at his own expense his or his spouse's widowed, separated or divorced mother, or any other relative of himself or his spouse, who is incapacitated through age or infirmity from looking after himself, he is entitled to an additional allowance of £100 for 1984–85 for each such dependent, unless the dependent has income in excess of the basic retirement pension. If such income exceeds the pension by less than £100, a lower allowance is given to bring the total up to that level.

Should the claimant be a woman (excluding a married woman living with her husband) the allowance is (for 1984–85) £145 reduced by £1 for each £1 of the dependent's own income in excess of the retirement pension. When there is more than one claimant for the same relative (for instance, when they share the care and maintenance of mother-in-law), the one allowance is apportioned between them in proportion to their contributions to the dependent's maintenance.

Children's services relief (TA 1970 s 17)   A taxpayer who is forced through age or infirmity to rely on the services of a son or daughter, living with and maintained by him, is entitled to an allowance (for 1984–85) of £55.

Housekeeper allowance (TA 1970 s 12)   A widow or widower is entitled to an allowance (for 1984–85) of £100 for a resident housekeeper who is either a relative or some other person employed as housekeeper. The allowance can only be claimed for a relative if any other person who may be entitled to claim an allowance in respect of that relative relinquishes his claim. Thus, where the relative is a married woman, her husband must relinquish the married element of his personal allowance. A male claimant cannot claim the married and housekeeper allowances in the same year (ie year of his wife's death or his remarriage).

Blind person's allowance (TA 1970 s 18)   A taxpayer who is a registered blind person for the whole or part of the year of assessment receives an additional relief (for 1984–85) of £360. This also applies for a married man where he or his spouse (living with him) is a registered blind person. If both spouses are blind, his additional allowance (for 1984–85) is £720. This allowance is an alternative to the children's services allowance (see above).

Child benefit   As from April 1979, the mother (usually) receives tax-free child benefit for each child who is under 16, or under 19 and receiving full-time education at a recognised educational establishment. There are no child tax allowances.

VI   METHOD OF CHARGING TAXABLE INCOME *(Step 5)*

1   Rates of tax

Income tax is charged on an individual's taxable income for 1984–85 at the following rates:

	Income Band
On the first £15,400 at 30% (basic rate)	£1 –£15,400
At higher rates	
on the next £2,800 at 40%	£15,401–£18,200
on the next £4,900 at 45%	£18,201–£23,100
on the next £7,500 at 50%	£23,101–£30,600
on the next £7,500 at 55%	£30,601–£38,100
on the remainder at 60%	Excess over £38,100

Since 1982–83 increases in the rate bands have been linked to the increase in the Retail Prices Index between the December before the year of assessment and the previous December. The indexed rises are, however, subject to a negative resolution of Parliament (ie they occur 'unless Parliament otherwise determines'; FA 1980 s 24(4)). So far, the bands have never been raised in line with the Retail Prices Index.

It should be remembered that where payments are made by the taxpayer under deduction of tax at source (eg annual payments and certain interest payments) those payments are added back to the taxpayer's taxable income for basic rate tax purposes, thereby effectively increasing the figure chargeable to basic rate tax above £15,400. When payments are received by the taxpayer after deduction at source, the tax due from the payee will be reduced by the basic rate tax already paid on his behalf by the payer.

EXAMPLE 22

Brian has a statutory income for 1984–85 of £30,000. He pays maintenance to his ex-wife of £2,000 pa and is entitled to personal reliefs of £4,000. His income tax calculation is as follows:

	£
Statutory income	30,000
Less charge on income	2,000
Total income	28,000
Less personal reliefs	4,000
Taxable income for basic and higher rates	£24,000

	£
Tax payable:	
First £15,400 at 30%	4,620
next £2,800 at 40%	1,120
next £4,900 at 45%	2,205
final £900 at 50%	450
	£8,395

2   Dates for payment of tax

Tax is collected either by direct assessment or by deduction at source. Tax collected by direct assessment is generally due on 1 January in the year of assessment or within 30 days of a notice of assessment (if later). Tax under Schedule D Cases I and II, however, is payable in two equal instalments on

1 January in the year of assessment and 1 July following (subject to a later notice of assessment as above: see TA 1970 s 4).

Where income is received after deduction of basic rate tax, eg dividends, the recipient taxpayer is assessed to higher rate tax on 1 December following the year of assessment.

Tax is collected under the PAYE system of Schedule E at basic and higher rates on a current year basis (TA 1970 s 204). If the taxpayer's only source of income is from Schedule E, the correct amount of tax can be collected under this system necessitating no further adjustment. Otherwise, where the taxpayer has other sources of income, either too much or too little tax may be deducted, thereby necessitating an adjustment.

3 Specimen income tax calculation

Applying the steps listed at p 23 it is now possible to calculate an individual's income tax liability for a tax year.

EXAMPLE 23

Benjamin has the following income for 1984–85:

(i)	Lecturer (Schedule E)	£7,500
(ii)	Author (Schedule D Case II)	£2,000
(iii)	Part-time barman (Schedule E)	£9,500
(iv)	Rents from houses (Schedule A)	£11,000
(v)	Dividends (Schedule F) from Tenko Ltd (gross—including tax credit of £600)	£2,000

Benjamin is married to Bertha who has income from part-time employment as a nurse (Schedule E) of £2,500. He is liable to make interest payments of £3,000 pa to the Wonky Building Society and £1,000 small maintenance payment to his ex-wife Holly.

		£
Schedule E (own income)		17,000
Schedule E (wife's income)		2,500
Schedule D Case II		2,000
Schedule A		11,000
Schedule F		2,000
Step 1: Statutory income from all sources		34,500
Step 2: Deduct charges on income:		
*Building society interest	£3,000	
Small maintenance payment	£1,000	4,000
Step 3: Total income		30,500
Step 4: Deduct personal reliefs:		
Married man's allowance	£3,155	
Wife's earning's relief (unrestricted)	£2,005	5,160
Step 5: Taxable income for basic and higher rates		£25,340

	£
Tax chargeable at *Step 5:*	
First £15,400 at 30%	4,620
Next £2,800 at 40%	1,120
Next £4,900 at 45%	2,205
Final £2,240 at 50%	1,120
Tax on £25,340 at basic and higher rates	9,065

Step 6: Give credit for tax deducted at source, ie from
   dividends   600
                                                                            ‾‾‾‾‾
                                                                           8,465
*Step 7: * Add back* for basic rate tax only sums paid after
   deduction of basic rate tax ie building
   society interest of £3,000 at 30%   900
   Total tax due   £9,365
                                                                          ‾‾‾‾‾‾

Notes: (1) Tax would have been deducted at source under the PAYE system in respect of the employments—his own and his wife's. Credit would be given for this tax in *Step 6*, thereby affecting the actual tax due from Benjamin by direct assessment. Nevertheless, Benjamin is actually liable (howsoever it is collected) for tax of £9,365 in 1984–85.

   * (2) The interest paid to the Wonky Building Society falls within the MIRAS scheme with the result that as Benjamin is subject to excess liability, the gross payments will operate as a deduction from his income for the purposes of his higher rate assessment, but must be added back to ensure that the Revenue collect basic rate tax on the payments.

VII   MISCELLANEOUS MATTERS (not affecting the income tax calculation)

1   Life Assurance Premium Relief (TA 1970 ss 19–21, Sch 1; FA 1976 Sch 4 paras 4, 5)

Tax relief is available for premiums paid by a UK resident on a 'qualifying' life assurance policy made *before* 14 March 1984 (TA 1970 ss 19–21). The relief is given by allowing the policyholder to deduct and retain 15% of the premium, provided that the total annual premiums payable do not exceed the greater of £1,500 and $\frac{1}{6}$th of his total income. The insurer reclaims the deduction from the Inland Revenue. The relief is not available for policies made after 13 March 1984, nor to those made before that date where the holder subsequently alters the policy to increase the benefits secured or to extend the term. In such cases premiums will be paid without the 15% deduction. The proceeds of a qualifying policy are not normally subject to income tax.

   In contrast, premiums on non-qualifying policies receive no tax relief and any gain, net of premiums paid, on encashment (on surrender or death) may be subject to higher rate (but not basic rate) income tax, subject to top-slicing relief. During the term of the policy tax-free withdrawals up to the value of the original investment can be made so long as those withdrawals do not exceed 5% of the premium paid for each year that the policy has been held.

   The single premium insurance bond is the commonest example of a non-qualifying policy. There is little life cover and the bond is linked to units in one of the insurer's funds (typically in a property fund or possibly in equity, gilts or cash). The insurer is taxed on the income and gains shown by the investments (at rates from 30% to $37\frac{1}{2}$%), whilst the policyholder is not charged on the accumulating profits but can make the annual tax-free withdrawal. Single premium bonds therefore provide shelter for income in the case of higher rate taxpayers and are used as part of the inheritance trust (see further Chapter 37).

2   Exemptions from income tax

There are a number of exemptions from income tax including the following. It should also be noted that many items are exempted from tax by virtue of

Revenue Extra-Statutory Concessions (see generally pamphlet IRI (1980) and supplements).

a) *Exempt organisations*

Certain organisations are exempt (see generally TA 1970 ss 360–374). In particular, the Crown is not within the tax legislation at all, whilst charities are exempt from income tax in respect of:
(a) woodlands chargeable under Schedule B;
(b) income from land and investment income provided that it is applied for charitable purposes only; and
(c) trading profits applied purely for charitable purposes where either the trade is part of the main purpose of the charity, or the work is carried out mainly by the beneficiaries (for instance Christmas cards made by the handicapped and sold for their benefit).
Foreign diplomats and members of overseas armed forces stationed in the UK are exempt.

b) *Exempt income*

Some of the more important items that are exempt from income tax include:
(a) scholarship income in the hands of the scholar (TA 1970 s 375—see further the discussion of this exemption in *Wicks v Firth* (1983));
(b) certain social security benefits and child benefit (TA 1970 s 219). Notice that, as from 6 April 1982, maternity pay and statutory sick pay, and, as from 5 July 1982, unemployment benefit, are all taxable under Schedule E (TA 1970 s 219A);
(c) interest on National Savings Certificates and SAYE schemes (TA 1970 s 415);
(d) the first £70 of interest each year from ordinary accounts at the National Savings Bank. Spouses are treated as separate persons, so that each may qualify for the £70 exemption (TA 1970 s 414);
(e) interest on damages for personal injuries or death (TA 1970 s 375A);
(f) interest paid by a building society (and, as from 6 April 1985, banks and certain other institutions) is received free of tax at basic rate only. However, the grossed-up equivalent must enter into the individual's income tax computation for the purposes of liability to higher rate tax (TA 1970 s 343).

EXAMPLE 24

Zia receives £70 interest from the Wailshire Building Society. This is treated as received by her after deduction of basic rate income tax. She must, therefore, gross up the receipt to £100 for the purpose of her income tax calculation. She receives a tax credit for the £30 basic rate tax, which is treated as having been paid, although she will not be entitled to any refund of that tax. Only the net income (£70) is available to cover any charges on Zia's income.

5 Schedule E—offices and employments

I INTRODUCTORY

The emoluments derived from an 'office or employment', after deducting any allowable expenditure, are charged to income tax under one of the three Cases of Schedule E (TA 1970 s 181). Tax is levied on a current year basis and is usually collected at source under the PAYE system. Insofar as the Cases of Schedule E involve a foreign element, the matter is considered in Chapter 13. This chapter will be limited to the charge under Case I which applies when the person holding the office or employment is resident or ordinarily resident in the UK.

Schedule E has a crucial significance in the income tax system since it raises, mainly through PAYE, some 75% of total income tax per annum. High rates of tax have led to the proliferation of fringe benefits designed to minimise, or avoid the PAYE net. Accordingly a characteristic feature of the Schedule in the past decade has been regular legislation seeking to close loopholes in its operation. Thus, it is now an area where detail has come to swamp principle.

II 'OFFICE OR EMPLOYMENT'

1 Meaning of 'office' and 'employment'

The term 'office' is not statutorily defined, but it has been described by Rowlatt J in *Great Western Rly Co v Bater* (1920) as 'a subsisting, permanent, substantive position which has an existence independent of the person who fills it, and which is filled in succession by successive holders . . .'. Although this dictum has been approved in cases over the years, in *Edwards v Clinch* (1981) the emphasis on permanence and continuity was played down in favour of the requirement of some continuity and of a position with an existence independent of the individual holding it. In that case a civil engineer who received ad hoc appointments as a planning inspector was held not to be an office holder because the position had no independent existence, but lapsed when the particular assignment was completed.

Typical examples of office holders would include trustees, PRs, company secretaries and auditors. It is generally assumed that a company director, whether full-time and salaried or part-time and in receipt of fees, is an office holder under Schedule E (*McMillan v Guest* (1942)). Often the directorship will continue regardless of the person who occupies it; but it may still be an office, it appears, even if it is created for a particular person (see *Taylor v Provan* (1974) cp *Edwards v Clinch* (1981)). The employment law case of *Parsons v Parsons* (1979) casts a disturbing light on the status of a director. In that case Denning MR held that a full-time director of a family company was not an employee for the purposes of claiming compensation for unfair dismissal since he and his fellow directors had regarded themselves as self-employed; there was no written or implied contract of service, and his remuneration had been paid without deduction of tax under PAYE.

Difficulties arise when a taxpayer acquires an office by reason of his particular profession; eg solicitor partners (taxable under Schedule D Case II) often acquire trusteeships. Each office will be separately assessed under Schedule E and not taxed under Schedule D, unless that office had been acquired as an integral part of the trade or profession (see *IRC v Brander and Cruickshank* (1971)). In practice, the Revenue allow partnerships which receive directors' fees to enter those fees in their Schedule D Case II assessment so long as the directorship is a normal incident of the profession and of the particular practice; the fees form only a small part of total profits; and under the partnership agreement the fees are pooled for division amongst the partners (see ESC A40).

The term 'employment' is not statutorily defined. It connotes a job or a post: a position where there is a written or implied contract of service. If the taxpayer works for more than one person, the difficulty is to know whether he holds a number of separate employments (taxable under Schedule E) or is making a series of engagements carried out as part of a profession or vocation. The basic division is between a contract of service (Schedule E) and a contract for services (Schedule D) and each case depends on all its circumstances. In *Davies v Braithwaite* (1931), for instance, an actress who made a series of separate engagements to appear on film, stage and radio was held to be taxable under Schedule D. Rowlatt J looked at her total commitments during the year and, as the number was considerable, decided that each was a mere engagement in the course of exercising her profession. Compare *Fall v Hitchen* (1973) where the taxpayer was employed as a professional ballet dancer by Sadlers Wells under a contract which only allowed him to take other work with their consent (which was not to be unreasonably withheld). Pennycuick V-C looked at the characteristics of the contract in isolation and held that the taxpayer was taxable under Schedule E; undoubtedly one reason for the decision was that the taxpayer had only one contract.

2   Taxing a partner/consultant

An equity partner in a firm is self-employed and, therefore, assessable under Schedule D Case I or II. Difficulties may arise, however, as to the status of a salaried partner. Whether he is an employee or is self-employed does not depend upon the labels used or whether his salary is taxed at source under PAYE. Instead, all the facts and in particular the terms of the agreement between the parties must be considered. Thus, in *Stekel v Ellice* (1973), although the agreement referred to 'salaried partner' and a 'fixed salary', it was, in substance, a partnership agreement rather than a contract of employment. However, provided that the partnership determines the new partner's status in advance and drafts the agreement accordingly, its terms will be conclusive unless there is strong factual evidence to the contrary (*BSM Ltd v Secretary of*

State for Social Services (1978)). If the partners are in any doubt on the matter, they should seek confirmation of status from the Revenue.

Similarly, whether a consultant is an employee or self-employed is largely a matter of arrangement. If the firm provides for him to receive annual remuneration and to work fixed hours, this points to a Schedule E assessment, whereas if he is to receive fees for *ad hoc* consultations an assessment under Schedule D Case II will be more likely. In practice, the Revenue look particularly at the direction and control of the taxpayer; at his freedom to choose his own methods of working, and at his ability to subcontract the work.

III   THE TAX IS ON 'EMOLUMENTS'

'Emoluments' are partially defined in TA 1970 s 183 as including 'all salaries, fees, wages, perquisites and profits whatsoever'. To be an emolument the payment must possess two characteristics:
(a) it must be in the nature of a reward for services present and future (and possibly past), and
(b) it must be derived from the office or employment.

Basic pay or salary is clearly an emolument. Additional cash payments (bonuses, for instance) will generally be emoluments, although in exceptional circumstances a gift of cash from an employer may escape tax if it can be shown to be for the personal qualities of the employee rather than for any services which he performs (see p 59). Major problems are, however, caused by benefits in kind (or fringe benefits); this term encompasses all non-cash benefits received by an employee in connection with his job (see *Beecham Group Ltd v Fair* (1984)). To the extent that the benefit is provided gratuitously by the employer the benefit in kind rules and the gift rules interlink.

IV   BENEFITS IN KIND

1   **General principles**

The legislature has steadily widened the Schedule E net to tax fringe benefits by introducing numerous intricate provisions, the details of which are beyond the scope of this book. All that this section attempts is a summary of the general principles and of the more important provisions. The legislation distinguishes between two categories of employee:
(a) lower-paid employees, and
(b) higher-paid employees and (most) directors.

There are also certain benefits in kind where the rules apply to both categories of employee. Some benefits are specifically excluded from Schedule E by Revenue concession; the best known examples are probably luncheon vouchers of up to 15p per working day (ESC A2) and free coal provided for mineworkers (ESC A6; a cash allowance in lieu of free coal is also untaxed).

2   **Lower-paid employees**

Lower-paid employees are those whose total emoluments do not exceed £8,500 pa and who are not directors. In theory, the rules that follow apply to all employees. In practice, however, the special code that applies to higher-paid employees (see p 50) will normally supersede these rules save in exceptional cases.

a) *Basic principles*

There are two basic principles. First, a benefit in kind is taxable in the hands of the employee if it is convertible into money; it need not be saleable. In the case of *Tennant v Smith* (1891) the House of Lords held that the benefit of a house which the employee was required by his employment to occupy but which he could not assign or sublet did not constitute an emolument since it was not convertible into money (for the other ratio of the case see p 55). The test is whether the benefit *could* be converted; it is irrelevant whether the employee actually converts it into money. Consider, for instance, a British Rail season ticket which cannot be sold because it is non-assignable, but which can be converted into cash by surrender.

Secondly, if the benefit is convertible into money, tax is levied on the value of the benefit to the employee: ie on the secondhand value. In *Wilkins v Rogerson* (1961), the company arranged with Montague Burton that each employee would be permitted to obtain clothes of up to £15 in value. The contract provided for payment directly by the company. When the Revenue sought to tax an employee on a suit costing £14.50 the court held that the benefit was convertible into money, because the taxpayer could sell the suit, but that he could only be taxed on the secondhand value estimated at £5 (see also *Jenkins v Horn* (1979), where this test operated to the taxpayer's disadvantage).

The practical application of these two principles can cause problems. For instance, the provision of a non-convertible benefit, such as the free use of a car, is not chargeable whereas the provision of money to enable the employee to purchase such a benefit is an emolument (see *Bird v Martland* (1982)). A further problem is that it may be difficult to decide whether particular facts involve the rules on benefits in kind or not. This is illustrated by the case of *Heaton v Bell* (1970) where a company operated a voluntary car loan scheme for its employees who were offered the use of fully insured company cars. If they accepted the offer they thereupon received slightly reduced wages. An employee could withdraw from the scheme on giving 14 days' notice whereupon he would revert to his original wage. The House of Lords by a majority of four to one decided that the case did not involve the benefit in kind rules (but see Lord Reid's dissenting judgment). Instead they concluded that an employee who joined the scheme was entitled to his original unamended wage and that he had merely chosen to spend a portion of that wage on the hire of a car. Thus tax was charged on the full wage since what the taxpayer chooses to spend his wages on is not tax deductible!

EXAMPLE 1

Simon is employed as a butler at a wage of £10 pw. He is required to 'live in' and 50p is deducted per week for board and lodging. Simon is assessed to tax on £10 pw (see *Machon v McLoughlin* (1926)). Compare the case of Rosie who is employed as a housemaid and is paid a weekly wage of £9.50. She is required to live in but is not charged for board and lodging. She is taxed on £9.50; the board and lodging is a non-convertible benefit in kind which, therefore, escapes tax.

Difficulties may also arise when the employer discharges debts incurred by his employee. In *Nicoll v Austin* (1935) a managing director told his employer company that he would have to sell his imposing house where he entertained potential customers because he could no longer afford to pay for its upkeep. To prevent the sale, the company paid the outgoings on the house and the employee was taxed on this sum as if he had been given the money to pay the bills himself.

EXAMPLE 2

(1) Employees are given £14.50 to buy clothes to wear to work. The sum is an emolument (cp *Wilkins v Rogerson* (1961)).
(2) Employees choose clothes and they send the bills to the employer for payment. As the debt has been incurred by the employee tax will be charged in accordance with *Nicoll v Austin* (1935).

b) *Expenses*

If a lower-paid employee receives an 'expense allowance' it will be presumed to be a genuine reimbursement for deductible expenses unless the Revenue can show it to be an emolument. Where an employee incurs expenses which the employer reimburses, those reimbursements will not be taxed as emoluments provided that the employee derives no personal profit from them. Therefore, so long as the repayment matches the expense no tax will be charged even though the original expenses would not have been deductible from the emoluments of the employee under TA 1970 s 189 (see p 64). In *Pook v Owen* (1970) a doctor holding a part-time hospital appointment who had to attend the hospital several times a week was reimbursed two-thirds of his travelling expenses. It was held that the reimbursements were not emoluments because he was no 'better off' as a result of them. They were (partial) repayments of actual expenditure.

Similarly, in *Donnelly v Williamson* (1982) a teacher, who was reimbursed for travelling expenses incurred in attending out-of-school functions, was not taxable on the reimbursements. The court held that they were not emoluments because they were not derived from her employment (she attended the functions voluntarily) and that they were a genuine attempt to compensate her for actual expenditure. Compare *Perrons v Spackman* (1981) where a mileage allowance paid by the council to one of its rent officers was held to be an emolument because it contained a profit element.

Exactly what expenses may be reimbursed is not entirely clear because there is no correlation between the reimbursement rules and the test for deductibility of expenditure under Schedule E. Presumably, the expense must be directly connected with the employment (see also *Hochstrasser v Mayes* (1960) discussed on p 61).

EXAMPLE 3

Justinian, a law lecturer, attends a legal conference in Edinburgh and his University employers refund his expenses. The reimbursements are not emoluments. If the University had instead paid for the conference so that he had received a benefit in kind Justinian would be taxed on it if it was convertible. If Justinian had borne the expenses himself he would have been unable to deduct them from his emoluments under TA 1970 s 189 (see p 61).

3   Higher-paid employees and directors (FA 1976 ss 60–72)

a) *Who is a higher-paid employee or director?*

The relatively lenient rules applicable to lower-paid employees will not be applied to employees falling within FA 1976 ss 60–72 which apply to any employee with emoluments of at least £8,500 pa. To determine whether the employee has emoluments of £8,500, it is assumed that the employee is higher-paid, the appropriate rules for valuing benefits are applied, and only if the resultant figure for emoluments is below £8,500 is he taxed as lower-paid.

EXAMPLE 4

Aziz receives a salary of £8,100 pa and an expense allowance of £400 (which is a benefit in kind for a higher-paid employee). He is treated as receiving emoluments of £8,500 pa and is, therefore, a 'higher-paid employee'.

Sections 60–72 also apply to a director whose emoluments are less than £8,500 pa unless he has no material interest in the company (ie unless he controls less than 5% of the ordinary share capital) *and* either works full-time for the company, or the company is non-profit making or a charity (FA 1976 s 72).

b) *The purpose of the special rules*

The object of the general charging provision of FA 1976 s 61 is to tax all benefits (other than those specifically excluded or charged elsewhere) provided by reason of the employment by any person (not just the employer) to the employee or his family *and whether or not convertible into cash.* Generally, the cost incurred by the employer in providing the benefit is treated as an emolument, subject to a deduction for any payment made by the employee (FA 1976 s 63). In *Rendell v Went* (1964) the managing director of a company had a car accident and was prosecuted at the Old Bailey for dangerous driving. The company paid for the best available legal services for him and he was acquitted. He was taxed on the cost to the company of providing the legal services (a non-convertible benefit in kind) although he did not request the benefit and could have found cheaper services elsewhere.

c) *Operation of the special rules*

When the benefit consists of the use of an asset owned by the employer, the cash equivalent included in the employee's emoluments is the higher of the actual cost to the employer in providing the asset (eg the cost of hiring it) and the 'annual value' of the use of the asset. In the case of land, its annual value is the rent that it might be expected to fetch on a yearly letting and will usually be the rateable value (see TA 1970 s 531). For any other asset, the annual value is 20% of its market (capital) value when it is first put at the employee's disposal (FA 1976 s 63(5)). If assets are given to an employee, the cash equivalent is the market value of the asset at the date of transfer less any sum paid by the employee (FA 1976 s 63(3)). If, however, the employee had previously had the use of the asset, he is taxed on its market value at the date when he first used it less the sum of the annual value(s) on which he has already been taxed (FA 1976 s 63(3A)).

EXAMPLE 5

On 6 April 1983, Mr C Rash was given by his employer the use of a hi-fi system costing £2,000. In October 1985 the employer transferred the system to Mr Rash free of charge when its market value was £800.

Market value at the date when first used by Mr Rash, ie cost	£2,000
*Benefit in kind in 1983–84: 20% × £2,000	£ 400
*Benefit in kind in 1984–85: 20% × £2,000	£ 400
Benefit in kind in 1985–86: £2,000 – £800 (£400 + £400)	£1,200

*If the employer had rented the system at £500 pa, this higher figure would be taxed as an emolument.

If the employee receives an expense allowance he is taxed on it in full as an emolument unless he can claim any allowable expenses under TA 1970 s 189 (see p 64). This forces the employee to justify his expenses.

EXAMPLE 6

Andy has a salary of £9,000 pa and an expense allowance of £4,000 pa. He is taxed on emoluments of £13,000 pa unless he can deduct any expenses under s 189.

d) *Exemptions from the charge*

Certain benefits are exempted from charge under FA 1976 s 61 namely:
(1) The provision of accommodation, supplies or services used by the employee purely in performing his work; for instance, the provision of an office or secretarial services (FA 1976 s 62(3)).
(2) The provision of a pension (or similar benefit) for the employee's family or dependents on his death or retirement (FA 1976 s 62(6)).
(3) The provision of meals in any canteen in which meals are provided for employees generally (FA 1976 s 62(7)). In practice, this provision is generously construed to enable different categories of staff to enjoy separate dining rooms (hence, 'two tier' canteens).
(4) The provision of medical treatment, or insurance against the cost of such treatment, outside the UK where the need for the treatment arises because the employee is performing his job outside the UK (FA 1976 s 62(8)).
    The cost of providing medical insurance within the UK is a taxable benefit for higher-paid employees and directors under FA 1976 s 61.

e) *Specific benefits*

Cars (FA 1976 ss 64, 65): These provisions tax higher-paid employees and directors on the benefit that they derive from a firm or company car which is available for their private use. Tax is not, therefore, charged if the employee can prove that he was forbidden to use the car for private use and did not so use it (*Gilbert v Hemsley* (1981)). A lower-paid employee will not be taxed on this benefit because it is not convertible into cash.

The legislation distinguishes between two categories of car: the pooled car and all others. A pooled car is one which is made available to various employees; is garaged overnight at the employer's premises; and any private use is purely incidental to its business use (FA 1976 s 65). The benefits of using such cars are not taxable.

If a non-pooled car is available for the private use of an employee or his family, he is taxed on a cash equivalent of the car as fixed by statute (FA 1976 s 64 and see the Tables in FA 1976 Sch 7, as amended by statutory instrument. These rates have been increased by about 10% for 1985–86). The cash equivalent depends upon the original market value of the car, its cylinder capacity and its age at the end of the year of assessment.

The tax charge varies according to the degree of business user. If the business use does not exceed 2,500 miles in the relevant year, the cash equivalent is increased by 50%; if the business use exceeds 18,000 miles in the relevant year, the cash equivalent is reduced by 50%.

There is a separate scale charge on the provision of petrol for private use in an employer's car (FA 1976 s 64A). The cash equivalent for 1984–85 is either £375, £480 or £750 depending upon the cylinder capacity and original market value of the car.

The provision of a personal chauffeur for an employee is a taxable benefit under the usual rules of FA 1976 s 61.

The employee is not taxed on any other benefits provided in connection with the car such as insurance and road fund tax (FA 1976 s 62(1)).

Despite these rules, cars remain an enormously valuable 'perk': for instance tax at the highest rate (60%) on the use of a new Rolls Royce by the employee where the business use is minimal is only £1,710 (for 1985–86).

Beneficial loan arrangements (FA 1976 s 66): Interest-free (or cheap) loans to employees are not caught under FA 1976 s 61 because the cost to the employer in providing the loan is nil. Accordingly, s 66 provides that where a higher-paid employee or director obtains a loan by reason of his employment, either interest-free or at a low rate of interest, he is taxed on the cash equivalent of that loan. This is defined as the difference between interest for the year calculated at the official rate (currently 12% pa) and any interest actually paid by the employee.

EXAMPLE 7

Day, a consultant with Digday Ltd, borrows £25,000 in order to purchase a suite of Italian furniture. He pays interest at 2% pa and the capital is to be repaid on demand. For 1984–85 Day has received an emolument equal to:

	£
Interest at official rate: 12% of £25,000	3,000
Less: interest paid at 2% pa	500
Taxable emolument	£2,500

A loan to a relative of the employee is also taxed under FA 1976 s 66 unless the employee can show that he derived no benefit from it.

If a loan to a higher-paid employee or director is released or written off, he is treated as receiving an emolument equivalent to that amount, even if the release is made on the termination of his employment (unless the termination is due to his death); 'golden handshakes' given in the form of the release of a loan will not have the benefit of the £25,000 exemption under TA 1970 s 187 (see p 62) and should, therefore, be avoided.

There is no charge to tax where the cash equivalent of a loan is £200 or less, or where the loan is made for a 'qualifying purpose', ie it is eligible for tax relief under FA 1972 s 75 (see Chapter 4). These exclusions ensure that the two most common loans found in practice, to purchase a dwelling house and to purchase a season ticket to travel to work, are not charged. The employee cannot obtain double tax relief, however, on a loan to purchase a dwelling house.

EXAMPLE 8

Dan, a higher-paid employee, is loaned £25,000 (interest-free) by his employer to enable him to buy a house. He borrows a further £25,000 from the Building Society to finance the purchase.

FA 1976 Sch 8 deems the loans to be made in the order (1) building society loan, (2) employer's loan, thereby ensuring that Dan is taxed at the 'official rate' of interest on £20,000 of the loan under FA 1976 s 66.

Shares (FA 1976 s 67): FA 1976 s 67 extends the loan provisions to catch shares acquired at an undervalue (as defined in s 67(2)). The difference between the sum actually paid and the full market value is treated as a loan.

EXAMPLE 9

Sandy the buying manager of Cosifabrics Ltd is allotted 10,000 £1 shares in the company in 1984. The market value of the shares is £2.25 each, but Sandy only pays 50p per share. Accordingly, the shares are issued partly paid. In 1987 he pays a further 50p per share to the company. The tax position is as follows:

(i) *From 1984 to 1987:* the notional loan per share is £2.25 − 50p = £1.75. This amounts to £17,500 so that interest on that sum at the official rate is treated as an emolument each year.

(ii) *After 1987:* the payment of a further 50p per share reduces the notional loan by £5,000 to £12,500. Henceforth, the official rate of interest on that figure is treated as an emolument.

Generally, the deemed loan remains outstanding until either the employee dies (CTT may then be charged on the shares as part of his estate on death); until the 'loan' is repaid (when liability to income tax will cease); or until the 'loan' is released or the beneficial interest in the shares is transferred (when tax is charged as if the 'loan' were written off). These rules do not apply to the extent that the acquisition of the shares is already taxed as an emolument under other provisions.

Scholarships (FA 1976 s 62A as amended): Scholarship income is exempt from tax (see p 45). However, scholarships awarded to the children of higher-paid employees and directors are taxed as emoluments of the parents unless not more than 25% of the total payments from the fund are to children of employees (whether or not higher-paid or directors) and the award is fortuitous, ie not resulting from the employment.

f) *Returns*

Employers are required to make an annual return in respect of each higher-paid employee and director on IR Form P11D detailing all benefits, including expense allowances, and payments made to that employee. The employer can apply for a blanket dispensation from having to include routine items such as travelling and hotel expenses which need not then be included in Form P11D, nor in the employee's income tax return.

4   Special cases—for all employees

The following benefits, which are not convertible into cash or which would have a low convertible value, are specifically taxed as emoluments under Schedule E for all employees.

a) *Living accommodation* (FA 1977 s 33)

If an employer provides his employee with living accommodation, the employee is taxed under FA 1977 s 33 on the value to him of that accommodation less any sum that he actually pays. The value is the higher of the annual value of the premises (defined in TA 1970 s 531 as the rateable value) and the rent paid by the employer for that accommodation (FA 1977 s 33(2)). As a result, tax under s 33 is frequently on a nominal sum since the annual value bears little relationship to the rent that would be received if the property were actually let, and, if the employer owns the premises, the alternative charge cannot apply.

FA 1983 s 21 amends FA 1977 s 33 for higher-paid employees in cases where the cost of providing the accommodation exceeds £75,000. Broadly, the employee will in such circumstances be charged to tax on an additional emolument calculated by applying the official rate of interest (as under beneficial loans; see FA 1976 s 66; p 53) to the excess by which the actual cost of providing the accommodation exceeds £75,000. That actual cost will usually be the cost of acquiring the property.

EXAMPLE 10

Giles, the managing director of Clam Ltd sells to the company his house in Chelsea for its market value of £150,000. He is granted an option to buy the property back in ten years time for its present value. The annual value of the house is £750 and Giles continues to live in the property. Giles is assessed to tax under Schedule E on an emolument of £750 pa plus 12% of £75,000 (£150,000 − £75,000) ie £9,000 pa.

The charge under FA 1977 s 33 does not catch the provision of ancillary services such as cleaning, heating and lighting unless the employee is higher-paid or a director when tax is charged on the cost to the employer of providing the services (but limited to a maximum of 10% of the emoluments of the employment) less any amount paid by the employee for those services (FA 1976 s 63A).

No charge arises under FA 1977 s 33 for 'representative occupation'. This is defined as occupation which is:
(1) necessary for the proper performance of the employee's duties (eg a caretaker and see *Tennant v Smith* (1891) p 49); or
(2) customary for the better performance of the employee's duties (eg a policeman who occupies a police house adjacent to the police station); or
(3) where there is a special threat to his security and special security arrangements are in force as a result of which he resides in that accommodation.

It should be noted that a director who falls within the provisions of FA 1976 ss 60–72 cannot be a representative occupier under (1) or (2) above.

b) *Vouchers (non-cash and cash) and credit tokens* (F (No 2) A 1975 s 36; FA 1981 ss 70, 71; FA 1982 ss 44, 45)

An employee (or his family) who receives a benefit in the form of a voucher or credit token will be charged to tax under one of various provisions.

Where he receives a non-cash voucher (ie a voucher or similar document, which can be exchanged for goods or services) he is taxed on the cost to the employer of providing the voucher rather than on its exchange value. The same rule applies to a transport voucher (such as season tickets and rail passes) except for lower-paid employees of transport undertakings who are exempted from the charge. Cheque vouchers (ie a cheque provided for an employee to be used by him to obtain goods or services) are similarly charged as emoluments.

Where the employee receives a cash voucher, ie a voucher which can be exchanged for a sum of money not substantially less than the cost to the person providing it, he is taxed on its exchange value.

Where the employee receives a credit token (including a credit card) he is taxed on the cost to the employer in providing the goods, money and services obtained by the use of that credit token (F (No 2) A 1975 s 36A).

5 Conclusions on the treatment of benefits in kind

The present system is neither logical nor fair and presents a bewildering range of alternatives. Consider, for instance, the following:

EXAMPLE 11

Rod wants his computer operator, Julie, to work overtime two evenings per week. Her salary is £4,500 pa. He plans to provide her with meals or a meal allowance on those two evenings. So far as Rod is concerned, the sum that he expends will be a deductible business expense, but for Julie taxation under Schedule E depends upon how the provision is made:

(1) If Rod, the employer, pays a cash allowance, that sum is an emolument.

(2) If Rod pays the bill incurred by Julie, that sum is an emolument (*Nicoll v Austin* (1935) p 49).

(3) If Rod gives Julie a voucher exchangeable at a restaurant, the cost incurred by Rod in providing the voucher is an emolument.

(4) If Julie buys the food herself and is reimbursed, it may be that there is no charge (see *Donnelly v Williamson* (1982); p 50).

(5) If the employer has an arrangement with the restaurant so that food is provided and the expense is directly met by the employer there is no charge (see *Wilkins v Rogerson* (1961); p 49).

V SICK PAY

Sick pay (defined under the Social Security and Housing Benefits Act 1982 s 1) is a taxable emolument for all employees whether paid by the employer, a Friendly Society, an insurance company or a third person if it is paid as a result of arrangements entered into by the employer (FA 1982 s 31). Where an employer runs an insured sick pay scheme to which both employer and employee contribute, the employee is taxed under Schedule E on sums paid to him or his family due to his absence from work because of disability or sickness (FA 1981 s 30) except (by concession) to the extent that the sums reflect contributions made by the employee (these sums will be taxed under Schedule D Case III unless exempted under ESC A26 which excludes from charge payments in the first 12 months of sickness). Maternity payments are also a taxable benefit.

VI SHARE OPTION AND INCENTIVE SCHEMES

Share schemes have been operated by companies in favour of their employees for a number of years. Legislation in 1972 and 1974, which subjected any capital profits to income tax, made the schemes unfashionable, but in 1978, 1980 and 1984 legislation was passed offering relief for approved schemes set up for employees. The main attraction of share schemes is that they bring together the interest of the employee and the company, so long as those shares are held by the employee, since the employee's shareholding is likely to become his most valuable disposable asset after his house.

1 Unapproved schemes

Option and incentive schemes designed purely for the directors or higher-paid employees, fell outside the three approved schemes because they were not open to all employees with the following income tax consequences. First, if shares are allotted to any employee at an undervalue, that undervalue constitutes an emolument, if convertible, (see *Weight v Salmon* (1935)).

Secondly, income tax may be charged on the grant of the option (see FA 1972 s 77) and on any release or assignment of it (TA 1970 s 186) and on the exercise of the option (TA 1970 s 186), with no instalment facility for tax due on the exercise of such options after 5 April 1984.

Arrangements whereby employees receive shares by reason of their employment will normally fall within FA 1972 s 79 which was introduced to prevent companies from issuing low value non-voting shares which could be converted into higher value ordinary shares, thereby giving the employee an untaxed windfall. Generally, s 79 imposes a charge to income tax on any increase in value of the shares between the date when they were acquired and seven years after that date or, if earlier, the date when the shares are disposed of or when any 'restrictions' laid upon them are lifted.

It is now possible for share option schemes benefitting only certain employees to be approved under FA 1984. Even when a scheme is unapproved, or the option is exercised outside the terms of a 1984 approved scheme, an employee will still be left with 40% of the profit after income tax at the highest rate.

2 Schemes approved in 1978, 1980 and 1984

a) *Approved profit sharing schemes* (FA 1978 ss 53–61 and Sch 9 as amended by FA 1982 s 42 and FA 1983 s 25)

Under approved profit sharing schemes all employees may be given shares in the company free from any income tax charge and with only an eventual CGT liability if the shares increase in value and are disposed of.

The schemes involve a company in setting up a trust fund with trustees acquiring shares in the company (either by subscription or purchase) which are then appropriated to individual employees (ie they are held by the trustees for a particular employee). The trustees receive the necessary funds from the company; in practice, the amount set aside by a company may vary according to the company's profitability.

The conditions for approval are complex. A major condition is that the market value of shares appropriated to an employee in any one year must not be less than £1,250 nor more than £5,000, but subject to these limits should be 10% of the employee's salary for the appropriate year (or for the previous year if greater). Further, the shares appropriated must be retained by the trustees for at least two years or until the earlier death or retirement of the employee (through injury, disability, redundancy or because he has reached pensionable age).

No tax charge arises on the appropriation or on any subsequent increase in the value of the shares. After the appropriation any dividends belong to the employee.

Once the two year period has expired, the employee can direct the trustees to sell the shares. No income tax liability arises if the shares are disposed of seven or more years after the appropriation date. If sold within seven years, income tax is payable on the lower of actual sale proceeds and a percentage of the original market value of the shares (ie at the date of appropriation) as follows:

Up to 4 years after appropriation	100%
4–5 years after appropriation	75%
5–6 years after appropriation	50%
6–7 years after appropriation	25%

Where the employment ceases or the employee reaches retirement age within the seven year period, the percentage of the original market value charged is 50% for the first six years and 25% in the seventh year. These schemes are tax-free for employers who can deduct sums paid to such a scheme as a business expense (or an expense of management) for corporation tax, provided that the sums are spent on acquiring the shares within the following nine months or are used to pay the trustees' expenses.

EXAMPLE 12

Eric, an employee, is a basic rate taxpayer to whom trustees appropriate shares when their market value is £1,000. His employer pays corporation tax at 50%.
(1) The company transfers £1,000 to the trust and this sum is then used by the trustees to subscribe for a new issue of shares by the company. The company obtains tax relief of £500 (50% of £1,000) so that the net cost is £500. There is a net inflow of £500 into the company.
(2) When the shares are sold after six and a half years for £2,000 Eric will be subject to income tax of £75 (30% of £250), but there is unlikely to be any CGT liability because of Eric's annual exemption.

The company has, therefore, incurred a net cost of £500 and the employee has received £1,925 (£2,000 – £75).

b) *Approved savings-related share option schemes* (FA 1980 s 47)

A share option scheme which is genuinely open to all employees may be approved under FA 1980 s 47 (for the detailed conditions for approval see FA 1980 Sch 10). Ordinary shares have to be acquired from the proceeds of SAYE savings contracts to which the maximum monthly contribution by an employee is currently £100. The price of the shares must be fixed at the time when the employee is granted the option and must not be less than 90% of the value of the shares at that time. Provided that the option is not exercisable or not exercised within three years of its acquisition (normally it will be exercisable when the SAYE contract matures at the end of five years) the employee is exempt from any charge to income tax (under TA 1970 s 186 or FA 1972 s 77) on the grant or exercise of the option. It is a condition of approval that the option rights cannot be transferred.

c) *Approved share option schemes* (FA 1984 s 38 and Sch 10)

FA 1984 introduced a new type of approved share option scheme not linked to savings under SAYE. If the scheme (including an existing unapproved scheme which either satisfies the necessary conditions or incorporates them) is approved, there is no income tax charged on the exercise of an option to acquire ordinary shares in the employer company where that option is granted after 5 April 1984. The only charge is to CGT if and when the shares are sold. There are detailed conditions for approval (see Sch 10), in particular: first, the price charged for the shares must not be less than their market value at the date when the option was granted; secondly, the scheme must be restricted to employees and full-time directors, save that employees who exercise the option after they have left full-time employment and their PRs (who exercise the option within one year of death) may be included; thirdly, the option must be exercisable after three but within ten years of its grant; and finally, the aggregate market value (generally at the time of the grant) of the total shares available per employee must not exceed the greater of £100,000 and four times his current or previous year's salary (or, in the absence of a preceding year salary, his annual salary).

It should be stressed that these schemes may be selective and that part-time employees may be included (eligibility depends upon working a minimum of 20 hours per week). Directors and employees of a close company who hold or within the previous year have held more than 10% of the company's ordinary share capital are not, however, eligible. Finally, notice that an option may be validly exercised outside the conditions of the scheme but subject to the income tax charge (1 above).

VII PROBLEM CASES

The fact that a payment made to an employee is connected with his employment does not automatically render it an emolument taxable under Schedule E. To be chargeable, it must be a reward for services. Three types of payment cause particular problems: gifts; contractual benefits unconnected with the services performed; and payments made on or after the termination of the employment. In all cases, whether the payment is chargeable must be considered from the position of the recipient regardless of whether it is tax-deductible by the payer.

1 Gifts

There is a basic distinction between a payment which is a reward for services and which is, therefore, taxable and one which is made in appreciation of an individual's personal qualities, which is not taxable.

Various factors are relevant in drawing this distinction. First, whether the payment is made once only or whether it is recurring (in the former case it is more likely to escape tax). Secondly, whether it is made to only one employee or to a whole class of employees. In *Laidler v Perry* (1966), for instance, all the employees received a £10 voucher at Christmas instead of the turkey that they had received in previous years. The employees were taxed on the cash value of the voucher. Thirdly, if the payment is by the employer there is a strong presumption that it is an emolument, whereas if it is from a third party, it is easier to show that it is a gift for personal qualities. However, tips are generally regarded as being in return for services and so taxable, even though made voluntarily by someone other than the employer. In *Calvert v Wainwright* (1947), a taxi driver was taxable on tips received from customers although the court suggested that a particularly generous tip from a special customer (at, eg Christmas) might escape tax (see also *Blakiston v Cooper* (1909)). Fourthly, a payment to which the employee is entitled under the terms of his contract of employment will be taxable as a part of his emoluments.

EXAMPLE 13

(1) Ham has played cricket for Gloucestershire for many years. At the end of his distinguished career the county grants him a benefit match (ie he is entitled to all the receipts from a particular game). The benefit is a tax-free testimonial paid for Ham's personal qualities (see *Seymour v Reed* (1927)). Compare:

(2) Mercenary plays as a professional in the Lancashire League and under the terms of his contract is entitled to have the 'hat passed round' (ie a collection taken) every time he scores 50 runs or takes 5 wickets in an innings. The sums that he receives will be taxed as emoluments because he is entitled to them in his contract of employment (see *Moorhouse v Dooland* (1955)).

Finally, it should be noted that the gift rules overlap with the benefit in kind rules. In deciding whether tax is chargeable under Schedule E, the gift rules should be applied first and then the benefit in kind rules.

EXAMPLE 14

Free Range Ltd gives all its employees a 25lb turkey at Christmas. In deciding whether tax is charged, (i) apply the gift rules (ie is the turkey given in return for services or is it for personal qualities?); then (ii) apply the benefit in kind rules (ie is the turkey convertible into money, in the case of lower-paid employees, or caught by FA 1976, in the case of higher-paid employees and directors). If it is decided that the benefit is a gift, no tax is charged. If it is decided that it is in return for services, tax may be charged in accordance with the benefit in kind rules. It is likely in this example that tax would be chargeable.

2   Signing-on fees and the reimbursement of expenditure or losses

Payments made to compensate the taxpayer for some sacrifice that he has made by taking up an employment are generally not taxable because they are not in return for services. In *Jarrold v Boustead* (1964) an international rugby union player was not taxable on a £3,000 signing-on fee paid to him when he turned professional. The payment was not an emolument, but was to compensate him for permanent loss of his amateur status.

The same principle was applied in *Pritchard v Arundale* (1971) where a chartered accountant was not taxed on a large shareholding transferred to him in return for signing a service contract as managing director of the company. The benefit was held to accrue to him, not for future services as managing director which were to be adequately rewarded, but as compensation for loss of his professional status as a chartered accountant. It may also be noted that the shares were to be transferred in return for the taxpayer's signing the service contract. Hence, even if he had died without performing any services for the company, the shares would have been transferable to his estate. Further, they were given by a third party not by the new employer (see also *Vaughan Neil v IRC* (1979); p 61).

Two features of these cases are, first, that the payment was compensation for a permanent loss to the taxpayer; if the loss is merely restricted to the period of the contract the payment is more likely to be viewed as advance remuneration. Secondly, the taxpayer was fully rewarded for his services under the contract. Therefore, the payments in the following example would probably be taxable.

EXAMPLE 15

(1) Josh who has been unemployed for 10 years agrees to work for Workplan Ltd and is paid a £10,000 'signing-on fee' for giving up his life of leisure on the dole.
(2) Jason agrees to work for Workplan Ltd for 5 years at a salary of £100 pa but with a 'signing-on' fee of £60,000.

In *Glantre Engineering Ltd v Goodhand* (1983) an inducement payment made to a chartered accountant was held to be an emolument as the taxpayer failed to show that he had provided consideration in return for the payment since he was merely moving from one Schedule E employment to another. Once the taxpayer fails to show that he has been permanently deprived of something akin to amateur status or the status of being a partner, it must follow that the payment is a reward for future services in the new employment.

The rule that compensation for loss caused to the employee escapes tax is not limited to signing-on fees. In *Hochstrasser v Mayes* (1960), ICI paid compensation to married (lower-paid) employees who suffered a loss on having to move house because of a re-location of their jobs. The compensation was not taxable as a reward for services. It may be that compensation paid for a personal loss suffered by an employee will be non-taxable provided that the employer benefits.

EXAMPLE 16

Num Ltd pays its employee, Sid, £1,000 to compensate him for the anguish he suffers as a result of his wife running off with the milkman. The company may argue that the payment is necessary and, therefore, a deductible expense of the company, because otherwise Sid may suffer a mental and physical collapse. Further, the payment may be non-taxable in Sid's hands as compensation for his suffering rather than a reward for services.

3 Payments for entering into restrictive covenants (TA 1970 s 34)

TA 1970 s 34 provides that if an employer pays money to an employee in return for an undertaking by the employee to restrict his activities before, during, or after his employment, the sum paid is charged under Schedule E, but only to excess liability. It is treated in the employee's hands as a sum net of basic rate tax so that it must be grossed up to calculate his liability (if any) to higher rate tax.

EXAMPLE 17

Ararat Ltd pays an employee, Thomas, £14,000 which is caught by TA 1970 s 34. Thomas must gross up the £14,000 to £20,000 (ie £14,000 × 100/70) and add it to his total income for the year of receipt. He must pay any higher rate tax due on that sum (treated as the top slice of his income) but receives a credit for the basic rate, ie £6,000 (£20,000 − £14,000).

Note that if the employee is not liable to basic rate tax he cannot claim a repayment of the basic rate tax.

The limitations of s 34 are illustrated by *Vaughan Neil v IRC* (1979). The payment of £40,000 to a barrister to induce him to leave the planning bar and work for a company was not taxed. It was not a reward for services, being in effect a compensation payment (see *Pritchard v Arundale*, p 60), nor was it caught by s 34 because the barrister had given no undertaking to the company not to practise at the bar. His inability to do so was not caused by accepting the particular terms of employment, but rather by accepting the employment itself; the payment was merely recognition that the job would prevent his practising at the bar. Finally, notice that s 34 could apply to a payment given at any time before or during, as well as on termination of, the employment.

For the employer, a payment for a restrictive covenant will usually be treated as a capital payment (since it brings into existence an enduring asset: the benefit of the covenant) and will not be deductible in arriving at his income profits (see *APC v Kerr* (1946); p 83).

4   Payments after the termination of employment

a) *General*

Certain lump sum payments made to the holder of an office or employment on its termination are taxable in full under Schedule E as a reward for services past, present or future. For instance, a deferred payment for services is spread back and taxed as the emoluments of the years when it was earned. In *Heasman v Jordan* (1954) a non-contractual bonus payment at the end of the Second World War for overtime during the war was spread back over the years of work.

A sum paid for the variation of a continuing contract of employment is prima facie taxable as a payment in anticipation of future services under the varied contract. In *Cameron v Prendergast* (1940), a payment of £45,000 made to a director to persuade him not to retire, but to continue working on reduced hours and for a reduced salary was held to be advance remuneration. (See also *Holland v Geoghegan* (1972): compensation for dustmen's loss of totting rights taxed as advance remuneration.)

Any payment made under a contractual obligation will be taxed in full, even though it is paid because of the termination of the employment. In *Dale v de Soissons* (1960) (followed in *Williams v Simmonds* (1981)), a director's service agreement provided for him to be paid £10,000 if it should be prematurely terminated. The taxpayer argued that the payment was not in return for services. It was held, however, that, as the payment was one to which he was contractually entitled, it was an emolument. In view of the generous taxation of non-contractual payments on a termination of employment (below), it is advisable to omit such compensation clauses from contracts of employment.

b) *Compensation for loss of office* (TA 1970 ss 187, 188)

Lump sum payments, not falling within the above categories, formerly escaped tax as the sum was not a reward for services ('golden handshakes').

TA 1970 s 187, however, applies a special scheme of taxation to 'any payment (not otherwise chargeable to tax) in connection with the termination of the holding of an office or employment or any change in its functions or emoluments'. This extremely wide section includes payments made by a person other than the employer to someone other than the employee (eg to his spouse or PRs). It also catches payments in kind, eg, the receipt by a dismissed employee of a company car as compensation.

Accordingly, s 187 catches golden handshakes, compensation and damages for wrongful dismissal and redundancy payments. The first £25,000 of any payments within s 187 is exempt from tax.

Redundancy payments can only be taxed under s 187 and not under the usual Schedule E rules (TA 1970 s 412), although tax is unlikely to arise because the payments will usually come within the exempt £25,000 limit. The Revenue have issued a Statement of Practice indicating what they regard as a genuine redundancy payment which qualifies for the £25,000 exemption (see SP 1/81).

Section 187 does not apply (TA 1970 s 188 and Sch 8) to:

(a) payments otherwise chargeable to tax under Schedule E (hence to payments caught by *Dale v de Soissons*);
(b) payments charged to higher rate tax under TA 1970 s 34 (p 61);
(c) benefits received under approved retirement pension schemes (or un-approved schemes, if the employee was taxed on his contributions);
(d) payments because of death or disability; and
(e) certain payments for foreign service.

Payments caught by s 187 are taxed as follows:

Step 1 The first £25,000 of the payment is tax-free.

Step 2 The next £25,000 is taxed at 50% of the taxpayer's marginal tax rate on that taxable slice (ie the tax is reduced by one-half). Hence, the tax on the £25,000 will be one-half of the difference between:

(a) the amount of tax payable if the £25,000 is not included as income, and

(b) tax payable if the £25,000 is included as income.

Step 3 The next £25,000 is taxed at 75% of the taxpayer's marginal tax rate on that taxable slice (ie the tax is reduced by one-quarter).

Step 4 Any excess over £75,000 is taxed in full.

EXAMPLE 18

During the year A (a married man) has the following income:

Earnings from employment	£25,000
Other income	nil
Lump sum on termination of employment	£80,000
Personal allowances	£3,155

Tax payable disregarding the terminal payment:

Taxable income: £25,000 – £3,155   =   £21,845

Tax payable:	£
£15,400 at 30%	4,620
£ 2,800 at 40%	1,120
£ 3,645 at 45%	1,640.20
	£7,380.20

Tax payable including the terminal payment:

(i) Calculate taxable slice: £80,000 – £25,000 exempt = £55,000

(ii) Calculate tax at marginal rate on first £25,000 of taxable slice and reduce it by one-half:

	£
£1,255 at 45%	564.75
£7,500 at 50%	3,750
£7,500 at 55%	4,125
£8,745 at 60%	5,247
	£13,686.75

Relief is £13,686.75 ÷ 2 = £6,843.38

Therefore, tax payable is £13,686.75 – £6,843.38 = £6,843.38.

(iii) Calculate tax at marginal rate (now 60%) on next £25,000 of taxable slice and reduce it by one-quarter:

	£
£25,000 at 60%	15,000
Relief is £15,000 ÷ 4	3,750
Therefore, tax payable is £15,000 – £3,750	£11,250

(iv) Remaining £5,000 taxed in full with no relief:

£5,000 at 60%	£3,000

Final liability is:

Tax on termination payment	
£6,843.38 + £11,250 + £3,000	£21,093.38
Tax on other income	£7,380.20
	£28,473.58

Terminal payments caught by TA 1970 s 187 are treated as earned income from which tax at the basic rate must be deducted under PAYE in the year when the job is lost (not the year when the money is paid in cases when the two are different). (For the relationship between s 187 and the 'Gourley principle', see Appendix I.)

VIII   DEDUCTIBLE EXPENSES (TA 1970 s 189)

Tax under Schedule E is charged on emoluments after deducting allowable expenditure. Allowable expenditure is defined in TA 1970 s 189 which draws a distinction between travelling and other expenses.

1   Expenses other than travelling expenses

Expenses will be deductible only if incurred '. . . wholly exclusively and necessarily in the performance of the said duties . . .'. These provisions may be contrasted with the more generous expenditure rules of Schedule D Cases I and II (see Chapter 6).

Three requirements must be satisfied if an expense is to be deductible: first, it must be incurred 'in performing' the duties. No deduction is allowed for expenses which enable the employee to prepare for his duties or to be better equipped to carry them out. In *Shortt v McIlgorm* (1945), for instance, the taxpayer could not deduct the fee that he paid to an employment agency. (See also *Simpson v Tate* (1952) where a medical officer could not deduct the cost of joining learned societies which would enable him to perform his duties better and note the partial reversal of this decision by TA 1970 s 192.) Secondly, the expense must be 'necessarily' incurred in the performance of the duties. This is an objective test; therefore, to satisfy it, every employee in the particular job would need to incur the expenditure. Nor is it sufficient that the employer requires the expenditure; the nature of the duties must require it.

In *Brown v Bullock* (1961) a bank manager was required by his employer to join a London club. He could not deduct his subscription because it was not necessary for the performance of his duties. It seems odd that the employer is not allowed to decide what is necessary to the particular office or employment!

The third requirement is that the expense should be incurred 'wholly and exclusively' in the performance of the duties. This same requirement is found in Schedule D Cases I and II and the meaning of these words is discussed in Chapter 6.

Few expenses will satisfy all three conditions. However, the harshness of TA 1970 s 189 is, in practice, mitigated in relation to various employments by a number of Revenue concessions (for instance, the flat rate allowance for the cost of tools and special clothing: ESC A1).

2   Travelling expenses

If travelling expenses are to be deductible they must be 'necessarily' incurred 'in the performance' of the duties (or be 'expenses of keeping or maintaining a horse to perform the same . . .'). There is no 'wholly and exclusively' requirement. The expense of travelling to work is not, therefore, deductible because it is incurred before, rather than in the performance of, the duties. In contrast, travelling between places of work is deductible.

EXAMPLE 19

(1) Sally is employed as a lecturer by the Midtech Poly and gives seminars at both the branches of the Poly which are two miles apart. Her travelling costs between both branches are deductible.

(2) Jim works as a postman and as a barman in a local pub. The cost of travelling between the sorting office and the pub is not deductible.

The requirement that travelling expenditure be 'necessarily incurred' has been considered in three House of Lords cases. In *Ricketts v Colquhoun* (1926) the travelling expenses of a barrister to and from Portsmouth where he had been appointed Recorder were not deductible. In *Pook v Owen* (1970), a general medical practitioner was allowed to deduct the expenses of travelling to a hospital where he held a part-time appointment, because some of the functions of that post were performed at his home so that he was travelling between two centres of work. Finally, in *Taylor v Provan* (1974) a Canadian director of Bass Charrington was allowed to deduct his travelling expenses to the UK, again, because he performed part of his duties at places outside the UK. What emerges from these cases is that travelling expenses for getting to work will not be deductible. Further, a job will not be treated as having two centres just because the taxpayer chooses to perform some of its functions at his home. Just how far an employment can be tailored to the particular personal circumstances of the employee is slightly unclear after *Taylor v Provan*, although it should be stressed that the qualities of that particular taxpayer were quite unique!

Travelling expenses raise two further problems. First, allowable expenditure has to be reasonable. In *Marsden v IRC* (1965) an Inland Revenue investigator could not deduct the full cost of travelling by car to perform his duties because he could have used a cheaper form of transport. This is not to say that the cheapest form must always be used, since the matter is one of fact and degree and allowance must be made for the inconvenience of certain forms of transport and for the dignity of the employee or office holder. Presumably, a company director will not be consigned to the local bus service! Secondly, the relationship between the rules for deductibility of expenditure and the taxation of reimbursements should be carefully noted (see p 50). In the case of higher-paid employees and directors such reimbursements are automatically treated as emoluments (FA 1976 s 60).

IX   METHOD OF ASSESSMENT: PAYE

Tax is charged under Schedule E on a current year basis usually in the year of payment (but see *Heasman v Jordan* (1954) p 62). It is collected by a sophisticated method of deduction at source operated by the employer and known as the PAYE system. The system generally applies to all income assessable under Schedule E except where the employer is non-resident, when the Revenue assess the employee directly. It must be applied by any employer who pays an employee more than £34 per week or £149 per month.

For directors and higher-paid employees, the employer must also complete Form P11D giving details of benefits in kind and payments by way of expenses (save, in the latter case, those for which a dispensation has been granted).

Before 1975, workers supplied through agencies who were generally self-employed could escape tax on earnings on a particular assignment by disappearing once it was completed. Accordingly, F(No 2)A 1975 s 38,

"Tax having been deducted at source, your net emoluments amount to two pieces of silver."

provides that where a worker receives remuneration under a contract with an agency to render personal services under supervision to a client he is taxable under Schedule E with the agency operating **PAYE**.

Certain workers (such as entertainers) are excluded from the operation of s 38 (s 38(5)) and special rules also apply to self-employed persons working in the construction industry. Tax must be deducted by the contractor unless the sub-contractor has a tax certificate (see IR 40).

PAYE is an extremely effective tax collector which reduces both the opportunity and the incentive for tax evasion. It can also be used to collect underpayments of tax in previous years by reducing or withholding completely allowances in the current year. In the event of an overpayment of tax in a previous year, this will be corrected either by direct repayment or by set-off against other tax liabilities of that year.

In an attempt to ensure that remuneration paid to directors is subject to deduction of tax at source, FA 1976 s 66A deals with the situation where a gross sum is paid to the director and the tax thereon is accounted for to the Revenue by a person other than the director. In such cases, unless the director makes good the sum overpaid, he shall be treated as receiving a further emolument equal to the amount of tax that has been accounted for to the Revenue. This provision applies to directors falling within the provisions of FA 1976 ss 60–72.

X   PENSIONS

1   Introduction

The provision of financial security in old age is a major concern not only for the employee and his dependents, but also for the state. The state discharges its duty in this area by providing a statutory pension scheme which is available to all who make National Insurance Contributions (mainly employees).

However, occupational pension schemes (private schemes provided by an employer for his employees) have become increasingly important and represent a significant (albeit hidden) part of an employee's remuneration, quite apart from providing better benefits than the state scheme. How these private schemes are set up and managed involves a highly complex area of law that is outside the scope of this book. The aim of this section is to outline the tax advantages of the private scheme in comparison with the state scheme.

A pension is treated as earned income in the hands of the employee and is taxed under Schedule E unless it is paid by a non-UK resident in which case it is taxed under Schedule D Case V (TA 1970 s 182). Pensions paid as a result of death on active service are exempt from income tax (F(No 2)A 1979 s 9).

2 The state scheme

The state scheme is funded by national insurance contributions from both employer and employee and is in two parts: the first part from which employers cannot contract out is the flat rate pension, payable from the age of 65 for males, 60 for females who have contributed to it for 9/10ths of their working lives. The second part is an earnings-related pension, which, is an additional pension related to individual employees' earnings and which employers may 'contract out' of by providing an appropriate private scheme. The main disadvantages of the state scheme are that:

(1) The retirement age is not flexible, but is restricted to 65 for a man and 60 for a woman.
(2) Although the employer's contributions are not taxed as the emoluments of the employee (FA 1970 s 24), there is no income tax relief for the employee's own contributions.
(3) For the tax year 1984–85, earnings above £12,999.96 are unpensionable.

3 Private occupational pension schemes (FA 1970 ss 19–26)

Private schemes can be 'contracted-out' of the second tier of the state scheme. National insurance contribution payments are reduced and payments are instead made to the private scheme. Contracting out is a complicated process, but, basically, the private scheme must be approved by the Occupational Pensions Board and, if it is to enjoy tax advantages, by the Revenue's Superannuation Fund Office.

Private schemes are funded by contributions from employer and employee. The fund is generally administered by trustees who are responsible for making the investments and paying the pensions. Alternatively, responsibility for providing the pensions may be passed to an insurance company which receives premiums in the form of employer/employee contributions.

All such 'retirement benefit schemes' (schemes for the provision of 'relevant benefits') are governed for tax purposes by a code introduced in FA 1970. The term 'relevant benefits' is widely defined to cover virtually any kind of payment to an employee or his widow, children or dependants generally in connection with retirement or death (FA 1970 s 25). Most private schemes will be governed by this code, but only if the scheme is 'exempt approved' within the meaning of FA 1970, will it enjoy all the following tax advantages:

(1) The employer's contributions will not be taxed as the employee's income. (The same is true for contributions to the state scheme or by a foreign government for its employees in the UK; or where the contributions are for a non-UK resident working wholly abroad).

(2) The employer's contributions are deductible from his profits as a business expense.
(3) The employee obtains income tax relief on his own contributions (through PAYE).
(4) The pension fund is not charged to income tax on the investments (except any income from commercial trading), nor to CGT on any disposal of investments.
(5) Any payments made to the employee's dependants on his death will not be charged to CTT provided that they are made at the trustees' discretion and not as of right (in practice, an employee may make a 'declaration of wish' as to whom he would like to benefit on his death, and the trustees pay attention to this when exercising their discretion).

4 Meaning of 'exempt approved'

If the retirement benefits scheme satisfies the requirements in FA 1970 ss 19(2) and 19(2A) it must be approved. These requirements are narrow and under FA 1970 s 20 the Revenue have a wide discretion to approve schemes which do not satisfy all the requirements (see IR 12 'Practice Notes'). Detailed study of ss 19(2) and 19(2A) and IR 12 is advised, but the main conditions which the scheme must meet relate to who can benefit; who administers the scheme; the levels of contributions; the minimum and maximum benefits payable; and specification of retirement age.

Besides being approved, a private scheme must be exempt if it is to receive all the above tax benefits. This requires the scheme to be established under 'irrevocable trusts'; ie it must be of a permanent nature so that it cannot be interfered with by the employer. Most schemes will be set up formally with a trust deed and a set of rules.

5 Personal pension schemes

An employee who cannot take advantage of an occupational pension scheme, or the earnings-related state scheme, should make his own pension arrangements in the same way as must the self-employed. This will usually take the form of an approved retirement annuity scheme under TA 1970 s 226 which will afford him some tax relief (see Chapter 29). Generally these schemes compare badly with occupational pension schemes because they enjoy fewer tax advantages; there are no employer's contributions and the benefits payable are less generous, being calculated by reference to the one individual concerned and not by reference to all the contributions in a fund.

6 Schedule D—trades and professions

'. . . take a gang of burglars. Are they engaged in trade or an adventure in the nature of trade? They have an organisation. They spend money on equipment. They acquire goods by their efforts. They sell the goods. They make a profit. What detail is lacking in their adventure? You may say it lacks legality, but it has been held that legality is not an essential characteristic of a trade. You cannot point to any detail that it lacks. But still it is not a trade, nor an adventure in the nature of trade. And how does it help to ask the question: If it is not a trade, what is it? It is burglary and that is all there is to say about it'. (Lord Denning in *Griffiths v Harrison* (1963))

I INTRODUCTION

Tax is charged under Schedule D Case I on the annual profits or gains arising to a UK resident from a trade carried on in the UK or elsewhere and under Case II from a profession or vocation (TA 1970 ss 108, 109). These cases, therefore, charge the self-employed and apply equally to sole traders, trading partnerships, sole practitioners, and professional partnerships. (For partnerships see Chapter 29.) Generally, the same principles operate under both Case I and Case II so that the two Cases may be treated together. The following differences should, however, be noted:

(1) An isolated transaction may be a trade (under Case I), but it can never be the exercise of a profession or vocation (under Case II), and so may attract income tax only under Schedule D Case VI (Chapter 9).

(2) Certain capital allowances are available only to traders (see Chapter 7).

(3) The rule in *Sharkey v Wernher* (p 81) applies only to traders.

(4) Damages or compensation obtained for any wrong or injury suffered by an individual in his profession or vocation are not chargeable gains (CGTA 1979 s 19(5)).

In most cases it will be clear whether the taxpayer is self-employed or whether he is an employee holding a post or office under Schedule E (but see p 47).

II WHAT IS A TRADE?

1 The problems involved

'Trade' is not defined. According to TA 1970 s 526(5) it 'includes every trade, manufacture, adventure, or concern in the nature of a trade'. This provision, although unhelpful, indicates that a single adventure may constitute a trade (see eg *Martin v Lowry* (1927) below). In *Ransom v Higgs* (1974) Lord Wilberforce considered that a trading transaction would usually exhibit the following features:

> 'Trade normally involves the change of goods or services for reward . . . there must be something which the trade offers to provide by way of business. Trade moreover presupposes a customer'. ([1974] 3 All ER at 964)

In the absence of a satisfactory statutory definition the meaning of trade must be sought from the voluminous case law in this area. The Final Report of the Royal Commission on the Taxation of Profits and Income (1955: CMD 9474) concluded that there would be no single test but suggested certain objective tests 'the badges of trade'.

Before considering these 'badges of trade', two general matters should be noted in connection with the case law. First, when the case is concerned with whether a taxpayer carried on a trade or not, caution needs to be exercised in citing it as precedent since the findings of the commissioners are decisions of fact which will rarely be overturned on appeal (see *Edwards v Bairstow and Harrison* (1956): p 9). The appeal court is often and reluctanty forced to conclude that facts exist to justify the findings of the commissioners. Secondly, before the introduction of CGT in 1965, the question whether or not a person had engaged in a trade was of fundamental significance. If he had, any profit was charged under Case I; if not income tax was inapplicable so that the resultant (capital) profit escaped tax altogether. Since 1965 the choice is not between a charge under Case I and no tax, but, normally, is between paying income tax and CGT or, for companies, corporation tax on their income and capital profits.

2   The 'badges of trade'

The Royal Commission identified six 'badges' designed to determine whether or not the purchase and resale of property is a trading transaction.

The subject matter of the transaction   Property which neither yields an income nor gives personal enjoyment to its owner is likely to form the subject matter of a trading transaction. Other property (typically land, works of art, and shares) may be acquired for the income and/or enjoyment which it provides.

In *Rutledge v IRC* (1929), the taxpayer was a businessman connected with the film industry. Whilst in Berlin he purchased one million toilet rolls for £1,000 which he resold in the UK for about £11,000 profit. The Court of Session held that the taxpayer had engaged in an adventure in the nature of a trade so that the profits were assessable under Case I. They stressed that such quantity of goods must have been intended for resale. Similarly, in *Martin v Lowry* (1927) the gigantic speculation involved in purchasing and reselling forty four million yards of government surplus aeroplane linen, at a profit of £1,600,000 amounted to a trade largely because of the nature of the subject matter and the commercial methods employed to sell it.

The purchase and resale of land inevitably causes more difficulty since owning land in quantity does not raise a presumption that trading is intended. In *IRC v Reinhold* (1953), for instance, despite the taxpayer having bought four houses over two years admittedly for sale, the Court of Session concluded that 'heritable property is not an uncommon subject of investment' and that the taxpayer was not trading. The result may be seen as a borderline decision and should be contrasted with *Cooke v Haddock* (1960).

Similar difficulties arose in *Taylor v Good* (1974) where the taxpayer was held not to be trading when he resold at a vast profit, because of planning permission, a house which he had purchased with the original intention of living there. The Court of Appeal took the view that a person intending to resell property is entitled to take steps to ensure that he obtains the best possible price for it! (Today that profit would be subject to CGT.)

Length of ownership This is a weak 'badge' because the presumption that, if property is sold within a short time of acquisition, the taxpayer has traded will often be rebutted on the facts.

Frequency of similar transactions Repeated transactions in the same subject matter point to a trade. Since a single adventure may amount to a trade this 'badge' will be applicable only in circumstances where that would not otherwise be the case. In *Pickford v Quirke* (1927) the court held that although a single purchase and resale by a syndicate of four cotton mills did not amount to trading, the series viewed as a whole did. Hence, subsequent transactions may trigger a Case I liability on earlier transactions (see *Leach v Pogson* (1962) in which the founding and subsequent sale of 30 driving schools consecutively, was held to be trading).

Work done on the property When work is done to the property in order to make it more marketable, or when an organisation is set up to sell the asset, there is some evidence of trading (see *Martin v Lowry* (1927): compare *Taylor v Good* (1974)). In *Cape Brandy Syndicate v IRC* (1921) three individuals engaged in the wine trade who formed a syndicate and purchased some 3,000 casks of Cape brandy which they blended (with French brandy), recasked, and sold in lots over an 18 month period were held to be trading.

Circumstances responsible for the realisation A forced sale to raise cash for an emergency raises a presumption that the transaction is not a trade. Sales by executors in the course of winding up the deceased's estate and by liquidators and receivers in the administration of an insolvent company will often fall into this category (see *Cohan's Executors v IRC* (1924) and *IRC v The 'Old Bushmills' Distillery Co Ltd* (1927) and p 72).

Motive If the transaction was undertaken in order to realise a profit, that is some evidence of trading. The absence of a profit motive does not prevent a commercial operation from amounting to a trade, however, (see, for instance, dividend stripping; Chapter 32) and, conversely, the mere fact that an asset is purchased with the intention of ultimate resale at a profit will not of itself lead to a finding of trading. Often the subject matter involved will be decisive. In *Wisdom v Chamberlain* (1968) the taxpayer who bought £200,000 of silver bullion as a 'hedge' against an expected devaluation of sterling and three months later sold it realising a profit of £50,000 was held to be trading. His claim that he had made no profit, but rather that the pound had fallen in value, was rejected.

3 Mutual trading

No man can trade with himself (but see the rule in *Sharkey v Wernher* p 81). Thus, when persons join together in an association and jointly contribute to a common fund for their mutual benefit, any surplus received by the members on a division of that fund is tax-free. (See *New York Life Insurance Company v Styles* (1889).)

If the association trades with non-members, however, the profits attributable to that activity are taxable. In *Carlisle & Silloth Golf Club v Smith* (1913), fees paid by visitors for the use of the club facilities were held to be trading receipts. TA 1970 s 347 prevents the mutual trading doctrine from being used to avoid tax, by imposing a charge on the return of surplus assets in circumstances when the original contributions were tax deductible.

4 Trading after a discontinuance

The mere realisation of assets after the permanent discontinuance of the business is not trading. Hence, in *IRC v Nelson* (1938) income tax under Case I was not charged when a whisky broker, who because of ill health had closed his business, sold the entire business including the stock in trade. By contrast, a sale of stock with a view to the cessation of trading (a 'closing-down sale') is chargeable because the trade is still continuing (see *J & R O'Kane & Co Ltd v IRC* (1922)). Special rules operate for the valuation of trading stock held at the date of cessation of a business (TA 1970 s 137, see p 80).

III MEANING OF 'PROFESSION' AND 'VOCATION'

In common with 'trade', neither 'profession' nor 'vocation' are statutorily defined. 'Profession' has been judicially described as involving 'the idea of an occupation requiring either purely intellectual skill or manual skill controlled by the intellectual skill of the operator' (see Scrutton LJ in *IRC v Maxse* (1919)). This definition can be misleading, because a person exercising an occupation in those terms (such as a solicitor) may, as a question of fact, be an employee assessable under Schedule E (see Chapter 5). As already mentioned, a profession is unlike a trade in that it involves an element of continuity. Hence, casual profits and fees arising from an isolated transaction are taxed under Schedule D Case VI.

'Vocation' has been judicially defined by Denman J in *Partridge v Mallandaine* (1886) as '. . . the way in which a man passes his life'. This definition is somewhat unhelpful, but the term embraces self-employed bookmakers, jockeys, authors and photographers.

IV COMPUTATION OF PROFITS

1 The accounts

Tax under Cases I and II is on the 'annual profits of the trade, profession or vocation' (TA 1970 s 108). 'Annual' in this context means of an income, as opposed to of a recurring nature (*Martin v Lowry* (1927)). From the profit and loss account income profits are calculated as income receipts less income expenditure. For instance, a trader whose income receipts are £40,000 and income expenses £25,000 has income profits of £15,000 (£40,000 − £25,000).

The taxpayer's profits as shown in his accounts must be agreed for tax purposes with the inspector of taxes. Accounts prepared for commercial purposes and according to standard accountancy practice will rarely show the taxable profits. Some items which have been deducted in the accounts may not be deductible for income tax purposes (such as entertainment expenses: see p 85). Other items are treated differently for taxation purposes: expenditure on a capital asset, for instance, is written off annually over the life of the asset as depreciation under standard accounting practice but is only deductible for income tax purposes if it falls within the system of capital allowances (see Chapter 7). As a result the taxpayer's accounts must be adjusted by adding back deductions which are not allowable and, where appropriate, by making permitted deductions (such as capital allowances).

2 The different bases

In drawing up accounts for taxation purposes, the taxpayer must use one of three bases: the earnings; the cash; or the bills delivered (the cash and bills delivered bases are known as the 'conventional' bases).

"Not the 'Yet-another-record-breaking-year' set, you fool! I want the 'Just-about-keeping-our-heads-above-water' figures!"

a) *The earnings basis*

Profits are calculated by deducting the expenses incurred during the accounting period from the income earned during that period. It is irrelevant whether the expenses have been paid or the income received. If accounts are rendered on this basis stock-in-trade and work-in-progress must be valued (for the rules governing the valuation of trading stock see p 78).

EXAMPLE 1

Jasper runs a bookshop in Covent Garden. He makes up his accounts each year to 31 December. For the year ending in 1984 his sales of books amount to £25,000, although he has not received payment from a valued customer, Leo, for a set of

Dickens (sold for £5,000); nor from the Astery Gallery for a set of art books sold for £3,500. His expenditure incurred during the year includes rent and rates on the bookshop of £3,000; staff wages, heating and lighting of £6,000; and expenditure on books (trading stock) of £13,000. Out of this incurred expenditure, Jasper owes rates of £1,000 and an electricity bill of £250. He further owes some £2,500 on the books purchased. He estimates that he owns stock at the end of the year which cost him £6,000. His opening stock was valued at £4,000. Jasper's accounts, computed on an earnings basis, will be:

	£	£
Total sales		25,000
+ closing stock		6,000
		31,000
Less total of:		
Opening stock	4,000	
Rent/rates	3,000	
Stock bought	13,000	
Wages, lighting etc	6,000	
		26,000
Jasper's taxable profit		£5,000

Note: In drawing up the account it is irrelevant that £3,750 of the incurred expenditure is unpaid and that customers owe £8,500.

A sum cannot be treated as earned, or an expense as incurred, until all the conditions precedent to earning or incurring it have been fulfilled (see *J P Hall & Co Ltd v IRC* (1925)). This does not mean, however, that the legal date for payment must have arisen. Thus, where goods are supplied or services rendered in year 1 which are not to be paid for until year 2, the price (even if it has to be estimated) must be included in the accounts for year 1. If the figure proves to be inaccurate, the assessment for year 1 must be reopened (see *IRC v Gardner, Mountain and D'Ambrumenil Ltd* (1947)).

This doctrine of relating back gives rise to two difficulties; first, if the goods or services are never paid for the bad debt cannot be related back to the year when the goods were supplied, but is only deductible in the year when it is shown to be bad (see p 86); and secondly, if the estimated payment was agreed between the Revenue and the taxpayer at the time as being correctly stated, the accounts cannot subsequently be adjusted if the amount proves inaccurate. Any adjustment will be made in a subsequent account when the error is discovered.

b) *The cash basis*

Profits are calculated by deducting payments actually made from sums actually received during the accounting period ('cash in minus cash out'). This basis presents a misleading picture of the state of the business when the taxpayer gives and receives credit, and carries trading stock. Further, it can be manipulated by the taxpayer to reduce his taxable profits.

EXAMPLE 2

Justinian, a barrister, makes up his accounts to 31 December each year. For 1984 he received fees of £12,000 and is owed a further £50,000; and he has paid bills of £5,000, but owes a further £4,000. On a cash basis his accounts show a profit of £7,000 (£12,000 – £5,000), but that profit would be reduced to £3,000 were he to pay off all his outstanding liabilities on 31 December.

c) *The bills delivered basis*

Profit is calculated on this basis by deducting bills received from bills sent out during the accounting period. Unlike the earnings basis, this does not involve the taxpayer in valuing work-in-progress and is, therefore, particularly appropriate for solicitors and accountants.

d) *Choice of basis*

Although there is no statutory authority stating whether the Revenue or the taxpayer can insist on using a particular basis, in practice the basis has to be agreed with the Revenue. As a general principle, the accounts should be drawn up on the basis which presents an accurate picture of the state of the business during the year. Most self-employed persons render accounts on the earnings basis, although solicitors, for instance, are usually allowed to change to the bills delivered basis after their first three years provided that they agreee to bill clients regularly. The Revenue are reluctant to accept the cash basis except, eg, for authors whose royalties are only earned when received and for barristers, who cannot sue for their fees. Once the Revenue have assessed the taxpayer on one basis, they cannot supplement that assessment by an assessment on an alternative basis (see *Rankine v IRC* (1952)).

The taxpayer may, however, change his basis for a later period. On a change from the earnings (or bills delivered basis) to the cash basis, the taxpayer may suffer the penalty of a double charge to tax, because in year 1 he is taxed on the earnings basis on sums owed (or on sums billed) and in year 2 (on the cash basis) he is taxed on that same money when received. Although there is no relief against this double charge, the taxpayer may as a corollary obtain a benefit because the same expenses may be deducted in years 1 and 2.

On a change from the cash to the earnings or bills delivered basis, the taxpayer could profit, because in year 1 (on the cash basis) he is only taxed on receipts, whereas in year 2 (on the earnings basis) he is taxed on sums earned. Earnings not received in year 1, therefore, formerly escaped tax altogether; they are now taxed as post-cessation receipts under TA 1970 s 144.

3 Post-cessation receipts

TA 1970 s 143 (re-enacting FA 1960 s 32) provides that where profits were calculated on the earnings basis, sums received in respect of the trade, profession or vocation after its discontinuance, which would not otherwise be charged to income tax because the source of the income no longer exists, are taxed under Schedule D Case VI. For this purpose, a debt released after a discontinuance is treated as a receipt (TA 1970 s 143(4)). Certain sums are excluded; in particular, receipts on the transfer of stock or work-in-progess in order to avoid an overlap with TA 1970 ss 137 and 138 (see TA 1970 s 143(3) and p 80).

Where profits were assessed on the cash basis, TA 1970 s 144 (re-enacting FA 1968 s 18) imposes a similar charge to tax on post-cessation receipts, except that sums received for the transfer of work-in-progress after a discontinuance are brought within the charge. Section 144 also catches receipts that would otherwise escape tax on a change from the cash to the earnings basis.

Receipts charged under ss 143 or 144 are taxed as earned income under Schedule D Case VI, generally in the year of receipt or, if the taxpayer elects, in the year of discontinuance so long as that discontinuance has not occurred more than six years before the receipt.

V   TRADING RECEIPTS

To be a 'trading receipt' a sum must possess two characteristics.

1   **The sum must be derived from the trade**

If the payment is in return for services or goods the payment is a trading receipt, whereas if it is made voluntarily in recognition of some personal quality of the taxpayer it is not (compare the rules for Schedule E: p 59). In *Murray v Goodhews* (1976), for instance, Watneys took back tied tenancies (mainly pubs) from their tenant traders as they fell vacant and made ex gratia lump sum payments to the traders which were held not to be trading receipts; they were paid voluntarily, by Watneys to acknowledge the good relationship with the traders and to maintain their good name. (As to whether the payments are deductible expenditure of the payer, Watneys, see p 83). As a contrast, in *McGowan v Brown and Cousins* (1977) the taxpayer, an estate agent, found sites for a company for which he was paid a low fee because it was expected that he would handle the subsequent lettings for the company. The company, however, found another agent to do the letting and 'paid off' the taxpayer with £2,500. This was held to be a trading receipt: it was a reward for services even though paid in pursuance of a moral rather than a legal obligation.

In *Higgs v Olivier* (1952) Laurence Olivier starred in the film of Henry V which did not achieve instant commercial success. As a result, the film company paid him £15,000 not to be involved in any film for 18 months. The payment was held not to be a receipt of his profession but, rather, compensation for not exercising that profession and, therefore, escaped tax.

2   **The sum must be income not capital**

The difficulty of determining whether payments are income receipts (taxable under Case I or II) or capital receipts (when the only liability is to CGT) was forcibly expressed by Greene MR in *IRC v British Salmson Aero Engines* (1938):

> '. . . in many cases it is almost true to say that the spin of a coin would decide the matter almost as satisfactorily as an attempt to find reasons'.

A number of tests have been suggested. The classical test is the distinction between a sale of the fixed capital of the business and of its circulating capital. Sale of the circulating capital produces income receipts.

The defect with this test is that the classification of the asset (is it fixed or circulating?) depends upon the particular trade.

EXAMPLE 3

(1) Koob, a bookseller, owns a freehold bookshop in Covent Garden. The books are his circulating capital (his stock-in-trade) so that the sale proceeds are trade receipts. The bookshop is his fixed capital, the sale of which would give rise to a CGT liability.

(2) Seisin buys vacant premises in Covent Garden which he renovates and sells as bookshops. He is trading in the sale of bookshops which are his circulating capital so that the receipts are income reciepts.

Other tests are but variations on the original theme and contain the same defect. For example, whether the expenditure brings into existence an enduring asset for the benefit of the trade (capital) or not, and the 'trees and fruit' test (the tree is the capital producing the fruit which is income).

The case law in this area is considerable and characterised by subtle distinctions. Many cases involve compensation receipts where the question is, usually, whether the receipt is for the loss of a permanent asset (capital), or is in lieu of trading profits (income). In *London and Thames Haven Oil Wharves Ltd v Attwooll* (1967), the taxpayer owned jetties used by oil tankers. A tanker crashed into and badly damaged a jetty. The taxpayer received compensation of £100,000, £80,000 to rebuild the jetty (capital) and £20,000 to compensate him for lost tanker fees (income). See also *Lang v Rice* (1984) discussed in Appendix V. The decided cases will be considered under six headings:

Restrictions on activity If, as part of his trading arrangements, the taxpayer agrees to restrict his activities in return for payments made to him, the payments are trade receipts. In *Thompson v Magnesium Elektron Ltd* (1944), the taxpayers manufactured magnesium which required chlorine, a by-product of which is caustic soda. ICI agreed to supply the chlorine at below market value and paid the taxpayers a lump sum to prevent them from making their own chlorine and caustic soda, sales of which would compete with those of ICI. The sum was a taxable receipt paid as compensation for profits that the taxpayers would have made on the sale of caustic soda. In *IRC v Biggar* (1982), a payment to a farmer, under EEC regulations, to compensate him for changing from milk to meat farming was a trade receipt (it was compensation for lost profits).

Sterilisation of an asset A payment for the permanent restriction on the use of an asset is capital even though the sum is computed by reference to loss of profits. In *Glenboig Union Fireclay Co Ltd v IRC* (1922), fireclay manufacturers who received compensation for the permanent loss of their right to work fireclay under neighbouring land were held to have received a capital sum. If the compensation is for the temporary loss of an asset, however, it is a trade receipt. Hence, in *Burmah Steamship Co Ltd v IRC* (1931), repairers of a vessel over-ran the contractual date for completion of the work and paid compensation for the lost profits of the owners. The payments were held to be trade receipts.

EXAMPLE 4

Hercules arranges to have his new cargo ship built in a Liverpool shipyard by 31 December 1983. The agreed price is £2m, but this is to be reduced by £10,000 per day if the ship is not ready on time. The ship is delivered ten days late, so that the price is reduced by £100,000. Although this reduction is calculated on the basis of Hercules' lost profits, it would seem that he has not received a sum in lieu of trading receipts.

Cancellation of a business contract or connection When a taxpayer receives compensation for the cancellation of a contract, the nature of the receipt depends upon the significance of the cancelled contract to the business. If it relates to the whole structure of the profit-making apparatus, the compensation is capital. Thus in *Van den Berghs Ltd v Clark* (1935) a Dutch and an English company (both manufacturing margarine) had contracted to trade in different areas so as to avoid competition. The Dutch company cancelled the contract, which had 13 years to run, and paid £450,000 in compensation. It was held to be a capital receipt because the contract had provided the means whereby profits were produced; the English company had, therefore, lost the equivalent of a fixed asset of the business.

If, however, the contract is merely one of many and of short duration, the compensation received is income. In *Kelsall Parsons & Co v IRC* (1938) the taxpayer was a manufacturers' agent who had contracts with different manufacturers and received commission on a sale of their products. One such contract was terminated a year early and the manufacturer paid £15,000 compensation. It was held to be a trade receipt. The contract was the source of profits and the compensation equalled the estimated profit that the taxpayer would have made. Likewise in *Rolfe v Nagel* (1982) a payment to compensate a diamond broker for a client transferring his business elsewhere was taxable as a payment in lieu of profits.

Appropriation of unclaimed deposits and advances   Sums are often received from customers as deposits to be used later in part payment towards the price of goods supplied. If they are forfeited, because of the customer's failure to take delivery of the goods, they are trade receipts in the year of payment (*Elson v Price's Tailors Ltd* (1962)). If at the time of receipt, a deposit is not a trade receipt, however, it does not later become one by appropriation, unless its nature has been changed by statute. Thus in *Morley v Tattersall* (1938), deposits taken by auctioneers remained clients' money and were not trading receipts even though unclaimed and appropriated by the auctioneers. Contrast *Jays the Jewellers Ltd v IRC* (1947) where pawnbrokers' pledges, although originally customers' money, became trading receipts when rendered irrecoverable by statute.

Sale of information ('know-how')   TA 1970 s 386 provides that where a trader disposes of know-how but continues to trade, any receipt is a trading receipt (TA 1970 s 386(2)), but that, where he disposes of know-how as one of the assets of his business which he is selling as an entity, it is treated as a sale of goodwill. In the latter case liability will be to CGT, unless the trader elects to treat the sum as a trading receipt (TA 1970 s 386(3)). Any sum received as consideration for a restriction on the vendor's freedom of activity (following a sale of know-how) is treated as a payment for know-how (TA 1970 s 386(8)).

Release of debts   A debt owed by the trader which has been deducted as a trade expense and which is later released, becomes a trade receipt in the year of its release (TA 1970 s 136).

EXAMPLE 5

Bill, a greengrocer, obtains lettuces from his brother Ben who runs a market garden. In 1984–85 he incurs debts of £3,000 to Ben which on the earnings basis is a trading expense. In 1985–86 Ben agrees to forego the debt because of the critical state of Bill's business, so that the £3,000 will be a trading receipt in the 1985–86 accounts.

3   Valuation of trading stock

a) *Why value stock (work-in-progress)?*

When the taxpayer calculates his profits on the earnings basis, he must value his unsold stock at the end of the accounting period, otherwise he could spend all his receipts on the purchase of new stock, thereby increasing his deductible expenses and reducing his taxable profits to nil. The same principle applies to unbilled work-in-progress.

EXAMPLE 6

In year 1 Zac, a trader buys 10,000 units of stock at £1 each. During the year he sells 5,000 units at £2 each.

	£
Receipts (sales)	10,000
Less Expenses (purchases)	10,000
Profit	£Nil

The trader appears to have made no profit whereas, in fact, his profit is £5,000. Therefore, at the end of the accounting year, his unsold (closing) stock must be treated as a receipt of the trade (ie it is treated as if he had sold it). Hence, the account becomes:

	£
Sales	10,000
Plus Value of closing stock	5,000
	15,000
Less Purchases	10,000
Profit	£5,000

At the start of the next accounting period the stock-in-hand (opening stock) or work-in-progress, must be entered into the accounts for that year at the same figure (ie £5,000 from *Example 6*) as an expense in order to avoid the stock being taxed twice.

EXAMPLE 7

Continuing *Example 6*, in year 2, Zac has opening stock of 5,000 units valued at £1 each. His purchases during the year are 15,000 units of stock at £1 each and he sells 10,000 units at £2 each.

	£
Sales	20,000
Plus Closing stock	10,000
	30,000
Less Purchases	15,000
Profit	£15,000

Failure to value opening stock as an expense produces too much profit (£15,000): his true profit is only £10,000:

	£	£
Sales		20,000
Plus Closing stock		10,000
		30,000
Less Opening stock	5,000	
Purchases	15,000	20,000
Profit		£10,000

b) *Method of valuation*

Each item of unsold stock must be valued at the lower of its cost price and market value. This follows from *IRC v Cock Russell and Co Ltd* (1949) which, in effect, allows losses but not profits to be anticipated: ie the trader can apply 'cost' to items that have increased in value and 'market value' to items that have fallen in value. 'Cost' is the original acquisition price; 'market value' means the best price obtainable in the market in which the trader sells—for instance, a retailer in the retail and a wholesaler in the wholesale market (*BSC Footwear v Ridgway* (1972)).

'Cost' is more difficult to calculate where the price of stock has altered during the accounting period so that it is necessary to identify which stock is left. The only method acceptable to the Revenue is for the trader to treat the stock sold as the stock first bought ('first in first out' ie 'FIFO'). This rule is applied despite evidence that goods were sold on the basis of last in first out ('LIFO').

Unlike stock, work-in-progress cannot be valued as individual items. Instead, it is usually valued by adding to 'direct costs' (such as labour) a proportion of indirect overhead expenses (the 'on-cost' method). However, the taxpayer is allowed to value work-in-progress at direct cost only (see *Duple Motor Bodies v Ostime* (1961)). Because of the difficulty of valuing work-in-progress, professional persons often prefer to draw up their accounts on the bills delivered basis.

c) *Valuation on a discontinuance*

On discontinuance of a trade (which includes a deemed discontinuance under TA 1970 ss 154 and 251) the rule in *IRC v Cock Russell* does not apply and trading stock unsold must be entered into the final accounts at market value (TA 1970 s 137 and see *Moore v R J Mackenzie & Sons Ltd* (1972)). A similar rule applies to work-in-progress. This provision is designed to prevent tax avoidance by the taxpayer discontinuing his business, entering his unsold stock at cost in the final accounts and then selling it privately at a tax-free profit.

Section 137 does not apply:

(1) where the stock is sold to another UK trader for valuable consideration so that it will appear in his accounts for tax purposes anyway; and

(2) where the trade is discontinued because of the death of the single individual who carried it on.

4   Gifts and dispositions for less than market value

A trader has no duty to make the maximum profit and normally tax is assessed according to the actual sum received on a disposal of his stock. There are, however, certain exceptions to this rule.

Transfer pricing (TA 1970 s 485)   TA 1970 s 485 is aimed at transfer-pricing arrangements entered into by multi-national corporations. It provides that on a sale between 'associated' bodies, the Revenue can substitute market value for the sale price if the sale is at an undervalue (TA 1970 s 485(1)). This provision aims to prevent the vendor company realising a tax deductible loss and the buyer company a profit which might be free from tax or charged at a lower rate than that applicable to the vendor. It, therefore, does not apply if the buyer is a resident UK trader.

For similar reasons, market value can be substituted where a sale is at an over value, unless the seller is a UK resident trader (TA 1970 s 485(2)).

Bodies are associated for this purpose if one controls the other or both are controlled by a third party (for the definition of 'control' see TA 1970 s 534).

In cases where the exception applies (ie where the seller is a UK resident trader and the sale is at an overvalue, or the buyer is a UK resident trader and the sale is an undervalue), the transaction may fall within the rule in *Sharkey v Wernher* (1956).

Rule in Sharkey v Wernher (1956) If an item of trading stock is disposed of otherwise than in the ordinary course of the taxpayer's trade, it must be brought into account as a trading receipt at its market value at the date of the disposal. In *Sharkey v Wernher* (1956) the taxpayer carried on the trade of a stud farm. She also raced horses for pleasure and she transferred five horses from the stud farm to the racing stable. The House of Lords held that the market value as opposed to the cost price of the horses at the date when they left the stud farm must be entered in the accounts of the trade as a receipt.

EXAMPLE 8

(1) Rex is a diamond merchant and on the occasion of his daughter's wedding he gives her his choicest diamond which cost him £80,000 and has a market value of £110,000. As the disposal is not a trading transaction, the market value (£110,000) is a trading receipt. The result is that Rex is treated as making a taxable profit of £30,000 on the stone. (There is no distinction between the trader using the goods himself and giving them away to a friend or relative: see *Petrotim Securities Ltd v Ayres* (1964)).

(2) Company A sells securities for which it had paid £400,000 to an associated UK trading company (company B) for £200,000. The securities then had a market value of £800,000. The following points should be noted:

(a) TA 1970 s 485 is inapplicable since the purchaser company is a UK resident trading company.

(b) The sale will be caught by the rule in *Sharkey v Wernher* which applies to both gifts of trading stock and to sales at undervalue (see *Petrotim v Ayres* (1964)).

(c) The recipient of trading stock caught by the rule in *Sharkey v Wernher* is treated as receiving the goods for their market value. Hence, company B is treated as having paid £800,000 for the securities (see *Ridge Securities Ltd v IRC* (1963)).

(d) In extreme cases both the purchase and the resale may be expunged from the accounts of the trader if neither constitutes a genuine trading transaction (see the Y transaction in *Petrotim v Ayres* (1964)).

The market value rule is subject to two major qualifications. First, it is only appropriate when the disposal of stock is not a genuine trading transaction. So long as the disposal can be justified on commercial grounds the general principle remains that a trader is free to charge what he likes for his goods.

EXAMPLE 9

Cutthroat runs a hi-fi business. In an attempt to encourage custom he gives away a cassette player (market value £40) to any customer who purchases goods costing more than £250. The gift is a commercial disposition and outside the scope of *Sharkey v Wernher*. Accordingly, Cutthroat is not required to enter the market value of the player as a trading receipt.

Secondly, the rule does not apply to professional persons (Case II taxpayers). In *Mason v Innes* (1967), Hammond Innes, the novelist, began writing *The Doomed Oasis* in 1958 and incurred deductible travelling expenses in obtaining background material. When the manuscript was completed in 1960 he assigned it to his father in consideration of natural love and affection when it had a market value of about £15,000. Innes was taxed under Case II and rendered accounts on the cash basis. When the Revenue sought to tax the market value of the copyright as a receipt of his profession the Court of Appeal held that the market value rule was limited to traders and to dispositions of trading stock. The fact that Innes was assessed on the cash basis was a further, but not the decisive reason, for excluding the rule. In rejecting the Revenue's argument, Lord Denning MR said:

> 'Suppose an artist paints a picture of his mother and gives it to her. He does not receive a penny for it. Is he to pay tax on the value of it? It is unthinkable. Suppose he paints a picture which he does not like when he has finished it and destroys it. Is he liable to pay tax on the value of it? Clearly not. These instances . . . show that . . . *Sharkey v Wernher* does not apply to professional men.'

EXAMPLE 10

Lex is a partner in the solicitors' firm of Lex, Lax & Lazy and he purchases a house in Chelsea. All the conveyancing work is done by his firm free of charge. The rule in *Sharkey v Wernher* does not apply.

VI   DEDUCTIBLE EXPENSES

1   Basic principles

An expense will be deductible in arriving at the taxpayer's profits under Cases I and II only if:
(a) It is an income and not a capital expense.
(b) It is incurred wholly and exclusively for the purpose of the trade, profession or vocation.
(c) Its deduction is not prohibited by statute (see generally TA 1970 s 130).

Deductible expenses are allowed under Schedule D only by implication from the charging section which imposes tax on 'profits' and from TA 1970 s 130 which contains a list of prohibited deductions. Generally, the rules for deductible expenditure under Schedule D are more generous than under Schedule E (see TA 1970 s 189 and Chapter 5).

Notice that a distinction is drawn between expenses incurred in earning the profits (which may be deductible) and expenses incurred after the profits have been earned, which are not deductible. For example, the payment of income tax is an application of profit which has been earned and is, therefore, not deductible (*Ashton Gas Co v A-G* (1906)). Other taxes, however, such as rates and stamp duty may be paid in the course of earning the profits and so may be deductible.

The professional costs involved in drawing up the trader's accounts and fees paid for tax advice are, in practice, deductible, but expenses involved in contesting a tax assessment are not. In *Smith's Potato Estates Ltd v Bolland* (1948), Viscount Simonds stated that:

> '. . . His [the trader's] profit is no more affected by the exigibility to tax than a man's temperature altered by the purchase of a thermometer, even though he starts by haggling about the price of it.'

2   The expense must be income not capital

Similar tests are applied in classifying expenditure as income or capital as in deciding whether a receipt is income or capital (see p 76). Hence, a distinction is drawn between the fixed and the circulating capital of the business. A payment is therefore capital if it is made to bring into existence an asset for the enduring advantage of the trade (see *British Insulated and Helsby Cables v Atherton* (1926)). The asset may be intangible as in *Walker v Joint Credit Card Co Ltd* (1982) where a payment by a credit card company to preserve its goodwill was held to be a capital payment.

A once and for all payment, even though it brings no enduring asset into existence, is more likely to be of a capital nature than a recurring expense. In *Watney Combe Reid & Co Ltd v Pike* (1982), ex gratia payments made by Watneys (the brewers) to tenants of tied houses to compensate them for the termination of their tenancies were held to be capital, because their purpose was to render capital assets (the premises) more valuable.

Payments to employees are generally deductible in computing the profits of the employer, so long as they are paid in the interests of the business. In *Mitchell v B W Noble Ltd* (1927), a company deducted the sum of £19,500 paid to a director to induce him to resign. It was held to be in the interests of the company to get rid of him and to avoid undesirable publicity by encouraging him to 'go quietly'.

Similarly, in *Heather v PE Consulting Group* (1978) payments made by a company to a trust created in order to acquire shares in that company for the benefit of employees and to prevent outside interference in the affairs of the company were deductible expenses because, inter alia, they encouraged the recruitment of well-qualified staff. Contrast, however, *APC v Kerr* (1946), where payments to two retiring directors in return for covenants that they would not compete with the company for the rest of their lives were held not to be deductible. It was a capital expense being a payment to enhance the company's goodwill. Two further points should be mentioned in connection with the *Kerr* case. First, that the tie was for life and it does not follow that the result would have been the same if the restrictive covenant had been for a shorter period. Secondly, although the payment was a capital expense of the employer, it would today be subject to higher rate income tax in the hands of the recipients (see TA 1970 s 34 at p 61).

Although capital expenditure is not generally deductible, tax relief may be given in accordance with the rules governing capital allowances (see Chapter 7).

3 Expense must have been incurred 'wholly and exclusively' for business purposes (TA 1970 s 130(a))

The courts have generally interpreted the requirement strictly, so that the sole reason for the expenditure must be a business purpose. In *Bentleys, Stokes & Lowless v Beeson* (1952) it was held that the expense incurred in entertaining clients to lunches was deductible. (TA 1970 s 411 generally disallows such expenditure today; see p 85). Romer LJ explained the requirements that have to be satisfied for an expense to be deductible as follows:

'. . . it is quite clear that the purpose must be the sole purpose. The paragraph says so in clear terms. If the activity be undertaken with the object both of promoting business and also with some other purpose, for example, with the object of indulging an independent wish of entertaining a friend or stranger or of supporting a charitable or benevolent object, then the paragraph is not satisfied though in the mind of the actor the business motive may predominate. For the statute so prescribes. Per contra, if, in truth, the sole object is business promotion, the expenditure is not disqualified because the nature of the activity necessarily involves some other result, or the attainment or furtherance of some other objective, since the latter result or objective is necessarily inherent in the act.'

Dual purpose expenditure is not deductible and there are numerous cases where this rule has been strictly applied. In *Caillebotte v Quinn* (1975) a self-employed carpenter worked on sites 40 miles from home. He ate lunch at a nearby café which cost him 40p per day instead of the usual 10p which it cost him at home. His claim to deduct the extra 30p per day as an expense was disallowed on the grounds that he ate to live as well as to work so that the expenditure was incurred for dual purposes. Similarly, in *Prince v Mapp* (1970) a guitarist in a pop group could not deduct the cost of an operation on his little finger because he played the guitar partly for business, but partly for pleasure. In *Mallalieu v Drummond* (1983) the House of Lords held that expenditure on clothing to be worn in court by a female barrister was not deductible. Although she only wore the clothes for business purposes and that was her sole conscious purpose when she purchased the garments, Lord Brightman concluded that 'she needed the clothes to travel to work and clothes to wear at work . . . it is inescapable that one object though not a conscious motive, was the provision of the clothing that she needed as a human being'. (In practice the cost of protective clothing is deductible and the Revenue have concluded 'clothing and tool allowances' with a number of Trade Unions.)

"I hardly think it's worth claiming for your work clothes, Mabel."

The 'dual purpose' cases show that it is not possible to split a purpose: ie if the taxpayer incurs the expenditure for two purposes, one business and the other personal, the expenditure is not deductible. It may, however, be possible to split a payment into a portion which is incurred for business purposes and a portion which is not. This approach was apparent in *Copeman v Flood* (1941) where the son and daughter of the managing director of a small private company were employed as directors at salaries of £2,600 each pa. The son was aged 24 and had some business experience, but the daughter was only 17 and incompetent. Although both performed duties for the company, the Revenue successfully claimed that the entire salary was not an expense incurred by the company 'wholly and exclusively' for business purposes. Lawrence J remitted the case to the commissioners for them to decide, as a question of fact, to what extent the payments were deductible expenses of the trade. He accepted that the expenditure could be apportioned into allowable and non-allowable parts.

In practice, payments are regularly split in this fashion when a car is used both for business and private use and when a business is run from the taxpayer's home and he claims to deduct a proportion of the overheads of the house.

4 Deduction of the expense must not be prohibited by statute

The deduction of expenses under Cases I and II is permitted by implication because TA 1970 s 130 contains a list of expenses which are stated not to be deductible. For instance, under s 130(k) no deduction is allowed for any sum 'recoverable under an insurance or contract of indemnity' whilst expenditure incurred for private as opposed to business purposes is made non-deductible by s 130(b). The deduction of business gifts and entertainment expenses is severely curtailed by TA 1970 s 411 which is drafted widely enough to catch hospitality of any kind (TA 1970 s 411(5)). A number of exceptions are permitted; the entertainment of an overseas customer, for instance, is a deductible expense so long as that entertainment is of a kind and on a scale which is reasonable in all the circumstances (TA 1970 s 411(2)). The entertainment of bona fide members of staff is permitted (TA 1970 s 411(5); and it does not even have to be reasonable!). Small gifts carrying conspicuous advertisements are permissible (TA 1970 s 411(7)), whilst there is an exception for the provision of that which it is in the ordinary course of the taxpayer's trade to provide (TA 1970 s 411(9) and see *Fleming v Associated Newspapers Ltd* (1972) where the House of Lords struggled to make sense of this all but incomprehensible provision).

5 Illustrations of deductible expenditure

Expenditure in heating and lighting business premises; rates on those premises and the wages paid to employees are obvious examples of allowable expenditure. Other expenditure may be more problematic, as the examples considered below show.

Rent paid for business premises   TA 1970 s 130(c) accepts that rent is deductible and it may be apportioned if part of the premises are used for non-business activities. An individual's private house may, of course, be used in part for business purposes and a portion of the overheads may be claimed as allowable expenditure. So long as no part of the house is used exclusively for business purposes the full CGT main residence exemption will still be available (see Chapter 16).

When the taxpayer pays a premium in return for the grant of a lease, a portion of the premium (corresponding to the portion that is charged under Schedule A; see Chapter 8) may be deducted as an expense (TA 1970 s 134).

Specific provisions have been enacted to deal with the problems caused by sale and leaseback, and surrender and leaseback arrangements. The attraction of such schemes stemmed from booming land values which encouraged the owner of the land (or of an interest therein) to sell (or surrender) it, thereby realising a capital sum, and immediately to take a lease-back of the same property. TA 1970 s 491 prohibits the deduction of rent in excess of a commercial level and in certain circumstances FA 1972 s 80 imposes a charge to income tax on a capital sum received in return for surrendering a lease which has less than 50 years to run, when a lease-back for a term not exceeding 15 years is taken.

EXAMPLE 11

Jake runs a pub on leasehold premises in Covent Garden. The lease has 30 years to run and property values have recently boomed in that area. The landlord offers Jake £50,000 to surrender the existing lease and agrees to grant him a new seven year lease at a dramatically increased rent:
  (i) The new rent will be deductible save for any excess above a commercial rent.
  (ii) A portion of the capital sum received by Jake will be subject to income tax and the balance may be subject to CGT (Jake has disposed of a chargeable asset).

Repairs and improvements   Sums expended on the repair of business assets are deductible (TA 1970 s 130). The cost of improvement is not, however, allowable being seen as capital expenditure (TA 1970 s 130(g)). The borderline between the two is a difficult factual question which depends upon the nature of the asset and the importance of the work in relation to it (see *Lurcott v Wakely and Wheeler* (1911) on the duty to repair and *O'Grady v Markham Main Colliery Ltd* (1932)).

The cost incurred on initial repairs carried out to a business asset may cause difficulties. In *Law Shipping Co Ltd v IRC* (1924), a vessel purchased for £97,000 was in such a state of disrepair that a further £51,000 had to be spent before it could obtain its Lloyd's Certificate. The Court of Session disallowed most of the subsequent expenditure; as Lord Cullen stated:

> 'It is in substance the equivalent of an addition to the price. If the ship had not been in need of the repairs in question when bought, the appellants would have had to pay a correspondingly larger price'.

By way of contrast in *Odeon Associated Theatres Ltd v Jones* (1972) subsequent repair work on a cinema which had been purchased in a run-down condition after the war, was allowed. There are three points of distinction from the *Law Shipping* case: first, the cinema was a profit-earning asset when purchased despite its disrepair; secondly, the purchase price was not reduced because of that disrepair; and thirdly, the Court of Appeal accepted that the expenses were deductible in accordance with the principles of proper commercial accounting. (For the precise significance of the evidence of accountants see *Heather v PE Consulting Group* (1973)).

Damages, losses, and bad debts   Damages and losses are deductible if 'connected with and arising out of the trade' (TA 1970 s 130(e)). Bad debts are deducted when shown to be bad (TA 1970 s 130(i)); if later paid they are treated as a trading receipt for that later year. In *Strong & Co of Romsey Ltd v Woodifield* (1906) damages paid to an hotel guest injured by the fall of a chimney from the building were not deductible. Lord Loreburn, somewhat unsympathetically, observed that 'the loss sustained by the appellants . . . fell upon them [sic] in their character not of traders but of householders' whilst Lord Davey rejected the claim because 'the expense must be incurred for the purpose of earning the profits'. Had the guest suffered food poisoning from the hotel restaurant any compensation would have been deductible! In practice, the *Strong v Woodifield* case will be avoided by the trader carrying insurance to cover compensation claims; further, the premiums that he pays for such insurance will be deductible.

Theft by employees causes particular difficulties. Petty theft by subordinates, so that money never finds its way into the till, will result in reduced profits for tax purposes, but defalcations by directors will not be similarly allowable (*Curtis v Oldfield* (1933); *Bamford v ATA Advertising* (1972)).

Travelling expenses   The cases establish two general propositions. First, that the cost of travelling to the place of business is not deductible; and secondly, that the cost of travelling in the course of the business is deductible. In *Horton v Young* (1971), for instance, a labour-only sub-contractor who operated from his home was entitled to deduct expenses incurred in collecting his team of bricklayers and travelling to the building site.

EXAMPLE 12

Wig is a barrister who travels into chambers each day from his home in Isleworth. He also travels from chambers to courts in the London area.
 (1) The cost of travelling from Isleworth to chambers is not deductible because chambers is his base. It does not matter that he does a substantial amount of work at home and that he claims a deduction for a portion of the expenses of the house (see *Newsom v Robertson* (1953)).
 (2) Expenses in travelling from chambers to court are deductible (contrast *Horton v Young* (1971): travelling between two centres of work).
 (3) If he were regularly to go from Isleworth to a case at Bow Street Magistrates Court and then on to chambers could he deduct all the travelling expenses? The difficult case of *Sargent v Barnes* (1978) in which a dental surgeon was unable to deduct travelling expenses to collect false teeth from a laboratory on his way to work, suggests that the answer is no, although it should be noted that the laboratory was not a place of work whereas the court is. A claim for travelling from the court to chambers might, therefore, succeed.

Stock relief   One effect of inflation in the 1970s was to increase the value of a taxpayer's stock over his accounting period thereby increasing his (taxable) paper profit without a corresponding increase in stock levels. To mitigate this problem, a special allowance known as 'stock relief' was introduced in 1975 (FA 1975; F(No 2)A 1975) and applied to companies and individuals assessed under Schedule D Cases I and II in respect of their stock and work-in-progress. The 1975 system was replaced with a simpler one in FA 1981, but, in view of the fall in inflation and the ability of the taxpayer to manipulate the relief, it has been abolished without any clawback of relief for accounting periods beginning on or after 13 March 1984 (FA 1984 s 48(1)). For periods which end on or include 13 March 1984 restricted relief is available (FA 1984 s 48(2)) and the provisions regulating the uses of surplus stock relief remain effective. Special rules apply where a new business begins before 13 March 1984 but its first accounting period ends after that date.

VII   THE BASIS OF ASSESSMENT

1   The normal basis

A taxpayer can commence or cease his business at any time, but he must draw up his accounts over a 12 month period known as the 'accounting year' which need not coincide with the tax year (6 April to 5 April). This gives rise to two difficulties:
 (1) The actual profits made in each year of assessment can only be arrived at by splitting two accounting years and taking the proportions which fall into the assessment year.
 (2) The calculation of the taxpayer's liability has to await the completion and agreement of the accounts with the inspector of taxes.

Because of these problems and as an incentive to business, tax is assessed under Schedule D Cases I and II on the 'preceding year basis' ie in any year of assessment tax is charged on the profits of the 12 month accounting period which ended in the previous year of assessment (TA 1970 s 115(1)). This is the *normal basis.*

EXAMPLE 13

Ernest's accounting year runs from 6 October to 5 October following. He has made the following profits in recent years:

Accounting year ending	Profits
5 October 1983	£ 5,000
5 October 1984	£ 8,000
5 October 1985	£10,000

In the year of assessment 1986–87 Ernest will be assessed on the profits of the 12 month accounting period ending in the preceding year of assessment (ie ending between 6 April 1985 and 5 April 1986). This will be the accounting year to 5 October 1985 which shows £10,000 profit. Assessments on Ernest for the earlier years would be:

Year of assessment	Assessment
1985–86	£8,000
1984–85	£5,000

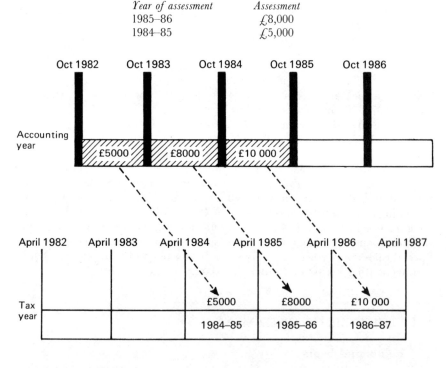

The taxpayer's duty to produce annual accounts is imposed indirectly. No time limit is provided in the legislation for making up accounts. However, if the taxpayer has not made up accounts in the three years preceding the relevant year of assessment, the Revenue take his accounting period to be the previous tax year (ie 6 April to 5 April) and make an estimated assessment (TA 1970 s 115(1)(2)). The only way for the taxpayer to appeal successfully against such an assessment will be by rendering accurate accounts. Further, the taxpayer must render accounts over a 12 month period; if he produces accounts which relate to a period other than 12 months, the Revenue can assess him to tax on the profits of any 12 month period ending in the previous year of assessment (TA 1970 s 115(2)(b)). This provision does not apply to the first or second years of a business (see below).

Tax is assessed directly on the taxpayer under Schedule D Cases I and II and, as a general rule, is payable in two equal instalments on 1 January in the year of assessment and on 1 July following (TA 1970 s 4(2)). The preceding year basis makes possible an assessment raised on the basis of accounts agreed before 1 December in that tax year. If, however, the assessment is not made until after 1 December, but before 1 June following, the first instalment of tax is due 30 days after the assessment and the second instalment on 1 July following; if the assessment is not made until after 1 June in the following year of assessment, all the tax is payable 30 days after the assessment (for details of appeals and related matters see Chapter 2).

To maximise the delay in paying tax, a taxpayer should choose his accounting period carefully. If that period coincides with the tax year, it will form the basis of charge for the tax year immediately following so that there will be a delay of only 9 and 15 months between the end of the accounting period and the payment of tax. If he chooses an accounting period which runs from 7 April to 6 April following, however, the maximum possible delay of 21 and 27 months will apply. Delay in paying tax is especially attractive when the profits of the business are rising. Not only will the taxpayer have the use of the tax for a considerable period of time but, additionally, he will be able to avoid immediate taxation on the current (higher) profits. If profits are constant the advantage is much reduced whilst, if they are falling, a large tax bill will have to be met out of current (smaller) profits.

Corporations are subject to current year assessment and the Revenue are studying the feasibility of a tax assessment on a current year basis for unincorporated businesses ([1978] STI 480).

2 Exceptions to the normal basis

It is impossible to apply the normal basis in the opening years of the business and where the taxpayer changes his accounting date. In the closing years of the business, although it would be possible to use the normal basis, an exceptional basis is applied to prevent the closure being manipulated to avoid tax.

a) *The opening years* (TA 1970 ss 116, 117)

For the year of assessment in which the business commences, the taxpayer is charged on his actual profits from the date of commencement to the end of the tax year (TA 1970 s 116(1)). If his accounting period straddles the end of the tax year, the profits are apportioned on a time (straight-line) basis.

In the second year of assessment the taxpayer is taxed on the profits of his first 12 months trading.

In the third and subsequent years of assessment, the normal basis of assessment under TA 1970 s 115 applies so he is taxed on the profits of the accounting period ending in the previous year of assessment.

EXAMPLE 14

Popeye begins trading on 6 October 1982 and makes the following profits:

Accounting period	Profit
6 October 1982–5 October 1983	£ 3,000
6 October 1983–5 October 1984	£ 9,000
6 October 1984–5 October 1985	£12,000

His first year of assessment is 1982–83 in which he is taxed on his actual profits from 6 October 1982 to 5 April 1983

ie $\dfrac{6}{12} \times £3,000 = £1,500$

In his second year (1983–84) Popeye is taxed on his first 12 months of trading: ie on profits from 6 October 1982 to 5 October 1983 = £3,000.

In his third year (1984–85) Popeye is taxed on the preceding year basis on the profits from 6 October 1982–5 October 1983 = £3,000 (again). In 1985–86 he is therefore taxed on £9,000.

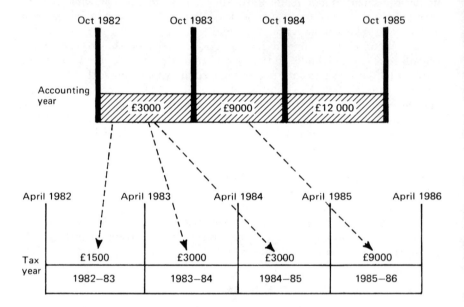

If the taxpayer's first accounting period is longer or shorter than 12 months (which may well be the case) this will not affect the assessment of his first and second years. However, in the third year, the normal basis cannot be applied, because there is not a 12 month accounting period ending in the previous year of assessment. The Revenue can, therefore, take any period of 12 months ending in the previous year of assessment. In practice, they will take the 12 months ending on the taxpayer's chosen accounting date.

EXAMPLE 15

Pluto begins trading on 6 August 1983 and makes up his first accounts to 5 October 1984 (14 months). The accounts show a profit of £14,000.

In 1983–84 (first year) Pluto will be assessed on his actual profits for the 8 month period ending 5 April 1984 ie £8,000. In 1984–85 (second year), Pluto will be assessed on his profit of the first 12 months of trading to 5 August 1984 ie £12,000.

In 1985–86 (third year), as Pluto intends to make up accounts to 5 October each year, the assessment will be on the 12 month period ending 5 October 1984, ie £12,000.

The effect of TA 1970 s 116 (the opening year rule) is to use the profits of the first 12 months of trading as the basis for the tax assessment in each of the first three years of assessment. This is not, however, double (or even triple) taxation because those profits are *deemed* to be the profits of the years of assessment. The taxpayer will be content with this duplication where the profits are low in relation to current profits, but not where the first year profits are higher than current profits. TA 1970 s 117 allows him to elect to have the assessments of the second and third years made on the basis of *actual* profits earned in those years. The election must cover both years and be made within seven years of the end of the second year of assessment. It can be withdrawn within that period to cover the case where the taxpayer makes low profits in year two, elects for the actual basis, but then discovers that because of high profits in the third year, the election has made him worse off.

EXAMPLE 16

Olive begins trading on 6 October 1982 and makes up accounts to 5 October each year. Her profits are (see diagram p 92)

Accounting period	Profits
6 October 1982–5 October 1983	£12,000
6 October 1983–5 October 1984	£ 4,000
6 October 1984–5 October 1985	£ 2,000

Assessment under TA 1970 s 116 produces profits of £30,000:

Tax year	Basis period	Profits £
Year 1 1982–83	Actual: 6 October 1982–5 April 1983	
	$=\dfrac{6}{12} \times £12,000 =$	6,000
Year 2 1983–84	12 months to 5 October 1983	12,000
Year 3 1984–85	Preceding year to 5 October 1983	12,000
Year 4 1985–86	Preceding year to 5 October 1984	4,000
		£30,000

An election under TA 1970 s 117 produces profits of £17,000:

Tax year	Basis period	£	Profits £
Year 1 1982–83	Actual: (no change)		6,000
Year 2 1983–84	Actual: 6 April 1983–5 April 1984		
	ie $\dfrac{6}{12} \times £12,000 =$	6,000	
	Plus $\dfrac{6}{12} \times £4,000 =$	2,000	
			8,000
Year 3 1984–85	Actual: 6 April 1984–5 April 1985		
	ie $\dfrac{6}{12} \times £4,000 =$	2,000	
	Plus $\dfrac{6}{12} \times £2,000 =$	1,000	
			3,000
			£17,000

Olive should make a s 117 election. Whenever profits are falling the election should be made. When the trend is upwards it should be ignored.

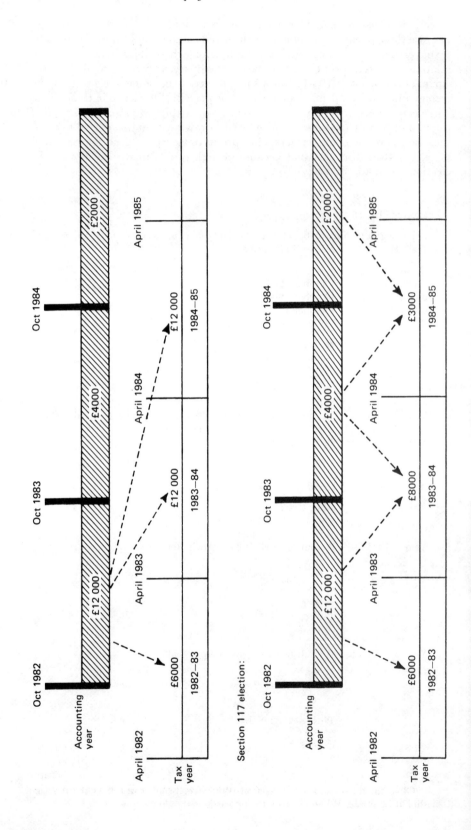

b) *Change of accounting date*

If the taxpayer decides to change his accounting date, there will be at least one year which does not fit the normal assessment basis since he must make up a set of accounts for one period of less or more than 12 months in order to effect that change.

In this case, the Revenue may take 'any period of 12 months ending in the preceding year of assessment' as the basis period *and* if they think that the year before that should be dealt with on the same basis they have the power to do so (TA 1970 s 115(2)(b) and (3)). As a matter of practice, the Revenue normally take as a basis the period of 12 months ending on the date in the preceding year which the taxpayer has chosen as his new year-end date.

EXAMPLE 17

Unlucky changes his accounting date from 5 October to 31 December. His profits are:

Accounting period	*Profits*
	£
Year ended 5 October 1982	20,000
Year ended 5 October 1983	6,000
14 months ended 31 December 1984	21,000
Year ended 31 December 1985	10,000

Assessments		*Profits*
		£
1983–84	(Normal Basis) Year ended 5 October 1982	20,000
*1984–85	(Normal Basis) Year ended 5 October 1983	6,000
1985–86	(No Normal Basis) Revenue will take 12 months to 31 December 1984	
	ie $\dfrac{12}{14} \times £21,000$	18,000
1986–87	(Normal Basis) Year ended 31 December 1985	10,000

The Revenue can revise the last normal assessment before the change (1984–85) to an assessment based on the new accounting date which results in tax on additional profits of £2,000:

		£
*1984–85	Twelve months to 31 December 1983	
	ie $\dfrac{10}{12} \times £6,000$	5,000
	Plus $\dfrac{2}{14} \times £21,000$	3,000
		£8,000

The taxpayer may appeal against the revised assessment under TA 1970 s 115(3). The principles on which the commissioners should act in considering such appeals were considered in *IRC v Helical Bar Ltd* (1972). Any appeal will not succeed merely because the Revenue are assessing profits of the same period twice since that is the effect of the legislation. In practice, the Revenue operate an 'averaging procedure' (see IR 26) which affects the revision year only (ie 1984–85 in *Example 17*) and aims to be fair to both parties.

c) *Closing year rules* (TA 1970 s 118(1)(a))

In the year of assessment in which the business terminates, the taxpayer is assessed on his actual profits from the beginning of that tax year (6 April) to the date of discontinuance. This normally involves apportioning the profits of an accounting period on a time basis (TA 1970 s 127). The two years of assessment preceding the final year (penultimate and pre-penultimate years of assessment) are taxed on the normal basis. However, the Revenue can elect under TA 1970 s 118 to assess the taxpayer on his actual profits of those years. The election is needed since under the preceding year basis the actual profits of those years would never be charged, so that taxpayers could ensure that large profits were channelled into that period.

EXAMPLE 18

B ceased to trade on 5 July 1985. His profits for years ended 31 December were:

$$£\ 9,000 \text{ for } 1981$$
$$£15,000 \text{ for } 1982$$
$$£12,000 \text{ for } 1983$$
$$£18,000 \text{ for } 1984$$
$$\text{and } £6,000 \text{ to } 5 \text{ July } 1985$$

Tax year	Basis period	£	Profits £
1985–86 *Final*	Actual: 6 April 1985–5 July 1985 $\text{ie} = \dfrac{3}{6} \times £6,000$		3,000
1984–85 *Penultimate*	Preceding year: year ended 31 December 1983		12,000
1983–84 *Pre-penultimate*	Preceding year: year ended 31 December 1982		15,000
1982–83	Preceding year: year ended 31 December 1981		9,000
			£39,000

TA 1970 s 118 Revenue election:

		£	£
1985–86 *Final*	Actual: (as above)		3,000
1984–85 *Penultimate*	Actual: 6 April 1984–5 April 1985 $\text{ie} = \dfrac{3}{6} \times £6,000$	3,000	
	Plus: $\dfrac{9}{12} \times £18,000$	13,500	16,500
1983–84 *Pre-penultimate*	Actual: 6 April 1983–5 April 1984 $\text{ie} = \dfrac{3}{12} \times £18,000$	4,500	
	Plus: $\dfrac{9}{12} \times £12,000$	9,000	13,500
1982–83	Preceding year (as above)		9,000
			£42,000

The Revenue would exercise their option to amend the assessments of 1983–84 and 1984–85 to an actual basis. Otherwise, the higher profits of the period from 1 January 1984 to 5 April 1985 escape tax completely.

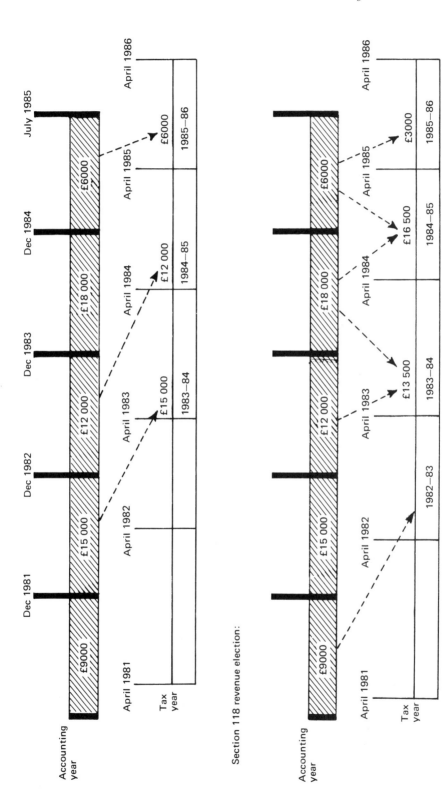

Section 118 revenue election:

The Revenue must exercise their election for both years. Therefore, (as with the s 117 taxpayer's election) it will only be made if the total profits of both years on an actual basis is higher than the total on the preceding year basis. Generally, if profits are rising the election will be made, if falling it will not.

3　When to apply opening and closing year rules

a) *Commencement of a business*

The taxpayer must apply the opening year rules from the date that he commences business. This date is a question of fact and acts preparatory to carrying on the business do not constitute commencement. For example, in *Birmingham and District Cattle By-Products Co Ltd v IRC* (1919) the construction of a factory, the purchase of machinery, and the making of contracts to purchase raw materials were preparatory acts. Business only commenced once the machinery was installed and the raw materials received. Expenditure is normally only deductible after that date, although expenses incurred in the three years before the business starts are treated as a loss of the year of commencement (FA 1980 s 39).

When the taxpayer who already runs an existing business takes up new business activities, it is a question of fact whether he is merely extending his existing business or starting a new one (see *Seldon v Croom-Johnson* (1932) where a barrister who took silk was held to be continuing his existing profession). In the former case, the normal preceding year basis continues to apply to all activities. In the latter case, he must apply the opening year rules to the new business.

EXAMPLE 19

Lenny owns a health food shop which he extends to serve morning coffee (decaffeinated) and brown sugar (only) doughnuts. This is an extension of his existing business and he continues to be assessed on the normal basis.

If Lenny turns his health food shop into a restaurant specialising in French cuisine, he must apply the closing years rules to the health food shop and the opening year rules to the restaurant business.

b) *Change of ownership*

When an existing business is transferred (including the incorporation of the business) the change of ownership results in the closing year rules being applied (TA 1970 s 154(1)). There are certain exceptions to this rule. First, where a business is transferred by a sole trader to a partnership in which he is a partner, or there is a change in the composition of an existing partnership (but with at least one continuing partner), all the persons concerned in the business before and after the change can elect for the business to be treated as continuing (TA 1970 s 154(2) and Chapter 29). Secondly, by concession, a change of ownership due to the death of the owner where the business passes to his spouse is not a discontinuance, unless claimed by that surviving spouse (ESCA7).

If the purchaser of the business is already running an existing business, he will have acquired either an entirely new business or assets to be used in the (expanded) old business (see also a) above). If the former, the opening year rules will apply to that enterprise but, at the end of the first three years of account, the businesses can normally be merged unless they are of a totally different nature. A mere purchase of assets does not trigger the opening year rules and the enlarged business continues on the normal basis. The question is one of fact. If a business and not just assets is transferred there will be a transfer of, inter alia, custom, staff and goodwill. (Compare *Reynolds Sons and Co Ltd v Ogston* (1930) and *Thomson and Balfour v Le Page* (1923).) There cannot be a succession to part of a trade; or through the accidental acquisition of another trader's custom; or, to a trade which ceased before the new owner took over (typically the purchase of a trader's assets on his bankruptcy).

c) *Discontinuance of a business*

It is a question of fact whether the particular change results in a discontinuance. A trade which is in abeyance or quiescent has not necessarily ceased. One test is whether it still generates expenditure and loss. (Compare *Kirk and Randall Ltd v Dunn* (1924) with *Ingram and Son Ltd v Callaghan* (1969).)

If a business is discontinued within two to five years of its commencement so that the opening and closing year rules overlap, the closing year rules prevail (TA 1970 s 118(1)).

4 Relief for fluctuating profits

The profits earned from certain businesses are so irregular that it would be unfair to tax them all in the year of receipt. Instead, they are deemed to have been received over a longer period ('averaged').

Farmers and market gardeners FA 1978 s 28 allows farmers and market gardeners to compare the profits of two consecutive years of assessment and, if the profits of either year are nil or one is less than 70% of the other, the profits of both years are equalised. ('Profit' means profit before deducting loss relief and capital allowances.) The relief is tapered where the profits in one year are between 70% and 75% of the other. The trader must claim the relief within two years of the end of the second year of assessment and he may not claim it for his opening or closing years.

EXAMPLE 20

A farmer's profits in Year 1 are £600 and in Year 2 £16,000. £600 is less than 70% of £16,000. Therefore profits are equalised and in years 1 and 2 he is taxed on profits of £8,300 (£16,600 ÷ 2).

Authors and artists Two provisions afford relief to authors who receive lump sums for copyright or royalties. TA 1970 s 389 provides that lump sums received for royalties within two years of the work's first publication, or for the assignment of copyright or in respect of non-returnable advances, may be spread back and taxed over either two or three years depending upon the length of time spent by the author on producing the work. This relief applies in respect of literary, dramatic, musical and artistic works.

By TA 1970 s 390, any sum received for the assignment of a copyright more than ten years after publication can be spread forward and taxed over a maximum of six years depending on the duration of the assignment. Special provisions apply where the author dies or retires within that six year period. This provision does not apply to artistic works.

Notice that by TA 1970 s 392 commissions, fees and similar payments received by an artist for a sale of his work can be spread back over two or three years.

Inventors   Similar provisions apply to lump sums received by inventors for the exploitation of their patents. By TA 1970 s 380, a sum received in return for patent rights is spread over the year of receipt and the next five years. By TA 1970 s 384, sums received for the use of a patent for a period of at least six years may be spread back over six years.

7 Capital allowances and loss relief

'. . . there is little evidence that these incentives [capital allowances] have strengthened the economy or improved the quality of investment. Quite the contrary . . . Too much investment has been made because the tax allowances make it look profitable . . . We need investment decisions based on future market . . . not future tax assessments.' (the Rt Hon Nigel Lawson MP, Chancellor of the Exchequer, Budget Statement 13 March 1984).

1 CAPITAL ALLOWANCES—INTRODUCTION

The cost of fixed assets and the depreciation of those assets due to gradual wear and tear are not allowable deductions from profits for income tax purposes although such expenditure is an unavoidable cost of a business and is incurred in earning its profits. Accordingly, a limited and controlled rate of depreciation for certain types of fixed assets is given in the form of capital allowances which are deductible in arriving at taxable profits. The allowances may have the effect of replacing a trading profit with an allowable loss for which the taxpayer will be entitled to loss relief (see p 119ff). The mere fact that capital expenditure has been incurred does not, however, mean that a capital allowance is available. Allowances are only given for items of expenditure prescribed by statute, the most important of which are given for plant and machinery and industrial buildings.

   The relevant legislation was consolidated in the Capital Allowances Act 1968 and has been replaced by FA 1971 for plant and machinery purchased after 26 October 1970. Later Finance Acts have further amended the system; in particular, FA 1984 in phasing out certain of the allowances as part of an overall policy to encourage capital investment by business for genuine commercial reasons (see further Appendix V).

II PLANT AND MACHINERY

1 Definition

The terms 'plant' and 'machinery' are not defined in the legislation and are to be given their ordinary meaning. The plethora of cases in this area indicates, however, that the meaning is not always obvious! Recent cases, although adopting a more robust view of what constitutes plant and machinery, emphasise that the answer in each case must depend on the particular facts. When considering the meaning of these terms, the usual starting point is the oft-quoted dictum of Lindley LJ in *Yarmouth v France* (1887):

> 'There is no definition of plant in the Act: but in its original sense, it includes whatever apparatus is used by a businessman for carrying on his business, not his stock-in-trade which he buys or makes for sale; but all goods and chattels, fixed or moveable, live or dead, which he keeps for permanent employment in his business'.

'Permanent' means that only durable (capital) items can be plant. Expenditure on non-durable items must be of a revenue nature. In *Hinton v Maden and Ireland Ltd* (1959), for instance, knives and lasts used by a shoe manufacturer, with a useful life of only three years, were considered plant whilst in *McVeigh v Arthur Sanderson and Sons Ltd* (1969) designs used by wallpaper manufacturers lacked 'materiality' and were of a revenue (income) nature.

If the expenditure is on a capital item, the test propounded in *Yarmouth v France* for deciding whether that item is plant is a functional one (the 'functional test') ie is the item in question used for carrying on the particular business (in which case it is plant), or is it used to provide a setting for carrying on the business (the 'setting test') in which case it is not plant.

In *Munby v Furlong* (1977) a barrister's law books were plant because they constituted an 'intellectual warehouse' used by him in carrying on his profession. In contrast, various cases illustrate that premises which 'house' the trade (provide its setting) cannot be plant. In *St John's School v Ward* (1974), prefabricated buildings that served as a gymnasium and laboratory for the school were not plant; they merely provided shelter. Similarly, in *Brown v Burnley Football and Athletic Club Ltd* (1980) a stadium was not plant because it served no function; the spectators watched within, rather than by means of, the stadium.

Various problems have arisen in connection with expenditure on structures. Are they plant or merely part of the setting? In *Benson v Yard Arm Club* (1979) the taxpayer's arguments that a ship which was used as a floating restaurant was plant because it attracted customers were rejected on the grounds that the ship was merely the setting in which his trade of restaurateur was carried on.

A suggested test in these cases is whether the structure performs an 'active' or 'passive' role in the business. If the former, it may be plant. Thus, in *Barclay Curle & Co Ltd v IRC* (1969) a dry dock used by shipbuilders and repairers was held to be plant as it performed the active role of positioning vessels for repair. In *Cooke v Beach Stations Caravans Ltd* (1974) a swimming pool constructed by a caravan owning and operating company was held to be plant although it performed the purely passive role of a container of water! In that particular trade, the pool was part of the means by which the company carried on its business and did not merely provide a setting for the trade (the passive test was inapplicable).

Such cases indicate that the functional/setting test is a guideline which must be looked at in the light of the particular trade so that what might be plant for one trade is merely part of the setting of another. (Compare, for instance, *J Lyons & Co Ltd v A-G* (1944) with *Jarrold v John Good & Sons Ltd* (1962).) This approach was applied in *Barclay Curle & Co Ltd v IRC* and *Cooke v Beach Station Caravans Ltd* and has been endorsed in the House of Lords in *IRC v Scottish & Newcastle Breweries* (1982), where expenditure by an hotelier on (inter alia) decor was expenditure on plant because the creation of a suitable atmosphere was a function of an hotelier's particular trade. Also, in *Leeds Permanent Building Society v Proctor* (1982) the court applied the functional test in relation to the business in question, so that decorative screens placed in the windows of a building society's premises to attract customers were plant.

The two recent House of Lords cases (*IRC v Scottish & Newcastle Breweries* (1982) and *Cole Bros Ltd v Phillips* (1982)) have effectively reduced the question of what constitutes plant into two propositions; first, the question is one of fact and degree to be decided by the commissioners, whose decision will not be reversed unless it is wrong in law. Secondly, the functional/setting and the active/passive tests are relevant, but only as applied to the facts of the particular trade and not in the abstract.

2 Who can claim the capital allowance?

The capital allowance is available for taxpayers assessed as follows:
(a) under Schedule D Cases I or II for companies, sole traders and partnerships; extended to furnished holiday lettings under Schedule D Case VI;
(b) under Schedule E where an employee purchases plant or machinery 'necessarily provided for use in the performance of the duties' (FA 1971 s 41(1)). The difficulty of satisfying this test is illustrated in *White v Higginbottom* (1983) where a vicar was unable to claim an allowance for a slide projector used in parish work since Vinelott J applying the test in TA 1970 s 189 (p 64) concluded that, as another vicar could manage without a projector, the expenditure had not been 'necessarily' incurred for the performance of his duties;
(c) under Schedule D Case I (but not under Schedule B) to the occupier of woodlands if managed on a commercial basis and with a view to profit;
(d) under Schedule A to a landlord who provides plant and machinery for use in the repair, maintenance or management of the property (TA 1970 s 78).

3 When will the allowance be claimed?

The allowances are deductible from the taxable profits of the accounting period ending in the previous tax year; or, for a company, the current accounting period. If the taxpayer is taxed under Schedule D Case I or II he will be assessed on a preceding year basis. Therefore, his capital allowances for the year of assessment are given for assets owned on the last day of the accounting period.

EXAMPLE 1

A & Co, solicitors, make up their accounts to 31 December 1984. They show income profits of £15,000. During that year they purchased assets for which they are entitled to capital allowances of £2,000. The Schedule D Case II assessment for 1985–86 will be £15,000 – £2,000 = £13,000.

Under the opening year rules an accounting period may be used as the basis of assessment for more than one year of assessment. In that event any allowable capital expenditure is allocated to the earlier tax year.

4 How are the allowances used?

The allowances are deductible from taxable profits in the relevant tax year. If the allowance exceeds those profits or if there were no profits, the unused allowance can be carried forward and set against future profits. Alternatively, the taxpayer may elect to treat the surplus as a loss and deduct it from his other income under TA 1970 s 169, or carry it back under FA 1978 s 30 if appropriate. For companies, the effect of TA 1970 s 177(3A) is broadly similar to s 169 save that it enables the allowance to be carried back for a period of three years to obtain a refund of tax. In cases other than trades, the allowance is deducted from the appropriate income (eg rent under Schedule A). With the phasing out of the first-year allowance by 1 April 1986 (FA 1984 s 58), the government is seeking to encourage genuine investment only and to prevent the taxpayer from manipulating his taxable profits by purchasing items of plant and machinery in a year of high profit simply to reduce that profit, and often in the case of small companies to take them out of the marginal corporation tax rate.

5   **Types of allowance**

Capital allowances on plant and machinery (new or secondhand) purchased after 26 October 1970 and before April 1986 consists of a first-year allowance which is available in the year the expenditure is incurred together with a writing-down allowance for subsequent years until the cost of the asset is written off. From 1 April 1986 only the WDA will be available.

a) *First-year allowance (FYA)*

The trader can deduct a percentage (FYA) of the cost of acquiring the asset from the profits of the basis period in which he acquires it, provided he incurred the expenditure for the purposes of his trade, and the asset belonged to him during the basis period of the year of assessment. This FYA is being reduced in stages from 100% to 75% on expenditure incurred after 13 March 1984, to 50% on expenditure incurred after 31 March 1985 and to nil on expenditure incurred after 31 March 1986. Expenditure incurred before 1 April 1987 under a binding contract entered into before 14 March 1984 qualifies for the 100% FYA. The 100% FYA remains available on future expenditure incurred on projects in development or special development areas where an offer of special assistance was made between 1 April 1980 and 13 March 1984. Where the date on which expenditure is incurred (under a contract made after 13 March 1984 and on or before 31 March 1986) is artifically advanced solely or mainly to claim a higher FYA, FA 1984 Sch 12 restricts that higher FYA to expenditure calculated on a time apportionment basis.

EXAMPLE 2

In the year ending 31 December 1985, Albert a solicitor has taxable profits of £15,000. On 31 July 1985 he pays for and uses in his firm a word processor costing £40,000. If Albert claims the maximum 50% FYA his taxable profits for 1986–87 are reduced to NIL (£15,000–£20,000 (50% × £40,000)). The £5,000 unused FYA can be carried forward against his profits in 1987–88 and subsequent years or can be treated as a loss in the year expenditure was incurred (1985–86) and deducted from his Schedule D Case I profits (if any) and then from any other income he has that year.

The taxpayer need not claim a full FYA and he should not do so if this will so reduce his taxable income as to result in a loss of personal allowances. If he disclaims or takes a reduced FYA, the balance of the cost price is subject to a writing-down allowance.

To prevent a taxpayer from obtaining a tax advantage through the exploitation of the FYA, it is not available: if the expenditure is incurred in a period when the business ceased to trade; if the asset is sold before being used; if the purchase is of a private motor car (post); in certain leasing transactions (post); and where the vendor and purchaser are connected persons or the arrangement is an artificial one (FA 1971 Sch 8 para 3).

Additionally, if the asset is to be only partially used for business purposes, the FYA is similarly restricted (FA 1971 Sch 8 para 5).

b) *Writing-down allowances (WDA)*

The WDA is a depreciation allowance of 25% of the 'qualifying expenditure': ie original cost of asset less any allowances already given. It is available for each year in which the asset belongs to the taxpayer and is or has been in use in the business in the relevant accounting period (other than the year when the trade permanently discontinues) until the cost is written off (FA 1971 s 44(1)). It is also available for assets such as cars which are not entitled to FYAs and it will be the only allowance available for expenditure incurred after 1 April 1986. It is proposed in the Finance Bill 1985 to relax the rules relating to the WDA by making it available in the case of expenditure incurred in a chargeable period commencing on or after 1 April 1985 even though the asset has not been brought into use in the business in that period. This change will advance the allowance particularly for assets which are paid for in instalments prior to delivery.

Where the FYA is 75% or 50%, the balance of the expenditure qualifies for a 25% WDA in subsequent years provided the above conditions are complied with. If the full FYA is not taken for expenditure incurred after 13 March 1984, the unrelieved proportion of that expenditure qualifies for an immediate WDA in that year (FA 1984 s 59).

EXAMPLE 3

Albert and Bertie are sole traders who make up their respective accounts to 31 December. In July 1984 each purchases a machine for £20,000. They each claim capital allowances as follows:

	A		B		
Assessment year 1985–86					
	£			£	£
Machine bought for	20,000	Machine bought for			20,000
Less 75% (full) FYA	15,000	*Less* FYA 60%			
Qualifying expenditure	£5,000	(reduced)		12,000	
		WDA of:			
		25% × £20,000 –			
		$\dfrac{60}{75} \times £20,000$		1,000	
					13,000
		Qualifying expenditure			£7,000
Assessment year 1986–87					
Qualifying expenditure		Qualifying expenditure			
b/f	5,000	b/f			7,000
Less WDA		*Less* WDA			
25% × £5,000	1,250	25% × £7,000			1,750
Qualifying expenditure		Qualifying expenditure			
c/f (to 1987–88 *et seq*)	3,750	c/f (to 1987–88 *et seq*)			£5,250

Like the FYA, the WDA may be claimed in whole or in part by individuals; for chargeable periods ending after 13 March 1984, it may be disclaimed by companies in whole or in part (FA 1971 s 44(2A) inserted by FA 1984 s 59(1)). One attraction of disclaiming the allowances is to maintain a higher pool (see below) of qualifying expenditure, thereby reducing the likelihood of a balancing charge (p 105).

c) *Pooling*

An item of plant or machinery purchased by a trader after 26 October 1970 is treated for the purpose of the WDA as falling into a 'pool' of machinery and plant. The value of the pool (also termed 'qualifying expenditure') is written down by 25% (or less) each year (see *Example 4(1)*). Certain items, such as cars, are not pooled. If there is a disposal of an item of plant or machinery from the pool (for instance, by sale or destruction) the qualifying expenditure in the pool is reduced by the disposal value of the item (for instance, by the sale price or insurance moneys). This reduction is known as a balancing adjustment (see *Example 4(2)*).

EXAMPLE 4

(1) Albert, a trader, makes up his accounts to 31 December and purchases (for immediate use in the business):

20 December 1984: machine A for £600
31 August 1985: machine B for £800
30 June 1986: machine C for £1,000

	First Year	Pool
Assessment year 1985–86	£	£
Purchase machine A on 20 December 1984	600	
FYA at 60% (part claim of 75%)	360	
Qualifying expenditure carried forward	240	
Transfer A to pool		240
Assessment year 1986–87		
Qualifying expenditure brought forward		240
WDA on pool at 25%		60
		180
Purchase machine B on 31 August 1985	800	
FYA at 50% (full claim)	400	
Qualifying expenditure carried forward	400	
Transfer B to pool		400
Assessment year 1987–88		
Qualifying expenditure brought forward		580
Purchase machine (on 30 June 1986)	1,000	
No FYA available	—	
	1,000	
Qualifying expenditure transferred to pool		1,000
		1,580
WDA on pool at 25%		395
Qualifying expenditure carried forward		£1,185

(2) Continuing (1) above on 1 June 1987 Albert sells machine A for £185.

	Pool
Assessment year 1988–89	£
Qualifying expenditure brought forward	1,185
Sale of machine A on 1 June 1987	185
	1,000
WDA on pool at 25%	250
Qualifying expenditure carried forward	£750

So long as the business continues, it is unlikely that a balancing adjustment will exceed the qualifying expenditure in the pool, so as to give rise to a balancing charge (below). If the sale proceeds of an item of plant or machinery exceed its cost price the excess is charged not to income tax but to CGT (see Chapter 14). Thus, in *Example 4(1)*, if machine A were sold for £700, the qualifying expenditure in the pool for the WDA would be £585 with a chargeable gain of £100 (£700 – £600).

d) *Balancing allowances and charges*

In the year when a business terminates there is no WDA; instead the proceeds received on the sale of the plant and machinery are deducted from the qualifying expenditure in the pool. If they are less than the value in the pool, the taxpayer receives a 'balancing allowance' for the difference which is deductible from his profits for the basis period. If the proceeds of sale are greater than the value left in the pool, however, the excess is a 'balancing charge' and is taxed as a receipt of the business (this is called the 'claw-back' of capital allowances). This procedure ensures that allowances equal the cost of the items to the business.

EXAMPLE 5

A trader sells his computer business for £50,000 of which £10,000 is paid for the plant and machinery. At the time of sale the qualifying expenditure in the pool of plant and machinery is £12,000. A, therefore, has a balancing allowance of £2,000 (£12,000 – £10,000) which he can deduct from his final trading profits.
   If A had instead received £14,000 for the plant and machinery his trading profits would be increased by a balancing charge of £2,000 (£14,000 – £12,000). The purchaser will claim capital allowances on the £14,000 paid for the (secondhand) plant and machinery.

The amount of the purchase money attributed to the plant and machinery in the sale of a business is a matter for hard bargaining between the parties with the vendor wanting a low figure (to reduce the risk of a balancing charge) and the purchaser a high figure for the purpose of FYA (if any) and WDA. In practice, the Revenue will normally accept the figure that the parties agree, since they cannot lose!

Capital allowances cannot be carried forward on the cessation of a business. In the case of deemed discontinuances under TA 1970 s 154 (for instance on a change in partners) balancing allowances and charges will be calculated as if the assets were sold for their market value at that time. If, however, there is an election under TA 1970 s 154(2) to treat the business as continuing, capital allowances continue as if the new owners had carried on the business throughout (Capital Allowances Act 1968 s 48 and FA 1971 Sch 8 para 15). When the transferor and the transferee are connected persons (see TA 1970 s 533) they can elect not to treat the business as discontinued so that the transferee can take over the allowances of the transferor. This election will normally be used when a business is incorporated (FA 1971 Sch 8 para 13).

EXAMPLE 6

A, who has carried on a trade for many years, owns plant and machinery on which the qualifying expenditure at the end of 1984–85 is £5,000. On 1 June 1984, he transfers the business to A Ltd, a company controlled by him. A and A Ltd may elect for A Ltd to receive the allowances as if there had been no discontinuance. Hence, in financial year 1984, A Ltd receives a WDA on plant and machinery of $25\% \times £5,000 = £1,250$.

6   Motor cars

The allowances for motor cars are restricted because they can (and usually will) be used for private as well as business purposes. By FA 1971 s 43, FYAs are given on motor vehicles used for business purposes only. The vehicle must, therefore, be designed to carry goods (eg lorries); or unsuitable for use as a private car (eg taxis and buses); or a hire vehicle which is not hired to any one person for more than 30 consecutive days nor for more than 90 days in any period of 12 months.

Any other vehicles are not eligible for a FYA, but qualify for 25% WDA subject to a maximum of $25\% \times £8,000 = £2,000$ pa. Because of this restriction on the WDA for non-business vehicles, they are not pooled but are written down individually so increasing the likelihood of a balancing charge or allowance.

To avoid businesses leasing expensive cars (ie which cost at least £8,000) and circumventing the allowance restriction by claiming to deduct the entire rental as a business expense, it is provided that a deduction under TA 1970 s 130 shall be limited to the proportion that £8,000 plus one-half of the excess above £8,000 bears to the total original cost.

EXAMPLE 7

Footsore hires a car, which cost £12,000, for business use at a rent of £1,020 for one year. The hire charge that he can treat as a business expense is limited to:

$$\frac{£8,000 + \frac{1}{2}(£12,000 - £8,000)}{£12,000} \times £1,020 = £850.$$

7   Miscellaneous

Leasing plant and machinery   FA 1980 ss 64–65 contain restrictions on, and sets out the conditions for, the availability of capital allowances where plant and machinery is bought in order to be leased. Generally, FYAs are only available if the asset is used for a 'qualifying purpose' (see FA 1980 s 64) and WDAs in cases where the assets are not so used are restricted (FA 1980 ss 65, 70). Some of the attractions of purchasing assets for leasing have been reduced by the phased withdrawal of FYAs.

Tenants purchasing plant and machinery   Where a lessee of trade premises incurs expenditure on the installation of plant and machinery for use in his trade, he can only claim allowances for the items which 'belong' to him. This will be the case if they are tenant's fixtures (ie removable by him at the end of the lease) or they are landlord's fixtures (eg lifts) which are treated for capital allowances as belonging to the tenant if he was required by the terms of his lease to incur the expenditure (FA 1971 s 46(2)). (In such a case, on the termination of the lease any balancing adjustment is levied on the landlord in recognition of the fact that the asset really belongs to him.) In *Stokes v Costain Property Investments Ltd* (1984) the unfortunate lessee incurred massive expenditure on the installation of lifts and central heating under a separate agreement to develop the site *before* the commencement of his lease. He could not claim allowances in respect of them as they did not 'belong' to him within the meaning of s 46(2) and neither could the landlord claim the allowances as he was not trading. Such a restrictive interpretation of s 46(2) represented a departure from the former Revenue practice which had permitted the tenant to claim the allowance in such cases. The section is to be amended in the Finance Bill 1985 (for expenditure incurred after 12 July 1984) to ensure that someone will be entitled to the allowance (see *Simon's Tax Intelligence* 1984 p 529).

Hire purchase   The acquisition of plant or machinery on hire purchase is treated as an outright purchase so that capital allowances are granted on the capital element of the purchase price as soon as the asset is brought into use in the business. The interest element is a deductible business expense in the year it is paid.

III   INDUSTRIAL BUILDINGS

Capital allowances are available under the Capital Allowances Act 1968 for the construction of an industrial building or structure used for manufacturing (not distributive) trades.

1   Definition

Unlike plant and machinery, an industrial building is defined at length in the legislation. It includes a building used as a mill, factory or similar premises and a building used for the storage of manufactured goods or raw materials (see *Copol Clothing Co Ltd v Hindmarsh* (1984) and generally the Capital Allowances Act 1968 s 7). This definition includes a workers' canteen but not normally a retail shop, house, showroom or office. Expenditure on acquiring the land itself is not allowed except for costs of tunnelling, preparing and levelling. Subsequent expenditure on improvements to the industrial building is allowable (Capital Allowances Act 1968 s 8).

If part of an industrial building is used for a non-industrial purpose, the full allowance is still available so long as expenditure on that part does not exceed 25% of the expenditure on the whole building.

2   Form of the allowance

a) *Initial allowance*

An initial allowance (IA) is available which is being reduced in similar stages to the FYA (see p 102). Thus, it is reduced from 75% to 50% on expenditure incurred before 1 April 1987 under a binding contract entered into before 14 March 1984 qualifies for the 75% IA, but relief is restricted where the date on which the expenditure is incurred under a contract made after 13 March 1984 and before 31 March 1986 is artificially advanced. As with plant and machinery the 75% IA will continue for certain assisted projects. The IA is granted for the construction or purchase of a new (as opposed to a secondhand) building. Like the FYA, the IA may be disclaimed in whole or in part at the choice of the taxpayer. It is also available to a landlord where the building is let, provided that he is the owner (Capital Allowances Act 1968 s 1(3)) or where it is occupied by licensees (Capital Allowances Act 1968 s 1(1A),(3A)). In these cases the allowances are deducted from any rent (or like payment) that the owner receives. Any balancing charge that arises is taxed under Schedule D Case VI.

b) *Writing-down allowance*

A WDA is available at 4% of the original cost of construction for every year when the building is in use, including the first year when an IA is granted.

EXAMPLE 8

A purchases a new building in September 1984 for £100,000.

	£	£
Year 1:		
Purchase		100,000
IA at 50%	50,000	
WDA at 4% × £100,000	4,000	
		54,000
Year 2:		
Qualifying expenditure brought forward		46,000
WDA at 4% × £100,000		4,000
Qualifying expenditure carried forward		£42,000

c) *Balancing allowances or charges*

When the building is disposed of, the qualifying expenditure left on the building is compared with the disposal consideration and a balancing allowance or charge is made. A balancing charge can never recover more than the allowances given, so that if the disposal value exceeds the original cost of the building, the excess represents a capital gain chargeable to CGT or, in appropriate circumstances, to DLT.

The building is regarded as having been written down to nil value after 25 years (4% × 25 = 100% of cost). As a result, no WDA is available after 25 years (maximum), nor will a disposal after 25 years give rise to a balancing charge or allowance.

d) *Purchase of a secondhand industrial building*

A WDA is available to a purchaser whose use of a secondhand building qualifies as industrial. The WDA is calculated by spreading the 'residue of expenditure' over the balance remaining of the 25 year life of the building. The residue of expenditure is the written down value of the vendor plus any balancing charge (or less any balancing allowance).

3 Miscellaneous

Hotel buildings Expenditure on the construction or improvement of hotel buildings where the hotel has at least ten letting bedrooms, provides beakfast and an evening meal, and is open for at least four months between April and October, qualifies for an IA of 20% and annual WDA of 4% of the cost. This IA will be reduced to nil from 1 April 1986.

Enterprise zones To stimulate development in deprived areas, the Secretary of State has designated a small number of enterprise zones wherein expenditure on certain industrial buildings, hotels and commercial buildings (including shops and offices) qualifies for 100% IA which remains unaltered. A WDA of 25% of the cost is also available where less than the full IA is claimed.

Small workshops Relief as for enterprise zones is available for expenditure between 27 March 1980 and 26 March 1983 on small workshops of 2,500 square feet or less and between 27 March 1983 and 26 March 1985 on those of 1,250 square feet or less. The 100% IA can also be claimed when certain existing buildings are converted into individual self-contained workshops the average size of which does not exceed 1,250 square feet (see FA 1983 s 31).

IV OTHER CATEGORIES OF EXPENDITURE ELIGIBLE FOR CAPITAL ALLOWANCES

Agricultural or forestry buildings Allowances are available for capital expenditure by the owner or tenant of agricultural or forestry land used for the sole purposes of husbandry and forestry. The expenditure must be incurred on the 'construction' of, inter alia, farm or forestry buildings including farmhouses (for which only one-third of the cost is allowed); farm cottages; fences and walls; and drainage and sewerage works.

The allowances comprise an IA of 20% of the cost which may be disclaimed in whole or in part, and a WDA of 10% of the cost for every year (including the first) that the building is in use until the cost is written off. As from 1 April 1986, the IA will be reduced to nil and the WDA to 4%.

Assured tenancies Special allowances are available as expenditure from 9 March 1982 to 1 April 1987 on dwellings let on assured tenancies by bodies approved by the Secretary of State under the Assured Tenancies Scheme. The expenditure is limited to £40,000 (£60,000 in Greater London) on each house or flat and the same IA and WDA is available as for industrial buildings (see p 107).

Scientific research Capital expenditure on scientific research carries a 100% allowance.

Patents and 'know-how' The cost of purchasing a patent for use in a business is at present relieved by equal instalments over 17 years. This system will be replaced in 1986 by an annual WDA of 25% on a reducing balance basis. If the patent is subsequently sold a balancing charge or balancing allowance arises in relation to the qualifying expenditure left. Any excess of sale proceeds over original cost, is chargeable to income tax under Schedule D Case VI over six years, or over the remainder of the life of the patent, if less.

The cost of acquiring 'know-how' is at present allowable over 6 years. From 1986 an annual WDA of 25% will be given on a reducing balance basis. Any sale is a taxable trading receipt.

Residual Capital allowances are also available for mines and oil wells and mineral rights (at present under review) and for cemeteries and crematoria. The present IA of 15% on dredging will be reduced to nil from 1 April 1986 but the annual WDA will remain at 4% of cost.

V   LOSSES IN TRADES, PROFESSIONS OR VOCATIONS—
THE MAIN RELIEFS

1   **Introductory**

Whenever an individual or partnership makes a loss: ie where allowable expenses in an accounting period exceed taxable income, there are two repercussions. First, any year of assessment using as its basis period one in which the loss was incurred will have a nil tax assessment. Secondly, the loss is, in tax terms, an asset which may be used to cancel out or relieve tax assessments of that or other years, so that the taxpayer will either pay less tax or be able to reclaim tax which he has previously paid.

Where the loss is made by a trading company, it is not available for use by individual shareholders (even in a 'one man' company). Hence, where it is proposed to start a business, and early losses are anticipated, the advantages of income tax relief must be weighed against the protection of limited liability (see Chapter 33).

In addition to the main reliefs other income tax reliefs are available for losses in the early years (p 113ff) and for losses in the final years of a business (p 117ff).

When seeking to apply the reliefs it is important to realise that a loss may be eligible for relief under more than one provision and that the choice will usually rest with the taxpayer. It should be noted that certain of the reliefs are available against the taxpayer's earned before unearned income; this order of set-off is significant where a wife's earnings election is in force.

2   **Relief under TA 1970 s 171: carry-forward**

A loss which is sustained in carrying on a trade, profession or vocation can be carried forward under s 171 and set off against the first available profits of the same trade, profession or vocation without time limit. The loss must be deducted as far as possible from the earliest subsequent profits with the result that the taxpayer may lose his personal allowances.

EXAMPLE 9 *(see diagram opposite)*

Scrooge's accounts are as follows:

Accounting period

Year to 31 December 1981	£2,000 profit
Year to 31 December 1982	(£6,000) loss
Year to 31 December 1983	£1,600 profit
Year to 31 December 1984	£3,600 profit
Year to 31 December 1985	£4,000 profit

The income tax assessments are:

Tax year	*Taxable profit (loss)*
1982–83:	£2,000
1983–84:	NIL (£6,000 loss carried forward)
1984–85: (£1,600 – £1,600)	NIL (s 171: £4,400 loss carried forward)
1985–86: (£3,600 – £3,600)	NIL (s 171: £800 loss carried forward)
1986–87: (£4,000 – £800)	£3,200 (s 171)

Scrooge would lose the benefit of his personal allowances in 1983–84, 1984–85 and 1985–86 if he has no other income against which to set them.

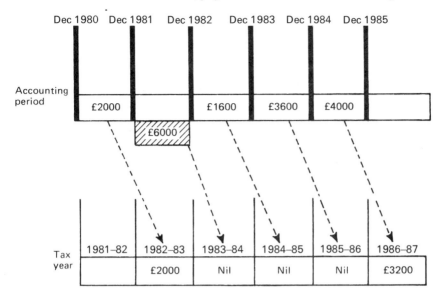

Where a business receives income which has already been taxed at source (eg dividends) any loss brought forward under s 171 can be used against that taxed income and a repayment claim made (TA 1970 s 171(3)).

In calculating the loss to be carried forward under s 171, certain items may be treated as losses. For instance, by s 173 an annual payment which is made wholly and exclusively for the purpose of the business and assessed under TA 1970 s 53 (because the taxpayer has no income) and which cannot be relieved because there are no profits against which to set it, may be treated as a loss for s 171. The same principle applies to unrelieved interest payments (TA 1970 s 175).

EXAMPLE 10

Oliver makes a loss of £10,000 in his accounting year ended 31 March 1984. He makes an annual payment each year on 1 March of £1,000. In 1984–85 there will be a nil assessment on his business profits, but under TA 1970 s 53 the Revenue require Oliver to pay basic rate income tax on £1,000 at 30% (£300). As he made a loss of £10,000 and has paid out £1,000 in total, Oliver's loss to be carried forward under s 171 is £11,000.

Losses can only be carried forward under s 171 against future profits from the same business. Thus, if the nature of the business changes in a future year, there can be no carry-forward of losses. In *Gordon and Blair Ltd v IRC* (1962) brewing losses could not be carried forward against bottling profits. Similarly, if the business ceases, there can be no carry-forward, although special rules operate on a change of partners (see Chapter 29).

There are two major drawbacks to loss relief under s 171. First, it is only available against profits from the same business and not against any other income of the taxpayer. Secondly, the relief is not immediate. Even assuming that the business makes profits in the future, loss relief may not be obtained for some years (see *Example 9*). In inflationary times, this delay renders the loss relief less valuable in real terms (cp TA 1970 s 168).

3   Relief under TA 1970 s 168: carry-across

Section 168 enables loss relief to be claimed in the year of assessment in which the loss is actually sustained. In theory, the relief should be apportioned when an accounting period straddles two tax years but, in practice, the Revenue give relief for the tax year in which the accounting period showing a loss ends. Relief under s 168 is given against the taxpayer's total income for the relevant year of assessment, earned before unearned income. Insofar as any loss remains unrelieved in that year, it can be carried forward and set against his non-trading income for one further year provided that the business is still being carried on for at least part of that year (TA 1970 s 168(2)).

EXAMPLE 11 *(see diagram opposite)*

Bertrand makes up his accounts to 30 September each year as follows:

Accounting period
Year to 30 September 1982   £5,000 profit
Year to 30 September 1983   £10,000 loss
Year to 30 September 1984   £2,000 profit

In each of the tax years 1983–84 and 1984–85 Bertrand also has other income which is assessed on a current year basis: viz £2,000 Schedule E (employment) income and £1,000 Schedule A (rental) income.

Under s 168 the loss of £10,000 can be relieved in the tax year 1983–84, in which it is made, and in the following tax year as follows, but with a loss of Bertrand's personal allowance in 1983–84.

Tax year	*Total income*	*Losses*
1983–84:	£	£
Schedule D Case I		
(Preceding Year Basis (**PYB**))	5,000	
Schedule E	2,000	
Schedule A	1,000	
	8,000	
Loss made in 1983–84		(10,000)
Section 168(1) relief	(8,000)	8,000
	NIL	(2,000)
1984–85:		
Schedule D Case I loss (PYB)	—	
Schedule E	2,000	
Section 168(2) relief	(2,000)	2,000
	—	—
Schedule A	£1,000	

Once the taxpayer has exhausted his total income in the relevant year, any surplus loss can be set against the total income (earned before unearned) of his spouse. The taxpayer can, however, elect for this set-off not to apply and should do so if this will preserve his personal allowances (TA 1970 s 168(3)). Thus, if in *Example 11* Bertrand's wife Bertina had Schedule E income in 1983–84 of £2,000, he should elect not to set off the balance of his loss (£2,000) against her income in order to preserve their personal allowances. If spouses have elected for the separate taxation of the wife's earnings and the husband is the trader, he has no right of set-off against his wife's earned income. If the wife is the trader, her trading loss can only be set off against her earnings from another source (FA 1971 Sch 4 para 4(1)).

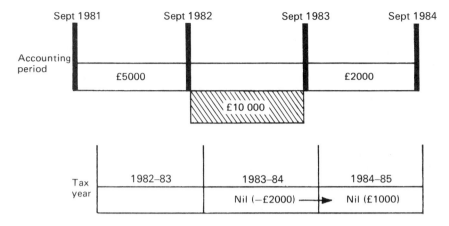

The taxpayer must make a specific written election for s 168 relief for each of the two years and must do so within two years of the end of the relevant year of assessment. Election may be made for the first and not for the second year or vice versa or for both years. When the election is made for both years and the business suffers a further loss in the next accounting period, the loss carried forward from the earlier year is set off first.

Certain restrictions are placed on the availability of s 168 relief in order to prevent a taxpayer indulging in a 'hobby' trade. TA 1970 s 170 denies the relief unless the taxpayer can show that the loss-making business was carried on on a commercial basis with a view to profit (although a reasonable expectation of profit is deemed conclusive evidence of this). By TA 1970 s 180, a farmer or market gardener will automatically lose the relief if he incurs a loss in each of the preceding five years unless he can show that any competent farmer or market gardener would have made the same losses. The moral here is 'let your losses be those of the reasonable man or make a profit every sixth year!'

4   Relationship between TA 1970 ss 168 and 171

Section 168 requires a specific election, otherwise there is automatic carry-forward under s 171. To the extent that s 168 is chosen, it is only the balance of the loss remaining unrelieved under that section that can be carried forward under s 171.

The two advantages possessed by s 168 are that the relief is given immediately and against all income of the taxpayer. It follows that an unprofitable trade can be 'nursed' by a wealthy taxpayer. Section 168 may also be advantageous when it is likely that the business will close with the result that s 171 will cease to be available. However, s 168 should not be chosen if it would result in the loss of personal allowances or when profits or rates of tax are likely to rise and the taxpayer can afford to wait for his relief.

VI   RELIEF FOR LOSSES IN THE EARLY YEARS OF BUSINESS

1   FA 1978 s 30: initial loss relief

A business will often make losses in its early years and FA 1978 s 30 provides relief where a loss is sustained in the year of assessment in which the business is first carrried on, or in any of the next three years of assessment, as an alternative to relief under TA 1970 ss 168 and 171.

Losses must be calculated on an actual basis in each year and the relief is obtained by a set-off against the taxpayer's total income of the three years of assessment preceding the year of loss. The set-off is against earlier years before later years and in each year is against the taxpayer's earned before unearned income and then against his spouse's earned before unearned income. As under TA 1970 s 168, a married person can elect to limit the set-off to his income only. The effect of the relief is to revise earlier income tax assessments and to obtain a tax refund. Section 30 is available to individuals (including partners) for a maximum of four years only and is not available to a limited company. Therefore, where early losses are envisaged, it may be worth starting as a sole trader (or partnership) and at a later stage incorporating the business (see Chapter 33).

As with TA 1970 s 168, FA 1978 s 30 relief requires a specific election within two years from the end of the year of assessment in which the loss is sustained. In an attempt to prevent hobby trades the relief is denied unless it can be shown that the business was carried on on a commercial basis with a view to profit (FA 1978 s 30(4)). Further the relief cannot be extended to eight years by the taxpayer transferring the business to his spouse after the first four years (FA 1978 s 30(5)).

EXAMPLE 12 *(see diagram opposite)*

Fergus began business as a sole practitioner on 1 July 1983. His results for the first two years of assessment were:

1983–84: loss £14,000 (ie 1 July 1983–5 April 1984)
1984–85: loss £3,000 (calculated on the actual basis ie 6 April 1984–5 April 1985).

Before beginning his own business, Fergus was employed as an assistant solicitor. He also has income from dividends. This other income comprised:

	Salary (Schedule E)	Dividend (Schedule F)
1980–81	£9,600	£6,000
1981–82	£10,000	£6,400
1982–83	£12,000	£7,000
1983–84	—	£4,000
1984–85	—	£5,000

Fergus makes two separate elections for relief under FA 1978 s 30: first, for the £14,000 loss and subsequently for the £3,000 loss. The position is as follows:

1980–81	£
Schedule E income	9,600
Less part of 1983–84 loss carried back (under s 30)	(9,600)
	NIL
Schedule F income	6,000
Less balance of 1983–84 loss (s 30)	(4,400)
Revised assessment	£1,600

1981–82	
Schedule E income	10,000
Less 1984–85 loss carried back	(3,000)
	7,000
Schedule F income	6,400
Revised assessment	£13,400

1982–83	£
Schedule E income	12,000
Schedule F income	7,000
No revision of assessment of	£19,000

1983–84	
Schedule E income (Schedule D)	NIL
Schedule F income	4,000
No revision of assessment of	£4,000

1984–85	
Schedule D income	NIL
Schedule F income	5,000
No revision of assessment of	£5,000

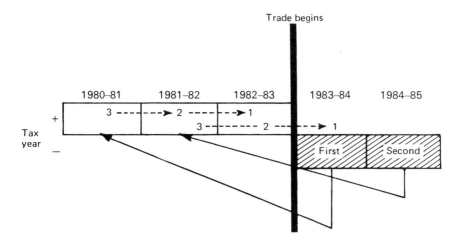

2   Relationship of FA 1978 s 30 with TA 1970 ss 168 and 171

As with s 168, relief under s 30 requires a specific election. The election need only be made for one year of loss, but, once made, that loss must be carried back against the taxpayer's income in the earlier years without limit, which may result in a loss of personal allowances.

FA 1978 s 30 and TA 1970 s 168 are alternatives so that the same portion of any loss cannot be relieved under both sections (ie twice). Where, however, relief has been given as far as possible under one section, any surplus loss remaining can be relieved by a specific election under the other section (see *Butt v Haxby* (1983)). Any surplus loss still unrelieved will then be carried forward under s 171.

EXAMPLE 13

Angus begins trading on 1 August 1983 and in the period to 5 April 1984 makes a loss of £15,000. His income in the preceding three years (1980–81 onwards) amounted to £10,000. If Angus elects for s 30 relief he will have wasted his personal allowances in the preceding years. He will be left with an unrelieved loss of £5,000 which can be relieved under s 168 against any other income which he may have in 1983–84 and (by a further election) in 1984–85. To the extent that relief is not given under s 168, the surplus loss will be carried forward under s 171.

Which relief the taxpayer chooses will depend upon the facts. FA 1978 s 30 relief is highly advantageous when the taxpayer has a large pre-trading income, since it will ensure a cash refund. Alternatively, if his other income in the year(s) of loss is large, relief under TA 1970 s 168 may be more attractive.

3   Losses and the opening year rules

The opening year rules of TA 1970 ss 116 and 117 are concerned only with the taxation of profits and do not affect the treatment of losses which are relieved in accordance with the above provisions.

In the case of a new business, as a result of the opening year rules, a period of loss may form the basis period of two or three years of assessment. However, the loss available for relief is limited to the actual loss sustained as reduced by any amount used to reduce profits in those basis periods. Compare two examples:

EXAMPLE 14

(1) Tartan began trading on 6 June 1983 with the following results:

6 June 1983–5 December 1983	£10,000 loss
6 December 1983–5 December 1984	£6,000 profit

Assessments (ignoring s 117 election)
1983–84: (actual)

6 June 1983–5 December 1983	£10,000 loss
6 December 1983–5 April 1984 ie $\frac{4}{12} \times £6,000$	£2,000 profit
Schedule D Case I assessment	NIL

Note that a portion of the £10,000 loss is in effect used to offset the £2,000 profit (therefore £8,000 loss unused).

1984–85: (first 12 months)

6 June 1983–5 December 1983	£10,000 loss
6 December 1983–5 June 1984 ie $\frac{6}{12} \times £6,000$	£3,000 profit
Schedule D Case I assessment	NIL

Note that £3,000 of the £8,000 surplus loss is used to offset the profit (leaving £5,000 loss).

1985–86: (PYB)

Profit of the year ending 5 December 1984	£6,000
Less s 171 loss (unused)	£5,000
Schedule D Case I assessment	£1,000

(2) Now assume that Tartan had the following results:

6 June 1983–5 December 1983	£3,000 loss
Year ending 5 December 1984	£6,000 profit

Assessments (ignoring s 117 election)
1983–84: (actual)

6 June 1983–5 December 1983	£3,000 loss
6 December 1983–5 April 1984	£2,000 profit
Schedule D Case I assessment	NIL

1984–85: (first 12 months)
6 June 1983–5 December 1983   £3,000 loss
6 December 1983–5 June 1984   £3,000 profit

Schedule D Case I assessment   NIL

1985–86: (PYB)
Year ending 5 December 1984   £6,000 profit

Notice in *Example 14(2)* that although no loss relief has been given under any of the specific loss provisions, the 'notional' losses (ie £5,000) used in arriving at assessments comes to more than the actual loss of £3,000. This notional use of losses is permissible (*Westward Television Ltd v Hart* (1968)). It is only when the loss is to be carried forward under s 171 (or used for s 168 or s 30 relief) that relief is restricted to the actual loss.

VII RELIEFS FOR LOSSES IN THE FINAL YEARS

1 TA 1970 s 172: transfer of a business to a company

The general rule is that loss relief is personal to the taxpayer who sustains the loss; it cannot be 'sold' with the business or otherwise transferred. Thus, if a business is incorporated, any unabsorbed loss of the old business which ceases to trade cannot be carried forward under s 171 by the company. However, TA 1970 s 172 provides that where the business of a sole trader or a partnership is transferred to a company and the whole or main consideration for the transfer is the allotment of shares to the former proprietor, he can set his unabsorbed losses against income which he receives from the company for any year throughout which he owns the shares allotted to him and during which the company continues to trade. He will normally be able to set the losses against either dividends on the shares or salary if he is a director or employee of the company in the order of earned before unearned income.

EXAMPLE 15

Evans sells his business to a company in return for an allotment of shares on 30 September 1983. His unused losses from the trade amount to £4,200.
In the period from 1 October 1983 to 5 April 1984, he receives a salary of £3,000 and dividends (gross) of £400 from the company. In 1984–85 he receives a salary of £5,000 and dividends of £600. Evans obtains relief under s 172 as follows:

	Total income £	Losses £
1983–84		
Unabsorbed Schedule D Case I loss		(4,200)
Salary	3,000	
Dividends	400	
	3,400	
Less s 172 relief	(3,400)	3,400
	NIL	(800)
1984–85:		
Salary	5,000	
Less s 172 relief	(800)	800
	4,200	
Dividends	600	
	£4,800	

Relief under s 172 is given automatically (as an extension of s 171) as if the original business had not ceased and as if the income derived from the company were profits of that business. However, for all other purposes the business has discontinued and, if the taxpayer wants relief for his business loss in the year of discontinuance under s 168(1), or terminal relief under s 174 (see below), he must make a specific election to that effect. Notice that s 172 relief is given to the taxpayer who sustains the loss and affords no relief for losses made by the newly-formed company.

2   TA 1970 s 174: terminal loss relief

If a loss is sustained in the last 12 months of a business, the unabsorbed loss of that period, so far as not otherwise relieved (eg under TA 1970 s 168, in the year of discontinuance) may be relieved by set-off against the business profits of the three years of assessment preceding the one in which the business terminates. Relief is given as far as possible against later rather than earlier years.

The loss is calculated on an actual basis and includes (i) unrelieved capital allowances within that 12 month period, (ii) any annual payments charged under TA 1970 s 53, (iii) any unrelieved interest payments so long as they are incurred wholly and exclusively for the purposes of the business. If any part of that period produces a profit (because it falls within a different accounting period) it is treated as nil in the computation of the terminal loss.

If profits of a preceding year are insufficient to absorb the loss, dividends and other income taxed at source in that year (and which are received in the course of carrying on the business) are treated as profits for the purposes of obtaining a repayment of income tax (TA 1970 s 171(3)).

Relief may be claimed under TA 1970 s 174 as an alternative to relief under TA 1970 s 172 (transfer to a company). If s 174 relief is claimed, any unused loss cannot be relieved under s 172.

EXAMPLE 16 *(see diagram opposite)*

Dolly closes down her hairdressing business on 5 June 1985. Her results for the four years ending 5 December 1984 and for her final six months of business were:

Accounting period	Profit/loss	Tax years	original assessments
Year to 5 December 1981	£11,000 profit		
Year to 5 December 1982	£7,000 profit	1982–83	£11,000
Year to 5 December 1983	£3,000 profit	1983–84	£7,000
Year to 5 December 1984	£1,000 profit	1984–85	£3,000
Six months to 5 June 1985	£12,000 loss	1985–86	£1,000

The 1985–86 assessment will be revised to nil under TA 1970 s 118 (the actual profits of the period 6 April 1985–5 June 1985 (none)). As the Revenue would not make a s 118 election in respect of 1983–84 and 1984–85 the assessment for these years remains unaltered. The 'terminal loss' is calculated as:

1985–86

6 April 1985–5 June 1985 ie $\frac{2}{6} \times$ £12,000 loss   £4,000 loss

1984–85

6 June 1984–5 December 1984 ie $\frac{6}{12} \times$ £1,000 profit   NIL

6 December 1984–5 April 1985 ie $\frac{4}{6} \times$ £12,000 loss   £8,000 loss
                                                                                    £12,000 loss

This terminal loss can be relieved first in 1984–85 then in 1983–84 and finally in 1982–83 resulting in the following revised assessments (and repayments of tax):

Final assessments

1982–83	£9,000	(£11,000 – £2,000)
1983–84	NIL	(£7,000 – £7,000)
1984–85	NIL	(£3,000 – £3,000)
1985–86	NIL	(£12,000)

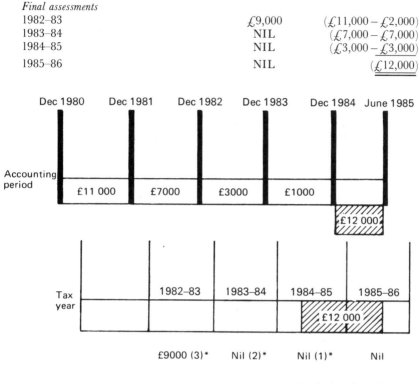

* = Order of set off

VIII PROBLEMS AND SPECIAL CASES

1 Capital allowances and losses

Capital allowances are deductible from profits. They may be used to create or increase a loss under TA 1970 s 168 or FA 1978 s 30 in the year that the expenditure is incurred (TA 1970 s 169 and FA 1978 s 30(7)). Alternatively, any unused capital allowances may be carried forward and deducted from the profits of the next and subsequent accounting periods.

EXAMPLE 17

In the year ended 31 December 1983 Albert made a profit of £3,000 and in the year ended 31 December 1984 a loss of £2,000. In addition, on 1 December 1984 he bought a machine for which he is entitled to capital allowances of £200.

Ignoring the availability of loss relief, Albert's Schedule D Case I assessments will be:

1984–85 (year ending 31 December 1983):	£3,000 profit
1985–86 (year ending 31 December 1984):	NIL

In the accounting year 1984 Albert has made a loss of £2,000. If he elects for s 168 relief, he can treat his unused capital allowances of £200 as an additional loss to be relieved against his profits of 1984–85 resulting in a revised assessment for 1984–85 on a £800 profit (ie £3,000 – [s 168 relief of £2,000 + capital allowances of £200]).

Insofar as capital allowances are carried forward they may not be used to increase or create a s 168 or s 30 loss. However, as they may be deducted from profits in preference to the current capital allowances this restriction is usually of reduced importance.

2 Partnerships

The above reliefs apply to a member of a partnership in respect of his share of any loss in a year of assessment. Difficulties may arise, however, in deciding which reliefs are available on a deemed discontinuance under TA 1970 s 154 whether or not the partners make an election under TA 1970 s 154 to be taxed on the preceding year basis (for details see Chapter 29).

3 Woodlands

A person who manages woodlands on a commercial basis with a view to the realisation of profit and who has elected to be taxed under Schedule D Case I (rather than under Schedule B; see Chapter 8) is assumed not to be carrying on a trade. Relief for losses is, however, given to him specifically under TA 1970 ss 168, 171 and 174. He is not entitled to relief under FA 1978 s 30.

4 Investment in corporate trades (FA 1980 s 37)

As a general rule, a person who subscribes for shares in a company and later disposes of them at a loss can only claim CGT relief for his loss. In an attempt to stimulate investment in corporate trades, FA 1980 enables the taxpayer to obtain income tax relief for his loss in certain circumstances under the 'venture capital scheme'. Broadly, FA 1980 s 37 allows an individual who has made a loss on the disposal of shares in a 'qualifying trading company' to deduct the loss from his total income in the year of assessment in which the loss is incurred. This relief is hedged about with restrictions:
(1) It is available only to an individual who subscribes for shares in a company for money or money's worth, including one who acquires the shares from a subscribing spouse; it is not available to a subsequent purchaser of the shares.
(2) The disposal giving rise to the loss must be a sale at arm's length for full consideration; or a distribution from the company on a dissolution or a winding up; or a deemed disposal under CGTA 1979 s 22(2) where the shares have become of negligible value.
(3) The company must satisfy the complex requirements of FA 1980 s 37(5) and (12). Basically, it must be an unquoted trading company, resident in the UK which does not trade in certain prohibited items such as land or shares.

If these conditions are satisfied, the allowable loss is calculated on CGT principles and is deducted in priority to relief under TA 1970 s 168 or FA 1978 s 30 from the individual's earned, before unearned, income and then subject to contrary election from his spouse's income.

The deduction is given in the year of assessment in which the loss arises and in one following year. The taxpayer must make an election in each case within two years of the relevant year of assessment.

Where the taxpayer has elected for s 37 relief for year 1 (when the loss occurs) any surplus loss can be set off against capital gains in year 1. If he subsequently elects to relieve that surplus loss under s 37 in year 2 instead, his CGT assessment for year 1 must be revised to prevent him from relieving the same loss twice. Any loss still unrelieved after the s 37 election in year 2 can be set off against capital gains (only) of that and subsequent years.

To prevent the taxpayer from obtaining total tax relief on his investment, any income tax relief he received on the acquisition of the shares under the Business Expansion Scheme (FA 1983 s 26; p 36) must be deducted from the base value of the shares when calculating an allowable loss for CGT and therefore, for s 37 (see *Example 19(2)*; p 38).

8 Schedules A and B—land

'Land, it has been said, is the perfect subject for taxation. This is undoubtedly true' (C Clark *Taxmanship* Hobart Paper (1964)).

I SCHEDULE A

1 Ambit

TA 1970 s 67 charges to tax the 'annual profits or gains arising in respect of rents and certain other receipts from land'. The charge is, therefore, on:

(1) Rents under leases of land in the UK. Rent is not defined, but is given its ordinary meaning of a payment by an occupier of land to his landlord for the use of the land. 'Lease' includes an agreement for a lease but not a mortgage by way of lease. Rents are the most common form of receipt under Schedule A.

(2) Rentcharges and other forms of recurrent payment derived from land. A rentcharge is an annual sum which can last for ever and is payable otherwise than by a tenant to his landlord, eg by one freeholder to another.

(3) Most other kinds of income that a person receives by virtue of his ownership of land, eg, fees for easements and profits à prendre. (See for instance *Lowe v J W Ashmore Ltd* (1971) which held that payments received for the sale of turves fell within this provision.)

It should be noted that tax is charged under TA 1970 s 67 on annual profits and gains ie only on so much of the receipt as is left after making certain deductions. 'Annual' means that the receipt must be income as opposed to capital, although in certain circumstances premiums (capital payments made on the grant of a lease) are deemed to be income (see below).

Although the ambit of TA 1970 s 67 is very wide, the following types of income are not taxed under Schedule A:

Income expressly excluded from Schedule A (TA 1970 s 67(1) para 3)   This includes yearly interest; profits and gains arising from mines, quarries and certain other concerns such as markets, tolls, bridges and ferries which by TA 1970 s 112 are taxed under Schedule D Case I; mineral rents and royalties (which are taxed half as income under Schedule D and half as capital) and miscellaneous receipts of income from, eg, wayleaves or tolls, in all of which cases the income is received after basic rate tax has been deducted at source by the payer under TA 1970 s 156.

Furnished lettings   Where a landlord receives rent from furnished lettings that sum will include a payment for the use of the furniture. The whole rent is charged under Schedule D Case VI unless the landlord elects within two years from the end of the year of assessment to be assessed under Schedule A for the portion attributable to the rental of the land. The use of the furniture continues to be taxed under Schedule D Case VI (TA 1970 s 67(2)). A landlord will make this election if the loss relief provisions or the allowable deductions under Schedule A are more favourable to him.

Receipts from trading on land   Only income which arises from the ownership of land is assessed under Schedule A. Thus, income received from a trade carried out on land is charged under Schedule D Case I as earned income (*Lowe v J W Ashmore Ltd* (1971)). This distinction will not always be obvious; eg, theatre or cinema receipts and profits from an hotel are receipts of a trade, but money received by a car park proprietor is arguably a receipt arising from the ownership of land.

If a landlord lets premises and provides services for the tenants he is prima facie assessable under Schedule A (or Schedule D Case VI if the premises are furnished) unless the receipts for services are receipts of a trade and assessable under Schedule D Case I. If the services amount to activities which are more than a mere exploitation of proprietary rights in the land, the receipts are trading receipts. In the case of let premises this is a question of fact and degree; it was thought that services over and above those provided by an ordinary landlord would be trading receipts (see *Fry v Salisbury House Estate Ltd* (1930)). Recent cases suggest, however, that it will be very difficult for a landlord who provides services to succeed in establishing that they are anything more than a mere exploitation of proprietary rights. In *Webb v Conelee Properties Ltd* (1982), the court held that there was no such trade as 'the letting of properties producing a rent' since that is precisely what is charged to tax under Schedule A and the taxpayer had conducted no other activities which could have amounted to a trade.

In *Griffiths v Jackson* (1983), income from letting furnished flats or bed-sitting rooms to students was held to be income from land assessable under Schedule D Case VI rather than the earned income of a trade with the attendant benefits of the capital allowances, the generous loss relief provisions and the capital tax reliefs available to a trader (see also *Gittos v Barclay* (1982)). FA 1984 amended these rules (with effect from 6 April 1982) by treating the profits of furnished holiday lettings as trading income and by extending CGT retirement and roll-over relief to such landlords (see further p 136).

2   Basis of assessment and collection of tax

Tax is charged under Schedule A on the profits of the current year of assessment and is due on or before 1 January of the tax year. As a result, the Revenue raise a provisional assessment on the taxpayer based on the previous year's rent which is later corrected when the true rent for the year is known. A landlord is, therefore, taxed on rent owing as well as rent received. He can claim relief for any rent that he never received so long as either he took reasonable steps to recover that rent or deliberately waived it to avoid hardship to a tenant (TA 1970 s 87).

Tax should be paid by the landlord. If he fails to pay, it may be collected from any tenant in occupation, who can re-imburse himself by deduction from subsequent payments of rent to the landlord. If the tenant is left out of pocket he can reclaim that sum from the Revenue (TA 1970 s 70(1)). Alternatively, unpaid tax can be collected from any agent of the person in default who has received rent or receipts from any land on behalf of that person (TA 1970 s 70(2)). If a tenant pays rent to a non-UK resident landlord, he must deduct basic rate income tax from the rent and account for it to the Revenue (TA 1970 s 89). Similarly, where part of any premium paid to a non-resident landlord is treated as income in the landlord's hands (see below), the tenant must deduct basic rate income tax from that part and account for it to the Revenue.

3   Deductions from rent

Income tax under Schedule A is charged on receipts less certain deductions. Allowable expenditure can only be deducted when it has been paid; the mere incurring of the liability is insufficient. The major deductions available against rental income, under TA 1970 s 72, are as follows:

Payments in respect of maintenance, repairs, insurance or management   Maintenance and repairs must be distinguished from improvements which are capital expenditure and, therefore, not deductible from rent. In general, repairs are only deductible if they would be deductible under Schedule D Case I. Thus the cost of repairs is, for instance, usually disallowed (and treated as a capital expense) where the disrepair arose before the period of the relevant lease (see *Law Shipping Co Ltd v IRC* (1924) and *Odeon Associated Theatres Ltd v Jones* (1971) p 86); a landlord must, therefore, have regard to the state of repair of premises when bought for letting. (Note ESC A21 which is available where property passes between spouses on death.)

Insurance expenses, to be deductible, must relate to the cost of insuring the building and not its contents.

Management expenses include the expenses of managing the property (eg advertising for tenants and collecting rent). For property companies the expenses of managing the land are deductible in arriving at Schedule A profits whereas the cost of managing the company is subject to the special corporation tax rules for management expenses (Chapter 28).

Services   The cost of providing services, where payment for the services is included in the rent, is deductible. Strictly, the services must be required by the lease, but in practice, the Revenue allows a landlord to deduct all his commercial expenses of a revenue nature in providing services or amenities for tenants eg the provision of central heating and the cleaning and lighting of the common parts (see IR 27).

Rates   Payments for general and water rates by the landlord are deductible expenses.

Superior rent   Payments of rent to a superior landlord, and rentcharges for which the landlord is responsible, are deductible.

Interest relief   Interest on a loan to purchase or improve the property is deductible from rent under FA 1974 Sch 1 para 4 provided that the property is let at a commercial rent for at least 26 out of the 52 weeks in the tax year; or when the property is not let, it is available for letting, owner-occupied or under repair.

Provided that these conditions are all satisfied, interest on a loan of any amount is deductible; there is no £30,000 ceiling as for a qualifying loan in connection with a private residence. Further, the interest is deductible from rent that the landlord receives from *any* property. Surplus interest can be carried forward and deducted from rent in future years so long as the above conditions remain satisfied in those years.

EXAMPLE 1

H owns a house which he lets to a tenant at a rent of £200 per month, payable in advance, commencing on 1 January 1984. He incurs the following expenses:

		£
15 December 1983	advertising for a tenant	60
10 February 1984	repair to burst pipe	40
10 February 1984	installing central heating	500
30 March 1984	rates	300

		£
H's 1983–84 Schedule A assessment will be:		
Rent receivable (January–April inclusive 4 × £200) =		800

		£	
Less	Advertising	60	
	Repairs	40	
	Rates	300	400
			£400

Notes:

(1) April's rent is included because it is receivable on 1 April 1984, ie within the year of assessment 1983–84.

(2) Expenditure on central heating is an improvement, ie capital expenditure and not deductible. Capital allowances are not available for plant or machinery bought for use in a dwelling house. They are available against Schedule A profits where machinery and plant is provided for the purpose of maintaining or managing the premises which are let (TA 1970 s 78). Central heating is not plant for these purposes.

4 Deductions from other receipts (TA 1970 s 74)

The expense rules in TA 1970 s 74 are more generous than those for rent in that they allow the taxpayer to deduct any expense of an income nature which is directly connected with the source of the income.

EXAMPLE 2

(1) A owns a piece of land which acquired in order to preserve the amenities of his home. The land is subject to a rentcharge of £2 pa. He derives no income from it. He contracts with B, in return for an annual payment of £5 pa, to allow B a right of way across the land, and to keep the path clear. It costs him £3 pa to keep the path clear. The £3 is an allowable expense. The rentcharge is not allowable, because it is not an expense of the transaction under which B has a right of way. The income chargeable under Schedule A will, therefore, be £5 − £3 = £2.

(2) C owns a field which is subject to a rentcharge of £10 pa. He uses it exclusively for profit by charging holiday-makers for the right to put tents there for short periods. The rentcharge is allowable as an expense of these transactions.

(From the Inland Revenue booklet 'Notes on the taxation of income from real property' (IR 27 (1980).)

5 Capital allowances

Capital allowances are available to the Schedule A taxpayer for expenditure on machinery and plant used in the management of property, eg, where a machine is bought to repair the property (TA 1970 s 78). The taxpayer must elect for the allowances in accordance with s 78(3).

6   **Rules for excess expenditure; loss relief** (TA 1970 s 72(2)–(4))

Schedule A losses can only be set off against Schedule A income and there is no carry-back of losses against Schedule A profits of a previous year. The extent to which Schedule A losses can be carried forward or set against profits on other premises depends upon the type of lease involved.

A 'lease at a full rent' is one where the rent, on average, is sufficient to cover the landlord's expenses under the lease but need not be a full commercial rent.

A 'tenant's repairing lease' is one under which the tenant is responsible for maintaining or repairing the whole or substantially the whole of the premises. Such a lease may or may not be at a full rent.

A lease which is not a tenant's repairing lease is one where the landlord is obliged to do some or all of the repairs (landlord's repairing lease). This lease also may or may not be at a full rent.

The theory underlying the following rules seems to be that a lease at a full rent is not acquired as a loss-making asset so that the loss relieving provisions are relatively generous. By contrast, a lease which is not at a full rent qualifies for a much restricted relief.

Carry-forward of losses   Losses arising under any kind of lease may always be carried forward and set off against rents from the same lease of the same premises in a subsequent year (TA 1970 s 77(1)).

Losses arising from a previous lease of the premises or from a 'void period' (a period when the property was not let) can be carried forward against rent from the same premises under a subsequent lease, provided that both leases are at a full rent; that the property was available for letting during any void period; and was not owner-occupied. Expenses in this case include making good any dilapidations incurred during a previous lease or void period.

EXAMPLE 3

Property is let subject to a lease at a full rent running from 1983–1993 (lease 1). Expenses are incurred in repairing the premises in 1992–93 which are not fully relieved against the rent of that year. The property is empty from 1993 to 1995 whilst the landlord looks for suitable tenants. During this time he incurs expenditure in insuring and repairing the property. In 1995 he lets it (lease 2) under a tenant's repairing lease at a full rent.

Leases 1 and 2 are both leases at a full rent albeit lease 2 is a tenant's repairing lease. Accordingly, the unrelieved expenses of lease 1 in 1992–93 and of the void period can be carried forward and set against the first available rent received from lease 2 without time limit.

Pooling of losses (TA 1970 s 72(4))   If the same landlord has granted leases of different premises, excess expenditure incurred in one lease can be set against profits arising from a lease on another property in the same tax year, provided that both leases are let at a full rent and that the lease showing the profit is not a tenant's repairing lease.

7   **The taxation of premiums under Schedule A** (TA 1970 ss 80–85)

A premium is a capital sum paid by a tenant to a landlord in connection with the grant of a lease. To understand the taxation of premiums, it should be noted that Schedule A was introduced before CGT so that a landlord could have avoided paying any tax by extracting a capital sum from the tenant instead of rent. Accordingly, certain premiums are deemed to be income and so chargeable to income tax. Insofar as a premium is not chargeable as income it may be subject to CGT. As the maximum rate of income tax on that part of the premium treated as income is 60%, it is important for a landlord to ensure that no part of the premium is so treated.

a) *The charge* (TA 1970 s 80)

If a lease is granted for a period not exceeding 50 years and the consideration includes a premium, a proportion of that premium is treated as additional rent taxable under Schedule A. This proportion is the amount that is left after deducting 2% of the premium for each complete year of the lease other than the first. The effect of the 2% discount is that the amount of premium charged to income tax falls with the length of the lease. For a one year lease all the premium is taxed and for a 50 year lease 2%.

EXAMPLE 4

Lease 16 years; premium £3,000.

Discount 2% of £3,000 over 15 years $= £3,000 \times \dfrac{2}{100} \times 15 = £900$

Chargeable slice: $£3,000 - £900 = £2,100$

The grant of a sub-lease of 50 years or less will, as a general rule, be taxed in the same way as the grant of a head lease. If, however, a premium on the grant of the head lease was taxed under Schedule A, this is taken into account when taxing any premium on the grant of the sub-lease (TA 1970 s 83).

b) *Anti-avoidance provisions*

There are elaborate provisions designed to prevent the charge to income tax on premiums from being circumvented. First, a landlord cannot avoid the TA 1970 s 80 charge by disguising the length of the lease. If its length can be extended by an option to renew or shortened by an option to surrender or to terminate, those options will be taken into account only insofar as they are likely to be exercised (TA 1970 s 84).

EXAMPLE 5

L grants a lease to T for 60 years at a premium of £20,000 and a rent of £1,000 pa for the first ten years and thereafter at an annual rent of ten times the then market rent. T has an option to surrender the lease after ten years. For the purposes of Schedule A this is treated as a ten year lease since the tenant is likely to exercise the option to surrender in view of the penal increase in the rent after ten years.

Secondly, where a landlord, instead of taking a premium on the grant of a lease for 50 years or less, requires the tenant to make improvements to the premises, the amount by which the value of the landlord's reversion is increased as a result of those improvements is treated as a premium (TA 1970 s 80(2)). This provision does not, however, apply if the tenant is required to make improvements to another property of the landlord; if the obligation is not imposed by the lease; or if the expenditure would have been a deductible expense of the landlord.

EXAMPLE 6

Property is let from 1 June 1984, for 7 years. Under the terms of the lease the tenant is required to carry out certain structural alterations as a result of which the value of the landlord's interest in the premises is increased by £2,000.

Increase:	£2,000
Less discount: $\dfrac{2}{100} \times £2{,}000 \times 6$:	240
Included in 1984–85 Schedule A profits:	£1,760

Thirdly, TA 1970 s 80(3) and (4) charge 'delayed premiums' as income. If a premium becomes payable at some date during the currency of the lease or the tenant has to pay a sum for the waiver or variation of any terms of the lease, the sum is treated as a premium and in both cases the premium is taxed in the year of receipt as a premium for the then unexpired period of the lease. If a tenant has to pay a sum for the surrender of a lease it is taxed as a premium on a lease running from the date of commencement to the date of surrender.

Fourthly, the assignment of a lease, which has been granted at an undervalue is charged under TA 1970 s 81. The charge under s 80 could be circumvented by a landlord granting a lease to, say, his spouse or to a company which he owns. No premium would be charged on the grant but the lease could then be assigned to the intended tenant and a premium taken. Section 80 only applies to a premium paid on the grant of a lease not on its assignment. However, s 81 provides that, when a lease is granted for less than its market premium, tax is charged under Schedule D Case VI on assignors of the lease up to the amount of premium foregone by the landlord and to the extent that such assignors have made a profit on that assignment.

EXAMPLE 7

A grants B a 21 year lease at a premium of £2,000 although he could have charged £3,000. Therefore, the 'amount forgone' is £1,000. A is chargeable under Schedule A on the premium that he actually receives.

Two years later B assigns the lease to C charging a premium of £2,800. B receives £800 more than he paid; that is within the 'amount forgone'.

B is, therefore, chargeable under Schedule D Case VI on:

$$£800 - \left(\frac{2}{100} \times 20 \times £800 \right) = £480$$

Notice that the 'amount forgone' still outstanding is £200 and that the period of the lease remains at the original length (viz 21 years) for the purpose of discounting. Two years later C assigns the lease to D charging a premium of £3,200. He has received £400 more than he paid but only £200 of that is caught under TA 1970 s 81 since that exhausts the 'amount forgone' by A. C is chargeable, therefore, under Schedule D Case VI on:

$$£200 - \left(\frac{2}{100} \times 20 \times £200 \right) = £120$$

An assignee should, therefore, ensure (so far as possible) that the lease was not granted at an undervalue, and if necessary should take advantage of the clearance procedure under TA 1970 s 81(2).

The final anti-avoidance provision prevents the grant of a lease from being disguised as a sale (TA 1970 s 82(1)). If D sells land (freehold or leasehold) to E with a right to have the property reconveyed to him in the future, any difference between the price paid by E and the reconveyance price payable by D is treated as a premium on a lease for the period between the sale and the reconveyance and is taxed under Schedule D Case VI.

TA 1970 s 82(3) extends TA 1970 s 82(1) so that if D sells land to E with a right for him (or a person connected with him) to take a leaseback of the property in the future, any difference between the price paid by E and the aggregate of the premium (if any) payable on the grant of a lease by E, together with the value of the reversion in E's hands, is treated as a premium on a lease for the period between the sale and leaseback and is taxed under Schedule D Case VI. So as not to prejudice a commercial sale and leaseback, this provision does not apply where the leaseback is within one month of the sale.

EXAMPLE 8

D sells land to E for £40,000 with a right to take a 20 year lease of the property after 11 years for a premium of £8,000. The value of E's reversionary interest subject to the lease is £2,000. There is a deemed premium under TA 1970 s 80(3) of £30,000 (£40,000 − [£8,000 + £2,000]) on a lease of 11 years. D is chargeable under Schedule D Case VI on:

$$£30,000 - \left(\frac{2}{100} \times £30,000 \times 10 \right) = £24,000$$

c) *Top-slicing relief* (TA 1970 Sch 3)

If part of a premium is chargeable to income tax under any of the above provisions, it is treated as rental income in the year that it is received. Some relief is given to an individual (not to a company), in the form of top-slicing, to prevent the premium being swallowed up in tax (TA 1970 s 85(2) and Sch 3).

The provisions of Sch 3 are detailed but generally top-slicing relief operates as follows:

(1) The discounted premium (for instance £10,000) is divided by the length of the lease (say ten years) to find the 'yearly equivalent' (here £1,000).
(2) Expenses are only set against the yearly equivalent insofar as they cannot be set against rent.
(3) The balance of the yearly equivalent after deducting allowable expenses is added to the top of the taxpayer's other income for the year to work out the highest rate of tax applicable. That rate of tax (say 40%) is charged in that year on the whole of the chargeable premium (here 40% × £10,000 = £4,000).
(4) If the yearly equivalent is completely used up by outgoings, the chargeable premium is taxed at the rate applicable to the highest part of the taxpayer's other income for the year. The whole premium is taxed after deducting allowable expenses.

d) *Premium payable in instalments*

If the premium is payable in instalments, tax is charged on the total of the instalments in the tax year when the first instalment is payable. Top-slicing relief is available. In addition, the tax may be paid by instalments over the shorter of the period of the instalments of the premium and eight years if the taxpayer can satisfy the Revenue that to pay the tax in one lump sum would cause him 'undue hardship' (undue hardship is not defined; TA 1970 s 80(6)). This claim must be made within the tax year following the one when the first instalment of the premium became payable (FA 1970 Sch 4 para 1(2)).

e) *Relief for traders paying a premium on trading premises* (TA 1970 s 134)

Rent is an allowable deduction from the trading income of a trader (TA 1970 s 130). If a trader is granted a lease of business premises for 50 years or less at a premium, he can treat a portion of the premium as an annual rent and deduct it from his trading income. This portion is the amount of the premium that is charged to income tax in the landlord's hands under Schedule A divided by the unexpired term of the lease. The rest of the premium is a capital expense.

A premium paid by a trader who takes an assignment of a lease is not allowable as a deduction from trading income.

EXAMPLE 9

L grants T a lease of business premises for ten years at an annual rent of £100 and a premium of £10,000.

L is chargeable under Schedule A on £8,200 of the premium (see TA 1970 s 80). The yearly equivalent of this sum, £820 (£8,200 ÷ 10), can be treated by T as additional rent so that each year he can deduct rent of £920 (£820 + £100) from his trading receipts.

II   SCHEDULE B: TAXATION OF INCOME FROM WOODLANDS

Income from woodlands is taxed either under Schedule B or, at the taxpayer's election, under Schedule D Case I. The taxpayer is given the choice because of the peculiar nature of woodlands as a source of income.

Tax is levied under Schedule B on the occupier of woodlands managed on a commercial basis with a view to the realisation of profit (TA 1970 s 91). If they are not so managed, there will be no liability to income tax but the capital taxes may apply. 'Occupier' does not include a person who has the use of woodlands for felling and removing timber in connection with his trade and who is taxed on his actual profits under Schedule D Case I (FA 1984 s 51).

The tax is on a notional income equivalent to one-third of the 'annual value' of the land. This is the rent that the occupier would receive if the land were let in its natural and unimproved state (ignoring any planted trees) under a lease whereby the tenant paid the rates and the landlord the cost of repairs and insurance. Although this calculation may produce a low taxable income, it is still likely to exceed the occupier's actual income whilst the trees mature. Expenses and capital allowances may not be claimed under Schedule B.

The occupier can elect to be taxed on his profits calculated under Schedule D Case I (TA 1970 s 111). This election is irreversible as regards that taxpayer's period of occupation, but on a change of occupation a new occupier is automatically assessed under Schedule B pending a s 111 election. An occupier cannot be selective in his election; it applies to all woodlands on the same estate. Woodlands planted or replanted within the ten years prior to the election may be treated as a separate estate.

Under Schedule D Case I, the profits from the occupation of the woodlands constitute a trade. Felled timber is treated as stock-in-trade, but not the growing timber which is a fixed asset. If the taxpayer carries on a trade in products derived from the woodlands, this is treated as a separate trade taxed under Schedule D Case I. In *Collins v Fraser* (1969) the occupier of woodlands who manufactured and sold crates made from the timber was held to be carrying on a separate trade (cp *Russell v Hird* (1983); see FA 1984 s 51 (above)).

Generally, the taxpayer will want to be taxed under Schedule D Case I when the trees are immature and non-income producing (so that he can claim capital allowances and loss relief). Once the trees are mature and income-producing he can then transfer them to a partnership or company which he controls in order to revert to the Schedule B basis. There is no requirement that the new occupier should be unconnected with the previous one.

III   ARTIFICIAL TRANSACTIONS IN LAND (TA 1970 s 488)

1   Application of TA 1970 s 488

TA 1970 s 488 is an anti-avoidance measure and if it catches a transaction income tax will be charged on the profit under Schedule D Case VI. Therefore, the maximum rate of charge will be 60% for individuals (in the case of companies the highest rate is 50%). When there is a possibility of a s 488 liability, the taxpayer may apply for a clearance (s 488(11)).

Section 488(2) specifies the conditions to be satisfied if the charge is to arise:

'This section applies wherever—
(a) land, or any property deriving its value from land, is acquired with the sole or main object of realising a gain from disposing of the land, or
(b) land is held as trading stock, or
(c) land is developed with the sole or main object of realising a gain from disposing of the land when developed,
and any gain of a capital nature is obtained from the disposal of the land—
(i) by the person acquiring, holding or developing the land, or by any connected person, or
(ii) where any arrangement or scheme is effected as respects the land which enables a gain to be realised by any indirect method, or by any series of transactions, by any person who is a party to, or concerned in, the arrangement or scheme;
and this subsection applies whether any such person obtains the gain for himself or for any other person.'

Property deriving its value from land includes shares in a landowning company, or a partnership interest in a landowning partnership. For these purposes land includes buildings and any estate or interest in land or buildings situated in the UK. The section is generally limited to land held or acquired by a dealer or developer.

a) There must be a disposal of the land so as to realise a gain of a capital nature

Disposal is not defined for TA 1970 s 488 but it will include the disposal of a controlling shareholding in a land-owning company, or an interest in a land-owning partnership or trust. The gain must be of a capital nature so that any gain which is treated as a trading profit for income tax or corporation tax will not be assessable under s 488.

b) *The gain must be realised by a chargeable person*

A chargeable person is either the person who acquires, holds or develops the land, or any person connected with him; or any person involved in any arrangement or scheme affecting the land which enabled the gain to be realised in an indirect way or by a series of transactions. This definition is extremely wide and it appears that a person can become involved in a scheme falling within TA 1970 s 488 without having an intention of realising a gain. In *Winterton v Edwards* (1980) L was a property developer who acquired land in order to realise a gain and W and B had small interests ($4\frac{1}{2}\%$ and 5% respectively) in any proceeds of sale. W and B were not involved in the complicated transactions entered into by L in an attempt to avoid any liability to CGT on his gains, but were assessed to tax under s 488 on their respective shares of the gain because they were concerned in L's transactions by virtue of their interests in the proceeds of sale.

A person will also be chargeable even if he makes no gain, but merely provides another person with the opportunity to make a gain (s 488(8); there is a similar provision in s 488(5)(a)) ie he is taxed on the gain of the person who makes the gain. In *Yuill v Wilson* (1980) the taxpayer was charged under s 488 because he had provided two Guernsey companies with the opportunity to realise a gain. The taxpayer is given the right to recover the tax from the person who realises the gain.

c) *When is a gain realised?*

Before a gain can be assessed, it must be 'realised'; ie the consideration for the disposal must be quantifiable in money terms (see TA 1970 s 489(13)). If, as in *Yuill v Wilson*, the consideration is a future contingent sum which cannot be valued, then to that extent no gain has been realised and there can be no s 488 charge. Hence, in *Yuill v Wilson* only the small cash sum actually received by the companies for the sale could be assessed. A further charge arose when the future contingent sums became payable (see *Yuill v Fletcher* (1984)).

A gain is, however, realised when the taxpayer has an enforceable right to the proceeds of sale even though they are only received in a later year (*Winterton v Edwards* (1980)).

d) *Motive*

According to s 488(1) the 'section is enacted to prevent the avoidance of tax by persons concerned with land or the development of land'. Whether this subsection is merely a statement of intent or whether it lays down a requirement that the taxpayer must have had a particular motive in carrying out the relevant transaction is not entirely clear; nor is it clear which tax the taxpayer must have tried to avoid, but certainly income tax or corporation tax on a trading gain (*Chilcott v IRC* (1982)) and possibly CGT also (*Winterton v Edwards* (1980)). An intention to avoid tax will be inferred if the taxpayer enters into an 'artificial' scheme or arrangement which resulted in a gain not otherwise chargeable to tax. Thus in *Yuill v Wilson* this intention (considered necessary by the Court of Appeal) was satisfied because the taxpayer entered into complicated transactions enabling gains to be realised by non-residents. In *Winterton v Edwards* (1980) the question of motive was not discussed, but the taxpayer had entered into a complicated CGT avoidance scheme. However, in *Page v Lowther* (1983) Warner J and the Court of Appeal applied s 488 to a transaction where there was no proven intention on behalf of the taxpayers to avoid tax and where the arrangement which resulted in the gain was not artificial; the fact that land was developed with the main aim of realising a gain by an indirect method on disposal was sufficient to bring the gain under s 488(2).

2 Calculation of the gain

The amount of the gain chargeable to income tax is the value received for the disposal less the disposal expenses, but subject to a 'just and reasonable' test (TA 1970 s 488(6)). Thus, although the legislation makes no specific provision for relief from a double charge to tax with DLT, it is thought that any profit chargeable to DLT would be excluded from charge under s 488. As s 488 applies only because the taxpayer has developed land with the intention of realising a profit, it does not charge any part of the gain attributable to a period before he decided to develop the land (TA 1970 s 488(7)). The land must, therefore, be valued at the time that the necessary intention is formed which poses considerable problems of valuation; eg, should the value be with or without the hope of planning permission?

3 Exemptions from TA 1970 s 488

Principal private residence Section 488 does not apply to a gain arising to an individual on the disposal of his principal private residence which is exempt from CGT (CGTA 1979 ss 101–105) or (generously) which would be exempt from CGT were it not that the property was acquired with the intention of making a gain on its disposal (CGTA 1979 s 103(3)).

Certain share sales Section 488 does not apply to any gain made on the disposal of shares in a company which holds land as trading stock, provided that the company sells the land in the usual course of its trade so as to be liable to corporation tax on the whole of the profit (TA 1970 s 488(10)). This exemption could produce anomalous results where the sale of shares precedes the sale of land. In *Chilcott v IRC* (1982) the taxpayer contracted to sell his shares in the company on condition that the company sold its land in the usual course of trading. As a result the company was assessable to corporation tax on the profit made on the sale of the land so that the taxpayer was not assessable on his profit on the sale of the shares under s 488. Vinelott J emphasised that this exemption from s 488 would not apply where the sale of the shares was part of an artificial scheme or arrangement. Thus, if the condition had not been imposed the taxpayer could have been assessed to tax under s 488(2) since by selling the shares he has sold the land and avoided a charge to corporation tax on the company. If, however, the company six years later sold the land for market value, so that corporation tax is charged on the whole profit, the taxpayer should be able to reclaim the income tax paid and be charged to CGT instead.

9 Schedule D Case VI—residual

   I   Scope
  II   Basis of assessment
 III Territorial scope

I SCOPE

Schedule D Case VI is a residual or sweeping-up Case. The charging provision of Case VI is TA 1970 s 109(2), which provides for tax to be charged on 'any annual profits or gains not falling under any other case of Schedule D and not charged by virtue of Schedules A B C or E'. Apart from this general charge, certain categories of income are specifically charged under Schedule D Case VI.

1 The general charge (TA 1970 s 109(2))

Although potentially very wide, catching any profits not otherwise charged to income tax, the ambit of Schedule D Case VI has been limited by the courts in a series of cases which are not always consistent. In common with Schedule D Cases I and II, the word 'annual' in s 109(2) means of an income nature rather than recurring each year. Capital receipts are not, therefore, caught. In *Scott v Ricketts* (1966) £39,000 was paid voluntarily to an estate agent (in addition to his fee) to persuade him to withdraw from participating in a property development scheme. It was held that the payment was a capital receipt and so not taxable under Schedule D Case VI.

The expression 'annual profits and gains' is construed *ejusdem generis* with other profits and gains under Schedule D. Therefore, if a receipt is not income profit for Schedule D Case I it cannot be for Schedule D Case VI either. This follows from *Jones v Leeming* (1930) which held that an isolated purchase and sale of property (here rubber estates acquired for re-sale at a profit) is either 'an adventure in the nature of a trade', in which case the profit is a trading receipt taxable under Schedule D Case I or a capital transaction. But in neither case is Schedule D Case VI relevant. Similarly, gifts, gambling winnings and findings do not constitute profits under Case VI.

The major example of profits falling within Case VI are profits received from the performance of casual services, which are neither derived from an office or employment, nor from a profession or vocation under Schedule D Case II because the element of regularity is missing. However, the profit must be substantially derived from the performance of services rather than from the sale of property. This distinction is sometimes blurred. In *Hobbs v Hussey* (1942) a solicitor's clerk (who was not an author by vocation) contracted with a newspaper to write his memoirs and then to assign the copyright; the payment that he received was taxable under Schedule D Case VI since it was substantially in return for the performance of services. The fact that there was a subsidiary sale of property (the copyright) was irrelevant and did not make the payment a receipt of capital (see also *Housden v Marshall* (1958) and *Alloway v Phillips* (1980)). By contrast, in *Earl Haig's Trustees v IRC* (1939), trustees who owned the copyright in the Earl's diaries allowed an author to use the diaries to write a biography in return for a half share of the profits from the book. This payment was not taxable under Schedule D Case VI since it was not a payment for services, but a capital receipt from the part-disposal of an asset (the diaries).

A payment that is partly in return for services and partly for the sale of property, will, it appears, be wholly taxable under Schedule D Case VI unless it can be apportioned. In *Hale v Shea* (1964), a payment to a retiring partner for future services (income) and for his share of the partnership assets (capital) was all taxed under Schedule D Case VI.

The payment must be made under an enforceable contract for ascertainable services, otherwise it is a gift and escapes income tax. Thus, in *Dickinson v Abel* (1969) a farm was owned by a trust and the taxpayer was a relation of a beneficiary. Because of this family connection, prospective purchasers offered him £10,000 if they managed to buy the farm for £100,000 or less. The taxpayer never agreed to provide services, but merely 'made the introduction' and eventually received £10,000. This payment was held to be a gift and escaped tax under Schedule D Case VI (see also *Scott v Ricketts* (above)). Notice, however, that once there is a contract for services, any receipt under it will be taxable even though it is not received for the particular services contracted for (see *Brocklesby v Merricks* (1934)). For other examples of payments for isolated services outside the normal business of the taxpayer and caught by Schedule D Case VI see *Ryall v Hoare* (1923) (payment of commission by a company to one of its directors for guaranteeing the company's overdraft) and *Lyons v Cowcher* (1916) (commission received from an isolated act of underwriting an issue of shares).

Casual profits received from activities which are analogous to a trade but which lack a fundamental characteristic are caught by Schedule D Case VI. In *Cooper v Stubbs* (1925) profits received by a cotton broker from dealings in 'futures' were taxable under Schedule D Case VI as the profits of speculation rather than of trade. There are also cases where the profits from stud fees have been taxed under Schedule D Case VI rather than Schedule D Case I (see for instance *Leader v Counsell* (1942)).

2 Specific charges

The categories of income specifically charged under Case VI include:
  (1) Income from furnished lettings (TA 1970 s 67; see below).
  (2) Premiums on leases received by an assignor of the lease and not by a landlord (TA 1970 s 81; see Chapter 8).
  (3) Sale and reconveyance of property (TA 1970 s 82(1); see Chapter 8).
  (4) Sale and lease-back of property (TA 1970 s 82(3); see Chapter 8).
  (5) Payments received for 'know-how' if not taxed as a trade receipt or as a capital gain (TA s 386(4); see Chapter 6).
  (6) Certain balancing charges (CAA 1968 s 6(6); see Chapter 7).
  (7) Certain receipts after a change of accounting basis (TA 1970 s 144; see Chapter 6).
  (8) Post-cessation receipts (TA 1970 ss 143; see Chapter 6).
  (9) Income from certain settlements which is taxed as that of the settlor (for example, under TA 1970 s 449; see Chapter 11).
 (10) Transactions in securities (TA 1970 ss 460–468; see Chapter 32).
 (11) Transfer of assets abroad (TA 1970 s 478; see Chapter 13).
 (12) Artificial transactions in land (TA 1970 s 488; see Chapter 8).
 (13) Gain on disposal by UK investor of a material interest in an offshore fund after 31 December 1984 (FA 1984 ss 92–100; see Chapter 32).

3 Furnished holiday lettings

It is established that the letting of property can rarely amount to a trade (see eg *Griffiths v Jackson* (1983); p 123). However, FA 1984 s 49 and Sch 11 (effective from 6 April 1982) provide for income from furnished holiday lettings in the UK to be treated as trading income and for the CGT business reliefs to be available for such properties. The provisions apply to lettings by individuals and by companies.

Definition   The accommodation must be available for letting to the public commercially as furnished holiday accommodation for at least 140 days in the tax year and must be actually let for at least 70 days. These periods need not be continuous and accordingly both winter and summer holiday accommodation may qualify. To ensure a 'genuine' holiday letting, it must not 'normally' (undefined) be let to the same person continuously in any seven months of the year (but including the 70 day period above) for more than 31 days. In the remaining five months of the tax year, therefore, the landlord may do what he wishes with the property, eg let it continuously; keep it empty; go into occupation himself. Hence, student accommodation will usually be excluded.

The term 'holiday' accommodation is undefined; presumably, if the above conditions are satisfied, it will be deemed to be a holiday letting (see eg *Gittos v Barclay* (1982) where these requirements are satisfied). Letting means occupation by a person other than the landlord and includes granting a licence to occupy.

Whether the accommodation qualifies as a holiday let in any tax year is judged on the facts of that year (for company landlords, the financial year). However, where the letting begins in a tax year (eg on 1 August 1984), it may qualify as a holiday let for that year if it satisfies the above requirements within the following 12 months (ie between 1 August 1984 and 31 July 1985). Likewise, a letting which ends in a tax year, must satisfy the necessary conditions during the previous 12 months.

Tax treatment   The income profits for the whole year will be assessed under Schedule D Case VI, but treated as trading profits for the purposes specified in FA 1984 Sch 11 para 1(2) and, therefore, receives most of the benefits of assessment under Schedule D Case I. Thus, the income is earned income and the deductible expenses, loss relief and capital allowances rules of Case I apply. However, the basis of assessment remains Case VI so that profits are assessed on income received not receivable in the current year (see below) and neither the preceding year basis nor the opening or closing year rules of Case I apply. The tax is, however, payable in two equal instalments in January and July as under Case I (see TA 1970 s 4(2)).

For CGT purposes the letting is treated as a trade in any year when it satisfies the above conditions or would do so but for the fact that the property is under construction or repair. Thus, roll-over (replacement of business assets) relief (CGTA 1979 s 115); hold-over relief on a gift of business assets to a company (CGTA 1979 s 126); and retirement relief (CGTA 1979 s 124) may be available on a disposal (see generally Chapter 16). However, a landlord who claims roll-over relief and occupies the property may not claim the main residence exemption against the entire gain on a subsequent disposal. In such a case the rolled-over gain is chargeable and the exemption applies only to any remaining gain. No special relief is given from CTT and holiday accommodation does not qualify for business property relief.

EXAMPLE 1

'Seaview' is purchased for £40,000 in 1984 and let as furnished holiday accommodation until 1990. It is then sold for £60,000 and the proceeds used in the purchase of 'Belvedere' for £85,000 which is also let. In 1992 the landlord takes possession and lives there until 1996 when he sells it for £145,000.

In 1990, the gain on 'Seaview' is rolled over into the purchase of 'Belvedere' giving it a base cost for CGT of £65,000. On the sale of 'Belvedere' in 1996 the gain is £80,000 of which £20,000 (rolled over from 'Seaview') is chargeable. The remaining gain is apportioned between the period of occupation which is exempt (ie 4/6 = £40,000) and the let period (ie 2/6 = £20,000) which is chargeable, unless eliminated under FA 1980 s 80 (see p 231).

If instead, Belvedere is sold in 1992 at the end of the season for £115,000, the gain of £50,000 might be eliminated by any retirement relief available to the landlord (he must show that the disposal is of a business or part of a business).

Where the same landlord lets several 'qualifying' properties, they are taxed as one trade. Should one or more properties qualify in the tax year and others not, because they fail to satisfy the 70 day requirement, the landlord can claim, within two years of the end of the relevant tax year, for the days of letting to be averaged between all or any of the properties thereby enabling all the properties to qualify. Thus, if property A is let in 1984–85 for 90 days and properties B and C for 50 days each respectively, A and B or A and C can be averaged so that two properties qualify; there are insufficient letting days for all three to qualify.

II BASIS OF ASSESSMENT

Tax is calculated under Schedule D Case VI on all profits or gains actually received (not receivable) in the current year of assessment or (depending on the circumstances) according to the average profits of a period not greater than one year (TA 1970 s 125). There are no express rules for deductible expenses, but the words 'profits or gains' imply a surplus of income after deducting expenses. A loss that is made on one Schedule D Case VI transaction can only be used, however, against profits from other Case VI transactions in the same tax year and any surplus carried forward against profits from Case VI transactions in future years (TA 1970 s 176). There is no set-off against income from other sources (cp the loss rules under Schedule D Cases I and II and note 3 above).

Whether Schedule D Case VI income is treated as earned or unearned income depends on its source. Casual profits from services for instance, are earned income, whereas rent from furnished lettings (other than in 3 above) is, generally, unearned.

III TERRITORIAL SCOPE

The usual principles apply (see TA 1970 s 108 at p 178). Thus, in *Alloway v Phillips* (1980) a Canadian resident contracted with an English newspaper to provide information about her husband Charles Wilson, the Great Train Robber. She was taxed under Schedule D Case VI on the £39,000 that she received, since the source of her income was her rights under the contract (a chose in action) which was enforceable and situated in the UK.

10 Schedule D Case III—annual payments

I   Introductory
II   Terminology
III   The machinery of tax collection (TA 1970 ss 52–53)
IV   Annual payments and anti-avoidance legislation
V   Taxation of interest payments
VI   Miscellaneous matters

I   INTRODUCTORY

Schedule D Case III charges income tax in respect of:

> '(a) any interest of money, whether yearly or otherwise, or any annuity or other annual payment, whether such payment is payable within or out of the United Kingdom, either as a charge on any property of the person paying the same by virtue of any deed or will or otherwise, or as a reservation out of it, or as a personal debt or obligation by virtue of any contract, or whether the same is received and payable half-yearly or at any shorter or more distant periods, but not including any payment chargeable under Schedule A, and
> (b) all discounts, and
> (c) income, except income charged under Schedule C, from securities bearing interest payable out of the public revenue.' (TA 1970 s 109(2)).

Income under Schedule D Case III is often referred to as 'pure income' because it will never be reduced by any deductible expenses; it is pure profit. It is also an area that abounds in complexity. In part, this is because of the variety of transactions that fall within its scope; in part, it is because of the stringent anti-avoidance provisions that seek to prevent the saving or avoiding of tax. Annuities and annual payments are sometimes referred to as settlements of income. This is because they operate to reduce the income of the payer and increase that of the payee. Hence, the payer can be seen as settling an income sum on the payee.

Income tax is charged on the income received (or credited) in the preceding tax year. Special rules, therefore, apply for the years when a new source of income is acquired and impose tax on the actual income for the first two tax years (the current year basis). The preceding year basis then operates for the third tax year, but the taxpayer is given the option to be assessed on a current year basis. In the final tax year when the income is paid tax is charged on a current year basis. The Revenue have an option to assess the taxpayer on the current year basis for the penultimate tax year if that would result in a larger assessment to tax than on the preceding year basis (PYB).

EXAMPLE 1

Judy covenants to pay £200 on 1 January and 1 July each year to Happy so long as Happy is registered as unemployed. The first payment is made on 1 January 1984 and payments continue until September 1991 when Happy obtains employment as a social worker. The final payment is accordingly made on 1 July 1991.

Happy's income under Schedule D Case III is as follows:

1983–84	£200	(1 January 1984)
1984–85	£400	(1 July 1984; 1 January 1985)
1985–86	£400	(PYB; no difference if current year basis is chosen).
1986–87/1989–90	(PYB).	
1990–91	£400	(PYB; no difference if current year basis is chosen and, therefore, the Revenue need not exercise their election).
1991–92	£200	(1 July 1991)

It is proposed to consider only the three main examples of payments falling within Schedule D Case III (interest, annuities and other annual payments).

As the taxation of interest is subject to special rules, interest payments are discussed separately at p 153.

II TERMINOLOGY

1 Interest

'Interest' is not statutorily defined, but was described as 'payment by time for the use of money' (per Rowlatt J in *Bennett v Ogston* (1930)). More precisely interest

> 'may be regarded either as representing the profit [the lender] might have made if he had had the use of the money, or conversely, the loss he suffered because he had not that use. The general idea is that he is entitled to compensation for the deprivation' (per Lord Wright in *Riches v Westminster Bank Ltd* (1947) 28 TC at 189).

Interest generally presupposes the idea of a debt to be repaid. The *Riches* case established that interest awarded by the court under the Law Reform (Miscellaneous Provisions) Act 1934 fell within the Schedule D Case III charge.

EXAMPLE 2

Bigco Ltd executes a debenture deed in favour of Mr Big who has made a secured loan to the company of £10,000. The deed provides for repayment of the loan together with a 'premium' of £2,000 by the end of 1990 and interest at 10% pa on the full redemption figure (£12,000) until 1990. The interest falls within Schedule D Case III and the repayment of £10,000 is a capital sum. The so-called 'premium' may be seen as deferred interest or, alternatively, as a capital sum paid as compensation for the capital risk taken by Mr Big.

Generally, the true nature of the payment is a matter of fact and the terms used by the parties are not conclusive (see *Lomax v Peter Dixon & Son Ltd* (1943) and *Davies v Premier Investment Co Ltd* (1945)). So long as the rate of interest charged is commercial, it is likely that the sum on which the interest is calculated will be treated as capital and will escape both income tax and CGT unless the debt is a 'debt on a security' within the meaning of CGTA 1979 s 134 (see Chapter 16). For the taxation of deep discount stock (see FA 1984 s 36 and Sch 9 at p 387) and for the taxation of investment in certain offshore funds (see FA 1984 ss 92–100, Schs 19, 20; and Chapter 32).

Finally, it should be noted that if the principal debtor defaults so that the moneys are paid under a contract of indemnity the sum will still be taxed as interest; if paid by a guarantor, the position is unclear (see *Re Hawkins, Hawkins v Hawkins* (1972) on indemnities and contrast *Holder v IRC* (1932) on guarantors).

2 Annuities

Annuities fall into two broad categories. First, a purchased annuity usually arising from a contract with an insurance company under which a capital sum is paid in return for a right to income (an annuity) for a stated period of time. Secondly, annuities payable under an instrument; for instance, an annuity that is bequeathed in a will.

3 Other annual payments

'Other annual payments' comprise a residual category, although the term is wide enough to include an annuity. Hence, all annuities may be described as annual payments but not all annual payments as annuities. The main features of an annual payment within Schedule D Case III were laid down by Jenkins LJ in *IRC v Whitworth Park Coal Co Ltd* (1958):

'(1) To come within the rule as an "other annual payment" the payment in question must be *ejusdem generis* with the specific instances given in the shape of interest of money and annuities . . .

(2) The payment in question must fall to be made under some binding legal obligation as distinct from being a mere voluntary payment . . .

(3) The fact that the obligation to pay is imposed by an order of the court and does not arise by virtue of a contract does not exclude the payment . . .

(4) The payment is question must possess the essential quality of recurrence implied by the description "annual" . . .

(5) The payment in question must be in the nature of a "pure income" profit in the hands of the recipient.'

The following matters should be borne in mind when applying the above propositions:

A legal obligation (propositions (2) and (3))   The legal obligation must arise from a contract, a court order, or a deed of covenant. Gifts, therefore, are not annual payments.

It does not matter that the payments are not of the same amount each year nor that the payments are contingent (*Moss Empires Ltd v IRC* (1937); contrast *British Commonwealth International Newsfilm Agency Ltd v Mahany* (1962)).

EXAMPLE 3

(1) Willie has two rich uncles, Feisal and Kemal, and they each wish to give him £1,000 every Christmas. Feisal is a very precise man and executes a deed of covenant to pay Willie £1,000 every year on 25 December. Kemal merely hands over a cheque each year.

The £1,000 paid under covenant by Feisal is an annual payment within Schedule D Case III, whereas the gift from Kemal is not (and is not Willie's income despite its recurrent quality). (See also the contrast between 'voluntary' maintenance and enforceable maintenance agreements; Chapter 36.)

(2) Aunt Lucy covenants to make Paddington's income up to £3,000 pa for the rest of his life. In some years she has to pay him money, in other years not. The sums are still annual payments although the amount paid each year varies.

Income sums paid to a beneficiary by the trustees of a discretionary trust fund are annual payments.

The payment must be 'annual' (proposition (4))   A payment is 'annual' if it is recurrent or is capable of recurrence. Payments made at intervals of less than a year will still be 'annual' provided that they may continue beyond a year. Periodic payments on divorce or separation are typical annual payments.

Only payments which are income in the hands of the recipient are included (see for instance *Martin v Lowry* (1927) for the meaning of 'annual profits' under Schedule D Case I). Payments may, therefore, be annual income payments; or they may represent instalments of a capital sum; or they may represent part income and part capital (in the latter case the income element will usually be interest on a debt which is being repaid in instalments). The interest element of any payment will be subject to charge under Schedule D Case III.

In considering whether payments constitute capital and/or income, the form of the document drawn up by the parties is not conclusive and a payment may represent a capital expenditure of the payer, but an income receipt for the payee and (presumably) vice versa.

EXAMPLE 4

Denis wants to sell his dental practice (which is worth £30,000) to Flossie and retire. The contract could be drawn up in a variety of different forms, eg:
(1) Flossie is to pay the purchase price of £30,000 over five years, at £6,000 pa. Each payment is a capital sum (see generally *IRC v Ramsay* (1935)).
(2) Flossie is to pay by instalments as in (1) above, but is to pay five instalments of £6,250 (so that the total sum to be paid will be £31,250). Each payment probably represents a capital and an income element and must accordingly be dissected. £6,000 is an instalment of capital and £250 interest on the unpaid balance (see *Secretary of State in Council of India v Scoble* (1903)).
(3) Denis agrees to be paid by Flossie either 15% of the profits of the business each year for the rest of his life or £1,000 pa whichever is the higher. Denis is in effect purchasing a life annuity so that the payments each year will be income in his hands (see *IRC v Church Comrs for England* (1977)); Flossie's payments are probably instalments of capital (see *IRC v Land Securities Investment Trust Ltd* (1969)).

The payment must be pure income profit in the hands of the recipient (proposition (5))   If the income is to be pure profit to the recipient, he must not have incurred allowable income expenditure in return for the payment.

This proposition prevents any attempt to disguise trading receipts as annual payments (see Scrutton LJ in *Howe v IRC* (1919)).

The rule is relatively easy to apply in the case of payments to traders. Far more difficult is the position when the payments are to a charity (consider for instance *IRC v National Book League* (1957) and *IRC v Campbell* (1968)). It would appear that a payment will still fall within Schedule D Case III in cases where the recipient promises something in return so long as that promise does not relate to the provision of goods or services, ie does not involve expense (see eg Lord Upjohn in the *Campbell* case: 'pure profit' had no relation to 'pure bounty').

EXAMPLE 5

Jason enters into a covenant with his old public school to pay £4,000 pa for seven years in return for the school agreeing to take Jason's son who is a dunce. It is further agreed that Jason will pay the full fees for his son's education (see the discussion in *Campbell v IRC* (1968) 45 TC at 427). The payment represents pure income profit to the school since the counter-stipulation costs it nothing. The position would be different if fees were not paid by Jason, when the annual payment would be treated as a payment in return for the son's education.

III   THE MACHINERY OF TAX COLLECTION (TA 1970 ss 52–53)

One of the characteristic features of Schedule D Case III is the provision under TA 1970 ss 52, 53 (and s 3) for the deduction and collection of tax at source from the payer. Both s 52 and s 53 are designed to achieve the same objective: under both, the Revenue collects basic rate income tax from the payer on the annual payment and the payer is permitted to deduct that sum from the amount paid to the payee. Generally, therefore, the payee will receive a net sum together with a credit for the basic rate income tax which has been deducted at source and paid to the Revenue on his behalf and will be assessed directly to higher rate tax, if appropriate; he is not entitled to claim by reason of the deduction that he has been underpaid (TA 1970 ss 52(1)(d), 53(1)).

1   The operation of TA 1970 s 52 for the payer

Section 52 will apply 'where any annuity or other annual payment charged with tax under Case III of Schedule D, not being interest, is payable wholly out of profits or gains brought into charge to income tax . . .'. It is, therefore, confined to the payer who has income ('profits and gains') on which he is subject to income tax. Accordingly, it cannot apply to companies as they do not pay income tax. When the payer satisfies these requirements, it is presumed (in the absence of contrary evidence) that the payment is made out of his income.

EXAMPLE 6

Wilbur, with an income of £10,000 pa from investments, covenants to pay his impecunious nephew Watson £1,000 pa for the next ten years.

Step 1: Wilbur is permitted under s 52(1)(c) to deduct from the £1,000 a sum equal to the basic rate tax thereon. Hence, at present rates, Wilbur can deduct £300 (30% × £1,000). He will, therefore, give Watson £700 together with a certificate showing that tax has been deducted (TA 1970 s 55; the appropriate form is IR 185).

Step 2: Wilbur's income is reduced from £10,000 to £9,000 because the covenanted sum operates as a charge on his income (he is settling £1,000 pa on Watson). It, therefore, follows that his 'total income' is £9,000 (TA 1970 s 528) and that he can set his personal allowances only against that sum (TA 1970 s 25). Wilbur's own tax will, therefore, be calculated on the taxable income that is left.

Step 3: In addition, Wilbur is also charged on the covenanted sum at the basic rate of income tax (see TA 1970 s 3).

The result is that the total cost of the covenant to Wilbur is £1,000 since he handed £700 to Watson at *Step 1* and £300 to the Revenue at *Step 3*.

As Viscount Simon explained in *Allchin v Coulthard* [1943] AC at 619, by the payer deducting the tax from the covenant at source (*Step 1*) 'the payer recoups himself for the tax which he has paid or will pay on the annual payment'. It is, therefore, in the interests of the payer to make the deduction of tax and does not directly concern the Revenue since they will collect the basic rate tax under TA 1970 s 3 at *Step 3* in any event. Hence, s 52(1)(c) *permits* the payer to make the deduction, but does not compel deduction. The whole process in *Example 6* may be represented diagrammatically thus:

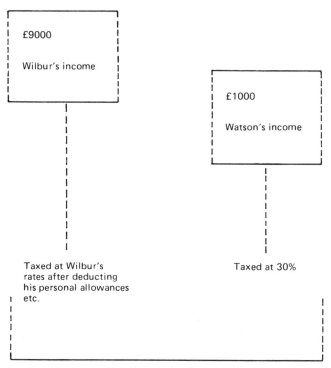

£9000

Wilbur's income

£1000

Watson's income

Taxed at Wilbur's rates after deducting his personal allowances etc.

Taxed at 30%

Total tax paid by Wilbur

2 The operation of TA 1970 s 53 for the payer

TA 1970 s 53 provides as follows:

'Where:—
(a) any annuity or other annual payment charged with tax under Case III of Schedule D, not being interest, . . . is not payable, or not wholly payable, out of profits or gains brought into charge to income tax, the person by or through whom any payment thereof is made shall, on making the payment, deduct out of it a sum representing the amount of income tax thereon . . .'

Section 53 will apply when the payer has no income or insufficient income to cover the amount of the annual payment and when he is not subject to income tax. Annual payments made by companies are, therefore, payable subject to the deduction of income tax under s 53. Unlike under TA 1970 s 52, deduction from the covenanted sum is compulsory.

As soon as a relevant annual payment is made there is an obligation on the payer to notify the Revenue who will then assess him to basic rate income tax on the annual payment. The annual payment net of basic rate income tax is made to the recipient who receives a certificate of tax deducted on form IR 185.

Under s 53 tax may be collected from agents of the payer (on the dangers of being held liable as an agent see *Rye and Eyre v IRC* (1935)). This difference in collection machinery from that under s 52 is necessary because the payer will not normally be subject to income tax when a s 53 payment is made. It will not, therefore, be possible to collect the basic rate tax on the annual payment at the same time as the rest of his income tax.

EXAMPLE 7

Wilbur (see *Example 6*) falls on hard times and receives no income. He remains bound by his covenant to pay Watson £1,000 pa. When he makes the next annual payment:

Step 1: Wilbur should deduct the basic rate tax (£300) on that annual sum and pay Watson £700 only.

Step 2: In accordance with s 53(2) Wilbur should notify the Revenue that the payment has been made. He will, therefore, receive an assessment to income tax for £300.

The total cost of the covenant is, therefore, £1,000, made up of £700 paid to Watson and £300 to the Revenue.

3   The position of the recipient of annual payments

The position of the recipient of an annual payment is broadly the same whether that payment is made under TA 1970 s 52 or s 53. He will have income under Schedule D Case III equivalent to the gross value of the payment (not just of the sum that he actually receives) and will be given a tax credit equal to the basic rate income tax deducted at source by the payer. Accordingly, he may be entitled to reclaim that tax (if he has unused personal allowances, for instance); or, the tax may exactly discharge his tax liability; or, he may be liable to extra income tax at the higher rates. This third possibility (more tax owed by the recipient) is comparatively rare since annual payments are seldom made to higher rate taxpayers and, in any event, TA 1970 s 457 will, in the majority of cases, deem the annual payment to be the income of the payer for the purpose of higher rate income tax (see p 151).

EXAMPLE 8

Watson received £700 from Wilbur in payment of a covenant for £1,000. He is also given an IR 185 certificate of tax deducted.

Watson's income under Schedule D Case III is £1,000 and he has a credit for income tax paid of £300. Therefore, his tax position will be as follows:

(1) If he is subject to tax at the basic rate (ie if he has no unused allowances or charges), there is no further liability to tax and no question of a refund.

(2) If he has no other income and so has available personal allowances he can reclaim the £300 tax paid on his behalf by Wilbur. If he had (say) £200 of unused allowances he would have taxable income of £800 (£1,000 − £200) on which tax at 30% would be £240. As the tax credit of £300 exceeds his tax liability by £60, he can obtain a refund of £60 of the tax deducted at source.

(3) If he has other income so that he is paying income tax at the top rate (currently 60%) he would have a tax liability of £600 and would therefore owe a further £300 tax.

4   Principal problems arising in connection with the deduction of tax at source

a) *The effect of failure to deduct tax at source*

The payer of an annual payment is allowed to deduct tax from the payment under s 52 and bound to do so under s 53. Failure to do so will not lead to any penalty. It will not generally concern the Revenue when the payment is made under s 52 since they will assess the payer to tax on the whole of his income without distinguishing the annual payment and if they fail to recover tax from the payer in a case where s 52 applies, the payee may be assessed.

Where there is a failure to pay the tax under s 53, however, the Revenue will seek to recover the sum either from the payer or by direct assessment from the payee. When an assessment is made upon the recipient the burden is on him to show that he was only paid a net sum. If he discharges that burden he cannot be assessed to tax (see eg *Hume v Asquith* (1969)).

Failure to deduct tax will of course affect the parties *inter se*. In general, if the payee has been overpaid, that overpayment cannot be reclaimed or corrected from later payments; it is a payment made under a mistake of law and the excess is treated as a perfected gift which cannot be undone (*Re Hatch* (1919)). There are a few exceptions to this general principle: if the mistake is one of fact recovery is possible (*Turvey v Dentons (1923) Ltd* (1953)); if the basic rate of tax increases after the payment, the excess can be recovered (TA 1970 s 521), but it appears that underdeductions cannot be recouped from later payments made in that tax year (*Johnson v Johnson* (1946) explaining *Taylor v Taylor* (1938)). There is of course nothing to stop a recipient who has been overpaid from reimbursing the payer!

EXAMPLE 9

Wilton has trading profits of £5,000 (on the preceding year basis) for the tax year 1984–85. He makes an annual payment to Watmore of £1,000 from which he fails to deduct basic rate income tax.

(1) The Revenue may assess Wilton under the s 52 machinery.
(2) If Wilton fails to pay, the Revenue may assess Watmore. Note that in the event of Wilton paying the tax, Watmore's income is £1,000 with a credit for £300 tax paid. The extra £300 that he has received is ignored; it is a tax-free gift.

b) *The use of formulae*

TMA 1970 s 106(2) provides that 'every agreement for payment of interest . . . or other annual payment in full without allowing any such deduction shall be void'. The parties may not, therefore, agree not to operate s 52 and s 53. If s 106(2) is infringed, the instrument is void only as to the provision seeking to oust the deduction machinery. The section is also limited in that it only applies to 'agreements', so that payments under court orders and wills are outside its terms (see Chapter 12).

Despite s 106, the parties will often wish to ensure that a fixed sum is paid each year to the recipient regardless of fluctuations in the basic rate of income tax. Say, for instance, that Felix is making annual payments to his aged mother, Felicity, and wants to ensure that she receives £700 each year. Whilst the basic rate is 30% a covenant to pay £1,000 pa would achieve this result. Were the basic rate to rise to 35% Felicity would only receive £650. As it is not possible to agree to pay £700 and not to deduct tax, the only way of achieving what Felix wants is to use a formula in the covenant. The standard formula would be that 'Felix agrees to pay Felicity such sum as will after deduction of income tax at the basic rate for the time being in force leave £700'. This takes effect as an undertaking to pay the gross sum which after deducting the appropriate income tax leaves Felicity with £700. What she receives is, therefore, constant; what will vary with the rate of tax is the sum paid to the Revenue and, therefore, the total cost of the covenant to Felix.

An alternative formula would be to promise Felicity £700 'free of tax', which takes effect as an undertaking to pay such sum as after deduction of income tax leaves £700 (*Ferguson v IRC* (1969); a similar rule applies to court orders that are so worded).

One danger if a formula is to be employed is that it is arguable that a promise to pay £700 free of tax means that the recipient should in any event end up with neither more nor less than £700. It follows that if the recipient is liable to higher rate income tax on the annual payment the payer must reimburse him for that tax, whilst conversely, any repayment of tax should be returned to the payer (the rule in *Re Pettit* (1922); see Chapter 12). In view of these difficulties great care should be taken in drafting formulae.

c) *Which section applies: TA 1970 s 52 or s 53?*

Difficulties will arise, for instance, if an annual payment falls due in a year when the payer has no income, but is finally paid in a year when he does have taxable income and vice versa (see generally *Luipaard Vlei's Estate and Gold Mining Co Ltd v IRC* (1930) and ESC A16). Which section applies is of considerable significance; it will, for instance, determine the ownership of the sum deducted from the annual payment since under s 52 it belongs to the payer whereas under s 53 it should be handed to the Revenue. In general, if the payer has taxable income for the appropriate year, it is presumed that the payment is made out of that income. This provision is normally advantageous to the taxpayer as the following example illustrates.

EXAMPLE 10

Hank has taxable income of £10,000 for 1984–85 and executes a deed of covenant to pay Hiram £1,000 pa for the next ten years.
(1) *If s 52 operates* Hank will be assessed to income tax on £10,000 at 30% = £3,000. (£9,000 is Hank's income and £1,000 is Hiram's).
(2) *If s 53 operates* Hank will be assessed on £10,000 at 30% (£3,000) together with £1,000 at 30% (£300). The total sum payable to the Revenue will be £3,300.

The presumption that s 52 applies if income is available is displaced when the payer has secured some fiscal or other advantage from charging the payment to capital (as in *Corp of Birmingham v IRC* (1930)), or where he has made a deliberate decision to charge the sum to capital (see, for instance, *Chancery Lane Safe Deposit and Offices Co Ltd v IRC* (1966)). In such cases despite the availability of income profits, s 53 will be applied. (Special rules for interest payments made by companies and charged to a capital account are considered at p 385.)

IV   ANNUAL PAYMENTS AND ANTI-AVOIDANCE LEGISLATION

Annual payments may be used for tax avoidance. Quite simply, a taxpayer subject to the higher rates of tax could alienate a part of his income to a taxpayer with lower rates of tax (or, better still, to someone who pays no income tax). In *IRC v Duke of Westminster* (1936) gardeners were paid by means of a deed of covenant in lieu of wages with advantageous tax results.

EXAMPLE 11

Homer is subject to income tax at the highest rate (currently 60%). He pays his son Hiram an allowance of £400 pa. Hiram has no other income. At Homer's marginal rates the total cost in gross terms of that allowance is £1,000 (since £1,000 − [60% × £1,000] = £400).

As an alternative, Homer might covenant to pay Hiram £1,000 pa. As an annual payment the result would be:
(1) Homer's income is reduced by £1,000 (ie he does not pay 60% tax on that sum).
(2) Homer pays basic rate tax at source under TA 1970 s 52.
(3) Hiram receives £700 net and reclaims (because of his unused allowances) the £300 paid at source by Homer.

The total cost to Homer is the same (£1,000), but Hiram receives an extra £600 and the Revenue loses £600 of tax.

Not surprisingly, legislation was introduced to nullify many of the avoidance possibilities. It is found in TA 1970 Pt XVI, but originated in piecemeal enactments. As a result, the provisions overlap with each other and contain minor inconsistencies. It must also be borne in mind that the legislation is concerned with capital as well as income settlements. This breadth of coverage is inevitable since, if it is desired to stop a particular income settlement from attracting fiscal benefits, it is necessary to cover a settlement of income-producing assets (ie capital) which might otherwise achieve the same result. The provisions relating to capital settlements are considered in Chapter 11.

1 The general principles

If an annual payment is caught by any of the anti-avoidance provisions of TA 1970 Pt XVI, it remains subject to the machinery of TA 1970 s 52 (so that a net sum will be handed to the payee) but the income is deemed to be the income of the settlor so long as he lives. The result, therefore, is that he has failed to alienate the slice of income and so will remain subject to tax on it.

The rules operate by treating the income as leaving the settlor (thereby allowing the deduction under s 52), and then deeming that income to return to him as settlement income. This follows from the decision in *Ang v Parrish* (1980) which, although only concerned with one particular provision in TA 1970 Pt XVI (s 457), probably applies to all the other provisions of that Part as well. Thus, if the settlor had only earned income when he made an annual payment which was caught by one of the provisions in TA 1970 Pt XVI, the settlement income that is deemed to be his returns to him as unearned income.

As the relevant income is deemed by TA 1970 Pt XVI to be the settlor's, his rates of income tax will apply to it resulting, frequently, in a charge to tax on that sum in excess of the basic rate. Generally the settlor may recover the extra tax (ie the excess above basic rate) that he has suffered (calculated on the basis that the settlement income is the top slice of his income) from the payee. Further, if the settlement income remains that of the payer it must follow that the payee has received no income. For tax purposes, therefore, any sum that remains in the payee's hands is ignored; it is in effect a tax-free gift.

EXAMPLE 12

Iain has earned income of £100,000 pa. He covenants to pay £10,000 pa to Alec, his impecunious neighbour, for the next four years. The covenant is caught by

TA 1970 Pt XVI (under s 434; see below) with the result that it is rendered ineffective for tax purposes. The consequences are as follows:

(1) Iain will deduct basic rate tax from the payment under TA 1970 s 52 ie £3,000.

(2) The £10,000 will be treated as unearned income in Iain's hands so that he will suffer 60% tax (at the highest rates) on the £10,000 (treated as the top slice of his income). Thus, tax on the £10,000 will be £6,000 (£10,000 at 60%) so that after deducting the basic rate tax paid under (1) Iain will suffer an extra assessment of £3,000 (£6,000 − £3,000).

(3) Iain can claim back the £3,000 (the extra tax) from Alec so that Alec will be left with £4,000 (ie £7,000 − £3,000).

(4) Alec will suffer no income tax on £4,000 as this sum is not his income for tax purposes.

The above discussion is accurate in respect of all the provisions in TA 1970 Pt XVI with the exception of s 457. Under that section, which is a sweeping up provision, the general principles are modified in two important respects. First, the annual payment is treated as partly effective (for basic rate income tax it becomes the income of the payee) and only as partly ineffective (for higher rates it remains the income of the payer); and secondly, the extra tax (at higher rates) which the settlor may suffer cannot be reclaimed from the payee.

2   Terminology

'Settlement' is given a wide definition for income tax. It 'includes any disposition, trust, covenant, agreement or arrangement' (TA 1970 s 454(3)) whilst, so far as settlements on infant unmarried children of the settlor are concerned, it also includes a transfer of assets (TA 1970 s 444(2)). All annual payments and capital settlements are within the definition.

'Settlor' is likewise widely defined to cover any person by whom the settlement was made, whether directly or indirectly. There can be infant settlors (see *IRC v Mills* (1974)); reciprocal settlors, as where A makes B's settlement and vice versa; and a settlement created by a person who surrenders an interest (*IRC v Buchanan* (1957)). The width of this definition may result in a settlement having more than one settlor which in turn may lead to the difficulty of deciding which settlor shall be deemed to own the income of that settlement (see, for instance, *IRC v Mills* (1974) and *D'Abreu v IRC* (1978)).

Despite the width of these terms, TA 1970 Pt XVI is generally subject to the important limitation that there must be an element of bounty if the transaction is to be treated as a settlement (see generally *IRC v Plummer* (1979) and note that the 'reverse annuity scheme' was stopped by FA 1977 s 48). The transaction must be looked at as a whole to discover whether bounty is present (see *Chinn v Collins* (1981)). The bounty requirement presumably explains why court orders in favour of the infant unmarried children of the payer, because they cannot be said to be 'voluntary', are outside TA 1970 Pt XVI, although similar orders directing payments to be held in trust for such children create settlements which are subject to Pt XVI (see generally *Yates v Starkey* (1951) and p 505; it may be questioned whether *Yates v Starkey* remains good law).

3   Dispositions for short periods (TA 1970 ss 434–436)

Section 434(1) provides as follows:

'. . . any income which, by virtue or in consequence of any disposition made, directly or indirectly, by any person (other than a disposition made for valuable and sufficient consideration), is payable to or applicable for the benefit of any other person for a period which cannot exceed six years shall be deemed for all the purposes of the Income Tax Acts to be the income of the person, if living, by whom the disposition was made, and not to be the income of any other person.'

First, the section does not apply if valuable and sufficient consideration is given. Secondly, it only applies if the relevant payments are payable for a period which *cannot* exceed six years (three years in the case of covenants to charity). The section can, therefore, be avoided either if a fixed period in excess of six years is chosen by the settlor (hence, the popularity of the seven year (or, for charities, four year) covenant) or, alternatively, if a period of uncertain duration is chosen which *might* exceed six years. The possible duration of the annual payment must be considered in the light of circumstances prevailing at the start. So long as it is capable of lasting more than six years at that time, subsequent events are ignored. If, however, a covenant reserves to the settlor (or any other person) a power of revocation which could be exercised to bring it to an end before the expiration of six years, the annual payment is caught by TA 1970 s 445 (see further p 150). It may sometimes be difficult to determine whether a period can exceed six years.

EXAMPLE 13

(1) Frances covenants to pay £1,000 pa to her cousin Donald so long as he is studying law at London University. The covenant is for an uncertain duration which could exceed six years. The likelihood of it doing so is probably remote, but the mere possibility that it might (Donald might after all spend the rest of his life researching into the rôle of the praetor in Roman Law) is sufficient. The covenant, therefore, escapes TA 1970 s 434 (see *IRC v Black* (1940)). If Donald ended his legal studies after only three years, s 434 would not be applied retrospectively.

(2) Judy executes a covenant on 1 February 1984 to pay Jason £1,000 pa for a period of seven years running from 1 August 1983 with the final payment falling due on 1 August 1989. The covenant will fall within TA 1970 s 434(1) because:
(a) The period of six years cannot begin to run until the obligation arose (on 1 February 1984); so that
(b) the final payment (on 1 August 1989) would fall due less than six years from the execution of the deed (see *IRC v St Luke's Hostel Trustee* (1930)).

If an annual payment specifies that different sums shall be paid each year it is only the constant element which will escape TA 1970 s 434. If, on the other hand, the payments are calculated by reference to a formula which may result in different amounts becoming payable, all the payments will escape s 434.

EXAMPLE 14

Bernard executes two covenants.
Covenant 1 in favour of Kilroy, is to last for seven years, and is for £10 in year 1, £20 in year 2 and so on in progressive steps until £70 is payable in year 7.
Covenant 2 is in favour of Sufi for seven years and is to consist of 1/7th of Bernard's gross salary each year as a motor mechanic.
For income tax, only £10 in *Covenant 1* will be outside the provisions of s 434 as this amount is constant in each of the seven payments; the remaining amounts paid each year will, however, be caught and taxed as Bernard's income. *Covenant 2* wholly escapes s 434 despite the fact that fluctuating sums may be paid depending on changes in Bernard's salary.

If s 434 applies to an annual payment, the income is treated as that of the settlor for all income tax purposes. Hence, the recipient is treated as having no income from the covenant and TA 1970 s 435 provides for the settlor to recover from the payee any extra tax payable by him as a result of the application of s 434.

4 Settlements on children (TA 1970 ss 437–444)

The income of an infant is not aggregated with that of his parents. As a separate taxable individual with his own personal allowances he would be an ideal recipient of a deed of covenant executed by his parent enabling tax to be saved on the covenanted sum at the parent's highest rate. However, TA 1970 s 437(1) provides as follows:

> 'Where, by virtue or in consequence of any settlement and during the life of the settlor, any income is paid to or for the benefit of a child of the settlor in any year of assessment, the income shall, if at the time of the payment the child was unmarried and below the age of 18 be treated for all the purposes of the Income Tax Acts as the income of the settlor for that year and not as the income of any other person.'

The section applies only to settlements on an infant and unmarried child of the settlor. It does not apply to adult children and, hence, will not usually catch covenants in favour of children at university; nor does it apply to the precocious infant who is married; nor to a covenant which does not exceed £5 pa (see s 437(3)); nor to covenants by grandparents in favour of grandchildren. Reciprocal settlements are caught by the definition of settlor in TA 1970 s 444(2).

The definition of 'settlement' in the case of a person's infant unmarried children is extended to include a transfer of assets. In *Thomas v Marshall* (1953) a father who opened Post Office accounts and bought Defence Bonds in the names of his infant children was caught by s 437.

If a covenant is caught by s 437 the consequences are the same as those for TA 1970 s 434 (see p 149), ie the income is taxed as that of the settlor who can recover any extra tax he has to pay on the covenant from the payee (TA 1970 s 441).

EXAMPLE 15

Siegfried executes two covenants in favour of his infant children:
Covenant 1 is in favour of his 16 year old daughter who has just married and provides for her to receive £1,000 pa until she attains the age of 21.
Covenant 2 is in favour of his 13 year old son; the covenant is also for £1,000 pa and is expressed to last until the son attains 21.

Siegfried has failed to dispose of any income since *Covenant 1* will not be capable of lasting for more than six years (and falls within TA 1970 s 434(1)) whilst *Covenant 2* is in favour of his infant child and so falls within s 437(1).

5 Revocable settlements (TA 1970 s 445)

If the terms of a settlement give any person the power to revoke the settlement, to cease payments, or to diminish payments thereunder, TA 1970 s 445 applies to treat the sums payable under the settlement (or the amount of any diminution) as the income of the settlor for all tax purposes.

Section 445 will not apply if the power of revocation cannot be exercised for at least six years (or three years in the case of charity) from the date when the first annual payment is payable (TA 1970 s 445(1) proviso). In that event the section will only apply when the power becomes exercisable.

Two other matters should be mentioned in connection with the operation of the provision. First, it is only a power of revocation contained in the settlement itself which brings s 445 into operation. As the wide definition of settlement includes an arrangement, it would seem that a separate document which gave the settlor this power would be treated as a part of one arrangement. Secondly, power to revoke is not the same as the use of a formula. If, therefore, the settlor's liability to pay under the covenant ceases because of the drafting of a formula it would seem that s 445 does not apply.

The result of falling within s 445 is broadly the same as under TA 1970 ss 434 and 437 although the assessment to tax on the settlor is under Schedule D Case VI (TA 1970 s 449(1)). Section 449(3) contains provisions enabling the settlor to recover from the payee any extra tax that he has to pay.

EXAMPLE 16

(1) Samson covenants to pay Delilah £1,000 pa for the rest of her life, but reserves a power to revoke the covenant at any time on payment to her of a £20 penalty.
  The settlement would be outside the provisions of TA 1970 s 434 because it is for an uncertain period which could exceed six years. The reservation of the power to revoke the agreement causes s 445 to operate, however, so that the £1,000 remains Samson's income.
(2) Judy covenants to pay Sandy one-half of the income that she receives each year from her family discretionary trust. The covenant is to last for seven years, but after two years, on Judy's request, the trustees cease to make payments to her. In effect, Judy has revoked the settlement, but s 445 would not apply (compare *IRC v Wolfson* (1949)).

6   Settlements rendered ineffective for the purposes of higher rate tax (TA 1970 s 457)

Section 457 is probably the most important of the anti-avoidance provisions in its application to income settlements and possesses features distinguishing it sharply from the anti-avoidance provisions discussed above. In particular, it will only apply if the other provisions do not. Further, the above provisions are designed to apply in relatively limited circumstances, whereas s 457 applies to all income settlements with only four exceptions.

Section 457(1) provides that:

'Where, during the life of the settlor, income arising under a settlement made on or after 7 April 1965 is, under the settlement and in the events that occur, payable to or applicable for the benefit of any person other than the settlor, then, unless, under the settlement and in the said events, the income . . . is income from property of which the settlor has divested himself absolutely by the settlement . . . the income shall, for the purposes of excess liability, be treated as the income of the settlor and not as the income of any other person'.

It applies unless the source of the income has been transferred from the settlor. In the case of income settlements this cannot occur because the settlor is only creating a settlement of the income once it has arisen; the source, whatever that may be, will always be retained by him. 'Excess liability' is defined as a liability to income tax at the higher rates.

There are four specific exclusions from s 457: the first two are concerned with annuities payable in connection with partnership arrangements (see Chapter 29); the third is for maintenance payments on divorce or separation (see Chapter 36), and the final exclusion is for covenanted payments to charity, so long as they do not exceed £5,000 in total in any one tax year (if the payments exceed £5,000 pa there will be an apportionment so that only the excess over £5,000 is caught by s 457).

The normal meaning of settlement applies to s 457 so that it will only be relevant where an element of bounty is present (*IRC v Plummer* (1979) see p 148).

An annual payment that is caught by s 457 (and, of course, most are) is treated quite differently from one that is caught by the anti-avoidance provisions discussed above. The payment is not wholly ineffective for tax purposes, but only for the purposes of 'excess liability'. It remains valid, therefore, for the purposes of basic rate tax. Annual payments caught by s 457 may, therefore, have tax advantages so long as the payee is not subject to tax at the basic rate. However, there will be no tax saving at the settlor's higher rates.

EXAMPLE 17

Jasper is a widower with income of £25,000. He covenants to pay his granddaughter, Camilla (aged 19), £1,000 pa whilst she is training to be a doctor. Camilla is a single woman and has no other income. The income tax consequences of the covenant are:

(1) It is not caught by TA 1970 ss 434, 437, or 445, but it does fall within s 457 (not being within one of the four exceptions) with the result that it is effective for basic rate income tax but not for excess liability.

(2) *Position of Jasper*   As Jasper is subject to the higher rate of income tax his income tax position is:

	£
Total income	25,000
Less: personal allowance	2,005
Taxable income	£22,995

Income tax payable	£
First £15,400 at 30%	4,620.00
Next £2,800 at 40%	1,120.00
Final £4,795 at 45%	2,157.75
Total income tax payable	£7,897.75

The result, for Jasper, is the same as if he had never made the covenant. He achieves no tax saving. Theoretically, the slice of income represented by the covenant has returned to Jasper as unearned income (see *Ang v Parrish* (1979)).

(3) *Paying the covenant*   The payment will be made under TA 1970 s 52 so that Jasper will deduct and retain income tax at the basic rate on £1,000. £700 will, therefore, be paid to Camilla.

(4) *The position of Camilla*   The £1,000 she is entitled to under the covenant is treated as her income, but only for the purposes of basic rate income tax. Furthermore, she has a credit for the basic rate income tax paid at source. Therefore, if she is subject to excess liability the covenant will be ignored in computing that sum. If she is a basic rate taxpayer, the sum will be included in

her income but as that amount of tax has already been paid on the £1,000 by Jasper there will be no practical consequence. However where she has no other income (as here) the result is as follows:

	£
Income under the covenant	1,000
Less personal allowance	2,005
Taxable income	nil
Tax deducted at source	300
Tax (refund)	£(300)

Camilla, therefore, reclaims the basic rate tax and ends up with £1,000. She has obtained £300 more than she would have received if a gift of £700 had been made to her. The benefit of the covenant lies in the tax reclaimed by the recipient and not directly in any saving of tax by the payer.

There are no provisions enabling the payer to recover his higher rate tax from the payee as under the other anti-avoidance provisions.

7   Conclusions: the advantages of covenants today

Despite the anti-avoidance provisions of TA 1970 Pt XVI, annual payments remain attractive vehicles for tax saving and offer advantages in the following circumstances:

Fully valid covenants   Few covenants escape TA 1970 s 457, but for those that are potential exceptions care should be taken to ensure that the conditions appropriate to the relevant exception are complied with. In particular, the opportunities offered for a reduction of income tax on matrimonial breakdown should be utilised (see Chapter 36).

Charities   Covenants in favour of charities need only be capable of lasting for more than three years and if the payer's total payments do not exceed £5,000 they will be fully valid. Since charities are generally exempt from income tax, they will be able to reclaim the basic rate income tax deducted at source by the payer.

Covenants effective at the basic rate level   Although a covenant falls within s 457, in appropriate circumstances a refund of the basic rate income tax will be made to the payee. The most widely used covenants are those in favour of children (over 18) at college and the Revenue have issued a form which may be used for that purpose (Form IR 47 issued on 24 September 1982, set out in Appendix II).

V   TAXATION OF INTEREST PAYMENTS

1   When is interest deductible by the payer as a charge on income?

TA 1970 ss 52 and 53 do not apply to interest payments, with the result that they should generally be paid gross and the recipient directly assessed to income tax under Schedule D Case III. In a limited number of cases, however, basic rate tax must be deducted at source and only a net amount paid. The main examples are: first, mortgage interest that is within the **MIRAS** scheme (see

Chapter 4); and secondly, yearly interest chargeable to tax under Schedule D Case III and which is paid either:

  (i) by a company or local authority otherwise than in a fiduciary or representative capacity, eg debenture interest; or
 (ii) by or on behalf of a partnership of which a company is a member; or
(iii) by any person to another person whose usual place of abode is outside the UK (see TA 1970 s 54).

In cases (i)–(iii) above, the payer must deduct a sum equal to the basic rate of income tax from the payment and the provisions of TA 1970 s 53 apply so that the payer is under a duty to notify the Revenue that the payment has been made. Generally, interest must be 'yearly' if these provisions are to operate. The distinction between 'yearly' and 'short' interest depends upon the degree of permanence of the loan. The crucial question is whether it is stated, or expected, that the loan will last, or is capable of lasting, for 12 months or longer.

Even if the payment falls within one of the three categories of interest payments listed in s 54, it must still be paid gross if it is interest payable in the UK on an advance from a bank carrying on a bona fide banking business in the UK or if the interest is paid by such a bank in the ordinary course of its business (on the meaning of 'bona fide banking business' see *United Dominions Trust Ltd v Kirkwood* (1965)). Notice, however, that as from 1985–86, banks and certain other institutions will be subject to the same composite rate scheme for most interest payments to UK residents as currently applies to Building Societies (see p 25). The payee will, therefore, be treated as receiving such interest payments after deduction of basic rate tax and will be assessed directly to any higher rate tax on the payments under Schedule D Case III, but will not, normally, be entitled to any refund of the tax deducted at source.

Finally, interest payments only operate as charges on the payer's income when the interest is 'protected' under FA 1972 s 75 and Sch 9; and FA 1974 Sch 1 (see Chapter 4).

VI   MISCELLANEOUS MATTERS

1   **Small maintenance payments** (TA 1970 s 65)

These payments which satisfy all the requirements for an annual payment are paid gross (see Chapter 36).

2   **Purchased life annuities** (TA 1970 s 230)

Purchased life annuities were formerly taxed as income with no allowance being given for their capital cost. TA 1970 s 230 permits the amount of any annuity payment which falls within its scope to be dissected into an income and a capital amount. The capital amount in each payment is found by dividing the cost of the annuity by the life expectancy of the annuitant at that time, calculated according to government mortality tables. The balance is treated as income taxable under the rules of Schedule D Case III.

Generally, s 230 does not apply if the annuity is already given tax relief (as is the case with purchased annuities for a fixed term of years which have always been dissected in a similar fashion); or, if the annuity was not purchased by the annuitant but by a third party; or, finally, if the premiums qualified for tax relief under TA 1970 ss 19, 20 or 227 when they were paid.

Annuities purchased in pursuance of a direction in a will fall outside the section (see Chapter 12); as do annuities provided under a superannuation scheme.

3 Patents and copyrights

Patent royalties are payable subject to the deduction provisions of TA 1970 ss 52 and 53. Such payments may be annual payments, but will usually fall within Schedule D Cases I and II as receipts of a trade or profession. There are 'spreading provisions' in certain cases where lump sums are received (TA 1970 ss 384, 380, see p 98).

Copyright royalties do not fall within ss 52 and 53 and are payable without deduction of tax. The recipient will be taxed under either Schedule D Case II (if a professional author) or otherwise under Schedule D Case VI. Again, spreading provisions are available for certain of these lump sum payments (TA 1970 ss 389–390; see p 97).

11 Trusts and settlements

   I   General principles
  II Trusts where the trustees are liable to a 15% surcharge
 III The taxation of beneficiaries
 IV The anti-avoidance provisions
  V Charitable trusts

I GENERAL PRINCIPLES

The general principles that apply to trustees resemble those affecting PRs. During the life of a trust the trustees will be subject to basic rate income tax under the appropriate Schedule on all the income produced by the fund. They are not allowed to deduct their personal allowances (the trust income is, after all, not their property) nor those of any beneficiary. Furthermore, expenses incurred in administering the fund may not be deducted and are, therefore, paid out of taxed income.

EXAMPLE 1

The trustees of the Jenkinson family trust run a bakery. The profits of that business will be calculated in accordance with the normal rules of Schedule D Case I and be subject to basic rate income tax in the trustees' hands. A change of trustees will not result in the discontinuance rules applying (TA 1970 s 154(7)).

Trustees will not be assessed in cases where the trust income accrues directly to a beneficiary who is not liable to pay income tax. The scope of this exception is limited and would appear to apply only where there is no liability to tax (for instance, because of non-residence or charitable status) and not where the income is untaxed merely because of the personal allowances of the beneficiary.

The theory behind this system of taxing trustees is that they are entitled to the income (because they can sue for it) and they will receive it in their fiduciary capacity. Furthermore, as a policy matter, it is essential to levy income tax on the trustees since otherwise, were income to be accumulated (turned into capital) as it arises, rather than distributed, it would escape income tax altogether.

II TRUSTS WHERE THE TRUSTEES ARE LIABLE TO A 15% SURCHARGE (FA 1973 ss 16–17)

1 The charge imposed by FA 1973 s 16

Trustees are not liable to income tax at the higher rates because they are not individuals. There is, however, a special surcharge of 15% which applies to the income arising in certain trusts after deducting administrative expenses. (This 'additional rate' is the difference between basic rate tax for the year (30%) and the second of the higher rates (45%): see FA 1971 s 32(1) as amended by FA 1984 s 17.)

FA 1973 s 16(2) provides as follows:

'This section applies to income arising to trustees in any year of assessment so far as it—

(a) is income which is to be accumulated or which is payable at the discretion of the trustees or any other person (whether or not the trustees have power to accumulate it); and

(b) is neither (before being distributed) the income of any person other than the trustees nor treated for any of the purposes of the Income Tax Acts as the income of a settlor; and

(c) is not income arising under a trust established for charitable purposes only; and

(d) exceeds the income applied in defraying the expenses of the trustees in that year which are properly chargeable to income (or would be so chargeable but for any express provisions of the trust)'.

Broadly, trusts which contain a power for trustees to accumulate income, and trusts which give the trustees a discretion over the distribution of the income are caught. The purpose of the surcharge is to increase the cost of accumulating income in trusts.

EXAMPLE 2

(1) Magnus is a wealthy individual who pays income tax at the highest rate (currently 60%). He creates a settlement of income-producing assets on discretionary trusts for his children giving the trustees power to accumulate the income for 21 years. Under the general principles discussed above, the income which was accumulated would suffer tax at only 30% (instead of 60% in Magnus' hands) and would subsequently be paid out as capital and so be free from any further income tax. As a result of FA 1973, however, the trustees have to pay an extra 15% rate of tax (making a 45% rate in all) so that the attractions of the settlement to Magnus are reduced (although not wholly removed).

(2) Trustees of a discretionary trust have income of £10,000 and incur administrative expenses of £1,000. Their income tax assessment will be—

	£
Basic rate on £10,000 (30% of £10,000)	3,000
Section 16 surcharge on £9,000 (15% of £9,000)	1,350
Total tax liability	£4,350

Section 16(2)(a) was considered in *IRC v Berrill* (1981) where the settlor's son was entitled to the income from the fund unless the trustees exercised a power to accumulate it. Vinelott J held that s 16 applied since the income was 'income . . . which is payable at the discretion of the trustees'. 'Discretion' is apparently wide enough to cover a discretion or power to withhold income. The phrase 'income which is to be accumulated' in para (a) presumably refers to income which the trustees are under a positive duty to accumulate. A mere power to accumulate is not sufficient, although it will usually mean that the income 'is payable at the discretion of the trustees' within para (a).

In *Carver v Duncan* (1984) trustees paid premiums on policies of life assurance out of the income of the fund as they were permitted to do under the trust deed. The Court of Appeal held that the payments did not fall to be deducted under s 16(2)(d) which was limited to expenses which were properly chargeable to income under the general law. Accordingly, the express authority in the instrument did not bring the sums within the section.

The surcharge will not apply to income which is treated as that of any person other than the trustees; for instance, to trusts where a beneficiary has a vested interest in the income (eg a life tenant) and also to cases where the anti-avoidance provisions of TA 1970 Pt XVI operate to deem the income to be that of the settlor (see |p 163ff). Presumably the *Pilkington* settlement (see Chapter 24), in which the income of a life tenant could be taken from him after it had arisen by the exercise of a power to accumulate it, would be subject to the surcharge as the income still 'belongs' to the trustees.

Two final points should be noted: first, s 16 does not apply to the income of an estate of a deceased person during administration (though it may, of course, apply to a subsequent will trust). Secondly, the tax is due from the trustees on 1 December following the appropriate year of assessment.

2　The charge imposed by FA 1973 s 17

The purpose of FA 1973 s 17 is to impose a further charge to income tax on income payments made at the trustees' discretion where the rates have increased between the time of the income arising (and trustees being taxed on it), and its distribution to beneficiaries. Section 17(2) provides that:

> 'The payment shall be treated as a net amount corresponding to a gross amount from which tax has been deducted at a rate equal to the sum of the basic rate and the additional rate in force for the year in which the payment is made; and the sum treated as so deducted shall be treated, so far as not set off under the following provisions of this section, as income tax assessable on the trustees.'

The set-off referred to allows the trustees to deduct from the tax now payable the tax that was charged at basic rate under FA 1973 s 16 on that income when it arose.

EXAMPLE 3

In 1984–85 the Trust produces £2,000 income. The income tax assessment (at 45%) will be for £900. In 1985–86 the trustees in the exercise of their discretion pay a net sum (£1,100) to a beneficiary. In that year the basic rate remains at 30% but the surcharge is 20%. The net payment must be grossed up in accordance with s 17(2) as follows:

$$£1,100 \times \frac{100}{100 - 50*} = £2,200$$

*The grossing up formula deducts the rate of tax in force in 1985–86 from 100— that rate is $30 + 20 = 50$.

Hence, the tax liability is £1,100 which can be reduced by setting off the £900 paid in 1984–85. £200, therefore, remains payable.

III　THE TAXATION OF BENEFICIARIES

1　Taxing a beneficiary who is entitled to trust income

A beneficiary who is entitled to the income of a trust as it arises (or is entitled to have it applied for his benefit) is subject to income tax for the year of assessment in which that income arises, even if none of the money is paid to him during that year (*Baker v Archer-Shee* (1927)). The sum to which the beneficiary is entitled is that which is left in the trustees' hands after they have paid administration expenses and discharged their income tax liability. The beneficiary is, as a result, entitled to a net sum which must be grossed up by the basic rate of income tax in order to find the sum which enters his total income computation and to a credit for some of the income tax paid by the trustees; not, it should be noted, for the full amount in cases where management expenses have been deducted (*Macfarlane v IRC* (1929)).

Depending upon his other income and allowances, a beneficiary may be entitled to reclaim all or some of the tax paid by the trustees. Alternatively, he may be liable for tax at the higher rates. The income that he receives from the trust will be unearned even if it arises from a trade run by the trustees (see *Fry v Shiels' Trustees* (1915) and TA 1970 s 530 but note also *Baker v Archer-Shee* (1927) which indicates that if a beneficiary is entitled to the income as it arises, he will be taxed according to the rules of the Schedule appropriate to that source of income).

EXAMPLE 4

Zac is entitled to the income produced by a trust fund. In 1984–85 £6,000 is produced and the trustees incur administrative expenses of £1,000. The trustees will be subject to tax at 30% on the income of £6,000. The balance of the income available for Zac will be:

	£	£
Gross income		6,000
Less: tax	1,800	
expenses	1,000	2,800
		£3,200

Zac is, therefore, taxed on £3,200 grossed up by tax at 30% ie:

$$\frac{£3,200 \times 100}{70} = £4,571$$

He will be given a credit for that portion of the basic rate tax paid by the trustees which is attributable to £4,571—this is £1,371.

Zac does not receive a credit for the rest of the tax paid by the trustees (£1,800 − £1,371 = £429) and the result is that management expenses have been paid out of taxed income so that the total cost of these expenses is £1,429. (An alternative way of dealing with management expenses is considered at p 162.)

2 Taxing an annuitant

An annuitant under a trust is not entitled to income of the trust as it arises; he is taxed under Schedule D Case III on the income that he receives. As income tax will be deducted from the annuity by the trustees under TA 1970 s 52, an assessment for basic rate tax on the beneficiary will be precluded. He has a tax credit for the basic rate tax deducted at source in the usual way.

3 Taxing a discretionary beneficiary

A discretionary beneficiary is merely entitled to be considered. Any payments that he receives will be charged as his income under Schedule D Case III (they are annual payments since they may recur) and he will receive a credit for the tax paid by the trustees and attributable to that payment. As the trust is discretionary, that tax will be at a rate of 45% (FA 1973 s 16). The effect of FA 1973 s 16 is, therefore, to encourage trustees to distribute income to beneficiaries who are subject to income tax at less than 45% so that all or a part of the surcharge can be repaid.

Once an irrevocable decision has been taken by the trustees to retain income as a part of the capital of the fund, the sum accumulated loses its character as income and is treated in the same way as the original fund, ie as capital. It follows, therefore, that the income tax suffered by that income (at 45%) is irrecoverable and that no further income tax will be charged on the accumulations when they are eventually paid out to the beneficiaries as capital (although such distributions will have CGT and CTT consequences). In deciding whether it is more advantageous to accumulate income or to pay it out to beneficiaries under their discretionary powers, trustees need to consider, inter alia, the tax position of the individual beneficiaries.

EXAMPLE 5

Trustees receive trust income of £10,000. There are three discretionary beneficiaries (all unmarried), Ding, Dang and Dong. Ding has no other income and has an unused personal allowance; Dang is a basic rate taxpayer; and Dong is subject to tax at a marginal rate of 60%. The trustees are deciding whether to pay income to any one or more of the beneficiaries or whether to accumulate it. The following tax consequences will ensue:

(1) The trustees are subject to 45% tax on the trust income (ie £4,500 tax).
(2) If the trustees decide to pay all the income to Ding (who has no other income) he will be entitled to a partial repayment of tax as follows:

	£
Income (Schedule D Case III)	10,000
Less: single person allowance	2,005
Taxable income	£ 7,995
Income tax	
£7,995 at 30%	2,398.50
Less: tax credit	4,500.00
Tax refund	£(2,101.50)

(3) If the trustees pay the income to Dang (the basic rate tax payer), he will not be entitled to a refund of any basic rate tax, but, depending upon the amount of his other income, he may obtain a refund of part of the 15% surcharge.
(4) If the trustees pay the income to Dong (the higher rate tax payer), extra tax will be levied as follows:

	£
Income	10,000
Tax at 60%	6,000
Less: tax credit	4,500
Tax owing	£ 1,500

(5) If the trustees accumulate the income, the £4,500 tax paid will be irrecoverable and the net income of £5,500 will be converted into capital.

Ideally, the trustees will avoid payments to Dong, will consider appointing all or part of the income to Ding and Dang and accumulate any balance.

4 The dangers of supplementing income out of capital

Capital payments will not generally be subject to income tax. If a beneficiary is given a fixed amount of income each year and is entitled to have that sum made up out of capital should the trust fail to produce the requisite amount of income, such 'topping up' payments will be taxed as income in the hands of the beneficiary (see *Brodie's WT v IRC* (1933) and *Cunard's Trustees v IRC* (1946)).

EXAMPLE 6

(1) The settlor's widow is given an annuity of £4,000 pa; the trustees have a discretion to pay it out of the capital of the fund if the income is insufficient. The widow will be assessed to income tax on the payments that she receives whether paid out of income or capital since they will be annual payments (TA 1970 s 53 will apply to the extent that there is insufficient income in the trust and they are paid out of capital).

(2) The settlor's widow is given an annuity of £4,000 pa and, in addition, the trustees have the power 'to apply capital for the benefit of the widow in such manner as they shall in their absolute discretion think fit'. Any supplements out of capital will now escape income tax since the widow has an interest in both income and capital, and payments out of capital will, therefore, be treated as advances of capital rather than as income payments.

The danger of capital payments being treated as income in the hands of the beneficiary is illustrated in the area of school fees. Where trustees pay the fees of an infant beneficiary by a lump sum payment, the Revenue take the view that the payment is taxable as income in the hands of the beneficiary for the year when the sum is paid. The correctness of this approach is questionable where the beneficiary is entitled to both income and capital from the fund and, even more so, when his sole entitlement is to capital advances. In the present uncertain state of the law, however, trustees are advised to exercise caution in making such payments. If the Revenue's view is correct, it will be better to make the payments annually rather than in a single lump sum which may be subject to income tax wholly in the year of payment (see generally LS Gaz (1982) p 692).

5   The divesting effects of Trustee Act 1925 s 31

The effects of s 31 (which may be excluded by the trust instrument) may be dealt with in two propositions: first, if an infant has a vested interest in the capital of a fund and the income is accumulated with the capital, the income belongs to the infant. Hence, the surcharge under s 16 is inapplicable since the income is that of a person other than the trustees (p 157 above); were the infant to die, both capital and income accumulations would belong to his estate. Secondly, if an infant has a vested interest in income only, eg to Albert for life where Albert is seven, the trustees will accumulate that income with the capital of the fund. Were the infant to die the accumulations would not pass to his estate. In this case s 31 has a divesting effect and for income tax purposes the accumulating income is subject to the FA 1973 s 16 surcharge because it does not belong to any particular beneficiary as it arises. In *Stanley v IRC* (1944) it was stated that 's 31 has effected a radical change in the law. [The beneficiary] is, in fact, for all practical purposes in precisely the same position as if his interest in surplus income were contingent'.

EXAMPLE 7

(1) Shares are settled for Amanda absolutely. She is aged six. Income produced by the shares (dividends) will be taxed as Amanda's income and grossed up at 30% with a credit for the basic rate tax deducted at source.

If, instead, the fund was held for Amanda contingent upon her attaining the age of 21, the surcharge would apply to the income, as it is not Amanda's, and only sums paid out to her by the trustees in the exercise of their powers of maintenance would be taxed as her income (in which case she would, of course, have a credit for the 45% tax paid by the trustees). When Amanda becomes 18 she will be entitled to the income by virtue of s 31 (despite her interest remaining contingent until 21).

(2) Shares in a settlement are held on trust for Barbara (aged six) for life with remainder to her Uncle Silus. As Barbara, the life tenant, has only a vested interest in income the trustees will pay 45% tax (the dividends will have already suffered basic rate deduction at source). Barbara will not be subject to tax on the income and will not, therefore, be able to reclaim any of the tax paid by the trustees, except to the extent that income is applied for her maintenance.

6   The taxation of management expenses

Management expenses, as already discussed, are deductible in calculating the 15% surcharge but not for basic rate purposes and the beneficiary is only entitled to the income that is left after deducting those expenses. Where a beneficiary has unused allowances (and, hence, will obtain a refund for any income tax paid by the trustees) the treatment of trustees' expenses results in a partial loss of that refund. A settlor should, therefore, give trustees a power to charge all expenses to capital or, in the absence of such a clause, trustees should consider paying the whole income to the beneficiary in return for an undertaking by him to reimburse the trustees for their expenditure. If the beneficiary entitled to the income is a higher rate taxpayer, the effect of the management expense rules is that he will be treated as entitled to less income, so that less tax will be paid and it will, therefore, be cheaper if the expenses are paid out of the trust income.

EXAMPLE 8

Assume that the beneficiary has no other income and unused allowances.
(1) Expenses borne by the trustees:

	£
Gross income of trust	1,000
Less: tax at 30%	300
	700(a)
Less: expenses paid by trustees	100
Net income of beneficiary	600

Gross income of beneficiary $\left(£600 \times \dfrac{100}{70} \right) = £857$

Tax refund (30% × £857)	257
Income retained by beneficiary	£857

(2) Contrast (1) with the case where the whole income is given to the beneficiary:

	£
Net income of beneficiary ((a) above)	700
Tax refund	300
Income received by beneficiary	1,000
Less: management expenses	100
Income retained by beneficiary	£900

IV THE ANTI-AVOIDANCE PROVISIONS

1 Introductory

Many of the anti-avoidance provisions in TA 1970 Pt XVI affecting income settlements (see Chapter 10) apply equally to capital settlements. However, TA 1970 s 434 is concerned with income settlements (see p 148) and will only apply to a capital settlement which is limited to six years or less. When they operate, the provisions generally deem the income of a capital settlement to be that of the settlor and provide for him to recover from the trustees any tax that he suffers on that income in excess of the basic rate.

EXAMPLE 9

Bonzo is a wealthy man paying income tax at the highest marginal rate (60%). He wishes to alienate part of his investment income (say £2,000 pa) to his godson Lucus. He could do so in one of two ways—
(1) By deed of covenant to pay Lucus £2,000 pa (ie an income settlement)
(2) By transferring capital assets that produce the £2,000 pa to trustees to hold on trust for Lucus for the appropriate time period (ie a capital settlement)
    Hence, legislation seeking to restrict the efficacy of a covenant ((1) above) must also deal with capital settlements ((2) above).

2 Parental settlements in favour of infant unmarried children (TA 1970 ss 437–438)

The income produced by settlements in favour of the settlor's own infant unmarried child will normally be treated as the income of the settlor during his lifetime. If income is accumlated, however, under an irrevocable capital settlement in favour of such beneficiaries, the income is not treated as that of the settlor (TA 1970 s 438(2)), but payments out of the fund will be treated as the settlor's income up to the amount of the accumulations (TA 1970 s 438(2)(b)).

EXAMPLE 10

Darien settles shares for the benefit of his three children: Amien, Darien Jr and Arres in equal shares contingent upon them attaining the age of 21. They are all infants and unmarried. If the income of the fund is £10,000 pa the income tax position is as follows:
(1) The trustees will be liable for income tax at a rate of 45% on that income (FA 1973 s 16).
(2) If the balance of the income (after the payment of tax) is accumulated, as the settlement is an irrevocable settlement of capital it will not be treated as the income of the settlor. Hence, so long as the income is retained in the trust no further income tax is payable. (Note: an irrevocable settlement depends upon both the general law and the provisions of TA 1970 s 439: see p 164.)
(3) If any of the income is paid to a child, it is treated as income of Darien. Say, for instance, that £1,100 is paid to, or for the benefit of, Amien. The result will be that Darien's income is increased by £2,000 (£1,100 grossed up at 45%). He has a tax credit for the £900 tax paid by the trustees. If he is charged to further income tax on that sum, TA 1970 s 441 contains tax recovery provisions that will enable him to claim a refund from the trustees or from any other person to whom the income is payable (in this case Amien, Darien Jr and Arres, although recourse would only be had to the beneficiaries to the extent that they

had received income). If Darien is subject to a marginal rate of income tax of 60% the result is:

	£
Deemed income	2,000
Damien's tax (highest rate) at 60%	1,200
Less: tax credit (tax paid by trustees)	900
Tax owing	£300

(4) If all the net income (£5,500) is distributed amongst the three beneficiaries (and, therefore, treated as Damien's income), any further distributions to the beneficiaries will be capital advancements.

(5) This settlement will normally be an accumulation and maintenance trust for CTT purposes (see Chapter 26); but this does not bestow any income tax advantages.

Three other general matters should be noted. First, that income covenants by the settlor/parent in favour of trustees will be caught as income settlements in accordance with the rules discussed in Chapter|10. Secondly, 'child' is widely defined to include 'a stepchild, an adopted child, and an illegitimate child' (TA 1970 s 444(1)), but does not, presumably, include a foster child. Finally, the definition of settlement is widened to include a transfer of assets (see *Thomas v Marshall* (1953) see p 150).

If the settlor is not the parent of the infant beneficiary, TA 1970 s 437 is not applicable; grandparental settlements are, therefore, advantageous from an income tax point of view. Even if the settlor is the parent, so long as the income is accumulated, there will still be an income tax saving if the parent is subject to income tax at rates in excess of 45%. In particular, notice the income tax saving where capital is settled for an infant absolutely as illustrated in the following example:

EXAMPLE 11

Dad's marginal rate of income tax is 60%. He settles shares, which produce an income of £1,000, upon trust for his infant daughter absolutely. The income is accumulated.

(1) If Dad had received the income, the income tax payable would have been £600, so that he would have been left with £400.

(2) As the income is settled upon trust for his daughter absolutely, the income will be treated as belonging to her so long as it is accumulated. As a result, she will be able to set her allowances against the income which will result in no income tax being charged. (The 15% surcharge does not apply because the income belongs to a beneficiary.) The sum of £1,000 is, therefore, retained in the settlement. However, there must be no payments out of the fund until the daughter attains 18 (or marries under that age), otherwise the sums paid out will be taxed as Dad's income.

To avoid the application of TA|1970 s 437, the settlement must be irrevocable. There must, therefore, be no power to terminate the trust, whether that power is given to the settlor or to a stranger. Furthermore, TA 1970 s 439 requires that income or assets from the fund must not be payable, according to the terms of the settlement, to or for the benefit of the settlor or his spouse except for such payments made after the death of the child beneficiary or on the bankruptcy of the child, or on a purported charge or assignment of assets by the child. Thus a settlement will be irrevocable if the child is given a protected life interest under the standard trusts (found in Trustee Act 1925 s 33); and if the settlement is to revert to the settlor on the death of the infant beneficiary. Finally, under s 439, a settlement will not be irrevocable if it can be determined by act or default of any person. For example, a settlement that will terminate if the settlor ceases to be employed as Chief Executive of British Rail is not irrevocable.

3 Revocable settlements where the fund will revert (TA 1970 s 446)

If there is a power to revoke the trusts (whoever possesses that power) and as a result the fund may revert to the settlor or his spouse, the income of the fund is treated as belonging to the settlor. It is all the income from the start of the trust which is so treated regardless of whether or not the power of revocation is exercised. However, if the power cannot be exercised for at least six years the income is not deemed to be the settlor's until the power becomes exercisable. If the power to revoke extends to only a portion of the fund, it is only the appropriate proportion of the income which is attributable to the amount of capital subject to the power of revocation which is treated as the settlor's. For these purposes, an ex-spouse is not a spouse and neither is the widow or widower of a deceased settlor (*Lord Vestey's Executors v IRC* (1949)).

If s 446 applies, the entire income of the settlement will be taxed as the settlor's unearned income under Schedule D Case VI despite the fact that he has received no income from the fund. It is treated as the top slice of his income but he can recover any excess tax charged, either from the trustees or from any person who has received income from the settlement (TA 1970 s 449).

4 Settlements in which the settlor is a discretionary beneficiary (TA 1970 s 448)

All the income arising under a settlement is treated as that of the settlor if, under the terms of that settlement, any person has, or may have, the power to pay that income or property to the settlor or his spouse. This provision does not apply if the discretionary power does not arise for at least six years from the creation of the settlement (but it will apply when the power becomes operative) and interests which are excluded under TA 1970 s 447 are excluded under this provision as well (they are listed on p 166).

Tax paid by the settlor as a result of s 448 may be recovered from the trustees or from any beneficiary who receives income from the fund.

5 Settlements with undistributed income (TA 1970 ss 447, 450, 451)

Undistributed income is the total income of the trust less income payments to beneficiaries and expenses properly charged to income (TA 1970 s 455).

a) *Settlements in which the settlor retains an interest* (TA 1970 s 447)

If the settlor is a discretionary beneficiary, the income is taxed as his income when it arises, in accordance with TA 1970 s 448 (above). TA 1970 s 447 provides that when the settlor (or his spouse) retains an interest in the settlement the undistributed income of the fund is taxed as the settlor's to the extent of his retained interest. An interest is retained if income or property in the fund will, or may, become payable to, or for the benefit of the settlor or his spouse. Presumably, therefore, if the settlor retains a reversionary interest in the whole of the capital of the fund, all the undistributed income is taxed as his under Schedule D Case VI. The settlor may recover any tax paid as a result of s 447 from the trustees or the beneficiaries.

EXAMPLE 12

Tim creates a settlement in favour of his two adult daughters Tina and Tanya, as concurrent life tenants, and he gives the trustees an overriding power to accumulate the income. Because he has not disposed of the remainder interest, Tim has retained an interest in the fund with the result that any accumulated income is taxed as his.

The nature of the interest which the settlor must retain, in order for TA 1970 s 447 to apply, has given rise to some discussion. A power to participate in the management of the trust is not, for instance, a sufficient interest (see *Lord Vestey's Executors v IRC* (1949)); likewise, the possibility that a beneficiary might make a gift back to the settlor is to be ignored; and recently, the Revenue have accepted that if the trustees agree to pay the CTT bill that arises on the creation of the settlement, this will not amount to a reservation of an interest (SP 1/82 and see Chapter 24). Section 447(2) further provides that if any interest of the settlor is dependent upon the happening of certain events, income will not be deemed to be that of the settlor. The events are:

'(a) if and so long as that income or property cannot become payable or applicable as aforesaid except in the event of:
(i) the bankruptcy of some person who is, or may become, beneficially entitled to that income or property; or
(ii) any assignment of, or charge on, that income or property being made or given by some such person; or
(iii) in the case of a marriage settlement, the death of both the parties to the marriage and of all or any of the children of the marriage; or
(iv) the death under the age of twenty-five or some lower age of some person who would be beneficially entitled to that income or property on attaining that age; or
(b) if and so long as some person is alive and under the age of twenty-five during whose life that income or property cannot become payable or applicable as aforesaid except in the event of that person becoming bankrupt or assigning or charging his interest in that income or property.'

Events (i) to (iv) in (a) above are alternatives but all the conditions in (b) must be satisfied if the settlor is not to retain an interest.

EXAMPLE 13

Harry settles property on trust for his godson Charles as protected life tenant (so that his interest will determine, inter alia, upon bankruptcy) contingent upon his attaining the age of 40. In the event of Charles' life interest being forfeited the fund is to pass to Harry's wife, Ruth. Charles is currently aged 19 and the settlement contains a power to accumulate the income for 21 years.

Although the settlor's wife, Ruth, is the beneficiary entitled in default, Harry, the settlor, is not treated as reserving an interest because of (b) above. Once Charles becomes 25, however, the accumulated income will be taxed as Harry's.

b) *Covenants to settlements* (TA 1970 s 450)

Covenants will not be a charge on income if made by a settlor in favour of the trustees of (or a body corporate connected with) a settlement which the settlor has made and which has undistributed income. In view of the ambit of TA 1970 s 457 (see p 168) this provision is of small practical significance.

c) *Receipt of a capital sum by the settlor* (TA 1970 s 451 as amended by FA 1981 ss 42, 43 and FA 1982 s 63)

The purpose of this provision is to prevent the settlor obtaining any benefit from a settlement in which the income may be taxed at a lower rate than that which would have applied had the settlor retained the income. In effect, capital payments to the settlor (or his spouse) from the fund are matched with undistributed income of the fund and taxed as the settlor's income under Schedule D Case VI. The sum is grossed up at basic and the 15% additional rate but the settlor is entitled to a credit for tax paid by the trustees—although not to any repayment! There are no provisions enabling the settlor to recover any tax that he may have to pay.

A 'capital sum' covers any sum paid by way of loan or a repayment of a loan and any sum paid otherwise than as income and which is not paid for full consideration in money or money's worth (TA 1970 s 451(8)). A capital sum is treated as paid to the settlor if it is paid at his direction or, as a result of his assignment, to a third party (TA 1970 s 451(9)).

The capital sum will only be caught by s 451 to the extent that it is less than, or equals, the income available in the settlement; this means the undistributed income of the fund from any relevant year ie any year of assessment after 1937–38. Any excess will not be charged in the year of receipt but it may be charged later if income becomes available in any of the next 11 years (TA 1970 s 451(1)(b)).

EXAMPLE 14

The undistributed net income of a settlement is as follows:

Year 1   £10,000
Year 2   £ 2,500
Year 3   £15,000
Year 4   £ 6,000
Year 5   £ 7,000

In year 3, the trustees lend the settlor £45,000. That loan is a capital sum and, therefore, the settlor is charged to income tax in year 3 on that sum to the extent that it represents available income. As the available income is £27,500 (years 1–3) he will be taxed on £27,500 grossed up at 45%—ie on £50,000. He will not be subject to basic or additional rate tax on that income so that if his marginal rate is 60% he will be taxed at 15% (60% – 45%).

The remaining £17,500 is carried forward to be taxed in succeeding years when income becomes available; in year 4, for instance, £6,000 is available. If the loan is repaid, there will be no further charge on available income in subsequent years, but any tax paid during the loan period cannot be recovered (s 451(3A)).

Section 451 also applies to a capital sum received by the settlor from a body corporate connected with the settlement. Generally, a company will be connected with a settlement if it is a close company and the participators include the trustees of the settlement (TA 1970 s 454(4)). The width of s 451 and its somewhat capricious nature (see for instance *De Vigier v IRC* (1964)) means that settlements will often contain a clause prohibiting the payment of capital sums to the settlor or his spouse.

6   Charging the settlor to excess liability (TA 1970 s 457)

Income which arises from property of which the settlor has not divested himself absolutely, is taxed as his for the purpose of excess liability. It is irrelevant that the income is distributed to another person. The section will only apply if the income is not caught by any of the anti-avoidance provisions discussed above and does not apply to matrimonial settlements (see p 501). A settlor will be treated as not having divested himself of the property (ie as continuing to have an interest in the property) in a wide range of circumstances (see, for instance, *Vandervell v IRC* (1967)), although the four exceptions under TA 1970 s 447(2)(a) (see p 166) apply equally to s 457.

7   General conclusions

So long as the settlor is prepared to sever all direct connection with his settlement, the above anti-avoidance provisions need not cause any problems.

Hence, so far as income tax is concerned capital settlements remain a viable way of disposing of family wealth. The attraction of accumulation settlements for minor children should be noted particularly as they may also have a privileged status for CTT purposes.

V   CHARITABLE TRUSTS

Income and capital gains accruing to charities receive privileged treatment and are generally exempt from tax so long as they are applied for charitable purposes only. There are also reliefs for covenanted donations to charities: for instance, basic rate income tax may be recovered by the charity on covenanted payments, whilst such covenants are deductible from the income of the donor for higher rate tax purposes so long as the sums covenanted do not exceed £5,000 pa (see the exceptions to TA 1970 s 457 in Chapter 10). Finally, charitable covenants need only be capable of lasting for more than three years to avoid TA 1970 s 434.

12 Estates in the course of administration

I   The deceased's income
II The administration period
III Taxation of distributions to beneficiaries

PRs (ie executors, where there is a will, and administrators on an intestacy) are under a duty to administer a deceased's estate. This involves considering:
(1) A duty to settle the deceased's outstanding income tax to the date of death. Although this Chapter is concerned primarily with income tax, notice that there may be an outstanding CGT liability (see Chapter 15) and that the PRs cannot obtain a grant of probate until any CTT, payable on their application for a grant, has been accounted for (see Chapter 22).
(2) Liability to income tax during the administration period. In addition, the PRs may incur a CGT liability (see Chapter 15). Further, the original CTT bill may require adjustment as a result of events happening after the death (see Chapter 22).
(3) The liability of beneficiaries to income tax on any income distributed to them from the estate.

I   THE DECEASED'S INCOME

The PRs are liable for any income tax owed by the deceased (TMA 1970 s 74(1)). They should report the death to the appropriate inspector of taxes and complete an ordinary income tax return (Form 11) on behalf of the deceased for the period from 6 April preceding his death to the date of death, and for earlier tax years (if necessary!). In computing the income tax of the deceased, normal principles operate and full personal allowances are available for the year of death.

Any outstanding income tax is a debt of the estate thereby reducing the chargeable value for CTT. Conversely, any repayment of income tax will swell the assets of the estate and may increase the CTT bill on death. Failure to make the appropriate returns means that the Revenue can assess the PRs, at any time within three tax years from the end of the tax year of death, for any tax that is owing for a period that is within six years of the date of that assessment (not the date of death).

EXAMPLE 1

A died on 28 September 1984 (tax year 1984–85). If the Revenue assess his PRs on 2 January 1986 (tax year 1985–86) they can relate it back to the tax year 1979–80.

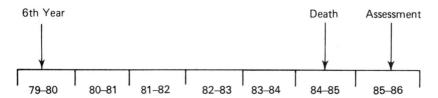

169

1 **Dividends**

Dividends received before the deceased's death form part of the deceased's income. For CTT purposes the quoted securities in the deceased's estate must be valued at death; if that quotation was 'ex div' (ie it did not include the value of a declared dividend) the dividend that is to be paid must be added to the value of the security. This problem does not arise when the shares were valued at death 'cum div' since the quotation includes any accruing dividend to date.

If the dividend is paid after the death but relates to a period partly before and partly after death, it may have to be apportioned (Apportionment Act 1870 s 2) for succession purposes.

However, whether or not the dividend is apportioned for succession purposes any dividend paid after the deceased's death is treated as the income of the estate and not of the deceased and must not be included in the deceased's tax return (*IRC v Henderson's Executors* (1931)). This rule follows from the fact that as the dividends were never owed to the deceased they never became a part of his income. In exceptional cases a dividend declared due before death, but paid after that death will be taxed as the deceased's income (see, for instance, *Re Sebright* (1944) and contrast *Potel v IRC* (1971)). Similarly, certain other investment income paid after death but relating to the period before death (for instance bank deposit interest) should be apportioned for succession purposes, but included as estate income for tax purposes. This rule may lead to some double taxation in that the income which is deemed for succession purposes to accrue before death is charged both to CTT (as part of the deceased's estate on death) and also to income tax in the hands of the PRs and beneficiaries. TA 1970 s 430 affords some relief against such double taxation but only to an absolutely entitled residuary beneficiary who is a higher rate taxpayer (see p 176).

EXAMPLE 2

T died on 30 May 1984 leaving his residuary estate (including 1,000 shares in B Ltd) to his brother B absolutely. On 15 June 1984 B Ltd declared a dividend on those shares of £420 (£600 gross) in respect of the year ending on 30 June. The dividend was paid on 28 July 1984.

Of this dividend 11/12 (£385) is deemed to have accrued before T's death and will be reflected in the value of the shares in T's estate which will have been valued 'cum div'. It will, thus, be taxed as part of the capital in T's estate.

However, for income tax purposes the whole dividend is taxed as the income of the estate, albeit with some relief for double taxation against any higher rate liability of B under TA 1970 s 430.

2 **Trust income**

Where the deceased was a life tenant under a trust, any income which was received by the trustees before his death is treated as his income and must be included in the PRs' tax return to the date of death. If income was paid to the trustees after the death but is attributable in part to the period before death tax is payable according to the actual apportionment. Any income that is apportioned to the deceased life tenant is taxed as the income of the estate—and not of the deceased (*Wood v Owen* (1941)).

Income that is apportioned to the deceased life tenant forms an asset of his estate, thereby increasing his CTT liability. This may result in an element of double CTT because the apportioned income may affect the value of the trust assets on which the trustees pay CTT on the life tenant's death. This double taxation will be avoided by deducting the apportioned income from the value of the settled assets.

EXAMPLE 3

T who died on 30 June 1984 was life tenant of a trust. Included in the settled assets was debenture stock in Blank Ltd. On 31 December 1984 B Ltd paid to the trustees the annual interest of £70 (£100 gross). This interest was apportioned by the trustees as to half (£35) to T and half (£35) to the remainderman X. The £35 apportioned to the deceased is estate income. Notice, also, that the £35 besides forming an additional asset of T's estate for CTT purposes also swells the value of the trust fund on which the trustees pay CTT at T's rates (see Chapter 22). To avoid the £35 being charged twice to CTT, it is deducted from the value of the settled assets. (If T's free estate passed to a residuary beneficiary absolutely, the latter may be entitled to relief under TA 1970 s 430 above.)

If the Apportionment Act 1870 is excluded so that all the income is paid to either a subsequent life tenant or a remainderman, income tax follows the actual apportionment made. That income therefore, is not taxed as part of the deceased's estate.

3 Sole traders and partners

As a general rule the death of a sole trader involves a discontinuance of the business so that the closing year rules must be applied (see TA 1970 ss 117, 118 and Chapter 6). If the business passes on death to a spouse, however, the discontinuance provisions are not applied, unless they are claimed (ESC A7). Therefore, for the year of his death, PRs must (unless ESC A7 applies) include in the deceased's tax return the actual profits of the business from the preceding 6 April to the date of death. They are liable for any extra tax arising from the exercise of the Revenue's election under TA 1970 s 118. Terminal loss relief under TA 1970 s 174 (see Chapter 7) may be available.

The death of a partner effects a discontinuance of the partnership so that the closing year rules must be applied, unless the PRs join in an election under TA 1970 s 154(2) (see generally Chapter 29).

4 Husband and wife

A husband (or his PRs if he is dead) may, within two months of a grant of probate being taken out to his wife's estate, disclaim liability for unpaid income tax in respect of her income for any year when they were living together (TA 1970 s 41).

II THE ADMINISTRATION PERIOD

The administration period is the period from the date of death until the date when the residue is ascertained and ready for distribution. Until that date no beneficiary is entitled to the income or to any property comprised in the estate and, accordingly, is not liable to income tax unless income is actually distributed to him. During the administration period, the PRs are liable, in a representative capacity, to income tax on all the income of the estate computed in the usual way. Their liability is only for basic rate income tax, never to higher rates. As they are not individuals, they have no personal reliefs. Tax relief is available, for one year, for interest on a loan raised to pay the CTT payable on delivery of the PRs' account, which is attributable to personal property owned beneficially by the deceased and which vests in his PRs, provided that the loan is on a loan account not merely by way of overdraft (FA 1974 Sch 1 para 17).

PRs may also claim mortgage interest relief for a house which was the only or main residence of the deceased and is now that of his widow or dependents (FA 1974 Sch 1 para 8).

If the PRs receive income from which basic rate tax has been deducted at source (such as dividends) they need not include such income in their tax return as they are subject to no further tax liability on it. Hence, they need only return details of income that they receive gross, such as bank interest (on IR Form 1).

Dividends and certain other income received by the PRs after the death in respect of a period wholly or partly before death is taxed as the income of the estate whether or not it is apportioned for succession purposes (see p 170). Similarly, trust income received by the trustees after the deceased life tenant's death and apportioned to him is taxed as the income of the estate (see p 170).

When the PRs carry on a business after the death of a sole trader in order to sell it as a going concern; or, to transfer it to a beneficiary, they must pay basic rate tax on any profits calculated in the usual way. Hence, they can deduct business expenses (TA 1970 s 130) and claim loss relief (normally under TA 1970 s 168 or s 171; FA 1978 s 30 does not apply). If the death effected a discontinuance of the business, the opening year rules apply as from the date of death (TA 1970 ss 115, 116 and see Chapter 6).

When property which produces no income is left to persons in succession (eg, to A for life, remainder to B) part of the capital sum realised on the sale of that property may be treated as income under the rule in *Re Earl of Chesterfield's Trusts* (1883) since, otherwise, the life tenant would receive nothing. Such equitable apportionment involves no income tax liability for the PRs (or the beneficiaries) because the apportionment is of a capital sum.

III   TAXATION OF DISTRIBUTIONS TO BENEFICIARIES

All income received by the PRs suffers basic rate tax either by deduction at source or by direct assessment in their hands. From this taxed income the PRs deduct administration expenses chargeable against income, leaving a net sum available for distribution to beneficiaries entitled to the income from the estate in one or more of the capacities considered below.

If the PRs have a discretion whether to deduct administration expenses from income or capital they should carefully consider the tax position of the beneficiary (if any) entitled to the income. When that beneficiary has a large income, they should deduct their expenses from income so as to reduce his income and, therefore, his tax bill. Conversely, if the beneficiary has only a small income, they should deduct expenses from capital so as not to prejudice any claim that he may have for a repayment of basic rate tax.

1   General legatees

A general legatee is a person who is entitled to a sum of money (a pecuniary legacy) not charged on any particular fund. This sum is capital and the legatee is generally not entitled to any income unless:
(1) the will directs the PRs to pay him interest; or

(2) the legacy remains unpaid at the end of the executor's year, in which case he is entitled to interest at 5% pa in the absence of a contrary direction; or

(3) the legacy is a 'statutory legacy' arising on intestacy (eg, to a surviving spouse) in which case he is entitled to interest at 6% pa from the date of death to the date of payment.

Any interest is paid gross by the PRs from the estate and the legatee is assessed directly to tax under Schedule D Case III on the interest in the year of receipt. If that interest is neither claimed nor paid, there is no income to be assessed in the beneficiary's hands (*Dewar v IRC* (1935)). Once a sum has been set aside to pay the legacy it may, however, be too late to disclaim the income (*Spens v IRC* (1970)).

2 Specific legatees

A specific legatee is entitled to a particular item of property and to any income produced by it as from the date of death. Therefore, once the PRs vest the legacy in the beneficiary, any income from it which arose during the administration period, is related back and taxed as the legatee's income for the tax year(s) when it arose. It will have suffered basic rate tax either through deduction at source or as a result of direct assessment on the PRs. Accordingly, the net income will be passed to the beneficiary together with a tax deduction certificate completed by the PRs (Form IR 185E).

EXAMPLE 4

A died in September 1984 leaving his 1,000 shares in B Ltd to his nephew T. A dividend of £70 is paid in respect of the shares in January 1985. The administration is completed and the shares vested in T in May 1985 together with the dividend and tax credit for the £30 basic rate tax which has been deducted. T must include the £100 in his income tax return for the tax year 1984–85 (when the dividend was paid) and not 1985–86 (when T received it).

3 Annuitants

An annuity is a pecuniary legacy payable by instalments. The payments are income from which the PRs must deduct basic rate income tax. The net sum will be paid to the annuitant who will be given a certificate of tax deducted (IR 185).

A testator usually wants the annuitant to receive a constant sum despite fluctuations in the tax rates. The two methods most commonly employed are:

(1) The testator provides for the payment of 'such sum as will after deduction of income tax at the basic rate for the time being in force leave £70 pa'.

The PRs must pay £70 grossed-up at the current basic rate, but they are not liable to indemnify the annuitant against any higher rate income tax for which he may be liable. Conversely, if the annuitant can reclaim all or any of the basic rate tax paid, he need not account for it to the PRs.

(2) If the testator provides for the payment of '£70 pa free from income tax' this imposes an obligation on the PRs to pay such sum as after deducting basic rate income tax leaves £70. However, it also means that the annuitant can recover from the PRs any higher rate tax that he may have to pay on the annuity and any basic rate tax that he can reclaim must be repaid to the PRs. In effect, he will never be left with more nor with less than £70 (see *Re Pettit, Le Fevre v Pettit* (1922), and Chapter 10).

An annuitant can insist on a capital sum being set aside to provide for his annuity. If the capital in the estate is insufficient he can demand that the actuarial value of the annuity be paid to him, abated if necessary (*IRC v Lady Castlemaine* (1943)). This capitalised annuity is not subject to income tax either in the PRs', or in the annuitant's hands.

If the will directs the PRs to purchase an annuity for the beneficiary, he will be charged to income tax on the full amount of each annual payment and cannot claim relief under TA 1970 s 230 whereby only the income element is subject to income tax (see Chapter 10). The beneficiary should therefore demand that the PRs give him the appropriate capital sum so that he can buy the annuity himself and claim s 230 relief.

Where there is insufficient income in the estate to pay the annuity in full, the will may direct the PRs to make up the income from capital. If they do so, that capital is treated as income from which basic rate tax must be deducted (*Brodie's WT v IRC* (1933)). The unfortunate result of such 'top-up' provisions is to convert capital into income. It is, therefore, better to give the PRs a discretion to make good any shortfall in the annuity by capital advances.

4   Residuary beneficiaries

A beneficiary may have a limited or an absolute interest in residue. A limited interest exists where he is entitled to the income only, eg if the will leaves residue to 'my wife for life, remainder to my children', the wife is entitled only to income from the estate. An absolute interest exists when the beneficiary is entitled to both the income and capital of the residue, as where the residue is left to 'my wife absolutely'. PRs normally have to provide the Revenue with details of the residuary beneficiaries and the nature of their interests (on Form IR 920).

a) *Beneficiary with a limited interest in residue*

The total income produced by the residue during the administration period cannot be calculated accurately until the residue is finally ascertained and the administration completed. Any income paid to the beneficiary during that period will be paid net of basic rate income tax deducted by the PRs. The beneficiary must gross up these sums as part of his total income in the year of receipt for the purposes of his excess liability or to obtain a repayment of basic rate tax (as appropriate).

When the administration is completed, the total net income payments of the period are aggregated and are deemed to have been paid out to the beneficiary at a uniform rate over the administration period. This may necessitate adjustments to his original income tax liability. Such adjustments must be made within three years of the end of the tax year in which the administration is completed.

EXAMPLE 5

Mildred dies on 6 April 1984 leaving the residue of her estate to her son, Sonny, for life, remainder to her daughter, Dotty, absolutely.

The PRs make payments to Sonny net of basic rate tax at 30% in 1984–85; 35% in 1985–86 and 25% in 1986–87. The administration is completed on 5 October

1986 when Sonny received a final payment of £980. Sonny receives the following sums:

Year	Net income received	Grossed-up amount
	£	
1984–85	70	£100 (inc tax credit £30)
1985–86	350	£538 (inc tax credit £188)
1986–87	980	£1,307 (inc tax credit £327)
	£1,400	

Sonny's total receipts are £1,400 (net) which sum is deemed to have been paid on a day to day basis over the administration period. Hence, Sonny's total income for the administration period is adjusted as follows:

Year	Adjusted net receipt	Grossed-up amount
	£	
1984–85	560	£800 (inc tax credit £240)
1985–86	560	£862 (inc tax credit £302)
1986–87 (6 months)	280	£373 (inc tax credit £93)
	£1,400	

Notice (1) That the income paid to Sonny will be the total income of the estate after deducting basic rate tax, any interest on legacies and interest on late payments of CTT, and any administration expenses properly charged to income.

(2) Although Sonny's total net income receipts (£1,400) will equal the net income of the estate his grossed-up income will differ from the total gross income of the estate for a number of reasons, but, in particular, because of changes in the basic rate of income tax and because of the payment of administration expenses by the PRs out of income net of basic rate tax.

b) *Beneficiary with an absolute interest in residue*

Such a beneficiary is entitled to receive both income and capital from the estate. He can, of course, only be charged to income tax insofar as any payments that he receives represent income. For the purpose of calculating to what extent the payments constitute income the following rules are applied (see TA 1970 ss 427(3) and (4), 430, 431).

First, sums paid to the beneficiary in any one year are deemed to be income (net of basic rate income tax) up to the amount of 'net residuary income' available and must be grossed up in order to calculate his total income for the year. 'Residuary income' is the total gross income received by the PRs in the relevant tax year less interest on legacies and on loans to pay CTT and less management expenses properly chargeable against income. 'Net residuary income' is the residuary income of the estate less basic rate tax for that year.

Secondly, any payment in excess of net residuary income is deemed to be capital.

Finally, within three years of the end of the tax year when the administration is completed, the initial assessments are revised as necessary so that the beneficiary is deemed to have received the full net residuary income for each tax year. Any balance that he has received is capital.

EXAMPLE 6

Carlos dies on 6 April 1984 leaving his residuary estate to his son, Carl.

The administration is completed on 5 April 1987 when Carl receives a final payment of £1,000.

During the course of the administration, Carl receives the following payments:

Year	Basic rate of income tax	Net residuary income	Carl's receipts
1984–85	30%	£700	£350
1985–86	35%	£700	£1,300
1986–87	25%	£700	£1,200

The income tax calculation proceeds as follows:

(1) *1984–85:* £350 is income in Carl's hands which he must gross up to £500. It will be taxed as part of his total income for that year. £350 of the net residuary income for 1984–85 is unapplied.

(2) *1985–86:* £700 is treated as income up to the net residuary income of that year (1985–86) which gives Carl total income of £1,071 (gross) for inclusion in his income tax return. The remaining £600 (£1,300 – £700)) is capital.

(3) *1986–87:* £700 of the £1,200 paid to Carl is income (and is, therefore, £824 gross).

(4) *5 April 1987:* Adjustments have to be made so that Carl is deemed to have received all the net residuary income produced by the estate over the administration period. Thus, in 1984–85 his income will be adjusted from £500 (£350 grossed up) to £1,000 (the £700 net residuary income grossed up).

Building Society interest is deemed to be paid net of basic rate income tax, but generally with no right for the recipient to recover that tax. (Notice the extension of this 'composite rate scheme' to interest paid by banks and other institutions as from 1985–86.)

Where this income forms part of the 'residuary income' of the estate, a beneficiary with an absolute interest in residue is treated as receiving the income not from its underlying source (ie the building society) but from the estate. Since all residuary income of the estate is paid net of basic rate tax with a tax credit, the beneficiary can, therefore, recover any basic rate tax for which he is not liable (see SP 7/80).

Income which accrued before death, but is received by the PRs after death, is included in the value of the deceased's estate for CTT purposes and is also taxed as the income of the estate (see p 170). Some relief against this double taxation is provided by TA 1970 s 430 which allows a reduction in the residuary income for the purposes of any liability to higher rate tax of a residuary beneficiary absolutely entitled to residue. The reduction is of an amount equal to the CTT chargeable on that income at the estate rate and the resultant sum is then grossed up at the basic rate of income tax.

EXAMPLE 7

X died on 30 April 1984. He left his residuary estate including 1,000 debentures in B Ltd to his daughter D. His PRs received interest of £140 (£200 gross) from B Ltd in November 1984 in respect of that company's accounting year ending 31 October 1984. The whole interest is taxed as the income of the estate, but as half the interest accrued before death, that portion is included in X's estate for CTT purposes. Under TA 1970 s 430 if D is a higher rate taxpayer one-half of the interest is eligible for relief. Assume that the estate rate of CTT is 20%.

	£
Interest (gross)	£200

Sum accrued before death	100
Less income tax for year of death	30
	£70

The relief is calculated as:

£70 × 20% (CTT estate rate)	14
Add income tax	6
Grossed-up amount that can be deducted from the residuary income to reduce D's liability to higher rate income tax only	£20

13 The overseas dimension

I Residence and ordinary residence
II Taxation of foreign income
III The taxation of the foreign taxpayer
IV Double taxation relief
V Anti-avoidance legislation: transfer of assets abroad (TA 1970 s 478; FA 1981 s 45)

Liability to UK income tax is determined by the source of the income and the residence of the recipient. Thus, as a general rule, a UK resident is subject to UK income tax on all his income wherever its source, including income arising abroad ('foreign income'), whereas a non-UK resident is only liable to UK income tax on income arising to him in the UK (the 'foreign taxpayer'). However, when considering an employee's liability to income tax under Schedule E, the domicile of the employee and the residence of the employer may also be relevant factors.

I RESIDENCE AND ORDINARY RESIDENCE

These terms, which are important for both income tax and CGT, are not statutorily defined.

Residence and ordinary residence is usually determined for a particular tax year and applies for the whole year. By concession, however, an individual who ceases to be permanently resident in the UK (ie who goes abroad for at least three years) is treated as non-resident from the date of his departure; conversely a person who takes up permanent residence in the UK (ie who comes for at least two years) is treated as resident from the date of his arrival in the UK.

" 'An individual is resident and ordinarily resident in the
United Kingdom if he is living in the ordinary course
of his life, or for an extended period; also though normally
he lives here, if he is abroad for occasional residence
only; or if he visits the United Kingdom, year by year,
even though his main home is abroad' . . . who on earth
wrote this, Harold Pinter?"

1   Individuals

Residence means, broadly, the country where a person lives. Residence (and ordinary residence) is a question of fact and degree determined according to a voluminous body of case law and a Revenue Statement of Practice (IR 20).

TA 1970 s 51 states that a temporary visitor to the UK will not be regarded as resident in the UK in any year of assessment provided that he does not spend more than 183 days here in that year taken as a whole and, provided that he has no intention of remaining permanently in the UK. The 183 days is construed strictly so that fractions of a day are included. Thus, an individual who is present in the UK in a tax year for more than six months will be resident. Even if he is in the UK for less than six months in the year, he may still be resident, despite s 51, if his presence has 'residential qualities', the most important of which are considered below:

Physical presence   If an individual is absent from the UK for the whole tax year he is unlikely to be regarded as resident (*Turnbull v Foster* (1904)); some physical presence is necessary. He may, however, be ordinarily resident.

Nationality   An individual who is a UK national is more likely than a national of another country to be regarded as UK resident.

Frequency and purpose of visits   An individual who visits the UK regularly, albeit with no abode here, may be regarded as resident if these visits form part of his habits and way of life. The Revenue's practice is to treat an individual as UK resident here once his visits average three months a year for four consecutive years. If it is clear at the outset that he will be making such visits (eg where he comes to attend university here) he is treated as resident from the start.

The fact that a person has no freedom of choice concerning his visits to the UK is irrelevant. In *IRC v Lysaght* (1928), a director of a UK company who was living in Ireland returned to the UK for about one week each month on company business and stayed in hotels. It was held that he was resident in the UK (see also *Levene v IRC* (1928)).

Family ties in the UK will also be some evidence of UK residence.

Former residence   By TA 1970 s 49 a British citizen (or citizen of the Republic of Ireland) who has been ordinarily resident in the UK and who leaves for occasional residence abroad will be treated during his absence as remaining resident in the UK unless he can prove to the contrary (see *Levene v IRC* (1928)).

Accommodation in the UK   The 'accommodation test' is a crucial factor in determining residence. An individual who has any accommodation in the UK available for his use, is treated as resident even if he only visits the UK for one day in the relevant tax year. If he visits the UK in each of four or more consecutive years, he will also be treated as ordinarily resident. The accommodation need not be owned by the individual. Whether it is available for his use is a question of fact; it will not be so available if it is let on terms that give him no right of occupation.

This test is qualified by TA 1970 s 50 in relation to a person who works abroad full-time and all of whose duties are performed abroad. Whether such an individual is resident in the UK must be decided independently of whether he maintains accommodation in the UK.

'Ordinary residence' has been held to mean habitual residence, ie where residence in the UK is part of the individual's way of life (*Levene v IRC* (1928)).

A person may be resident without being ordinarily resident and vice versa. Thus, where an individual who has resided in the UK for many years is absent for one year, he ceases to be resident for that year, but may remain ordinarily resident.

2   Corporations, partnerships and trusts

A corporation is resident where its central management and control are located. This is usually the place where board meetings are held and not necessarily where the company is incorporated or registered (see also SP 6/83).

A similar rule applies for partnerships. If the management and control of the business is exercised abroad, the firm is deemed to be non-resident even though individual partners may be resident in the UK (TA 1970 s 153). However, to the extent that some of the business is carried on in the UK, profits will be taxed under Schedule D Case I.

The residence of a trust is determined by reference to the trustees who are treated as resident in the UK if any one of them is so resident (cp residence rules for CGT).

II   TAXATION OF FOREIGN INCOME

1   Profits of a trade, profession or vocation (Schedule D)

a) *General*

A UK resident is assessed under Schedule D Cases I or II on all his profits arising from a trade, profession or vocation ('trade') carried on by him in the UK, despite some of the profits being attributable to overseas business: TA 1970 s 109(2). However, until 1984–85 he was entitled to a 25% deduction from his 'relevant income' (ie profits before deducting loss relief) in any tax year that he spent at least 30 qualifying days (see FA 1978 s 27(2)) abroad on business. This deduction is reduced to $12\frac{1}{2}\%$ for 1984–85 and thereafter abolished (FA 1984 s 30(2).

Where it applies, the deduction is calculated as $12\frac{1}{2}\%$ of the proportion of the traders' profits that the qualifying days of absence bear to 365.

EXAMPLE 1

In 1984–85 a UK resident trader with relevant income from the trade of £20,000 (calculated on the preceding year basis) spends 60 qualifying days abroad. His deduction is:

$$\frac{12\frac{1}{2}}{100} \times \frac{60}{365} \times £20,00 = £411$$

b) *Trade carried on wholly abroad (Schedule D Case V)*

Non-resident trade   For a trader to be assessed under Schedule D Case V, he must be resident in the UK, but the trade must be carried on wholly abroad. This is a question of fact, and for the sole trader who is resident in the UK and who has the sole right to manage and control the business it will be difficult to argue that the trade is wholly carried on abroad (*Ogilvie v Kitton* (1908)).

A UK resident company may, however, be able to show that it is trading wholly abroad (*Mitchell v Egyptian Hotels Ltd* (1915)). Where the company establishes a foreign subsidiary (as opposed to a branch) it is a question of fact whether that subsidiary is carrying on its own trade or acting merely as agent for the parent company. The answer appears to depend upon where the head and brains of the trade are to be found and not on who owns the shares. To avoid the risk of the subsidiary being treated as UK resident it is, therefore, prudent to ensure that UK resident directors are not in a majority on the subsidiary's board; that the non-resident directors of the subsidiary are men of substance who are capable of independent thought and judgment; and that board meetings (where 'real' decisions and not just 'rubber stampings' occur) should be held outside the UK. (Note, however, the rules taxing controlled foreign companies under FA 1984 ss 82–91; see p 409).

If a non-resident partnership trades in the UK, any UK resident partner will be assessed under Case I on the UK profits although he will be charged under Case V on his share of any foreign profits.

Although 'trade' is used here to include professions and vocations, in practice, profits arising from a profession will rarely be taxed under Case V because the individual exercising his profession wholly abroad is unlikely to be a UK resident and hence will escape UK income tax completely (see *Davies v Braithwaite* (1931)).

Computation of profits Tax is assessed under Case V on income arising in the preceding tax year whether or not it is remitted to the UK ('the arising basis'). If, however, the taxpayer is not domiciled or not ordinarily resident in the UK he is taxed under Case V on the remittance basis only ie on actual sums received in the UK in the preceding tax year . . . 'from remittances payable in the UK or from property imported or from money or value arising from property not imported . . .' (TA 1970 s 122(3)).

The opening and closing year rules of Case I (TA 1970 ss 115–118) do not apply to income taxed under Case V. Instead in the tax year when the source of the income first arises and for the following tax year, the taxpayer is taxed on the actual profits (or remittances if applicable) of the first tax year which puts him onto the preceding tax year basis by year 3.

When the source ceases, the taxpayer is taxed in the final year on the actual profits of that year and in the penultimate year on actual profits or the preceding year basis whichever shows the greater profit.

The rules are the same for a partnership except that TA 1970 s 154 does not apply so that there is no deemed discontinuance on a change of partners.

Deductible expenses (which do not include the trader's travelling costs), capital allowances and losses are calculated as under Case I, but loss relief is only given against other foreign (and not UK) income.

Where, despite the endeavours of the taxpayer, income which is taxed on the arising basis cannot be remitted to the UK because of foreign laws, executive action abroad, or the non-availability of foreign currency, the payment of tax is postponed until the problem passes.

Until 1984–85, 25% of income earned abroad was tax free. By FA 1984 s 30(3), (4) that proportion is reduced to $12\frac{1}{2}$% for 1984–85; thereafter relief is abolished. As a corollary, loss relief (including capital allowances) is restricted in the same proportions until 1985–86. Losses incurred before 1984–85 and not yet relieved still attract the 25% restriction.

The remittance basis There is no definition of remittance for income tax; tax is levied under Case V on actual sums received or treated as received in the UK by the taxpayer on the preceding year basis which includes the proceeds from property representing a remittance, but does not include investments of the income which are brought into this country so long as they are not realised in the UK by the taxpayer (TA 1970 s 122).

EXAMPLE 2

Carlos, domiciled and ordinarily resident in Spain, but resident in England carries on his business in Peru. Out of the profits of his business he buys a Picasso painting in France which he brings to England. This is property in kind and not a remittance under Case V. Were he to sell the Picasso in the UK, he would be taxable under s 122.

The sum must be received as the income of the trader and not, eg, as a gift, nor as the income of someone else, nor as capital. This is a question of fact.

TA 1970 s 122 also contains anti-avoidance provisions designed to catch disguised remittances, eg, where a UK loan is repaid from a remittance.

If the income is not remitted in the year when it arises, the trader cannot be taxed until the sums are remitted whereupon he is taxed by reference to the year of remission. As this could result in a large tax bill, he can elect to be taxed by reference to the year when the particular remittances arose.

2   Other categories of income

Income other than from a trade or employment which accrues to a UK resident from a foreign source will be taxed under Schedule C or under Schedule D Case IV or V.

a) *Schedule C*

Schedule C taxes dividends received from investments in UK and foreign public funds and foreign public authorities or institutions which are payable in the UK and dividends payable in the Republic of Ireland in respect of UK government securities registered with the Bank of Ireland.

Under Schedule C, basic rate tax is deducted at source from the dividends by the person entrusted with making the payment in the UK (the paying agent) and the taxpayer is assessed to any higher rate tax on a current year basis.

Certain payments out of public funds are specifically not charged under Schedule C (eg interest from trustee savings banks and War Loan is taxable in the recipient's hands under Schedule D Case III).

b) *Schedule D Cases IV and V*

Today the operation of Schedule D Cases IV and V is identical and it is merely an historical anachronism that certain income is chargeable under one Case rather than the other. Strictly, Case IV taxes income arising to a UK resident from foreign securities other than those charged under Schedule C and Case V charges income from possessions outside the UK.

Tax is charged under both Cases on income arising in the preceding tax year but such income is taxed only on the remittance basis when the recipient is not domiciled in the UK, or resident but not ordinarily resident in the UK (TA 1970 s 122(2)(a)).

The following categories of income are taxed under Cases IV or V:

Distributions from companies   Distributions are charged under Case V unless they relate to a secured debt eg a debenture (Case IV).

The distribution will only be taxable under either Case if it is income. This is decided by applying the local law to see whether or not the corpus of the asset is left intact after the distribution: if it is the payment will be taxed as income; if not, it is capital (*IRC v Reid's Trustees* (1947)).

Income from land and unsecured loans   Such income is taxable under Case V.

Income from a foreign trust   If a UK resident beneficiary has an absolute right to all or part of the income of the foreign trust (one where the trustees are non-UK resident and the assets are abroad), he is taxed under Case V as it arises and whether or not he receives it. Similar principles apply to a discretionary beneficiary in whose favour the trustees have exercised their discretion to appoint income.

Miscellany   Certain pensions (see p 186) and alimony ordered by a foreign court are taxed under Case V.

3   Employment income (Schedule E)

The three Cases of Schedule E aim to tax the emoluments wherever earned of a person resident or ordinarily resident in the UK.

The expression 'foreign emoluments' used in all three Cases means the emoluments of a person not domiciled in the UK whose employer is not a UK resident. The employee may be resident or ordinarily resident in the UK (such as a French domiciled journalist employed by a French newspaper in England as their foreign correspondent).

a) *Individual resident and ordinarily resident: Case I*

Where a person is resident and ordinarily resident in the UK, but is required by his employment to perform duties wholly or partly outside the UK, he is charged on all his emoluments (under the usual principles of Schedule E; see Chapter 5) with limited reliefs.

Long absence (FA 1977 Sch 7 para 1)   Where the duties are performed wholly or partly abroad during a qualifying period of absence of at least 365 days the employee can deduct 100% of the emoluments earned during that period. This 365 day period is unlikely to fall all within one tax year—if it did the employee would probably be regarded as non-resident so that Case I would not apply. Accordingly, when it straddles tax years, the 100% deduction is given against so much of the total emoluments of that year as were earned during the part of the qualifying period falling within that year (see *Example 4* below).

However, FA 1977 Sch 7 para 4 contains anti-avoidance provisions which apply whenever the duties of that employment or any other 'associated employment' held by the employee are not performed wholly abroad; this is to prevent an abuse of the relief by the loading of emoluments onto the foreign duties. Employments are 'associated' if they are with the same employer or with different companies in the same group (see para 4(5)).

A qualifying period of 365 days means that the employee must be abroad for a continuous period of 365 days. A period abroad will be continuous for these purposes unless visits back to the UK exceed 62 consecutive days for any single period, or 1/6th of the total days in that period.

Terminal leave spent abroad will count as a qualifying period; if spent in the UK it will not. Some duties (such as reporting back to base in the UK) can be regarded as incidental to overseas duties but the days so spent in the UK nevertheless count as 'days in the UK' in calculating the 1/6 and 62 day rules.

EXAMPLE 3

(1) A spends 300 days abroad before returning to the UK for 65 days. He then goes abroad for a further 300 days. A does not have a qualifying period of 365 days absence because, although his period in the UK does not exceed 1/6th of the total, it exceeds 62 days.

(2) A has the following periods of absence from, and presence in, the UK.

	Period	Days
1	Absent from UK	70
2	Present in UK	8
3	Absent from UK	105
4	Present in UK	26
5	Absent until final return	160
	Total days	369

A has a qualifying period of 365 days which is not broken by the two periods in the UK. Period 2 can be amalgamated with 1 and 3 because 8 days is less than 1/6th of that total period of 183 days. Presence in the UK on 34 days (2 and 4) is less than 1/6th of the final total period of 369 days.

EXAMPLE 4

Wanderer is employed as the export sales manager of Worldwide Enterprises PLC. He is absent from the UK on a sales promotion campaign in the Far East from 1 October 1984 to 31 December 1985 (458 days). During this period he returned to the UK to visit his mother for 21 days in 1984–85 and 30 days in 1985–86. His salary in 1984–85 was £16,000 and in 1985–86 £18,000. His duties are performed wholly abroad:

The whole period qualifies for the 100% deduction.

	1984–85 £	1985–86 £
Salary	16,000	18,000
Less: relief for overseas duties		
1984–85 $100\% \times \left(£16,000 \times \dfrac{188}{365}\right)$	8,241	
1985–86 $100\% \times \left(£18,000 \times \dfrac{270}{365}\right)$		13,315
Schedule E assessment	£7,759	£4,685

Short absences (FA 1977 Sch 7 para 2)   Where the duties of an office or employment are performed wholly or partly abroad, but there is no qualifying period of 365 days, the employee may deduct a percentage of his emoluments, provided that he accumulates at least 30 qualifying days of absence in any tax year. A qualifying day is defined as for Schedule D Case V (FA 1977 s 27(2)). Until 1984–85, this percentage was 25%; for 1984–85, it is reduced to 12½%; and thereafter it is abolished (FA 1984 s 30(1).

Where the duties of the employment or an associated employment are not performed wholly abroad the anti-avoidance provisions of FA 1977 Sch 7 para 4 apply (see p 183 and *Varnam v Deeble* (1984)).

In applying both the long and short absence reliefs, FA 1977 Sch 7 para 8 provides that, if overseas duties are merely incidental to a main UK employment, they are deemed to be performed in the UK. Even where the duties are performed substantially abroad, *any* duties in the UK will be taken into account in calculating the relief (para 9 construing TA 1970 s 184(2)).

Notice also that the percentage deductions are applied to the emoluments (including benefits) as reduced by any allowable expenses.

Foreign employments (FA 1977 s 31 and Sch 7)   Where the duties of the employment are performed wholly outside the UK and the employer is resident outside the UK, the employee is entitled to the same deductions from his emoluments as for short absences above (ie for 1984–85, $12\frac{1}{2}$%) regardless of periods of absence; he is also subject to the anti-avoidance provisions of FA 1977 Sch 7 para 4 (p 183).

Foreign emoluments (FA 1974 Sch 2 para 3)   Where the employee who receives foreign emoluments (see p 183) performs duties partly in the UK, he can deduct 50% of the foreign emoluments unless, (for 1984–85 onwards) he has been resident in the UK for nine out of the previous ten years and is now resident, when there is no deduction (FA 1984 s 30(9). This 50% is reduced by FA 1984 s 30 to 25% for 1987–88 and 1988–89 and withdrawn thereafter. Further, no employee can claim the relief from 1984–85 unless he took up the relevant UK duty before 1 August 1984 under an obligation incurred before 14 March 1984.

EXAMPLE 5

(1) A is domiciled abroad and employed in Exeter by a foreign company. On 6 April 1984 he has been UK resident in eight of the ten preceding years. He will qualify for a 50% deduction in 1984–85 but will be taxed on all his earnings in 1985–86 onwards (because he has now been resident nine out of ten years).
(2) B is like A, but arrived in the UK only in 1983–84. Provided he fulfils all the necesssary conditions for relief in each year, he will be entitled to the deductions available from 1984–85 until 1988–89.
(3) C is like A, but is only informed of his transfer to the UK on 1 May 1984. He assumes his duties on 1 October 1984. He is entitled to no deductions.

'Golden handshakes' paid before 1 August 1984, to such employees on termination of their employment, pursuant to an obligation incurred before 14 March 1984 are entitled to a 50% deduction, but thereafter are taxed under the usual rules for Schedule E (see p 62) with no further relief (FA 1984 s 30(7).

b) *Individual resident but not ordinarily resident: Case II*

Where a person is resident, but not ordinarily resident in the UK, he is assessed under Case II on emoluments for duties performed in the UK only. The foreign emoluments relief (above) may be available in appropriate cases.

c) *The remittance basis of Schedule E: Case III*

Case III applies to an employee who is resident (whether or not ordinarily resident) in the UK to tax emoluments which would otherwise escape tax under Cases I or II, but only if the emoluments are remitted to the UK.

Hence, Case III applies in two instances. First where the emoluments received in the UK are foreign emoluments and the duties of the employment are performed wholly abroad (so that neither Cases I or II can apply). Secondly, it applies where the emoluments received in the UK are for duties performed abroad (so that Case II cannot apply) and the employee, although resident, is not ordinarily resident in the UK (so that Case I cannot apply).

Remittances, for Schedule E, are governed by TA 1970 s 184(4) and, basically, bear the same meaning as for Schedule D Case V (see p 181 and TA 1970 s 122), Remittances under Schedule E are, however, assessed on a current year basis and may include the transmission to the UK of property in kind.

Notice that where an employee is potentially liable under both Cases I and II in respect of emoluments paid partly in the UK and partly abroad from a single employment performed inside and outside the UK, any emoluments paid in, enjoyed in, or remitted to the UK after 5 April 1983 will only be taxed under Case III to the extent that they exceed the Case II emoluments for the year (SP 5/84).

4   Place of work

In deciding whether the duties of an employment are in substance performed wholly abroad, merely incidental duties performed in the UK are ignored (TA 1970 s 184(2)). This is a question of fact, and the rule is restrictively construed (see *Robson v Dixon* (1972)). However, such incidental duties are included in applying the deductions in Case I.

Also by TA 1970 s 184(3) specific duties are always deemed to be performed in the UK; in particular Crown employments and certain duties of seamen and aircrew. The rules regarding the latter are, however, relaxed in applying the Case I deductions. Generally, crews of ships and aircraft will be treated as performing their duties abroad in respect of any part of a voyage that does not begin *and* end in the UK (FA 1977 Sch 7).

For the purposes of income tax generally, areas designated under the Continental Shelf Act 1964 are regarded as part of the UK (eg workers on oil rigs in the UK sector of the North Sea are deemed to work in the UK).

5   Deductible expenses

An employee who is taxed under Case I and performs his duties wholly abroad is allowed more generous deductions from his emoluments than would otherwise be allowed under TA 1970 s 189 provided that the emoluments are not foreign (FA 1977 s 32). He can deduct his costs of travelling to and from the UK to take up or leave the employment. If the expenses of board and lodging incurred in carrying out the duties abroad are paid or reimbursed by the employer, the employee will be entitled to a deduction so that those payments will not be emoluments. In addition where he spends 60 or more continuous days outside the UK, the expenses of travel of his spouse and children under 18 are not taxable if met by his employer (limited to two trips in each year of assessment). If the employee has two employments, the duties of which are performed wholly or partly abroad, the cost of travelling from one to the other is allowable provided that at least one of the places is overseas. An employee in receipt of 'foreign emoluments' may deduct travel expenses for duties performed in the UK (ESC A23). Some relaxation of these rules is proposed in a Consultative Document (March 1984).

6   Foreign pensions and annuities

Income from foreign pensions and annuities is taxed under Schedule D Case V on 90% of the income arising in the preceding year. However, such income will be taxable under Schedule E if it is payable in the UK through a department or agent of a Commonwealth government.

7 Collection of tax

Tax on an employee's Schedule E emoluments is generally collected at source by the employer under the PAYE system (TA 1970 s 204 and see Chapter 5).

Where an employer is resident in the UK he must as a general rule operate PAYE in respect of all his employees assessable under Schedule E, except for those entitled to a 100% deduction whose emoluments can be paid gross.

The application of TA 1970 s 204 to a non-resident employer, whose employees were assessable under Schedule E was considered in *Clark v Oceanic Contractors Inc* (1983). In that case a non-resident company made payments abroad to employees engaged in performing duties in the UK sector of the North Sea so within the UK for the purpose of liability under Schedule E (see FA 1973 s 38(6)). The House of Lords held that s 204 applied to the employer company so that it should have operated PAYE in respect of the payments. When employees are assessable under Schedule E, the only limit on the territorial scope of s 204 is whether it can effectively be enforced. It will, therefore, apply to the non-resident employer who maintains a 'trading presence' in the UK. This was so in the particular case: the company carried on activities in the UK and in the UK sector of the North Sea; was liable to corporation tax on its profits (TA 1970 s 246); and had an address for service in the UK.

If Schedule E emoluments are paid overseas by a non-UK resident employer with no trading presence in the UK, it appears from the *Oceanic* case that the employer cannot be made to deduct tax under s 204 on making the payments. In these circumstances, the Revenue are empowered to collect the tax from the relevant employees, in four equal instalments, by direct assessment under the 'direct collection' method (TA 1970 s 205 and 1973 Regulations.)

III THE TAXATION OF THE FOREIGN TAXPAYER

When in any given tax year, an individual is not a UK resident, he will be liable to UK income tax on income which has its source in the UK, unless that income is exempt from income tax (eg TA 1970 s 99).

Income arising in the UK to the foreign taxpayer is generally taxed at basic and higher rates with no personal reliefs or allowances. However, a proportion of the personal reliefs may be available to a foreign taxpayer who is a British subject or citizen of the Irish Republic; or is or has been a British Crown employee; or is employed in the service of a missionary society; or is employed in the service of any state under Her Majesty's protection; or is a resident of the Isle of Man or Channel Islands; or comes within a double taxation agreement providing for such relief; or has previously resided in the UK and is resident abroad for health reasons (of self or family); or is a widow whose late husband was a British Crown employee (TA 1970 s 27(2)).

The tax payable by such persons is calculated as the higher of *Step 2* and *Step 3* below.

Step 1 Calculate liability as if all income were UK income and all reliefs were given.

Step 2 Take the proportion of the liability in *Step 1* that the income liable to UK tax bears to that person's total (worldwide) income.

Step 3 Calculate UK tax liability on income liable to UK tax giving the same reliefs as for a UK resident.

EXAMPLE 6

Christian, who is married to Esther, works in Zambia for the Missionary Society of Eastern Zambia (and is, therefore, not a UK resident). His income from the Society for the relevant tax year is £8,000 and he also receives £2,100 dividends from UK companies and £2,000 (gross) UK debenture interest. The UK married man's personal allowance for the year is (say) £3,000.

UK income tax liability

		£	
Step 1	Salary	8,000	
	Dividends (plus tax credit)	3,000	
	Interest	2,000	
		13,000	
	Less personal allowance	3,000	
	Tax at 30% on	£10,000	= £3,000

$$Step\ 2\quad \frac{£5,000}{£13,000} \times £3,000 \qquad = £1,154\ less\ \text{tax credit of }£900 \quad = \quad £254$$

Step 3	Dividends and interest	5,000	
	Less personal allowance	3,000	
	Tax at 30% on	£2,000 (£600) less credit (£900) =	NIL

The income tax payable will be the higher of *Step 2* and *Step 3*, ie £254.

Where the taxpayer's total income in *Step 1* above comprises UK income only, he is entitled to full personal allowances; in calculating his total income, his wife's income is not deemed to be his if it is not chargeable to UK income tax (see *IRC v Addison* (1984)).

1   Profits of a trade, profession or vocation

As an application of the source doctrine, the foreign taxpayer will be taxable under Schedule D Case I on the profits of any trade carried on *within* as opposed to *with* the UK. For these purposes, however, maintaining an administrative or representative office as opposed to a branch in the UK will not constitute trading within the UK. The same principle applies to the exercise of a profession or vocation except that the exercise of either in the UK would normally render the taxpayer a UK resident (TA 1970 s 108(1)(a)(iii)).

The majority of cases have been concerned with the sale of goods by a non-resident to a person in the UK. The courts have tended to say that the trade is carried on in the place where, under English law, the contract is made. This is the place where acceptance of the offer is communicated. However, the place where contracts are made is only one (albeit important) factor to be considered. The better test is probably whether the trade which gives rise to the profits takes place in the UK (*Firestone Tyre and Rubber Co Ltd v Lewellin* (1957)).

When a trade is carried on within the UK, the profits are computed under the normal rules for Schedule D Case I. If it proves difficult to determine the profits attributable to that trade, the Revenue tax the proportion of the profits that the UK turnover bears to the trader's total turnover.

Some relief is afforded by TMA 1970 s 81 to the foreign manufacturer who sells goods in the UK through a branch or agency to ensure that tax is charged on only the merchanting profit.

Where a foreign taxpayer is assessed to tax under Schedule D Case I, it can be levied on the branch and agency within the UK although certain agents, eg independent brokers, are excepted from this provision (TMA 1970 ss 79, 82).

2 Employment income

The foreign taxpayer is assessed under Schedule E Case II on emoluments he receives for duties performed in the UK. Case II, in effect, treats the UK duties as a source of income which would otherwise escape tax completely. If the emoluments are foreign emoluments (see p 183), some relief from tax may be available in appropriate cases (see p 185).

IV DOUBLE TAXATION RELIEF

Overseas income may be taxed in its country of origin and if UK tax is also chargeable on the same income, the taxpayer is entitled to relief in one of three ways. First, the UK has a number of double taxation agreements (treaties) with other countries. They differ in details, but generally provide that certain categories of income will be taxed in only one of the countries concerned (usually where the taxpayer is resident). Other income will be taxable in both countries, but with a credit for one amount of tax against the other.

Secondly, if there is no treaty in force, 'unilateral relief' is given under TA 1970 s 498. This takes the form of a credit against the UK tax equal to the foreign tax paid.

Thirdly, if neither of the above applies, unilateral relief may be given under TA 1970 s 516 by way of deduction (from the foreign income which is assessable to UK tax) of the amount of foreign tax paid. Relief by deduction is less advantageous to the taxpayer than relief by credit.

V ANTI-AVOIDANCE LEGISLATION: TRANSFER OF ASSETS ABROAD (TA 1970 s 478; FA 1981 s 45)

1 General

A person who is neither resident nor ordinarily resident in the UK cannot be assessed to UK income tax on income which arises from a source outside the UK. Accordingly, an individual resident in the UK could transfer income-producing assets to a connected non-resident who is not subject to income tax. Section 478, therefore, provides that if an individual who is ordinarily resident in the UK transfers assets so that as a result of that transfer, or of associated operations, income becomes payable to any person resident or domiciled outside the UK and the transferor has either power to enjoy that income (TA 1970 s 478(1)) or receives a capital sum (TA 1970 s 478(2)), the income of the non-resident is taxed as the individual's income under Schedule D Case VI.

The apparently wide scope of s 478 was limited, in the case of *Vestey v IRC* (1980), to the original transferor of the assets or his spouse. As a result, FA 1981 s 45 was introduced to 'fill the gaps' in s 478.

An individual will avoid liability under both sections if he can prove that the transfer or associated operation was not made for the purpose of avoiding any tax or, that it was a bona fide commercial transaction the purpose of which was not to avoid tax. There is no clearance procedure for either section and the onus of proof is on the taxpayer.

2 TA 1970 s 478

a) *General*

Two factors are essential to the operation of both s 478(1) and (2). First, there must be a transfer of assets by an individual. This means a transfer of property or rights of any kind eg the incorporation of a company. The assets need not be situated in the UK.

Secondly, as a result of the transfer, either alone or together with associated operations, income must become payable to a non-UK resident or non-UK domiciled person. The person to whom the income becomes payable need not be non-resident at the time of transfer (*Congreve v IRC* (1948)).

'Person' includes a corporation and, for these purposes, a corporation incorporated outside the UK is always considered non-resident (TA 1970 s 478(7); the UK does not include the Channel Islands or Isle of Man).

'Associated operations' is widely defined in s 478(4) and case law. Basically, any operation (except death) which is carried out by any person (not necessarily the transferor) is capable of being an associated operation, provided only that, together with the transfer, it results in income becoming payable in accordance with s 478 (for a case where this did not happen see *Fynn v IRC* (1958)). Whether the operation has this result is judged objectively without regard to the intention of the person effecting the operation.

EXAMPLE 7

(1) A transfers assets to a company resident in the UK. Subsequently it becomes non-resident and receives income from the assets which A has the power to enjoy. The removal of the company overseas is an associated operation which triggers s 478 (*Congreve v IRC* (1948)).

(2) A transfers assets to a UK resident company, B Ltd, in consideration for an allotment of shares. Some years later B Ltd sells the assets to a non-resident company, C Ltd, in return for shares in C Ltd. The transfer by B Ltd to C Ltd is associated with the transfer of assets from A to B Ltd (*Corbett's Executrices v IRC* (1943)).

(3) A sells foreign investments to an overseas company in return for shares in that company. He makes a will leaving his residuary estate (which includes the shares) to his daughter. The making of the will, although not the death, is an operation associated with the transfer of the assets abroad. Hence, on the death of A the daughter becomes entitled to dividends on those shares and falls (today) within FA 1981 s 45 (cp *Bambridge v IRC* (1955)).

b) *Section 478(1)*

Section 478(1) will only apply if, given that the above two conditions are satisfied, an individual resident and ordinarily resident in the UK has 'power to enjoy the income of a person resident or domiciled outside the UK'. The income caught by the section need not be derived directly from the assets transferred, but the power of enjoyment must be held by the transferor or his spouse (*Vestey v IRC* (1980); TA 1970 s 478(8)(a)).

EXAMPLE 8

X, a UK resident, transfers assets to Z, a Greek resident, and as a result X has the power to enjoy the income of Y, a resident of Yugoslavia. Y's income will be deemed to be X's for the purposes of s 478(1).

An individual has the power to enjoy income if any of the five circumstances in s 478(5) are satisfied. Generally, they apply to any situation whereby the transferor receives, or is entitled to receive, any benefit in any form from the income:

(1) Where he receives a benefit (including a payment in kind) from the use of the income by any person.

EXAMPLE 9

A non-resident company uses its income profits to redeem the debentures of a UK resident individual. The capital received is a benefit within (1) because it results from a use of the income (*Latilla v IRC* (1943)).

(2) Where assets that he holds, or which are held for him, increase in value as a result of the income becoming payable to the non-resident.

EXAMPLE 10

X Ltd, a non-resident company, is in debt to A, a UK resident. When income becomes payable to X Ltd, A's chose in action (the debt) increases in value (unless X Ltd had sufficient funds to repay the debt) because X Ltd is more likely to be able to honour its obligations (*Lord Howard de Walden v IRC* (1941)).

(3) Where he directly receives, or is entitled to receive, a benefit from the income or the assets representing the income.

EXAMPLE 11

(a) C a UK resident holds 90% of the issued shares of a non-resident company, B Ltd, which gives him the right to a dividend when declared. C is entitled to receive a benefit within (3) (*Lee v IRC* (1941)).
(b) Trustees of a non-resident trust exercise their discretion to pay income to a UK resident beneficiary B. B has received a benefit within (3) above.

(4) Where he is a member of a class of discretionary beneficiaries who may become entitled to some of the income as a result of the exercise of a power by any person. Even if the power is never exercised so that the transferor never benefits, he is within (4). Thus, in *Example 11(b)*, B has power to enjoy the income whether or not he receives a benefit.
(5) Where he can control the application of the income in any way, not necessarily for his own benefit. This does not include a right to direct the investments nor a power of appointment which is concerned with capital rather than income payments (*Lord Vestey's Executors v IRC* (1949)). Thus in *Example 11(a)* C has power to enjoy B Ltd's income through his ability to replace the existing directors by virtue of his 90% shareholding (contrast the power to appoint trustees; *IRC v Schroder* (1983)).

When applying these tests regard must be had to the overall effect of the transfer and anything to do with it (TA 1970 s 478(6)).

c) *Section 478(2)*

Section 478(2) applies where, in connection with a transfer of assets abroad, the transferor or his spouse receives or is entitled to receive a capital sum, whether before or after the relevant transfer. 'Capital sum' is defined as a sum paid or payable by way of loan; or any sum (not being income) which is paid or payable otherwise than for full consideration in money or money's worth.

EXAMPLE 12

B, a UK resident, who has transferred income-producing assets to a non-resident trust has power to direct the investments of the trust. He authorises a loan to be made to Mrs B. B and Mrs B fall within s 478(2).

d) *Computation of the income chargeable under TA 1970 s 478(1) and (2)*

When a transferor is caught by s 478(1), he can be assessed to income tax under Schedule D Case VI on the whole of the non-resident's income from any source, not just the income which he has the power to enjoy or the income arising from the assets which he transferred (this aspect of *Congreve v IRC* (1948) was not overruled by the House of Lords in *Vestey v IRC* (1980)).

If s 478(2) applies the transferor can only be assessed on the income arising as a result of the transfer of assets. The assessment is not limited to the amount of the capital sum, however, and includes income arising before the capital sum was paid or payable and all such income arising thereafter.

Should the Revenue assess both the transferor and his spouse under either subsection, they cannot tax the same income twice (FA 1981 s 46(1)), but must charge it in such proportions as they consider 'just and reasonable'.

In computing the income of the non-resident which is chargeable under s 478(1) or (2), the transferor is only entitled to such deductions and reliefs as he would have been allowed had he, and not the non-resident, actually received the income (see *Lord Chetwode v IRC* (1976); management charges of a non-resident company were not deductible by a UK resident individual, and see TA 1970 s 480(2)). If, however, the income has already suffered basic rate tax, this will not be collected again from the UK resident (TA 1970 s 480).

3   FA 1981 s 45

This provision was designed to fill the gaps in TA 1970 s 478 revealed by the *Vestey* case. Hence, it operates when the same conditions are satisfied as for s 478, whereupon it catches any individual ordinarily resident in the UK (other than the transferor or his spouse who are already caught by s 478) who receives a benefit from the assets transferred. The important limitation in s 45 is that such an individual is only assessed to income tax under Schedule D Case VI to the extent of any benefit that he receives.

The benefit is taxed under Schedule D Case VI as the income of the UK resident in the year of receipt to the extent that it does not exceed the 'relevant income' of the non-resident in the tax years up to and including the year when the benefit is paid. In so far as it exceeds the relevant income of those years, any excess is carried forward and set against the first available relevant income of future years until it is finally absorbed.

'Relevant income' means, in relation to an individual, income arising in any year of assessment to the non-resident and which, as a result of the transfer of assets, can be used to provide a benefit to that individual (FA 1981 s 45(3)).

The same income cannot be charged to tax twice (FA 1981 s 46(1)). Therefore, where several beneficiaries receive benefits, the relevant income is allocated amongst them by the Revenue in such proportions as may be just and reasonable. The taxpayer may appeal against the apportionment to the Special Commissioners.

EXAMPLE 13

A non-resident discretionary trust has relevant income in three consecutive years of £6,000, £6,000 and £12,000 respectively. It makes payments to two UK resident beneficiaries in *Year 2*. It is assumed that the apportionment provisions would be applied pro rata and not according to the order in which the payments are made.
   The benefits are taxed as follows:

			A £	B £
Year 1				
Benefits paid			NIL	NIL
Relevant income £6,000 (unapportioned)				
Year 2				
Benefits paid			6,000	12,000
Relevant income	£6,000			
Plus income brought forward	£6,000			
	£12,000	apportioned	4,000	8,000
Untaxed benefit carried forward			2,000	4,000
Year 3				
Benefits paid			NIL	NIL
Relevant income	£12,000			
	£6,000	apportioned	2,000	4,000
Relevant income carried forward	£6,000		NIL	NIL

In *Year 2* A and B are assessed to income tax under Case VI on £4,000 and £8,000 of their respective benefits. The balance is assessed in *Year 3*.

If the benefit is of a capital nature and results from a capital gain made by the non-resident, the same sum is not charged to both income tax under s 45 and CGT under FA 1981 s 80. To the extent that the benefit exceeds relevant income it is charged to CGT, in which case, it cannot be treated as income in a subsequent year under s 45 (FA 1981 s 45(6); see p 272).

4 Powers of the Revenue to obtain information (TA 1970 s 481)

The Revenue have wide investigatory powers for the purposes of both TA 1970 s 478 and FA 1981 s 45 which are exercisable against a taxpayer, and also against his advisers. They can demand, at 28 days notice, such particulars as they deem necessary.
   A solicitor is exempted from these powers in that he can only be compelled to state that he was acting on his client's behalf and to give the client's name and address. However, he is only exempt to the extent that he is acting qua solicitor. Thus, where he acts, eg as a tax consultant he cannot use the exemption.
   A bank is also exempted from providing details of ordinary banking transactions (TA 1970 s 481(4)), except to the extent that it has acted for a customer in connection with the formation and management of a non-resident company which would be close if resident in the UK and is not a trading company, or the creation or execution of a trust which may be used for schemes under s 478 or s 45. The banks' exemption has been narrowly construed in *Royal Bank of Canada v IRC* (1972) and in *Clinch v IRC* (1973). Other advisers, eg barristers and accountants, have no exemption from s 481.

Section 3   Capital gains tax

Chapters

14 CGT—basic principles

'It is impossible to draw an unambiguous distinction between "capital" gains and "income" gains and the attempt to do so necessarily results in great uncertainty for the taxpayer because a particular transaction may or may not be found by the courts to fall on one side of the line or the other' (Carter Commission, Canada, 1966).

I INTRODUCTION

1 Background

Capital gains tax (CGT) was introduced in the Finance Act 1965 and was consolidated in the Capital Gains Tax Act 1979 (CGTA 1979). It was largely introduced to tax profits left untaxed by income tax. Income tax, in the much quoted dictum of Lord Macnaghten, was and is a tax on income. Thus, it does not tax the profit made on a disposal of a capital asset. However, since 1965, the taxpayer will be charged to CGT on his gain, after deducting any available exemptions and reliefs, at a flat rate of 30%.

As the then Chancellor of the Exchequer Mr James Callaghan in his 1965 Budget speech, introducing CGT, explained:

'Yield is not my main purpose . . . The failure to tax capital gains is . . . the greatest blot on our system of direct taxation. There is little dispute nowadays that capital gains confer much the same kind of benefit on the recipient as taxed earnings more hardly won. Yet earnings pay tax in full while capital gains go free . . . This new tax will provide a background of equity and fair play . . .'

Since CGT aims to tax only what is untaxed by income tax, there will normally be no CGT on a transaction that is chargeable to income tax. Hence, in the case of certain transactions which might attract both taxes, CGT is chargeable on only so much of the transaction as is not charged to income tax. Two principal areas where this overlap of taxes is evident are the purchase and sale of assets which qualify for capital allowances (see p 105 and p 211) and the grant of leases at a premium where part of the premium is assessable to income tax under Schedule A (see Chapter 8).

The ambit of CGT has been substantially reduced since 1965. The charge on death was removed in 1971 (see Chapter 15); the charge on lifetime gifts and, therefore, overlap with CTT may generally be avoided by the use of the hold-over election under FA 1980 s 79 (see Chapter 17) whilst the criticism that the tax was levied on inflationary gains was removed by the indexation allowance introduced in FA 1982 (see p 203).

As a result of these changes to CGT over the years, the tax now need be paid only on a sale of assets which have increased in value by more than the rate of inflation. These will usually be speculative assets, such as shares and land.

One wonders, therefore, whether this rump tax with its vastly complicated body of rules and exemptions is worth retaining for such speculative profits.

It is estimated that the yield from CGT in 1983–84 will represent a mere 1.3% of the total revenue raised in direct taxes and in his 1984 Budget Speech the Rt Hon Nigel Lawson MP commented that 'the tax continues to attract criticism—not least for its complexity—and that is a matter to which I hope to return next year'.

2 Basic principles

CGT is charged on any gain resulting when a chargeable person makes a chargeable disposal of a chargeable asset. This gain is taxed on a current year basis at a flat rate of 30% on so much of the gain as is left after taking into account any exemptions or reliefs and after deducting any allowable losses. The tax is payable on 1 December following the year of assessment.

Only gains that are made after 6 April 1965 are charged. Thus, where an individual acquired an asset in 1960 for £10,000 and sold it in 1970 for £20,000, thereby making a gain of £10,000, only such part of the gain as accrued since 6 April 1965 is charged (see p 204). The tax is not, therefore, retrospective.

a) *Who is a chargeable person?* (CGTA 1979 ss 2, 12–18)

Chargeable persons include individuals who are resident or ordinarily resident in the UK; trustees, personal representatives and partners. In the case of partners, each partner is charged separately in respect of his share of the partnership gains (CGTA 1979 s 60, see Chapter 29).

Companies are not chargeable persons and, therefore, do not pay CGT. Instead they pay corporation tax on chargeable gains included in their profits at an effective rate of 30% (see p 381).

b) *What is a chargeable asset?* (CGTA 1979 s 19(1))

All forms of property are assets for CGT purposes including options, debts, incorporeal property, any currency (other than sterling) and property that is created by the person disposing of it (eg goodwill which is built up from nothing by a trader). An asset which cannot be transferred by sale or gift is within the definition. In *O'Brien v Benson's Hosiery (Holdings) Ltd* (1978) a director under a seven year service contract paid his employer £50,000 to be released from his obligations under the contract. The employer was assessed to CGT on the basis that the contract, despite being non-assignable, was an asset under s 19(1) so that the release of those rights resulted in 'a capital sum being received in return for the forfeiture or surrender of rights' (CGTA 1979 s 20(1)(c); see further p 214).

In *Marren v Ingles* (1980) shares in a private company were sold for £750 per share payable at the time of the sale plus a further sum if the company obtained a Stock Exchange quotation and the market value of the shares at that time was in excess of £750 per share. Two years later a quotation was obtained and a further £2,825 per share was paid. The House of Lords held that the taxpayers were liable to CGT on the original sale price of £750 per share plus the value of the contingent right to receive a further sum (their Lordships did not attempt to put a value on it; was it nominal?). That right was a chose in action (a separate asset) which was disposed of for £2,825 per share two years later, leading to a further CGT liability. Despite this extremely wide definition of asset for CGT purposes, CGTA 1979 lists a number of assets which are non-chargeable and provides for the gain on the disposal of certain other assets to be exempt. In both these cases the result is the same in that the gain will not be taxed.

II CALCULATION OF THE GAIN

The gain on which CGT is chargeable is found by taking the disposal consideration of the asset and deducting from that figure any allowable expenditure (often called the 'base cost'). The disponer's acquisition cost is usually the main item of expenditure. If the allowable expenditure exceeds the disposal consideration, the disponer has made a loss for CGT purposes which may be used to reduce the gains that he has made on disposals of other assets (see p 210 ff).

EXAMPLE 1

A sells a painting for £20,000 (the disposal consideration). He bought it six months ago for £14,000 (the acquisition cost). His chargeable gain is £6,000. If A sold the picture for £10,000 he would have an allowable loss of £4,000.

However, the calculation of disposal consideration and allowable expenditure is not always as simple as in the above example.

1   What is the consideration for the disposal?

a) *General*

The term 'disposal' is not defined but covers a number of transactions. Where the disposal is by way of a sale at arm's length, the consideration for the disposal will be the proceeds of sale. For disposals between husband and wife the disposal consideration is deemed to be of such a sum that neither gain nor loss results (CGTA 1979 s 44), irrespective of whether actual consideration is given.

Where the disposal is not at arm's length, however, the consideration for the disposal is taken to be the market value of the asset at that date. This applies to gifts, to disposals between 'connected persons' (where the disposal is always deemed to be otherwise than by bargain at arm's length), to transfers of assets by a settlor into a settlement and to certain distributions by a company in respect of shares (CGTA 1979 s 29A(1)(a)).

EXAMPLE 2

A gives a Ming vase worth £40,000 to the milkman. The consideration for the disposal is taken to be £40,000. If, instead, A sold the vase to his son B for £10,000, B is a 'connected person' and the consideration for the disposal is taken to be £40,000.

The market value of the asset is taken to be the disposal consideration whenever the actual consideration cannot be valued or the consideration is services (CGTA 1979 s 29A(1)(b)).

EXAMPLE 3

A, an antique dealer, gives B, a fellow dealer, a Ming vase worth £40,000 in consideration of B entering into a restrictive covenant with A, whereby he (B) agrees not to open an antique shop in competition with A. The consideration for the disposal is taken to be £40,000.

This market value rule can work to a taxpayer's advantage by giving the recipient a high acquisition cost for any future disposal in a transaction where the disponer is not charged to CGT on the gain (known as 'reverse Nairn Williamson arrangements'). To some extent this is prevented from happening by CGTA 1979 s 29A(2) which provides that, where there is an acquisition without a disposal (eg the issue of shares by a company) and either no consideration is given for the asset, or the consideration is less than its market value, the actual consideration (if any) given prevails.

In the case of disposals after 6 April 1983 by excluded persons who are exempt from CGT (including charities, friendly societies, approved pension funds, and non-residents) the recipient is taken to acquire the asset at market value. When the disposal is before 6 April 1985 and is by an excluded person, who is otherwise within the charge to CGT, both parties may elect that the actual consideration (if any) should prevail, eg gains made on the incorporation of the UK branch of an overseas company (FA 1984 s 66).

EXAMPLE 4

(1) A Ltd issues 1,000 £1 ordinary shares to B at par when their market value is £2 per share. The issue of shares by a company is not a disposal. This is, therefore, an acquisition by B without a disposal. Were it not for s 29A(2), B's acquisition cost of the shares would be £2,000. As it is, the transaction is caught so that B's acquisition cost is what he actually paid for the shares: ie £1,000.

(2) In 1984, A, a resident of Peru, gives a house in Mayfair worth £150,000 and which he had acquired in 1970 for £20,000 to his son B who is a UK resident. A is not chargeable to CGT on his gain of £130,000 because he is an excluded person and B acquires the property at a base value of £150,000.

b) *Connected persons*

'Connected persons' for CGT fall into four categories (CGTA 1979 s 63).

(1) An individual is connected with his spouse, his or her relatives and their spouses. Relatives include siblings, direct ancestors (parents, grandparents), and lineal descendants (children, grandchildren) but not lateral relatives (uncles, aunts, nephews and nieces). Marriage continues for the purpose of this provision until final divorce (see *Aspden v Hildesley* (1981)).

(2) A company is connected with another company if both are under common control. A company is connected with another person if he (either alone or with other persons connected with him) controls that company.

(3) A partner is connected with a fellow partner and his spouse and their relatives except in relation to acquisitions and disposals of partnership assets under bona fide commercial arrangements (for example, where a new partner is given a share of the assets).

(4) A trustee is connected with the settlor, any person connected with the settlor and any close company in which the trustee or any beneficiary under the settlement is a participator (for the definition of close company and participator see Chapter 28). He is not connected with a beneficiary.

c) *The market value of assets*

Where assets fall to be valued at market value, market value is taken as the price for which those assets could be sold on the open market with no reduction for the fact that this may involve assuming that several assets are to be sold at the same time (CGTA 1979 s 150).

Special valuation rules apply for shares and securities listed in The Stock Exchange Daily Official List (CGTA 1979 s 150(3)). Their market value is taken as the lesser of:

(a) the lower of the two prices quoted for that security in the Daily Official List, plus 1/4 of the difference between the two prices ('quarter-up');

(b) half way between the highest and lowest prices at which bargains were recorded in that security on the relevant date excluding bargains at special prices ('mid price').

Unquoted shares and securities are valued on a number of criteria including the size of the holding and, therefore, the degree of control of the company.

Where the asset transferred is subject to a restriction, for example, land which is mortgaged, the value of the asset is reduced to take account of the restriction (CGTA 1979 s 62(6)). However, as an anti-avoidance measure, artificial and non-commercial restrictions in favour of connected persons are ignored (CGTA 1979 s 62(5)).

The market value rule is modified where a person acquires, by a series of transactions from a connected person, assets which are worth more when valued together than as individual items. The value of each asset is taken as a proportion of the aggregate market value of all the assets (CGTA 1979 s 151). The aim of this provision is to prevent a transferor from obtaining a tax advantage and is similar to the rule for sets of chattels (see p 227).

EXAMPLE 5

A owns 52 of the 100 issued shares in X Ltd (an unquoted company). A controlling shareholding in the company is valued at £10 per share and a minority holding at £2 per share. A acquired his shares in 1966 for £1 each. He gives 26 of his shares to his son B and later makes him a further gift of the remaining 26 shares. Both gifts are of minority holdings valued at £52 (ie at £2 per share). In each case, therefore, A appears to have made a gain of only £26 (£52 – £26). However, under s 151 each holding transferred is valued as a proportionate part (1/2) of the aggregate holding which, being a controlling interest, is valued at £520. Accordingly, A has made gains of £234 on both occasions (£260 – £26).

One difficulty in the operation of s 151 is that each time the transferee receives a further acquisition, the earlier transaction has to be revalued and the transferor's gain on that transaction recalculated (subject to the six year rule for assessments: see Chapter 2). A further problem is whether the acquisition must be from the same connected person or merely from any person with whom the transferee is connected. The Revenue take the latter view which could have the anomalous result of increasing the chargeable gains of transferors who are unconnected with one another simply because they happen to transfer an asset to the same transferee with whom each is connected. However, s 151 clearly does not apply to transfers by one person to different transferees with whom he is connected.

d) *Deferred consideration* (CGTA 1979 s 40)

Where the consideration for the disposal is known at the date of the disposal but is payable in instalments or is subject to some contingency, the disponer is taxed on a gain calculated by reference to the full amount of the consideration receivable with no discount for the fact that payment is postponed. If, in fact, he never receives the full consideration his original CGT assessment is adjusted.

EXAMPLE 6

A bought land 5 years ago for £50,000. He sells it today for £100,000 payable in 2 years time. A is taxed now on a gain of £50,000 despite the fact that he has received nothing and with no discount for the fact that the right to £100,000 in 2 years time is not worth £100,000 today.

It may be that the deferred consideration cannot be valued because it is dependent on some future contingency. In *Marren v Ingles* (1980) part of the payment for the disposal of shares was to be calculated by reference to the price of the shares if and when the company obtained a Stock Exchange quotation. The taxpayer's gain on the disposal of the shares could not be calculated by reference to such an unquantifiable consideration. Accordingly he was treated as making two separate disposals. The first was the disposal of the shares. The consideration for this was the payment that the taxpayer actually received plus the value (if any) of the right to receive the future deferred sum (a chose in action). The value of the chose in action then formed the acquisition cost of that asset. Hence, once the deferred consideration became payable, the taxpayer was treated as making a second disposal, this time of the chose in action. He was, therefore, chargeable on the difference between the consideration received and whatever was the acquisition cost of that asset.

In *Marren v Ingles* the House of Lords did not attempt to value the chose in action. In all probability its value would have been nominal, with the result that on the first disposal (of the shares) the gain would have been calculated by reference only to the cash received, whilst on the second disposal (of the chose in action) the entire consideration received would constitute a gain. There is no element of double taxation involved in the *Marren v Ingles* situation. Instead, the CGT is collected (in effect) in two instalments with the result that the taxpayer may be better off than A, in *Example 6* above, who is taxed on money years before receiving it. (Where the taxpayer is entitled to retirement relief on the disposal of the shares, however, the relief may not be exhausted on the share disposal, in which case the balance cannot be used against the gain on the disposal of the chose in action.)

2 What expenditure is deductible?

Once the disposal consideration is known, the gain (or loss) can be calculated by deducting allowable expenditure. This is defined in CGTA 1979 s 32 as 'expenditure incurred wholly and exclusively' in:

(i) *Acquiring the asset* The purchase price or market value, including any allowed incidental costs, or where the asset was created rather than acquired (for example, a painting) the cost of its creation may be deducted (CGTA 1979 s 32(1)(a)).

(ii) *Enhancing the value of the asset* 'Expenditure on improvements must be reflected in the state or nature of the asset at the time of its disposal. Thus, the costs of an application for planning permission which is never granted would not be deductible, whereas the costs of building an extension would be. Also deductible under this head are the costs of establishing, preserving or defending title to the asset (for example, the costs of a boundary dispute and, in the case of PRs, a proportion of probate expenses) (CGTA 1979 s 32(1)(b)).

(iii) *Disposing of the asset*   The incidental costs of disposal which are deductible include professional fees paid to a surveyor, valuer, auctioneer, accountant, agent or legal adviser; costs of the transfer or conveyance; costs of advertising to find a buyer and any costs incurred in making a valuation or apportionment necessary for CGT (CGTA 1979 s 32(1)(c)). Other taxes, such as CTT on a gift, are not deductible and neither is the cost of appealing against any CGT assessment!

The requirement in CGTA 1979 s 32 that expenditure must be 'wholly and exclusively' incurred makes use of the same test for allowable expenditure as that found for income tax under Schedule D Cases I and II. For CGT purposes, however, these words have been interpreted relatively liberally. In the case of *IRC v Richards' Executors* (1971), PRs who sold shares at a profit claimed to deduct from the sale proceeds the cost of valuing the relevant part of the deceased's estate for probate. The House of Lords held that they could do so even though the valuation was for the purposes of estate duty as well as for CGT.

'Expenditure' within CGTA 1979 s 32 must be something that reduces the taxpayer's estate in some quantifiable way. Thus in *Oram v Johnson* (1980) the taxpayer who bought a second home for £2,500, renovated it himself and later sold it for £11,500 could not deduct the notional cost of his own labour.

On a deemed disposal and reacquisition (see p 251) notional expenses are not deductible (CGTA 1979 s 32(4)), but actual expenses are. Thus, in *IRC v Chubb's Settlement Trustees* (1971), where the life tenant and the remainderman ended a settlement by dividing the capital between them so that there was a deemed disposal under (now) CGTA 1979 s 54(1), the costs of preparing the deed of variation of the settlement were deductible (the result of this case is to leave s 32(4) as a prohibition on the deduction of imaginary expenses!).

Certain items of expenditure are not deductible despite appearing to fall within s 32. These include interest on a loan to acquire the asset (CGTA 1979 s 32(3)); premiums paid under a policy of insurance against risks of loss of, or damage to, an asset; and, most important, any sums which a person can deduct in calculating his income for income tax. Additionally, no sum is deductible for CGT purposes which would be deductible for income tax, if the disponer were in fact using the relevant asset in a trade; in effect therefore, no items of an income, as opposed to a capital, nature will ever be deductible. For example, the cost of repair (as opposed to improvement) or of insurance of a chargeable asset, both of which are of an income nature, are disallowed as deductions for CGT.

EXAMPLE 7

A buys a country cottage in 1977 for £11,000 to rent to arab sheiks. He spends £6,000 in installing a gold plated bathroom and £4,000 on mending the leaking roof. Over the following 6 years he spends a further £500 on repairing leaking radiators and £400 on general maintenance. He pays a total of £3,000 on property insurance. He sells it in 1983 for £25,000.

His chargeable gain is:

	£	£
Sale proceeds		25,000
Less:		
Acquisition cost	11,000	
Cost of improvements	6,000	17,000
		£ 8,000

The cost of repairs, maintenance and insurance are not deductible for CGT because they are deductible in computing his income under Schedule A. The insurance premiums are specifically disallowed under CGTA 1979 s 141.

If A had bought the cottage as a second home, his gain on sale would still be £8,000; the other items are still disallowed as deductions for CGT because they are of an income nature.

3 The indexation of allowable expenditure

A major criticism of capital gains tax over the years has been its failure to make any allowance for the effects of inflation. Hence, the tax has charged both 'real' and 'paper' gains, and has to some extent operated as a wealth tax.

FA 1982 attempts to deal with such criticism by introducing an indexation allowance which operates for disposals of assets on or after 6 April 1982 as a further allowable deduction. Items of allowable expenditure will be index-linked (to rises in the RPI), so that the eventual gain on disposal should represent only 'real' profits.

a) *Operation of the allowance for assets acquired after 6 April 1982*

The indexation allowance is calculated by comparing the RPI for the twelfth month after the month in which the allowable expenditure was incurred with the index for the month in which the disposal of the asset occurs. Assuming that the RPI has increased, the allowable expenditure is multiplied by the fraction

$$\frac{RD - RI}{RI}$$

where RD is the index for the month of disposal and RI is the index for the twelfth month after the month in which the item of expenditure was incurred. The resultant figure (known as the 'indexation allowance') is a further allowable deduction in arriving at the chargeable gain on disposal of the asset.

It should be noted that the first 12 months of ownership do not qualify for indexation, although any gain realised in that period will, of course, be reduced by the annual exemption (£5,600 index-linked).

As the allowance is linked to allowable expenditure, it follows that, where an asset has a nil base cost (for instance, goodwill built up by the taxpayer) there can be no indexation allowance.

EXAMPLE 8

A painting was bought for £20,000 on 10 April 1983 and sold for £100,000 on 30 June 1987. RPI for April 1984 is 300; RPI for June 1987 is 500. Indexation allowance is: $£20,000 \times \dfrac{(500 - 300)}{300} = £13,333$

Therefore, the chargeable gain is:

	£	£
Sale proceeds		100,000
Less:		
Acquisition cost	20,000	
Indexation allowance	13,333	33,333
Chargeable gain		£ 66,667

Assume that the painting was restored on 12 November 1985 for £2,000. RPI for November 1986 is 400. Indexation allowance is £13,333, as above, plus:

$$£2,000 \times \frac{(500-400)}{400} = £500$$

Therefore, the chargeable gain is £64,167 (£66,667 − £2,000 − £500)

In the case of disposals between spouses the normal rules are modified to allow the recipient spouse to have the benefit of the period of ownership of the other. Hence, if a man gives an asset to his wife seven months after the acquisition she will obtain the benefit of the allowance five months later (ie twelve months from her husband's date of acquisition).

b) *Assets already owned on 6 April 1982*

Items of expenditure on assets already owned on 6 April 1982 will be index-linked only from March 1982 (subject to 12 months having elapsed since the expenditure was incurred). The indexation provisions are not retrospective and, in the case of assets already pregnant with gain, offer only extremely limited relief.

c) *Comments*

Although the indexation allowance is to be welcomed on the grounds of fairness to taxpayers, the rules introduce yet more complexity into an already complex tax; for instance, simple—if alarming—rises in the RPI have been assumed in the above examples whereas in practice, the indexation formula must be calculated to three decimal places. The rules dealing with shares are often excessively technical, and the attack on 'bed and breakfasting' cannot be justified by reference to indexation alone (see Chapter 19). Further, nothing has been done for the taxpayer who has owned an asset for a number of years with allowable expenses which have been rendered derisory by subsequent inflation.

4   Calculation of gains for assets acquired before 6 April 1965

Only gains after 6 April 1965 are chargeable (CGTA 1979 s 28(3)). Thus, for assets acquired before 6 April 1965, the legislation contains rules determining how much gain is deemed to have accrued since 6 April 1965.

Generally, the gain is deemed to accrue evenly over the whole period of ownership (the so-called straight line method: CGTA 1979 Sch 5 para 11(3)). The chargeable gain is, therefore, a proportion of the gross gain calculated by the formula:

$$\text{Gross gain} \times \frac{\text{years of ownership since 6 April 1965}}{\text{total years of ownership}} = \text{chargeable gain}$$

EXAMPLE 9

(In *Examples 9–11* it is assumed that no indexation allowance is available.)

	£
A bought a picture on 6 April 1964 for	5,000
He sells it on 6 April 1984 for	19,000
His gain is	£14,000

His chargeable gain is: $£14,000 \times \dfrac{18}{20} = £12,600$

In applying this formula, the ownership of the asset can never be treated as beginning earlier than 6 April 1945 (CGTA 1979 Sch 5 para 11(6)). If it was acquired before then it is deemed to have been acquired on that date. The same time-apportionment formula applies for the calculation of allowable losses. Where various items of expenditure were incurred on an asset before 6 April 1965, each item must be separately time-apportioned.

EXAMPLE 10

	£
A bought an antique desk in 1960 for	4,000
He restored it in 1964 for	1,000
He sold it in 1985 for	15,000
His total gain is	£10,000

The total gain is apportioned as follows:

(i) Gain attributable to acquisition cost: $\dfrac{£4,000}{£5,000} \times £10,000 = £8,000$

Chargeable part (time-apportioned): $£8,000 \times \dfrac{20}{25} = £6,400$

(ii) Gain attributable to restoration cost: $\dfrac{£1,000}{£5,000} \times £10,000 = £2,000$

Chargeable part (time-apportioned): $£2,000 \times \dfrac{20}{21} = £1,905$

Total chargeable gain is £8,305 (£6,400 + £1,905)

Where the original cost of the asset was low but the asset had appreciated substantially in value before subsequent expenditure was incurred, the application of these rules would produce an unfair result. Hence, an alternative method of apportionment is available. The amount of the gain attributable to the subsequent expenditure is established as a question of fact and the balance of the gain is then treated as derived from expenditure at the original date of acquisition. Each part of the gain can then be time apportioned.

As an alternative to the time-apportionment formula, the taxpayer can elect (within two years of the disposal) that the acquisition cost of the asset is taken as its market value on 6 April 1965 (CGTA 1979 Sch 5 para 12). The chargeable gain is then computed in the usual way. However, it must be noted that, although this election can be made to reduce a gain, it cannot be used to turn a gain into a loss or to increase a loss. In the former case there is deemed to be neither a gain nor a loss; in the latter case the taxpayer is restricted to the smaller loss.

EXAMPLE 11

	Case A	Case B
	£	£
A bought a picture in 1963 for	5,000	20,000
Its market value on 6 April 1965 was	20,000	22,000
He sells it in 1984 for	19,000	10,000

In *Case A*, if A elects for market value on 6 April 1965, he cannot turn his gain (total £14,000) into a loss of £1,000. The 1984 disposal is treated as producing neither gain nor loss.

In *Case B*, if A elects for market value on 6 April 1965 his loss of £12,000 is restricted to his actual loss made during his period of ownership, ie £10,000 (note that this loss is not time-apportioned—see CGTA 1979 Sch 5 para 12(2)).

Disposals on or after 6 April 1982 will have the benefit of an indexation allowance. Where the gain is time-apportioned any indexation allowance will be deducted from the gross gain before it is apportioned. If the election is made, however, the allowance will be deducted from the chargeable gain. This may be an argument in favour of making the election.

EXAMPLE 12

	£
A bought a picture in April 1960 for	6,000
Its market value on 6 April 1965 was	10,000
A sells it in April 1985 for	15,000

RPI for March 1982 is 250; RPI for April 1985 is 300.

(i) *Time-apportionment method:*

	£
Gain is:	
Sale proceeds	15,000
Less: acquisition cost	6,000
	9,000

Less: indexation allowance

$$£6,000 \times \frac{300-250}{250} = \qquad 1,200$$

$$\underline{\underline{£7,800}}$$

Chargeable gain is:

$$£7,800 \times \frac{20}{25} \qquad \underline{\underline{£6,240}}$$

(ii) *Election for market value:*

Gain (£15,000 − £10,000) =	5,000

Less: indexation allowance

$$£10,000 \times \frac{300-250}{250} = \qquad 2,000$$

$$\underline{\underline{£3,000}}$$

A would make the election here.

This general rule for calculating a gain since 1965 does not apply in two cases: first, on land with a development value the chargeable gain (or loss) is calculated by reference to its market value at 6 April 1965 except that the resulting gain or loss is restricted to the actual gain or loss over the whole period of ownership. Secondly, on the disposal of quoted securities see Chapter 20.

5 Part disposals

The term disposal includes a part disposal. Whenever part of an asset or an interest in an asset is disposed of it is necessary to calculate the original cost of the part sold before any gain on it can be computed. This applies, for instance, to a sale of part of a land-holding or of part of a shareholding, or to the grant of a lease (for leases see 7 below).
   The formula used for calculating the original cost of the part sold is:

$$C \times \frac{A}{A+B}$$

Where   C = all the deductible expenditure on the whole asset
        A = sale proceeds of the part of the asset sold
        B = market value of the part retained (at the time when the part is sold).

The indexation provisions are applied in the same way for part disposals as for disposals of the whole, except that only the apportioned expenditure is index-linked.

EXAMPLE 13

10 acres of land were bought for £10,000 on 1 January 1978. 4 acres of land were sold for £12,000 on 1 October 1984 (the remaining 6 acres are then worth £18,000). RPI for March 1982 is 250. RPI for October 1984 is 340.
   Acquisition cost of the 4 acres sold is:

$$£10,000 \times \frac{£12,000}{£30,000} = £4,000$$

Indexation allowance is:

$$£4,000 \times \frac{(340-250)}{250} = £1,440$$

Therefore, the chargeable gain is:

	£	£
Sale proceeds		12,000
Less:		
Acquisition cost	4,000	
Indexation allowance	1,440	5,440
		£ 6,560

The part disposal formula need not be used (thereby removing the need to value the part of the asset not disposed of), when the cost of the part disposed of can be easily calculated. In particular, on a part disposal of shares of the same class in the same company the cost of each individual share can be worked out as a fraction of the total number owned by the taxpayer.

The rules will not be applied to small part disposals of land (CGTA 1979 ss 107–108) if the taxpayer so elects. Where the consideration received is 5% or less of the value of the entire holding and does not exceed £20,000 (or without limit for a disposal to an authority with compulsory powers of acquisition) the transaction need not be treated as a disposal. Instead, the taxpayer can elect to deduct the consideration received from the allowable expenditure applicable to the whole of the land. Similar principles apply to small capital distributions made by companies (see Chapter 19).

6 Wasting assets (CGTA 1979 ss 37–39)

A wasting asset is one with a predictable useful life not exceeding 50 years. If the asset is a wasting chattel (ie an item of tangible moveable property such as a television or washing machine), there is a general exemption from CGT. In the case of plant and machinery qualifying for capital allowances there are special rules (see p 211). Short leases of land are likewise subject to their own rules; freehold land, needless to say, can never be a wasting asset. Accordingly the main types of asset subject to the wasting asset rules are:

(a) commodities dealt with on a terminal market;
(b) options (CGTA 1979 s 128(6)) with the exception of quoted options to subscribe for shares in a company; all traded options quoted on a recognised stock exchange or on the London Financial Futures Exchange (FA 1984 s 65); and options to acquire assets for use in a business (CGTA 1979 s 138 amended by FA 1980 s 84);
(c) purchased life interests in settled property where the predictable life expectation of the life tenant is 50 years or less (CGTA 1979 s 37);
(d) patent rights;
(e) copyrights in certain circumstances; and
(f) leases for 50 years or less (other than of land: see p 209).

On disposal of any of the above assets any gain is calculated on the basis that the allowable expenditure on the asset is written down on a uniform basis over its expected useful life so that any claim for loss relief will be limited. Consistent with the general principles which apply to such assets, it is only the written down expenditure which is entitled to the indexation allowance.

EXAMPLE 14

Copyright (20 years unexpired) of a novel is bought for £3,000 on 1 April 1975. The copyright is sold for £2,600 on 1 April 1985. RPI for March 1982 is 250. RPI for April 1985 is 350. The written down acquisition cost is:

$$£3,000 \times \frac{10 \text{ years}}{20 \text{ years}} = £1,500$$

The indexation allowance is:

$$£1,500 \times \frac{(350-250)}{250} = £600$$

Therefore, the chargeable gain is:

	£	£
Sales proceeds		2,600
Less:		
acquisition cost	1,500	
indexation allowance	600	2,100
Chargeable gain		£ 500

7 Rules for leases of land

The grant of a lease out of a freehold or superior lease is a part disposal. The gain is, therefore, computed by deducting from the disposal consideration (ie the premium) the cost of the part disposed of, calculated as for any part disposal (see 5 above). Included in the denominator of the formula as a part of the market value of the land undisposed of is the value of any right to receive rent under the lease.

A lease which has 50 or less years to run is a wasting asset. It does not depreciate evenly over time, however, so that on any assignment of it, its cost is written down, not as described in 6 above, but according to a special table in CGTA 1979 Sch 3 para 1.

Where a sub-lease is granted out of a lease which is a wasting asset, the ordinary part disposal formula is not applied. Instead, any gain is calculated by deducting from the consideration received for the sub-lease, that part of the allowable expenditure on the head lease which will waste away over the period of the sub-lease.

EXAMPLE 15

A acquires a lease of premises for 40 years for £5,000 (that lease is, therefore, a wasting asset). After 10 years he grants a sub-lease to B for 10 years at a premium of £1,000.

A's gain is calculated by deducting from the consideration on the part disposal (ie £1,000), such part of £5,000 as will waste away (in accordance with CGTA 1979 Sch 3 para 1) on a lease dropping from 30 years to 20 years.

Any part of a premium that is chargeable to income tax under Schedule A (see Chapter 8) is not also charged to CGT. Thus, on the grant of a short lease out of an interest that is not a wasting asset (for example, the freehold) there must be deducted from the premium received such part of it as is taxed under Schedule A. The part disposal formula is then applied and in the numerator the sum representing the consideration received on the part disposal is the premium received less that part taxed under Schedule A.

EXAMPLE 16

A buys freehold premises for £200,000. He grants a lease of the premises for 21 years at a premium of £100,000 and a rent. The value of the freehold subject to the lease and including the right to receive rent is now £150,000.

Of the premium of £100,000 20/50ths is discounted (ie £100,000 × 20 × 2/100) and the balance (ie £100,000 × 30/50) is taxed under Schedule A = £60,000.

	£
A's chargeable gain is, therefore:	
Consideration received	100,000
Less: amount taxed under Schedule A	60,000
	40,000
Less: cost of the part disposed of	
$£200,000 \times \dfrac{£40,000}{£100,000 + £150,000} =$	32,000
Chargeable gain (ignoring indexation)	£ 8,000

III   LOSSES FOR CGT

1   When does a loss arise?

A loss arises for CGT whenever the consideration for the disposal of a chargeable asset is less than the allowable expenditure incurred by the taxpayer (but ignoring any indexation allowance).

> **EXAMPLE 17**
>
> If an antique desk was bought for £12,000, restored for £1,000 and then sold for £11,000, a loss of £2,000 would result.

Where a loss arises no indexation allowance is available to increase further that loss. Hence the allowance can only be used to reduce a gain; it cannot be used to increase a loss, and neither can it replace a gain with a loss.

> **EXAMPLE 18**
>
> A painting was bought for £50,000 on 1 November 1982 and sold for £60,000 on 4 May 1986. RPI for November 1983 is 320; RPI for May 1986 is 400. Indexation allowance:
>
> $$£50,000 \times \frac{(400-320)}{320} = £12,500$$
>
> Without any indexation allowance the gain is £10,000 (£60,000 − £50,000) but the full indexation allowance would produce a loss of £2,500.
>
> Accordingly, the gain of £10,000 is cancelled and the disposal is deemed to be on a no gain/no loss basis. Had the picture been sold for £40,000 the loss of £10,000 could not be increased by the indexation allowance.

Although the disposal of a debt (other than a debt on a security) is usually exempt from CGT, a loss that is made on a qualifying loan to a trader may be treated as a capital loss (see p 228).

If an asset is destroyed or extinguished; abandoned, in the case of options that are not wasting assets (p 208); or if its value has become negligible (see p 215), the taxpayer may claim to have incurred an allowable loss.

2   Use of losses

Losses must be relieved primarily against gains of the same year, but any surplus loss can be carried forward and set against the first available gain of future years without time limit.

Losses cannot be carried back and set against gains of previous years except for the net losses incurred by an individual in the year of his death (CGTA 1979 s 49(2)). Losses cannot be set against the taxpayer's income except under the so-called venture capital scheme: see p 120.

A loss that is incurred on a disposal to a connected person can only be set against any gains on subsequent disposals to the same person (CGTA 1979 s 62(3)).

3 Restriction of losses: capital allowances

Generally, chattels which are wasting assets are exempt from CGT (see p 208). Plant and machinery which are tangible moveable property are always classified as wasting assets, but will not be exempt from CGT if they are used in a trade and qualify for capital allowances. Other assets which qualify for capital allowances, such as industrial buildings, will be chargeable assets because they are not wasting.

As CGT does not generally overlap with income tax, a gain which is charged to income tax will not be charged to CGT; and a loss will not be allowable for CGT if it is deductible for income tax. Thus, the gain or loss on a disposal of plant and machinery and other assets qualifying for capital allowances is calculated in the usual way (and not written down in the case of wasting assets) and any gain is charged to CGT to the extent that it exceeds the original cost of the asset.

EXAMPLE 19

	£
Year 1: Machine bought for	10,000
First year allowance claimed 75%	7,500
Year 2: Machine sold for	12,000

There is a balancing charge for income tax of £7,500 (ie to the extent of the capital allowance given—see further Chapter 7). The excess of the sale price over the acquisition cost (£2,000) is chargeable to CGT.

However, it is rare for plant and machinery to be sold at a gain; it is more likely to be sold at a loss, in which case the loss is not allowable for CGT to the extent that it is covered by capital allowances. They may reduce a loss to nil, but they cannot produce a gain.

EXAMPLE 20

	£
Machine bought for	4,000
Sold later for	2,000
Capital allowance given of	2,000
Loss for CGT is:	
Disposal proceeds	2,000
Less: acquisition cost	4,000
Capital loss	(2,000)
Credit for capital allowances	2,000
Allowable loss	£ NIL

IV RATE OF CGT

CGT is charged at a flat rate of 30% on the chargeable gains of a person after deducting allowable losses (if any) and his annual exemption.

1 The annual exemption

The amount of the annual exemption depends on the capacity in which the person made a gain. The amount is index-linked.

Individuals   The first £5,600 (for 1984–85) of the total gains in a tax year are exempt from CGT.

EXAMPLE 21

	£	£
A sells a painting for		16,000
Original cost of painting	8,700	
Indexation allowance (say)	1,000	9,700
Chargeable gain		6,300
Less: annual exemption for 1984–85		5,600
Gain charged to CGT		£ 700

If the exemption is unused in a tax year it is lost since there is no provision to carry it forward (contrast the CTT annual exemption).

Personal representatives   In the tax year of the deceased's death and the two following tax years, PRs have the same annual exemption as an individual. In the third and following tax years they have no annual exemption and so are charged to CGT on all chargeable gains they make (see p 221).

Trustees   Trustees have half the annual exemption available to an individual, ie £2,800 (for 1984–85). Where the same settlor has created more than one settlement after 6 June 1978 the annual exemption is divided equally between them. Three settlements for instance would each have an exemption of £933.33. This is subject to a minimum exemption per trust of one-tenth of the individual's annual exemption, ie £560. Thus, if a settlor creates 10 settlements they will each have an exemption of £560.
   Where the settlement is for the mentally or physically disabled, the trustees have the same exemption as an individual, ie £5,600 (subject to the same rules for groups of settlements).

Husband and wife   Husband and wife who are living together share the one annual exemption of £5,600 which is divided between them in proportion to their respective gains. This method of apportioning the exemption may not apply where losses are involved (see below).

EXAMPLE 22

H and W have chargeable gains in the tax year 1984–85 of £2,000 and £8,000 respectively. The £5,600 exemption is apportioned between them as follows:

$$H = \frac{£2,000}{£10,000} \times £5,600 = £1,120$$

$$W = \frac{£8,000}{£10,000} \times £5,600 = £4,480$$

H is taxed on £2,000 − £1,120 = £880
W is taxed on £8,000 − £4,480 = £3,520

2   Order of set-off of losses

Current year losses must be deducted from current year gains in full.

EXAMPLE 23

A makes chargeable gains of £4,000 and incurs allowable losses of £3,000 in the tax year. His gain is reduced to £1,000 and is further reduced to zero by £1,000 of his annual exemption. He is forced to set his loss against gains for the year which would in any event have escaped tax because of the annual exemption.

Unrelieved losses in any tax year can be carried forward to future tax years without time limit though they must be deducted from the first available gains. However, the loss need only be used to reduce later gains to £5,600 (the amount covered by the annual exemption) and not to zero.

EXAMPLE 24

A makes the following gains and losses:

Tax year	Gain	Loss
	£	£
Year 1	4,000	9,000
Year 2	7,500	3,000
Year 3	11,000	NIL

In *Year 1* A pays no CGT and carries forward an unused loss of £5,000. His annual exemption for that year is wasted. In *Year 2* A's gain is reduced to £4,500 and he pays no CGT as this is covered by his annual exemption. The £5,000 loss from year 1 does not reduce his gain to zero. It is carried forward to year 3. In *Year 3* A can use the £5,000 loss that he is carrying forward from year 1 to reduce his gain to £6,000. After deducting his annual exemption he pays CGT at 30% on £400 (£120).

The same rule applies to spouses in respect of their individual gains and losses except that any losses of one spouse can be set against the gains of the other unless either spouse elects to the contrary before 6 July in the following tax year.

Further, where the spouses' combined chargeable gains in any tax year do not exceed the annual exemption and either spouse is carrying forward an unused loss from a previous year, they can elect to divide the exemption in the way most favourable for utilising the loss.

EXAMPLE 25

H and W have the following chargeable gains and allowable losses:

	H		W	
	£	£	£	£
Current year gains		10,000		2,000
Less: current losses	4,000		1,000	
Loss b/f	3,000		NIL	

H and W can agree to divide the £5,600 exemption as to £4,600 to H and £1,000 to W so that H need only use £1,400 from his £3,000 loss brought forward leaving him £1,600 to carry forward to subsequent years, ie:

	H		W	
	£	£	£	£
Current year gains		10,000		2,000
Less: current year losses	4,000		1,000	
Less: £1,400 of loss b/f	1,400	5,400	NIL	1,000
		4,600		1,000
Less: exemption		4,600		1,000
Taxable amount		£ NIL		£ NIL

3   **When is CGT payable?**

CGT is assessed on a current year basis and is generally payable in full on 1 December following the year of assessment or thirty days after assessment, if that is later. Interest is charged (currently at 8% per annum) on tax remaining unpaid after the due date.

CGT may be payable in instalments when the consideration for the disposal is paid in instalments over a period exceeding 18 months running from the date of the disposal or later and the Revenue are satisfied that payment of tax in one lump sum would cause undue hardship. The instalments of tax can be spread over a maximum of eight years provided that the final instalment of tax is not payable after the final instalment of the disposal consideration has been received. Undue hardship is not defined—arguably it will always be undue hardship for a taxpayer to have to pay CGT before he has received all the disposal money.

V   MEANING OF 'DISPOSAL'

1   **General**

A 'disposal' is not defined for CGT. Giving the word its natural meaning, there will be a disposal of an asset whenever its ownership changes or whenever an owner divests himself of rights in, or interests over, an asset (for example, by sale, gift or exchange). Additionally, the term is extended by the legislation to cover certain transactions which would not fall within its commonsense meaning. Thus, in certain circumstances, trustees of a settlement are treated as disposing of and immediately reacquiring settlement assets at their market value ('deemed disposals': see p 251).

A part disposal of an asset is charged as a disposal according to the rules consider earlier (p 207). Death is not a disposal for CGT purposes (see Chapter 15).

2   **Capital sums derived from assets** (CGTA 1979 s 20)

Whenever a capital sum is derived from an asset there is a disposal for CGT. This is so whether or not the person who pays the capital sum receives anything in return for his payment (see *Marren v Ingles* (1980)).

It appears that all legal rights which can be turned to account by the extraction of a capital sum are assets for CGT purposes. The test is whether such rights can be converted into money or money's worth and the mere fact that they are non-assignable does not matter so long as consideration can be obtained in some other way (for instance, by surrendering the right). This is apparent from the case of *O'Brien v Benson's Hosiery (Holdings) Ltd* (1978) (see p 197). In *Marren v Ingles* (1980) (see p 201) the right to receive an unquantifiable sum in the future was an asset, a chose in action, from which a capital sum was derived when the right matured.

The rights must, however, be legally enforceable. Thus, a sum derived from a personal agreement, for example, by a person to restrict his future activities, is not a disposal because it is not a disposal of an asset (the right to work is not a legal right, although it may be a right of man!).

Where a restrictive agreement is entered into by a trader or by a taxpayer exercising a profession it might be argued that there is a disposal of his goodwill (see *Higgs v Olivier* (1952)).

Four specific instances of disposals are given in s 20:

(1) where a capital sum is received by way of compensation for the loss of, or damage to, an asset (for instance, the receipt of damages for the wrongful destruction of an asset). It should be noted that there is only a disposal where a capital sum is received. Thus, in accordance with the general principles of CGT, if the receipt is of an income nature, it is charged to income tax and not to CGT (an example is compensation received by a trader for loss of trading profits—see, for instance, *London and Thames Haven Oil Wharves Ltd v Attwooll* (1967) and *Lang v Rice* (1984)).

(2) where a capital sum is received under an insurance policy for loss of or damage to an asset.

(3) where a capital sum is received in return for the forfeiture or surrender of rights. This category includes payments received in return for releasing another person from a contract (*O'Brien v Benson's Hosiery (Holdings) Ltd* (1978)); from a restrictive covenant; but not a statutory payment on the termination of a business tenancy (*Drummond v Austin Brown* (1984)).

(4) where a capital sum is received for the use or exploitation of assets, for example, for the right to exploit a copyright or for the right to use goodwill created by another person.

The receipt of a capital sum from an asset under categories (1) and (2) above need not be treated as a disposal or part disposal provided that the asset has not been totally lost or destroyed. Instead, the taxpayer can elect to deduct compensation money from the acquisition cost of the asset thereby postponing a charge to CGT (CGTA 1979 s 21). However, this relief, which does not apply to wasting assets, is only available if one of three conditions is satisfied. First, the sum must be wholly used to restore the asset. Secondly, if the full amount of the capital sum is not used to restore the asset, the amount unused must not exceed 5% of the sum received. Where the sum unused exceeds 5%, the asset is treated as being partly disposed of for a consideration equivalent to the unused sum. Thirdly, the capital sum must be small (5% or less) compared with the value of the asset.

EXAMPLE 26

A buys a picture for £20,000 which is now worth £30,000. It is damaged by rain from a leaking roof and A receives £8,000 compensation with which he restores the picture. The £8,000 is deducted from the cost of the asset (£20,000), but it also qualifies as allowable expenditure on a future disposal so that for CGT the cost of the asset remains £20,000 and A is in the same position as if the damage had never occurred.

Assume, however, that A restores the picture for £7,600. The £400 unused does not exceed 5% of £8,000. It is, therefore, deducted from the acquisition cost of the picture (£20,000).

Alternatively, if A received compensation of £1,500 which he does not use to restore the picture, A need not treat this receipt as a part disposal as it does not exceed 5% of the value of the picture (£30,000). Instead, he can elect to deduct £1,500 from his acquisition cost, so that the picture has a base value of £18,500 on a subsequent disposal.

3 **Total loss or destruction of an asset** (CGTA 1979 s 22(1))

Total loss or destruction of an asset is a disposal for CGT purposes and, where the owner of the asset receives no compensation, it may give rise to an allowable loss equal to the base costs of the taxpayer. Where the asset is tangible moveable property, however, the owner is deemed to dispose of it for £3,000 thereby restricting his loss relief. This limitation derives from the fact that gains on such assets are exempt from CGT insofar as the consideration does not exceed £3,000 (see p 227). As a corollary, therefore, loss relief on the disposal of such assets is not available where the consideration received is less than £3,000.

EXAMPLE 27

A buys a picture for £10,000 which is destroyed by fire; A is uninsured. Although the picture is now worthless, A's allowable loss is restricted to £7,000.

Land and the buildings on it are treated as separate assets for these purposes. Where the building is totally destroyed both assets are separately deemed to have been disposed of and reacquired, and it is the overall gain or loss which is taken into account.

Where the taxpayer later receives compensation or insurance moneys for an asset which is totally lost or destroyed, this is strictly a further disposal for CGT purposes under CGTA 1979 s 20(1) since it is a capital sum derived from an asset (the right under the insurance contract). In practice, however, the Revenue treat both disposals (ie the entire loss of the asset and the receipt of capital moneys) as one transaction. If the taxpayer uses the capital sum within one year of receipt to acquire a replacement asset, he may claim to roll over any gain made on the disposal of the destroyed asset against the cost of the replacement asset; this relief does not apply to wasting assets. If only part of the capital sum is used in replacement, only partial roll-over is available (CGTA 1979 s 21(4), (5).

EXAMPLE 28

A buys a picture for £6,000 which is destroyed when its value is £10,000. He receives insurance money of £10,000 and uses it towards the purchase of a similar picture for £12,000. A has made a gain of £4,000 on the original picture (£10,000 − £6,000) on which he need not pay CGT. He may deduct the gain from the cost of the new picture so that his base cost becomes £8,000 (£12,000 − £4,000).

Assume that A buys the new picture for only £8,000 and claims roll-over relief. Amount of insurance money not applied in replacement = £2,000 (£10,000 − £8,000).

His chargeable gain is, therefore, £2,000 and £2,000 is rolled over so that A's base value for the new picture is £8,000 − £2,000 = £6,000.

The same relief applies where the asset destroyed is a building. The gain on the old building can be rolled over against the cost of the new building. Any gain deemed to have been made on the land cannot, however, be so treated and will, therefore, be chargeable.

4   Assets becoming of negligible value (CGTA 1979 s 22(2))

Where an asset becomes of negligible value (for example, shares and securities in an insolvent company) the taxpayer is deemed to have disposed of and immediately reacquired the asset at its market value (nil) thus enabling him to claim loss relief. This disposal is deemed to occur in the tax year in which the

Revenue accept the claim which may not be the same as the year in which the asset became of negligible value. In practice, a claim will be accepted for a tax year which ended within two years of the date of the claim, provided that the loss occurred before or in that earlier year (SP D13). The timing of the claim is, therefore, important (*Williams v Bullivant* (1983)).

Should the value of the asset subsequently increase, the result of claiming relief under s 22(2) will be that on a later disposal the base value will be nil so that all the consideration received will be treated as a gain and there will be no question of claiming any indexation allowance.

5 Options (CGTA 1979 ss 137–139)

The grant of an option (whether to buy or to sell an asset) is a disposal, not of a part of the asset which is subject to the option, but of a separate asset, namely, the option itself at the date of the grant. The gain will be the consideration paid for the grant of the option less any incidental expenses (see *Strange v Openshaw* (1983)).

EXAMPLE 29

(1) A grants to B for £3,000 an option to buy A's country cottage in 2 years time for £30,000 which is its current market value. A has made a gain of £3,000 from which he can deduct any incidental expenses involved in granting the option. (This is an option to buy.)

(2) A pays B £3,000 in return for an option to sell that country cottage to B in 2 years time for £30,000. (This is an option to sell.) B has made a gain of £3,000 less any incidental expenses.

If the option is exercised, the grant and the exercise are treated as a single transaction for both grantor and grantee.

EXAMPLE 30

As in *Example 29*, assuming that A had deductible expenses of £15,000.

(i) when B exercises the option and pays A £30,000 for the house, A's gain is:

	£
Proceeds from sale of house	30,000
Consideration for option	3,000
	33,000
Less: deductible expenses	15,000
Chargeable gain	£18,000

B's acquisition cost is £30,000 plus the cost of the option, ie £33,000 (both items will be index-linked 12 months after the expenditure was incurred).

(ii) where A exercises the option and sells the house to B for £30,000, A's gain is:

	£	£
Proceeds of sale		30,000
Less: cost of option	3,000	
deductible expenses	15,000	18,000
Chargeable gain		£12,000

B's acquisition cost of the cottage is only £27,000 (ie £30,000 reduced by the amount that he received for the option).

An option is a chargeable asset so that, if disposed of, there may be a chargeable gain or allowable loss. It will be a wasting asset unless it is an option to subscribe for shares which is quoted on The Stock Exchange; a traded option; or it is an option to acquire assets to be used in a trade. The abandonment of an option which is a wasting asset is not a disposal.

6   Appropriations to and from a trader's stock-in-trade

There are two cases to consider. First, where a trader acquires an asset for private use and later appropriates it to his trade. As a general rule, this is a disposal and CGT is payable on the difference between the market value of the asset at the date of appropriation and its original cost.

EXAMPLE 31

A owns a picture gallery. He buys a picture for private use for £5,000 and transfers it to the gallery when it is worth £15,000. He has made a chargeable gain of £10,000. Later he sells the picture to a customer for £30,000. The profit on sale of £15,000 (£30,000 − £15,000) is chargeable to income tax under Schedule D Case I.

However, the trader can elect to avoid paying CGT at the date of appropriation by transferring the asset into his business at a no gain/no loss value. When the asset is eventually sold, the total profit will be charged to income tax under Schedule D as a trading receipt. So, in the above example, were A to make the election he would pay no CGT, but instead he would be liable to income tax on a profit of £25,000 (£30,000 − £5,000).

Whether the election should be exercised or not must depend upon the particular facts of each case. CGT may be more attractive as a choice of evils with its annual exemption and flat rate charge. Income tax, on the other hand, will be paid later (on eventual sale) and the profit so made may be offset against personal allowances or unused capital allowances.

Secondly, where an asset originally acquired as trading stock is taken out for the trader's private use. In this case, there is no election and the transfer is treated as a sale at market value for income tax purposes (see *Sharkey v Wernher* (1956) p 81). The taxpayer will have market value as his CGT base cost.

EXAMPLE 32

One of the pictures in A's gallery cost him £6,000. He removes it to hang it in his dining room when its market value is £16,000. He later sells it privately for £30,000.

On the appropriation out of trading stock, A is treated as selling the picture for its market value (£16,000) and the profit (£10,000) is assessed to income tax. The gain on the subsequent sale (£30,000 − £16,000 = £14,000) is chargeable to CGT.

7   Miscellaneous cases

Hire purchase agreements   Although the purchaser does not own the asset until he pays all the instalments, the vendor is treated as having disposed of the asset at the date when the purchaser is first able to use it (usually the date of the contract). The consideration for the disposal is the cash price payable under the contract. These transactions rarely give rise to a CGT charge, however, either because the asset is exempt (eg, a private car or a chattel worth less than £3,000) or because it is a wasting asset. Further, the contract will normally be a trading transaction falling within the income tax charge.

In the rare case where there is a CGT charge and the contract is subsequently rescinded there will be repayment of CGT.

Mortgages and charges (CGTA 1979 s 23) Neither the grant nor the redemption of a mortgage is treated as a disposal. Where the property is sold by a mortgagee or his receiver, the sale is treated as a disposal by the mortgagor.

Settled property On the happening of certain events the trustees are deemed to have disposed of the trust assets and immediately reacquired them (see Chapter 8).

Value-shifting (CGTA 1979 s 25) There are anti-avoidance provisions intended to charge a person who passes value to another without actually making a disposal (see Chapter 19).

8 Time of disposal

A disposal under a contract of sale takes place for CGT purposes at the date of the contract, not completion, with an adjustment of tax if completion never occurs (CGTA 1979 s 27). If the contract is conditional, the disposal takes place when the condition is fulfilled. Where a local authority compulsorily acquires land (other than under a contract), the disposal occurs when the compensation is agreed or when the authority enters the land (if earlier). In the case of gifts, disposal occurs when the ownership of the asset passes to the donee (usually the date of the gift). Where a capital sum is derived from an asset, the disposal occurs when the sum is received.

15 CGT—death

I GENERAL

Since 1971, CGT has not been charged on a death in order to avoid a double charge to tax with, formerly estate duty, and, now CTT. On death the assets of the deceased are deemed to be acquired by the personal representatives (PRs) at their market value at death. There is an acquisition without a disposal or, as it is otherwise known, an uplift but no charge (CGTA 1979 s 49(1)). Hence, death wipes out capital gains.

EXAMPLE 1

Included in T's estate on his death in October 1984 is a rare first edition of 'Ulysses' which T acquired in 1967 for £10,000. It is worth £100,000 at death. The gain of £90,000 is not chargeable on T's death. Instead his PRs acquire the asset at a new base value of £100,000.

II VALUATION OF CHARGEABLE ASSETS AT DEATH

The assets of the deceased are valued at their open market value at the date of death. The CTT valuation applies for CGT (CGTA 1979 s 153) even though property may have been valued under the special CTT related property provisions (see Chapter 22). The market value for CGT is not, however, reduced by any CTT business or agricultural property relief.

Where land or property valued on death as 'related property' (see p 283) is sold within three years after the death, or quoted securities within one year, for less than the death valuation, the PRs may substitute a lower figure for the death valuation and so obtain a reduction in the CTT paid on death. Not surprisingly, this lower figure will also form the death value for CGT so that the PRs cannot claim CGT loss relief. As an alternative to reducing the estate valuation, the PRs may simply claim a CGT loss on the disposal. This would be advantageous where they have made chargeable gains on disposals of other assets in the estate and where no repayment of CTT would result from amending the value of the death estate.

Ideally, for CGT, the PRs want a high value for the assets on death because of the tax-free uplift, whereas for CTT they want as low a value as possible. Generally, of course, CTT will take precedence with the result that low valuation is usually the goal.

III CGT LOSSES OF THE DECEASED

Any losses of the deceased in the tax year of his death must be set primarily against gains of that year. Unused losses can then be set against the chargeable gains of the widow or widower for the whole of that tax year subject to an election by that person for this set-off not to apply. Any surplus loss at the end of the year of death can be carried back and set against chargeable gains of the deceased in the three tax years preceding the year of death, taking the most recent year first (CGTA 1979 s 49(2)). Any tax thus reclaimed will, of course, fall into the deceased's estate for CTT purposes!

IV SALE OF DECEASED'S ASSETS BY PRs

Any sale of the deceased's assets by his PRs is a disposal for CGT purposes and they are chargeable to CGT on the difference between the sale consideration and the market value at death. The normal deductions for the incidental expenses of sale are available and PRs can deduct an appropriate proportion of the cost of valuation of the estate for probate purposes (*IRC v Richards' Executors* (1971)). The Revenue publish a scale of allowable expenses for the cost of establishing title (see SP7/81). However, PRs may claim to deduct more than the 'scale' figure in cases when higher expenses have been incurred. PRs have an annual exemption from CGT of £5,600 in the tax year of death and in each of the two following tax years. Thereafter they have no exemption, so that any sales likely to produce a chargeable gain should be made within that time or the assets vested in the appropriate beneficiaries who can take advantage of their annual exemption.

For deaths after March 1982, the PRs have the benefit of the indexation allowance, although (in line with general principles) not for the first 12 months of their ownership.

EXAMPLE 2

Continuing *Example 1*, if the PRs sell the book in May 1986 for £130,000, they have made a gross gain of £30,000 from which they can deduct their annual exemption of £5,600 (if unused); the incidental expenses of sale; a proportionate part of the cost of valuing the estate for probate in November 1984; and an indexation allowance, calculated on £100,000 as from October 1985, and on the relevant part of the cost of valuation as from November 1985.

Where the PRs dispose of a private dwelling house which, both before and after the death, was occupied by a person who is entitled on death to the whole, or substantially the whole, of the proceeds of sale from the house, either absolutely or for life, by concession PRs have the benefit of the private residence exemption from CGT (ESC D5).

EXAMPLE 3

Bill and his brother Ben live in Bill's house. On his death Bill leaves the house to Ben who goes on living in it. The property has to be sold by the PRs to pay for Bill's funeral. Any gain will be exempt.

V   LOSSES OF THE PRs

Losses made by the PRs on disposals of chargeable assets during administration can be set off against chargeable gains only on other sales made by them. Any surplus losses at the end of the administration period cannot be transferred to beneficiaries (cp trustees). Accordingly, where PRs anticipate that a loss will not be relieved, they may prefer to transfer the loss-making asset to the relevant beneficiary so that he can sell it and obtain the loss relief.

VI   DISPOSALS TO LEGATEES (CGTA 1979 s 49(4))

On the disposal of an asset to a legatee, the PRs make neither gain nor loss for CGT purposes, and the legatee acquires the asset at the PRs' base value plus the expenses of transferring the asset to him. The legatee must, however, wait a further 12 months after acquiring the asset before he can obtain the benefit of any indexation allowance.

EXAMPLE 4

The PRs transfer the book (see *Example 1*) to the legatee (L) under the will in May 1986 when it is worth £130,000. The cost of valuing the book as a part of the whole estate in November 1984 was £1,000 and the PRs incurred incidental expenses involved in the transfer of the book in May 1986 of £150. L sells the book in July 1986 for £140,000. On the disposal by the PRs to L, no chargeable gain accrues to the PRs and L's base value is:

	£
Market value at death	100,000
Valuation cost	1,000
Indexation allowance:	
On £100,000 from October 1985 to May 1986 (say)	300
and on £1,000 from November 1985 to May 1986 (say)	10
Expenses of transfer	150
Base cost of L	£101,460

When L sells the book in July 1987 for £140,000 he is charged to CGT on his gain which is £38,540 (£140,000 – £101,460) as reduced by any allowable expenditure that he has incurred, including an indexation allowance on £101,150 from May 1987 to July 1987. Note that the indexation allowance of £310 may not itself be index-linked.

A legatee is defined in CGTA 1979 s 47(2) as any person taking under a testamentary disposition or on intestacy or partial intestacy, whether beneficially or as a trustee. A '*donatio mortis causa*' is treated for these purposes as a testamentary disposition and not as a gift, so that the donee acquires the asset at its market value on the donor's death and the donor is not treated as having made a chargeable gain.

It is unclear from the legislation whether a person who receives assets under a trust created by will or on intestacy receives them as a legatee (in which case there is no charge to CGT) or as a beneficiary absolutely entitled as against the trustee, in which case there is a deemed disposal under CGTA 1979 s 54 which is chargeable (see Chapter 18). In practice this question is of less importance today since any gain under s 54 can be held over under FA 1980 s 79 (as amended). The answer appears to depend upon the status of the executors and the terms of the will (see *Cochrane's Executors v IRC* (1974) and *IRC v Matthew's Executors* (1984)). During the course of administration they are the sole owners of the deceased's assets, albeit in a fiduciary capacity (*Commissioner of Stamp Duties v Livingstone* (1965)) so that until they have transferred assets to other persons as trustees, or completed the administration (so that they are deemed to have assented to themselves as trustees), any transfer of assets to a beneficiary is probably treated as a distribution to a legatee and not chargeable. Once one of the above events has happened, however, the capacity in which a beneficiary receives the asset depends on the nature of the trust. If it is a trust for sale where the beneficiary is absolutely entitled to the proceeds of sale, the property is not settled for CGT (CGTA 1979 s 46; see p 248), so that he receives any distribution as a legatee with no CGT charge. If, however, the will creates a strict settlement or a trust for sale under which the property is settled, any beneficiary who then receives trust property does so as a beneficiary absolutely entitled as against the trustee and any gain is chargeable (subject to s 79 hold-over relief).

EXAMPLE 5

(1) T dies leaving his property to executors on trust for sale for his three children absolutely, all of whom are over 18. Whether the children receive the assets before the administration is completed or after the executors have assented to themselves as trustees does not matter since they take as legatees. In the former case the trust has not yet arisen, in the latter case the property is not settled.

(2) T dies leaving his property to executors on trust for sale for his widow for life and then for his three children absolutely, all of whom are over 18. If the widow dies before the executors become trustees, any distributions to the children will be received as legatees for the reasons given above. If, however, the widow dies after the executors have become trustees, then the property is settled, so that the children receive assets as persons absolutely entitled as against the trustees with a consequent deemed disposal under CGTA 1979 s 54 (there will, however, be no charge because the event leading to their entitlement was the death of the life tenant—see Chapter 18).

In conclusion, therefore, no CGT need be paid when a beneficiary becomes absolutely entitled to property under a will trust. Either he will take qua legatee or a hold-over election under s 79 will be available.

When the former matrimonial home of the deceased passes to his surviving spouse there is an uplift in the base value of the property on death in the usual way. On a subsequent disposal by that spouse, any gain since death will be exempt from CGT if the house has been occupied as that spouse's main residence. Even if it has not, by CGTA 1979 s 101(7), the deceased's period of ownership is deemed to be that of the surviving spouse in deciding what proportion of the gain (if any) is chargeable (see p 232).

EXAMPLE 6

T bought a house in 1968 for £5,000. It was his main residence until his death in 1983 when it was worth £15,000. His wife (W) never lived there with him, but became entitled to the house on his intestacy. T's administrators transferred the house to W in 1984. She thereupon occupied it as her main residence for one year and then went abroad until 1993 when she returned and sold the house for £25,000.

For the purpose of the main residence exemption, W can claim that she has occupied the house as her main residence for 19 out of the 25 years that it has been in the ownership of herself or T, ie:

1968–83 (15 years)   Occupied by T as his main residence
1983–84* (1 year)   Occupation by administrators treated as that of W
1984–85* (1 year)   Occupied by W
1991–93* (2 years)   Last two years of ownership disregarded (CGTA 1979 s 102)

W is, therefore, charged on a proportion of the gain:
(1) sale consideration ($£25,000$) – base cost ($£15,000$) = $£10,000$ (assuming no other allowable expenses).

(2) fraction chargeable: $£10,000 \times \dfrac{6}{25} = £2,400$

Were it not for s 101(7), she would be charged on a larger proportion of the gain, ie: $£10,000 \times \dfrac{4 \text{ (see*)}}{10 \text{ (length of her ownership)}} = £4,000$

VII   DISCLAIMERS AND VARIATIONS (CGTA 1979 s 49(6))

Subject to certain conditions, which are the same as for CTT (see p|321), any variation of the deceased's will or of the intestacy rules, or any disclaimer, made in both cases within 2 years of the deceased's death can be treated for CGT (as for CTT) as if it were made by the deceased and is consequently not a chargeable disposal.

EXAMPLE 7

Facts as in *Example 1*. L is entitled under T's will to the book worth $£100,000$. Within two years of T's death L varies the will so that the book (now worth $£140,000$) passes to his brother B. This need not be a disposal for CGT. Instead, it can be treated as if T's will had so provided. Accordingly, B acquires the asset at its market value at death ($£100,000$) plus any additional expenses of the PRs.

The election that is available for CGT is identical to that available for CTT purposes. In most cases it is likely that both the elections will be exercised so that the variation will be read back into the original will for both CGT and CTT purposes. This is not necessary, however, since the elections are quite independent of each other with the result that the CTT election can be exercised without the CGT election and vice versa. Careful thought should be given to this problem; consider the following:

EXAMPLE 8

(1) A will leaves shares worth $£100,000$ to the testator's daughter. She transfers the shares within the permitted period to her mother (the testator's surviving spouse). The shares are then worth $£105,000$.
    For CTT the election will probably be desirable as the result will be to reduce the testator's chargeable estate at death by $£100,000$ since the shares are now an exempt transfer to a surviving spouse.
    For CGT the election probably should not be made since, if the daughter makes a chargeable transfer, her gain will be $£105,000 – £100,000 = £5,000$

which will be covered by her annual CGT exemption. Her mother will then acquire the shares at the higher base cost of £105,000.

(2) A will leaves shares worth £100,000 to the testator's surviving spouse. After they have risen in value to £140,000 she decides (within the permitted time limit) to vary the will in favour of her daughter.

For CTT it is by no means obvious that the election should be made. If it is, £100,000 will constitute a chargeable death transfer (if it is not, the surviving spouse will have made a chargeable life transfer of £140,000). Hence, a careful consideration of the total chargeable transfers of the testator and the widow will be necessary and the different life and death rates of CTT must be borne in mind.

For CGT it would seem much more likely that the disposal should be read back into the will since otherwise there will be a chargeable gain of £140,000 − £100,000 = £40,000. (Notice, of course, that the effect of a s 79 hold-over election would be much the same as a 'reading back' into the will. The consent of the donee would be an additional requirement but the base cost of the daughter would then include the costs of the transfer by the PRs to the spouse: for a consideration of the inter-relationship between s 79 and the variation rules see LS Gaz (1984) p 99.)

Finally, it should be mentioned that even if the CGT election is exercised, the result will not affect the indexation allowance. The ultimate legatee will still have to serve the standard qualifying period with no credit for the period of ownership of either the PRs or of the original legatee.

16   CGT—exemptions and reliefs

In many cases a gain on the disposal of an asset will not be chargeable either because the gain itself is exempt or because the asset is not chargeable. Even if a gain is chargeable, there are various reliefs whereby the tax can be minimised or deferred indefinitely. As already noted on p 211, there is an annual exemption for an individual whose gains do not exceed £5,600 in the tax year.

I   MISCELLANEOUS EXEMPTIONS

Exempt assets   Certain assets are not chargeable for CGT. The taxpayer, therefore, realises no chargeable gain or, often more significantly, no allowable loss on their disposal. Non-chargeable assets include sterling (CGTA 1979 s 19(1)), National Savings Certificates, Premium Bonds and Save As You Earn deposits (CGTA 1979 s 71), private motor vehicles (CGTA 1979 s 130) and betting winnings (CGTA 1979 s 19(4)).

Exempt gains   The following gains are exempt from CGT:
(a) damages for personal injuries (CGTA 1979 s 19(5));
(b) gains on the disposal of decorations for valour unless the decoration was acquired for money or money's worth (CGTA 1979 s 131);
(c) gains on the disposal of foreign currency obtained for private use (CGTA 1979 s 133);
(d) gains on the disposal of certain gilt-edged securities held for at least 12 months (CGTA 1979 ss 64, 67). There is a similar exemption for corporate bonds issued or transferred after 13 March 1984 where either the issuing body or the bond is listed on The Stock Exchange or dealt in on the Unlisted Securities Market (FA 1984 s 64).
(e) the disposal of pension rights, annuity rights and annual payments will not generally give rise to a chargeable gain (CGTA 1979 s 144);
(f) any gain on the disposal of a life policy, a deferred annuity policy, or any rights under such policies, unless the disposal is by someone other than the original beneficial owner and that person acquired the interest or right for money or money's worth (CGTA 1979 s 143(1)); and
(g) gains are exempt if made by such bodies as authorised unit trusts and investment trusts (FA 1980 s 81); and charities, provided that the gain is applied for charitable purposes (CGTA 1979 s 145(1)).

Charities   Disposals to charities and to certain national institutions are treated as made on a no gain/no loss basis (CGTA 1979 s 146 and FA 1975 Sch 6 para 12).

Heritage property and woodlands The exemptions for heritage property are basically the same as for CTT (see Chapter 23). First, where property of national interest is given (or sold by private treaty) to a non-profit making body (including a charity or other national institution mentioned in CGTA 1979 s 146) any gain will be exempt from CGT provided that the Treasury so directs (see FA 1975 Sch 6 para 13). Secondly, any gain on a disposal of such property may be conditionally exempt from CGT in the same way as for CTT (CGTA 1979 s 147; see FA 1976 ss 76, 77). Thirdly, the gain on any property that is accepted by the Treasury in satisfaction of CTT is exempt from CGT (CGTA 1979 s 147(2)(b)).

Where the occupier of woodlands is charged to income tax under Schedule B, any consideration that he receives for the disposal of the trees is excluded for CGT purposes. If the woodlands are sold, that part of the consideration attributable to the timber is excluded from any CGT calculation (CGTA 1979 s 113).

II CHATTELS

A gain on the disposal of a chattel that is a wasting asset is exempt from CGT. A wasting asset is one with a predictable useful life of 50 years or less and includes yachts, caravans, washing machines, animals and all plant and machinery (see Chapter 14).

In the case of non-wasting chattels, if the disposal consideration is £3,000 or less, any gain is exempt (CGTA 1979 s 128(1)). CGT is as a result easier to administer as there is no need to calculate gains and losses on assets of minimal value. Insofar as the disposal consideration exceeds £3,000, the chargeable gain is limited to 5/3 of the excess of that consideration over £3,000.

Where a loss is made on the disposal of a chattel and the disposal consideration is less than £3,000, the sum of £3,000 is substituted for that consideration so as to limit a claim for loss relief.

EXAMPLE 1

(1) A bought a necklace for £2,600 and later sold it for £3,300 so making a total gain of £700. The chargeable gain is reduced to $5/3 \times £300$ ($£3,300 - £3,000) = £500$.

(2) A bought a brooch for £4,000 and sold it for £2,600 so making an actual loss of £1,400. He is deemed to have sold it for £3,000 so that his allowable loss is restricted to £1,000 ($£4,000 - £3,000$).

The taxpayer cannot dispose of a set of articles by a series of separate transactions so as to take advantage of the £3,000 exemption on each disposal. Whether the disposals are to the same person or to connected persons (albeit on different occasions) they are regarded as a single transaction (see also CGTA 1979 s 151, p 200).

EXAMPLE 2

A owns three Rousseau paintings which, as a set, have a market value of £12,000. He paid £2,000 for each of the paintings which individually are worth £3,000. He sells all three paintings at different times to his sister B for £3,000 each. He thereby appears to fall within the chattel exemption on each disposal. The Revenue can treat the three disposals as a single disposal of an asset worth £12,000 with a base value of £6,000 so that A has made a chargeable gain of £6,000.

III   DEBTS

1   What is a debt?

A debt is a chargeable asset (CGTA 1979 s 19(1)). It is not defined, so that it bears the common law meaning of 'a sum payable in respect of a liquidated money demand recoverable by action' (*Rawley v Rawley* (1876)). It can include a right to receive a sum of money that is not yet ascertained (*O'Driscoll v Manchester Insurance Committee* (1915)) or a contingent right to receive a definite sum (*Mortimore v IRC* (1864)). However, for the purposes of CGT, it cannot include a right to receive an unidentifiable sum at an unascertained date; there must be a liability, either present or contingent, to pay a sum which is ascertained or capable of being ascertained (*Marren v Ingles* (1980)).

EXAMPLE 3

Barry agrees to sell his Ming vase to Bruce for £5,000 plus one half of any profits that Bruce realises if he resells the vase in the next ten years. The disposal consideration received for the vase is £5,000 plus the value of a chose in action. As that chose is both contingent (on resale occurring) and for an unascertained sum (half of any profits) it is not a debt.

---

2   The general principle

A disposal of a debt by the original creditor, his personal representatives or legatee is exempt from CGT unless it is a debt on a security (below). 'Disposal' includes repayment of the debt (CGTA 1979 s 134(1)(2)). Since a contractual debt will normally give a creditor merely the right to repayment of the sum lent, together with interest, the disposal of a debt will rarely generate a gain and the aim of CGTA 1979 s 134(1) is to exclude the more likely claim for loss relief, particularly where the debt is never repaid. This provision only applies to the original creditor so that an assignee of a debt can claim an allowable loss if the debtor defaults, unless the assignee and the debtor are connected persons (CGTA 1979 s 134(4)).

If the debt is satisfied by a transfer of property, that property is acquired by the creditor at its market value. Since this could operate harshly for an original creditor who can claim no allowable loss, s 134(3) provides that on a subsequent disposal of the property, its base value shall be taken as the value of the debt.

EXAMPLE 4

A owes B £30,000 and in full satisfaction of the debt he gives B a painting worth £22,000. B does not have an allowable loss of £8,000. However, if B later sells the painting for £40,000 he is taxed on a gain of £10,000 only (£40,000 − £30,000).

The harshness of CGTA 1979 s 134(1) is mitigated by CGTA 1979 s 136, allowing original creditors to claim loss relief in respect of a 'qualifying loan'. The debt must have become irrecoverable and the creditor must not have assigned his rights. Creditor and debtor must not be married to each other nor be companies in the same group.

A 'qualifying loan' must be used by a UK resident borrower wholly for the purpose of a trade (not being moneylending) carried on by him and the debt must not be 'on a security' (CGTA 1979 s 136; for time limits for claims see SP 3/83).

3 Debts on a security

The legislation distinguishes between debts which can normally only decrease in value and those with such characteristics that they may be disposed of at a profit. It, therefore, provides that a 'debt on a security' is chargeable to CGT even in the hands of the original creditor (CGTA 1979 s 134(1)).

Unfortunately, the term 'debt on a security' lacks both statutory and satisfactory judicial interpretation despite three cases (see *Cleveleys Investment Trust Co v IRC* (1971); *Aberdeen Construction Group Ltd v IRC* (1978); *W T Ramsay Ltd v IRC* (1981)). Apparently, the phrase 'debt on a security' has a limited and technical meaning and '[it] is not a synonym for a secured debt' per Lord Wilberforce in *Aberdeen Construction Group Ltd v IRC*. Thus, a mortgage which is a debt secured by an estate in land is not a debt on a security for the purposes of CGT. The word 'security' is defined in CGTA 1979 s 82(3) as including 'any loan stock or similar security whether of the government of the UK or elsewhere, or of any company, and whether secured or unsecured'. Despite the word 'including' the Revenue have stated that they regard the definition as exhaustive (SP 11 June 1970) and their view has been generally accepted by the courts.

There are various requirements that a debt must fulfil in order to qualify as a debt on a security. As a minimum, the security should be marketable or capable of being dealt in, embodied at the very least in a contract and preferably in a document or certificate which must be either loan stock or similar to the loan stock of a government, local authority or company. It should have ordinary terms for repayment, with or without a premium and contain a provision for the payment of interest *(W T Ramsay Ltd v IRC)*. If a debt satisfies these very narrow requirements, any disposal of it, whether or not by the original creditor will result in a chargeable gain or allowable loss.

IV THE MAIN RESIDENCE (CGTA 1979 ss 101–105)

Perhaps the most important exemption for the individual taxpayer is from any gain that he makes on the disposal of his principal private residence. This exemption, combined with mortgage interest relief, provides government encouragement for the investment of private capital in home ownership.

1 When is the exemption available?

The exemption is available for any gain arising on the disposal by gift or sale by a taxpayer of his only or main residence, including grounds of up to one acre (or such larger area as is required for the reasonable enjoyment of the dwelling house).

The question of whether a particular property is a taxpayer's 'only or main residence' is sometimes a difficult one to answer. If only one property is occupied by him as a residence the exemption *prima facie* applies. Where the taxpayer has two residences, only the residence which is his main residence can qualify for relief.

EXAMPLE 5

A owns one property in the country and he rents a flat in London. Any gain that A makes on the country property is not automatically exempt just because A owns only that property; A must be able to show that it is his 'main' residence.

Which of two residences is the main residence is a question of fact which is not decided simply by the periods of time spent in each. For a discussion of the courts' approach, see the income tax case of *Frost v Feltham* (1981) (see p 30).

When the taxpayer has two residences, he can elect for one to be treated as his main residence (CGTA 1979 s 101(5)). This election should be made even though one of the residences is not owned by the taxpayer (it may, for instance, be tied accommodation). The election can be backdated for up to two years and should be made within two years of acquiring a second residence. Failure to do so means that the inspector of taxes can decide which is the main residence, subject to the right of appeal by the taxpayer. The election can be varied.

2   How many residences can qualify for exemption?

A maximum of two houses may qualify for exemption; the only or main residence and a property owned by the taxpayer but used as a residence by a dependent relative, rent-free and for no other consideration (CGTA 1979 s 105). A 'dependent relative' is any relative of the taxpayer or his spouse who is incapacitated, through age or infirmity, from maintaining himself and the taxpayer's mother or mother-in-law if separated or widowed. Only one house can qualify so that if the taxpayer has a number of dependent relatives they must all live together (compare interest relief for income tax: p 30).

Husband and wife can have only one main residence between them and, in contrast to the income tax rules for interest relief, there is no CGT exemption for a house occupied by a former or separated spouse.

3   Miscellaneous problems

Land used with the house   The exemption for land of up to one acre only applies if it is used in connection with the residence. Thus, a gain made on a disposal of the land will not be exempt if the residence is sold before the land. In *Varty v Lynes* (1976) the taxpayer sold the house and part of the garden. Later he sold the remaining part of the garden with the benefit of planning permission. It was held that this second disposal was chargeable. Had the taxpayer sold the garden before or at the same time as the house, any gain would have been exempt. The Revenue have stated that they will not seek to charge CGT on such disposals unless the land (as in the *Varty* case) has development value.

What is a dwelling house?   This is a question of fact. In *Makins v Elson* (1977) the taxpayer bought land intending to build a house on it. In the meantime, he lived there in a caravan which was connected to the mains services. He never built the house and later sold both land and caravan at a profit. The caravan was held on the facts to be a dwelling house.

What is a residence? This is also a question of fact and degree. In *Batey v Wakefield* (1981) a separate bungalow which was used by a caretaker within the grounds of the taxpayer's house was exempt from CGT on sale, on the basis that a residence can comprise several dwellings which need not necessarily be physically joined. The problem is whether the dwelling in question forms part of the residence (see also *Green v IRC* (1982)).

Sale by trustees Where trustees dispose of a house which is the residence of a beneficiary who is entitled to occupy it by the terms of the settlement (CGTA 1979 s 104) or under a discretion exercised by the trustees, any gain is exempt. The latter point was decided in *Sansom v Peay* (1976) and has repercussions for CTT since the Revenue argue that the beneficiary in whose favour the discretion has been exercised thereby acquires an interest in possession in the settlement (see Chapter 24).

Use of a house for a business If part of the house is used exclusively for business purposes, a proportionate part of the gain on a disposal of the property becomes chargeable (CGTA 1979 s 103). However, as long as no part is used exclusively for business purposes no exemption will be lost. Doctors and dentists who have a surgery in their house are advised to hold a party in that surgery at least once a year (and to invite the local tax inspector!).

Letting part of the property Where the whole or part of the property has been let as residential accommodation this may result in a partial loss of exemption. However, the gain attributable to the letting (calculated according to how much was let and for how long) will be exempt from CGT up to the lesser of £20,000 and the exemption attributable to the owner's occupation. This relief does not apply if the let portion forms a separate dwelling (FA 1980 s 80 and SP 14/80). The Revenue have stated that the taking of lodgers will not result in a loss of any of the exemption provided that the lodger lives as part of the family and shares living accommodation (SP 14/80).

EXAMPLE 6

A sells his house which he has owned for 20 years realising a gain of £120,000. He occupied the entire house during the first ten years. For the next six years he let $\frac{1}{3}$ of it and for the final four years the entire property.

	£	£
Total gain		120,000
Less exemptions		
(i) 10 years occupation	60,000	
(ii) 6 years occupation of $\frac{2}{3}$ ($£60,000 \times \frac{2}{3} \times \frac{6}{10}$)	24,000	
(iii) final 2 years ownership ($£60,000 \times \frac{2}{10}$)	12,000	
		96,000
Gain attributable to letting		24,000
Less exemption		20,000
Chargeable portion		£4,000

Disposal by PRs Concessionary relief may be available to PRs (see ESC D5 discussed on p 221).

4   Effect of periods of absence

To qualify for the exemption, the taxpayer must occupy the property as his only or main residence throughout the period of his ownership. As a general rule, therefore, the effect of periods of absence is that on the disposal of the residence a proportion of any gain will be charged. That proportion is calculated by the formula: $\text{Total gain} \times \dfrac{\text{period of absence}}{\text{period of ownership}}$.

Special rules operate for husband and wife since in deciding whether a house has been occupied as a main residence throughout the period of ownership one spouse can take advantage of a period of ownership of the other (CGTA 1979 s 101(7)(a): see p 223 for an illustration of this rule).

Despite the general rule that absences render part of the gain chargeable, certain absences are ignored. These include, by concession, the first 12 months of ownership in cases where occupation was delayed because the house was being built or altered (SP D4).

The last two years of ownership are likewise ignored and this often proves highly beneficial on a matrimonial breakdown (see generally Chapter 36). It also means that a taxpayer owning two houses can by careful use of his election obtain a tax advantage.

EXAMPLE 7

Judith has owned for many years a flat in London and a cottage in Wales. She has elected for the flat to be her main residence. In 1984 she sells the flat. She should, therefore, elect retrospectively for her Welsh cottage to be her main residence from 1982 onwards.

CGTA 1979 s 102 allows other periods of absence to be ignored provided that the owner had no other residence available for the exemption during these periods and that he resided in the house before and after the absence in question. These periods are:
(a) any period or periods of absence not exceeding three years altogether;
(b) any period when the taxpayer was employed abroad; and
(c) a maximum period of four years where the owner could not occupy the property because he was employed elsewhere.

ESC D3 gives relief when the absence results from a non-owning spouse's employment and the Revenue also accept that, if the absence exceeds the permitted period in (a) and (c), it is only the excess which does not qualify for the exemption. The requirement that the taxpayer should reside after the period of absence will not apply in (b) and (c) if it is prevented by the terms of his employment (ESC D4). If he is required either by the nature of his employment or as the result of his trade or profession to live in other accommodation ('job related accommodation'—see p 30) he will obtain the exemption if he buys a house intending to use it in the future as a main residence. It does not matter that he never occupies it and that it is let throughout, provided that he can show that he intended to live there. He should, of course, make the election since he is occupying other (job-related) property.

5   Expenditure with profit-making motive

The exemption does not apply if the house was acquired wholly or partly for the purpose of realising a gain, nor to a gain attributable to any expenditure which was incurred wholly or partly for the purpose of realising a gain (CGTA 1979 s 103(3)). Presumably, the acquisition of a freehold reversion by a tenant with a view to selling an absolute title to the property would fall within this provision. If so, the portion of the gain attributable to the reversion would be assessable. The requirement of motive makes this provision difficult to apply.

V BUSINESS RELIEFS

1 The problems and the taxes

A number of CGT reliefs relate to businesses both incorporated and unincorporated. Their aim is to enable businesses to be carried on and transferred without being threatened by penal taxation. Although this chapter is concerned only with CGT reliefs, a disposal of a business will normally involve other taxes. It may be by way of gift (including death) or by sale. If by way of gift, the relevant taxes will be CGT, stamp duty, income tax and CTT. For CGT, hold-over relief under CGTA 1979 s 126 or FA 1980 s 79 will usually be available on a lifetime gift; on a death, there will be neither stamp duty nor CGT. Where the transfer is a sale, stamp duty, income tax and CGT may apply.

The reliefs apply to a disposal of:
(a) a sole trade/profession;
(b) a part of a trade/profession (eg a partnership share);
(c) shares in a company; and
(d) assets used by a company or partnership in which the owner of the assets either owns shares or is a partner.

2 Roll-over (replacement of business assets) (CGTA 1979 s 115)

Where certain assets of a business are sold and the proceeds of sale wholly re-invested in acquiring a new asset to be used in a business, the taxpayer can elect to roll over the gain and deduct it from the acquisition cost of the new asset. Tax is, therefore, postponed indefinitely.

EXAMPLE 8

A makes a gain of £50,000 on the sale of factory 1, but he immediately buys factory 2 for £120,000. He can roll the gain of £50,000 into the purchase price of factory 2 thereby reducing it to £70,000 (actual cost £120,000 minus rolled over gain of £50,000).

The old and the new asset must be comprised in the list of business assets in CGTA 1979 s 118. These are land and buildings; fixed plant and machinery; ships; aircraft; hovercraft; and goodwill. The assets need not be of the same type; eg, a gain on the sale of an aircraft can be rolled over into the purchase of a hovercraft. Further, although the old asset must have been used in the taxpayer's trade during the whole time that he owned it (otherwise only partial roll-over is allowed), it could have been used in successive trades provided that the gap between them did not exceed three years.

EXAMPLE 9

A inherited a freehold shop in 1975 when its value was £25,000. The shop was kept empty until 1979 when he decided to start a fish and chip shop. He sold the shop in 1984 for £60,000 and purchased new premises for £75,000.

His total gain is £35,000. The premises have been used for trading purposes during one-half of his ownership period. Hence, £17,500 can be rolled over so that the cost of the new premises becomes £57,500, but the balance of the gain (£17,500) will be taxed.

Land and buildings that are sold must be occupied as well as used for the purposes of the taxpayer's business. If the property is occupied by his partner or employee, he must be able to show that their occupation is representative (ie attributed to him) to obtain the relief. For occupation to be representative it must either (i) be essential for the partner or employee to occupy the property to perform his duties; or (ii) be an express term of the employment contract (or partnership agreement) that he should do so, and the occupation must enable him to perform his duties better. If either of these conditions is proved, the Revenue accept that the property is used for the purpose of the owner's trade (see *Anderton v Lamb* (1980)).

The new asset must be bought within one year *before* or three years *after* the disposal of the old one. The new asset need not be used in the same trade as the old but can be used in another trade carried on by the taxpayer simultaneously or successively, provided in the latter case that there is not more than a three year gap between the ceasing of one trade and the start of another (see SP 8/81). There is nothing to prevent the taxpayer from rolling his gain into the purchase of more than one asset or to require him to continue to use the new asset in a trade throughout his period of ownership.

This relief is also available to partnerships and to companies. It can also be claimed for an asset which is owned by an individual and used by his partnership or family trading company (for the definition of such a company see p 236). In such cases the relief is only available to the individual and the replacement asset cannot be purchased by the partnership or company.

There are certain restrictions on the relief. First, if the new asset is a depreciating asset (defined as a 'wasting asset' or one which will become a wasting asset within ten years such as a lease with 60 years unexpired) the gain on the old asset cannot be deducted from the cost of the new. Instead, tax on the gain is postponed until the earliest of the three following events:

(a) ten years elapses from the date of the purchase of the new asset; or
(b) the taxpayer disposes of the new asset; or
(c) the taxpayer ceases to use the new asset for the purposes of a trade.

If, before the deferred gain becomes chargeable, a new asset is acquired (whether the depreciating asset is sold or not), the deferred gain may be rolled into the new asset (see CGTA 1979 s 117).

EXAMPLE 10

Sam sells his freehold fish and chip shop for £25,000 thereby making a gain of £12,000. One year later he buys a 55 year lease on new premises for £27,000 and seven years after that acquires a further freehold shop for £35,000.

(1) *Purchase of 55 year lease:* this lease is a depreciating asset. The gain of £12,000 on the sale of the original shop is, therefore, held in suspense for ten years.

(2) *Purchase of the freehold shop:* as the purchase occurs within ten years of the gain, roll-over relief is available so that the purchase price is reduced to £23,000.

Secondly, if the whole of the proceeds of sale are not re-invested in acquiring the new asset there is a chargeable gain equivalent to the amount not re-invested and it is only the balance that is rolled over. Accordingly, if the purchase price of the new asset does not exceed the acquisition cost of the old, all the gain is chargeable and there is nothing to roll over.

EXAMPLE 11

A buys factory 1 for £50,000 and sells it for £100,000 thereby making a gain of £50,000. A buys factory 2 for £80,000. The amount not reinvested (£20,000, ie £100,000 − £80,000) is chargeable. The balance of the gain (£30,000) is rolled over so that the acquisition cost of factory 2 is £50,000. If factory 2 had only cost £50,000 the amount not re-invested would equal the gain (ie £50,000) and be chargeable.

If the taxpayer knows that the price of the new asset will be too low to enable him to claim roll-over (or full roll-over) relief and he is married, it may be advantageous to transfer a share in the old asset to his wife before it is sold although this ruse could be challenged under the *Ramsay* principle (Chapter 32).

EXAMPLE 12

H buys factory 1 for £50,000 and transfers 2/5 of it to his wife W. The factory is sold for £100,000. H's gain is £30,000 ([3/5 × £100,000] − [3/5 × £50,000]). W's gain is £20,000 ([2/5 × £100,000] − [2/5 × £50,000]).
   H's share of the proceeds of sale is £60,000. H then buys factory 2 for £50,000. The proceeds of sale are not wholly re-invested in factory 2 and, therefore, H is charged to CGT on £10,000 (£60,000 − £50,000). The balance of his gain £20,000 (£30,000 − £10,000) can be rolled over, leaving him with a base value for factory 2 of £30,000. H and W between them are taxed on a gain of £30,000 instead of (as in *Example 11*) H being taxed on a gain of £50,000.

Finally, roll-over relief should not be claimed where the taxpayer makes an allowable loss on the sale of the old asset since he cannot add this loss to the base value of the new asset. Nor should he claim the relief where the gain does not exceed his annual exemption. Even if his gain does exceed the exempt limit, it may not be worth claiming the relief, as the claim cannot be to hold over only a part of the gain and the effect of reducing the base cost of an asset is to depress any indexation allowance.

3 Retirement relief (CGTA 1979 s 124)

Retirement relief exempts from CGT up to £100,000 of gains made by taxpayers on a disposal of a business or part of a business and shares in a 'family trading company'. It is available to individuals (not to trustees) on sales and gifts and is subject to two requirements. First, the transferor must be at least 60 at the date of the disposal, although he does not actually need to retire. It then exempts from charge £20,000 of the gain for each year that the transferor's age exceeds 60 up to a maximum of £100,000 at 65. The relief is calculated in terms of months and days. Secondly, the assets must have been owned by the transferor for a minimum of one year for any relief to apply, but for ten years to qualify for full relief. The relief is, therefore, reduced by 1/10th for each year of ownership less than ten years down to a minimum of one year.

EXAMPLE 13

A is aged 63 and has owned the assets for eight years.

His relief is £60,000 (because of age) but is reduced by $2/10 \times 60{,}000$ (ie £12,000) to £48,000.

The maximum relief is £100,000 per individual not per business. A taxpayer can claim relief for different disposals (up to a maximum of £100,000) so long as the other conditions are satisfied.

Disposal of an unincorporated business　The disposal may be of a business owned by a sole trader or of part of a business, including the share of a partner. 'Business' bears its ordinary meaning and includes trades, professions or vocations assessable to income tax under Schedule D Case I or II.

The difficult distinction is between disposals of a business or part of a business (which qualify for relief) and a disposal of assets used in a business (which does not). In *McGregor v Adcock* (1977) a farmer sold about $\frac{1}{6}$ of his farming land with planning permission and continued farming the remainder. His claim for retirement relief failed because it was held that he had only sold a business asset and not a part of the business which continued unchanged after the disposal.

The assets in respect of which the relief is claimed must be business assets, including goodwill, used for the purpose of the business and not investment assets (eg, a valuable picture or a shareholding). However, it is the business and not the asset that must have been owned for ten years to obtain maximum relief. Thus, the taxpayer can purchase assets, put them into a business that he has owned for many years and claim the relief, provided that he can show that they are used in the business and, where they have not been so used for very long, that they are not merely investment assets.

By concession the relief is given to a transferor who has owned consecutive businesses provided that there has been only a short interval between them. There will be no break in continuity for the purpose of calculating the transferor's length of ownership (ESC D8). Also by concession, the relief is available where the business has been closed down and the assets later sold at a gain, provided that they were disposed of within three years of the closure and were not used in the interim. The amount of the relief is calculated according to the transferor's age at the date of the closure |(ESC D14).

Relief is given to a partner who disposes of his share in the partnership assets; it can also apply where a partner disposes of an asset owned by him but used in the partnership, provided that the disposal is associated with the disposal of his partnership share and that no rent has been charged to the partnership for its use (SP D5). (Insofar as a rent is charged the relief is proportionately reduced.)

Disposal of shares or securities in a 'family trading company'　The relief applies on a disposal of shares or securities in a family trading company of which the taxpayer is a full-time working director.

A 'family trading company' is a trading company in which the transferor owns a minimum of 25% of the shares conferring voting rights or in which he owns at least 5% and he and his family together own 51% (CGTA 1979 s 124).

'Family' comprises the transferor's spouse, parent or ancestor, child or descendant, brother or sister and the same relatives of his spouse.

EXAMPLE 14

The 200 issued shares of Prang Ltd are owned as follows:

80 by Arthur Wonderstone, a rich American financier
10 by Bernard Pringshein
38 by Sally Pringshein (sister)
38 by Erma Pringshein (aunt)
15 by Ella Pringshein (mother)
<u>19</u> by Julius John (a family friend of the Pringsheins)
<u>200</u> total shares

Arthur and Bernard are full-time working directors; both have owned their shares for ten years and are aged 65.

Prang Ltd is the family trading company of Wonderstone since he owns over 25% of the shares. Note that in no literal sense is it his family company. He will be entitled to retirement relief. However, it is not Bernard's family trading company since although he possesses 5% of the shares and although together with other members of his family he will have over 50% of the shares (101 out of 200), nevertheless they do not own 51% of the shares. No retirement relief is available.

To be a full-time working director the transferor must devote 'substantially the whole of his time to the service of the company in a managerial or technical capacity' (CGTA 1979 s 124(8)). If the transferor divides his time between associated companies of which he is a director he will not get any relief unless they are in a group (ESC D9).

To obtain any relief the shares must have been owned for at least one year prior to the disposal and all the other criteria satisfied for the same length of time up to the date of the disposal. However, there is no requirement that the actual shares disposed of should have been held for a minimum period, provided that the necessary shareholding has been owned throughout.

EXAMPLE 15

A is a shareholder and working director in A Ltd. He is aged 62 and has owned 25% of the shares in A Ltd for 8 years. Two years ago he acquired a further 10% of the shares. He now sells all the shares for £90,000; he has allowable expenses (ie the cost of the shares) of £10,000. A's gain is £80,000 (£90,000 − £10,000) and he is entitled to retirement relief of £32,000 (£40,000 × 8/10). A's chargeable gain is £80,000 − £32,000 = £48,000.

Relief is only given against so much of the gain as is related to the chargeable business assets of the company. Such assets will include land, goodwill and plant and machinery which qualifies for capital allowances (see Chapter 7). Cash, debts and stock are not chargeable assets, whilst shares held in another company, although chargeable, are investment not business assets. In order to calculate the gain that is eligible for retirement relief, first calculate the total gain on the shares, and then multiply by the fraction of chargeable business assets (CBA) divided by total chargeable assets (TCA):

ie total gain on shares $\times \dfrac{\text{CBA}}{\text{TCA}}$.

EXAMPLE 16

A who qualifies for retirement relief makes a gain of £140,000 and is entitled to retirement relief of £32,000. If the chargeable business assets of the company are valued at £200,000 and chargeable investment assets at £600,000, the amount of the gain against which retirement relief can be set is:

$$£140,000 \times \frac{\text{CBA}}{\text{TCA}} = £140,000 \times \frac{£200,000}{£800,000} = £35,500.$$

Thus the balance of the gain of £108,000 (£140,000 − £32,000) is chargeable.

By concession a gain on the disposal of an asset owned by a shareholder but used by his family trading company is eligible for retirement relief if it was provided rent-free, the shareholder had been a full-time working director throughout his period of ownership and the disposal of the asset was connected with a disposal of shares eligible for relief (ESC D11).

EXAMPLE 17

A is aged 62 and acquired 60% of the shares in A Ltd at a cost of £40,000 ten years ago. He has been a full time working director of A Ltd throughout this time.

Five years ago A bought land for £100,000 which the company has used rent-free for the whole of that time. A gives the shares (now worth £100,000) and the land worth £140,000 to his son.

A is entitled to retirement relief of £40,000 which he can use against his total gain of £100,000 (£60,000 on the shares and £40,000 on the land) leaving him with a chargeable gain of £60,000 (this may be held over if the appropriate election is made).

When a company is liquidated, distributions made by the liquidator to a shareholder could result in the latter having a chargeable gain. Despite the fact that the company will not be trading at this time and will not have chargeable business assets, the Revenue give retirement relief by reference to the facts at the date of closure of business (SP 6/79). Finally, when a business is transferred to a company in exchange for shares, the two ownership periods (of the unincorporated business and of the shares) can be aggregated for the purposes of the ten year rule.

Husband and wife   Spouses each have £100,000 retirement relief available for their disposals. By concession (ESC D7) where one spouse transfers his entire business interest or shareholding to the other spouse who within ten years disposes of it, their two periods of ownership can be aggregated to enable the disponer to obtain maximum relief. This concession will not apply to a spouse who transfers part only of his interest to the other spouse in an attempt to enable them both to obtain maximum retirement relief.

Losses   Where the transferor has made a gain eligible for retirement relief, but also has unused losses, the retirement relief is given first against the gain, so as to preserve the losses.

Consultative Document (March 1984)   A government consultative document proposes to extend the relief to shares in the family holding company of a family trading group and to extend 'family trading company' to include ownership of more than 50% of the shares (cp p 236). It also considers extending the relief to trusts where the business is carried on by the life tenant; the justifications for reducing the age requirement; permitting relief where the disposal occurs because of ill health; and limiting the relief to only one occasion.

4 Postponement of CGT on gifts and undervalue sales
(CGTA 1979 s 126; FA 1980 s 79)

On a gift or sale at an undervalue, any gain can usually be held over under FA 1980 s 79 at the joint election of the donor and donee (see Chapter 17). However, s 79 does not apply to gifts to a company, so that CGTA 1979 s 126 remains important. It provides that a gain on a gift may be held over if the gift is to a company and consists of either (i) assets used in the business of the transferor, or used by a company which is his family trading company, or (ii) shares or securities in the transferor's family trading company. Such gifts are unusual and only likely to occur on an incorporation of a business where the transferor, instead of rolling over his gain into shares in the company under CGTA 1979 s 123 (below), chooses to roll it into the company (see Chapter 34). The relief applies to a disposal of assets, whether or not the business is being disposed of at the same time.

The asset need not have been owned for a minimum period of time (compare CGTA 1979 s 124), although it must have been used for business purposes throughout its period of ownership, otherwise the relief is proportionately reduced.

The relief requires a joint election of donor and donee. It differs from s 79 relief in two respects; first, any CTT that is paid on the disposal may not be added to the donee's base cost and secondly, if the donee subsequently emigrates the held-over gain does not then become chargeable.

EXAMPLE 18

H is a sole trader aged 58. On 9 March 1984 he sells his business to his family company at an undervalue. There are chargeable business assets valued at £160,000 having allowable base costs of £50,000 and for which the company pays £75,000.

	£	£
Chargeable gain (£160,000 – £50,000)		£110,000
Held-over gain:		
Unrelieved gain		110,000
Less: actual proceeds	75,000	
Less cost	50,000	
Chargeable immediately		25,000
Relief limited to undervalue of		£85,000
Company's acquisition cost		160,000
Less: held-over gain		85,000
		£75,000

Where the disposal is by a transferor over the age of 60, both retirement relief and hold-over relief under FA 1980 s 79 or CGTA 1979 s 126 may be available. In such cases the transferor should deduct his retirement relief first (to eliminate a part of the gain) and then hold over any remaining gain under s 79 or s 126 as appropriate (see *Example 5* on p 244).

5   Hold-over relief on the incorporation of a business
(CGTA 1979 s 123)

This relief also takes the form of a postponement of, rather than an exemption from, CGT. It applies when there is a disposal of an unincorporated business (whether by a sole trader, a partnership, or trustees) to a company and that disposal is wholly or partly in return for shares in that company. Any gains made on the disposal of chargeable business assets will be deducted from the value of the shares received (the gain is 'rolled into' the shares).

The business must be transferred as a going concern; a mere transfer of assets is insufficient. Further, all the assets of the business (excluding only cash) must be transferred to the company. As only a gain on business assets can be held over, it will be advisable to take investment assets out of the business before incorporation.

EXAMPLE 19

On the incorporation of his business for shares, there is a gain on business assets of £50,000. The market value of the shares is £150,000. The gain is rolled over by deducting it from the value of the shares so that the acquisition cost of the shares is £100,000 (£150,000 − £50,000).

Where only a part of the total consideration given by the company is in shares (the rest being in cash or debentures), only a corresponding part of the chargeable gain can be rolled forward and deducted from the value of the shares. That part is found by applying the formula:

$$\text{Gain rolled forward} = \text{total gain} \times \frac{\text{market value of shares}}{\text{total consideration for transfer}}$$

EXAMPLE 20

A transfers his hotel business to Strong Ltd in return for £160,000, consisting of 10,000 shares (market value £120,000) and £40,000 cash. The chargeable business assets transferred are the premises (market value £130,000) the goodwill (market value £10,000) and furniture, fixtures etc. (market value £20,000). On the premises and the goodwill A makes chargeable gains of £35,000 and £5,000 respectively.

Thus A's chargeable gain is:

$$£40,000 - \left(£40,000 \times \frac{£120,000}{£160,000}\right) = £40,000 - £30,000 = £10,000$$

and the acquisition cost of the shares is £120,000 − £30,000 = £90,000 (ie £9 per share).

Section 123 is a mandatory provision and results in the entire gain being held over so that it is not possible to deduct retirement relief first. So long as the company is the taxpayer's family trading company, relief will be given on a disposal of the shares. If not, the taxpayer should consider transferring the business, at least in part, for a cash consideration to obtain the benefits of retirement relief.

17 CGT—gifts and sales at under-value

'Mr Turner has really argued his case on broader lines than I have so far indicated, and has used language, though moderate and reasonably temperate, as to the ways of Parliament in misusing language and in effect "deeming" him into a position which on any ordinary use of the words "capital gains" was impossible to assert. He in effect says "Here is a discreditable manipulation of words. The Statute is not truthful. Words ought to mean what they say".' (Russell LJ in *Turner v Follett* (1973) 48 TC at 621).

I INTRODUCTORY

A disposal of an asset, otherwise than by way of a bargain at arm's length, is treated as a disposal at the open market value of that asset (CGTA 1979 s 29A). A donor is, therefore, deemed to receive the market value of the property that he has given away even though he has received nothing (*Turner v Follett* (1973)). A transaction between connected persons is always treated as a disposal at market value (CGTA 1979 s 62(2); for the definition of connected persons see p 199).

EXAMPLE 1

Jackson sells a valuable Ming vase to his son Pollock for £10,000 which is the price that he had paid for it ten years before. The market value of the vase at the date of the sale is £45,000. This disposal between connected persons is deemed to be made otherwise than by way of bargain at arm's length so that market value is substituted for the price actually paid and Jackson is deemed to have received £45,000. Pollock is treated as acquiring the vase for a cost price of £45,000

In addition to being treated as a disposal at market value for CGT purposes, a gift of assets will be chargeable to CTT. (The interrelation between CGT and CTT is considered further on p 244.)|When the gift has to be effected by a written instrument of transfer, stamp duty may also be chargeable.

II HOLD-OVER RELIEF ON GIFTS (FA 1980 s 79 as amended)

For disposals, otherwise than by way of bargain at arm's length, made after 5 April 1980 it is possible to avoid paying CGT by an election to hold over the chargeable gain. The result is not to exempt any gain from CGT, but to postpone the incidence of the tax.

1   The conditions for relief

Four conditions have to be satisfied if hold-over relief is to apply to the disposal.

First, there must be a disposal 'otherwise than under a bargain at arm's length' (FA 1980 s 79(1)). Thus, gifts, sales at an under-value, and all disposals between connected persons are covered. The relief may be useful in making property adjustments between divorced or separated spouses (p 508) and for transactions between partners (p 422).

Secondly, the donee must be resident or ordinarily resident in the UK (see Chapter 13). This limitation prevents CGT from being avoided by passing chargeable gains to a donee who is a non-UK resident and not subject to the tax. The effect of the subsequent emigration of a transferee who has made an election under s 79 is considered at p 246.

Thirdly, both the transferor and the transferee must make a claim for relief under this section. No time limit is specified in s 79 so that the general six year period laid down in TMA 1970 s 43 will apply. Although the transferee will 'take over' the transferor's gain in the asset, it is unlikely that this will deter him from joining in the election!

Fourthly, the disposal must be between certain persons. It applies to a disposal between individuals; by a settlor into a settlement (where the election can be made by the settlor alone); and by the trustees of a settlement (so that it is available on deemed disposals of settled property; see Chapter 18).

However, the election is not available for a gift by an individual to a company. CGT will accordingly be charged unless the asset concerned is a business asset and hold-over relief under CGTA 1979 s 126 is available (see Chapter 16).

2   Operation of the relief

The relief reduces the consideration deemed to have been paid on a disposal by the amount of the chargeable gain that would otherwise arise. Hence, the market value of the asset is reduced by the 'held-over gain'.

As the transferee acquires the asset at a reduced base cost, when he later disposes of it, CGT may be charged on both the gain made during his period of ownership and on the held-over gain.

EXAMPLE 2

Smiley gives Karla an antique snuff box worth £35,000. Smiley's allowable expenditure for CGT purposes is £10,000. They make a joint election under s 79 so that the disposal consideration deemed to have been received by Smiley is reduced by the held-over gain, ie £35,000 − £25,000 = £10,000. Hence, Smiley is treated as disposing of the box for £10,000 and, as his expenses are £10,000, he has made neither gain nor loss. Karla is treated as acquiring the box for the same consideration (£10,000).

Within 12 months of the gift Karla sells the snuff box at an auction for £41,000 incurring deductible expenses of £2,000. Karla will be assessed to CGT on a gain calculated as follows:

	£	£
Sale proceeds		41,000
Less:		
Acquisition cost	10,000	
Disposal expenses	2,000	
		12,000
Chargeable gain		£29,000

Note: Of this gain, £4,000 is attributable to Karla's period of ownership (£29,000 − £25,000) and £25,000 represents the gain held over on the gift from Smiley.

3 Subsequent gifts and the death of the transferee

While the asset continues to be disposed of by way of gift, further s 79 elections can be made so that CGT will only become chargeable if the asset is sold by a bargain at arm's length. In the case of a family which intends to keep an heirloom in the family, the danger of a CGT assessment is largely removed.

EXAMPLE 3

The Wippet family have always owned Sir Alfred Munning's painting 'The Sleeping Heifer'. In 1982 grandpa Wippet gave it to his son, Rab, when it was worth £50,000 (grandpa's base cost was £6,000). Five years later (in 1987) Rab gave the picture to his son, Hal, when the picture had further risen in value to £85,000 (Rab's allowable deductions amounted to £9,000). Both disposals are subject to a right of election under s 79:

(1) *The 1982 gift:* grandpa and Rab must jointly elect to hold over grandpa's gain of £44,000 (£50,000 – £6,000). As a result the disposal is for £6,000 which becomes Rab's acquisition cost.

(2) *The 1987 gift:* Rab and Hal must elect for hold-over. Rab's gain of £76,000 (£85,000 – £9,000) will be held over and Hal will acquire the picture at a base cost of £9,000.

CGT is not charged on a death (see Chapter 15). The assets of the deceased are deemed to be acquired by his PRs at their market value at death (probate value). Accordingly, if the deceased had owned property on which a charge to CGT had been postponed as a result of the s 79 election, the effect of the death is to wipe out that gain.

EXAMPLE 4

In *Example 3* above the picture was given to Hal in 1987 for a consideration equal to £9,000 and with held-over gains of £76,000. If Hal were to die in 1990 when the Munning had further risen in value to £92,500 the result would be:

(1) for CTT purposes £92,500 will form part of Hal's estate on death; and

(2) for CGT purposes Hal's PRs will acquire the asset at a value of £92,500 and all the gain (some £83,500 at the time of Hal's death) will be untaxed.

4 Hold-over relief and the annual exemption

Section 79 relief is for 'the amount of any chargeable gain which . . . would accrue to the transferor'. The annual exemption is deducted from the individual's 'taxable amount' (CGTA 1979 s 5(1) which is the total chargeable gains for the year after deducting losses (CGTA 1979 s 4(1)). As the annual exemption is deducted from chargeable gains, it is not possible, therefore, to combine it with an election under s 79. Either the whole chargeable gain is held over, or it is subject to CGT with an exemption (for 1984–85) of £5,600. For gifts where the gain would not exceed the annual exemption, the s 79 election should not be made; even if the gain just exceeds the exempt limit it may be preferable to pay the small CGT charge that arises.

5 Section 79 and retirement relief

Retirement relief reduces the gains made by the taxpayer on the disposal of a business (see Chapter 16). Unlike the annual exemption, this relief operates by reducing the gross gain so that only the balance after deducting retirement relief is chargeable gain (CGTA 1979 s 124(4)). Retirement relief and s 79 relief can, therefore, be combined so that the gain is first reduced by retirement relief and any remaining chargeable gain can be held over.

EXAMPLE 5

Magnus gives his greengrocer's business to his daughter, Minima. There is a gain of £90,000 on the value of the chargeable assets that are transferred. Magnus has retirement relief of £40,000 which reduces his gain to £50,000 (£90,000 − £40,000). The balance of the chargeable gain of £50,000 can be held over if he and Minima make a joint election under s 79.

6   Sales at under-value

If the consideration paid exceeds the allowable deductions of the transferor, the excess is subject to CGT. The balance of any gain (ie the amount by which the consideration is less than the full value of the asset) may be held over under FA 1980 s 79(3).

EXAMPLE 6

Julius sells his country cottage, worth £25,000, to his brother Jason for £16,500. Julius has allowable deductions for CGT purposes of £11,000. The CGT position is:
(1) Total gain on disposal: £25,000 − £11,000 = £14,000.
(2) Excess of actual consideration over allowable deductions:
       £16,500 − £11,000 = £5,500.
(3) Gain subject to CGT ((2) above) is £5,500 so that after deducting Julius' annual exemption tax is nil.
(4) Balance of gain, £8,500, ((1) minus (2)) can be held-over under s 79.

If the partial consideration is less than the allowable deductions, it is ignored (a loss cannot be created).

If retirement relief is available, it is deducted first from any chargeable gain actually realised; any remaining relief is then deducted from the notional gain which arises as a result of treating the disposal as being at market value; any remaining gain may then be held over.

EXAMPLE 7

Moira transfers her newsagent business to her son Michael. The base costs of the chargeable business assets total £50,000; their market value is £225,000. Michael is to pay his mother £100,000. Moira is entitled to retirement relief of £50,000. The CGT position is as follows:
(1) Total gain on disposal: £225,000 − £50,000 = £175,000.
(2) Excess of actual consideration over base costs: £100,000 − £50,000 = £50,000.
(3) Deduct retirement relief from (2). The actual gain is, therefore, wiped out.
(4) Balance of gain, £125,000 ((1) minus (2)) will be held over if a s 79 election is made.

III   THE INTERRELATION OF HOLD-OVER RELIEF AND CTT

Gifts and sales at under-value will commonly lead to a CTT charge. A considerable overlap, therefore, exists between CGT and CTT necessitating certain specific provisions.

First, in calculating the fall in value of the transferor's estate for CTT purposes, any CGT for which he becomes liable is ignored. CTT is not, therefore, charged on any CGT paid. Secondly, if CGT is paid on a gift by the transferee, the amount of that CGT will reduce the value transferred for CTT (FA 1975 Sch 10 para 4). Normally, of course, CGT is paid by the transferor, but there is nothing to stop the parties from agreeing that the transferee shall discharge the burden. This reduction in the value transferred applies whoever pays the CTT.

EXAMPLE 8

Michele gives a Persian carpet valued at £50,000 to her cousin Nicole. Michele's allowable deductions for CGT purposes are £8,000. The tax position is as follows:
(1) Ignoring s 79 hold-over relief, Michele is treated as having made a capital gain of £42,000. The CGT payable after deducting her annual exemption of £5,600 will be £10,920 (30% of £36,400). This may be paid by either Michele or Nicole.
(2) CTT will be charged on the fall in value of Michele's estate. This will be:
    (a) £50,000 plus the CTT (grossing-up), if Michele pays the CTT; or
    (b) £50,000, if Nicole pays the CTT.
    If Nicole pays the CGT of £10,920, the fall in Michele's estate for CTT becomes:
    (a) £50,000 − £10,920 = £39,080 plus CTT thereon, if Michele pays the CTT; or
    (b) £39,080, if Nicole pays the CTT.
It is far more likely that Michele and Nicole will elect to hold over the capital gain of £42,000. As no CGT is then payable, there is obviously no question of claiming relief for the CGT paid against the value transferred for CTT.

Thirdly, where the gain is held over the transferee can add all or part of the CTT paid on the value of the gift to his base cost (s 79(5)). This is so whoever pays the CTT. There are two limits upon the amount of CTT that can be so used:
(1) The maximum amount is the CTT attributable to the gift. If CTT had been paid by the transferor, so that 'grossing-up' occurred, it is only the CTT charged on the value of the gift received by the donee which can be used (grossing-up is discussed in Chapter 21).
(2) The CTT that is added to the transferee's base cost cannot be used to create a CGT loss on later disposal by the transferee.

EXAMPLE 9

Francoise is given a diamond brooch worth £35,000. A chargeable gain of £15,000 is held over as a result of a s 79 election and Francoise pays CTT of £12,000. Her base cost for CGT purposes is £20,000 (£35,000 less the held-over gain of £15,000) plus the CTT of £12,000 making £32,000. If she sells the brooch for £25,000 incurring allowable expenditure of £2,000 it might appear that she had made a CGT loss since:

$$£25,000 \text{ (sale proceeds)} - £34,000(£32,000 + £2,000) = £(9,000)$$

However, the CTT can be added to the CGT base cost to reduce a gain, but not to generate a loss. Accordingly, £9,000 of the £12,000 CTT cannot be added to her base cost so that Francoise has made neither a gain nor a loss.

Finally, note that if extra CTT is payable by the transferee because the transferor dies within three years of the gift (see p 304), this sum (in so far as attributable to the original gift) may be added to the transferee's base costs (FA 1980 s 79(6)).

IV   THE INDEXATION ALLOWANCE AND THE HOLD-OVER ELECTION

So far as gifts are concerned, the general principle is that the donee will qualify for the indexation allowance (see Chapter 14) 12 months after the gift is made. Only items of allowable expenditure may obtain the benefit of an indexed rise. The CTT added to the donee's base cost (above) is not such an item (FA 1982 s 86(2)(b)) and neither is any indexation allowance which is added to the donee's acquisition costs. When considering whether or not to make the s 79 election, bear in mind that the effect is to give the donee a low acquisition cost for the asset and it is that low figure which is given the benefit of the allowance.

V   THE SUBSEQUENT EMIGRATION OF THE TRANSFEREE

The s 79 election is available only if the transferee is resident or ordinarily resident in the UK. If, after an election has been made, the transferee ceases to be so resident the gain that has been held over becomes immediately chargeable at the rate of tax then prevailing and whether or not the asset is retained (FA 1981 s 79).

EXAMPLE 10

In 1982 Imelda's father gives her a Fabergé easter egg. A gain of £8,000 is held over so that she has an acquisition cost of £10,000. In 1985 she takes up permanent residence in Spain. The held-over gain of £8,000 becomes chargeable 'immediately before' she ceases to be UK resident and will be assessed to tax at the rates in force in the tax year of emigration.

Even if the asset has increased in value to £20,000 by 1985, there is no question of charging that increase which is attributable to her period of ownership; any loss would likewise be ignored.

The CGT is payable primarily by the transferee, but if tax remains unpaid 12 months after the due date it can be recovered from the transferor (FA 1981 s 79(7)). In such an event the transferor is given a right to recover a corresponding sum from the transferee (FA 1981 s 79(9)) although, if the Revenue have not obtained payment from the transferee, the transferor is unlikely to succeed.

The emigration charge will only operate if the original disposal on which the gain was held over occurred after 5 April 1981 and the emigration occurred within six years of that disposal (FA 1981 s 79(4)). Further, the charge will not apply if the transferee has left the UK because of work connected with his office or employment and performs all the duties of that office or employment outside the UK. He must not dispose of the asset whilst outside the UK (if so the gain is charged unless the disposal is to a spouse) and must resume UK residence within three years of his initial departure otherwise the gain is charged (FA 1981 s 79(5)).

It will obviously be unnecessary to invoke this emigration charge if, before becoming non-resident, the transferee had made a disposal of the asset (FA 1981 s 79(2). That disposal will either have triggered the held-over gain or, if it was by way of gift and a s 79 election had been made, the asset pregnant with gain will now be owned by another UK resident, so that the Revenue are not threatened with a loss of tax. If that prior disposal is merely a part disposal, so triggering only a part of the held-over gain, the balance will be chargeable on emigration.

An exception to the principle that the transferor who emigrates after the disposal of the asset in the UK will not be subject to a charge, is when that prior disposal is to the emigrating transferor's spouse. If that spouse had further disposed of the asset, however, that further disposal will be treated as if it had been by the transferor so that the emigration charge will not apply (FA 1981 s 79(3)).

VI   COMMENTS AND CONCLUSIONS

The election under s 79 may be seen as a further example of the 'withdrawal' of CGT. The original wide ambit of the tax has been drastically curtailed in recent years. In 1971 it ceased to apply on death; in 1982 chargeable gains were limited to real, not just paper, profits; and the results of the hold-over election is largely to remove the tax from gifts and settlements and to limit its operation to sales at arm's length.

The technique of holding over a gain was not novel. It had been possible from 1965 to roll over the gain on disposals of business assets so long as the sale proceeds were reinvested in other assets (CGTA 1979 s 115) and, since 1969, to postpone CGT on transfers of businesses to companies in return for shares. In 1978, a relief similar to the present s 79 was introduced to hold over gains on gifts of business assets (CGTA 1979 s 126). However, the relief under s 79 is more generous than that under s 126; not only is it available irrespective of the type of asset transferred, but, in addition, any CTT paid on the same disposal can be added to the donee's base costs. Section 126 is now limited to gifts to companies, but it should be noted that it contains no provisions to charge the gain should the donee company emigrate.

Section 79 is irrelevant to gifts between husband and wife which are always on a no gain no loss basis irrespective of any actual consideration passing. Finally, note that the transferee acquires the asset at the time of the gift. There is no attempt to deem the transferor's ownership period to be that of the transferee. It, therefore, follows that s 79 may be used to avoid CGT in the following circumstances.

EXAMPLE 11

Hubert owns a country cottage in Norfolk for which he paid £5,000 in 1970. It is now worth £45,000. The main residence exemption does not apply so that there is a potentially chargeable gain of £40,000. Hubert could give the cottage to his student son Miles and they could elect under s 79. Miles could live in the cottage during the summer vacation. It would become his main residence so that when he sold it at the end of the holiday the gains could be safely harvested free of CGT!

18 CGT—settlements

    I   What is a settlement for the purposes of CGT?
    II   The creation of a settlement
    III Actual and deemed disposals by trustees
    IV Disposal of beneficial interests
    V   Resettlements
    VI Migration of settlements and beneficiaries
    VII Relief from and payment of CGT

The CGT provisions seek to tax the settled fund and not the value of the individual interests of the beneficiaries. Actual disposals by the trustees and certain deemed disposals may trigger a charge, but disposals of beneficial interests will normally be exempt. The extension of the FA 1980 s 79 hold-over election into settlements means that property can be rolled into and out of a settlement without any charge to CGT. As a result, the treatment of settlements is similar to that of a series of outright gifts.

I WHAT IS A SETTLEMENT FOR THE PURPOSES OF CGT?

1 'Settled property': the provisions of CGTA 1979 s 46

'Settlement' is not defined but 'settled property' is 'any property held in trust' (CGTA 1979 s 51) with the exception of certain trusts mentioned in CGTA 1979 s 46. In the following three instances given in s 46, although there is a trust of property, the property is not 'settled property' and is treated as belonging to the beneficiary.

First, property is not settled where 'assets are held by a person as nominee for another person, or as trustee for another person absolutely entitled as against the trustee'. The provision covers nomineeships and bare or simple trusts.

EXAMPLE 1

Tim and Tom hold 1,000 shares in DNC Ltd on trust for Bertram, aged 26, absolutely. This is a bare trust since Bertram is solely entitled to the shares and can at any time bring the trust to an end (see *Saunders v Vautier* (1841)). The shares are treated as belonging to Bertram so that a disposal of those shares by the trustees is treated as being by Bertram and any transfer from the trustees to Bertram is ignored.

Secondly, where the property is held on trust 'for any person who would be [absolutely] entitled but for being an infant or other person under a disability' it is not settled.

EXAMPLE 2

(1) Topsy and Tim hold property for Alex absolutely, aged 9. Because of his age Alex cannot demand the property from the trustees and the trust is not,

therefore, simple or bare. For CGT purposes, however, Alex is a person who would be absolutely entitled but for his infancy and he is, therefore, treated as owning the assets in the fund.

(2) Teddy and Tiger hold property on trust for Noddy, aged 9, contingent upon his attaining the age of 18. At first sight it would seem that there is no material difference between this settlement and that considered in (1) above since, in both, the beneficiary would be absolutely entitled were it not for his infancy. Noddy, however, is not entitled to claim the fund from the trustees because of the provisions of the settlement. Unlike in (1) above, Noddy's entitlement is contingent upon living to a certain age, so that, were he to ask the trustees to give him the property, they would refuse because he has not satisfied the contingency. This distinction would be more obvious if the settlement provided that the contingency to be satisfied by Noddy was the attaining of (say) 21 (see *Tomlinson v Glyns Executor and Trustee Co* (1969)). The fund in this example is, therefore, settled property for the purposes of CGT.

The third case mentioned in s 46 is where the fund is held for 'two or more persons who are or would be jointly [absolutely] entitled'. The word 'jointly' is not limited to the interests of joint tenants, but applies to concurrent ownership generally. It does not apply to interests which are successive, but only covers more than one beneficiary concurrently entitled 'in the same interest' (see *Kidson v MacDonald* (1974); *Booth v Ellard* (1980); and *IRC v Matthew's Executors* (1984)).

EXAMPLE 3

(1) Bill and Ben purchase Blackacre as tenants in common. The land is held on trust for sale pursuant to the Law of Property Act 1925 ss 34–36, but for the purposes of CGT the property is not settled and is treated as belonging to Bill and Ben equally (*Kidson v MacDonald* (1974)).

(2) Thal and Tal hold property on trust for Simon for life, remainder to Karl absolutely. Although Simon and Karl are, in common parlance, jointly entitled to claim the fund from the trustees, they are not 'jointly absolutely entitled' within the meaning of s 46. The property is settled for CGT purposes.

It is the concept of being 'absolutely entitled as against the trustee' which lies at the root of the three cases mentioned in s 46. Section 46(2) provides that:

'It is hereby declared that references in this Act to any asset held by a person as trustee for another person absolutely entitled as against the trustee are references to a case where that other person has the exclusive right, subject only to satisfying any outstanding charge, lien or other right of the trustees to resort to the asset for payment of duty, taxes, costs or other outgoings, to direct how that asset shall be dealt with'.

The various rights against the property possessed by trustees and mentioned in s 46(2) refer to personal rights of indemnity; they do not cover other beneficial interests under the settlement.

EXAMPLE 4

Jackson is entitled to an annuity of £1,000 pa payable out of a settled fund held in trust for Xerxes absolutely. The property is settled for CGT purposes (*Stephenson v Barclays Bank Trust Co Ltd* (1975)).

Section 46(2) does not offer any guidance on the question of when a beneficiary has 'the exclusive right . . . to direct how [the] asset in [the settlement] shall be dealt with'. Under general trust law beneficiaries will not be able to issue such directions unless they have the right to end the trust by demanding their share of the property (see eg *Re Brockbank* (1948)). Difficulties arise where one of a number of beneficiaries is entitled to a portion of the fund.

EXAMPLE 5

A fund is held for the three daughers of the settlor (Jane, June and Joy) contingent upon attaining 21 and, if more than one, in equal shares. Jane, the eldest is 21 and is, therefore, entitled to 1/3 of the assets. Whether she is absolutely entitled as against the trustees depends upon the type of property held by the trustees. The general principle is that she will be entitled to claim her 1/3 share, but not if the effect of distributing that slice of the fund would be to damage the interests of the other beneficiaries. When the settled assets are land or a substantial shareholding this would normally be the result since, in the case of land, the asset will often have to be sold to raise the necessary moneys, and, in the case of shares, the trustees may lose a controlling interest in the company (see *Crowe v Appleby* (1975)). It, therefore, depends upon the type of assets held on trust whether or not Jane is absolutely entitled to her share. If she is, the result is that that portion of the fund ceases to be settled (even though Jane leaves her share in the hands of the trustees). If the fund consists of land, Jane will not be absolutely entitled; hence, the settlement will continue until all three daughters either satisfy the contingency or die before 21. Only then will the fund cease to be settled since one or more persons will, at that point, become jointly absolutely entitled.

Finally, note that a person can become absolutely entitled to assets without being 'beneficially' entitled (see further p 255).

II   THE CREATION OF A SETTLEMENT

The creation of a settlement is a disposal of assets by the settlor whether the settlement is revocable or irrevocable, and whether or not the settlor or his spouse is a beneficiary (CGTA 1979 s 53). If chargeable assets are settled, a chargeable gain or allowable loss will result. As the settlor and his trustees are connected persons (CGTA 1979 s 62(3)), any loss resulting from the transfer will only be deductible from a subsequent disposal to those trustees at a gain. Since FA 1981, any gain made on the creation of the settlement may, at the election of the settlor alone, be held over.

EXAMPLE 6

Roger settles 100,000 shares in Adza Ltd at a time when they are worth £200,000. His allowable expenditure totals £50,000. He also settles his main residence. The beneficiaries are his wife Rena for life with remainder to their two children Robina and Rybina. For CGT purposes, the following rules apply:
(1) *Main residence*   This is exempt from CGT.
(2) *Shares*   These will be treated as disposed of for their market value (£200,000) and, hence, Roger will have made a gain of £150,000. From this figure, stamp duty which Roger pays may be deducted (1% of £200,000 = £2,000). Hence, the chargeable gain will be £148,000 and this may be held over at the election of Roger. If this election is made the shares will be acquired by the trustees at a base cost of £200,000 − £148,000 = £52,000.

III ACTUAL AND DEEMED DISPOSALS BY TRUSTEES

A charge to CGT may arise as a result of either actual or deemed disposals of that property by the trustees. Notice, however, that where trust property is transferred, on a change of trustees, from the old to the new trustees, there is no charge to CGT since they are treated as a single and continuing body (CGTA 1979 s 52(1)).

1 Actual disposals by trustees

When chargeable assets are sold by trustees normal principles apply in calculating the gain (or loss) and the trustees are chargeable at the usual 30% rate subject to an annual exemption of one-half of the allowance available to individuals, although, if the trust is for the disabled or for a person in receipt of an attendance allowance, the full allowance is available. If the disposal generates a loss it may be set off against gains of the same year or of future years made by the trustees. If the loss is still unrelieved at the end of the trust period, it may be transferred to the beneficiary who becomes absolutely entitled to the fund. If more than one beneficiary becomes so entitled, the loss is apportioned between them (CGTA 1979 s 54(2)). (Note that a trust loss is more favourably treated than losses made by PRs; see p 222.)

2 The exit charge: CGTA 1979 s 54(1)

a) *The general rule*

CGTA 1979 s 54(1) provides for a deemed disposal of the chargeable assets in the fund, whenever a person becomes absolutely entitled to any portion of the settled property ('exit charge'). The trust ends with respect to that portion since there will either be an appointment of assets to a beneficiary, or, if the fund is still held by the trustees, a bare trust will result (see CGTA 1979 s 46(1)). The section is a 'deeming' provision and treats the assets of the fund as being sold by the trustees for their market value at that date and immediately reacquired for the same value, thereby ensuring that any increase in value in the chargeable assets is charged (except in the two instances discussed below). The deemed reacquisition by the trustees is treated as the act of the person who is absolutely entitled to the fund as against the trustees (see CGTA 1979 s 46(1)).

EXAMPLE 7

Shares in Dovecot Ltd are held by trustees for Simone absolutely, contingent upon attaining the age of 25. She has just become 25 and the shares are worth £100,000. The trustees' base costs (including any indexation allowance) are £25,000. She is now absolutely entitled to the fund and the trustees are deemed to sell the shares (for £100,000) and to re-acquire them (for £100,000). On the sale they have realised a chargeable gain of £75,000 (£100,000 − £25,000). The shares are deemed to be Simone's property so that if she directs their sale and, say, £107,000 is raised she will have a chargeable gain of £7,000 (£107,000 − £100,000).

b) *Disposals triggered by the death of a life tenant*

The termination of a life interest in possession because of the death of the life tenant may result in a deemed disposal by the trustees under s 54(1). Although there is still a deemed disposal and re-acquisition, no CGT (or loss relief) is charged (or allowed) on any resultant gain (loss) (CGTA 1979 s 56). This corresponds to the normal CGT principle that on death there is an uplift but no charge (see Chapter 15; and for the CTT consequences Chapter 25).

EXAMPLE 8

Property consisting of shares in Zac Ltd is held on trust for Irene for life, or until remarriage and thereafter to Dominic absolutely.
(1) *If Irene dies* There will be a deemed disposal and re-acquisition of the shares by the trustees (CGTA 1979 s 54(1)), but CGT will not be charged. The property henceforth belongs to Dominic.
(2) *If Irene remarries* The life interest will cease with the same consequences as in (1), save that CGT will be chargeable.

If a life interest is in a part only of the fund, the death of the life tenant will result in there being an uplift on the appropriate portion of each asset in the fund without any CGT charge thereon (CGTA 1979 s 56(1A)).

If the death of the life tenant causes the property to result to the settlor the 'reverter to disponer' exception, which will be considered in more detail for CTT, applies (see p 349). The death of the life tenant in these circumstances does not lead to a charge to CTT and, hence, the normal uplift but no charge provisions of CGT must be modified to ensure that there is no double benefit. For CGT the death will cause a deemed disposal and reacquisition, but for such a sum as will ensure that neither gain nor loss accrues to the trustees (a no gain/no loss disposal).

EXAMPLE 9

In 1973 Sue settles property (worth £14,000) on trust for Samantha for life. In 1984 Samantha dies. There is deemed disposal and re-acquisition by the trustees under s 54(1) for £14,000 (to ensure neither gain nor loss).

c) *The hold-over election*

The second case where no charge results from a deemed disposal under s 54(1) is if an election is made by the trustees and the appropriate beneficiaries to hold over the gain (FA 1980 s 79 as amended by FA 1982 s 82). Hence, CGT need be paid neither on the creation nor on the termination of the trust and assets can be rolled into and out of a settlement without any charge; the position is comparable to a chain of absolute gifts.

EXAMPLE 10

Sarah creates a settlement in 1983 by transferring six Monet paintings to trustees on trust for her cousin Robin contingent upon his attaining 21. The pictures had cost Sarah £100,000 in 1981; they were worth £115,000 when settled and are worth £170,000 when Robin attains 21 in 1990. The CGT position (ignoring any incidental costs of disposal etc. and the indexation allowance) is:
(1) *On creation in 1983* Sarah's gain of £15,000 (£115,000 − £100,000) may be held over. The trustees will acquire the paintings at a base cost of £100,000.
(2) *When Robin becomes 21·* There will be a deemed disposal and reacquisition under s 54(1), but if the trustees and Robin jointly elect, the gain of £70,000 (£170,000 − £100,000) may be further held over.

d) *Hold-over relief and the tax-free death uplift*

Normally, a tax-free uplift occurs when the death of the life tenant gives rise to a s 54(1) disposal. This general rule is, however, subject to one limitation. If the settlor had made an election to hold over his gain when he created the settlement, that held-over gain may not be wiped out on the subsequent death of the life tenant. The held-over gain will either be chargeable at that point, or it may be further held over if trustees and beneficiaries agree (CGTA 1979 s 56A).

EXAMPLE 11

Property was settled on trust for Frank for life with remainder to Brian absolutely. The settlor elected to hold over the gain of £12,000 when he created the settlement. When Frank dies, the total gain on the deemed disposal made by the trustees is £40,000. The CGT position is:
(1) There will be a tax-free uplift on the death of Frank, but only for gains arising since the creation of the settlement. Of the total gain of £40,000, £28,000 is, therefore, free of CGT.
(2) The remaining £12,000 gain (the gain held over by the settlor) will be subject to tax on Frank's death unless an election to hold over that gain is made by the trustees and Brian.

The result of s 56A is a partial revival of the charge to CGT on death. This contrasts strikingly with the position that applies when there is a series of outright gifts. The different rule for settled property is, presumably, to be explained as an anti-avoidance measure. Assume that Bertha wishes to give her daughter Brenda an asset on which there is a large unrealised capital gain. They could both elect for hold-over relief, but that would result in Brenda taking over the gain. Alternatively, Bertha could settle the asset on an aged life tenant, who may die, and give the remainder interest to Brenda. No CGT will arise on the creation of that settlement if Bertha elects for hold-over relief and, were it not for the anti-avoidance provision, the death of the life tenant would wipe out all gains leaving Brenda with the asset valued at its then market value.

e) *Allowable expenditure on a deemed disposal*

By its very nature a deemed disposal should not lead to any expenditure. Hence, CGTA 1979 s 32(4) (which prohibits notional expenditure) seems somewhat redundant, especially in the light of *IRC v Chubb's Settlement Trustees* (1971) which permits the deduction of actual expenses incurred upon the partition of a fund (see p 202). The normal indexation allowance is available to trustees and, once the settlement ends, to the beneficiary subject, in both cases, to the twelve month ownership requirement being satisfied.

3 **The termination of a life interest on the death of the life tenant** (CGTA 1979 s 55(1))

The death of a life tenant in possession, in cases where the settlement continues thereafter (ie where CGTA 1979 s 54(1) does not operate), results in a deemed disposal and reacquisition of the assets in the fund by the trustees at their then market value (CGTA 1979 s 55(1)). CGT will not normally be imposed, and the purpose of s 55(1) is the familiar one of ensuring a tax-free uplift.

The termination of a life interest in a part of the fund, where the settlement continues thereafter, results in a proportionate uplift in the value of all the assets (but see SP D10).

A life interest is defined in s 55(4) as follows:

'(a) includes a right under the settlement to the income of, or the use or occupation of, settled property for the life of a person other than the person entitled to the right, or for lives,

(b) does not include any right which is contingent on the exercise of the discretion of the trustee or the discretion of some other person, and

(c) subject to subsection (5) below, does not include an annuity, notwithstanding that the annuity is payable out of or charged on settled property or the income of settled property.

(5) In this section the expression "life interest" shall include entitlement to an annuity created by the settlement if—

(a) some or all of the settled property is appropriated by the trustees as a fund out of which the annuity is payable, and

(b) there is no right of recourse to settled property not so appropriated, or to the income of settled property not so appropriated,

and . . . the settled property so appropriated shall, while the annuity is payable, and on the occasion of the death of the annuitant, be treated for the purposes of this section as being settled property under a separate settlement.'

EXAMPLE 12

Property is held on trust for Walter for life and thereafter for his son Vivian contingently on attaining 25. Walter dies when Vivian is 24. The CGT consequences are:

(1) *Death of Walter:*   There is a deemed disposal of the property under CGTA 1979 s 55(1); there is a tax-free uplift.

(2) *Vivian becomes 25:*   There is a further deemed disposal under s 54(1) and CGT will be charged on any increase in value of the assets since Walter's death, unless the trustees and Vivian elect for hold-over relief.

As with deemed disposals under s 54(1) on the death of a life tenant, the full tax-free uplift on death does not apply if a gain is held over on the creation of a settlement. The held-over gain will, therefore, be chargeable unless it can be further held over by a s 79 election. The election would presumably be by the trustees alone.

4   Conclusions on deemed disposals under CGTA 1979 ss 54 and 55

The changes made by FA 1982 have dramatically affected the CGT charge on settled property. The general availability of hold-over relief has the effect of equating settlements with a chain of lifetime gifts. Further, the amendments to s 55 ensure that if a life interest terminates, for a reason other than the death of the beneficiary and the settlement continues, there is no deemed disposal for CGT purposes. There is also no charge when a beneficiary merely acquires a right to the income of the fund.

EXAMPLE 13

Property is settled upon trust for Belinda for life or until remarriage, and thereafter for Roger contingent upon his attaining 25. If Belinda remarries when Roger is 10, the CGT position is:

(1) *The remarriage of Belinda:* Belinda's remarriage terminates her life interest, but there is no deemed disposal as Roger is not at that time absolutely entitled to the fund. Hence, there are no CGT consequences.

(2) *When Roger attains 18:* He will become entitled to the income from the fund as a result of Trustee Act 1925 s 31. There is no CGT consequence.

(3) *When Roger attains 25:* There is a deemed disposal under s 54(1), but any chargeable gain may be held over on the election of Roger and the trustees.

IV   DISPOSAL OF BENEFICIAL INTERESTS

There is no charge to CGT when a beneficiary disposes of his interest so long as that interest has not at any time been acquired for a consideration in money or money's worth other than another interest under that settlement (CGTA 1979 s 58(1)).

Once a beneficial interest has been purchased for money or money's worth, however, a future disposal of that interest will be chargeable to CGT.

When a life interest has been sold, the wasting asset rules (see p 208) may apply on a subsequent disposal of that interest by the purchaser.

EXAMPLE 14

Ron is the remainderman under a settlement created by his father. He sells his interest to his friend Algy for £25,000. No CGT is charged. If Algy resells the remainder interest to Ginger for £31,000, Algy has made a chargeable gain of £6,000 (£31,000 − £25,000).

The termination of the settlement may result in the property passing to a purchaser of the remainder interest. As a result, that purchaser will dispose of his interest in consideration for receiving the property in the settlement (CGTA 1979 s 58(2)). This charge does not affect the deemed disposal by the trustees (and the possible CGT charge) under s 54(1).

EXAMPLE 15

Assume, in *Example 14*, that Ginger becomes entitled to the settled fund which is worth £80,000. He has realised a chargeable gain of £49,000 (£80,000 − £31,000). In addition, the usual deemed disposal rules under s 54(1) operate.

An exchange of interests by beneficiaries under a settlement is not treated as a purchase so that a later disposal of the (new) interest will not be chargeable.

V   RESETTLEMENTS

When property is transferred from one settlement into another, different, settlement a CGT charge may arise under CGTA 1979 s 54(1) because the trustees of the second settlement (who may be the same persons as the trustees of the original settlement) will become absolutely entitled to that property as against the original trustees (see *Hoare Trustees v Gardner* (1979)). Such resettlements need not lead to a charge if the original trustees exercise the election under FA 1980 s 79 to hold over any gains on the property, but this election results in the property losing the indexation allowance for 12 months. Accordingly, it should only be made if a resettlement of the property has occurred and trustees should wait for the Revenue to establish this before electing. Exactly when a resettlement occurs is still a matter of uncertainty (see especially *Roome v Edwards* (1981) and *Bond v Pickford* (1983)). In *Roome v Edwards*, Lord Wilberforce stressed that the question should be approached 'in a practical and common sense manner' and suggested that relevant indicia included separate and defined property, separate trusts and separate trustees but he emphasised that such factors are helpful but not decisive and that the matter ultimately depends upon the particular facts of each case. Finally, he contrasted special powers of appointment which, when exercised, will usually not result in a resettlement of property, with wider powers (eg of advancement) which permit property to be wholly removed from the original settlement. The Revenue's Statement of Practice (SP 9/81), issued after *Roome v Edwards*, does not accurately reflect the judgments in that case and should be ignored.

VI   MIGRATION OF SETTLEMENTS AND BENEFICIARIES

The CGT rules that apply to non-resident trusts are dealt with in Chapter 20. If part of the fund is appointed to non-resident trustees who realise a chargeable gain and that part is still treated as comprised in the original settlement (see V above), it presumably follows that the original trustees can be made accountable for any CGT; if not, the rules dealing with overseas trusts will apply.

1   Sale of beneficial interests in non-resident trusts

FA 1981 s 88 modifies the basic exemption from CGT for disposals of beneficial interests. First, if the disposal occurs after the trust has become non-resident, the disposal will be chargeable to CGT. Secondly, if the trust becomes non-resident after the disposal (so that the exemption under CGTA 1979 s 58(1) applied to the disposal) the effect of the emigration is to trigger a charge which is payable by the emigrating trustees. (If the emigration is the result of new foreign trustees being appointed, it would seem that the resultant chargeable gain is that of the retiring UK trustees.) In a sense, therefore, the exempt gain under s 58(1) is held in suspense.

FA 1981 s 88 will not apply to the trustees if, before becoming non-resident, they dispose of all the assets which were subject to the trusts at the time when the disposal of the beneficial interest occurred. If some of those assets are retained, the chargeable gain for which they may be held liable is limited to the value of those assets (FA 1981 s 88(3)(4)).

If the trustees fail to pay tax under s 88 within 12 months of the due date, this can be charged at any time in the next 5 years on the former beneficiary who made a disposal of his interest, although he is given a right of recovery against the trustees (FA 1981 s 88(5)(6)).

EXAMPLE 16

Bloggs, the remainderman in a family trust, disposes of his interest for £50,000. Two years later the trustees become non-resident. For CGT purposes:
(1) The original sale by Bloggs is exempt (s 58(1)).
(2) Immediately before their emigration the trustees are treated as making a chargeable gain equal to that which had accrued to Bloggs.

2   The migration of the settlement

FA 1981 s 81 ensures that, if a settlement becomes non-resident and then realises chargeable gains and capital payments had been made in a year when it was resident, any capital payment, so long as it was paid in anticipation of the subsequent disposal of assets, will be brought into charge under FA 1981 s 80 (see Chapter 20).

3 Hold-over relief and migration

If a gain was held over on the making of a settlement, that gain will be triggered when the trustees become non-resident (either by ceasing to be resident or on the appointment of overseas trustees). As with the deferred s 58 charge discussed above, the chargeable gain is deemed to accrue immediately before the trustees cease to be resident, so that the old (UK) trustees will be liable (FA 1981 s 79). This triggering of the charge is obviously unnecessary if chargeable disposals have occurred after the creation of the settlement (FA 1981 s 79(2)).

If the trustees do not pay the tax within 12 months of the due date, at any time within the next 5 years the settlor may be charged with that tax at the rate prevailing on the date of migration. He then has a right of recovery against the trustees. If the hold-over election is claimed, the settlor should, therefore, be alive to the danger of foreign resident trustees being appointed at any time in the next 5 years. Perhaps he should reserve control over the appointment of trustees during that period.

Similar rules operate when a beneficiary emigrates after a gain arising on a deemed disposal under s 54(1) has been held over. The beneficiary becomes liable to CGT on the held-over gain immediately before ceasing to be resident. If he fails to pay the CGT, the trustees are accountable. Trustees are, therefore, at risk in making a s 79 election; their risk continues for five years. Some kind of indemnity or a retention of property may be a desirable safeguard for them.

Where a gain is subsequently triggered, the amount of gain is charged at the rate of CGT prevailing at the date of the triggering event.

VII RELIEFS FROM AND PAYMENT OF CGT

1 Payment

CGT attributable to both actual and deemed disposals of settled property is assessed on the trustees. If the tax is not paid within six months of the due date for payment, it may be recovered from a beneficiary who has become absolutely entitled to the asset (or proceeds of sale therefrom) in respect of which the tax is chargeable. The beneficiary may be assessed in the trustees' name for a period of two years after the date when the tax became payable (CGTA 1979 s 52(4)).

2 Exemptions and reliefs

Exemptions and reliefs from CGT have been discussed in Chapter 16, but note the following matters in the context of settled property:

Main residence exemption   May be available in the case of a house settled on both discretionary and on interest in possession trusts (see *Sansom v Peay* (1976)).

The annual exemption   Trustees are generally allowed half of the exemption appropriate to an individual (for 1984–85, half of £5,600 = £2,800).

Death exemption   The tax-free uplift will be available for trusts with a life interest, but not for discretionary trusts.

Retirement relief   Retirement relief is not available to trusts.

Hold-over relief on gifts   Is generally available on creation and termination of the trust.

Roll-over (reinvestment) relief   Only available if the trustees are carrying on an unincorporated business.

19 CGT—companies and shareholders

I   CGT problems involving companies
II   Capital distributions paid to shareholders
III   The disposal of shares
IV   Value shifting

I   CGT PROBLEMS INVOLVING COMPANIES

1   CGT and corporation tax

Companies and unincorporated associations are not subject to CGT; chargeable gains are assessed to corporation tax. Broadly, the principles involved in computing the chargeable gain (or allowable loss) are the same as for individuals and the effective rate of corporation tax charged on the gain is 30% (see Chapter 28).

Disposals within a group of companies (as defined) will generally be free of corporation tax. Any charge is held over until either the asset is sold outside the group or until the company which owns the asset leaves the group; see p 407.

2   Company takeovers and demergers

If the takeover is by means of an issue of shares by the purchasing company, CGT on the gain made by the disposing shareholder may generally be postponed until the consideration shares are sold. Where the assets of the target company are acquired for a cash consideration, a chargeable gain will result for the target company unless it obtains roll-over relief under CGTA 1979 ss 115–121 (see p 233). From the point of view of the target's shareholders, failure to obtain this relief would not only lead to a corporation tax charge on the gains raised by the sale of the assets, it would also leave them the problem of what to do with a 'cash shell' company (see further Chapter 34).

FA 1980 s 117 and Sch 18 contain provisions aimed at facilitating arrangements whereby trading activities of a single company or group are split up in order to be carried on either by two or more companies or by separate groups of companies ('demergers'; see p 487).

3   Incorporation of an existing business

CGTA 1979 s 123 affords relief in cases where a business is transferred to a company as a going concern in return for the issue of shares in the company (see p 240).

II   CAPITAL DISTRIBUTIONS PAID TO SHAREHOLDERS

A capital distribution (whether in cash or assets) is treated as a disposal or part disposal of the shares in respect of which the distribution is received (CGTA 1979 s 72(1)). A capital distribution is restrictively defined to exclude any distribution which is subject to income tax in the hands of the recipient (CGTA 1979 s 72(5)(b)). As the definition of a distribution for the purposes of Schedule F is extremely wide (see p 392) the CGT charge is confined to repayments of share capital and to distributions in the course of winding up.

EXAMPLE 1

(1) Prunella buys shares in Zaba Ltd for £40,000. Some years later the company repays to her £12,000 on a reduction of share capital. The value of Prunella's shares immediately after that reduction is £84,000.

The company has made a capital distribution for CGT purposes and Prunella has disposed of an interest in her shares in return for that payment. The part disposal rules must, therefore, be applied as follows:

(i) consideration for part disposal: £12,000

(ii) allocation of base cost of shares:

$$£40,000 \times \frac{A}{A+B} = £40,000 \times \frac{£12,000}{£12,000 + £84,000} = £5,000$$

(iii) gain on part disposal: £12,000 − £5,000 = £7,000.

(2) Stanley buys shares in Monley Ltd for £60,000. The company is wound up and Stanley is paid £75,000 in the liquidation. Stanley has disposed of his shares in return for the payment by the liquidator and, therefore, has a chargeable gain of £15,000 (£75,000 − £60,000).

If the company had been insolvent so that the shareholders received nothing Stanley should claim loss relief because his shares would have become of negligible value (see CGTA 1979 s 22(2); *Williams v Bullivant* (1983); and p 216.) He has an allowable loss of £60,000.

These rules are also applied when a shareholder disposes of a right to acquire further shares in the company (CGTA 1979 s 73). The consideration received on the disposal is treated as if it were a capital distribution received from the company in respect of the shares held.

Under s 72(2) if the inspector is satisfied that the amount distributed is relatively small, the part disposal rules are not applied but the capital distribution is deducted from the allowable expenditure on the shares. The result is to increase a subsequent gain on the sale of the shares (in effect the provision operates as a postponement of CGT). On that later disposal the indexation allowance will presumably be calculated on the reduced allowable expenditure. For these purposes, a capital distribution is treated as small if it amounts to no more than 5% of the value of the shares in respect of which it is made (see CGT 8 para 125). In practice, the Revenue will allow the taxpayer to be assessed on a part disposal (even when the distribution is small) if he so desires.

On a liquidation there will often be a number of payments made prior to the final winding-up and each is a part disposal of shares (subject to the relief for small distributions) so that the shares will need to be valued each time a distribution is made (see SP D3).

EXAMPLE 2

Mark purchased 5,000 shares in Rothko Ltd for £5,000. The company has now made a 1:5 rights issue at £1.25 per share. Mark is, therefore, entitled to a further 1,000 shares but, having no spare money, sells his rights to David for £250. At that time his 5,000 shares were worth £7,500. As the capital distribution (£250) is less than 5% of £7,500 the part disposal rules will not apply. Therefore, £250 will be deducted from Mark's £5,000 base cost (NB Mark may prefer the part disposal rules to apply since (i) any gain resulting may be covered by his annual exemption; and (ii) expenditure of £5,000 (rather than £4,750), will then be index-linked for the purpose of the indexation allowance).

III THE DISPOSAL OF SHARES

1 Background to FA 1982

A disposal of shares is a chargeable event. Before FA 1982, the CGT rules were relatively straightforward and involved treating identical shares as a single asset. This 'pooling' system involved a cumulative total of shares with sales being treated as part disposals from the pool and not as a disposal of a particular parcel of shares.

EXAMPLE 3 (Pre FA 1982 pooling)

Low acquires ordinary shares in XYZ Ltd as follows:

Date	Shares	Cost (£)
1966	100	100
1970	60	250
1976	500	400
1978 (1:1 bonus)	660	—
1980 (1:10 rights)	132	132
Total	1452	£882

In 1980 Low was treated as owing a single asset (1,452 shares) which cost him £882. In 1981 he sold 726 shares for £726, a part disposal of one half of the holding. His chargeable gain was £726 − £441 (one half of the total cost of the asset) = £285.

Special rules applied where all or part of a shareholding was acquired before 6 April 1965 (see further p 204).

Shares of the same class acquired on or after 6 April 1982 are not pooled. Instead, each acquisition is treated as the acquisition of a separate asset (FA 1982 s 88(1)). A disposal of shares can then be matched with a particular acquisition and this is done in accordance with detailed identification rules which apply even where the shares are distinguishable from each other by, for instance, being individually numbered. Shares are therefore treated as a 'fungible' asset.

The new identification rules were introduced because of the indexation allowance which makes it necessary to know whether the shares disposed of have been acquired within 12 months (so that no allowance is available) or, in other cases, to calculate the indexation allowance by reference to the original expenditure. The rules also seek to prohibit avoidance and saving schemes and as a result have seriously damaged bed and breakfasting arrangements (see further p 263). For companies the rules are operative from 1 April 1982.

2 Shares acquired on or after 6 April 1982

a) *The identification rules*

When a disposal of shares acquired on or after 6 April 1982 occurs there are two basic rules of identification:

Rule 1   The shares which are disposed of are identified, first, with shares acquired within the previous 12 months and, within that period, with shares acquired earlier rather than later (**FIFO**).

Rule 2   Once acquisitions within the 12 month period have been exhausted, the disposal is identified with shares acquired outside the 12 month period but with those acquired later rather than earlier (**LIFO**).

These two rules may be illustrated diagrammatically:

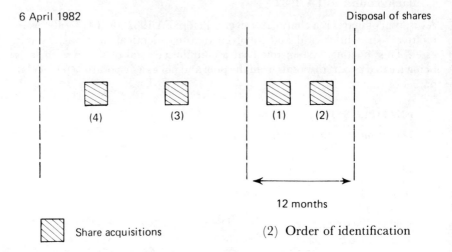

6 April 1982   Disposal of shares

(4)   (3)   (1)   (2)

12 months

◨ Share acquisitions   (2) Order of identification

EXAMPLE 4

Ian buys ordinary shares in Processor Ltd as follows:

	Shares	Cost (£)
in May 1982	1,000	1,000
in June 1984	2,000	3,000
in February 1986	1,000	2,000
in March 1986	2,000	2,400

He sells 1,500 shares in June 1986 for £3,750 and a further 2,000 shares in July 1986 for £5,000. The identification rules operate as follows:

(i) *The disposal in June 1986:* Applying *Rule 1*, this is a disposal of all the shares acquired in February 1986 and of 500 of the shares acquired in March 1986. Ian's chargeable gain is: $£3,750 - (£2,000 + (\frac{1}{4} \times £2,400)) = £1,150$.

No indexation allowance is available because none of the shares have been held for the qualifying 12 month period.

(ii) *The disposal in July 1986:* Applying *Rule 1*, this is a disposal of the remaining 1,500 shares acquired in March 1986. Applying *Rule 2*, the remaining 500 shares are attributed to the purchase in June 1984. The chargeable gain is:

$$£5,000 - (£1,800 + (\frac{1}{4} \times £3,000)) = £2,450.$$

Further, the 500 shares purchased in June 1984 will have an indexation allowance from June 1985 to July 1986.

b) *Bonus and rights issues*

Further acquisitions by means of a bonus or rights issue will be regarded as part of the original holding of shares acquired (for identification purposes) on the date when that holding was acquired. For the indexation allowance, however, expenditure incurred on a rights issue only qualifies 12 months from the date when it was incurred.

EXAMPLE 5

Barney acquires ordinary shares in Flintstone Ltd as follows:

	Shares	*Cost (£)*
June 1983	100	100
June 1984	200	350
August 1984	300	— (1:1 bonus issue)
June 1985	150	150 (1:4 rights issue)

In January 1986 he disposes of 350 shares for £525.

The identification rules provide:

(i) *The bonus shares* are attributed to the shares in respect of which they were issued; ie 100 to the June 1983 purchase and 200 to the June 1984 purchase.

(ii) *The rights issue shares* are similarly attributed so that 50 are attributed to the June 1983 purchase and the remaining 100 to the June 1984 purchase.

As a result of these attributions the position is as follows:

	Shares	*Cost (£)*	
June 1983	100	100	
	100	—	(bonus)
	50	50	(rights)
June 1984	200	350	
	200	—	(bonus)
	100	100	(rights)

(iii) *The disposal of 350 shares in January 1986:* this disposal comprises 350 shares from the June 1984 acquisition (treated as 500 shares). The chargeable gain (ignoring the indexation allowance) is £525 − (350/500 × £450) = £525 − £315 = £210.

For the indexation allowance expenditure incurred on the original 200 shares is index-linked as from June 1985, but that on the 100 rights issue shares only from June 1986. Hence, of the 350 shares sold:

140 are original shares (index-linked from June 1985)

140 are bonus shares (no index-linking)

70 are rights issue shares (no index-linking).

c) *Bear transactions and bed and breakfasting*

Normally, shares will be acquired before they are sold. So far as transactions on The Stock Exchange are concerned, however, the delivery of shares which have been sold need not take place until the end of a Stock Exchange account (usually a fortnightly period). Shares may, therefore, be disposed of and later acquired within the same account. This is a 'bear transaction' since the aim is to buy at a lower price to fulfil the earlier sale bargain. FA 1982 s 88(4)(b) provides that, when shares are disposed of for transfer or delivery on a particular date (such as the settlement date after a Stock Exchange account), they must be first identified with shares which are acquired on or after the date of disposal but which will be delivered on or before the date specified for the delivery of the shares sold. Shares dealt with under bear transactions are, therefore, matched before considering any earlier shares that might be used to fulfil the bargain. Note that if shares are acquired for delivery after the date for delivery of the shares sold this rule does not apply (FA 1982 s 88(4)(a)). One consequence of the above provision is to catch what is commonly known as 'bed and breakfasting'.

EXAMPLE 6

Alberich has unused CGT losses. He owns shares which have an unrealised gain and which he wishes to retain. He sells the shares at close of business one day and repurchases them at the start of business the next. Shares have been 'parked' overnight and the gain extracted. (Notice that 'b & b' transactions might equally be used to extract an allowable loss to set against realised gains.) If the two days are in the same Stock Exchange account, the sale and repurchase are matched for identification purposes; if the two days are in different Stock Exchange accounts, the identification rules are avoided (but at greater cost).

When a gain has been extracted by 'b & b', although the higher repurchase figure will form the basis for the indexation allowance, the usual 12 month period must first elapse. Further as a scheme which is artificial and designed to obtain a tax advantage, bed and breakfasting appears to fall within the *Ramsay* principle (see Chapter 32).

d) *Institutional investors*

Pressure from institutional investors resulted in amendments to the identification rules in FA 1983 s 34 (as amended), which allow an alternative method of calculating the allowance, known as 'parallel pooling'. The amendments seek to overcome the administrative problems that the rules posed for large institutional investors who relied upon computer records. Parallel pooling is, therefore, limited to companies and does not affect the basic principles of the indexation allowance; although on a particular disposal it might produce a slightly different tax liability, the final result of a sequence of disposals will be broadly the same under either method.

e) *Anti-avoidance*

FA 1982 s 89(3) aims to prevent the no gain/no loss rules which apply to disposals between husband and wife and between companies in a group from being used to exploit the identification rules. In the absence of this provision, shares not qualifying for indexation could be disposed of first (the no gain/no loss disposal) leaving shares which did qualify to be disposed of by a chargeable disposal to a third party. The normal identification rules are, therefore, amended so that the order of disposals is reversed when, but for the no-gain/no-loss provisions, a chargeable disposal would have consisted wholly or partly of shares not qualifying for the indexation allowance.

EXAMPLE 7

Jack acquired 100 ordinary shares in Rhyme Nurseries Ltd in August 1983 and a further 250 in September 1985. He then disposes of 200 to his wife, Jill, in December 1985 and a further 150 to his son, Humpty, in January 1986.

Under the general rules, the disposal to Jill would be out of the shares acquired in September 1985 and the transfer to Humpty would be of the remaining (unindexed) shares and the shares acquired in August 1983 which would qualify for the allowance. As a result of s 89(3) the order is reversed so that the disposal to Humpty is made up of shares acquired in September 1985 for which the indexation allowance is not available.

3 Shares acquired before 6 April 1982

Shares of the same class are treated as a single asset ('pooling') and are deemed to be acquired for indexation purposes at 6 April 1981. The allowance is then calculated on the RPI increase from March 1982.

EXAMPLE 8

Jackie acquired shares in Sas Ltd as follows:

	Shares	*Cost* ($£$)
1967	100	100
1970	50	75
1972	125	200
1975	25	40
1979	100	135
	400	£550

In March 1984 she sells 100 of the shares for £250. She is treated as acquiring 400 shares in April 1981 at a cost of £550. Accordingly, she is making a part disposal in March 1984 and her gain (ignoring indexation) is:
  £250 − (100/400 × £550) = £112.50.
She will be entitled to an indexation allowance from March 1982 to March 1984 on the expenditure of £137.50 (£250 − £112.50).

This general rule may require modification if shares have been acquired in the tax year 1981–82 (ie between 6 April 1981 and 5 April 1982). If the result of acquisitions in this period is that the total cost of the shares in the holding is greater on 5 April 1982 than it was on 5 April 1981, the acquisitions in 1981–82 are not pooled but are treated as separate holdings (FA 1982 Sch 13 para 9).

EXAMPLE 9

As the diagram (overleaf) shows, on 6 April 1981 the taxpayer owned a pool of 300 shares which had cost him £600. Between 6 April 1981 and 5 April 1982 he sold 150

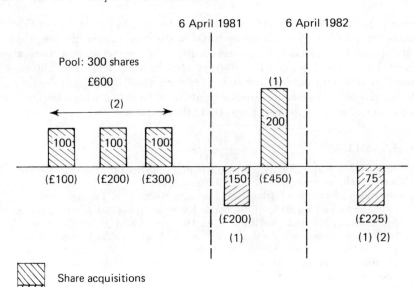

Share acquisitions
Share disposals   (1) Order of disposals

shares and acquired a further 200 shares so that on 6 April 1982 the total cost of the shares in the holding had increased (from £600 to £750). Therefore, the acquisitions in 1981–82 are not pooled but are treated as a separate holding. As a result the disposal of 75 shares after April 1982 is treated as exhausting the shares acquired in 1981–82 before reducing the share pool. Hence:

(1) The disposal in 1981–82 is matched with the acquisition in 1981–82 (so that 50 shares are left of the 1981–82 acquisition).

(2) The disposal after April 1982 is matched first with those remaining 50 shares and then is treated as coming out of the pool.

4   Shares acquired before 6 April 1965

For unquoted shares any gain is deemed to accrue evenly (the 'straight-line method') and it is only the portion of the gain since 6 April 1965 which is chargeable (see 204). The disponer may elect to have the gain computed by reference to the value of the shares on 6 April 1965. This election may only reduce a gain; it cannot increase a loss or replace a gain by a loss. Where different shares are disposed of on different dates the general rule of identification is first in, first out (CGTA 1979 Sch 5 paras 13–14).

For quoted shares and securities the general principle is that a gain is calculated by reference to their market value on 6 April 1965 (the rules for ascertaining the market value are laid down in CGTA 1979 Sch 6 paras 2(3), 3(2)). If, however, a computation based upon the original cost of the shares produces a smaller gain or loss, it is the smaller gain or loss which is taken. If one calculation produces a gain, and one a loss, there is deemed to be neither. Shares are identified on the first in, first out basis.

EXAMPLE 10

Norman bought ordinary shares in Woof PLC (a quoted company), as follows:

Date	Shares	Cost (£)
1962	100	2,000
1963	100	6,000
1964	100	3,500

On 6 April 1965 each share is worth £30. *On 24 December 1965* 250 shares are sold for £10,000 (ie £40 per share). As only some of the shares are sold, identification is on the basis of FIFO: therefore, the 1962 and 1963 shares are sold together with 50 of the 1964 shares.

(i) *The 1962 shares:*   cost price £2,000
                                   market value on 6 April 1965 £3,000
                                   sold for £4,000

If market value on 6 April 1965 is taken, there is a gain of £1,000.

(ii) *The 1963 shares:*   cost price £6,000
                                   market value on 6 April 1965 £3,000
                                   sold for £4,000

A calculation based on the market value on 6 April 1965 produces a gain; that based on the original cost price produces a loss. Therefore, there is deemed to be neither.

(iii) *50 of the 1964 shares:* cost price £1,750
                                   market value on 6 April 1965 £1,500
                                   sold for £2,000

The gain is £250 arrived at by taking the original cost price of £1,750 (a larger gain of £500 would be produced using the market value on 6 April 1965).

(iv) Norman's total gain is, therefore, £1,250.

As an alternative to the above procedure, the taxpayer may elect to be charged by reference to the market value of either all his shares or all his securities or both on 6 April 1965 (ie pooling on 6 April 1965). The original cost becomes wholly irrelevant and can neither reduce a gain; reduce a loss; nor result in neither gain nor loss (CGTA 1979 Sch 5 para 4(1)). If, in *Example 10*, Norman made such an election his gain would be
£10,000 – £7,500 (5/6 × £9,000) = £2,500.

IV VALUE SHIFTING

Complex provisions designed to prevent 'value shifting' are found in CGTA 1979 ss 25–26. Although the sections are not limited to shares, the commonest examples of value shifting involve shares.

Under CGTA 1979 s 25 three types of transaction are treated as disposals of an asset for CGT purposes, despite the absence of any consideration, so long as the person making the disposal could have obtained consideration. The disposal is deemed not to be at arm's length and the market value of the asset is the consideration actually received plus the value of the 'consideration foregone'. Instances of value shifting are:

Controlling shareholdings Section 25(2) applies when a person having control (defined in TA 1970 s 302) of a company exercises that control so that value passes out of shares (or out of rights over the company) in a company owned by him, or by a person connected with him, into other shares in the company or into other rights over the company. In *Floor v Davis* (1978) the House of Lords decided that the provision could apply where more than one person exercised collective control over the company, and that it covered inertia as well as positive acts.

EXAMPLE 11

Ron owns 9,900 ordinary £1 shares in Wronk Ltd and his son, Ray, owns 100. Each share is worth £40. At the instigation of Ron a further 10,000 shares are offered to the existing shareholders at their par value (a 1 : 1 rights issue). Ron declines to take up his quota and all the shares are subscribed by Ray. The value of Ron's shares has been substantially reduced as he now holds a minority of the issued shares. CGT will be charged under s 25(2).

Leases   Section 25(4) provides as follows:

'If, after a transaction which results in the owner of land or of any other description of property becoming the lessee of the property, there is any adjustment of the rights and liabilities under the lease, whether or not involving the grant of a new lease, which is as a whole favourable to the lessor, there shall be a disposal by the lessee of an interest in the property.'

EXAMPLE 12

Andrew conveys property to Edward by way of gift, but reserves to himself in the conveyance a long lease at a low rent. As the lease is valuable, the part disposal will give rise to a relatively small gain. Andrew later agrees to pay a rack rent so that the value of Edward's freehold is increased. When the rent is increased tax is charged on the consideration that could have been obtained for Andrew agreeing to pay that increased sum.

Extinction of rights   The extinction or abrogation, in whole or in part, of a right or restriction over an asset is treated as a disposal by the person entitled to enforce that right (CGTA 1979 s 26): eg the release of a restrictive covenant or easement over land.

In contrast to s 25, s 26 applies only if there is an actual disposal of an asset. It strikes at schemes or arrangements, whether made before or after that disposal, as a result of which 'a tax-free benefit has been or will be conferred on the person making the disposal or a person with whom he is connected; or on any other person'. When it applies, the inspector is given power to adjust, as may be just and reasonable, the amount of gain or loss shown by the disposal (s 26(4)). This widely drafted provision will not operate if the taxpayer shows that the avoidance of tax was not the main purpose, or one of the main purposes, of the arrangement or scheme. Further, it does not catch disposals between husband and wife (within CGTA 1979 s 44); disposals between PRs and legatees; or disposals between companies which are members of a group. It applies to disposals after 29 March 1977 and has not yet been subjected to judicial scrutiny.

20   CGT—the foreign element

I GENERAL

An individual who is resident or ordinarily resident in the UK in any year of assessment is taxed on his worldwide chargeable gains made during that year (CGTA 1979 s 2(1)). There are two qualifications to this general proposition. First, where the gain is on overseas assets and cannot be remitted to the UK because of local legal restrictions, executive action by the foreign government or the unavailability of the local currency, CGT will only be charged when those difficulties cease. Secondly, an individual who is resident, but not domiciled, in the UK is liable only to CGT on such gains on overseas assets as are remitted to the UK. For the location of assets, see p 372 and note that, as from 6 April 1983, a non-sterling bank account belonging to a non-UK domiciliary is located overseas (FA 1984 s 69). A person who is not resident in the UK is generally not liable to CGT on gains wherever made. The special rules that apply in the case of overseas corporations are considered on p 270.

Residence and ordinary residence bear the same meaning as for income tax (see Chapter 13). Notice, however, that for CGT a trust is not resident if a majority of the trustees are non-resident and the trust is administered outside the UK (contrast the position for income tax).

Gains may be taxed both in the UK and in a foreign country. Where the UK has a double taxation treaty with the relevant country, the matter is dealt with under the terms of the treaty. Otherwise, a person may claim unilateral relief from double taxation usually by receiving a tax credit against CGT for the foreign tax paid.

II REMITTANCE OF GAINS BY A NON-UK DOMICILIARY

An individual who is resident or ordinarily resident, but not domiciled, in the UK is chargeable to CGT only on the remitted gains from overseas assets, with no relief for any overseas losses. The definition of remittance is extremely wide and catches a sum resulting from the gains, which is paid, used or enjoyed in the UK or brought or sent to the UK in any form (CGTA 1979 s 14(2)) and a transfer to the UK of the proceeds of sale of assets purchased from the gain. Anti-avoidance provisions in TA 1970 s 122 designed to catch disguised remittances are extended to CGT. The section applies for example, where a loan (whether or not made in the UK so long as the moneys are remitted to the UK) is repaid out of the overseas gain.

III CGT LIABILITY OF NON-RESIDENTS

1 Individuals

A non-resident individual escapes tax even on disposals of assets situated in the UK except where he carries on a trade (but not a profession) in the UK through a branch or agency (CGTA 1979 s 12(1)). In such cases he is taxed on any gain that arises on a disposal of assets used or previously used for the trade or held or acquired for that branch or agency (eg a lease of premises).

2 Companies

A non-resident company is excluded from liability to CGT except where it trades in the UK through a branch or an agency (see Chapter 28). Thus, a non-resident investment company is never liable to CGT. However, UK domiciled individuals cannot form non-resident companies to avoid CGT on (inter alia) overseas gains. If a non-resident company would be a close company if it were resident in the UK, its chargeable gains are apportioned amongst UK resident shareholders in proportion to their entitlement to assets on a winding-up. There is no apportionment to a shareholder who is entitled to less than 5% of the assets or to a shareholder who is not domiciled in the UK. If the gains are already taxed in a foreign country with which the UK has a double taxation treaty, there is no apportionment. Otherwise the shareholder is charged on the apportioned gain with a claim for relief against double taxation (CGTA 1979 s 15).

The apportionment rule is not as great a disincentive to the formation of a non-resident company as it may appear since gains made on the disposal of most assets of a trading company that are used in the trade are not apportioned (CGTA 1979 s 15(5)). Thus, problems really arise only for the shareholder of a non-resident investment or holding company. Notice that the provisions whereby the profits of a 'controlled foreign company' including an investment company may be apportioned to its UK resident corporate members do not apply to its chargeable gains (see p 409: FA 1984 s 82(6)).

Losses made by the non-resident company cannot be used to reduce its gain before apportionment, nor can the losses as such be apportioned except to the extent that a shareholder has had a gain apportioned to him in that tax year and the apportioned loss would eliminate or reduce the gain. A shareholder can be reimbursed by the company for tax he has paid on apportioned gains without a further charge. Otherwise, he can deduct the tax paid from any gain made on a subsequent disposal of the shares.

3 Trusts

FA 1981 s 80 applies to non-resident trusts in respect of gains made from 1981–82 onwards where the trustees are not resident or ordinarily resident in the UK during the tax year, but the settlor is domiciled and resident in the UK at some time during the tax year or when the settlement was made. Hence, if the settlor was UK domiciled and resident at the date of its creation the apportionment rules of s 80 *always* apply, but if a settlement was originally created by a non-domiciled settlor, who subsequently becomes a UK domiciliary, it will be caught by these rules only for those years when the settlor is UK resident. As from 1984–85 'settlement' and 'settlor' are defined as for income tax (see TA 1970 s 454(3)) and settlor includes the testator or intestate where the settlement arises under a will or intestacy (FA 1981 s 83(7)).

When s 80 applies, the trustees calculate trust gains and losses in the usual way (but without any annual exemption) and the net gains are apportioned amongst beneficiaries who have received capital payments in that year. If a beneficiary is not domiciled in the UK during that year, he is not charged on his portion of the gain so that although the gains are apportioned in accordance with capital payments made to *all* beneficiaries, it is only the gains apportioned to UK beneficiaries which are subject to charge. Unused losses of the trust cannot be apportioned but are carried forward by the trust.

a) *Method of apportionment*

The net trust gains are apportioned to the beneficiaries rateably up to the amount of any capital payment made to them in that tax year. Insofar as gains cannot be apportioned in one year (because of insufficient capital payments) they are carried forward and added to the gains of the next and following years. Insofar as capital payments of previous years were not taken into account in apportioning gains (for example, because there were no gains in that year), they are carried forward and added to capital payments of a year when gains were made. A beneficiary to whom a trust gain is apportioned can set against it any allowable losses and his annual exemption.

A 'capital payment' is any payment received by a beneficiary otherwise than as income and the payment may be direct or indirect. Where trustees discharge an obligation of a beneficiary that will be a capital payment.

EXAMPLE 1

A non-resident discretionary settlement has four beneficiaries, two of whom (A and B) are UK domiciled. Over 3 years the fund has no income and makes the following net gains and capital payments. No capital payments have been made to the non-UK domiciled beneficiaries.

	£	A £	B £
Year 1			
Capital payments		10,000	5,000
Net gains £6,000 apportioned		4,000	2,000
Capital payments c/f		6,000	3,000
Year 2			
Capital payments		3,000	6,000
Including payments b/f		9,000	9,000
Trust gains	20,000		
Amount apportioned	18,000	9,000	9,000
Gains c/f	£2,000	—	—
Year 3			
Capital payments		15,000	5,000
Trust gains	10,000		
Gains b/f	2,000		
Amount apportioned	£12,000	9,000	3,000
Capital payments c/f		£6,000	£2,000

Where a beneficiary becomes absolutely entitled to an asset of the settlement he is treated as receiving a capital payment equivalent to the value of the asset so that the amount of trust gains apportioned to him is not limited to the gain (if any) shown by that asset. However, the beneficiary will receive the asset at its market value under CGTA 1979 s 54(1).

b) *Relationship with income tax*

What appears to be a capital payment by trustees may be treated as income in the hands of the beneficiary under the anti-avoidance provisions of TA 1970 s 478 or FA 1981 s 45 (see Chapter 13). Such payments are charged to income tax up to the trust income for that year; income from previous years is included to the extent that such income has not already been charged to a beneficiary. Any excess is treated as a capital payment for the purpose of the apportionment of trust gains.

EXAMPLE 2

The same settlement as in *Example 1*, except that the following payments made to A and B over three years are first treated as income under TA 1970 s 478 or FA 1981 s 45.

	£	A £	B £
Year 1			
Trust payments		20,000	10,000
Trust income	£12,000		
Charged to income tax on A and B		8,000	4,000
		12,000	6,000
Trust gains	£15,000		
Apportioned for CGT		10,000	5,000
Payments c/f		£2,000	£1,000
Year 2			
Payments b/f		2,000	1,000
Payments made		10,000	11,000
		12,000	12,000
Trust income	30,000		
Charged to income tax on A and B	24,000	12,000	12,000
Income c/f	£6,000	—	—
Trust gains c/f	£12,000		
Year 3			
Trust payments		10,000	10,000
Trust income	8,000		
Trust income b/f from year 2	6,000		
Charged to income tax on A and B	£14,000	7,000	7,000
		3,000	3,000
Trust gains	4,000		
Trust gains b/f from year 2	12,000		
	16,000		
Apportioned for CGT	6,000	3,000	3,000
Trust gains c/f	£10,000		

c) *Changes in residence*

Capital payments made to beneficiaries prior to the trustees becoming non-resident and in anticipation of a subsequent disposal, may be apportioned when that disposal occurs (FA 1981 s 81). Where trustees become UK resident and are carrying forward unapportioned gains (because of a lack of capital payments), tax is charged when the beneficiaries receive capital payments.

d) *Leedale v Lewis (1982) and FA 1965 s 42* (CGTA 1979 s 17)

The rules considered above apply to gains made by non-resident trusts from 1981–82 onwards. From 6 April 1965 to 5 April 1981 FA 1965 s 42 (later CGTA 1979 s 17) provided that the gains were to be apportioned amongst the beneficiaries on a just and reasonable basis and taxed as if the beneficiaries had made the gains. The House of Lords in *Leedale v Lewis* (1982) considered the position of beneficiaries who had received nothing from a discretionary trust. They were originally assessed to CGT by reference to their ultimate fixed interests, but it was held that CGT could also be assessed by reference to their discretionary interests. This decision is obviously significant for trusts where the discretionary and fixed interests are in different hands (see eg *Bayley v Garrod* (1983)). Net gains may be apportioned after deduction of losses realised by the trustees (see *Ritchie v McKay* (1984)).

As a result of the widespread criticism of the *Leedale v Lewis* decision (see eg (1983) LS Gaz 461), FA 1984 s 70 and Sch 14 modified the 1965 provisions so that where tax has not already been paid on pre 1981 gains a beneficiary, who has not benefited from the trust, may claim that any payment of CGT be postponed until he does benefit.

Section 4 Capital transfer tax

Chapters

21   CTT—lifetime transfers

'Taxation, as Colbert remarked more than 300 years ago, is like plucking a live goose: the art of it is to get the most feathers with the least hissing. Capital Transfer Tax yielded fewer feathers than Estate Duty, but the hissing was so formidable that the Chancellor had to make substantial concessions.' (Dymond *Capital Transfer Tax*).

I   INTRODUCTION TO CTT

1   Background

Most countries impose some kind of wealth tax, usually in the form of a death duty either levied on property inherited or on the value of a deceased's estate. Estate duty was first introduced in 1894 as a tax on a deceased's property whether passing under a will or on intestacy. It was preferred to an inheritance tax on the purely practical grounds that the tax was easier to calculate and collect as the deceased's estate had, in any event, to be valued on death for probate purposes. It was always criticised for being a voluntary tax in that it was easy to avoid by giving away property before death. This criticism was only countered to a limited extent by gradually extending the tax to embrace gifts made within seven years of death.

The Labour government introduced CTT in the 1974 Budget which had '. . . as its main purpose to make the estate duty not a voluntary tax, but a compulsory tax, as it was always intended to be' (Mr Denis Healey, the then Chancellor of the Exchequer).

Subsequent Conservative governments, whilst retaining the tax, have so reduced its effect in line with their pledged aim of alleviating the burden of direct taxes that if one compares the original tax as envisaged in 1974 with the present position only the skeleton remains. The original idea of a comprehensive cradle to grave gifts tax has been destroyed leaving a tax which lacks consistent principles and whose faults resemble those of the old estate duty regime.

Statistics reveal that in 1981 CTT produced barely one-third of the 1972 yield from estate duty (see Tables below). Since 1981, the bands of CTT have been widened; the top rates dramatically reduced; and the ten year limit on cumulation introduced. What is left, therefore, is an enormously complex tax which can often be avoided if professional advice is taken. Presumably the tax is more lucrative for professional advisers than it is for central government!

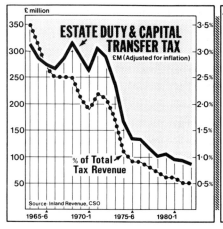

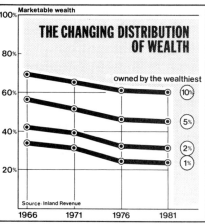

2 Nature of CTT

CTT was introduced by Finance Act 1975, heavily amended by subsequent Finance Acts and consolidated in the Capital Transfer Tax Act 1984 which becomes law on 1 January 1985. All references are to the pre-consolidation legislation: see pp xviii–xx for a destination table.

CTT aims to catch all gratuitous dispositions of wealth and, accordingly, charges:

(1) inter vivos gifts, in respect of which CTT is effective from 27 March 1974 (to prevent the tax from being avoided immediately following its announcement on 26 March 1974);

(2) property passing on death, in respect of which CTT is effective from 13 March 1975 (deaths prior thereto being subject to estate duty); and

(3) transfers relating to settled property.

There are four main principles of CTT: first, there must be a disposition of wealth which involves a reduction in the value of an individual's estate and CTT is charged on that reduction. Death is treated as a disposition of wealth whereby the individual's estate is reduced to zero so that CTT is charged on the full value of that estate. There are two different rates of CTT; one applies to lifetime transfers; the other to transfers on death and within three years before death (p 289).

Secondly, the disposition must normally involve an element of bounty or gift. Thus CTT is not usually charged on bona fide commercial transactions (nor on bad bargains!)

Thirdly, in order to calculate the rate at which CTT is levied dispositions are cumulated for ten years and the rates of CTT increase as the cumulative total of transfers increases with higher rates applying to dispositions on death; death for CTT purposes is merely the occasion of the final transfer.

Fourthly, CTT is levied on all dispositions of property worldwide by an individual who is domiciled in the UK and on all dispositions by an individual of property situated in the UK regardless of his domicile.

CGT like CTT is a tax on the movement of capital. It is charged on a gain made on the disposal of chargeable assets by an individual. A disposal includes a gift (see Chapter 17). Thus, gifts may attract both taxes: CGT on the profit deemed to have been made by the donor and CTT on the reduction in value in the donor's estate as a result of the gift. Today this double taxation rarely need occur. On death no CGT is charged whilst for lifetime gifts any CGT can be deferred until the asset is sold because of the hold-over election (FA 1980 s 79).

II   WHEN DOES THE CHARGE ARISE ON LIFETIME TRANSFERS?

The principal CTT charging provision is FA 1975 s 19(1) which states that 'CTT shall be charged on the value transferred by a chargeable transfer'. A chargeable transfer is defined in FA 1975 s 20(5) as having three elements: there must be a transfer of value; made by an individual; which is not exempt. A transfer of value is defined in FA 1975 s 20(2) as any disposition which reduces the value of the transferor's estate.

'Disposition' is not defined, but the ordinary meaning is wide and includes any transfer of property whether by sale or gift; the creation of a settlement; and the release, discharge or surrender of a debt. Further, by FA 1975 s 20(7), it includes an omission to exercise a right. The right must presumably be a legal right and the omission must satisfy three requirements:
(1) The estate of the person who fails to exercise the right must be reduced in value.
(2) Someone else's estate (or a discretionary trust) must be increased in value (ie contrary to the usual principle, there must be a positive benefit to another).
(3) The omission must be deliberate which is presumed to be the case in the absence of contrary evidence.

Examples of such omissions include failure to sue on a debt until after the limitation period has expired; failure to exercise an option either to sell or purchase property on favourable terms; and failure by a landlord to exercise his right to increase rent under a rent review clause. The omission will constitute a transfer of value at the latest possible time when it was possible to exercise the right, unless the taxpayer can show (1) that the omission was not deliberate but was a mistake of fact (eg he forgot) or of law (eg failure to realise the debt had become statute barred) or (2) that it was the result of a reasonable commercial decision involving no element of bounty (eg failure to sue a debtor who was bankrupt).

Examples of dispositions which reduce the value of the transferor's estate include:
(1) A gives his house worth £60,000 to his son B.
(2) A sells his car worth £4,000 to his daughter C for £2,000.
(3) A grants a lease of his factory to his nephew D at a peppercorn rent. The factory was worth £100,000; the reversion is worth only £60,000.
(4) A is owed £1,000 by a colleague E. A releases the debt so that his estate falls in value.

III   WHAT DISPOSITIONS ARE NOT CHARGEABLE TRANSFERS?

1   **Commercial transactions** (FA 1975 s 20(4))

A disposition is not a transfer of value and, therefore, is not chargeable if the taxpayer can show that he did not intend to confer a gratuitous benefit on another. This provision excludes from the CTT charge commercial transactions which are bad bargains.

The onus is on the taxpayer to prove that he had no gratuitous intent. Therefore, a disposition reducing the value of the transferor's estate will trigger a liability to CTT (by analogy to a crime the 'actus reus') unless the taxpayer can show that he did not have the necessary 'mens rea' for the liability to arise, ie that he had no gratuitous intent.

Notice that the transferor must not have intended to confer a gratuitous benefit on *any* person.

EXAMPLE 1

A purchases a holiday in the Bahamas in the name of C. A must show that he had no intention to confer a gratuitous benefit on C.

The burden of proving non-gratuitous intention differs according to whether the transaction is with a connected or unconnected person.

The definition of 'connected person' is the same as for CGT (FA 1975 s 51(4)) (for details see CGTA 1979 s 63 and p 199) and includes:

(1) relatives, extended for CTT to include uncle, aunt, nephew and niece;
(2) trustees, where the terms 'settlor', 'settlement' and 'trustees' have their CTT meaning (FA 1975 Sch 5 para 1; see Chapter 24);
(3) partners (for certain purposes only); and
(4) certain close companies.

In order for a disposition between two *unconnected* persons not to be chargeable, the transferor must show that he had no gratuitous intent and that the transaction was made at arm's length. In the case of a disposition to a *connected* person, in addition to proving no gratuitous intent, the taxpayer must show that the transaction was a commercial one such as strangers might make.

EXAMPLE 2

T sells his house worth £70,000 to his daughter for £60,000. T will not escape liability to CTT unless he can show that he never intended to confer a gratuitous benefit on his daughter and that the sale at an undervalue was the sort of transaction that he might have made with a stranger (eg that he needed money urgently and, therefore, sold at a reduced price).

For certain property there are special rules:

a) *Reversionary interests*

A beneficiary under a settlement who purchases for value any reversionary interest in the same settlement is charged to CTT on the price that he pays for the interest (FA 1975 s 20(4) proviso: for the rationale of this rule see p 349).

EXAMPLE 3

Property is settled on A for life, remainder to B absolutely. B has a reversionary interest. A buys B's interest for its commercial value of £50,000. He is chargeable to CTT on £50,000.

b) *Transfer of unquoted shares and debentures*

A transferor of unquoted shares and securities must show, in addition to lack of gratuitous intent, either that the sale was at a price freely negotiated at that time, or at such a price as might have been freely negotiated at that time. In practice, such shares are often not sold on an open market. Instead the company's articles will give shareholders a right of pre-emption if any shareholder wishes to sell. Provided that the right does not fix a price at which the shares must be offered to the remaining shareholders, but leaves it open to negotiation or professional valuation at the time of sale, the Revenue will usually accept that the sale is a bona fide commercial transaction satisfying the requirements of FA 1975 s 20(4).

EXAMPLE 4

The articles of two private companies make the following provisions for share transfers:
(1) *ABC Ltd:* the shares shall be offered pro rata to the other shareholders who have an option to purchase at a price either freely negotiated or, in the event of any dispute, as fixed by an expert valuer.
(2) *DEF Ltd:* the shares shall be purchased at par value by the other shareholders.
Position of shareholders in ABC Ltd: they will be able to take advantage of FA 1975 s 20(4) since the price is open to negotiation at the time of sale.
Position of shareholders in DEF Ltd: s 20(4) will not be available with the result that if the estate of a transferor falls in value (if for instance £1 shares have a market value of £1.50 at the time of transfer) CTT will be charged *even in the absence of gratuitous intent.* (Note that articles like those of DEF Ltd also cause problems for business property relief—see p 330.)

c) *Partnerships*

Partners are not connected persons for the purpose of transferring partnership assets from one to another.

EXAMPLE 5

A and B are partners sharing profits and owning assets in the ratio 50:50. They agree to alter their asset sharing ratio to 25:75. Although A's estate falls (he has transferred half of his interest in the partnership assets to B), he will escape liability to CTT under FA 1975 s 20(4) if he proves a lack of gratuitous intent. Assuming that A and B are not connected otherwise than as partners, lack of gratuitous intent will be presumed, since such transactions are part of the commercial arrangements between partners.

2 Other non-chargeable dispositions

Excluded property   No CTT is charged on excluded property (see Chapter 27). The most important categories are property outside the UK owned by someone domiciled outside the UK and reversionary interests under a trust.

Exempt transfers   Exempt transfers are not subject to charge (see Chapter 23). The most common exemptions are:
(1) transfers between spouses, whether inter vivos or on death;
(2) transfers up to £3,000 each tax year;
(3) outright gifts of up to £250 pa to any number of different persons.

Waiver of remuneration and dividends (FA 1976 ss 91, 92)   A waiver or repayment of salaries and other remuneration assessable under Schedule E by a director or employee is not a chargeable transfer provided that the Schedule E assessment has not become final; the remuneration is formally waived (eg by deed) or if paid, repaid to the employer; and the employer adjusts his profits or losses to take account of the waiver or repayment.

Similarly, a person may, in the 12 months before the right accrued (which time is identified in accordance with usual company law rules), waive a dividend on shares without liability to CTT. A general waiver of all future dividends is only effective for dividends payable for up to 12 months after the waiver and must, therefore, be renewed each year.

Mutual transfers   See below p 293.

Voidable transfers (FA 1976 s 88)   Where a transfer is voidable (eg for duress or undue influence) and is set aside, it is treated for CTT purposes as if it had never been made, provided that a claim is made by the taxpayer. As a result the CTT paid on the transfer may be reclaimed. Transfers made after the voidable transfer, but before it was avoided, must be recalculated and CTT refunded, if necessary.

IV   ON WHAT VALUE IS CTT CALCULATED?

1   General: what is the cost of the gift?

Where an individual makes a chargeable disposition which reduces the value of his estate CTT is charged on the amount by which his estate has fallen in value as a result of the transfer. For these purposes, a person's estate is the aggregate of all the property to which he is beneficially entitled (FA 1975 s 23(1)). Thus, it includes property over which he has a general power of appointment (because he could appoint the property to himself), but not property owned in a fiduciary or representative capacity eg as trustee or PR.

In theory, therefore, the transferor's estate must be valued both before and after the transfer and the difference taxed. In practice, it is normally unnecessary to do this since the transferor's estate will only fall by the value of the gift. However, the cost to the transferor of the gift may be more than the value of the property handed over.

EXAMPLE 6

A gives £50,000 to B. His estate falls in value by £50,000 *plus* the CTT that he has to pay, *ie* £50,000 must be grossed up at the appropriate rate of CTT to discover the full cost of the gift to A (see Part VI).

Were he to give B land worth £50,000 his estate falls in value by the value of the property (£50,000) and by any CGT, stamp duty and costs of transfer (such as conveyancing fees) that A pays. It also will fall by the CTT payable.

However, FA 1975 Sch 10 provides, that, for the purpose of calculating the cost of the gift, the transferor's estate is deemed to drop by the value of the property plus the CTT necessary to make such a gift, but *not* by any other tax nor by any incidental costs of transfer. Thus, in *Example 6*, A's estate drops in value by the value of the land and by the CTT that A has to pay.

When A gives property to B and B agrees to pay the CTT, the overall cost of the gift is reduced since A's estate will only fall by the value of the property transferred. B will be charged on the value of the property that he receives.

EXAMPLE 7

A gives property worth £50,000 to B. If A pays the CTT, the £50,000 is a net gift and if A is charged to CTT at 30% then that rate of tax is chargeable on the larger (gross) figure (here £71,429) which after payment of CTT at 30% leaves £50,000 in B's hands.

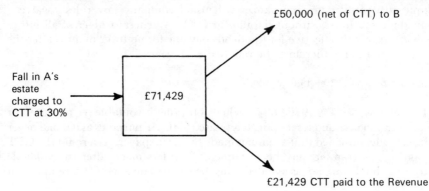

If, in this example, B had paid the CTT the result would be:

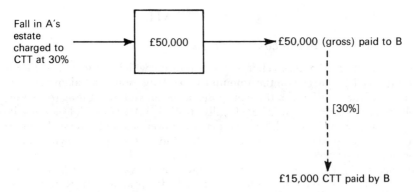

CTT is always calculated on the fall in value of the transferor's estate not on the increase in value in the transferee's estate. This can work to the taxpayer's advantage, or disadvantage.

EXAMPLE 8

Compare

(1) A gives B a single Picasso plate which is worth £20,000; B pays the CTT. In fact, B owns the remaining plates in the set (currently worth £150,000) and the acquisition of this final plate will give B's set a market value of £200,000. Although B's estate has increased in value by £50,000, he is only charged to CTT on the fall in value in A's estate (£20,000).

(2) A owns 51% of the shares in A Ltd. This controlling interest is worth £100,000. He gives 2% of the shares to B who holds no other shares. 2% of the shares are worth (say) £2 but A, having lost control, will find that his estate has fallen by far more than £2—say to £80,000. It will be the loss to A (£20,000) not the gain to B (£2) which is taxed.

2 Problems in valuing an estate

Any calculation of CTT on a transfer will require a valuation of the property transferred (see generally FA 1975 Sch 10). As a general rule it is valued at the price that it would fetch on the open market. No reduction is made for the fact that the sale of a large quantity of a particular asset might cause the price to fall.

a) *Examples of the value transferred*

Liabilities Incumbrances affecting property (to the extent that they were incurred for money or money's worth) reduce the value of the property (FA 1975 Sch 10 para 1).

> **EXAMPLE 9**
>
> A gives his house to his son B. The market value of the house is £80,000, but it is subject to a mortgage to the Halifax Building Society of £25,000. Hence, the property is valued for CTT at £55,000.

Co-ownership of land If land worth £100,000 is owned equally by A and B, it might be assumed that the value of both half shares is £50,000. In fact the shares will be worth less than £50,000 since it will be difficult to sell such an interest on the open market. Whoever purchases will have to share the property with the other co-owner and in practice a discount of 10–15% is reasonable.

Shares and securities When quoted shares and securities are transferred, their value is taken (as for CGT; see Chapter 14) as the smaller of the 'quarter up' and 'mid price' calculation.

Valuation of unquoted shares and securities is a large and complex topic beyond the scope of this book. A number of factors are taken into account, eg the company's profit record, its prospects, its assets and its liabilities. The percentage of shares which is being valued is a major factor. A majority shareholding of ordinary voting shares carries certain powers to control the affairs of the company (it will, for instance, give the owner the power to pass an ordinary resolution). A shareholding representing more than 75% confers greater powers, eg the power to pass special resolutions. Correspondingly, a shareholder who owns 50% or less of the voting power (and, even more so, a shareholding of 25% or less) has far fewer powers (he is a minority shareholder).

In valuing majority and substantial minority holdings it appears that the Revenue accept a net asset valuation as the starting point and then apply a discount (between 10–15%) in the case of minority holdings. In the case of shares and securities which are dealt in on the Unlisted Securities Market, although recent bargains through that market will be taken as a starting point, other factors may lead to a different value being finally adopted (see SP 18/80). When the shares are subject to a restriction upon their transfer they are valued on the basis of a sale on the open market with the purchaser being permitted to purchase the shares, but then being subject to the restrictions.

b) *Special rules*

FA 1975 Sch 10 contains special valuation rules designed to counter tax avoidance.

Related property (FA 1975 Sch 10 para 7) Some assets are worth more when valued together rather than separately, so that CTT advantages could result were they split between different taxpayers.

The effect of the related property provisions is to prevent this advantage by requiring such assets (eg shares, sets of articles and concurrent interests in land) to be valued as one holding. Such assets if held by spouses are valued as a proportion of the aggregate value.

EXAMPLE 10

X Ltd is a private company which has a share capital of £100 divided into 100 £1 shares. Assume that shares giving control (ie more than 50%) are worth £100 each and minority shareholdings £20 per share. If Alf has 51% of the shares the value of his holding is £5,100 (£100 per share) but, if that 51% holding were split so that Alf has 25% and Bess 26% the value of those holdings (at £20 per share) would be £500 and £520 respectively.

Suppose that Alf and Bess are married. Alf transfers 26% of the company's shares to Bess. Alf becomes a minority shareholder with shares worth £500 but pays no CTT because transfers between spouses are exempt. Bess also has a minority holding worth £520. If Alf and Bess then each transfer their respective holdings to their son Fred, they pay CTT on a value of £1,020, whereas if Alf had transferred his 51% holding to Fred directly he would have paid CTT on £5,100. Alf and Bess' holdings are valued together as a majority holding worth £5,100. When Alf transfers his 25% holding to Fred this is 25/51 of the combined holding and is valued, therefore, at £2,500 (ie 25/51 of £5,100). Once Alf has disposed of his holding, Bess's 26% holding is then valued in the normal way on a subsequent transfer ie as a minority holding worth £520 (in certain cases the associated operations rule or the '*Ramsay* principle' might be invoked; see p 285).

Inter-spouse transfers are the main instance of an exempt transfer. However, the related property provisions also catch the other exempt transfers (eg to a charity or political party) in circumstances where, without such provisions, the transferor could obtain a similar tax advantage.

EXAMPLE 11

As *Example 10*, Alf owns 51% of the shares in X Ltd. He transfers 2% to a charity paying no CTT because the transfer is exempt. He then transfers the remaining 49% to Fred. Alf is a minority shareholder and the loss to his estate is only £980 compared with £5,100 if he had transferred the entire 51% holding directly to Fred. Some time later Fred might purchase the 2% holding from the charity for its market value of £40. Unless the two transfers (ie to the charity and to Fred) are more than five years apart, the charity's holding is related to Alf's so that his 49% holding is valued at £4,900 on the transfer to Fred.

The related property rules also apply on death subject to the proviso that if the property is sold within three years after the death for a price lower than the related property valuation, the property may be revalued on death ignoring the related property rules (see Chapter 22).

Property subject to an option (FA 1975 Sch 10 para 5)   When property is transferred on the exercise of an option or other similar right created for full consideration, there should be no liability to CTT.

Where an option is granted for less than full consideration there will be a chargeable transfer at that time. A credit will be given against the value of the property transferred, when the option is exercised, for any consideration actually received and for the value that was charged to CTT on the grant of the option.

EXAMPLE 12

(1) Harold grants Daisy an option to purchase his house in three years time for its

present value of £12,000. Daisy pays £3,000 for the option. When Daisy exercises the option three years later the house is worth £25,000.

Harold has not made a transfer of value and is not liable to CTT since (as the option was granted for full consideration) the house is only worth £12,000 to him.

(2) Assume that Daisy gives no consideration for the option which is worth £3,000. CTT is, therefore, chargeable on that sum. On the exercise of the option CTT is payable on £13,000 (£25,000 – £12,000) minus the sum that was charged on the grant of the option (£3,000). Hence, the charge will be on £10,000.

Life assurance policies Life assurance policies normally involve the payment of annual premiums in return for an eventual lump sum payable either on retirement or on death. Special valuation rules (which do not apply on death (see p 302) or to mutual transfers (p 293)) are laid down by FA 1975 Sch 10 para 11 to prevent a tax saving when the benefit of such a policy is assigned.

EXAMPLE 13

A gives the benefit of a policy effected on his own life to B when its open market value is £10,000. A has paid five annual premiums of £5,000, so that the cost of providing the policy is £25,000 to date. For CTT purposes the policy is valued at the higher of its market value or the cost of providing the policy. As a result A is taxed on £25,000.

V 'ASSOCIATED OPERATIONS' (FA 1975 s 44)

The legislation contains complicated provisions which apply to any type of property, to prevent a taxpayer from reducing the value of a gift or the CTT chargeable by a series of associated operations.

'Associated operations' are defined in FA 1975 s 44 as:

'(1) ... any two or more operations of any kind, being—
(a) operations which affect the same property, or one of which affects some property and the other or others of which affect property which represents, whether directly or indirectly, that property, or income arising from that property, or any property representing accumulations of any such income; or
(b) any two operations of which one is effected with reference to the other, or with a view to enabling the other to be effected or facilitating its being effected, and any further operation having a like relation to any of those two, and so on; whether those operations are effected by the same person or different persons, and whether or not they are simultaneous; and "operation" includes an omission.

(2) The granting of a lease for full consideration in money or money's worth shall not be taken to be associated with any operation effected more than three years after the grant, and no operation effected on or after 27 March 1974 shall be taken to be associated with an operation effected before that date.

(3) Where a transfer of value is made by associated operations carried out at different times it shall be treated as made at the time of the last of them; but where any one or more of the earlier operations also constitute a transfer of value made by the same transferor, the value transferred by the earlier operations shall be treated as reducing the value transferred by all the operations taken together, except to the extent that the transfer constituted by the earlier operations but not that made by all the operations taken together is exempt under Sch 6 para 1 to this Act.'

The definition is extremely wide, and lacks authoritative judicial interpretation. Further, the Revenue have issued no general guidelines as to when they intend to invoke it. (Compare similar difficulties caused by the *Ramsay* principle which creates a judicial associated operations rule: see Chapter 32 and Appendix V for a discussion of the relationship between the two.)

Basically, the Revenue can tax as one transaction any number of separate transactions (including omissions) which, when looked at together, reduce the value of the taxpayer's estate. The transactions need not be carried out by the same person nor need they be simultaneous. Apparently the lifetime act of making a will can amount to an associated operation although the subsequent death will not be such an operation! (*Bambridge v IRC* (1955)). Intestacy would appear to be covered by the reference to an omission.

Section 44(1)(a) is concerned with the channelling of gifts, in particular between spouses (where the transfers are exempt).

In such dispositions the transferor is deemed to have made a transfer equivalent to the value of all the operations at the time when the last of them is made. If one of the operations involved a transfer of value by the same transferor, he is entitled to a credit for that value against the aggregate value of the whole operation unless the transfer was exempt because it was made to a spouse (FA 1975 s 44(3)).

EXAMPLE 14

H whose rate of CTT is 30% transfers £20,000 to his wife (W) who has made no chargeable transfers and whose CTT rate is, therefore, nil. W then passes the £20,000 to her son (S) and, as it is covered by her nil rate band, no CTT is payable. Contrast the position had H made the gift directly to S when a CTT bill would have resulted. Under FA 1975 s 44(1)(a) the Revenue can claim that the transfers (H to W and W to S) are 'associated'. H is deemed to have made a transfer of value equivalent to the value transferred by all the associated operations, ie £40,000, being £20,000 (H to W) and £20,000 (W to S). Furthermore, H receives no credit against the £40,000 for the transfer of £20,000 to W because it was an inter-spouse transfer. It is unclear whether under s 44(3) W is also chargeable on her gift of £20,000 to S. The preferable view is that she is not since the one charge on H should cover all the relevant transfers; but assume that H also gives £3,000 to his son which is exempt by his annual exemption. All three transfers (H to S, H to W and W to S) are associated at the time of the last of them (W to S). Under FA 1975 s 44(3) H is not charged on the aggregate value of all three transfers (ie £43,000) but on £40,000 only because he has a credit for any previous (associated) transfers of value (the £3,000 transfer to S) with the exception of inter-spouse transfers.

Commenting upon the associated operation provisions, Mr Joel Barnett (then Chief Secretary to the Treasury) stated that they would only be used to attack inter-spouse transfers in blatant tax avoidance cases

> 'where the transfer by a husband to a wife was made on condition that the wife should at once use the money to make gifts to others, a charge on a gift by the husband might arise under [s 44].' (Official Report, Standing Committee A; 13 February 1975 col 1596).

Thus, spouses may equalise their estates (see p 497 and channel gifts in order to utilise the poorer spouse's exemptions, eg the £3,000 annual exemption and the exemption of gifts on marriage of up to £5,000. As the charge under s 44 will not be invoked, it presumably follows that neither will the *Ramsay* principle.

EXAMPLE 15

H is wealthy, his wife, W, is poor. Both wish to use up their full CTT exemptions and to provide for their son who is getting married. It would be sensible for the following scheme to be adopted:

Stage 1 H transfers £11,000 to W which is exempt as an inter-spouse transfer. This will enable W to utilise two years annual exemption of £3,000 plus the £5,000 marriage exemption.

Stage 2 Both spouses then each give £11,000 to the son.

Apparently s 44 will not be invoked so long as the gift to W was not made on condition that she pass the property to S.

FA 1975 s 44(1)(b) enables the Revenue to put two separate transactions together.

EXAMPLE 16

(1) A owns two paintings which together are worth £60,000, but separately they are worth £20,000. A sells one picture for £20,000. This is a commercial transaction (s 20(4)) and, therefore, A pays no CTT. A then sells the second picture, also for £20,000, to the same purchaser.

As a result of the two transactions, the purchaser has paid only £40,000 but received value of £60,000 and A's estate has fallen in value by £20,000. The effect of s 44(1)(b) is that the Revenue can put the two transactions together and charge A on the loss to his estate (ie £20,000) provided there is a gratuitous intent. Where the transactions are with a connected person the presumption of gratuitous intent will be hard to rebut. In the example, if both sales were to a commercial art gallery it is likely that, despite s 44, no tax would be chargeable.

(2) A owns freehold premises worth £200,000. A gives the property to his nephew (N) in two stages. He grants a yearly tenancy of the premises to N at a full market rent thereby incurring no liability to CTT. Two years later, he gives the freehold to N which being subject to a lease is worth only £100,000. Hence, A pays CTT on £100,000 only, although he has given away property worth £200,000.

Under FA 1975 s 44(1)(b) the Revenue can tax A on the overall loss to his estate. FA 1975 s 44(2) provides an exemption where more than three years have elapsed between the grant of the lease for full consideration and the gift or sale of the reversion.

(3) A wants to give his annual exemption of £3,000 to B each year. Although he has no spare cash, he owns a house worth £30,000. Accordingly, A sells the house to B for £30,000 which is left outstanding as a loan repayable on demand. Each year A releases as much of the outstanding loan as is covered by his annual exemption. After ten years the loan is written off. The house is then worth £40,000 (the scheme is generally known as a 'sale and mortgage back'). A loan which is repayable on demand is not chargeable to CTT (see p 293 post) and the release of part of the loan each year although a transfer of value, is covered by A's annual exemption.

These may be associated operations under FA 1975 s 44(1)(b). The Revenue have intimated that they would regard the overall transaction as a transfer of value by A of the asset at its market value (£40,000) at the date when the loan is written off. A would have a credit for his previous transfers of value, ie £30,000 (s 44(3)) and would, therefore, be charged to CTT on the capital appreciation element only, ie £10,000.

For the Revenue's view in *Example 16(3)* to be upheld they would have to show that the donor retained ownership of the house throughout the period of ten years. In support, it could be argued that the transferor's estate must be valued immediately after the disposition and that in the case of a disposition effected by associated operations that means at the time of the last of those operations (see FA 1975 ss 20(2), 51(1) and 44(3)). The counter-argument is that the value transferred is the difference between the value of the house immediately before the first stage in the operation (ie £30,000) and the value of the debt after the last operation (nil) so that the loss to the transferor is £30,000 all of which is covered by the annual exemptions. In such a controversial area the practical advice must be to tread warily especially as the *Ramsay* principle may be used to attack any 'scheme' even one falling outside s 44 (see further Appendix V).

VI HOW IS CTT CALCULATED?

1 The principle of cumulation

Each individual must keep a cumulative account of all the chargeable transfers made by him because CTT is levied not at a flat rate but at progressively higher rates according to that total. It is the cumulative amount which fixes the rate of CTT for each subsequent chargeable transfer. The rates of CTT applicable to lifetime transfers are set out in *Table 1* and range from 0%–30%. The rate bands are index-linked.

Since 1981 an individual is required to cumulate over a ten year period with (as before) death constituting the final chargeable transfer (FA 1981 s 93).

> **EXAMPLE 17**
>
> (Ignoring exemptions, reliefs and assuming that current CTT rates apply throughout).
>   A makes the following chargeable transfers:
> (1) *June 1984* £100,000
>   Applying the rates of CTT in the lifetime table (*Table 1*) the £100,000 must be split up and taxed as follows:
>   The first £64,000: taxed at 0% (the nil rate band)
>   The next £21,000: taxed at 15%
>   The final £15,000: taxed at 17½%
>
> (2) *June 1990* £50,000
>   The starting point in using the lifetime table is £100,000 which was the point reached by the gift in 1984 and CTT is charged at rates applicable to transfers from £100,000 to £150,000:
>   ie first   £16,000 at 17½%
>   The next £32,000 at 20%
>   The final £ 2,000 at 22½%
>
> (3) *July 1994* £100,000
>   The 1984 gift of £100,000 drops out of the account as it was made more than ten years before. CTT is, therefore, charged at rates applicable to transfers from £50,000 to £150,000

The ten year limitation on cumulation, together with the £64,000 nil rate band and reduced rates of tax, has dramatically reduced the effect of CTT and provided an incentive for the making of lifetime gifts. A wealthy individual can plan to give away the nil rate band every ten years without paying any CTT. (Nor, of course, need he pay any CGT since it can be held over under FA 1980 s 79 (see Chapter 17)).

TABLE 1—CTT RATES FOR LIFETIME TRANSFERS ON OR AFTER 13 MARCH 1984

Gross cumulative transfers	Cumulative CTT to bottom of band	CTT rate on excess of transfers over bottom of band
£	£	
0– 64,000	—	Nil
64,000– 85,000	Nil	15%
85,000–116,000	3,150	$17\frac{1}{2}$%
116,000–148,000	8,575	20%
148,000–185,000	14,975	$22\frac{1}{2}$%
185,000–232,000	23,300	25%
232,000–285,000	35,050	$27\frac{1}{2}$%
Over 285,000	49,625	30%

2 Inter-relation of life and death rates

On death an individual is charged to CTT on the value of his estate immediately before death. The rates of tax on death are double the lifetime rates and range from 0% to 60%. The principle of cumulation applies so that CTT is levied at death rates on the value of the whole estate, starting at the point reached by the cumulative total of lifetime transfers.

TABLE 2—CTT RATES FOR DEATHS ON OR AFTER 13 MARCH 1984

Cumulative transfers	CTT to bottom of band	CTT rate on excess of cumulative transfers over bottom of band
£	£	
0– 64,000	—	Nil
64,000– 85,000	Nil	30%
85,000–116,000	6,300	35%
116,000–148,000	17,150	40%
148,000–185,000	29,950	45%
185,000–232,000	46,600	50%
232,000–285,000	70,100	55%
Over 285,000	99,250	60%

EXAMPLE 18

Take the same facts as in *Example 17* except that in August 1995 A dies leaving an estate worth £150,000. Using the death table CTT is charged at the death rates on a transfer of value from £150,000 (the point reached by the total of lifetime transfers) to £300,000:
ie £35,000 at 45%
The next £47,000 at 50%
The next £18,000 at 55%
(Note that for gifts made within three years of death—in this case the 1994 transfer—special provisions operate; see p 304).

3   Grossing-up

CTT is charged on the fall in value in the transferor's estate (FA 1975 ss 19, 20). Accordingly, tax is charged on the value of the gift *and* on the CTT on that gift, ie on the total cost of making the gift. To understand this principle, take the example of A, who has made no previous chargeable transfers and who transfers £68,000 to B. CTT payable by A can be calculated as follows:

Step 1   Deduct from the transfer any part of it that is exempt. A has an available annual exemption of £3,000: there is, therefore, a chargeable transfer of £65,000.

Step 2   Calculate the rate(s) of CTT applicable to the chargeable transfer. Using the lifetime table, the first £64,000 falls within the nil rate band and, therefore, CTT is payable only on the balance of £1,000 at 15%.

Step 3   If A pays the CTT on the gift, his estate falls in value by £65,000 *plus* the CTT payable on the £1,000, ie A is charged on the cost of the gift by treating the £65,000 as a gift *net* of tax.

Therefore, the part of the gift on which CTT is payable (here £1,000) must be 'grossed up' to reflect the amount of tax payable on the gift by using the formula:

$$\frac{100}{100 - R}$$

where R is the rate of CTT applicable to the sum in question. In A's case the calculation is:

$$£1,000 \times \frac{100}{85} = £1,176 \text{ gross.}$$

Thus, the cost of the gift to A is £65,176 of which B receives £65,000. The Revenue receive £176 in CTT. (Note that B also receives £3,000 free of CTT by virtue of A's annual exemption.)

Bearing in mind the principle of cumulation A must keep an account of his chargeable transfers: ie

Net gift	CTT	Gross gift
£	£	£
64,000	0	64,000
1,000	176	1,176
£65,000	£176	£65,176

The starting point on the lifetime table for A's next chargeable transfer is £65,176.

Grossing-up is a relatively straightforward procedure where it has to be done at only one particular rate of tax. However, it becomes more complicated where the relevant gift straddles two or more rate bands.

If, a few months later, A makes a further chargeable transfer to B of £50,000 (with no annual exemption available), the rate of CTT applicable to the gift is established by taking a starting point of £65,176 on the lifetime table. As before, if A pays the CTT his estate falls in value by £50,000 plus the CTT so that £50,000 must be grossed up at the appropriate rates. In this instance, there is more than one applicable rate. There are two methods of grossing-up. The first is mathematical (as before) but the second (and easier) method is by using a grossing-up table (*Table 3*; see opposite).

Step 1   Add the net gift of £50,000 to the cumulative total of net transfers to date, making a total of £115,000 (£65,000 + £50,000).

Step 2   Look in the left hand column of the table for the figure nearest to, but less than, the new total of net transfers to date (£115,000), ie £107,426.

Step 3   Read across that line of the table to take tax on £107,426 (viz £8,575) and apply the appropriate fraction as shown on the table
ie $\frac{1}{4} \times$ (£115,000 − £107,426)
$= \frac{1}{4} \times$ £7,574 = £1,894.

Therefore, the tax = £8,575 + £1,894 = £10,469. However, this figure includes the CTT paid on the previous transfer (viz £176) which must be deducted. CTT of £10,293 is, therefore, payable in respect of the net gift of £50,000. The gross gift is £60,293. A's total of gross chargeable transfers to date will now be £125,469.

TABLE 3—LIFETIME TRANSFERS—TRANSFEROR BEARING THE TAX

Cumulative total		Capital transfer tax payable			
£	£	£			£
0–	64,000	Nil			
64,001–	81,850	Nil + 3/17	(17.647%) for each £ over		64,000
81,851–107,425		3,150 + 7/33	(21.212%) for each £ over		81,850
107,426–133,025		8,575 + 1/4	(25%)	for each £ over	107,425
133,026–161,700		14,975 + 9/31	(29.032%) for each £ over		133,025
161,701–196,950		23,300 + 1/3	(33.333%) for each £ over		161,700
196,951–235,375		35,050 + 11/29	(37.931%) for each £ over		196,950
over 235,375		49,625 + 3/7	(42.857%) for each £ over		235,375

4   Effect of placing the tax burden on the donee

Grossing-up is necessary to establish the cost to a donor of making a gift where the donor is paying the CTT. There is no grossing-up, however, where the donee pays the CTT since the donor's estate falls only by the value of the gift. The donee, therefore, pays CTT on the gift that he receives and the tax will be calculated according to the previous chargeable transfers of the donor. As a result less CTT is paid.

EXAMPLE 19

(1) A has made no previous chargeable transfers but has used up his annual exemption. He gives £65,000 to B and B agrees to pay CTT. A has made a chargeable transfer of £65,000, on £1,000 of which CTT is payable at the rate of 15%. If B pays, A's estate falls in value by only £65,000. B is charged to CTT at A's rates. B, therefore, pays CTT at 15% on £1,000 (ie £150) so that £26

less tax is paid than if A had paid. However, B ends up with less than if A had paid the CTT receiving £64,850, instead of £65,000. A further result of B's paying the tax is that A's cumulative total of gross chargeable transfers is lower for the purposes of future chargeable transfers, ie 65,000, rather than £65,176.

Compare

(2) If B is to pay the CTT on A's gift to him and A wants B to retain a net sum of £65,000 after paying the tax, A must give B a larger sum £65,176 to enable B to pay the tax of £176. The result is that whether A or B pays the CTT, the Revenue will receive £176 tax and the total cost to A will be the same.

5   Transferring non-cash assets the cheapest way

Where the gift is of a non-cash asset such as land, the CTT is calculated as before, but the question of who pays the tax and how much has to be paid will be of critical importance since neither party may have sufficient cash to pay the CTT without selling the asset. If the donor pays the CTT, the value of the gift must be grossed up. In addition, the tax must be paid in one lump sum. If, however, the donee pays the tax, there is no grossing-up; so that the transfer attracts less CTT. Additionally, in the case of certain assets the tax can be paid by the donee in ten yearly instalments (FA 1975 Sch 4 para 13). One advantage of instalments is that, if the asset is itself income producing, the donee may have income out of which to pay, or contribute towards, the instalments. Alternatively, the donor can fund the instalments paid by the donee by gifts out of his annual exemption. The assets on which CTT may be paid by instalments are:

(1) land, whether freehold or leasehold;

(2) a controlling shareholding of either quoted or unquoted shares;

(3) a minority shareholding of unquoted shares provided the tax cannot be paid without undue hardship;

(4) a business or part of a business, eg, a share in a partnership.

However, in the case of a transfer of land ((1) above), interest on the outstanding tax is charged at 8% pa, when payment is made by instalments.

EXAMPLE 20

A wants to give B his business which is valued at £400,000. A has made no previous chargeable transfers. If A pays the tax (ignoring exemptions and reliefs) the gift (£400,000) must be grossed up so that the total cost to A is £520,178 and the CTT payable is £120,178; A must pay this in one lump sum. If B pays the tax, the £400,000 is a gross gift on which the CTT at A's rates is £87,125. Thus, there is a tax saving of £33,053. Further B can pay the tax in instalments out of income from the business.

6   Problem areas

a) *Transfers of value by instalments* (FA 1975 s 40)

Where a person buys property at a price greater than its market value, the excess paid will be a transfer of value (assuming that donative intent is present). If the price is payable by instalments, part of each is a transfer of value. That part is the proportion that the overall gift element bears to the price paid.

EXAMPLE 21

A transfers property worth £40,000 to B for £80,000 payable by B in eight equal yearly instalments of £10,000. Hence, after ten years there will be a transfer of value of £40,000. The part of each instalment that is a chargeable transfer is:

$$\text{Annual instalment} \times \frac{\text{value of gift}}{\text{price payable}} = \pounds 10,000 \times \frac{\pounds 40,000}{\pounds 80,000} = \pounds 5,000.$$

b) *Transfers made on the same day*

If a person makes more than one chargeable transfer on the same day and the order in which the transfers are made affects the overall amount of CTT payable, they are treated as made in the order which results in the least amount of CTT being payable (FA 1975 s 43(2)). This will only be relevant where the transfers taken together straddle different rate bands and the donor does not pay the tax on all the transfers. Where this is the case the overall CTT will be less if the grossed-up gift is made first.

c) *Transfers reported late* (FA 1976 s 114 (as amended))

When a transfer is reported late (for the due date for reporting transfers see p 298) after CTT has been paid on a subsequent transfer, tax must be paid on the earlier transfer and an adjustment may have to be made to the tax bill on the later transfer. The tax payable on the earlier transfer is calculated as at the date of that transfer and interest is payable on the outstanding tax as from the date that it was due. If there is more than ten years between the earlier and the later transfers, no adjustment need be made in respect of the later transfer since the ten year limit on cumulation means that the later transfer is unaffected by the earlier transfer. When there is less than ten years between the two transfers the extra tax charged on the later transfer is levied on the earlier transfer in addition to the tax already due on that transfer.

d) *Non-commercial loans* (FA 1976 ss 115, 116)

The rules are different for interest-free loans repayable after a fixed term and loans repayable on demand. If A lends B £20,000 repayable in five years time at no interest, A's estate is reduced in value because of the delay in repayment and A has made a transfer of value (assuming gratuitous intent). CTT is levied on the difference between £20,000 and the value of the present right to receive £20,000 in five years' time.

If, instead, A lent B £20,000 repayable on demand with no interest charged, A's estate does not fall in value because it includes the immediate right to £20,000. Accordingly, A has not made a transfer of value and no CTT is payable.

If a commercial rate of interest is charged on a loan, no CTT will be payable since the estate of the lender will not have fallen in value. Further, any interest may (normally) be waived without any charge to CTT by virtue of the exemption for regular payments out of income (see Chapter 23).

7 Mutual transfers

Problems arise when a gift is made by A to B (so that CTT is chargeable) and at some later stage B makes a gift back to A (a further chargeable occasion). In the absence of relieving provisions CTT would be charged on both gifts. Complex provisions in FA 1976 ss 86–87 provide for a measure of relief by enabling the gifts to be 'unscrambled'; s 86 is concerned with the donee's gift (the 'gift back') and s 87 with the original gift. For the provisions to apply both gifts must be actual transfers made during the lifetime of the relevant transferor and the gift back must occur either during the life of the original donor or within two years of his death. The gift back may be to either the donor, his spouse, or after his death to his surviving spouse so long as that spouse has not remarried.

The gift back   The donee need not return the original property, but the gift back must not exceed the amount by which the donee's estate had been increased by the donor's gift. It follows, therefore, that this will not be the value transferred on the occasion of the original gift (since grossing-up is ignored whilst, if the donee paid CTT, his estate will only have been increased by the sum remaining after that payment). Also, any change in the value of the property given is ignored. Such a gift back will not be subject to CTT so long as it is made not more than ten years after the original gift, but within two years after the donor's death.

The original gift   Tax can be recovered. A claim has to be made by the donor (or, if dead, his PRs or surviving spouse). To the extent that the original gift is cancelled, the cumulative total of the donor will be reduced thus affecting subsequent gifts (those made after the claim). How much of the original gift is cancelled (and, therefore, how much CTT is repaid) depends upon how long after the original gift the gift back occurs. If within one year there is a full cancellation and repayment; if later, for each complete 12 months the value restored is reduced by 4%. (In effect, the original gift is treated as a loan charged at 4% interest.) When the donor has made a number of gifts to the same donee, it is the later gifts which are cancelled first.

EXAMPLE 22

1979   Adolphus gives to Gustavus shares in Swede Ltd worth £20,000 (Adolphus paid CTT of £6,000).

1984   Gustavus gives Adolphus shares in Veg Ltd worth £30,000. He still has the shares in Swede Ltd which are worth £30,000.

(1) *The gift back:* it does not matter that identical property is not returned. Gustavus' gift back is exempt from CTT to the extent of £20,000 (the increase in his estate as a result of Adolphus' gift) and the remaining £10,000 is charged to CTT in the usual way. The fact that the Swede Ltd shares have increased in value since 1979 is irrelevant.

(2) *The original gift:* Adolphus cannot reclaim all the tax paid. As the gift back is exactly five years after the original gift there is a discount of 20% (5 × 4%) so that only 80% of the original gift has been restored. Only some of the £6,000 CTT paid by Adolphus can be recovered but this will be calculated as the top slice of the tax originally charged. It follows that *more* than 80% of the original tax paid may be recovered.

(3) *Change of tax rates:* if the rates of CTT have been reduced between the original gift and the gift back, any refund of CTT to the original donor will be calculated in accordance with the rates of CTT current at the date of the gift back. Hence, as the rates changed between 1979 and 1984, some recalculation will be necessary. For the purpose of reducing the cumulative total of the original donor, however, the reduction will be calculated using the old rates (those in force when the original gift was made).

VII SPECIAL RULES FOR CLOSE COMPANIES

Only transfers of value made by individuals are chargeable to CTT (FA 1975 s 20(5)). An individual could, therefore, avoid CTT by forming a close company and using that company to make a gift to the intended donee, or a controlling shareholder in a close company could transfer his ownership of the company's assets indirectly by altering the capital structure of the company or the rights attached to his shares, so as to reduce the value of his shareholding in favour of the intended donee.

EXAMPLE 23

(1) A transfers assets worth £100,000 to A Ltd in return for shares worth £100,000. A's estate does not fall in value so that there is no liability to CTT. The company then gives one of the assets (worth £50,000) to A's son B. The company and not A has made a transfer of value.

(2) A Ltd has an issued share capital of £100 all in ordinary £1 shares owned by A. The company is worth £100,000. The company resolves:
(a) To convert A's shares into non-voting preference shares carrying only the right to a repayment of nominal value on a winding-up.
(b) To issue to B a further 100 £1 ordinary shares at par value.
    The result is that the value has passed out of A's shares without any disposition by A. As a consequence CTT would not, prima facie, apply.

FA 1975 s 39 contains provisions designed to prevent an individual from using a close company to obtain a tax advantage in either of these ways. For the purposes of FA 1975 s 39, 'close company' and 'participator' have their corporation tax meaning (see Chapter 28) except that a close company includes a non-UK resident company and participator does not include a loan creditor.

1 Transfers of value by close companies (FA 1975 s 39(1))

Where a close company makes a transfer of value, it is apportioned amongst the participators in proportion to their interests in the company, so that they are treated as having made the transfer ('lifting the veil') (FA 1975 s 39(1)). Thus, in *Example 23(1)* above, A is treated as having made a transfer of value of £50,000. For s 39(1) to apply the company must have made a transfer of value, ie its assets must fall in value by virtue of a non-commercial transaction (FA 1975 s 20(4)). The value apportioned to each participator is treated as a net amount which must be grossed up at the participator's appropriate rate of CTT. Any participator whose estate has increased in value as a result of that transfer can deduct the increase from the net amount (ignoring the effect that the transfer may have had on his rights in the company).

EXAMPLE 24

A Ltd is owned as to 75% of the shares by A and 25% by B. It transfers land worth £100,000 to A. By FA 1975 s 39(1) A and B are treated as having made net transfers of value of £75,000 and £25,000 respectively. B will be charged to CTT on £25,000 grossed up at his rate of CTT. A, however, can deduct the increase in his estate (£100,000) from the net amount of the apportionment (£75,000), so that he pays no CTT. If A's shares (and B's) have diminished in value, the decrease is ignored.

Apportionment is not always as obvious as it may seem. For instance, in calculating a participator's interest in the company, the ownership of preference shares is usually disregarded. Further, where trustees are participators and the interest in the company is held in an interest-in-possession settlement (see Chapter 25) the apportioned amount is taxed as a reduction in the value of the life tenant's estate. In no-interest-in-possession trusts the apportioned amount is taxed as a payment out of the settled property by the trustees. Finally, where a close company is itself a participator in another close company any apportionment is then sub-apportioned to its own participators.

In two cases no apportionment occurs. First, if the transfer is charged to income tax or corporation tax in the donee's hands, there is no CTT liability. Secondly, where a participator is domiciled abroad, any apportionment made to him as a result of a transfer by a close company of property situated abroad is not charged to CTT.

EXAMPLE 25

(1) A Ltd (whose shares are owned 50% by A and 50% by B) pays a dividend. The dividend is not chargeable to CTT in A or B's hands because income tax is charged on that sum under Schedule F.

(2) A Ltd in (1) above provides A with free living accommodation and pays all the outgoings on the property. If A is a director or employee of A Ltd, these items are benefits in kind on which A pays income tax under Schedule E (see Chapter 5). If A is merely a shareholder in the company these payments are treated as a distribution by A Ltd and are charged to income tax in A's hands under Schedule F. However, if A was not a member of A Ltd, there would be no income tax liability, so that the participator, B, would be treated for CTT purposes as having made a chargeable transfer of value under FA 1975 s 39(1).

(3) An English company, A Ltd, in which B and C each own 50% of the shares, gives a factory in France worth £100,000 to B, who is domiciled in the UK. C is domiciled in France and, therefore, the amount apportioned to him (£50,000) is not chargeable under FA 1975 s 39.

Participators can reduce their CTT on sums apportioned by the usual lifetime exemptions with the exception of the small gifts exemption and the exemption for gifts on marriage. Insofar as the transfer by the company is to a charity or political party it is exempt. The company can also claim 50% business relief if it transfers part of its business or shares in a trading subsidiary.

The company is primarily liable for the tax. If it fails to pay, secondary liability rests concurrently with the participators and beneficiaries of the transfer. A participator's liability is limited to tax on the amount apportioned to him; for a non-participator beneficiary it is limited to the increase in value of his estate.

2   Deemed dispositions by participators (FA 1975 s 39(5))

Whenever value is drained out of shares in a close company by an alteration (including extinguishment) of the share capital or by an alteration in the rights attached to shares, this is treated as a deemed disposition by the participators and is apportioned in the usual way (FA 1975 s 39(5)). Liability for CTT under FA 1975 s 39(5) rests purely on the participators and not on the company.

EXAMPLE 26

Taking the facts of *Example 23(2)* above there is no actual transfer of value by A or A Ltd. However, under FA 1975 s 39(5) there is a deemed disposition by A equivalent to the fall in value of his shareholding. From owning all the shares and effectively all the assets he is left with a holding of 100 shares worth (probably) only their face value.

(2) A owns 60% and B 40% of the shares in A Ltd. Each share carries one vote. The articles of association of the company are altered so that A's shares continue to carry one vote, but B's shares are to carry three votes each. There is a deemed disposition by A to B equivalent to the drop in value in A's estate resulting from his loss of control of A Ltd.

VIII LIABILITY, ACCOUNTABILITY AND BURDEN

1 Liability for CTT (FA 1975 ss 25–27)

The person primarily liable for CTT on a lifetime transfer of unsettled property is the transferor, although in certain cases, his spouse may be held liable as a transferor to prevent him from divesting himself of property to that spouse so that he is then unable to meet a CTT bill (FA 1975 s 25(8)).

EXAMPLE 27

H makes a gross chargeable transfer to S of £100,000 and fails to pay CTT. He later transfers property worth £50,000 to his wife W which is exempt (inter-spouse). W can be held liable for CTT not exceeding £50,000.

If the Revenue cannot collect the tax from the transferor (or his spouse) they can then claim it, subject to specified limits, from one of the following:

(1) The transferee, ie any person whose estate has increased in value as a result of the transfer. Liability is restricted to tax (at the transferor's rates) on the value of the gross transfer after deducting any unpaid tax.

EXAMPLE 28

A makes a gross chargeable transfer to B of £40,000 on which CTT at A's rate of 30% is £12,000. A emigrates without paying the tax. The Revenue can only claim £8,400 in tax from B, ie

	£
Gross chargeable transfer by A	40,000
Less unpaid tax	12,000
Revised valued transferred	£28,000
B is liable for CTT at 30%	£8,400

(2) Any person in whom the property has become vested after the transfer. This category includes a person to whom the transferee has transferred the property; or, if the property has been settled, the trustees of the settlement and any beneficiary with an interest in possession in it; or a purchaser of the property unless he is a bona fide purchaser for money or money's worth and the property is not subject to an Inland Revenue charge. The liability of these persons is limited to tax on the *net* transfer only and liability is

further limited, in the case of trustees and beneficiaries, to the value of the settled property and, in the case of a purchaser, to the value of the property. Also included within this category is any person who meddles with property so as to constitute himself a *'trustee de son tort'* and any person who manages the property on behalf of a person under a disability.

(3) A beneficiary under a discretionary trust of the property to the extent that he receives income or any benefit from the trust. Liability is limited to the amount of his benefit after payment of any income tax.

If additional tax becomes due on a gift because of the transferor's death within three years, the transferee is primarily liable for the tax, but should he fail to pay, the Revenue can claim the tax from the persons in category (2) above.

Quite apart from those persons from whom they can claim tax, the Revenue have a charge for unpaid tax on the property transferred and on settled property where the liability arose on the making of the settlement or on a chargeable transfer of it. The charge takes effect in the same way as on death (see Chapter 22) except that for lifetime transfers it extends to personal property also. It will not bind a purchaser of land unless the charge is registered and in the case of personal property unless the purchaser has notice of the facts giving rise to the charge.

Once CTT on a chargeable transfer has been paid and accepted by the Revenue, liability for any additional tax ceases six years after the later of the date when the tax was paid or the date when it became due. However, if the Revenue can prove fraud, wilful default or neglect by a person liable for the tax (or by the settlor which results in an underpayment of tax by discretionary trustees), this six year period only starts to run once the Revenue know of the fraud, wilful default or neglect, as the case may be. When the Revenue are satisfied that tax has been or will be paid, they may, at the request of a person liable for the tax, issue a certificate discharging persons and/or property from further liability.

2 Accountability and payment

a) *Duty to account*

An account need only be delivered in respect of a chargeable transfer. Thus, the Revenue need not be notified of a transfer of excluded property or of a transfer that is wholly exempt (eg within the annual exemption or inter-spouse), with the exception of an exempt transfer of settled property which must be notified. As a general rule, the person who is primarily liable for the CTT must deliver the account. When the transfer is by a close company, nobody is under a duty to account, but in practice the company should do so in order to avoid interest on unpaid tax.

The account must be delivered within 12 months from the end of the month when the transfer was made or within three months from the date when that person first became liable to pay CTT (if later). In practice the account should be delivered earlier, since the tax is due before this date. Form C5 is used for all lifetime transfers including transfers of settled property with an interest in possession. Anyone who fails to deliver an account, make a return, or provide information when required may be subject to penalties and the Revenue have a wide general power to obtain information from 'any' person (FA 1975 Sch 4 para 5) by means of a notice. They cannot use this power to compel a solicitor or barrister to disclose privileged information concerning a client, but they can use it to obtain the name and address of a client.

b) *Payment of tax*

For all lifetime transfers of settled or unsettled property made between 6 April and 30 September, the tax is due on 30 April following and for transfers made between 1 October and 5 April it is due six months from the end of the month when the transfer was made. The best date to make a transfer is 6 April because there is 12 months in which to pay the tax! Extra tax due on transfers made within three years of death becomes payable six months after the end of the month in which the death occurred.

Payment by instalments   Generally CTT must be paid in one lump sum. FA 1975 s 28(3) provides that any person liable for the tax (except the transferor and his spouse) can sell, mortgage or charge the property even if it is not vested in him, so that if, for instance, A gives property to B who settles it on C for life, either B, the trustees, or C (if called upon to pay the tax) can sell, mortgage or charge the property in order to do so.

Despite the general rule, if the transferee pays the CTT he can elect in the case of certain assets only to pay the tax in ten yearly instalments; the first instalment becoming due when the tax is due. The lifetime instalment option is available for the same assets as on death (see p 307), except that in the case of a transfer of a minority holding of unquoted shares, the 20% alternative is not available to show undue hardship. Trustees or beneficiaries who are liable for the tax on transfers of settled property can elect to pay in instalments provided that the property falls within one of the specified classes. Despite this election, the outstanding tax (and any interest due) may be paid at any time. Furthermore, if the relevant property is sold or transferred by a chargeable transfer the tax must be paid at once (FA 1975 Sch 4 para 13(4)(6)).

Interest   Interest at 8% pa is charged on any tax which is not paid by the due date. Where the tax is to be paid by instalments, interest is charged on overdue instalments only, except in the case of land where interest is charged on all the oustanding tax.

Satisfaction of tax   The Revenue have a discretion to accept in satisfaction of tax (but not interest) any object that is pre-eminent for its national, scientific, historic or artistic interest (see further Chapter 23).

Adjustments to the tax bill   Subject to the six year limitation rule (see p 298) if the Revenue prove that too little tax was paid in respect of a chargeable transfer, tax underpaid is payable together with interest. Conversely, if too much tax was paid, the Revenue must refund the excess together with interest, which is free of income tax in the recipient's hands.

3 **Burden of tax**

The question of who, as between the transferor and the transferee, should bear the tax on a lifetime transfer is a matter for the parties to decide. The decision will affect the amount of tax payable (see p 291). The parties can agree at any time before the tax becomes due and the Revenue will accept their decision so long as the tax is paid. However, the agreement does not affect the liability of the parties, so that if the tax remains unpaid, the Revenue can collect it from persons liable under the legislation.

IX   ADMINISTRATION AND APPEALS (FA 1975 Sch 4)

1   Calculation of liability

CTT is not assessed by reference to the tax year. Instead, when the Revenue are informed of a chargeable transfer of value they raise an assessment called a determination. If they are not satisfied with an account or if none is delivered when they suspect that a chargeable transfer has occurred, they can raise a 'best of judgment' or estimated determination of the tax due. A determination of CTT liability is conclusive against the transferor and for all subsequent transfers, failing a written agreement with the Revenue to the contrary or an appeal.

If the taxpayer disputes the determination he can appeal to the Special Commissioners within 30 days of it. The appeal procedure is basically the same as under TMA 1970 for income tax, corporation tax and CGT, except that an appeal can be made direct to the High Court, thereby bypassing the commissioners, either by agreement with the Revenue or on application to the High Court. In this case, the appeal is not limited to points of law. Appeal then lies in the usual way to the Court of Appeal and, with leave, to the House of Lords (or by the 'leap frog' procedure direct to the House of Lords). The disputed tax is not payable at the first stage of the appeal. However, if there is a further appeal, the tax becomes payable; if this appeal is then successful, the tax must be repaid with interest.

Proceedings for the recovery of CTT can be taken by the Crown under the Crown Proceedings Act 1947 in the High Court. Straightforward cases may be taken in the County Court by Inland Revenue staff other than barristers or solicitors (**FA 1984 s 106(1)**).

2   Back duty

The penalties are much the same as for income tax, corporation tax and CGT. If a person is fraudulent (including wilful default) in producing accounts and other information, the penalty is £50 plus twice the difference between the liability calculated on the true and false basis. For negligence, the penalty is £50 plus that difference (**FA 1975 Sch 4 para 30(1)(2)**). Solicitors and other agents who fraudulently produce incorrect information are liable to a maximum penalty of £500 reduced to £250 in cases of neglect (**FA 1975 Sch 4 para 30(3)**).

Proceedings for these penalties may be taken before the Special Commissioners or the High Court within three years of the determination of the correct tax due.

Assessments to recover CTT lost through fraud, wilful default and neglect of a person liable for the tax (which for these purposes includes the settlor in the case of discretionary trusts) may be made up to six years from the discovery of the offence (**FA 1975 Sch 4 para 23(2)**).

22 CTT—death

I GENERAL

FA 1975 s 22(1) provides that

> 'on the death of any person (after 12 March 1975) tax shall be charged as if immediately before his death he had made a transfer of value and the value transferred by it had been equal to the value of his estate immediately before his death . . .'.

Hence, for CTT purposes death is seen as the final transfer of value to be cumulated with earlier chargeable transfers in the previous ten years and occurring, by a fiction, immediately before death.

1 CTT and estate duty

Up to 13 March 1975 the estate duty regime continued to operate. The various transitional provisions for estate duty and CTT are beyond the scope of this book although mention should be made of FA 1975 s 22(4) which preserves for CTT the old surviving spouse exemption. This exemption provided that, for estate duty purposes, where property was left to a surviving spouse in such circumstances that the spouse was not competent to dispose of it (for instance was given a life interest therein) estate duty would be charged on the first death but not again on the death of the survivor. With the advent of CTT it is provided that on the survivor's death after 12 March 1975 there shall be excluded from that person's estate 'the value of any property which, if estate duty were chargeable on that death, would be excluded from the charge by FA 1894 s 5(2) [relief on death of surviving spouse]'.

2 Meaning of 'estate'

The definition of 'estate' for CTT purposes has already been considered in connection with lifetime transfers (FA 1975 s 23(1); see p 282). On death, however, the estate does not include excluded property. As the transfer is deemed to occur immediately before the death, the estate includes any equitable joint tenancies of the deceased which pass by operation of law *(jus accrescendi)* at the moment of death.

EXAMPLE 1

Bill and his sister Bertha jointly own their home. The documents of title indicate that they are joint tenants so that on the death of either that share will pass automatically to the survivor and will not be transferred by will. For CTT purposes, however, the half share in the house will be subject to charge.

The estate at death also includes a gift made before death in anticipation of death and conditional upon it occurring (a donatio mortis causa). Hence, although the property may have been handed over, it is still treated as part of the deceased's estate at death.

3   Valuation

In general assets have to be valued at 'the price which the property might reasonably be expected to fetch if sold in the open market at that time'. No reduction is allowed for the fact that all the property is put on the market at the same time (FA 1975 s 38(1)). This hypothetical sale occurs immediately before the death and the value arrived at for CGT purposes becomes the value at death for CGT purposes and, hence, the legatee's base cost (CGTA 1979 s 153). Where reliefs reduce the CTT value (notably business property relief) that relief is ignored for CGT purposes. Accordingly, for CTT, low values ensure the least tax payable but will give the legatee a low base cost and so a higher capital gain when he disposes of the asset.

Although the general rule is that assets should be valued immediately before death, FA 1975 Sch 10 permits values to be amended in certain circumstances, eg reasonable funeral expenses can be deducted (including a reasonable sum for mourning for family and servants) and, in certain cases, where death causes a change in the value of assets.

EXAMPLE 2

(1) A took out a life insurance policy for £100,000 on his own life. Its value immediately before death would be equal to the surrender figure. As a result of A's death £100,000 will accrue to A's estate and hence the value of the policy for CTT purposes is treated as that figure (FA 1975 Sch 10 para 9(1)(a), (2)).

(2) A and B were joint tenants in equity of a freehold house worth £100,000. Immediately before A's death his joint interest would be worth in the region of £50,000. As a result of death that asset passes to B by survivorship (ie its value is nil to A's estate). In this case it is not possible to alter the pre-death valuation (FA 1975 Sch 10 para 9(2)).

In three cases the death valuation can be altered if the asset is sold within a short period of death for less than that valuation. Relief is not given merely because the asset falls in value after death; only if it is sold by bargain at arm's length is the relief available. Normally the sale proceeds will be substituted as the death valuation figure if an election is made by the person liable for the CTT on that asset (in practice this will be the PRs who should elect if CTT would thereby be reduced). Where such revaluations occur, not only must the CTT bill (and estate rate) on death be recalculated but also, for CGT purposes, the death valuation is correspondingly reduced so as to prevent any claim for loss relief. The three cases when this relief is available are:

Related property sold within three years of death   The meaning of related property has already been discussed (see Chapter 21).|So long as a 'qualifying sale' (as defined) occurs, the property on death can be revalued ignoring the related property rules (ie as an asset on its own). Although the sale proceeds need not be the same as the death value, if the sale occurs within a short time of death the proceeds received will offer some evidence of that value.

EXAMPLE 3

Sebastian's estate on death includes one of a pair of Constable watercolours of Suffolk sunsets. He leaves it to his son; the other is owned by his widow, Jemima. As a pair, the pictures are worth £200,000. Hence, applying the related property provisions, the watercolour is valued at £100,000 on Sebastian's death. If it were to be sold at Sotheby's some eight months after his death for £65,000, the death value could be recalculated ignoring the related property rules. It would be necessary to arrive at the value of the picture immediately before the death.

Quoted investments sold within 12 months of death If sold for less than the death valuation the sale proceeds can be substituted for that figure. It should be noted that if this relief is claimed it will affect *all* such investments sold within the 12 month period; hence, the aggregate of the consideration received on such sales is substituted for the death values. Special rules operate if investments of the same description are repurchased.

Land sold within three years of death The relief extends to all interests in land and is similar to that available for quoted shares. Hence, all sales within the three year period are included in any election.

4 Liabilities

In general, liabilities will only reduce the value of the deceased's estate if incurred for consideration in money or money's worth (FA 1975 Sch 10 para 1(3)), eg an outstanding building society mortgage and the deceased's outstanding tax liability.

II HOW TO CALCULATE THE CTT BILL ON DEATH

Tax on death is calculated according to the rates set out in the death table (*Table 2*; see p 289: FA 1975 s 37(3)). These rates are always double those in the lifetime table.

Hence, the top lifetime rate of CTT for inter vivos transfers is 30%—for death it is 60%. Not surprisingly, lifetime giving can be an attractive proposition especially since FA 1980 s 79 has made CGT on such gifts an optional tax (see further Chapter 17).

To work out CTT on death the following procedure should be adopted:

Step 1 Calculate total chargeable death estate; ignore, therefore, exempt transfers (eg to a spouse) and apply any available reliefs (eg reduce the value of relevant business property by the appropriate percentage).

Step 2 Join the death table at the point reached by the transferor on the lifetime table at the time of his death—ie cumulate the death estate with chargeable lifetime transfers made in the ten years before death.

Step 3 Calculate death CTT bill.

Step 4   Convert the tax to an average or estate rate—ie divide CTT *(Step 3)* by total chargeable estate (arrived at in *Step 1*) and multiply by 100 to obtain a percentage rate. It is then possible to say how much CTT each asset bears. This is necessary in cases where the CTT is not a testamentary expense but is borne by the legatee (see p 308ff).

EXAMPLE 4

Dougal has just died leaving property valued after payment of all debts etc at £80,000. A picture worth £10,000 is left to his daughter Diana (the will states that it is to bear its own CTT) and the rest of the estate is left to his son Dalgleish. Dougal made chargeable lifetime transfers in the ten years preceding his death of £120,000. To calculate the CTT on death:
(1) Join the death table at £120,000 (lifetime cumulative total).
(2) Calculate CTT at death rates on an estate of £80,000:

$$
\begin{array}{lr}
 & \pounds \\
\pounds 28,000 \times 40\% = & 11,200 \\
\pounds 37,000 \times 45\% = & 16,650 \\
\pounds 15,000 \times 50\% = & \underline{7,500} \\
 & \underline{\underline{\pounds 35,350}}
\end{array}
$$

(3) Calculate the estate rate

$$\frac{\pounds 35,350 \ (\text{CTT})}{\pounds 80,000 \ (\text{Estate})} \times 100 = 44.2\%$$

(4) Apply estate rate to picture (ie $44.2\% \times \pounds 10,000) = \pounds 4,420$. This sum will be payable by Diana.
(5) Residue ($\pounds 70,000$) is taxed at $44.2\% = \pounds 30,940$. The balance will be paid to Dalgleish.

As the difference in the life and death tables means that death-bed gifts would be a highly attractive way of substantially reducing the CTT bill, any gifts made within three years before death are subject to a supplementary CTT assessment. This is done in two stages. First, CTT will already have been charged at the lifetime rates. If it has not been paid at the date of the donor's death it will be a testamentary expense and should, unless the donee has agreed to pay, be paid by the PRs. Hence, the chargeable lifetime transfer is known and this figure is not affected by the subsequent death.

Secondly, the supplementary CTT is charged upon the donee (the PRs are not liable for this extra tax) and will be calculated according to the death rates that would have applied to that chargeable transfer, with the lifetime tax then being subtracted from that figure. The donee alone is responsible for this extra tax and a prudent donee will take out insurance to cover the risk of liability to CTT in these circumstances.

EXAMPLE 5

In *Example 4* above the testator had cumulative lifetime transfers of £120,000, including a chargeable transfer of £20,000 made within three years of his death. The extra tax will be assessed as follows:

Step 1   CTT (at death rates) on a transfer of £20,000 starting with a total on the cumulative clock of £100,000.

$$£16,000 \times 35\% \quad = \quad 5,600$$
$$£ \ 4,000 \times 40\% \quad = \quad 1,600$$
$$\overline{£7,200}$$

Step 2 Deduct tax at life rates on £20,000 starting at the same cumulative total on the life tables

$$£16,000 \times 17\% \quad = \quad 2,800$$
$$£ \ 4,000 \times 20\% \quad = \quad 800$$
$$\overline{£3,600}$$

Step 3 Extra CTT payable by the donee is £7,200 − £3,600 = £3,600

Notes:
(a) The £20,000 is not added to the death estate and does not affect the death estate rate. Hence, it is taxed at a lower point on the death table than that estate.
(b) If the property given away within three years of death has fallen in value some relief may be available. This relief is not available in the case of tangible moveables which are wasting assets (see below).
(c) In the event of a change in the lifetime CTT rates between the date of the gift and the death, the deduction in *Step 2* will be by reference to the rates in force when the gift was made.

Continuing this example, if the value of the gift had fallen by the time of Dougal's death from £20,000 to £17,000, the extra CTT on death would be charged as follows:
(1) CTT at death rates on a transfer of £17,000

$$£16,000 \times 35\% \quad = \quad 5,600$$
$$£ \ 1,000 \times 40\% \quad = \quad 400$$
$$\overline{£6,000}$$

(2) Deduct CTT at life rates on the original £20,000 chargeable transfer (£3,600):
ie £6,000 − £3,600 = £2,400

Therefore, the extra CTT on the death is £2,400.

Had the property been sold by the donee before Dougal's death for £3,000 less than its value when given away by Dougal, the extra (death) CTT would be charged on the sale proceeds with the same result as above. If, however, the property had been given away by the donee before Dougal's death, even though its value might at that time have fallen by £3,000 since Dougal's original gift, no relief is given, with the result that the extra charge caused by Dougal's death will be levied on the full £20,000.

III PAYMENT OF CTT—INCIDENCE AND BURDEN

If the deceased was domiciled in the UK at the time of his death, CTT is chargeable on all the property comprised in his estate whether situated in the UK or abroad. If, however, he was domiciled elsewhere, CTT is only chargeable on his property situated in the UK.

1 Who pays the CTT on death?

a) *Duty to account*

The deceased's PRs are generally under a duty to deliver to the Revenue within 12 months of the death an account specifying all the property that formed part of the deceased's estate immediately before his death and including property

(1) in which the deceased had a beneficial interest in possession (eg where the deceased was the life tenant under a settlement); and

(2) property over which he had a general power of appointment (this property is included since such a power would have enabled the deceased to appoint himself the owner so that in effect the property is indistinguishable from property owned by him absolutely).

In practice, the PRs will deliver their account as soon as possible because first, they cannot obtain probate and, therefore, administer the estate until an account has been delivered and the CTT paid; and, secondly, they must pay interest at 6% pa on any CTT payable on death and which is unpaid by the end of the sixth month after the end of the month in which the deceased died (for instance, a death in January would mean that CTT is due on 1 August and, thereafter, interest would be payable).

b) 'Excepted estates' (SI 1981/880 as amended by SI 1983/1039)

No account need be delivered in the case of an 'expected estate'. The taxpayer must die domiciled in the UK; must have made no chargeable lifetime transfers in the ten years before death; must not have been a life tenant under a settlement; and must not have owned at death foreign property amounting to more than 10% of the value of the estate (or £2,000 if greater). Subject thereto the estate will be expected if the gross value at death does not exceed £40,000. This figure takes account of all property passing under the will or intestacy; of nominated property; and, in cases where the deceased had been a joint tenant of property, requires the entire value of that property to be included (not just the value of the deceased's share).

The Revenue reserve the right to call for an account (on Form 204) within 35 days of the issue of a grant of probate, but if they do not do so, the PRs are then automatically discharged from further liability.

c) CAP forms

In cases other than b) above, to obtain a grant the PRs must submit an Inland Revenue account (a CAP Form). CAP Form 202 is a simplified form which proceeds on the assumption that there will be no CTT liability. The deceased must die domiciled in the UK; have made no chargeable lifetime transfers in the ten years before death; and have been neither entitled in an interest in possession trust nor have settled property in that ten year period. CAP Form 202 is then the appropriate form so long as the net estate at death does not exceed the current CTT threshold (£64,000). The estate must comprise property situated in the UK only and liabilities (including exemptions and reliefs from CTT) are deducted in arriving at the net figure. Accordingly, if a millionaire leaves his entire estate to his surviving spouse, CAP Form 202 will (assuming that the other requirements are met) be the appropriate form. Where the deceased had been a joint tenant at death it is only the value of his share of the property that is included.

If CAP Form 202 cannot be used, either CAP Form 200 or 201 (if the deceased died domiciled outside the UK) must be completed (see Appendix III for a completed CAP Form 200).

d) Liability for CTT (FA 1975 ss 25–27)

PRs must pay the CTT on assets owned beneficially by the deceased at the time of death and on land comprised in a settlement which vests in them as PRs.

Their liability is personal, but limited to assets which they received as PRs or might have received but for their own neglect or default (FA 1975 s 27 and see *IRC v Stannard* (1984)). If the PRs fail to pay the CTT other persons are concurrently liable, namely:

(1) Executors de son tort, ie persons who interfere with the deceased's property so as to constitute themselves executors. Their liability is limited to the assets in their hands (see *IRC v Stype Investments (Jersey) Ltd* (1982)).

(2) Beneficiaries entitled under the will or on intestacy in whom the property becomes vested after death. Their liability is limited to the property that they receive.

(3) A purchaser of real property if an Inland Revenue charge is registered against that property. His liability is limited to the value of the charge.

(4) Any beneficiary entitled to an interest in possession in the property after the death. Liability is generally limited to the value of that property.

Where the deceased had an interest in possession in settled property at the date of his death, it is the trustees of the settlement who are liable for any CTT on the settled property to the extent that they received or could have received assets as trustees. Should the trustees not pay the tax, the persons set out in (3) and (4) above are concurrently liable.

Where additional tax is due on chargeable transfers made by the deceased within three years before his death or, where tax is, because of the death, payable on a gift to a political party made within one year before death, the donee in each case is solely liable for that tax.

In addition to persons who are liable for CTT on death, real property is automatically subject to an Inland Revenue charge from the date of death until the date when the CTT is paid (FA 1975 Sch 4 para 20(1)(a)).

e) *Method of payment*

In order to obtain a grant of representation, PRs must pay all the CTT for which they are liable when they deliver their account (CAP Form) to the Revenue. Additionally, they may pay the CTT for which they are not liable (eg CTT on settled property in which the deceased had an interest in possession) if they are asked to do so by the persons liable. (They will then of course be entitled to reimbursement.) If they refuse to pay such CTT, they are still entitled to a grant of probate since they have paid all the tax for which they are liable.

As mentioned above, the general rule is that all the CTT payable must be paid in one lump sum within six months after the death. However, in the case of certain property the tax may, at the option of the PRs, be paid in ten yearly instalments with the first instalment falling due six months after the end of the month of death. The object of this facility is to prevent the particular assets from having to be sold by the PRs in order to raise the necessary CTT.

The instalment option is available on the following assets:

(1) land, freehold or leasehold, wherever situate;

(2) a controlling shareholding in a company whether quoted or unquoted ('control' is defined as voting control on all questions affecting the company as a whole);

(3) a non-controlling shareholding in an unquoted company where the Revenue are satisfied that payment of the tax in one lump sum would cause 'undue hardship'. Undue hardship is presumed where the tax on the shares and on other property carrying the instalment option comprises at least 20% of the tax due from that particular person (in the same capacity);

(4) other non-controlling shareholdings in unquoted companies, where the

value of the shares exceeds £20,000 and either their nominal value is at least 10% of the nominal value of all the issued shares in the company, or the shares are ordinary shares whose nominal value is at least 10% of the nominal value of all ordinary shares in the company; and

(5) a business or a share in a business, eg a partnership share.

An additional attraction of paying by instalments is that, generally, no interest is charged so long as each instalment is paid on the due date. In the event of late payment the interest charge is at 6% pa on the outstanding instalment. Interest is, however, charged on the total outstanding CTT liability (even if the instalments are paid on time) in the case of land which is not a business asset and shares in investment companies. If the asset subject to the instalment option is sold, the outstanding instalments of CTT become payable at once. Finally, it should be stressed that in the case of businesses the instalment option complements business property relief under FA 1976 Sch 10 (see Chapter 23).

If the instalment option is exercised the first instalment is, as already mentioned, payable six months after the month of death. Hence, PRs will normally exercise the option in order to pay as little CTT as possible before obtaining the grant. Once the grant has been obtained they may then decide to discharge the CTT on the instalment property in one lump sum. PRs should, however, bear in mind the following matters: first, some CTT will usually be payable before the grant. The necessary cash may be obtained from the deceased's account at either a bank or a building society, from property for which a grant is not necessary, or by means of a personal loan from a beneficiary. If a loan has to be raised commercially, the interest thereon will qualify for income tax relief for 12 months so long as the loan is on a loan account (not by way of overdraft) and is used to pay the tax attributable to personal property (including leaseholds and land held on trust for sale). The Keith Committee rejected suggestions that CTT should generally be made payable after a grant has been obtained (see Volume 3 Chapter 33).

Secondly PRs normally exercise the instalment option to defer CTT until after obtaining the grant. Where the CTT is a testamentary expense, the tax will then, usually, be paid off in one lump sum. If the residuary legatee objects (it may, for instance, be necessary to sell an asset to pay the CTT), PRs could arrange to vest the residue in that beneficiary and for him to discharge the future instalments. Adequate security should, however, be taken in such cases because if the beneficiary defaults, the PRs remain liable for the outstanding CTT.

Thirdly, in the case of a specific gift which bears its own CTT and which is subject to the instalment option, the decision whether to discharge the entire CTT bill once probate has been obtained should be left to the legatee. PRs should not make a unilateral decision (see further p 309). Once PRs have paid all the outstanding CTT they are entitled to a certificate of discharge under FA 1975 Sch 4 para 25(2).

2   Allocating the burden of CTT

The Revenue are satisfied once the CTT due on the estate has been paid. However, as far as the PRs and beneficiaries under the will are concerned, the further question arises as to how the tax should be borne as between the beneficiaries: eg should the tax attributable to a specific legacy be paid out of the residue as a testamentary expense or is it charged on the property, the specific legacy, itself? The answer to this question is particularly important whenever specific legacies are combined with exempt or partially exempt residue, since, if the CTT is to be paid out of that residue, the grossing-up calculation under FA 1975 Sch 6 Pt III (see p 310) will be necessary and will result in more CTT being payable.

As a general rule, a testator can, and should, stipulate expressly in his will where the CTT on a specific bequest is to fall. The one exception is that any direction in the will to pay the CTT attributable to a chargeable share of residue out of exempt residue will be void. Chargeable residue must bear its own tax (see p 311).

If the will makes no provision for the burden of tax, the general principle is that CTT on UK unsettled property is a testamentary expense payable from residue. Under the estate duty regime land had, in such cases, borne its own duty, but the Scottish case of *Re Dougal* (1981) decided that the CTT legislation drew no distinction between realty and personalty and the matter was put beyond doubt in F (No 2) A 1983 for deaths occurring after 25 July 1983.

In drafting wills and administering estates the following matters should, therefore, be borne in mind:

(1) When drafting a new will, expressly state whether bequests are tax-bearing or are free of tax.

(2) Old wills which have been drawn up but are not yet in force should be checked to ensure that provision has been made for the payment of CTT on gifts of realty. The will may have been drafted on the assumption that such gifts bear their own tax in which case amendments will be necessary.

(3) In the case of deaths before the clarifying legislation of F (No 2) A 1983, the administration of the estate may run into problems when there is a bequest of realty without any provision for the payment of CTT. The PRs should try to obtain the agreement of the beneficiaries concerned to the payment of CTT; failing such agreement they should treat the tax as a testamentary expense to be borne by the residue (see [1982] LS Gaz 1518).

(4) CTT on foreign property and joint property will always be borne by the beneficiary unless the will provides to the contrary.

Assuming that the will contains a specific tax-bearing legacy, how will the CTT, in practice, be paid on it? As the PRs are primarily liable to the Revenue for the CTT, they will usually pay in order to obtain probate and seek to recover it from the legatee concerned afterwards. Where the PRs pay CTT which is not a testamentary expense (ie on all tax-bearing gifts), they have a right to recover that sum from the person in whom the property is vested (FA 1975 s 28(1A)). In the case of a pecuniary legacy, the recovery of CTT will present no problems since the PRs can deduct the CTT from the legacy before handing over the balance to the legatee. For specific legacies of other property (ie land or chattels), the PRs have the power to sell, mortgage or charge the property in order to recover the tax. If they instead (usually at the legatee's request) propose to transfer the asset to the legatee, they should ensure that they are given sufficient guarantees that the tax will be refunded to them.

Problems can arise for PRs who pay the CTT on specific tax-bearing legacies to which the instalment option applies. If they choose to pay the CTT on such legacies in one lump sum, when they seek to recover that tax from the legatee he can elect to repay them in instalments (FA 1975 s 28(2)). Hence, the PRs should, after consulting the legatee, elect to pay the CTT on that property by instalments; if they do so, however, and if the legatee defaults in paying the instalments, the PRs remain concurrently liable for the outstanding CTT.

To avoid any dispute, when the PRs have paid CTT which they are entitled to recover from the legatee, they can obtain a certificate from the Revenue which is conclusive as to the amount of tax which they are entitled to recover (FA 1975 s 28(6)).

3   Cases where the CTT has to be recalculated

There are a number of instances where the CTT paid on a deceased's estate will need to be recalculated. In general this will be necessary when the value of that estate is altered for some reason, or where the destination of a bequest is varied. If the CTT has to be recalculated, the estate will be different and the burden of the CTT will be affected. The principal instances where recalculation is necessary are:

Cases where sale proceeds are substituted for the death valuation   (See above p 302).

The effect of variations and disclaimers   Such changes, if made within two years of the death, may be read back into the original will (see p 320).

Discretionary trusts under FA 1975 s 47(1A)   If broken up within two years of death, it is as if the testator had provided in his will for the dispositions of the trustees (see p 320).

Orders under the Inheritance (Provisions for Family and Dependants) Act 1975   When the court exercises its powers under s 2 of the 1975 Act to order financial provision out of the deceased's estate for his family and dependents, the order is treated as made by the deceased on death and may result in there having been an under- or over-payment of CTT on death. Any application under this Act should normally be made within six months of the testator's death, so at least the PRs will have some warning that adjustments to the CTT bill may have to be made. Further adjustments to the tax bill may have to be made if the court makes an order under s 10 of the Act reclaiming property given away by the deceased in the six years prior to his death with the intention of defeating a claim for financial provision under the Act. In this case, the deceased's cumulative total of chargeable lifetime transfers in the previous ten years is reduced by the gift reclaimed. This, of itself, may affect the rate at which tax is charged on the deceased's estate on death. Also the value of the reclaimed property and any tax repaid on it falls into the deceased's estate for calculating the CTT payable on death.

IV   PROBLEMS CREATED BY THE PARTIALLY EXEMPT TRANSFER (FA 1975 Sch 6 Pt III (AS AMENDED)

1   When does Pt III apply?

In many cases the calculation of the CTT bill on death will be relatively straightforward. Difficulties may, however, arise when a particular combination of dispositions are made in a will. FA 1975 Pt III provides machinery for resolving these problems with a method of calculating the gross value of the gifts involved and, accordingly, the CTT payable. The area is both highly technical and not readily comprehensible. Consider, first, a number of instances where the calculation of the CTT on death poses no special difficulties:

Where all the gifts are taxable   eg A leaves all his property to be divided equally amongst his four children. In this case the whole of A's estate is charged to CTT.

Where all the gifts are exempt   eg A leaves all his property to a spouse and/or a charity. In this case the whole estate is untaxed.

Where specific gifts are exempt and the residue is chargeable   eg A leaves £100,000 to his spouse and the residue of £50,000 to his children. Here the gift to the spouse is exempt, but CTT is charged on the residue of £50,000 so that only the balance will be paid to the children.

Where specific gifts are chargeable but bear their own tax under the terms of the will and the residue is exempt   eg A leaves a specific tax-bearing gift of £100,000 to his niece and the residue to his spouse. The spouse receives the residue after deduction of the £100,000 gift; CTT is calculated at death rates on the £100,000 and is borne by the niece.

Where there are no specific gifts and part of the residue is exempt, part chargeable   eg A leaves his estate to be divided equally between his son and his spouse. The widow receives half the residue which is, therefore, exempt. The son receives the other half of the residue after the CTT charged on that half has been deducted. It should be noted that the chargeable portion of residue must always bear its own tax; any provision in the will to the contrary is void.

There may be bequests where the calculation of the CTT is not so obvious and it becomes necessary to apply the rules in Pt III. Taking the simplest illustration, consider a will containing a specific gift which is chargeable but does not bear its own CTT and residue which is exempt, eg A's estate on death is valued at £150,000 and he leaves £100,000 tax-free to his son and the residue to a charity. The problem is to decide how much CTT should be charged on the specific gift of £100,000. Consider three possible solutions:

Solution 1   CTT is calculated as if it is only the specific gift of £100,000 that is taxable. This solution is inadequate because it ignores the fundamental CTT principle that a specific gift must be *net* of its CTT—ie that the £100,000 should represent what is left after deducting CTT from a larger sum (the gross sum).

EXAMPLE 6

Using the above facts, CTT on £100,000 is £11,550. Therefore, the son would receive £100,000 and the charity a residue of £50,000 − £11,550 tax = £38,450 (exempt).

If this method were adopted there would be scope for considerable tax savings. In *Example 6*, if A were to leave his entire estate of £150,000 to his son, the CTT would be £30,850 so that the son would be left with only £119,150 (£150,000 − £30,850). However, by amending the will to provide for a specific gift to the son coupled with an exempt residue the son could be given more than £119,150. Not surprisingly, *Solution 1* has never been adopted.

EXAMPLE 7

Leave the son £125,000 tax-free with the residue of the £150,000 estate going to a charity. CTT on £125,000 would be £20,750 payable out of the residue with the result that (1) the charity is left with £4,250 and (2) the son gets £5,850 more than if he had been left the entire estate.

Solution 2   CTT is calculated as if the entire estate (£150,000) is taxable and the specific gift is then grossed up at that estate rate. This method produces too much tax, because it assumed (wrongly) that the whole estate is chargeable whereas, in fact, part of it is exempt. *Solution 2* was adopted in 1975, but replaced in 1976 by *solution 3*.

EXAMPLE 8

As in *Example 6*, leave the son £100,000 tax-free. CTT on £150,000 is £30,850. The estate rate is, therefore:

$$\frac{£30,850}{£150,000} \times 100 = 20.57\%$$

£100,000 grossed up at 20.57% = £125,897. The son, therefore, receives £100,000. CTT is £25,897. The charity only receives £24,103 (£150,000 − £125,897).

Solution 3   Treat the specific gift as the only chargeable estate which must be grossed up at death rates using a Pt III (death) grossing-up table. The resultant sum is the gross estate which, after deducting CTT at death rates, will leave the net specific gift.

GROSSING-UP TABLE FOR USE ON DEATH

(FA 1975 Sch 6 Pt III para 19(3) as substituted by FA 1976 s 96)

Net value of chargeable gift	Capital transfer tax payable			£
£ £	£			
0– 64,000	Nil			
64,001– 78,700	Nil +3/7	(42.857%)	for each £ over	64,000
78,701– 98,850	6,300 +7/13	(53.846%)	for each £ over	78,700
98,851–118,500	17,150 +2/3	(66.667%)	for each £ over	98,850
118,501–138,400	29,950 +9/11	(81.818%)	for each £ over	118,500
138,401–161,900	46,600 +1	(100%)	for each £ over	138,400
161,901–185,750	70,100 +11/9	(122.222%)	for each £ over	161,900
over 185,750	69,925 +1½	(150%)	for each £ over	185,750

EXAMPLE 9

Out of an estate of £150,000, £100,000 is left tax-free to the son and the residue to charity.

Step 1   On the Pt III table find the figure immediately below £100,000 (ie £98,851).

Step 2   Reading across that line of the table, the tax on the net gift of £100,000 is, therefore, £17,150 + (2/3 × [£100,000 − £98,851]) = £17,916.

It should be emphasised that the object of this exercise is to attribute a gross value to the specific gift. Hence, the specific gift in this example is grossed up to become £117,916 and, therefore, the charity is left with £32,084.

Bearing in mind the frequency of specific tax-free legacies, Pt III will come into play wherever they are combined with an exempt or partly exempt residue.

Where the partly exempt transfer contains business or agricultural property eligible for 50% relief, the correct combination of gifts can achieve a substantial tax saving since the value transferred is reduced by the relief before applying Pt III. In general, the surviving spouse should be given a pecuniary legacy equal to the value of the business after CTT relief has been given (see further 1983 NLJ 769).

EXAMPLE 10

A who has made no previous chargeable transfers leaves a net estate of £600,000 of which £400,000 is attributable to business property and eligible for 50% relief. He leaves a pecuniary legacy of £400,000 to his widow and the residue to his children.

Step 1 Deduct the 50% relief ie £200,000 (£400,000 × 50%) from the value transferred of £600,000 = £400,000.

Step 2 Attribute the reduced value transferred to specific gifts first. Since the widow's gift exhausts the value transferred of £400,000, the residue passing to the children of £200,000 is untaxed.

2   Effect of previous chargeable transfers on the Pt III calculation

In considering the application of Pt III, it has so far been assumed that the deceased had made no previous chargeable lifetime transfers in the ten years before his death. If he has, the specific gift on death can only be grossed up after taking account of those cumulative lifetime transfers because they will affect the rate at which tax is charged on the estate on death.

EXAMPLE 11

A's estate on death is valued at £250,000 and he leaves £100,000 tax-free to his son and the residue to a charity. A had made gross lifetime transfers in the previous ten years of £110,000.
    To work out the CTT on the £100,000 specific legacy:

Step 1 Reduce the inter vivos transfer by the amount of tax that would be payable on the same transfer at the death rates in force at the date of the death. CTT on £110,000 at death rates = £15,050
£110,000 − £15,050 = £94,950

Step 2 Add the specific gift of £100,000 to £94,950 = £194,950.

Step 3 Gross up £194,950 at death rates using the death grossing-up table = £278,675.

Step 4 Deduct the gross lifetime chargeable transfers of £110,000 leaving £168,675. This figure is the grossed-up amount of the specific gift.

Step 5 £168,675 is the chargeable estate from which the son receives £100,000 and the CTT is £68,675.

3   Double grossing-up

Part III deals with the more complex problems that arise if specific tax-free gifts are combined with chargeable gifts bearing their own tax, and an exempt residue.

Assume that B makes a specific bequest of £100,000 tax-free to his son, and leaves a gift of £50,000 bearing its own tax to his daughter with residue of £300,000 going to his spouse. To gross-up the specific tax-free gift of £100,000 as if it were the only chargeable estate would produce insufficient CTT bearing in mind that there is an additional chargeable legacy of £50,000. On the other hand, if the £100,000 were grossed up at the estate rate applicable to £150,000 (ie the two gifts of £100,000 and £50,000) the resulting tax would be too high because the £50,000 gift should not be grossed up. Further, as previously discussed, to gross up £100,000 at the estate rate applicable to the whole estate including the exempt residue would produce too much tax because this assumes, wrongly, that the residue is also taxable.

The solution provided in Pt III is to gross up the specific tax-free gift at the estate rate applicable to a hypothetical chargeable estate consisting of the grossed-up specific tax-free gift and the gifts bearing their own tax. The procedure, known as double grossing-up, is as follows:

Step 1   Gross up the specific tax-free gift of £100,000 (using the death grossing-up table) as if it were the only chargeable estate. The result is £117,916.

Step 2   Add to this figure the tax-bearing gift of £50,000 making a hypothetical chargeable estate of £167,916.

Step 3   Calculate CTT on £167,916 using the death table = £38,912. Then convert to an estate rate: viz

$$\frac{£38,912}{£167,916} \times 100 = 23.17\%$$

Step 4   Gross up the specific tax-free gift a second time at this rate of 23.17%:

$$£100,000 \times \frac{100}{76.83} = £130,157$$

Step 5   The chargeable part of the estate now consists of the grossed-up specific gift (£130,157) and the gift bearing its own tax (£50,000) = £180,157.

Step 6   On the figure of £180,157, CTT is re-calculated at £44,421 and the final estate rate is found:

$$\frac{£44,421}{£180,157} \times 100 = 24.66\%$$

Step 7   The grossed-up specific tax-free gift (£130,157) is then charged at this rate (24.66%) = tax of £32,097.

It should be noted that the CTT on specific tax-free gifts (here £32,097) must always be paid from the residue and it is only the balance that is exempt. The tax-bearing gift of £50,000 will of course be taxed at £24.66%, but the tax (ie £12,330) will be borne by the daughter.

To conclude, Pt III is relevant whenever a tax-free specific gift is mixed with an exempt residue, and, if tax-bearing gifts are also included in the will, then a double grossing-up calculation is required. Logically, to gross up only twice is indefensible since the estate rate established at *Step 6* (24.66%) should then be used to gross up further the £100,000 (ie repeat *Step 4*) and so on and so on! Thankfully, the statute only requires the grossing-up calculation to be done twice with the consequence that a small saving in CTT results!

4 Problems where part of residue is exempt, part chargeable

So far we have been concerned with a wholly exempt residue. What, however, happens if part of the residue is chargeable? For example, A, whose estate is worth £300,000, leaves a specific tax-free gift of £100,000 to his son; a tax-bearing gift of £50,000 to his daughter; and the residue equally to his widow and his nephew.

The method of calculating the CTT is basically the same as in the double grossing-up example above in that the chargeable portion of the residue (half to nephew) must be added to the hypothetical chargeable estate in *Step 2* to calculate the assumed estate rate. The difficulty is caused because, although CTT on grossed-up gifts is payable before the division of residue into chargeable and non-chargeable portions, the CTT on the nephew's portion of the residue must be deducted from his share of residue after it has been divided. This must be done despite any stipulation to the contrary in the will. To take account of this, the method for calculating the CTT payable in such cases is amended as follows:

Step 1 Gross up the specific tax-free gift of £100,000 to £117,916.

Step 2 Calculate the hypothetical chargeable estate by adding to the grossed-up gift of £117,916: (1) the tax-bearing gift of £50,000 and (2) the chargeable residue:

	£	£
Estate		300,000
Less: grossed-up gift	117,916	
tax-bearing gift	50,000	167,916
		£132,084

The nephew's share (the chargeable residue) is half of £132,084 = £66,042.
This results in a hypothetical chargeable estate of
£117,916 + £50,000 + £66,042 = £233,958.

Step 3 Calculate the 'assumed estate rate' on £233,958:

CTT on £233,958 $= £71,177$

$$\left[\text{Estate rate is } \frac{£71,177}{£233,958} \times 100 \quad = 30.42\% \right]$$

Step 4 Gross up the specific tax-free gift at this rate of 30.42%

$$£100,000 \times \frac{100}{69.58} = £143,719$$

Step 5 The chargeable part of the estate now consists of:

	£	£
Chargeable residue, ie estate		300,000
Less: grossed-up gift	143,719	
tax-bearing gift	50,000	193,719
		£106,281

Nephew's share is $\frac{1}{2} \times £106,281 = £53,141$

Therefore, chargeable estate is
£193,719 + £53,141 = £246,860

Step 6 Calculate the estate rate on the chargeable estate of £246,860

CTT on £246,860   = £78,273

$$\left[\text{Estate rate is } \frac{£78,273}{£246,860} \times 100 \qquad = 31.71\%\right]$$

Step 7 The grossed-up specific tax-free gift of £143,719 is taxed at the rate of 31.71% = £45,573.

Then deduct the gross gift of £145,573 (£100,000 gift + £45,573 tax) from the estate of £300,000 leaving £154,427.

Step 8 The tax-bearing gift of £50,000 is taxed at £31.71% = £15,855. This tax is paid by the daughter, but the estate is further reduced by £50,000 to £104,427.

Step 9 The residue remaining of £104,427 is divided as to:

		£
Widow's share:	$\frac{1}{2} \times$ £104,427	£52,214 (exempt)
Nephew's share:	$\frac{1}{2} \times$ £104,427	52,214
Less: CTT at 31.71% on	£53,141	16,851
Nephew's share after tax:		£35,363

Note: that the nephew's share of the residue for the purpose of calculating CTT at 31.71% is the amount which forms part of the chargeable estate as calculated in *Step 5*.

V ABATEMENT

Although Pt III is mainly concerned with calculating the chargeable estate in cases where there is an exempt residue, it also deals with certain related matters:

Allocating relief where gifts exceed an exempt limit A transfer may be partly exempt only because it includes gifts which together exceed an exempt limit, eg a transfer to a non-UK domiciled spouse which exceeds £55,000 and gifts on death or within one year before death to political parties which exceed £100,000. To deal with these cases FA 1975 Sch 6 para 19(2) provides for the exemption to be allocated between the various gifts as follows:
(1) Specific tax-bearing gifts take precedence over other gifts.
(2) Specific tax-free gifts receive relief in the proportion that their values bear to each other.
(3) All specific gifts take precedence over gifts of residue.

Abatement of gifts If a transferor makes gifts in his will which exceed the value of his estate, those gifts must be abated in accordance with Pt III. There are two cases to consider:
(1) Where the gifts exceed the transferor's estate without regard to any tax payable, the gifts abate according to the rules contained in the Administration of Estates Act 1925 and tax is charged on the abated gifts.

EXAMPLE 12

A testator's net estate is worth £150,000. He left his house worth £50,000 to his nephew, the gift to bear its own tax, and a general tax-free legacy of £150,000 to a charity. Under FA 1975 Sch 6 para 17 the legacy must abate to £100,000 to be paid to the charity free of tax. The house will bear its own tax.

(2) Where the transferor's estate is only insufficient to meet the gifts as grossed-up under Pt III rules, abatement is governed by FA 1975 Sch 6 para 18. The order in which the gifts are abated depends on the general law.

VI SPECIFIC PROBLEMS ON DEATH

This section is concerned with a number of specific problems that should be considered when drafting wills. Points 1 to 3 are devoted to the difficulties that may arise when property is left to a beneficiary who dies either at the same time as the testator, or soon afterwards. In points 4 and 5 drafting flexible wills and amending the will after the testator's death are considered. Will planning involving the use of the spouse exemption is considered in Chapter 35.

1 **Commorientes**

Where A and B leave their property to each other and are both killed in a common catastrophe or otherwise die in circumstances such that it is not clear in what order they died, Law of Property Act 1925 s 184 stipulates that the younger is deemed to have survived the elder. Hence, if A was the elder, he is presumed to have died first so that his property passes to B (assuming no survivorship clause—see below, and CTT would be chargeable. B's will leaving everything to A will not take effect because of the prior death of A so that his assets (including his inheritance from A) will pass on intestacy. CTT would be chargeable. The result is that property bequeathed by the elder would (subject to quick succession relief) be charged to CTT twice. To prevent this double charge, FA 1975 s 22(9) provides that for CTT purposes A and B 'shall be assumed to have died at the same instant'. Hence, A's estate is only charged once—on *his* death, it is not taxed a second time on B's death since the gift is treated as lapsing. LPA 1925 s 184 is ousted only for CTT purposes; it still governs the actual destination of the property bequeathed by A.

2 **Survivorship clauses**

To inherit property on a death it is necessary only to survive the testator so that if the beneficiary dies immediately after inheriting the property, the two deaths could mean two CTT charges. Some relief is provided by quick succession relief (p 318), but the prudent testator may seek to avoid this risk by providing in his will for the property to pass to the desired beneficiary only if that person survives him for a stated period. Such provisions are referred to as survivorship clauses and FA 1975 Sch 5 para 22A permits such clauses for a period of up to six months.

EXAMPLE 13

T leaves £100,000 to A 'if he survives me by six months. If he does not the money is to go to B'.

The effect of FA 1975 Sch 5 para 22A is to leave matters in suspense for six months and then to read the will in the light of what has happened. Hence, if A does survive for six months it is as if the will had provided '£100,000 to A'; if he dies before the end of that period, it is as if the will had provided for £100,000 to go to B. The result is that two charges to CTT are avoided; there will merely be the one chargeable occasion when the testator dies.

In principle, it is prudent to use survivorship clauses, but they should be avoided when the bequest is to a surviving spouse and is made with the intention of equalising the couples' estates (see p 497). The danger of choosing a period in excess of six months is that FA 1975 Sch 5 para 22A will not apply so that the bequest will be settled property to which ordinary charging principles will apply. If a longer period is essential, insert a two year discretionary trust into the will (see p 320).

3   **Quick succession relief** (FA 1981 s 101)

Quick succession relief offers a measure of relief against two charges to CTT on the same property, when two chargeable events occur within five years of each other.

For unsettled property quick succession relief is only given on a death where the value of the deceased's estate had been increased by a chargeable transfer (inter vivos or on death) to the deceased made within the previous five years. It is not necessary for the property then transferred still to be part of the deceased's estate when he dies.

In the case of settled property the relief is only available (and necessary) for interest in possession trusts. It is given whenever an interest in possession terminates and hence can be deliberately activated by the life tenant assigning or surrendering his interest. The earlier transfer in the case of settled property will be either the creation of the settlement or a termination of some prior life interest.

EXAMPLE 14

In 1983 S settles property on trust for A for life, B for life, C absolutely. In 1984 A dies and in 1985 B surrenders his life interest.

1983   CTT will be chargeable.

1984   Quick succession relief is available on A's death. The chargeable transfer in the previous five years was the creation of the settlement in 1983.

1985   Quick succession relief is available on the surrender of B's life interest. The chargeable transfer in the previous five years was the termination of A's life interest.

The relief reduces the CTT on the second chargeable occasion. CTT is calculated in the usual way and then reduced by a sum dependent upon two factors. First, how long has elapsed since the first chargeable transfer was made. The percentage of relief is available as follows:

100%   if previous transfer one year or less before death
 80%   if previous transfer one–two years before death
 60%   if previous transfer two–three years before death
 40%   if previous transfer three–four years before death
 20%   if previous transfer four–five years before death

The second factor is the amount of CTT paid on the first transfer. FA 1981 s 101(3) states that the relief is 'a percentage [determined as above] of the tax charged on so much of the value transferred by the first transfer as is attributable to the increase [in the estate of the second transferor]'. Hence, if A transferred £55,000 to B who died within one year of that gift the appropriate percentage will be 100%; but if the transfer by A had been his first chargeable transfer and, therefore, had fallen into the nil rate band the relief is 100% × 0!

EXAMPLE 15

(1) *Tax-free legacy/death:* A, who has made no previous chargeable transfers, dies leaving an estate of £200,000 out of which he leaves a tax-free legacy of £100,000 to B. B dies 18 months later leaving an estate of £250,000.

(a) CTT on A's estate	= £37,450
Proportion paid in respect of tax-free legacy	= £18,725
(b) Quick succession relief 80% × £18,725	= £14,980

	£
(c) CTT on B's death	56,500
Less: Quick succession relief	14,980
CTT payable	£41,520

(2) *Life gift (grossed-up)/death:* A gives £94,225 to B and pays the CTT. £94,225 grosses up to £100,000 (CTT × £5,775, assuming it was A's first chargeable transfer). B dies 18 months later leaving an estate of £250,000.

(a) $\dfrac{£94,225 \text{ (gift less CTT borne by B)}}{£100,000 \text{ (value transferred)}} \times £5,775 \text{ (CTT)}$ = £5,441

(b) Quick succession relief 80% × £5,441   = £4,353.19

	£
(c) CTT on B's death on £250,000	56,500.00
Less: Quick succession relief	4,353.19
CTT payable	£52,146.80

(3) *Settled property:* S settled £134,575 on X for life remainder to Y. S agrees to pay the CTT.
£134,575 grosses up to £150,000 (CTT £15,425)
18 months later X (who has made no previous transfers) surrenders his life interst to Y when the property has risen in value to £250,000.

(a) $\dfrac{£134,575 \text{ (increase in X's estate)}}{£150,000} \times £15,425$ = £13,838.80

(b) Quick succession relief 80% × £13,838.80   = £11,071

	£
(c) CTT on surrender.	28,250
Less: Quick succession relief	11,071
CTT payable	£17,179

4   The two year discretionary trust on death (FA 1975 s 47(1A) as amended)

If a testator creates, by his will, a trust without an interest in possession so long as that trust is ended *within two years* of his death, the dispositions of the trustees are 'read back' into the original will. The normal charging provisions for settlements are inoperative so that there is no charge (see p 355ff) when the property leaves the trust. Such a trust is advantageous where, eg the testator is dying and desires his estate to be divided between his four children, but is not sure of the proper proportions. By inserting the two year trust a final decision about the exact distribution of the estate can be postponed for a further two years. Hence, the settlor can give all the assets to trustees and ensure that the settlement clause in the will provides: overriding powers of appointment exercisable for a period of not more than 23 months from the date of death (this ensures that the trust ends within two years of the testator's death); subject thereto a discretionary trust of income with a provision for accumulation; and finally, a provision that in default of the exercise of these appointment powers, the property shall be held for the beneficiaries equally.

CTT will be charged at the estate rate for the property settled but the 'reading back' of the ultimate distributions into the will may require the death CTT to be recalculated.

Consider, for instance, the position if one of the beneficiaries of a two year trust were a surviving spouse. At death the entire fund would be charged to CTT. Were the trustees ultimately to decide to distribute the assets to that spouse, the reading back provision would ensure that the CTT paid on death would be recovered (with interest at 6%) because of the spouse exemption (a distribution to a charity would have the same effect; FA 1984 s 103). Presumably, if it were obvious at the outset that the entire fund should be paid to the spouse, the trustees could execute an irrevocable appointment (even before any grant of probate) and thereby avoid paying CTT on the fund. operate for CGT, so that, unless it can be said that the beneficiaries who receive the fund take as legatees under the will, there will be a deemed disposal of settled property under CGTA s 54(1) (see p 222).

Secondly, this trust can be used as an alternative to a survivorship clause. Say, for instance, that the testator wants Eric to get the property if he survives the testator by 18 months failing which Ernie is to receive it. This cannot be achieved by a conventional survivorship clause (which must be limited to six months; see p 317). If Eric and Ernie are made beneficiaries of a discretionary trust however, and the trustees know the testator's wishes about the break-up of the fund, there is no risk of a double CTT charge in carrying out his wishes.

Finally, such a trust is obviously attractive as compared to variations and disclaimers. If there is any doubt about who should be given the deceased's estate, it is better to use such a trust than to rely upon an appointed legatee voluntarily renouncing a benefit under the will. All the most convincing fiscal arguments will often fail to persuade people to give up property and they cannot be compelled to vary or to disclaim!

5   Disclaimers and variations (post mortem tax planning)

It will often be desirable to effect changes in a will after the death of the testator, for instance, to rearrange the dispositions with a view to saving tax (and especially CTT). In practice, however, it is non-tax factors that are usually most significant—typically the need to provide for someone who is omitted from the will or who is inadequately provided for. It may even be that a beneficiary under the will decides that he does not want the bequest. In all these cases, persons named in the original will reject a portion of their inheritance; hence, they will (usually) be making a gratuitous transfer of value with the result that CTT will prima facie be chargeable on these dispositions. Other taxes too could be important—notably CGT, income tax and stamp duty.

These problems also arise on an intestacy—indeed the statutory intestacy provisions will often prove even less satisfactory than a will.

So far as both CTT and CGT are concerned certain changes to a will, or to the intestacy rules, are permitted, if effected within two years of death, to take effect as if they had been provided for in the original will (for CTT see FA 1978 s 68; for CGT, CGTA 1979 s 49(6)–(9)). The effect of 'reading back' these changes into the will or amending the intestacy rules is to avoid a second charge to CTT and any charge to CGT.

EXAMPLE 16

T by will leaves property to his three daughters equally. He omits his son with whom he had quarrelled bitterly. The daughters might agree to vary the will by providing that the four children take equally and, for the capital taxes, T's original will can be varied to provide for the four of them equally. Hence, no daughter need be taxed on the gift of a part of her share to her brother.

Notice that to take advantage of these provisions there must be a voluntary alteration of the testamentary provisions; in the case of enforced alterations (eg as a result of applications under the Inheritance (Provisions for Family and Dependants) Act 1975, see p 310) different provisions apply.

a) *Permitted ways of altering the will or intestacy*

There are two methods of altering a will or intestacy; by a disclaimer and by a variation. A disclaimer operates as a refusal to accept property and, hence, to be valid, should be made before any act of acceptance has occurred (such as receiving any benefit). When a disclaimer is effected the property passes according to fixed rules of law. It is not possible to disclaim in favour of a particular person. Hence, if a specific bequest is disclaimed the property falls into the residue of the will; if it is the residue itself which is disclaimed the property will pass as on an intestacy. Property can also be disclaimed on intestacy.

A disclaimer is, therefore, an all or nothing event; it is not possible to retain part and disclaim the rest of a gift. If, however, both a specific bequest and a share of residue are left to the same person, the benefit of one could be accepted and the other disclaimed.

In a variation, the deceased's provisions are altered at the choice of the person effecting the alteration so that the gift is redirected and the fact that some benefit had already accrued before the change is irrelevant. Any part of a gift can be redirected. The person who makes the variation has clearly owned the property of the deceased for the time up to the variation.

b) *The CTT rules on variations and disclaimers*

If the following conditions are satisfied the variation or disclaimer is not itself a transfer of value and instead takes effect as if the original will or intestacy had so provided:

(1) The variation or disclaimer must occur within two years of death. In the

case of disclaimers it is likely that action will need to be taken soon after the death otherwise the benefit will have been accepted.

(2) The variation or disclaimer must be effected by an instrument in writing (in practice a deed is often used) executed by the person who would otherwise benefit.

(3) In the case of variations, where it is desired to 'read them back' into the original will, an election in writing to that effect must be made to the Revenue (normally within six months of the variation). This election has to be made by the person making the variation and, where the effect of that election would be to increase the CTT chargeable on the death, also by the PRs. PRs can only refuse to join in such an election, however, if they have insufficient assets in their hands to discharge the extra CTT bill (for instance, where administration of the estate had been completed and the assets distributed). No election is necessary in the case of disclaimers which, assuming that the other requirements are satisfied, are automatically 'read back' into the will.

(4) A variation or disclaimer cannot be for money or money's worth, except where there are reciprocal variations or other beneficiaries are also disclaiming for the ultimate benefit of a third person.

(5) All property comprised in the deceased's estate immediately before death can be redirected under these provisions except for property which the deceased was treated as owning by virtue of an interest in possession in a settlement.

EXAMPLE 17

(1) A and T were joint tenants. On the death of T, A can redirect the half share of the property that he acquired by right of survivorship taking advantage of FA 1978 s 68.

(2) T by will created a settlement giving C a life interest. C can redirect that interest under FA 1978 s 68.

(3) T was the life tenant of a fund—the property now vests in D absolutely. D cannot take advantage of FA 1978 s 68 if he varies the terms of the settlement by disposing of his interest. (Notice, however, that FA 1975 s 47(4) permits a beneficiary to disclaim an interest in settled property without that disclaimer being subject to CTT.)

In the case of variations, the choice to elect or not to elect is with the taxpayer. A similar election operates for CGT but it is not necessary to exercise both CTT and CGT elections; they can be used separately (see p 224).

PRs of deceased beneficiaries can effect variations and disclaimers which can be read back into the original will whilst the estate of a beneficiary alive at the testator's death can be increased by such a variation or disclaimer (see '*Capital Taxes*' vol 1 p 22).

EXAMPLE 18

(1) T leaves property to his wealthy brother. The brother wishes to redirect it to grandchildren. An election for CTT purposes is advisable since (a) it will not increase the CTT charged on T's death and (b) it will avoid a second charge at the brother's rates (for which quick succession relief would not be available—see p 318).

(2) T leaves residue to his widow. She wishes to redirect a portion to her daughter. In this case it is not apparent without more information whether the election

should be made or not. If it is made, the CTT on T's death will be increased because an exempt bequest is being replaced with one that is chargeable. If the election is not made, on T's death the residue remains exempt but the widow will make a chargeable lifetime transfer. This may well be advantageous when compared with the CTT at T's death rates. The widow will, for instance, benefit from the lower lifetime rates of tax; may have unused exemptions and reliefs; and may have the £64,000 nil rate band available.

(3) H leaves £1m to his wife, W. She dies immediately and leaves everything to her only child, D. It might be advantageous for the PRs of W to vary H's will so that £500,000 is left to D and £500,000 to W (the consent of H's PRs would be needed). The result would be to equalise the estates of H and W (see further p 497).

(4) H leaves £1m to his only daughter, D. His widow, W, dies soon afterwards leaving a small estate to D. D should consider varying H's will so that (say) £500,000 is left to W. D will then receive that sum from W's estate.

c) *Other taxes*

Although variations and disclaimers can normally be safely employed for CTT and CGT, problems may exist in other areas. A variation, being a voluntary disposition, will normally attract 1% ad valorem stamp duty (unless the nil rate applies). Had the change been effected by a disclaimer which is neither a conveyance on sale nor a voluntary disposition (rather it is a refusal to accept), there will be no ad valorem duty. If the disclaimer is by deed, a 50p stamp should be affixed.

If a variation were made by a beneficiary in favour of his own infant unmarried child there would be a settlement for income tax purposes within TA 1970 Pt XVI (see Chapter 11). Hence, income arising (unless accumulated in a capital settlement) will be assessed as that of the parent. Again, a disclaimer would escape these problems since property has never been owned and, therefore, despite the wide definition of 'settlement' for income tax purposes, would appear to fall outside these provisions.

For the DLT consequences of variations and disclaimers see p 436.

23 CTT—exemptions and reliefs

I   Lifetime exemptions and reliefs
II   Death exemptions and reliefs
III   Exemptions for lifetime and death transfers

Instead of exempting whole categories of property from charge, as does CGT, CTT allows for certain exemptions and reliefs some of which are available on lifetime transfers only; some on death only; and some for all transfers, whether in lifetime or on death.

The exemptions may be justified on the grounds of necessity—some gifts must be permitted (eg Christmas and Wedding presents); or, in the case of reliefs applicable to particular property, because it is desirable that the property should be preserved and not sold to pay the tax bill (eg business and agricultural reliefs).

The nil rate band (currently £64,000) is not an exempt transfer. In fact transfers within this band are chargeable transfers, but taxed at 0%, and accordingly exemptions and reliefs should be exhausted first.

I   LIFETIME EXEMPTIONS AND RELIEFS

1   Transfers not exceeding £3,000 pa (FA 1975 Sch 6 para 2)

Up to £3,000 can be transferred free from CTT each tax year (6 April to 5 April). To the extent that this relief is unused in any one year it can be rolled forward for one tax year only, but only to the extent that the annual exemption for the second year is fully utilised.

EXAMPLE 1

A gives away £2,500 in 1982–83; £2,800 in 1983–84; and £3,700 in 1984–85.
For 1982–83: no CTT (£3,000 exemption) and £500 is carried forward.
For 1983–84: no CTT (£3,000 exemption) and £200 only is carried forward. The £500 from 1982–83 could only have been used to the extent that the transfer in 1983–84 exceeded £3,000.
For 1984–85: CTT on £500 (£3,200 is exempt).

The relief can operate by deducting £3,000 from a larger gift. Where several gifts are made in the same tax year, earlier gifts will be given the relief first; if several gifts are made on the same day there is a pro rata apportionment of the relief irrespective of the actual order of gifts. FA 1981 s 94 extended the relief to settlements with interests in possession; broadly the matter is one for the election of the life tenant (see p 350).

What should a would-be donor do who does not wish to transfer assets/money to the value of £3,000, but at the same time is reluctant to see the exemption lost? One solution is to vest an interest in property in the donee whilst retaining control of the asset, but the device of selling the asset with the purchase price outstanding and releasing part of the debt each year equal to the annual exemption may fall foul of the associated operations rules (Chapter 21).

2 **Normal expenditure out of income** (FA 1975 Sch 6 para 5)

To qualify for relief the relevant transfer must be part of the normal and regular expenditure of the transferor; taking one year with the next it must be payable out of income, and, after allowing for all such transfers, the transferor must be left with sufficient income to maintain his usual standard of living. The legislation does not define 'usual standard of living', whilst the requirement that there must be regular payments out of income makes it impossible to apply to gifts of chattels. A further problem may be caused by the requirement that the payments be normal and regular. A pattern of payments is most easily shown where the taxpayer is committed to making the payment ab initio as, for instance, where he enters into a deed of covenant. In other cases a couple of payments might have to be made before there is sufficient evidence of regularity.

EXAMPLE 2

A takes out a life insurance policy on his own life for £60,000 with the benefit of that policy being held on a trust for his grandchildren. A pays the premiums on the policy of £3,500 pa. A makes a transfer of value of £3,500 pa but he can make use of the normal expenditure exemption to avoid CTT so long as all the requirements for that exemption are satisfied. Alternatively, the £3,000 annual exemption would relieve most of the annual premium.

Anti-avoidance rules provide that:
(1) The normal expenditure exemption will not cover a life insurance premium unless the transferor can show that the life cover was not facilitated by and associated with an annuity purchased on his own life (FA 1975 Sch 6 para 5(2)).
(2) Under FA 1975 s 42 (unless the transferor can disprove the presumption of associated transactions, as above) a CTT charge can arise when the benefit of the life policy is vested in the donee. In general, if a charge arises, the sum assured by the life policy is treated as a transfer of value.

These special rules exist to prevent tax saving by the use of back-to-back insurance policies, as in the following example:

EXAMPLE 3

Tony pays an insurance company £50,000 in return for an annuity of £7,000 pa for the rest of his life. At the same time he enters into a life insurance contract on his own life written in favour of his brother Ted. The potential advantages are that on the death of Tony the sum of £50,000 is no longer part of his estate and the annuity has no value. The insurance proceeds will not attract CTT because they do not form part of his estate and Tony could claim that the premiums amounted to regular payments out of his income and so were free of CTT.

3 **Small gifts** (FA 1975 Sch 6 para 4)

Any number of £250 gifts can be made in any tax year by a donor provided that the gifts are to different donees. It must be an outright gift (not a gift into settlement) and the sum cannot be severed from a larger gift. Hence, if A wished to give his daughter £3,250 pa, it would be necessary to make separate gifts to her of £3,000 and £250 to secure full exemption.

4   Gifts in consideration of marriage (FA 1975 Sch 6 para 6)

The gift must be made before or contemporaneously with marriage and only after marriage if in satisfaction of a prior legal obligation. It must be conditional upon the marriage taking place so that should the marriage not occur the donor must have the right to recover the gift (if this right is not exercised, there may be a CTT charge on the failure to exercise that right under FA 1975 s 20(7)). A particular marriage must be in contemplation; it will not suffice, for instance, for a father to make a gift to his two year old daughter expressed to be conditional upon her marriage on the fatalistic assumption that she is bound to get married eventually!

The exemption can be used to settle property, but only if the beneficiaries are limited to (generally) the couple, any issue, and spouses of such issue (see FA 1975 Sch 6 para 6(3)(b)). Hence, a marriage cannot be used to effect a general settlement of assets within the family.

The sum exempt from CTT is:

(1) £5,000, if the donor is a parent of either party to the marriage. Thus, each of four parents can give £5,000 to the couple.

(2) £2,500, if the transferor is a remoter ancestor of either party to the marriage (eg a grandparent or great-grandparent) or if the transferor is a party to the marriage. The latter is designed to cover ante nuptial gifts since after marriage transfers between spouses are normally exempt without limit (see p 328).

(3) £1,000, in the case of any other transferors (eg a wedding guest).

5   Dispositions for maintenance etc (FA 1975 s 46)

Dispositions listed in FA 1975 s 46 are not transfers of value so that they are ignored for CTT purposes. The Revenue take the view that this exemption only applies to inter vivos dispositions, presumably because 'disposition' is not adequate to cover the deemed disposition on death.

Maintenance of a former spouse (FA 1975 s 46(1)(a))   Even without this provision such payments would in many cases escape CTT. If made before decree absolute, the exemption for gifts between spouses (see p 328) would operate and even after divorce they might escape CTT as regular payments out of income; or fall within the annual exemption; or be non-gratuitous transfers. What s 46 does is to put the matter beyond all doubt.

Two problems may be mentioned. First, maintenance is not defined, so that whether it could cover the transfer of capital assets (eg the former matrimonial home) is unclear. Secondly, if the payer dies but payment is to continue for the lifetime of the recipient, the position is unclear in the light of the Revenue's view that this exemption is limited to inter vivos dispositions.

Maintenance of children   Provision for the maintenance, education or training of a child of either party to a marriage (including stepchildren and adopted children) is not a transfer of value (FA 1975 s 46(1)(b)). The maintenance can continue beyond the age of 18 if the child is in full-time education. Thus, school fees paid by parents escape CTT. Similar principles operate where the disposition is for the maintenance of a parent's illegitimate child (FA 1975 s 46(4)). A similar relief is given for the maintenance of other people's children if the child is an infant and not in the care of either parent; once the child is 18, not only must he be undergoing full-time education, but also the disponer must (in effect) have been in loco parentis to the child during his minority (FA 1975 s 46(2)). Hence, payment of school and college fees by grandparents will seldom escape CTT under this provision.

Care or maintenance of a dependent relative   The provision of maintenance whether direct or indirect must be reasonable and the relative (as defined in FA 1975 s 46(6)) must be incapacitated by old age or infirmity from maintaining himself (although mothers and mothers-in-law, who are widowed or separated are always dependent relatives).

II   DEATH EXEMPTIONS AND RELIEFS

1   **Woodlands** (FA 1975 s 36 and Sch 9)

This relief takes effect by deferring CTT on growing trees and underwood forming part of the deceased's estate. Their value is left out of account on the death. An election must be made for the relief by written notice given (normally) within two years after the death. It is not available where the woodlands qualify for agricultural relief (see p 332). To prevent deathbed CTT saving schemes the land must not have been purchased by the deceased in the five years before his death (note, however, that the relief is available if the woodlands were obtained by gift or inheritance within the five year period). The relief does not apply to the land itself, but any CTT charged can be paid in instalments. The deferred tax on the timber may become chargeable as follows:

Sale of the timber with or without the land   CTT will be charged on the net proceeds of sale, but deductions can be made for costs of selling the timber and also for the costs of replanting. The net proceeds are taxed according to the death rates at the date of the disposal and the tax is calculated by treating those proceeds as forming the highest part of the deceased's estate. The 50% business property relief may be available where the trees or underwood formed a business asset at the date of death and, but for the deferment election, would have qualified for that relief. In such cases the relief is given against the net proceeds of sale.

A gift of the timber   Not only is the deferred charge triggered by a gift of the timber, but also the gift itself will be subject to CTT and, if it is merely a disposal of business assets (the timber) and not of the whole or a part of the business, business relief will not be available. In calculating the tax payable on the lifetime gift the value transferred is reduced by the triggered CTT charged on the death and the tax can be paid by interest-free instalments (whoever pays the CTT) spread over ten years (FA 1975 Sch 4 para 15).

EXAMPLE 4

(1)   Wally Wood dies in 1981 with a death estate of £100,000. In addition, he owns at death a woodlands business with the growing timber valued at £40,000 and the land etc valued at £30,000. The woodlands exemption is claimed by his daughter Wilma. In 1984 she sells the timber; the net proceeds of sale are £50,000.

(a) *Position on Wally's death:* The timber is left out of account. The value of the rest of the business (£30,000) attracts 50% business relief, so that, £15,000 will be added to the £100,000 chargeable estate.

(b) *Position on Wilma's sale:* The CTT charge is triggered. The net proceeds are reduced by 50% business relief to £25,000 which will be taxed according to the death rates of CTT in force in 1984 for transfers between £115,000 (ie Wally's total chargeable death estate) and £140,000.

(2) As in (1) above except that Wilma gives the timber to her brother Woad in 1984 when its net value is £50,000. The deferred charge will be triggered as in paragraph (b) of (1) above. CTT on Wilma's gift will be calculated according to her lifetime rates in force for 1984. She can deduct from the net value of the timber the deferred tax ((1) above) and any CTT can be paid by instalments whether it is paid by her or by Woad.

2   Death on active service (FA 1975 Sch 7 para 1)

FA 1975 Sch 7 para 1 ensures that the estates of persons dying on active service, including members of the UDR and RUC killed by terrorists in Northern Ireland, are exempt from CTT. This provision has been generously interpreted to cover a death arising many years after a wound inflicted whilst on active service, so long as that wound was one of the causes of death; it need not have been the only, or even the direct cause (*Barty-King v Ministry of Defence* (1979)). A *donatio mortis causa* is covered by the exemption but not lifetime transfers, whilst transfers within three years before death are still subject to the supplementary assessment (see p 304).

III   EXEMPTIONS FOR LIFETIME AND DEATH TRANSFERS

1   The inter-spouse exemption (FA 1975 Sch 6 para 1)

This most valuable exemption from CTT for transfers between spouses is only restricted where the donee spouse is not domiciled in the UK when the amount excluded from CTT is £55,000. The exemption is considered in different parts of this book and the following points represent a summary of those sections:

(1) For tax planning purposes the lowest total CTT bill is produced if the spouses ensure that they make equal chargeable transfers of value (see Chapter 35).

(2) Both should take advantage of the lifetime exemptions. The Revenue will normally not invoke the associated operations provisions to challenge a transfer between spouses even if it enables this to occur (Chapter 21).

(3) The rules for related property are designed to counter tax saving by splitting assets between spouses (see Chapter 21).

(4) CTT on a gift by one spouse to a third party may be collected from the other spouse in certain circumstances (see Chapter 21).

2   Business property relief (FA 1976 s 73 and Sch 10)

The stated purpose of this relief (and of agricultural relief (below)) is to prevent a business from having to be sold in order to pay the CTT bill. Any CTT that is payable after allowing this relief may often be paid by interest-free instalments (see Chapter 21). The relief if given automatically.

a) *Meaning of 'relevant business property'*

Business property relief is given in respect of transfers of 'relevant business property' which is defined as any of the following:

(1) *A business* Eg that of a sole trader or sole practitioner; or

(2) *An interest in a business* Eg the share of a partner in either a trading or professional partnership. The relief is available irrespective of the size of the transferor's interest in that enterprise. A sole trader who transfers a part of his trade falls within this category. (An interest in a business is distinct from assets used by such a business; for a similar problem in CGT see p 236.)

(3) *Shares or securities which give the transferor control of the company* Control does not have to be transferred; the requirement is simply that *at the time of transfer* the transferor should have such control (see p 331).

(4) *Shares in an unquoted company not falling within the above category* Hence, all shareholdings in private companies can qualify for relief.

(5) *Any land or building, plant or machinery which immediately before the transfer was used by a partnership in which the transferor was a partner or by a company of which he had control* The unjust result is that if the appropriate asset is used by a company in which the transferor owned 25% of the ordinary shares, no relief will be available. Had the asset been used by a partnership, however, in which he was entitled to 25% of all profits and surpluses, relief would be available. Relief also applies if the asset is held in a trust but is used by a life tenant for his own business or by a company which he controls.

Notice that the relief is available irrespective of whether a rent is charged for the use of the asset; in practice a nominal rent only should be reserved to preserve any CGT retirement relief (see p 238).

b) *Amount of relief*

Relief is given by percentage reduction in the value of the property transferred. The chargeable transfer will be of that reduced sum, grossed-up if the transferor is to bear the CTT. Business property relief is applied before other reliefs (for instance, the £3,000 inter vivos relief). The appropriate percentage depends upon which item of business property is transferred.

50% relief is available for businesses, interests in such business, and controlling shareholdings (ie categories (1), (2) and (3) above).

30% relief is available for minority shareholdings (category (4) above) and for assets used by a business (category (5) above).

EXAMPLE 5

Topsy is a partner in the firm of Topsy & Tim (builders). He owns the site of the firm's offices and goods yard. He gives to his daughter Teasy (1) his share of the business (value £500,000) and (2) the site (value £50,000). Business property relief will be available on the business at 50% so that the value transferred is £250,000 and on the site at 30% so that the value transferred is £35,000.

Notes:
  (i) Topsy's total transfers amount to £285,000 which may be further reduced if other exemptions are available.
 (ii) The effect of business property relief on the death of a transferor is to reduce the value of his estate and, hence, the estate rate.
(iii) CTT may remain payable on business property after deducting all available reliefs. Whether the transfer is made during lifetime or on death, it will usually be possible to pay the tax by interest-free instalments.

c) *Conditions if relief is to be available*

In general, relevant business property which has been owned for less than two years attracts no relief. Technical provisions deal with the problems caused by a succession of businesses, to ensure no loss of relief. Furthermore, the incorporation of a business will not affect the running of the two year period. Where a transfer of a business is made between spouses on death the recipient can include the ownership period of the deceased spouse. This is not, however, the case with an inter vivos transfer.

EXAMPLE 6

(1) Solomon incorporated his leather business by forming Solomon Ltd in which he held 100% of the issued shares. For business property relief the two year ownership period begins with the commencement of Solomon's original leather business.

(2) Solomon gave his shares to his wife and she gives them to her son within two years of that gift. The transfer to Mrs Solomon is exempt from CTT. The gift by Mrs Solomon attracts no business property relief, as the two year qualification period has not elapsed. If Mr Solomon leaves his shares in his will to her, his period of ownership can be included in calculating her two year period.

Other provisions exclude from relief certain businesses (eg those designed to hold investments or to deal in securities or land), whilst private assets cannot be disguised as a part of the business in an attempt to take advantage of the relief (see the same problem in CGT p 237).

As it is designed for businesses, relief is obviously not available for transfers of the sale proceeds from a business. Also the relief does not extend to a business subject to a 'buy and sell' agreement. Such arrangements are common in partnership agreements and amongst shareholder/directors of companies and provide that if one of the partners or shareholder/directors dies then his PRs are obliged to sell the share(s) and the survivors are obliged to purchase them. As this is a binding contract the beneficial ownership in the business or shares has passed to the purchaser so that business relief is not available (SP 12/80).

EXAMPLE 7

The shares of Zerzes Ltd are owned equally by the four directors. The articles of association provide that on the death of a shareholder his shares *shall* be sold to the remaining shareholder/directors who *must* purchase them. Business relief is not available on that death. If the other shareholders had merely possessed pre-emption rights, as no binding contract of sale exists, the relief would apply.

d) *Businesses held in settlements*

For interest in possession trusts the relief is given, as one would expect, by reference to the life tenant. So long as he satisfies the two year ownership test, relief will be given at the following rates:

50% relief for shares in companies controlled by the life tenant (taking into account both trust shares and any shares which he owns) and for businesses belonging to the trust;

30% relief for unquoted non-controlling shares held in the trust; and

30% relief for the assets listed in a) (5) above (see p 329) which are held in the trust and which are either used by the life tenant for his own business or by a company controlled by him.

For trusts without interests in possession the relief is given to the trust so long as the conditions are satisfied by the trustees, so that the beneficiaries are ignored. The relief will be given when the trust is subject to the anniversary charge and any resultant tax can be paid by instalments. When the business ceases to be relevant property (ie when it leaves the trust) business relief will again be available on fulfilment of the normal conditions.

e) *The problems of 'control'*

Control of a company means that the maximum 50% relief may be available. 'Control' is defined as follows:

> 'a person has control of a company at any time if he then has the control of powers of voting on *all questions* affecting the company as a whole which if exercised would yield a majority of the votes capable of being exercised thereon . . .' (FA 1975 Sch 4 para 13(7)).

Hence, control of 51% of the votes exercisable in general meeting will normally ensure that the transferor has 'control' for the purposes of business property relief. In calculating whether this figure has been attained a life tenant can aggregate shares held by the settlement with shares in his free estate, whilst the shares of husband and wife will be treated as one holding. In no other cases can shares of different persons or bodies be added together in order to discover whether an individual has control or not.

Care should be taken in reducing a controlling holding and where it is intended to make more than one transfer of the shares the transferor should keep control as long as possible.

EXAMPLE 8

Albert owns 80% of the issued ordinary shares in Albert Ltd. He transfers 30% of the company's shares to his son in 1984 and the remaining 50% to his daughter in 1985. On the transfer in 1984, 50% business property relief is available on the transfer of the 30% holding. Note that it is not necessary actually to transfer control. On the transfer in 1985 relief at 30% (only) is available since the 50% holding is not a controlling interest.

If he had transferred 29% of the shares in 1984 with the remaining 51% passing in 1985, 50% relief as above would be available on the transfer in 1984, and on the 1985 transfer, since Albert still has control.

Given that controlling shareholdings are worth significantly more than minority holdings the different percentage reliefs are explicable. Assume, for instance, that a controlling holding of 51 shares is worth £4 per share and the minority holding (49 shares) £3 per share. After reliefs, the majority shares are worth £2 each; the minority £2.10 each. In considering the reliefs, therefore, the valuation of the holding is obviously crucial, although it is disastrous to own a controlling interest (valued as such) and yet be deprived of 50% relief because of a technicality. This may occur if a company's articles contain a *Bushell v Faith* clause designed to prevent a director from being removed by ordinary resolution (hence circumventing the Companies Act 1948 s 184). For CTT purposes such clauses will mean that no shareholder can have control of that company since no one will control *'all questions* affecting the company as a whole'.

EXAMPLE 9

A company has two shareholders, A and B, holding 80% and 20% of the shares respectively. B is protected by a '*Bushell v Faith* clause' giving him five votes per share, whilst A has only one vote per share. Hence, for CTT purposes, despite his 80% stake, A does not have control on all questions affecting the company as a whole and his business relief is restricted to 30%.

In such cases it is worth exploring other ways of entrenching B's position. Consider, for instance, the use of a shareholders' agreement; giving B a life service contract; or inserting an article that on a s 184 resolution the general meeting shall not be quorate unless B attends. None of these alternatives should affect A's entitlement to 50% business property relief.

3   Agricultural property relief (FA 1981 s 96 and Sch 14)

FA 1981 s 96 and Sch 14 introduced new rules for giving relief in the case of transfers of agricultural property. As for business relief, this relief is given automatically. The old regime will not be considered save for a brief mention of the transitional provisions.

a) *Meaning of 'agricultural property' and 'agricultural value'*

Relief is given for transfers of value of agricultural property, defined as agricultural land or pasture including cottages, farm buildings and farmhouses together with land used with them so long as they are 'of a character appropriate to the property'. It is the 'agricultural value' of such property which is subject to the relief; 'agricultural value' is defined as the value which the property would have if subject to a perpetual covenant prohibiting its use otherwise than as agricultural property. Enhanced value attributable to development potential is not subject to the relief (although business property relief can apply to this excess value). Otherwise, normal valuation rules, eg on the basis of vacant possession, are applied. It is not necessary to transfer a farming business or part thereof in order to obtain relief; it can be given on a mere transfer of assets.

b) *The amount of relief*

As with business relief, agricultural relief is given by a percentage reduction of the transferred value. Other exemptions (eg the £3,000 lifetime exemption) can be set against the reduced figure. Where the transferor is to pay the CTT, this reduced figure must be grossed up. Any resultant tax may be paid by instalments and, unlike business property relief, this relief is unrestricted. There are two levels of relief:

50% relief for the occupier of agricultural property subject to a two year ownership requirement. Into this category fall owner occupiers and tenant farmers in possession. Exceptionally, the 50% relief is also available where the transferor is a landlord out of possession. He must have owned the property for the seven years before the transfer and that property must have been occupied (by himself or another) for the purposes of agriculture throughout that period. Furthermore, he must have the right to obtain vacant possession within 12 months of the transfer. (The existing tenant must not, therefore, enjoy the protection of the Agricultural Holdings Acts.)

30% relief is available in other cases and, therefore, covers a landlord owning a freehold reversion. The qualifying period of ownership is seven years immediately preceding the transfer and during this period the land must throughout have been occupied either by the transferor or by others for the purposes of agriculture. Although it was intended that the same amount of tax would be produced on the tenanted agricultural value after 30% relief as on the vacant possession agricultural value after 50% relief, it is probably advantageous to reduce the value of the land (eg by granting a lease to a family partnership) and opting for 30% relief.

EXAMPLE 10

Adam lets agricultural property to a partnership consisting of himself, Bertram, and Claud. So far as Adam is concerned: (1) the 30% relief will be available for his freehold reversion; and (2) the 50% relief will apply to his vacant possession interest in the land in his capacity as a partner.

The relief (at 50% or 30% as appropriate) is available in three further cases: first, where agricultural property is held on discretionary trusts (50% relief, if the trustees have been farming the land themselves); secondly, where 'agricultural property' is held on trust for a life tenant under an interest in possession trust; and finally, relief is available where agricultural property is held by a company in which the transferor of shares has control. 'Control' has the same meaning as for business property relief. To claim the relief the appropriate two or seven year period of ownership must be satisfied by the company (vis-à-vis the agricultural property) and by the shareholder/transferor (vis-à-vis the shares transferred).

c) *Technical provisions*

As with business property relief there are technical provisions relating to replacement property, transfers between spouses, and succession from a donor. Similarly, a binding contract for the sale of the property results in agricultural relief not being available. Furthermore, the grant of a tenancy of agricultural property will not be a transfer of value provided that the grant is for full consideration in money or money's worth (FA 1981 s 97). Hence, it will no longer be necessary for the lessor to show (particularly in the case of transfers within the family) that he had no gratuitous intent and that the transaction was such as might be made with a stranger. The change (surprisingly made retrospective) is explicable because of the end of double discounting in FA 1981.

d) *Transitional relief; double discounting*

Under the rules which prevailed up to 1981 agricultural property relief was available where L let Whiteacre to a partnership consisting of himself and his children M and N. On a transfer of the freehold reversion (valued on a tenanted, not a vacant possession, basis) 50% relief was available. The ingredient of 'double discounting' consisted of first reducing the value of the property by granting the lease and then applying the full (50%) relief to that discounted value. As a *quid pro quo* the Revenue argued that the grant of the lease could be a transfer of value even if for a full commercial rent.

Double discount is not available under the new system of agricultural relief and the grant of the tenancy will not be a chargeable transfer of value if for full consideration (FA 1981 s 97). On a transitional basis, however, where land was let, as in the above example, on 10 March 1981 so that any transfer by L immediately before that date would have qualified for the 50% allowance, on the next transfer of value, that old relief will still apply. (Note that the old relief was limited to £250,000 of agricultural value before giving relief or to 1,000 acres, at the option of the taxpayer.) It is only the first actual transfer of that reversion after 10 March 1981 that will obtain the benefit of double discounting, so that it is important to ensure that that transfer is not exempt (eg to a spouse). Also, the transitional relief will not apply in cases where the pre-10 March 1981 tenancy has been surrendered and regranted. Similar transitional relief applies where before 10 March 1981 the land was let to a company which the transferor controlled.

e) *Inter-relation of agricultural and business property reliefs*

The two reliefs are similar and overlap. The following distinctions are worthy of note:
(1) Agricultural relief must be given in priority to business relief (FA 1976 Sch 10 para 10).
(2) The instalment option is automatically available for agricultural relief (FA 1981 s 96(2)). For business property the facility is more restricted.
(3) Business relief is not available for a transfer of assets (eg some of a farmer's acreage) but only for a transfer of part of a business. Agricultural relief is not so limited.
(4) Differences exist in the treatment of woodlands, crops, livestock, dead-stock, plant and machinery, and farmhouses etc. Generally, in these areas business relief is more widely available.

4 Relief for heritage property (FA 1976 ss 76–83)

FA 1976 s 76 provides that in certain circumstances CTT can be postponed on transfers of value of heritage property. As tax can be postponed on any number of such transfers, the result is that a liability to CTT can be deferred indefinitely (similar deferral provisions operate for CGT: CGTA 1979 s 147(3)).

a) *Conditions to be satisfied if CTT is to be deferred*

In order to obtain this relief, first, the property must fall into one of two main categories designated by the Treasury:

Category 1 works of art (including pictures, prints and books) which are of 'national, scientific, historic, or artistic interest'.

Category 2 land and buildings which are (generally) of outstanding scenic, historic, or architectural interest.

Secondly, undertakings have to be given with respect to that property to take reasonable steps for its preservation; to secure reasonable access to the public (see '*Works of Art a basic guide*' published by the Central Office of Information); and (in the case of Category 1 property) to keep the property in the UK. In appropriate cases of Category 1 property, it is sufficient for details of the object and its location to be entered on an official list of such assets.

The undertaking must be given by 'such person as the Treasury think appropriate in the circumstances of the case'. In practice, this will mean a PR, trustee, legatee or donee.

A third requirement exists in the case of lifetime transfers of value. The transferor must have owned the asset for the six years immediately preceding the transfer if relief is to be given. Notice, however, that the six year requirement can be satisfied by aggregating periods of ownership of a husband and wife and that it does not apply in cases where the property has been inherited on a death and the exemption has then been successfully claimed. As an anti-avoidance provision it is surprising that the six year requirement is limited to inter vivos transfers since the result is that death bed schemes are permitted.

b) *Effect of deferring CTT*

Where relief is given the transfer is a 'conditionally exempt transfer'. So long as the undertakings are observed and the property is not further transferred CTT liability can be postponed. If there is a subsequent transfer, the exemption may be claimed a second time. Three 'chargeable events' cause the deferred CTT charge to become payable: first, a breach of the undertakings; secondly, a sale of the asset; and thirdly, a further transfer (inter vivos or on death) without a new undertaking. If a further transfer satisfies the requirements for a conditionally exempt transfer, not only will that transfer itself not be chargeable but it will not lead to any triggering of the deferred charge.

In the case where a fresh undertaking is given, but the transfer does not satisfy the other requirements for a transfer of heritage property (eg it is to a spouse or is made before the six year ownership requirement has been satisfied), no chargeable event occurs (see FA 1976 s 78(5)). Thus, any deferred charge is not triggered, but the transfer itself may be chargeable, if not to a spouse.

c) *Calculation of the deferred CTT charge*

Calculation of the deferred CTT charge will depend upon what triggers the charge. If there is a breach of undertakings, the tax is charged upon the person who would be entitled to the proceeds of sale were the asset then sold. The value of the property at that date will be charged according to the transferor's rates of CTT. Where he is alive, this is by reference to his cumulative total at the time of the triggering event; where he is dead, the property is added to his death estate and charged at the highest rate applicable to that estate but according to the lifetime table unless the conditionally exempt transfer occurred on his death.

EXAMPLE 11

In 1983 Aloysius gives a Rousseau painting (valued at £500,000) to his daughter Wilma. The transfer is conditionally exempt, but, two years later (when the picture is worth £650,000), Wilma breaks the undertakings by refusing to allow the painting to be exhibited in the Primitive Exhibition in London. If Aloysius is still alive in 1985, CTT is calculated on £650,000 at Aloysius' lifetime rates according to his cumulative total of chargeable transfers in 1985. Had Aloysius died in 1984 with a death estate of £1,000,000, £650,000 would be charged at the lifetime rates appropriate to the highest part of his death estate of £1,650,000.

If the deferred charge is triggered by a sale of the heritage property, the above principles operate, save that it is the net sale proceeds that will be subject to the deferred charge. Expenses of sale, including CGT, are deductible.

Calculation of the deferred charge is more complex where it is triggered by a gift of the heritage property since two chargeable transfers could occur; the first on the gift and the second by the triggering of the deferred charge. If the gift is a chargeable event the tax payable on that gift is credited against the triggered deferred charge. Where the gift is a chargeable transfer, but not a chargeable event, as the triggering charge does not arise (p 335) the credit will be available against the next chargeable event affecting that property.

EXAMPLE 12

Eric makes a conditionally exempt transfer to Ernie in 1982. Ernie in turn gives the asset to Erica in 1984 and Erica does not give any undertaking.
The gift to Erica is a chargeable transfer. CTT will be calculated at Ernie's lifetime rates in 1984.
The triggered charge: the value of the asset in 1984 will be subject to CTT at Eric's lifetime rates (assuming that he is still alive). A tax credit for the CTT paid on the 1984 gift which is attributable to the value of the asset is available.

If Erica had given an appropriate undertaking in 1984, the gift to Erica would be taxed as above (the six year requirement is not satisfied by Ernie). The transfer is not a chargeable event so that no triggering of the conditionally exempt transfer occurs. The tax credit is available when this charge is triggered, eg by Erica selling the asset.

Where there has been more than one conditionally exempt transfer of the same property, and a chargeable event occurs, the Revenue have the right to choose which of the earlier transferors (within 30 years before the chargeable event) shall be used for calculating the sum payable.

EXAMPLE 13

Z gives a picture to Y who gives it to X who sells it. There have been two conditionally exempt transfers (by Z and Y) and the Revenue can choose (subject to the 30 year time limit) whether to levy the deferred CTT charge according to Z or Y's rates.

d) *Settled property*

The exemption may be available for heritage property held in a discretionary trust (FA 1976 ss 81, 82, 82A). Where it is held in an interest in possession trust, it is treated as belonging to the life tenant and the above rules are applied.

e) *Maintenance funds*

FA 1982 ss 93–95 and Sch 16 provide for no CTT to be charged when property (whether or not heritage property) is settled on trusts to secure the maintenance, repair etc of historic buildings. Such trusts also receive special income tax treatment (FA 1980 ss 52–53) and, for CGT, the hold-over election under FA 1980 s 79 is available (the rules of CGTA 1979 s 148 are repealed for disposals after 6 April 1984; FA 1984 s 68).

f) *Private treaty sales and acceptance in lieu*

Heritage property can be given for national purposes or for the public benefit without any CTT or CGT charge arising. Alternatively, the property can be sold by private treaty (not at an auction) to a heritage body as listed in FA 1975 Sch 6 para 12. The transferor is offered a 'douceur' equal to 25% of the tax exemption (ie the sale price will be the value of the asset net of CTT plus 25% of that CTT saved). On such gifts or sales, any conditional exemption is made absolute, but any gain realised on a sale will be subject to CGT (FA 1975 Sch 6 paras 12, 13).

An asset can be offered to the Revenue in lieu of tax (see FA 1975 Sch 4 para 17(1). As with sales to heritage bodies, the credit allowed for the value of the asset surrendered will be that asset's net value plus 25% of the notional tax saved. The Secretary of State has to agree to accept such assets and it should be noted that the standard of objects which can be so accepted is very much higher than that required for the conditional exemption (for the difficulties surrounding *Calke Abbey* see 1984 CTT News p 52).

5 Gifts to political parties (FA 1975 Sch 6 para 11)

Such gifts are exempt from CTT, whether effected during life or on death, insofar as that they do not exceed £100,000 in total on death and within one year before death; the excess is chargeable. There are detailed provisions which deny relief where the gift is delayed, conditional, made for a limited period, or could be used for other purposes (see FA 1975 Sch 6 paras 11 and 15). There are no special CGT provisions for political gifts and the hold-over election (FA 1980 s 79) will not apply since a political party is not an individual.

6 Gifts to charities (FA 1975 Sch 6 para 10)

Gifts to charities are exempt without limit. As with gifts to political parties detailed provisions deny the exemption if the vesting of the gift is postponed; if it is conditional; if it is made for a limited period; or if it could be used for non-charitable purposes.

24 CTT—settlements: definition and classification

I   Introductory and definitions
II Classification of settlements
III Creation of settlements
IV Payment of CTT

I INTRODUCTORY AND DEFINITIONS

The objective when taxing settled property is to ensure that it is the capital of the settlement which is subject to tax and not just the value of the various beneficial interests. Further, successive governments have affirmed that the object of the CTT provisions is to ensure that settled property is taxed no more or less heavily than unsettled property. The original scheme in FA 1975 was considered to be defective in the area of trusts without interests in possession and FA 1982 introduced major amendments.

1 What is a settlement?

'Settlement' is defined in FA 1975 Sch 5 para 1:

'(2) "Settlement" means any disposition or dispositions of property, whether effected by instrument, by parole or by operation of law, or partly in one way and partly in another, whereby the property is for the time being—
(a) held in trust for persons in succession or for any person subject to a contingency; or
(b) held by trustees on trust to accumulate the whole or part of any income of the property or with power to make payments out of that income at the discretion of the trustees or some other person, with or without power to accumulate surplus income; or
(c) charged or burdened (otherwise than for full consideration in money or money's worth paid for his own use or benefit to the person making the disposition), with the payment of any annuity or other periodical payment payable for a life or any other limited or terminable period; . . .
(3) A lease of property which is for life or lives, or for a period ascertainable only by reference to a death, or which is terminable on, or at a date ascertainable only by reference to, a death, shall be treated as a settlement and the property as settled property, unless the lease was granted for full consideration in money or money's worth, and where a lease not granted as a lease at a rack rent is at any time to become a lease at an increased rent it shall be treated as terminable at that time'.

EXAMPLE 1

(1) Property is settled on X for life remainder to Y and Z absolutely (a fixed trust; see (2)(a) above).
(2) Property is held on trust for 'such of A, B, C, D, E and F as my trustees in their absolute discretion may select' (a discretionary trust; see (2)(b) above).
(3) Property is held on trust 'for A contingent on attaining 18' (a contingency settlement; see (2)(a) above).

(4) Property is held on trust by A and B as trustees for Z absolutely (a bare trust, although for CTT purposes there is no settlement and the property is treated as belonging to Z).

(5) A and B jointly purchase Blackacre. Under LPA 1925 ss 34–36 there is a statutory trust for sale with A and B holding the land on trust (as joint tenants) for themselves as either joint tenants or tenants in common in equity. For CTT purposes there is no settlement and the property belongs to A and B equally.

(6) A grants B a lease of Blackacre for his (B's) life at a peppercorn rent. This is a settlement for CTT purposes and A is the trustee of the property (FA 1975 Sch 5 para 1(7)). Under LPA 1925 s 149 the lease is treated as being for a term of 90 years which is determinable on the death of B.

(7) A owns Blackacre. He reserves a lease on the property for his life and sells the freehold reversion for full value. It would appear that the lease is granted for full consideration (in money or money's worth) with the result that there is no settlement for CTT purposes (see SP E10).

2 Settlors and trustees

In the majority of cases it is not difficult to identify the settlor, since there will usually be one settlor who will create a settlement by a 'disposition' of property (which may include a series of associated operations; see FA 1975 s 51). If that settlor adds further property, this creates no problems in the interest in possession settlement, but difficulties arise if the settlement is discretionary (see p 360) with further complications if the original property was excluded property and the additional property was not, or vice versa (see Chapter 27). A settlement may have more than one settlor:

EXAMPLE 2

(1) Bill and Ben create a settlement in favour of their neighbour Barum.

(2) Bill adds property to a settlement that had been created two years ago by Ben in favour of neighbour Barum.

FA 1975 Sch 5 para 1(8) states that: 'Where more than one person is a settlor in relation to a settlement and the circumstances so require, this Schedule [Sch 5] and Section 25(3)(d) of this Act [FA 1975] shall apply in relation to it as if the settled property were comprised in separate settlements'. *Thomas v IRC* (1981) indicates that this provision only applies where an identifiable capital fund has been provided by each settlor. The fund will be treated as two separate settlements in the case of discretionary trusts where both the incidence of the periodic charge and the amount of CTT chargeable may be affected. FA 1975 Sch 5 para 1(6) defines settlor (in terms similar to those for income tax purposes—see Chapter 11) thus:

> ' "Settlor", in relation to a settlement, includes any person by whom the settlement was made directly or indirectly, and . . . includes any person who has provided funds directly or indirectly for the purpose of or in connection with the settlements or has made with any other person a reciprocal arrangement for that other person to make the settlement'.

A further problem arises where there is only one settlor who adds property to his settlement; is this for CTT purposes one settlement or two? This question is significant in relation to discretionary trusts (especially with regard to timing and rate of the periodic and inter-periodic charges) and where excluded property is involved in a settlement. As a matter of trust law, there will be a single settlement where funds are held and managed by one set of trustees for one set of beneficiaries, so that such additions will usually not lead to the creation of separate settlements. When it would be advantageous for there to be two settlements, a separate settlement deed with (ideally) separate trustees should be employed.

The ordinary meaning is given to the term 'a trustee', although by FA 1975 Sch 5 para 1(7) it includes any person in whom the settled property or its management is for the time being vested. In cases where a lease for lives is treated as a settlement the lessor is the trustee.

II CLASSIFICATION OF SETTLEMENTS

1 The three categories

Since FA 1982 settlements for CTT purposes must be divided into three categories.

Category 1   A settlement with an interest in possession, eg where the property is held for an adult tenant for life who, by virtue of his interest, is entitled to the income and has 'an interest in possession'.

Category 2   A settlement lacking an interest in possession, eg where trustees are given a discretion over the distribution of the income so that no beneficiary has an interest in possession. At most, beneficiaries have the right to be considered when the discretion is exercised by the trustees; the right to ensure that the fund is properly administered; and the right to join with all the other beneficiaries to bring the settlement to an end.

This category also includes settlements where the property is held on trust for a minor contingent on his attaining a specified age. As long as the beneficiary is a minor there will be no interest in possession and the settlement will fall into Category 2, unless the trust satisfies the requirements for a Category 3 accumulation and maintenance settlement.

Category 3   Into this category fall special or privileged trusts. They lack an interest in possession, but are not subject to the Category 2 régime. The main example to be considered in this book is the accumulation and maintenance trust for children.

To place a particular trust into its correct category is important for two reasons. First, because the CTT treatment of each is totally different both as to incidence of tax and as to the amount of tax charged; and secondly, because a change from one category to another will normally give rise to a CTT charge. For example, if a life interest ceases, whereupon the fund is held on discretionary trusts, the settlement moves from Category 1 to Category 2, and a chargeable occasion (the ending of a life interest) has occurred.

2 The meaning of an 'interest in possession'

Normally trusts can easily be slotted into their correct category. Trusts falling within Category 3 are carefully defined so that any trust not specifically falling into one of those special cases must fall into Category 2. Problems are principally caused by the borderline between Categories 1 and 2 where the division is drawn according to whether the settlement has an interest in possession or not. In the majority of cases no problems will arise: at one extreme stands the life interest settlement; at the other the discretionary trust. However, what of a settlement which provides for the income to be paid to Albert, unless the trustees decide to pay it to Bertram, or to accumulate it; or where the property in the trust is enjoyed in specie by one beneficiary as the result of the exercise of a discretion (eg a beneficiary living in a dwelling house which was part of a discretionary fund)? To resolve these difficulties, the phrase an 'interest in possession' needs definition. The legislation does not assist; instead, its meaning must be gleaned from a Press Notice of the Revenue and *re Pilkington (Pearson v IRC)* (1980) which largely endorses the statements in the Press Release.

The Inland Revenue Press Notice (12 February 1976) provides as follows:

> '... an interest in settled property exists where the person having the interest has the *immediate entitlement* (subject to any prior claims by the trustees for expenses or other outgoings properly payable out of income) *to any income* produced by that property as the income arises; but ... a discretion or power, in whatever form, which can be exercised *after income arises* so as to withhold it from that person negatives the existence of an interest in possession. For this purpose a power to accumulate income is regarded as a power to withhold it, unless any accumulation must be held solely for the person having the interest or his personal representatives.
>
> On the other hand the existence of a mere power of revocation or appointment, the exercise of which would determine the interest wholly or in part (but which, so long as it remains unexercised, does not affect the beneficiary's immediate entitlement to income) does not ... prevent the interest from being an interest in possession'.

The first paragraph is concerned with the existence of discretions or powers which might affect the destination of the income after it has arisen and which prevent the existence of any interest in possession (eg a provision enabling the trustees to accumulate income or to divert it for the benefit of other beneficiaries). The second paragraph concerns overriding powers which, if exercised, would terminate the entire interest of the beneficiary, but which do not prevent the existence of an interest in possession (eg the statutory power of advancement). Administrative expenses charged on the income can be ignored in deciding whether there is an interest in possession, so long as such payments are for 'outgoings properly payable out of income'. A clause in the settlement permitting expenses of a capital nature to be so charged is, therefore, not covered and the Revenue consider that the mere presence of such a clause is fatal to the existence of any interest in possession.

Re Pilkington (Pearson v IRC) (1980)   In essence, the facts of the case are simple. Both capital and income of the fund were held for the settlor's three adult daughters in equal shares subject to three overriding powers exercisable by the trustees: (1) to appoint capital and income amongst the daughters, their spouses and issue; (2) to accumulate so much of the income as they should think fit; and (3) to apply any income towards the payment or discharge of any taxes, costs or other outgoings which would otherwise be payable out of capital. The trustees had regularly exercised their powers to accumulate the income. What caused the disputed CTT assessment (for a mere £444.73!) was the irrevocable appointment of some £16,000 from the fund to one of the daughters. There was no doubt that, as a result of the appointment, she obtained an interest in possession in that appointed sum; but did she already have an interest in possession the fund? If so, no CTT would be chargeable on the appointment (see p 348); if not, there would be a charge because the appointed funds had passed from a 'no interest in possession' to an 'interest in possession' settlement (Category 2 to Category 1).

The Revenue contended that the existence of the overriding power to accumulate and the provision enabling all expenses to be charged to income deprived the settlement of any interest in possession. It was common ground that whether such powers had been exercised or not was irrelevant in deciding the case. The overriding power of appointment over capital and income was not seen as endangering the existence of any interest in possession (see paragraph 2 of the Press Notice).

For the bare majority of the House of Lords the presence of the overriding discretion to accumulate the income was fatal to the existence of any interest in possession. 'A present right to present enjoyment' was how an interest in possession was defined and the beneficiary did not have a present right. 'Their enjoyment of any income from the trust fund depended on the trustees' decision as to accumulation of income' (per Viscount Dilhorne). No distinction is to be drawn between a trust to pay income to a beneficiary, but with an overriding power to accumulate and a trust to accumulate, but with a power to pay. Hence, in the following examples there is no interest in possession:

(1) to A for life but trustees may accumulate the income; and
(2) the income shall be accumulated but trustees may make payments to A.

3 Problems remaining after *Pilkington*

The test laid down by the majority in the House of Lords established some certainty in a difficult area of law and it is possible to say that the borderline between trusts with and without an interest in possession is reasonably easy to draw; where there is uncertainty about the entitlement of a beneficiary to income, it is likely that the settlement will fall into the 'no interest in possession' regime. In the light of the favourable changes made to the CTT treatment of discretionary trusts in FA 1982 that may be no bad thing for taxpayers!

The following are some of the difficulties left in the wake of *Pilkington*:

Dispositive and administrative powers   For there to be an interest in possession the beneficiary must be entitled to the income as it arises. Were this test to be applied strictly, however, even a trust with a life tenant receiving the income might fail to satisfy the requirement because trustees may deduct management expenses from that income, so that few beneficiaries are entitled to all the income as it arises. This problem was considered by Viscount Dilhorne as follows:

> '. . . Parliament distinguished between the administration of a trust and the dispositive powers of trustees . . . . A life tenant has an interest in possession but his interest only extends to the net income of the property, that is to say, after deduction from the gross income of expenses etc properly incurred in the management of the trust by the trustees in the exercise of their powers. A dispositive power is a power to dispose of the net income. Sometimes the line between an administrative and a dispositive power may be difficult to draw but that does not mean that there is not a valid distinction'.

In *Pilkington* the trustees had an overriding discretion to apply income towards the payment of any taxes, costs, or other outgoings which would otherwise be payable out of capital and the Revenue took the view that the existence of this overriding power was a further reason for the settlement lacking an interest in possession. It was, therefore, necessary to decide whether this power was administrative (in which case its presence did not affect the existence of any interest in possession) or dispositive (fatal to the existence of such an interest). Viscount Dilhorne decided that the power was administrative. Acceptable though this argument may be for management expenses, is it convincing when applied to other expenses and taxes (eg CGT and CTT) which would normally be payable out of the capital of the fund? It must be stressed that the House of Lords did not have to decide whether the Revenue's contention was correct or not; Viscount Dilhorne's observations are obiter dicta and the Revenue still adhere to their Press Notice (p 341). Would-be settlors should be advised not to insert such clauses.

Power to allow beneficiaries to occupy a dwelling house   This power may exist both in settlements which otherwise have an interest in possession and in those without. The mere existence of such a power is to be ignored; problems will only arise if and when it is exercised. SP 10/79 indicates that if such a power was exercised so as to allow, for a definite or indefinite period, someone other than the life tenant to have exclusive or joint right of residence of a dwelling house as a permanent home, there would be a CTT charge on the partial ending of a life interest. In the case of a fund otherwise lacking an interest in possession, the exercise of the power would result in the creation of such an interest and therefore, a CTT charge would arise. Whether this view is correct is arguable; in practice, any challenge could prove costly to the taxpayer and trustees who possess such powers should think carefully before exercising them.

Interest-free loans to beneficiaries   The Revenue's view is that a free loan to a beneficiary creates an interest in possession in the fund. As he is a debtor (to the extent of the loan), one wonders in what assets his interest subsists; the moneys loaned would appear to belong absolutely to him. Again, trustees should avoid making such loans and, if need be, the trust should guarantee a bank loan to the beneficiary.

EXAMPLE 3

The trustees of a discretionary trust lend £10,000 to beneficiary A in 1982. In 1985 he repays that sum in full. If the Revenue's view is correct, the result is that:
(1) *In 1982:* A has an interest in possession in £10,000. CTT is chargeable.
(2) *In 1985:* A's interest in possession ceases. CTT is chargeable.

Position of the last surviving member of a discretionary class   If the class of beneficiaries has closed, the sole survivor is entitled to the income as it arises so that there is an interest in possession. When the class has not closed, however, trustees have a reasonable time to decide how the accrued income is to be distributed and, if a further beneficiary could come into existence before that period has elapsed, the current beneficiary is not automatically entitled to the income as it arises so that there is no interest in possession (*Moore and Osborne v IRC* (1984)). Likewise, if the class has not closed and the trustees have a power to accumulate income.

III   CREATION OF SETTLEMENTS

The creation of a settlement will be a chargeable transfer of value by the settlor. If the burden of paying the CTT is put upon the trustees of the settlement, the

Revenue accept that the settlor will not thereby retain an interest in the settlement under the income tax provisions in TA 1970 Pt XVI (SP 1/82).

When an interest in possession trust is created no CTT is charged in the following examples.

EXAMPLE 4

(1) S settles £100,000 on trust for himself for life with remainder to his children. As S, the life tenant, is deemed to own the entire fund (and not simply a life interest in it) his estate has not fallen in value.

(2) S settles £100,000 on trust for his wife for life, remainder to his children. S's wife is treated as owning the fund so that S's transfer is an exempt transfer to a spouse.

IV PAYMENT OF CTT

Primary liability for CTT arising during the course of the settlement rests upon the settlement's trustees. Their liability is limited to the property which they have received or disposed of or become liable to account for to a beneficiary and such other property which they would have received but for their own neglect or default.

If trustees fail to pay, the Revenue can collect tax from any of the following (FA 1975 s 25(3)):

(1) Any person entitled to an interest in possession in the settled property. His liability is limited to the value of the trust property, out of which he can claim an indemnity for the tax he has paid.

(2) Any beneficiary under a discretionary trust up to the value of the property that he receives (after paying income tax on it) and with no right to an indemnity for the tax he is called upon to pay.

(3) The settlor, where the trustees are resident outside the UK, since, should the trustees not pay, the Revenue cannot enforce payment abroad. If the settlor pays he has a right to recover the tax from the trust.

25 CTT—settlements with an interest in possession

I   Basic principles
II When is CTT charged?
III The taxation of reversionary interests

I BASIC PRINCIPLES

1 General

The beneficiary entitled to the income of a fund (usually the life tenant) is treated as owning that portion of the capital of the fund. This rule is a fiction, since in no sense is the life tenant the owner of the capital in the fund. A number of consequences follow from this CTT fiction. First, as all the capital is treated as being owned by the life tenant, for CTT purposes it forms part of his estate, so that on a chargeable occasion CTT is charged at his rates. The settlement itself is not a taxable entity (contrast the rules for discretionary trusts), although primary liability for CTT falls upon the trustees.

Secondly, as the life tenant is treated as owning all the capital in the fund, other beneficiaries with 'reversionary interests' own nothing. FA 1975 defines reversionary interests widely to cover

> 'a future interest under a settlement, whether it is vested or contingent (including an interest expectant on the termination of an interest in possession which, by virtue of paragraph 3 of Schedule 5 to this Act, is treated as subsisting in part of any property)'.

Generally, reversionary interests are excluded property and can be transferred without a charge to CTT. Despite the breadth of this definition, the term would not appear to catch the interests of discretionary beneficiaries. Such rights as they possess (to compel due administration; to be considered; and jointly to wind up the fund) are present rights. Their interests are neither in possession nor in reversion. The interest in possession trust is thus, unique in having a special charging system based upon the fiction that the fund belongs to the person with the interest in possession. The CTT levy on other settlements operates by treating the settlement as a separate chargeable entity and by (generally) imposing a tax charge at regular intervals. There appears to be no reason why this method, if it achieves its stated object of 'neutrality', should not be applied across the board.

2 Who is treated as owning the fund?

Life interests   The beneficiary entitled to an interest in possession is treated as being beneficially entitled to the property, or to an appropriate part of that property; if there is more than one, it is necessary to apportion the capital in the fund (FA 1975 Sch 5 para 3(1)).

A beneficiary who has the right to the income of the fund for a period shorter than his lifetime (however short the period may be) is still treated for CTT as owning the entire settled fund. If the settlement does not produce any income, but instead the beneficiary is entitled to use the capital assets in the fund, para

3(1) suggests that he is treated as owning those assets. If the use is enjoyed by more than one beneficiary, the value of the fund is apportioned under para 3(5) in accordance with the 'annual value' of their respective interests. Annual value is not defined.

EXAMPLE 1

Bill and Ben, beneficiaries under a strict settlement, jointly occupy 'Snodlands', the ancestral home, which is worth £150,000. This capital value must be apportioned to Bill and Ben in proportion to the annual value of their respective interests. As their interests are equal the apportionment will be as to £75,000 each.

A beneficiary entitled to a fixed amount of income   Difficulties arise where one beneficiary is entitled to a fixed amount of income each year (eg an annuity) and any balance is paid to another beneficiary. If the amounts of income paid to the two were compared in the year when a chargeable event occurred a tax saving could be engineered. Assume, for instance, that the annuity interest terminates so that CTT is charged on its value. The proportion of capital attributable to that interest and, therefore, the CTT would be reduced if the trustees switched investments into assets producing a high income in that year. As a result a relatively small proportion of the total income would be payable to the annuitant who would be treated as owning an equivalently small portion of the capital. When a chargeable event affects the interest in the residue of the income (eg, through termination) the trustees could switch the assets into low income producers, thereby achieving a similar reduction in CTT.

FA 1975 Sch 5 para 3(4) is designed to counter such schemes by providing that the Treasury may prescribe higher and lower income yields which take effect as limits beyond which any fluctuations in the actual income of the fund are ignored (see SI 1980/1000).

EXAMPLE 2

The value of the settlement is £100,000; income per annum £25,000. A is entitled to an annuity of £5,000 pa; B to the balance of the income. If there is a chargeable transfer affecting the annuity, A is not treated as owning £20,000 of the capital ([£5,000 ÷ £25,000] × £100,000) but instead a proportion of the Treasury 'higher rate' yield. Assume that the higher rate is 15% on the relevant day; the calculation is, therefore:

Notional income = 15% of £100,000 = £15,000.
A's annuity is £5,000; as a proportion of income it is £5,000 ÷ £15,000; A's share of capital is, therefore, [£5,000 ÷ £15,000] × £100,000 = £33,333.

This calculation is used whenever the actual income yield exceeds the prescribed higher rate. The calculation cannot lead to a charge in excess of the total value of the fund!

When a chargeable transfer affecting the interest in the balance of the income occurs, if the actual income produced falls below the prescribed lower rate, the calculation proceeds as if the fund yielded that rate. If both interests in the settlement are chargeable on the same occasion, the prescribed rates do not apply because the entire fund is chargeable.

A lease treated as a settlement   When a lease is treated as a settlement (eg a lease for life or lives), the lessee is treated as owning the whole of the leased property save for any part treated as belonging to the lessor. To calculate the lessor's portion it is necessary to compare what he received when the lease was granted with what would have been a full consideration for the lease at that time (FA 1975 Sch 5 para 3(6), Sch 10 para 8).

EXAMPLE 3

(1) Land worth £100,000 is let to A for his life. The lessor receives no consideration so that A is treated as owning the whole of the leased property (ie £100,000). The granting of the lease is a chargeable transfer of value by the lessor of £100,000 (grossed-up if necessary).
(2) As above, save that full consideration is furnished. The lease is not treated as a settlement (see Chapter 24). No CTT will be charged on its creation as the lessor's estate does not fall in value.
(3) Partial consideration (equivalent to 40% of a full consideration) is furnished so that the value of the lessor's interest is 40% of £100,000 = £40,000. The value of the lessee's interest is £60,000 and the granting of the lease is a chargeable transfer.

II WHEN IS CTT CHARGED?

CTT is charged whenever the interest in possession terminates. This may occur during the life of the beneficiary (FA 1975 Sch 5 para 4(2)) or on the death of the life tenant (FA 1975 s 22 in conjunction with FA 1975 Sch 5 para 3(1)).

1 The charge on death

As the assets in the settlement are treated as part of the property of the deceased at the time of his death, CTT is charged on the settled fund at the estate rate appropriate to his estate. The tax attributable to the settled property should be paid by the trustees. Notice that although the trustees pay this tax, the inclusion of the value of the fund in the deceased's estate increases the estate rate, thereby causing a higher percentage charge on his free estate.

EXAMPLE 4

The settlement consists of securities worth £100,000 and is held for Albinoni for life with remainder to Busoni. Albinoni has just died and the value of his free estate is £75,000; he made chargeable lifetime transfers of £50,000. CTT will be calculated as follows:
(1) Chargeable death estate: £75,000 + £100,000 (the settlement) = £175,000.
(2) Join death tables at £50,000 (point reached by lifetime transfers).
(3) Calculate death CTT (£66,600).
(4) Convert to estate rate

$$\frac{\text{tax}}{\text{estate}} \times 100: \text{ ie } \frac{£66,600}{£175,000} \times 100 = 38.06\%.$$

(5) CTT attributable to settled property is 38.06% of £100,000 = £38,060.

2   **Inter-vivos terminations**

Actual terminations   A charge to CTT will arise when the interest of the life tenant ceases.

EXAMPLE 5

£100,000 is held on trust for Albinoni for life or until remarriage and thereafter for Busoni. If Albinoni remarries his life interest terminates and CTT will be charged at his lifetime rates on the value of the fund at that time.

   If Albinoni never remarried, but consented to an advancement of £50,000 to Busoni, his interest ends in that portion of the fund so that CTT will be charged at his life rates. Grossing-up does not apply because the value transferred is 'equal to the value of the property in which his interest subsisted' (ie £50,000 only: see para 4(2)). Three years later Albinoni surrenders his life interest in the fund, now worth £120,000. CTT is then charged on £120,000.

Deemed terminations   FA 1975 Sch 5 para 4(1) provides that if the beneficiary disposes of his beneficial interest in possession, that disposal 'shall not be a transfer of value but shall be treated as the coming to an end of the interest'. The absence of gratuitous intent does not prevent a CTT charge on the termination of beneficial interests in possession.

EXAMPLE 6

(1)   Albinoni assigns by way of gift his life interest to Cortot. CTT will be charged as if that life interest had terminated. Cortot becomes a tenant *pur autre vie* and when Albinoni dies his interest in possession terminates triggering another CTT charge on the fund calculated according to Cortot's lifetime rates.

(2)   If, instead of gifting his interest, Albinoni sells it to Cortot for £20,000 (full value) and the fund was then worth £100,000, Albinoni's interest terminates so that he has made a transfer of value of £100,000. However, as he has received £20,000, CTT is charged only on the fall in his estate of £80,000 (£100,000 – £20,000: FA 1975 Sch 5 para 4(4)).

Partition of the fund   A partition of the fund between life tenant and remainderman causes the interest in possession to terminate and CTT will be charged on that portion of the fund passing to the remainderman (FA 1975 Sch 5 para 4(3)).

EXAMPLE 7

Albinoni and Busoni partition the £100,000 fund in the proportions 40:60. Albinoni is treated as making a transfer of £100,000, but CTT will be charged on only £60,000 (£100,000 – £40,000). It should be remembered that CTT is payable out of the fund to be divided.

Advancements to life tenant/satisfaction of a contingency   If all or part of the capital of the fund is paid to the life tenant, or if he becomes absolutely entitled to the capital, his interest in possession will determine *pro tanto*, but no CTT will be charged since there will be no fall in the value of his estate (FA 1975 Sch 5 para 4(3)).

EXAMPLE 8

Property is settled upon Delibes contingent on his attaining the age of 30. At 18, he will be entitled to the income of the settlement (Trustee Act 1925 s 31); an interest in possession will, therefore, arise. At 30, that interest terminates, but, as he is now absolutely entitled to the capital, no CTT is charged.

Purchase of a reversionary interest by the life tenant (FA 1975 ss 20(4), 23(3))   As the life tenant owns the fund it follows that tax could be reduced were he to purchase a reversionary interest in that settlement. Assume, for instance, that B has £60,000 in his bank account and is the life tenant of a fund with a capital value of £100,000. For CTT he owns £160,000. If B were to purchase the reversionary interest in the same settlement, however, for its market value of £60,000, the result would be as follows: first, B's estate has not fallen in value. Originally it included £60,000; after the purchase it includes a reversionary interest worth £60,000 since, although excluded property, the reversionary interest must still be valued. Secondly, B's estate now consists of the settlement fund valued at £100,000 and has been depleted by the £60,000 paid for the reversionary interest so that a charge to CTT on £60,000 has been avoided.

To prevent such a loss of CTT, FA 1975 s 23(3) provides that the reversionary interest is not to be valued as a part of B's estate at the time of its purchase (thereby ensuring that his estate has fallen in value) whilst FA 1975 s 20(4) is excluded from applying in this case thereby ensuring that the fall in value is subject to charge even though there is no donative intent. Hence, the £60,000 paid for the reversionary interest is chargeable to CTT.

Transactions reducing the value of the property   When the value of the fund is diminished by a depreciatory transaction entered into between the trustees and a beneficiary (or persons connected with him) tax is charged as if the fall in value were a partial termination of the interest in possession (FA 1975 Sch 5 para 4(9)). A commercial transaction lacking gratuitous intent is not caught by this provision.

EXAMPLE 9

Trustees grant a 50 year lease of a property worth £100,000 at a peppercorn rent to the brother of a reversionary beneficiary. As a result the property left in the settlement is the freehold reversion worth only £20,000. The granting of the lease is a depreciatory transaction which causes the value of the fund to fall by £80,000 and as it is made with a person connected with a beneficiary, para 4(9) will apply and CTT will be levied as if the life interest in £80,000 had ended. (Contrast the position if the lease had been granted to the brother in return for a commercial rent.)

3   **Exemptions and reliefs**

Reverter to settlor/spouse (FA 1975 Sch 5 paras 4(5), 4(6))   If, on the termination of an interest in possession, property reverts to the settlor there is no charge to CTT unless the settlor (or his spouse) had acquired that interest for money or money's worth. This exemption also applies when the property passes to the settlor's spouse or (if the settlor is dead) to his widow or widower so long as that reverter occurs within two years of his death.

EXAMPLE 10

Janacek creates a settlement of £100,000 in favour of K for life. When K dies and the property reverts to the settlor no CTT will be charged.

Contrast the position, if the settlement provided that the fund was to pass to L on the death of the life tenant, but the settlor's wife had purchased that remainder interest and given it to her husband as a Christmas present. On the death of the life tenant, although the property will revert to the settlor, the normal charge to CTT will apply.

Use of the life tenant's exemptions The spouse exemption is available on the termination of the interest in possession if the person who then becomes entitled, whether absolutely or to another interest in possession, is the spouse of the former life tenant. FA 1981 s 94 permits the use of the life tenant's annual (£3,000 pa) exemption and the exemption for gifts in consideration of marriage on the inter vivos termination of an interest in possession if the life tenant so elects (see FA 1981 s 94(5)(6)). The exemptions for small gifts (£250) and normal expenditure out of income cannot be used.

EXAMPLE 11

Orff is the life tenant of the fund. His wife and son are entitled equally in remainder. If he surrenders the life interest, there will be no tax on the half-share passing to his wife (spouse exemption). Against the chargeable half-share passing to his son, Orff can use the annual exemption and, if surrender coincides with the marriage of the son, the £5,000 marriage gift relief.

The surviving spouse exemption The carry over of this estate duty relief is discussed on p 301. The first spouse must have died before 13 November 1974 (FA 1975 s 22(4), Sch 5 para 4(7)).

Excluded property If the settlement contains excluded property, CTT is not charged on that portion of the fund (FA 1975 s 23(1), Sch 5 para 4(11)).

FA 1975 s 46 dispositions If the interest in possession is disposed of for the purpose of maintaining the disponer's child or supporting a dependent relative, CTT is not charged (see Chapter 23).

Protective trusts The forfeiture of a protected life interest is normally not chargeable (see Chapter 26).

Variations and disclaimers Dispositions of the deceased may be altered after his death without incurring a second charge to CTT. Alterations are permitted for settlements created by the deceased, but not for settlements in which the deceased had been the life tenant (see Chapter 22).

EXAMPLE 12

Poulenc, the life tenant of the settlement created by his father, has just died. His brother Quercus is now the life tenant in possession and if he assigns his interest within two years of Poulenc's death, the normal charging provisions will apply. (Note (1) he could disclaim his interest without any CTT charge (FA 1975 s 47(4));

(2) see CTT News Vol 6 p 51 for problems caused to trustees when other property of the deceased is varied or disclaimed).

Quick succession relief (FA 1981 s 101)   This relief is similar to that for unsettled property. The first chargeable transfer may be either the creation of the settlement or any subsequent termination of an interest in possession (whether that termination occurs inter vivos or on death). Hence, it can be voluntarily used (by the life tenant surrendering or assigning his interest) whereas in the case of unsettled property it is only available on a death. The calculation of the relief in cases where there is more than one later transfer is dealt with in FA 1981 s 101(4).

EXAMPLE 13

(1) A settlement is created January 1982; (2) the life interest ends in half of the fund in March 1984; (3) the life interest ends in the rest of the fund in February 1985.
   Quick succession relief is available at a rate of 60% on event (2); and again at a rate of 40% on event (3). Generally, relief is given in respect of the earlier transfer first ((2) above). To the extent that the relief given represents less than the whole of the tax charged on the original net transfer ((1) above), further relief can then be given in respect of subsequent transfers ((3) above) until relief equal to the whole of the tax (in (1) above) has been given.

Business reliefs   In a settlement containing business property that property is treated as belonging to the life tenant who must fulfil the conditions for relief (FA 1976 Sch 10 as amended by FA 1981 s 100).

EXAMPLE 14

Satie is the life tenant of the settlement. He holds 30% of the shares in the trading company Teleman Ltd, and the trust holds a further 25%. Further, the trust owns the factory premises which are leased to the company. On death of Satie, CTT business relief is available as follows:
(1) *On the shares:* the relief (assuming that the two year ownership condition is satisfied) is at 50% on Satie's shares and on those of the fund. The life tenant is treated as having controlled the company since he held 30% (his own) and is treated as owning a further 25% of the shares.
(2) *On the land:* the relief is at 30% since the asset is used by a company controlled by the life tenant (For the pre-1981 rules, see *Fetherstonhaugh v IRC* (1984).)

   Similar principles operate for agricultural relief: ie the life tenant must satisfy the conditions of two years' occupation or seven years' ownership (ownership by the settlement being attributed to the life tenant).

III   THE TAXATION OF REVERSIONARY INTERESTS

As reversionary interests are generally excluded property their disposition does not lead to a CTT charge.

EXAMPLE 15

A fund is settled on trust for A for life (A is currently aged 88); B for life (B is 78); and C absolutely (C (A's son) is 70).

This settlement is likely to be subjected to three CTT charges within a fairly short period. The position would be much improved if B and C disposed of their reversionary interests:

(1) B should surrender his interest. Taking into account his age it has little value and is merely a CTT trap.

(2) C should assign his interest to (ideally) a younger person. He might for instance have minor grandchildren and an accumulation and maintenance trust in their favour would be an attractive possibility.

The result of this reorganisation is that the fund is now threatened by only one CTT charge (on A's death) in the immediate future.

In four cases a reversionary interest is not excluded property to prevent their use as a tax avoidance device.

First, a disposition of a reversionary interest to a beneficiary under the same trust, who is entitled to a prior interest, is chargeable (see p 349).

Secondly, a disposition of a reversionary interest which has at any time, and by any person, been acquired for a consideration in money or money's worth is chargeable to CTT. (For special rules where that interest is situated outside the UK see Chapter 27.)

EXAMPLE 16

Umberto sells his reversionary interest to Vidor (a stranger to the trust) for its market value, £20,000. If the general rules operated the position would be that:

(1) Vidor will not be charged to CTT, and as Umberto is disposing of excluded property no CTT is chargeable.

(2) Vidor has replaced chargeable assets (£20,000) with excluded property so that were he to die or make an inter vivos gift CTT would be avoided.

FA 1975 s 24(3)(a) and Sch 5 para 2 prevent this result. The reversion ceases to be excluded property once it has been purchased (even for a small consideration) with the result that a disposition by Vidor will lead to a CTT charge.

Thirdly, a disposition of a reversionary interest is chargeable if it is one to which either the settlor or his spouse is, or has been, beneficially entitled (FA 1975 s 24(3)(a)).

EXAMPLE 17

Viv settles property worth £100,000 on trust for his father Will for life (Will is 92). Viv retains the reversionary interest which he then gives to his daughter Ursula. If the general rules were not modified the position would be that:

(1) The creation of the settlement would be a chargeable transfer by Viv but the diminution in his estate would be very small (the difference between £100,000 and the value of a reversionary interest in £100,000 subject only to the termination of the interest of a 92 year old life tenant!).

(2) The transfer of the reversion by Viv would escape CTT since it is excluded property.

FA 1976 s 120 ensures that the reversion is chargeable so that Viv achieves no tax saving (and, indeed, is left with the danger of a higher CTT bill than if he had never created the settlement since the death of Will is a chargeable event).

Fourthly, the disposition of a reversionary interest is chargeable where that interest is expectant upon the termination of a lease which is treated as a settlement (typically one for life or lives; FA 1975 s 24(3)(b)). The result is that the lessor's reversion is treated in the same way as a reversionary interest purchased for money or money's worth so that on any disposition of it, CTT will be charged (see p 338).

26 CTT—settlements without an interest in possession

I   Introduction and terminology
II   The method of charge
III   Exemptions and reliefs
IV   Discretionary trusts created before 27 March 1974
V   Accumulation and maintenance trusts
VI   Other special trusts

I INTRODUCTION AND TERMINOLOGY

The method of charging settlements lacking an interest in possession is totally different from that for settlements with such an interest. Instead of attributing the fund to one of the beneficiaries, it is the settlement itself which is the taxable entity for CTT. Like an individual, it must keep a record of chargeable transfers made, although, unlike the individual, it will never die and so will only be taxed on the lifetime table. The method of charge was radically altered by FA 1982 in relation to events occurring after 8 March 1982. For convenience this chapter will discuss the taxing provisions of FA 1982 with reference to the discretionary trust which is the most significant of the 'no interest in possession' settlements. In fact the category of 'no interest in possession settlement' is wider than discretionary trusts catching for instance, the type of settlement in the *Pilkington* case (Chapter 24) and funds where the beneficiaries' interests are contingent.

EXAMPLE 1

(1) A fund of £100,000 is held upon trust for such of A, B, C, D, E and F as the trustees may in their absolute discretion (which extends over both income and capital) think appropriate. The trust is one without an interest in possession.
(2) Dad settles property on trust for son contingent on his attaining 30. Son is aged 21 at the date of the settlement and the income is to be accumulated until son attains 30. There is no interest in possession.

CTT is charged on 'relevant property' (FA 1982 s 102(1)) defined as settled property (other than excluded property) in which there is no qualifying interest in possession, with the exception of the 'special trusts' considered in Sections V and VI below.

A 'qualifying interest in possession' is one owned beneficially by an individual or, in restricted circumstances, by a company. If within one settlement there exists an interest in possession in a part only of the property, the charge to CTT under FA 1982 is on the portion which lacks such an interest.

II THE METHOD OF CHARGE

The central feature is the periodic or anniversary charge imposed upon discretionary trusts at ten yearly intervals. The anniversary is calculated from the date on which the trust was created (FA 1982 s 105(1)) subject to special rules when the trust follows a life interest in favour of the settlor's spouse (see *Example 3* below).

EXAMPLE 2

Silus creates a discretionary trust on 1 January 1984. The first anniversary charge will fall on 1 January 1994; the next on 1 January 2004 and so on. If the trust had been created by will and he had died on 31 December 1983, that date marks the creation of the settlement (FA 1982 s 123).

EXAMPLE 3

Silus creates (in 1984) a settlement in favour of his wife Selina for life; thereafter for such of his three daughters as the trustees may in their absolute discretion select. Selina dies in 1986. For CTT purposes the discretionary trust is created by Selina on her death (FA 1982 s 120). The ten year anniversary runs from the creation of the original settlement in 1984 (FA 1982 s 105(2)).

Apart from the anniversary charge, CTT will also be levied (the 'exit charge') on the happening of certain events. In general, the CTT then charged is a proportion of the last periodic charge. Special charging provisions operate for chargeable events which occur before the first ten year anniversary when the first periodic charge is levied.

1 The creation of the settlement

Normal principles operate so that there will, generally, be a chargeable transfer of value by the settlor for CTT purposes. The following matters should be noted: first, if the settlement is created inter vivos, grossing-up applies unless CTT is paid out of the fund.

Secondly, the cumulative total of chargeable transfers made by the settlor is crucial since it enters the cumulative total of the settlement on all future chargeable occasions (ie his transfers do not drop out of the cumulative total after ten years).

Thirdly, a 'related settlement' is one created by the same settlor on the same day as the discretionary trust (other than a charitable trust). Generally such settlements should be avoided (see below).

Fourthly, additions of property by the original settlor to his settlement should also be avoided (see p 360). If property is added by a person other than the original settlor, the addition will be treated as a separate settlement.

2 Exit charges before the first ten year anniversary

a) *When will an exit charge arise?*

A charge is imposed whenever property in the settlement ceases to be 'relevant property' (FA 1982 s 108). Hence, if the trustees appoint property to a beneficiary or if an interest in possession arises in any portion of the fund, there will be a CTT charge to the extent of the property ceasing to be held on discretionary trusts. If the CTT is paid out of the property that is left in the discretionary trust, grossing-up will apply. A charge is also imposed if the trustees make a disposition as a result of which the value of relevant property comprised in the settlement falls (a 'depreciatory transaction'; see p 349, but notice that there is no requirement that the transaction be made with a beneficiary or with a person connected with him).

The exit charge does not apply to a payment of costs or expenses (so long as 'fairly attributable' to the relevant property), nor does it catch a payment which is income of any person for the purposes of income tax (FA 1982 s 108(5)).

b) *Calculation of the settlement rate*

The lifetime rates of CTT apply in all cases, even if the trust was set up under the will of the settlor. The rate of CTT is calculated at 30% of the lifetime rates applicable to a hypothetical chargeable transfer.

Step 1   This postulated transfer is made up of the sum of the following:
(1) the value of the property in the settlement immediately after it commenced;
(2) the value (at the date of the addition) of any added property; and
(3) the value of property in a related settlement (valued immediately after it commenced (FA 1982 s 111(5)).
No account is taken of any rise or fall in the value of the settled fund and the value comprised in the settlement and in any related settlement can include property subject to an interest in possession.

Step 2   Tax at the lifetime rates on this hypothetical transfer is calculated by joining the lifetime table at the point reached by the cumulative total of previous chargeable transfers made by the settlor in the ten years before he created the settlement (ie tax starts at the total reached by the settlor when he created the settlement). Other chargeable transfers made on the same day as the settlement are ignored and, therefore, if the settlement was created on death, other gifts made in the will or on the intestacy are ignored (FA 1982 s 111(4)(b)).

Step 3   The tax is converted to an average rate (the equivalent of an estate rate) and 30% of that rate is then taken. The resultant rate (the 'settlement rate') is used as the basis for calculating the exit charge.

EXAMPLE 4

Justinian settles £100,000 on discretionary trusts on 1 April 1985. His total chargeable transfers immediately before that date stood at £60,000. He pays the CTT. If an exit charge arises before the first ten year anniversary of the fund (1 April 1995) the settlement rate would be calculated as follows:

Step 1   Calculate the hypothetical chargeable transfer. As there is no added property and no related settlement it comprises only the value of the property in the settlement immediately after its creation (ie £100,000).

Step 2   Cumulate the £100,000 with the previous chargeable transfers of Justianian (ie £60,000). Taking the lifetime tables, tax on transfers between £60,000 and £160,000 is £17,675.

Step 3 The tax converted to a percentage rate is 17.675%; 30% of that rate produces a 'settlement rate' of 5.30%.

c) *The tax charged*

The charge is on the fall in value of the fund. To establish the rate of charge, a further proportion of the settlement rate must be calculated equal to 1/40th of the settlement rate for each complete successive quarter that has elapsed from the creation of the settlement to the date of the exit charge. That proportion of the settlement rate is applied to the chargeable transfer (the 'effective rate').

EXAMPLE 5

Assume in *Example 4* that on 25 March 1987 there was an exit charge on £20,000 ceasing to be relevant property. The 'effective rate' of CTT is calculated as follows:

Step 1 Take completed quarters since the settlement was created, ie seven.

Step 2 Take 7/40ths of the 'settlement rate' (5.30%) to discover the 'effective rate = 0.93%.

Step 3 The effective rate is applied to the fall in value of the relevant property. The CTT will, therefore, be £186 if the tax is borne by the beneficiary; or £187.75 if borne by the remaining fund.

There is no charge on events that occur in the first three months of the settlement (FA 1982 s 108(4)) nor, where the trust was set up by the settlor on his death, on events occurring within two years of that death (see p 320).

3   The charge on the first ten year anniversary

a) *What property is charged?*

The charge is levied on the value of the relevant property comprised in the settlement immediately before the anniversary (FA 1982 s 107).

As the charge is on relevant property, no distinction appears to be drawn between capital and income. In a fund with substantial income the trustees should be advised to distribute the income before the relevant anniversary as such distributions will not be subject to any exit charge (see p 356). It might be argued that in the definition of 'settlement' for CTT purposes in Sch 5 para 1(2) (p 338) a distinction is drawn between the property in the settlement and the income produced by that property. Trustees caught with income in the fund at the anniversary might care to argue this point!

The assets in the fund are valued according to general principles and, if they include business or agricultural property, the reliefs appropriate to that property will apply, subject to satisfaction of the relevant conditions. Any CTT charged on such property will be payable in instalments.

b) *Calculation of the rate of CTT*

The lifetime table will be used and, as with the exit charge, the calculation depends upon a hypothetical chargeable transfer.

Step 1 Calculate the hypothetical chargeable transfer which is made up of the sum of the following:

(1) the value of relevant property comprised in the settlement immediately before the anniversary;
(2) the value, immediately after it was created, of property comprised in a 'related settlement'; and
(3) the value, at the date when the settlement was created, of any non-relevant property then in the settlement which has not subsequently become relevant property.

Normally the hypothetical chargeable transfer will be made up exclusively of property falling within category (1). Categories (2) and (3), which affect the rate of CTT to be charged without themselves being taxed, are anti-avoidance measures. Related settlements are included because transfers made on the same day as the creation of the settlement are normally ignored and, therefore, a CTT advantage could be achieved if the settlor were to set up a series of small funds rather than one large fund. Non-relevant property in the settlement is included because the trustees could switch the values between the two portions of the fund.

Step 2 Calculate tax at the lifetime rates on the hypothetical chargeable transfer by joining the lifetime table at the point reached by:
(1) the chargeable transfers of the settlor made in the ten years before he created the settlement; and
(2) chargeable transfers made by the settlement in the first ten years. Where a settlement was created after 26 March 1974 and before 9 March 1982, distribution payments (as defined by the CTT charging regime in force between those dates) must also be cumulated (FA 1982 s 110(7)).

Discretionary settlements will, therefore, have their own total of chargeable transfers with transfers over a ten year period being cumulated. The unique feature of a settlement's cumulation lies in the inclusion (and it never drops out!) of chargeable transfers of the settlor in the decade before the settlement is created.

Step 3 The CTT is converted to a percentage and 30% of that rate is then taken and charged upon the relevant property in the settlement.

The highest lifetime rate of CTT is 30%. The highest effective rate (anniversary rate) is, therefore, 30% of 30%, ie 9%. Where the settlement comprises business property qualifying for 50% relief, this effective rate falls to $4\frac{1}{2}$% and assuming that the option to pay in instalments is exercised, the annual charge over the ten year period becomes a mere 0.45%.

EXAMPLE 6

Take the facts of *Example 5* (viz, original fund £100,000, exit charge on £20,000; previous transfers of settlor £60,000). In addition, assume Justinian had created a second settlement of £15,000 on 1 April 1985.

The fund is worth £105,000 at the first ten year anniversary.

(1) Relevant property to be taxed is £105,000
(2) Calculate hypothetical chargeable transfer

	£
Relevant property, as above	105,000
Property in related settlement	15,000
	£120,000

(3) Settlement's cumulative CTT total: £

  Settlor's earlier transfers   60,000

  Chargeable transfers of trustees in preceding
  ten years   20,000

   £80,000

(4) Tax from the lifetime table on transfers from £80,000 to £200,000 (£120,000 + £80,000) = £24,650 so that, as a percentage rate, CTT is 20.54%.

(5) The 'effective rate' is 30% of 20.54% = 6.162%.
  Tax payable is £105,000 × 6.162% = £6,470.

4 Exit charges after the first anniversary charge and between anniversaries

The same events will trigger an exit charge after the first ten year anniversary as before it. The CTT charge will be levied on the fall in value of the fund with grossing-up, if necessary. The rate of charge is a proportion of the effective rate charged at the first ten year anniversary. That proportion is 1/40th for each complete quarter from the date of the first anniversary charge to the date of the exit charge (FA 1982 s 112).

EXAMPLE 7

Continuing *Example 6*, exactly 15 months later the trustees appoint £25,000 to a beneficiary. The CTT (assuming no grossing-up) will be:
  £25,000 × 6.162% × 5/40 (5 quarters since last ten year anniversary = £192,56,

If the lifetime rates of CTT have been reduced (including the raising of the rate bands) between the anniversary and exit charges, the lower rates will apply to the exit charge and, therefore, the rate of charge on the first anniversary will have to be recalculated at those rates (FA 1982 Sch 17 para 31). So long as the CTT rate bands remain linked to rises in the retail prices index (FA 1982 s 91) recalculation is likely to be the norm.

No exit charge is levied if the chargeable event occurs within the first quarter following the anniversary charge (see p 357).

5 Later periodic charges

The principles that applied on the first ten year anniversary operate on subsequent ten year anniversaries. So far as the hypothetical chargeable transfer is concerned the same items will be included (so that the value of property in a related settlement and of non-relevant property in the settlement are always included). The cumulative total of the fund will, as before, include the chargeable transfers of the settlor made in the ten years before he created the settlement and the transfers out of the settlement in the ten years immediately preceding the anniversary (earlier transfers by the settlement fall out of the cumulative total). The remaining stages of the calculation are unaltered.

6 Technical problems

The basic structure of the FA 1982 provisions is relatively straightforward. The charge to CTT is built upon a series of periodic charges with interim charges (where appropriate) which are levied at a fraction of the full periodic charge. The result is a system by no means unfavourable to the discretionary trust (see Chapter 37). A number of technical matters should be noted.

Reduction in the rate of the anniversary charge   If property has not been in the settlement for the entire preceding ten years there is a proportionate reduction in the charge (FA 1982 s 109(2)). The reduction in the periodic rate is calculated by reference to the number of completed quarters which expired before the property became relevant property in the settlement.

EXAMPLE 8

Assume in *Example 6* that £15,000 had become relevant property on 30 April 1991.
 The CTT charge on the first ten year anniversary (on 1 April 1995) would now be calculated as follows:
(1) £90,000 (£105,000 − £15,000) at 6.162% = £5,545.80.
(2) The £15,000 will be charged at a proportion of the periodic charge rate: *viz*—
6.162% reduced by 24/40 since 24 complete quarters elapsed from the creation of the settlement (on 1 April 1985) to the date when the £15,000 became relevant property. As a result the CTT charged is £15,000 × 2.465% × £369.75.

This proportionate reduction in the effective rate of the periodic charge will not affect the calculation of CTT on events occurring after the anniversary; ie any exit charge is at the full effective rate.

FA 1982 does not contain provisions which enable specific property to be identified. Thus, the reduction mentioned above applies to the value of the relevant property in the fund at the ten year anniversary 'attributable' to property which was not relevant property throughout the preceding ten years. Presumably, therefore, some sort of proportionate calculation will be necessary where the value of the fund has shown an increase. Furthermore, if accumulated income (or merely undistributed income) is caught by the anniversary charge, a separate calculation will have to be made with regard to each separate accumulation, as being property which has not been in the settlement for the whole of the previous decade.

Transfers between settlements   FA 1982 s 121 prevents a tax advantage from switching property between discretionary settlements, by providing that such property remains comprised in the first settlement. It would seem to follow that property cannot be moved out of a discretionary trust to avoid an anniversary charge; that property cannot be switched from a fund with a high cumulative total to one with a lower total; and that the transfer of property from one discretionary fund to another will not be chargeable.

Added property   Special rules operate if, after the settlement commenced (and after 8 March 1982), the settlor made a chargeable transfer as a result of which the value of the property comprised in the settlement was increased (FA 1982 s 110(1)). Note that it is only additions by the settlor that trigger these provisions and that it is the value of the fund which must be increased and not necessarily the amount of property in that fund. Transfers which have the effect of increasing the value of the fund are ignored if they are not primarily intended to have that effect and do not in fact increase the value by more than 5%.

EXAMPLE 9

Sam, the settlor, creates in 1986 a discretionary trust of stocks and shares in Sham Ltd and the benefit of a life insurance policy on Sam's life.
(1) Each year Sam adds property to the settlement, which is equal to his annual exemption.
(2) Sam continues to pay the premiums on the life policy each year.
(3) Sam transfers further shares in Sham Ltd.
  The special rules for added property will not apply in either cases (1) or (2), since Sam is not making a chargeable transfer; the first transfer is covered by the annual exemption and the second by the exemption for normal expenditure out of income. The transfer of further shares to the fund, however, is caught by the provisions of FA 1982 s 110, relating to added property.

If the added property provisions apply, the calculation of the periodic charge which immediately follows the addition will be modified. For the purposes of the hypothetical chargeable transfer, the cumulative total of the settlor's chargeable transfers will be the higher of the totals (1) immediately before creating the settlement plus transfers made by the settlement before the addition; and (2) immediately before transferring the added property, deducting from this latter total the transfer made on creation of the settlement and a transfer to any related settlement. Thus the settlor should avoid additions, since they may cause more CTT to be charged at the next anniversary and it will, therefore, be preferable to create a separate settlement.

III EXEMPTIONS AND RELIEFS

Many of the exemptions from CTT will not apply to property in discretionary trusts, eg the annual exemption, the marriage exemption, and the exemption for normal expenditure out of income. There is also no exemption if the settled fund reverts to either the settlor or his spouse. Business and agricultural property relief may, however, be available, provided that the necessary conditions for the relief are met by the trustees. There is no question of any aggregation with similar property owned by a discretionary beneficiary.
  Exit charges are not levied on certain property leaving the settlement, eg:
(1) Property ceasing to be relevant property within three months of the creation of the trust or of an anniversary charge, or within two years of creation (if the trust was set up on death), is not subject to an exit charge (p 357 and 320).
(2) Property may pass, without attracting an exit charge, to such privileged trusts as employee trusts (FA 1982 s 115); maintenance funds for historic buildings (FA 1982 Sch 16 para 1); permanent charities (FA 1982 s 119(1)); political parties in accordance with the exemption in FA 1975 (FA 1982 s 119(1); and see Chapter 23); national heritage bodies (FA 1982 s 119(1); and non-profit making bodies approved by the Treasury and holding heritage property (FA 1982 s 119(1)(2). There is no exemption in the case of property passing into an accumulation and maintenance trust.
  If a discretionary fund includes property which is excluded for CTT

purposes, the periodic and exit charges will not apply to that portion of the fund (FA 1982 s 108(8)).

IV DISCRETIONARY TRUSTS CREATED BEFORE 27 MARCH 1974

Discretionary settlements created before 27 March 1974 are subject to special rules for the calculation of tax which will generally result in less tax being charged (FA 1982 Sch 15).

1 Chargeable events occurring before the first ten year anniversary

The rate of CTT to be charged is set out in FA 1982 s 111 as modified by Sch 15 paras 4 and 5. As the settlement is treated as a separate taxable entity only transfers made by the settlement are cumulated. Such chargeable transfers will either be distribution payments (if made under the CTT regime in force from 1974 to 1982) or chargeable events under FA 1982 s 108. Once the cumulative total is known, the rate of tax will be calculated according to the lifetime table and the charge will be at 30% of that rate.

2 The first anniversary charge

No anniversary charge can apply before 1 April 1983. Thus, the first discretionary trust to suffer this charge is one created on 1 April 1973 (or 1963; 1953; 1943 and so on).

The amount subject to the charge is calculated in the normal way. In calculating the rate of charge, however, it is only chargeable transfers of the settlement in the preceding ten years that are cumulated and not any chargeable transfers of the settlor before he created the settlement. Property in a related settlement and non-relevant property in the settlement are ignored. As before, the rate of charge is reduced if property has not been relevant property throughout the decade preceding the first anniversary. The danger of increasing a CTT bill by an addition of property by the settlor (see p 360) is even greater with these old trusts. If such an addition has been made, the settlor's chargeable transfers in the ten year period before the addition must be cumulated in calculating the rate of tax on the anniversary charge (FA 1982 Sch 15 para 3). The effective rate of charge for the anniversary charge is (as for new trusts) 30% of the rate calculated according to the lifetime table.

3 Chargeable events after the first anniversary charge

The position is the same as for new trusts. The charge is based upon the rate charged at the last anniversary.

EXAMPLE 10

In November 1964 Maggie settled £200,000 on discretionary trusts for her family. The following events have since occurred:
In May 1977: a distribution payment of £50,000.
In May 1984: trustees distribute a further sum of £75,000 (tax borne by beneficiary).

In November 1984: the first ten year anniversary. The value of relevant property then in the fund is £100,000.

CTT will be charged as follows:

(*1*) *May 1984:* The distribution will be a chargeable event occurring before the first ten year anniversary. CTT will be calculated on the lifetime tables by cumulating the chargeable transfer of £75,000 with the earlier transfer made by the settlement (the distribution payment of £50,000). The rate of CTT is, therefore, 13.83% and the effective rate 4.15%. CTT is £3,112.50.

(Notice that there is no proportionate reduction in the effective rate for exit charges levied on old discretionary trusts before the first anniversary.)

(*2*) *November 1984:* The anniversary charge will be calculated on the relevant property in the settlement (£100,000). The cumulative total of transfers made by the settlement is £125,000 (£50,000 and £75,000) so that the rate of CTT according to the lifetime table is 22.925%. The effective rate is, therefore, 6.878%. CTT payable will be £6,878 (6.878% of £100,000).

V   ACCUMULATION AND MAINTENANCE TRUSTS (FA 1982 s 114)

1   The privileged treatment

Rather than make outright gifts to minor children, funds will frequently be settled in trust for their benefit. If special treatment were not accorded to such settlements the CTT charges would discriminate between gifts to adults and settled gifts to infants.

EXAMPLE 11

Simon makes two gifts: to his brother, Enrico, and to his two month old granddaughter, Frederica.

(1) *The gift to Enrico:* CTT will be charged only when the gift is made.

(2) *The gift to Frederica:* In view of her age, it is necessary to settle the property on trusts which give the trustees the power to maintain Frederica, but which give her no interest in possession. Under general principles, the creation of that settlement will be a chargeable transfer of value and the discretionary trust charging regime will thereupon operate. As a result there will be anniversary charges and, when Frederica obtains either an interest in possession or an absolute interest in the settled fund, there will be an 'exit' charge.

The objective of the special provisions that apply to accumulation and maintenance trusts is to prevent this double charge. The creation of an accumulation and maintenance settlement may lead to a CTT charge (the 'entry' charge), but thereafter the ten year anniversary charge will not apply and there will be no proportionate periodic charge when the property leaves the trust. As a result, the taxation of gifts to children is treated in the same way as gifts to adults.

2   The requirements of FA 1982 s 114

To qualify for the privileged CTT treatment, an accumulation and maintenance trust has to satisfy the three requirements considered below. Failure to do so means that the normal charging system applies. When the requirements cease to be satisfied CTT will not usually be charged save in exceptional cases (see p 368).

3   Requirement 1

'One or more persons (. . . beneficiaries) will, on or before attaining a specified age not exceeding 25, become entitled to, or to an interest in possession in, the settled property or part of it' (FA 1982 s 114).

Requirement 1 is concerned with the age at which a beneficiary becomes entitled either to the income from the fund or to the fund itself. The age of 25 is specified as a maximum age limit and this is a generously late age when one considers that the purpose of these rules is to deal with settlements for infant children.

EXAMPLE 12

(1)   Property is settled upon trust 'for A absolutely, contingent on attaining the age of 18'. A will become entitled to both income and capital at that age so that Requirement 1 is satisfied.

(2)   Property is settled upon trust 'for B absolutely, contingent upon attaining the age of 30'. At first sight Requirement 1 is broken since B will not acquire the capital in the fund until after the age of 25. However, the requirement will be satisfied if the beneficiary acquires an interest in possession before 25; B will do so, because the Trustee Act 1925 s 31 (if not expressly excluded) provides that when a beneficiary with a contingent interest attains 18, that beneficiary shall thereupon be entitled to the income produced by the fund even though he has not yet satisfied the contingency.

The requirement that a beneficiary *'will'* become entitled does not require absolute certainty; death, for instance, can always prevent entitlement. The word causes particular problems when trustees possess overriding powers of advancement and appointment (dispositive powers) which, if exercised, could result in entitlement being postponed beyond 25. So long as the dispositive power can only be exercised amongst the existing beneficiaries and cannot postpone entitlement beyond the age of 25, Requirement 1 is satisfied. Accordingly, a power to vary or determine the respective shares of members of the class, even to the extent of excluding some members altogether, is permissible.

EXAMPLE 13

Property is held on trust for the three children of A contingent upon their attaining the age of 25 and, if more than one, in equal shares. The trustees are given overriding powers of appointment, exercisable until a beneficiary attains 25, to appoint the fund to one or more of the beneficiaries as they see fit. Requirement 1 is satisfied since the property will vest absolutely in the beneficiaries no later than the age of 25. The existence of the overriding power of appointment is irrelevant since it cannot be exercised other than in favour of the class of beneficiaries and cannot be used to postpone the vesting of the fund until after a beneficiary has attained 25.

The mere existence of a common form power of advancement will not prevent Requirement 1 from being satisfied (see *Inglewood (Lord) v IRC* (1983)). It should be noted that powers of advancement can be exercised so as to postpone the vesting of property in a beneficiary beyond the age stated in the trust document and, hence, beyond the age of 25 (see *Pilkington v IRC* (1964)) and they can, in exceptional cases, result in property being paid to a non-beneficiary (as in *Re Clore's ST* (1966) where the payment was to the beneficiary's favourite charity). Obviously, if the power is so exercised a charge to CTT will result.

The effect of dispositive powers which, if exercised, would break Requirement 1, was considered in a Revenue Press Release of 19 January 1975 and is illustrated by the following example:

EXAMPLE 14

Property is settled 'for the children of E contingent on their attaining 25'. The trustees are given the following (alternative) overriding powers of appointment.
(1) *To appoint income and capital to E's sister F:* The mere existence of this power causes the settlement to break Requirement 1. There is no certainty that the fund will pass to E's children since the power might be exercised in favour of F.
(2) *To appoint income to E's brother G:* The same consequence will follow since the mere existence of this power means that the income could be used for the benefit of G and, hence, break Requirement 2 (for details of this Requirement see below).
(3) *To appoint capital and income to E's relatives so long as those relatives are no older than 25:* This power does not break Requirement 1 since whoever receives the settled fund, whether E's children or his relatives, will be no older than 25.

It may be difficult to decide whether or not the settlement contains a power of revocation or appointment which will break Requirement 1. In *Inglewood v IRC* (1981), Vinelott J distinguished between events provided for in the trust instrument and events wholly outside the settlor's control:

'. . . the terms of the settlement must be such that one or more of the beneficiaries, if they or one of them survive to the specified age, will be bound to take a vested interest on or before attaining that age . . . Of course, a beneficiary may assign his interest, or be deprived of it, by an arrangement, or by bankruptcy, before he attains a vested interest. But he is not then deprived of it under the terms of the settlement, so these possible events, unlike the exercise of a power of revocation or appointment, must be disregarded.' [1981] STC at 318 (see also Fox LJ [1983] STC at 138).

EXAMPLE 15

Sebag creates a settlement in favour of his second daughter, Juno, under which she will obtain the property if she attains the age of 18. If she marries before that age, however, the property is to pass to Sebag's brother, Sebastian.
   This provision in the settlement could operate to deprive Juno of the property in circumstances when, as a matter of general law, she would not be so deprived. The settlement does not satisfy Requirement 1 and so does not qualify for privileged treatment.

Two other matters should be noted in relation to Requirement 1. First, even if a trust instrument fails to specify an age at which the beneficiary will become entitled to either the income or capital, the Revenue accept that so long as it is clear from the terms of that instrument and the known ages of the beneficiaries that one or more persons will in fact become entitled before the age of 25, Requirement 1 will be satisfied (ESC F8).

Secondly, for an accumulation and maintenance trust to be created there must be a living beneficiary at that time. It is possible to set up a trust for a class of persons including some who are unborn ('the grandchildren of the settlor' for instance), but there must be at least one member of the class in existence at the date of creation (FA 1982 s 114(7)). If the single living beneficiary dies, the fund (assuming that it was set up for a class of beneficiaries) will remain in existence as an accumulation and maintenance trust until a further member of that class is born. If a further class member is never born, the fund will eventually pass elsewhere and at that stage a CTT charge may arise.

4   Requirement 2

'No interest in possession subsists in the settled property (or part) and the income from it is to be accumulated so far as it is not applied for the maintenance, education or benefit of such a person' (FA 1982 s 114).

There must be no interest in possession and once such an interest arises, the settlement breaks Requirement 2 and ceases to be an accumulation and maintenance trust.

If there is to be no interest in possession in the income, what is to be done with it? Two possibilities are envisaged by Requirement 2; it can either be used for the benefit of a beneficiary (eg under a power of maintenance), or it can be accumulated. It would appear that it is not essential for there to be either a power to maintain or to accumulate; Requirement 2 will be satisfied where trustees must use the income for the benefit of the beneficiaries and, at the other extreme, where the trustees must accumulate the income and have no power to maintain.

EXAMPLE 16

A trust is set up for Loeb, the child of the settlor, contingent on attaining the age of 25. So long as he is a minor the trustees will have a power to maintain him out of the income of the fund and a power to accumulate any surplus income (Trustee Act 1925 s 31). When Loeb becomes 18 he will be entitled to the income of the fund so that an interest in possession will arise and the settlement will cease to be an accumulation and maintenance trust. The ending of the trust will not lead to any CTT charge.

Care should be taken in choosing the appropriate period if the intention is to accumulate income beyond the minorities of the beneficiaries. Various periods are permitted under the LPA 1925 ss 164 and 165 and under the Trustee Act 1925 s 31, but some of them may cause the trust to fall outside the definition of an accumulation and maintenance settlement. In the case of an inter vivos trust, for instance, a direction to accumulate 'during the lifetime of the settlor' would mean that an interest in possession might not arise until after the beneficiaries had attained the age of 25; likewise, a provision to accumulate for 21 years when the beneficiaries are over the age of four would be fatal.

5   Requirement 3

'Either
 (i) not more than 25 years have elapsed since the day on which the settlement was made or (if later) since the time when the settled property (or part) began to satisfy [Requirements 1 and 2], or
 (ii) all the persons who are, or have been, beneficiaries are, or were, either grandchildren of a common grandparent, or children, widows or widowers of such grandchildren who were themselves beneficiaries but died before becoming entitled as mentioned in [Requirement 1]' (FA 1982 s 114).

Requirement 3 was first introduced in FA 1976 to stop the accumulation and maintenance trust from being used to benefit more than one generation. There are two ways in which it can be satisfied. First, the trust must not last for more than 25 years from the date when the fund became settled on accumulation and maintenance trusts. The second (alternative) limb of Requirement 3 is satisfied if all the beneficiaries have a common grandparent.

EXAMPLE 17

(1) Property is settled for the children and grandchildren of the settlor. As there is no grandparent common to all the beneficiaries, the trust must not last for longer than 25 years if an exit charge to CTT is to be avoided.
(2) Property is settled for the children of brothers Bill and Ben. As there is a common grandparent the duration of the settlement does not need to be limited to 25 years.

There is one case in which two generations can be benefited under an accumulation and maintenance trust since substitution *per stirpes* is permitted where the original beneficiaries had a common grandparent and one of the original beneficiaries has died.

6 Advantages of accumulation and maintenance trusts

No CTT is charged when property from an accumulation and maintenance trust becomes subject to an interest in possession in favour of one or more of the beneficiaries, or when any part of the fund is appointed absolutely to such a beneficiary (FA 1982 s 114(3)(4)). This exemption, together with the exclusion of the anniversary charge (FA 1982 s 102(1)(b)), means that once the property is settled on these trusts there should be no further CTT liability.

EXAMPLE 18

'. . . to A absolutely contingent on attaining 25'. This straightforward trust will satisfy the requirements so long as A is an infant. Consider, however, the position:
(1) *When A attains 18:* he will be entitled to the income from the fund (Trustee Act 1925 s 31) and, therefore, Requirement 2 is broken. No CTT is charged on the arising of the interest in possession.
(2) *When A attains 25:* ordinary principles for interest in possession settlements apply; A's life interest comes to an end, but no CTT is payable since the life tenant is entitled to all the property (see FA 1975 Sch 5 para 4(3)).
(3) *If A dies aged 19:* CTT will be assessed on the termination of an interest in possession (FA 1975 Sch 5 para 4(1)).

As already discussed, there is nothing to prevent an accumulation and maintenance trust from being created for an open class of beneficiaries, eg 'for all my grandchildren both born and yet to be born'. If such a trust is to be created, it is important to ensure that the class of beneficiaries will close when the eldest obtains a vested interest in either the income or capital. Failure to do so will result in a partial divesting of the beneficiary with the vested interest when a further beneficiary is born, and, as a result, a CTT charge. Class-closing rules may be implied at common law (see *Andrews v Partington* (1791)), but it is safer to insert an express provision to that effect.

FA 1982 s 114(4)(b) provides that 'tax shall not be charged . . . on the death of a beneficiary before attaining the specified age'. It follows that, if the entire class of beneficiaries is wiped out, an accumulation and maintenance trust will cease on the death of the final member, but, whoever then becomes entitled to the fund, no CTT will be payable. When it is necessary to wait and see if a further beneficiary is born, this provision will not operate, since it is not the death of the beneficiary which ends the accumulation and maintenance trust, but the failure of a further beneficiary to be born within the trust period.

EXAMPLE 19

(1) Property is settled upon trust for Zed's grandchild, Yvonne, contingent upon her attaining 18. If she were to die aged 16, the property would (in the absence of any provision to the contrary) revert to Zed and no CTT would be payable.

(2) Property is settled upon trust for Victor's children contingent upon their attaining 21 and, if more than one, in equal shares. Victor's one child, Daphne, died in 1983 aged 12 and Victor himself has just died.

  No charge to CTT arose on Daphne's death and the property continues to be held on accumulation and maintenance trusts until Victor dies when the trust ends with a charge to CTT.

7   Occasions when an 'exit charge' will arise

It will be rare for property to leave an accumulation and maintenance trust otherwise than by appointment to a beneficiary and so long as this happens no CTT is chargeable. Provision is, however, made for calculating an 'exit charge' in the following four circumstances (FA 1982 ss 113(6), 114(5)):

(1) When depreciatory transactions entered into by the trustees reduce the value of the fund (FA 1982 s 114(3)(b)).

(2) When the 25 year period provided for in Requirement 3 is exceeded and the beneficiaries do not have a common grandparent.

(3) When property is advanced to a non-beneficiary or resettled on trusts which do not comply with the three Requirements.

(4) If the trust ends some time after the final surviving beneficiary has died (see *Example 19(2)*).

CTT is calculated in these cases on the value of the fund according to how long the property has been held on the accumulation and maintenance trusts:

0.25% for each of the first 40 complete successive quarters in the relevant period;

0.20% for each of the next 40;

0.15% for each of the next 40;

0.10% for each of the next 40; and

0.05% for each of the next 40.

Hence, on expiry of the permitted 25 years CTT at a rate of 21% will apply to the fund. Thereafter, normal discretionary trust rules will apply, so that five years later there will be an anniversary charge.

8   The creation of accumulation and maintenance trusts

No special relieving provisions operate on the creation of accumulation and maintenance trusts; their creation normally involves a chargeable transfer of value. One possibility of avoiding CTT is to set up an accumulation and maintenance trust by a disposition falling with FA 1975 s 46 (see p 326). What has to be shown is that the whole of the capital is to be expended on the maintenance, education, or training of the child, and the trustees must, therefore, have the widest powers so to apply the fund. If this argument is successful, neither the creation nor the destruction of the trust are chargeable transfers.

VI OTHER SPECIAL TRUSTS

1 **Charitable trusts**

If a trust is perpetually dedicated to charitable purposes, there is no charge to CTT and the fund is not 'relevant property' (FA 1982 s 102). Transfers to such charities are exempt, whether made by individuals or by trustees of discretionary trusts (FA 1982 s 119). FA 1982 s 113 is concerned with temporary charitable trusts which that section defines as 'settled property held for charitable purposes only until the end of a period (whether defined by a date or in some other way)' and ensures that when the fund ceases to be held for such purposes an exit charge will arise. That charge (which is calculated in the same way as for accumulation and maintenance trusts; see p 368) will never exceed a 30% rate which is reached after 50 years.

2 **Trusts for the benefit of mentally disabled persons and persons in receipt of an attendance allowance**

These rules were recast by FA 1981. As from 10 March 1981, a qualifying trust for a disabled person is treated as giving that person an interest in possession. As a result the CTT regime for no interest in possession trusts does not apply.

3 **Pension funds** (FA 1975 Sch 5 para 16 as amended)

A superannuation scheme or fund approved by the Revenue for income tax purposes is not subject to the rules for no interest in possession trusts. A benefit payable out of that fund which becomes comprised in a discretionary trust is, however, subject to the normal charging rules; the person entitled to that benefit being treated as the settlor.

4 **Employee trusts** (FA 1975 Sch 5 para 17 as amended)

These trusts will not in law be charitable unless they are directed to the relief of poverty amongst employees (see *Oppenheim v Tobacco Securities Trust Co Ltd* (1951). They may, however, enjoy considerable CTT privileges. Their creation will not involve a transfer of value, whether made by an individual (FA 1978 s 67) or by a discretionary trust (FA 1982 s 115). Once created, the fund is largely exempted from the CTT provisions governing discretionary trusts, especially from the anniversary charge. To qualify for this treatment, the fund must be held for the benefit of persons employed in a particular trade or profession together with their dependents.

5 **Compensation funds** (FA 1982 ss 102, 126)

Trusts set up by professional bodies and trade associations for the purpose of indemnifying clients and customers against loss incurred through the default of their members are exempt from the rules for no interest in possession trusts.

6 Newspaper trusts

The provisions relating to employee trusts (above) are extended to cover newspaper trusts such as the Scott Trust (which owns the *Guardian*) and the Telegraph Newspaper Trust (owner of the *Daily Telegraph*).

7 Maintenance funds for historic buildings (FA 1982 ss 93–95, Sch 16)

CTT exemptions are available for maintenance funds where property is settled and the Treasury give a direction under FA 1982 s 93. Once the trust ceases, for any reason, to carry out its specialised function, an exit charge, calculated in the same way as for accumulation and maintenance trusts, occurs.

8 Protective trusts

A protective trust is set up either by using the statutory model provided for by the Trustee Act 1925 s 33, or by express provisions which closely resemble that provision.

These trusts have always been subject to special CTT rules and, as originally enacted, the rules offered considerable scope for tax avoidance (see eg *Thomas v IRC* (1981)). FA 1978 accordingly effected a change with effect from 11 April 1978 by providing that the life tenant is deemed to continue to have an interest in possession for CTT purposes despite the forfeiture of his interest. It, therefore, follows that the discretionary trust regime is not applicable to the trust that arises upon such forfeiture. Should the capital be advanced to a person other than the life tenant, a charge to CTT will arise and on the death of the beneficiary the fund will be treated as part of his estate for CTT purposes. As a result of these rules there is the curious anomaly that, after a forfeiture of the life interest, the interest in possession rules apply to a discretionary trust.

One cautionary note should be added; this system of charging only applies to protective trusts set up under Trustee Act 1925 s 33 or under trusts 'to the like effect'. Minor variations to the statutory norm are, therefore, allowed; but not perhaps the inclusion of different beneficiaries under the discretionary trust, nor a provision which enables a forfeited life interest to revive after the lapse of a period of time. In such cases, the normal rules applicable to interest in possession and discretionary trusts apply.

27 CTT—excluded property and the foreign element

I   Domicile and situs
II   What is excluded property?
III Double taxation relief for non-excluded property
IV   Miscellaneous points
V   Foreign settlements, reversionary interests, and excluded property

As a general rule, CTT is chargeable on all property within the UK regardless of its owner's domicile and on property, wheresoever situate, which is beneficially owned by an individual domiciled in the UK.

Any transfer of 'excluded property', however, is not chargeable to CTT (FA 1975 ss 20(3) and 23(1)). The main example of excluded property is 'property situated outside the UK . . . if the person beneficially entitled to it is an individual domiciled outside the UK' (FA 1975 s 24(2)). However, in determining whether property is excluded property the relevant factors include not only the domicile of the transferor who is the beneficial owner of the property and the situation of the property (situs), but also the nature of the transferred property, since certain property is excluded regardless of its situs or the domicile of its owner.

I   DOMICILE AND SITUS

1 Domicile

Whether property is excluded depends on the domicile (rather than the residence or nationality) of the transferor. An individual cannot, under English law, be without a domicile which connotes a legal relationship between an individual and a territory. There are three kinds of domicile: domicile of origin, domicile of choice and domicile of dependence.

A person acquires a domicile of origin at the moment when he is born. He will usually take the domicile of his father unless he is illegitimate or born after his father's death in which case he takes the domicile of his mother. A domicile of origin is never completely lost, but may be superseded by a domicile of dependency or choice; it will revive if the other type of domicile lapses.

A person cannot acquire a domicile of choice until he is 16 or marries under that age. Whether someone has replaced his domicile of origin (or dependence) by a domicile of choice is a question of fact which involves physical presence in the country concerned and evidence of a settled intention to remain there permanently or indefinitely.

Two categories of individual may acquire a domicile by dependence: unmarried infants under the age of 16 acquire their father's domicile by dependence and women who married before 1 January 1974 acquired their husband's domicile by dependence.

If a person's domicile under the general law is outside the UK, he may (as an anti-avoidance measure) be deemed to be domiciled in the UK, for CTT purposes only, in one of two circumstances (FA 1975 s 45(1)). First, if a person was domiciled in the UK on or after 10 December 1974 and within the three years immediately preceding the transfer in question, he will be deemed to be domiciled in the UK at the time of making the transfer (FA 1975 s 45(1)(a)). This provision is aimed at the taxpayer who moves his property out of the UK and then emigrates to avoid future CTT liability on transfers of that property. In such a case he will have to wait a further three years from the date of emigration for his property to become excluded property under FA 1975 s 24(2).

Secondly, a person will be deemed domiciled in the UK if he was resident in the UK on or after 10 December 1974 and in not less than 17 out of the 20 income tax years ending with the income tax year in which he made the relevant transfer (FA 1975 s 45(1)(b)). This provision aims to catch the person who has lived in the UK for a long time even though he never became domiciled here under the general law. Residence is used in the income tax sense (see Chapter 13), but without applying the accommodation test.

EXAMPLE 1

(1) Jack who was domiciled in England moved to New Zealand on 1 July 1981 intending to settle there permanently. Jack died on 1 January 1983 when according to the general law he had acquired a domicile of choice in New Zealand. However, because Jack had a UK domicile on 10 December 1974 and died within three years of losing it, he is deemed under s 45(1)(a) to have died domiciled in the UK. Accordingly, all his property wherever situated (excluding gilts; see below) is potentially chargeable to CTT. Jack would have had to survive until 1 July 1984 to avoid being caught by this provision.

(2) On 5 June 1984, Jim who is domiciled under the general law in Ruritania and who is a director of BB Ltd (the UK subsidiary of a Ruritanian company) gives a house that he owns in Ruritania to his son. In connection with his job he has been resident for income tax purposes in England since 1 January 1964, but he intends to return to Ruritania when he retires. For CTT purposes Jim is deemed to be domiciled in England under s 45(1)(b); the gift is, therefore, chargeable to CTT.

2   Situs

Subject to contrary provisions in double taxation treaties (and special rules for certain property) the situs of property depends on common law rules and on the type of property involved. For instance:

(1) An interest in land (including a leasehold estate or rentcharge) is situated where the land is physically located.

(2) Chattels (other than ships and aircraft) are situated at the place where they are kept at the relevant time.

(3) Registered shares and securities are situated where they are registered or, if transferable upon more than one register, where they would normally be dealt with in the ordinary course of business.

(4) Bearer shares and securities being transferable by delivery, are situated where the certificate or other document of title is kept.

(5) A bank account (ie the debt owed by the bank) is situated at the branch which maintains the account. (Special rules deal with non-residents' foreign currency bank accounts; FA 1982 s 96.)

"I'm not complaining, Henry, it's just that I always think of sunshine, palm-fringed beaches and villas whenever I think of taxhavens . . . ."

II WHAT IS EXCLUDED PROPERTY?

1 Property situated outside the UK and owned beneficially by a non-UK domiciliary (FA 1975 s 24(2))

All property falling into this category is excluded regardless of its nature. Settled property situated abroad will be excluded property if the settlor was domiciled outside the UK at the time when he made the settlement (FA 1975 Sch 5 para 2).

In deciding whether the transferor is a UK domiciliary at the time of the transfer the deeming provisions of FA 1975 s 45 will generally operate.

2 Property which is exempt despite being situated in the UK

Government securities Certain government securities (gilts) issued before 18 March 1977 and beneficially owned by a person neither domiciled nor ordinarily resident in the UK are exempt from CTT (F (No 2) A 1915 s 47 and F (No 2) A 1931 s 22(1)(b)). The deeming provisions of FA 1975 s 45 do not apply to such transferors. Such gilts also receive privileged treatment for CGT (CGTA 1979 s 67 and Sch 2) and for income tax (TA 1970 s 99). If these securities are settled they will be excluded property if either the person beneficially entitled to an interest in possession (eg a life tenant) is neither domiciled nor ordinarily resident in the UK, or, in the case of a discretionary trust, if none of the beneficiaries are domiciled or ordinarily resident in the UK (FA 1975 Sch 7 para 3).

FA 1978 s 72 introduced certain anti-avoidance provisions.

(1) If gilts are transferred from one settlement to another they will only be

excluded property if the beneficiaries of *both* settlements are non-UK resident or domiciled. This prevents gilts from being channelled from a discretionary trust where they were not excluded property (because some of the beneficiaries were UK domiciled and/or resident) to a new settlement with non-domiciled beneficiaries only, where they would be excluded property.

(2) Where a close company is a beneficiary of a trust, any gilts owned by the trust will be excluded property only if all participators in the company are non-UK domiciled and resident, irrespective of the company's domicile. This aims to prevent individuals from using a company to avoid CTT.

This privileged tax treatment only applies to gilts issued before 18 March 1977. Hence, all transfers of value of gilts issued thereafter are chargeable to CTT even if in the beneficial ownership of individuals domiciled and resident outside the UK.

Certain property owned by persons domiciled in the Channel Islands or Isle of Man
Certain savings (eg national savings certificates) are excluded property if they are in the beneficial ownership of a person domiciled and resident in the Channel Islands or the Isle of Man (FA 1975 Sch 7 para 5).

Visiting forces   Certain property owned in the UK by visiting forces and staff of allied headquarters is excluded property (FA 1975 Sch 7 para 6).

Overseas pensions   Certain overseas pensions (usually payable by ex-colonial governments) are exempt from CTT on the pensioner's death regardless of his domicile (FA 1975 Sch 7 para 4).

For the inter-relationship of excluded property and settlements see below.

III   DOUBLE TAXATION RELIEF FOR NON-EXCLUDED PROPERTY

Non-excluded property may be exposed to a double charge to tax (especially on the death of the owner); once to CTT in the UK and again to a similar tax imposed by a foreign country. Relief against such double charge may be afforded in one of two ways. First, the UK might have a double taxation treaty with the relevant country when the position is governed by FA 1975 Sch 7 para 7. The provisions of the treaty will override all the relevant CTT legislation and common law rules regarding the situs of property (for the individual provisions of each such treaty see Foster *Capital Taxes Encyclopaedia, foreign element, F4*).

Under these treaties, the country in which the transferor is domiciled is generally entitled to tax all property of which he was the beneficial owner. The other country involved usually has the right to tax some of that property, eg land situated there. In such cases the country of domicile will give relief against the resulting double taxation. Most of these treaties also contain provisions to catch the individual who changes his domicile shortly before death to avoid tax.

Secondly, where no double taxation treaty exists, unilateral relief is given in the form of a credit for the foreign tax liability against CTT payable in the UK (FA 1975 Sch 7 para 8). The amount of the credit depends on where the relevant property is situated; in some cases no credit is available if the overseas tax is not similar to CTT, although some relief is, effectively, given since, in valuing the reduction in the transferor's estate for calculating CTT, the amount of overseas tax paid will be disregarded (see FA 1975 Sch 10 para 1 (2)). This relief is naturally less beneficial than a tax credit as the transferor must still bear the double tax.

IV MISCELLANEOUS POINTS

1 Valuation of the estate—allowable deductions

Generally, certain liabilities of a transferor are deductible when calculating the value of his estate for CTT (see p 283). However, any liability to a non-UK resident is deductible as far as possible from a transferor's foreign before his UK estate. As a result, a foreign domiciliary who is chargeable to CTT on his UK assets cannot usually deduct his foreign liabilities from his UK estate. There are two exceptions to this rule. First, if a liability of a non-UK resident has to be discharged in the UK it is deductible from the UK estate; secondly, any liability which encumbers property in the UK, reduces the value of that property.

EXAMPLE 2

Adolphus dies domiciled in Ethiopia. His estate includes cash in a London bank account, shares in UK companies and a stud farm in Weybridge which is mortgaged to an Ethiopian glue factory. He owes a UK travel company £500 for a ticket bought to enable his daughter to travel around Texas and £200,000 to a Dallas horse dealer. CTT is chargeable on his UK assets. However, the loan is deductible from the value of his stud farm and £500 is deductible from the UK estate generally. There is no reduction for the debt of £200,000 assuming he has sufficient foreign property.

2 Expenses of administering property abroad

Administration expenses are not generally deductible from the value of the deceased's estate. However, the expense of administering or realising property situated abroad on death is deductible from the value of the relevant property up to a limit of 5% of its value.

3 Enforcement of tax abroad

On the death of a foreign domiciliary with UK assets, the deceased's PRs cannot administer his property until they have paid any CTT and obtained a grant of probate. However, the collection of CTT on lifetime transfers by a foreign domiciliary presents a problem if both the transferor and transferee are resident outside the UK and there is no available property in the UK which can be impounded.

V FOREIGN SETTLEMENTS, REVERSIONARY INTERESTS AND EXCLUDED PROPERTY

1 Foreign settlements

As a general rule settled property which is situated abroad is excluded property if the settlor was domiciled outside the UK when the settlement was made

(FA 1975 Sch 5 para 2). The domicile deeming provisions of FA 1975 s 45 only apply to a settlor who settled property after 10 December 1974. Therefore, the domicile of the individual beneficiaries under a foreign settlement is irrelevant, so that even if a beneficiary is domiciled in the UK, there will be no charge to CTT on the termination of his interest in possession nor on any payment made to him under a discretionary trust.

EXAMPLE 3

Generous, domiciled in the USA, settles shares in US companies on his nephew, Tom, for life. Tom is domiciled and resident in the UK. The property is excluded property, being property situated abroad settled by a settlor domiciled at that time outside the UK, so that there will be no charge to CTT on the ending of Tom's life interest.

If, however, those shares were exchanged for shares in UK companies, the property would no longer be excluded and there would be a charge to CTT on the termination of Tom's life interest.

If Generous had settled those same US shares on discretionary trusts for his nephews, all of whom were UK domiciled, the property would be, for the same reason, excluded property, so that the normal discretionary trust charges to CTT will not apply.

a) *Definition*

For CTT purposes any future interest in settled property is classified as a reversionary interest. The term, therefore, includes an interest dependent on the termination of an interest in possession, whether that interest is vested or contingent. A contingent interest where the settlement does not have an interest in possession is also a reversionary interest for CTT purposes.

EXAMPLE 4

Property is settled on the following trusts:
(1) A for life, remainder to B for life, remainder to C. B and C both have reversionary interests for CTT purposes.
(2) A for life, remainder to B for life, remainder to C if he survives B. C's contingent remainder is a reversionary interest for CTT purposes.
(3) To A absolutely contingent upon attaining the age of 21. A is currently aged six and has a reversionary interest for CTT purposes.

The interest of a discretionary beneficiary is not, however, a 'reversionary interest', being in no sense a future interest. Such a beneficiary has certain present rights, particularly the right to be considered by the trustees when they exercise their discretion and the right to compel due administration of the fund. The value of such an interest is likely to be nil, however, since the beneficiary has no right to any of the income or capital of the settlement. He has merely a hope ('spes').

b) *'Situs' of a reversionary interest*

A reversionary interest under a trust for sale is a chose in action rather than an interest in the specific settled assets be they land or personalty (*Re Smythe, Leach v Leach* (1898)). In other cases the position is unclear; but by analogy with estate duty principles it will be a chose in action if the settled assets are personalty; but an interest in the settled assets themselves if they are land. Since a chose in action is normally situated in the country in which it is recoverable (*New York Life Insurance Co v Public Trustee* (1924)), in some cases the reversionary interest will not be situated in the same place as the settled assets.

c) *Reversionary interests—the general rule*

A reversionary interest is excluded property for CTT (FA 1975 s 24(3); see p 351) with three exceptions designed to counter tax avoidance:
(1) Where it was purchased for money or money's worth.

> **EXAMPLE 5**
>
> There is a settlement on A for life, remainder to B. B sells his interest to X who gives it to his brother Y. X has made a chargeable transfer of value of a reversionary interest (which can be valued taking into account the value of the settled fund and the life expectancy of A).

(2) Where it is an interest to which the settlor or his spouse is beneficially entitled.
(3) Where a lease for life or lives is granted for no or partial consideration, there is a settlement for CTT (FA 1975 Sch 5 para 1(3)) and the lessor's interest is a reversionary interest (FA 1975 s 51(1)). Such a reversionary interest is only excluded property to the extent that the lessor did not receive full consideration on the grant (see FA 1975 Sch 5 para 3(b) for valuation of the lessee's interest in possession and Sch 10 para 8 for the valuation of the lessor's interest).

> **EXAMPLE 6**
>
> L grants a lease of property worth £30,000 to T for £10,000 for T's life. T is treated for CTT purposes, as having an interest in possession and, therefore, as absolute owner of two-thirds of the property (£30,000 – £10,000). L is treated as the owner of one-third of the property (because he received £10,000). Therefore, one-third of his reversionary interest is not excluded property.

d) *Reversionary interests—the foreign element*

Under FA 1975 s 24(3) a reversionary interest (with the three exceptions above) is excluded property regardless of the domicile of the settlor or reversioner or the situs of the interest. Where the settled property is in the UK, but the reversionary interest is situated abroad (see (b) above) and beneficially owned by a foreign domiciliary, the interest probably is excluded property in all cases under the general rule of FA 1975 s 24(2).

However, the status of a reversionary interest in settled property situated outside the UK is cast into some doubt by virtue of FA 1975 Sch 5 para 2 to which s 24 is expressly made subject (FA 1975 s 24(1)). Paragraph 2(1) states:

> 'where property comprised in a settlement is situated outside the UK
> (a) the property (but not a reversionary interest in the property) is excluded property unless the settlor was domiciled in the UK at the time the settlement was made; and
> (b) section 24(2) of this Act applies to a reversionary interest in the property, but does not otherwise apply in relation to the property.'

This provision appears to exclude the operation of s 24(3) by saying that a reversionary interest in settled property situated abroad is only excluded property (under the general rule in s 24(2)) if it is itself situated abroad and owned by a foreign domiciliary.

However, it has been suggested that para 2(1) only prevails over s 24 in cases of conflict and that there is no conflict here since the words 'but not a reversionary interest' in para 2(1)(a) simply mean that whether a reversionary interest is excluded property depends not on the situs of the settled property nor on the settlor's domicile, but on the general rule in s 24(3).

In summary, therefore, a reversionary interest is always excluded property regardless of situs or domicile with three exceptions (see p 377). Even if the interest falls within one of the exceptions, it will still be excluded property if the interest (regardless of the whereabouts of the settled property) is situated outside the UK and beneficially owned by a foreign domiciliary (FA 1975 s 24(2)); or if the reversionary interest is itself settled property, is situated abroad and was settled by a foreign domiciliary (FA 1975 s 24(2) and Sch 5 para 2(1)).

For a discussion of the tax planning opportunities afforded by reversionary interests see p 351.

Section 5 Business enterprise and stamp duty

Chapters

28   Corporation tax

'the current rates of corporation tax are far too high, penalising profit and success and blunting the cutting edge of enterprise'. Chancellor of the Exchequer, the Rt Hon Nigel Lawson MP, Budget Statement 13 March 1984.

I   INTRODUCTION

Corporaton tax was introduced by FA 1965 and applies to all bodies corporate including authorised unit trusts and unincorporated associations but not partnerships or local authorities. It is levied on the profits of a company which are made up of both income profits, computed according to income tax principles, and capital profits which will be assessed in accordance with CGT rules. The 1965 legislation was substantially amended by FA 1972 (with effect from 1 April 1973); it is common to refer to the system in force from 1966 to 1973 as the *classical* system and that introduced in 1973 (and still in force today) as the *imputation* system.

The classical system had two main features. First, dividends, and company distributions generally, were not allowed as deductions in arriving at profits; instead they were payable out of net profits and were further subject to income tax (and, if relevant, to surtax) in the hands of the recipient. Secondly, a special category of company, the close company, was created which was to be subject to special rules largely designed to frustrate the use of small companies in tax planning schemes.

The Conservative government (1970–74) introduced changes in the operation of corporation tax. The special penalties suffered by close companies were gradually reduced but, most significantly, the imputation system fundamentally altered the rules dealing with the taxation of distributions. In general, the new system was designed to achieve parity in the taxation of a company's profits whether those profits were retained or distributed to shareholders, since the classical system had resulted in the double taxation of distributions, first as profits of the company and then as dividends in the hands of the shareholder. The cornerstone of the new system was advance corporation tax (ACT) which is generally payable on all company distributions. ACT serves a dual purpose since it represents a payment of both corporation tax for the company and basic rate income tax for the recipient shareholder.

Although the imputation system has been retained in its essential aspects it has many critics. Inland Revenue statistics show that the revenue raised from companies amounts to only a small proportion of the total tax yield per annum.

Furthermore, there are inequalities of treatment as between the company and the individual and the small private company is able to avoid any substantial levy to corporation tax by paying out its 'profits' as salaries to the manager shareholders. The dramatic reduction in corporation tax rates in FA 1984 (discussed below) marks a further shift away from the classical system. For small companies the reduction will enable dividends to be (in effect) tax deductible and, for other companies, the element of double charge will be virtually eradicated by 1986. The Green Paper (Cmnd 8456: January 1982) which discusses alternatives to the present system, has so far not been proceeded with.

II GENERAL PRINCIPLES—RATES OF TAX

The tax is charged by reference to financial years (FY) which run from 1 April to 31 March and are referred to by the calendar year in which they commence. Hence, FY 1983 means the financial year running from 1 April 1983 to 31 March 1984. The rate at which corporation tax is charged has hitherto been fixed in arrears and for the last ten years has been 52%. However, FA 1984 has fixed the rate for 1983 at 50% and also provided that for FY 1984, 1985, and 1986 the rate shall be 45%, 40%, and 35% respectively (the special rate for small companies is discussed on p 382). Where companies are wound up the rate charged during their final financial year will be that fixed for the preceeding financial year (TA 1970 s 245(2)).

Corporation tax is charged on a current year basis on the company's profits of the financial year. Therefore, where a company's accounting period straddles two financial years the profits must be apportioned (TA 1970 s 243(3)). In the case of trading profits the apportionment will be on a time basis; in the case of other income and gains the apportionment will be according to actual income or chargeable gains of the financial year. Unlike for individual traders there is for a company no optimum date on which to make up accounts.

EXAMPLE 1

Grr Ltd makes up its accounts to 31 December. For the years ended 1983 and 1984 its trading profits were £240,000 and £360,000 respectively. The rate of corporation tax for FY 1982 is 52%; for 1983 50%; for 1984 45%.
   The tax will be calculated as follows:
(i) *Profits of £240,000 apportioned:*
January 1983–April 1983.
3/12 of £240,000 = £60,000 taxed at 52% (FY 1982)
April 1983–December 1983:
9/12 of £240,000 = £180,000 taxed at 50% (FY 1983)
(ii) *Profits of £360,000 apportioned:*
January 1984–April 1984:
3/12 of £360,000 = £90,000 taxed at 50% (FY 1983)
April 1984–December 1984:
9/12 of £360,000 = £270,000 taxed at 45% (FY 1984)

The tax is payable within nine months after the end of the accounting period on which it was assessed or (if later) within one month from the making of the assessment. Hence, in *Example 1* the tax will be due by 30 September in each year. An important exception applies to trading companies which were liable to income tax under the pre-1966 rules. For such companies the interval for payment under that earlier system is retained so that their corporation tax is payable on 1 January in the year following the financial year in which the company's accounting period ends.

FA 1972 introduced two reliefs from the full corporation tax rate. First, FA 1972 s 93 ensures that capital gains will, in effect, be charged at the same rate as that which applies to the gains of individuals. This equality is achieved by charging to corporation tax a fraction of the chargeable gain. For FY 1983 this fraction is 3/5 which is assessed at 50% thereby ensuring an average rate of charge of 30%.

Secondly, FA 1972 s 95 introduced a small companies rate of corporation tax for income but not capital profits of such companies. The rate for FYs 1983–86 is 30% which applies to companies whose profits do not exceed £100,000. Where profits exceed £100,000 but not £500,000 tapering relief is available to avoid a sudden leap to a higher overall tax rate. The corporation tax definition of a small company is purely related to its profits for any particular financial year. For this purpose profits include franked investment income (see p 383) and chargeable gains.

EXAMPLE 2

Zee Ltd makes up its accounts to 31 March each year. For the year ending 31 March 1984 the company had trading profits of £60,000 and had made chargeable gains of £52,000.

The profits of Zee Ltd for corporation tax purposes are:

	£
Trading profits	60,000
Chargeable gains (£52,000 × 3/5)	31,200
Chargeable profits	£91,200

Zee Ltd will, therefore, qualify for the small companies rate so that corporation tax will be charged as follows:

	£
Income profits (£60,000 at 30%)	18,000
Chargeable gains (£31,200 at 50%)	15,600
Total tax	£33,600

Were the trading profits of Zee Ltd to be £85,000 then, with the addition of chargeable gains, the small companies threshold of £100,000 would be exceeded so that a form of tapering relief would apply as follows:

(i) Corporation tax payable £116,200 (ie £85,000 + £31,200) at 50% = £58,100
(ii) *Less* tapering relief

$$(\text{upper relevant amount} - \text{profits}) \times \frac{\text{income profits}}{\text{total profits}} \times \text{statutory fraction}$$

		£
ie $(£500,000 - £116,200) \times \dfrac{£85,000}{£116,200} \times \dfrac{1}{20}$ (ie 5%)	=	14,037

(iii) Total tax =		£44,063

This tax can be analysed thus:

		£
Capital gains: £31,200 at 50%	=	15,600
Income:		
$\left(£100,000 \times \dfrac{£85,000}{£116,200}\right) = £73,150$ at 30%	=	21,945
plus £11,850 (£85,000 − £73,150) at (50% + 5%)	=	6,518
		£44,063

Two points should be stressed in connection with the small companies rate. First, anti-avoidance provisions exist to prevent the fragmentation of a business amongst subsidiaries in an attempt to create a whole series of small companies. Secondly, although tapering relief applies where profits fall into the range £100,000 to £500,000, this does not mean that the tax on profits in excess of £100,000 is at a rate below 50%. This is because the purpose of tapering relief is to increase gradually the average rate of corporation tax from the 30% payable by a company with income profits of £100,000 to the 50% payable by a company with profits of £500,000. To achieve this result the rate applicable to the slice of profits between £100,000 and £500,000 has to *exceed* 50%. At present this marginal rate is 55% calculated as follows:

Tax on £100,000 at 30%	=	£30,000
Tax on £500,000 at 50%	=	£250,000
Difference (£250,000 – £30,000)	=	£220,000

Therefore, £220,000 corporation tax has to be raised on profits falling between £100,000 and £500,000 (ie on £400,000).
Hence, as a percentage, tax on £400,000 will be

$$\frac{220,000}{400,000} \times 100 = 55\%$$

This point is of practical significance when considering how much money the directors of family companies should take by way of remuneration. The marginal corporation tax rate is only just below the highest rate of income tax so that it may be advantageous from a tax point of view to pay out such moneys in the form of salaries and will always be so in cases where the personal tax rates of the directors are not as high as 55% (see further Chapter 33).

III   HOW TO CALCULATE THE PROFITS OF A COMPANY

Profits of a company are defined as including both income profits and capital gains (TA 1970 s 238(4)(a)).

1   Income profits

Generally, income profits have to be computed in accordance with the income tax rules that apply in the year of assessment in which the company's accounting period ends (TA 1970 s 250(1)(2)). Each class of income will, therefore, be calculated under the same Schedules that apply for income tax. Thus, a trading company having no other income will compute its profits in accordance with the rules of Schedule D Case I and the salaries and fees paid to its directors and employees will be allowable expenses under TA 1970 s 130. It should be noted that TA 1970 s 251(2)(b) prohibits the deduction, as an expense, of annual payments, annuities, and yearly interest unless paid on a loan from a bank carrying on business in the UK. Such payments must be relieved, if at all, as charges on income (see p 385).
In calculating the income profits no account is taken of dividends and other distributions received by one UK company from another (franked investment income: TA 1970 s 239). The utilisation of such income is considered at p 398. Notice, however, that franked investment income (FII) is included in the profits of a company for the purpose of discovering whether the small companies rate is applicable; this income is not then taxed. Where income is received by a company net of income tax deducted at source (eg building society interest, debenture interest, and annuities received by companies) the

gross income is included in the profits of the company and a credit is given against the corporation tax payable for the tax deducted at source.

EXAMPLE 3

Lexo Ltd makes up its accounts to 31 March each year. The accounts for the period ending 31 March 1984 show the following:

		£
Trading profit		160,000
Profit from lettings		40,000
Building society interest received:		
net	£35,000	
tax credit	£15,000	
Gross		50,000
Total profits		£250,000

	£
Corporation tax payable:	
£100,000 at 30% + £150,000 at 55%	112,500
Less building society tax credit	15;000
	£97,500

Notes
(1) The trading profit is calculated according to the rules of Schedule D Case I, for 1983/84, and the profit from lettings according to Schedule A.
(2) Building society interest is not franked investment income, but is treated in the same way as other sums received subject to deduction of income tax at source. If the tax credit exceeded the corporation tax payable, the excess would be repaid to the company.

The income tax principles are relevant only in determining the amount of the company's income profits—other enactments of that legislation are not relevant. Thus the preceding year rules and the opening and closing year provisions of Schedule D have no application to companies and there is no question of any personal reliefs or allowances applying. The system of capital allowances applies to companies with suitable modifications. The specific difficulties that may arise when an existing business or partnership is converted into a company are dealt with separately in Chapter 34.

2   Capital gains

A company's chargeable gains are computed in the same way as for an individual. Hence, the definition of chargeable assets and the occasions when a disposal occurs are common to both individuals and companies. The annual exemption (currently £5,600) is not available for disposals by companies. In the case of disposals between companies in the same group the disposal is treated as giving rise to neither gain nor loss until either the asset is disposed of outside the group or until the recipient company leaves the group (see p|407). A disadvantage suffered by a company and its shareholders is that on any capital gain realised by the company there is an element of double taxation since not only will the company suffer corporation tax on the gain, but also the shareholder whose shares may have increased in value as a result of the capital profit (albeit, after tax) will suffer capital gains tax when he disposes of those shares.

EXAMPLE 4

Saloman Ltd (wholly owned by John Saloman) makes a chargeable gain of £100,000. It will suffer corporation tax of £30,000 on that gain. Saloman's shares will have increased in value by, say, £70,000 so that were he to sell them he would suffer capital gains tax of (ignoring exemptions and reliefs) £21,000. Effectively, therefore, the corporate gain has been subject to tax at 51% (30% paid by the company and 21% by Saloman).

Vesting appreciating assets in private companies may, therefore, be tax inefficient and it may be better for the shareholder to retain those assets and lease them to the company (see p 477).

3 Deducting charges on income

TA 1970 s 248(1) provides that

'. . . any charges on income paid by the company in the accounting period, so far as paid out of the company's profits brought into charge to corporation tax shall be allowed as deductions against the total profits for the period as reduced by any other relief from tax other than group relief'.

It follows that such charges may be set against all the company's profits, including chargeable gains; this is in contrast with the position of individuals who can never offset charges against their chargeable gains. As the charges reduce profits any deductions arrived at in calculating those profits cannot be deducted a second time as a charge (TA 1970 s 248(2)). Interest payments, for instance, which are deducted as a business expense in arriving at trading profits under the Schedule D Case I rules cannot be deducted a second time as a charge. As s 248(1) refers to sums actually paid, it is important for a company to organise, so far as possible, its payments which constitute charges on income to be made at the end of one accounting period rather than at the beginning of the next in order to obtain the earliest possible tax relief. Where charges exceed the total profits for the year, the excess will still qualify for a measure of tax relief (see p 387; contrast the position of individual taxpayers who obtain no relief).

a) *Meaning of 'charges on income'*

The following are the main charges on income:
(a) annual interest, annuities or any other annual payment;
(b) any other interest payable on a loan from a bank carrying on a bona fide banking business in the UK; and
(c) royalties and sums paid in respect of user of a patent and certain mining rents and royalties.

Hence, debenture interest falls under (a) above, whilst short term interest falls within (b), although the standard example, the bank overdraft, would usually be deducted as a business expense in arriving at profits. These permitted charges can only be deducted if:
(1) The payment is to be borne by the company. Thus, no deduction is allowed where a right to reimbursement exists.
(2) The payment must be charged to income in the company's accounts, except that, for interest payments made after 31 March 1981, deduction will be permitted even though the payment appears in the company's books as a capital expense (FA 1981 s 38).
(3) The payment, except for covenanted donations to charity, must be made under a liability incurred for valuable and sufficient consideration.

EXAMPLE 5

Zeus Ltd makes the following covenanted payments.
  (i) £5,000 pa to the Society to Promote Antiquarian Studies (a registered charity).
 (ii) £8,000 pa to the trustees of a trust fund set up by the company to educate the children of its employees and to provide evening classes in arts and crafts for its employees.

The payment of £5,000 pa: will be a charge on income so long as it is capable of lasting for more than three years (TA 1970 s 248(9)). The charity will obtain a full tax rebate so that basic rate income tax (deducted at source by the company under TA 1970 s 53) will be refunded.

The payment of £8,000 pa: is not a charitable payment (see *Oppenheim v Tobacco Securities Trust Co Ltd* (1951)) and will only be an allowable charge if incurred for suitable consideration. In *Ball v National & Grindlay's Bank Ltd* (1971) the Court of Appeal concluded that at the time when the covenant was made it must be possible to show that the company was receiving adequate consideration for the payments. Such consideration could be in the form of money or money's worth including an obligation to the company. Hence, it is likely that the £8,000 would not be deductible as a charge since it will not suffice to show that there was some business advantage in making the payment, and no consideration in money or money's worth is being received by the company. Such payments do not offer tax advantages, therefore, and the company might be advised to avoid the use of annual payments altogether and to argue that the costs of establishing and maintaining the trust are allowable business expenses and, therefore, deductible under TA 1970 s 130 in arriving at profits (see TA 1970 s 251(2)(b)).

(4) Interest payments must be paid by a company which exists wholly or mainly for the purpose of carrying on a trade (or alternatively the payment must be wholly and exclusively laid out for trading purposes); or the company must be an investment company (including an authorised unit trust); or the relevant loan must be to purchase land occupied by the company. These requirements are not particularly demanding since virtually all companies will be trading or investment companies (note, however, difficulties for an unincorporated association which does not trade; although it pays corporation tax, it cannot deduct interest payments).

b) *Shares, debentures and deep discount securities*

There are two major sources of corporate finance. Money can either be raised by an allotment of shares so that the contributors become members of the company and will generally expect to receive dividends on those shares. Alternatively, money can be borrowed with the company creating debentures and paying interest to the debenture holders. Such interest will qualify as a charge on a company's profits and so obtain tax relief at the full rate. Dividends, however, are not deductible from a company's profits since they are not charges on income. As a result of the imputation system a full double charge to tax is avoided and relief is given at 30%. Whilst the corporation tax rate exceeds the 30% level of relief, there remains a discrimination in favour of debentures and against raising funds by a share issue. For small companies, the corporation tax rate is now 30% so that there is no element of double taxation; for other companies, the 50% rate is to be reduced to 35% by FY 1986 when any discrimination against dividends will effectively disappear. Until 1986, therefore, those companies which possess a large preference share capital may obtain a tax advantage from converting such shares into loan stock. Two further innovations in the tax treatment of loan stock should also be noted. First, certain fixed interest stock, which is issued or transferred after 13 March 1984, will be exempt from CGT (or corporation tax) on disposal, so long as it has been held for at least 12 months. The stock must be either quoted on The UK Stock Exchange or dealt in on the Unlisted Securities Market or issued by a body with other securities so quoted or dealt in (FA 1984 s 64 and Sch 13).

Secondly, FA 1984 s 36 and Sch 9 provides that in the case of deep discount securities (defined as redeemable securities, excluding shares, issued after 13 March 1984 at a price substantially below their redemption price and carrying little or no interest) the discount is treated as deemed annual income accruing on a compound interest basis. The issuing company will deduct this deemed income each year as a charge on income (although it will only pay the discount on redemption), whilst the shareholder will be taxed under Schedule D Case III on the discount when he disposes of the security or when it is redeemed. A disposal has its CGT meaning, but if the holder dies he is treated as receiving the accrued income immediately before death (so that it enters in his final income tax return). As the discount is subject to income tax in a single year, holders should dispose of the security in their most advantageous year of assessment. If the disposal results in overall profits exceeding the accrued income, CGT may be charged on the excess; if a loss results, CGT loss relief will be available (there is no double charge to CGT and income tax; see CGTA 1979 s 31).

4 Loss relief

Differing relieving provisions apply depending upon the type of loss which the company has made. In all cases, however, it is only the company (or exceptionally another company in the same group) which is entitled to the relief and never the members of the company. The loss is thus 'locked into' the company and this is a matter of some significance in deciding whether to commence business as a company or partnership (see further Chapter|33).

Losses are deducted from the appropriate profits of the company in priority to charges on income.

a) *Relief for trading losses: 'carry-forward'* (TA 1970 s 177(1))

A trading loss can be carried forward and set against trading profits from the *same* trade in the future. (The equivalent relief for the unincorporated trader is found in TA 1970 s 171.) A claim for relief must be made within six years of the end of the accounting period in which the loss was incurred. The relief is given by reducing the trading income of the succeeding accounting period or periods. In cases where such trading income is insufficient to absorb the full loss, interest and dividends received by the company may be treated as trading income for the purpose of loss relief (TA 1970 s 177(7)) provided that such income would have been taxed as trading income if tax had not been assessed under other provisions. Dividends received by a company whose trade involves dealing in shares fall into this category.

Unrelieved charges on income may be carried forward as a trading expense but only to the extent that the charge was made 'wholly and exclusively for the purposes of the trade' (TA 1970 s 177(8)). Thus, any charges not so made should be relieved against current year profits in priority, leaving only those payments to be carried forward which satisfy the 'wholly and exclusively' test.

EXAMPLE 6

Hee Ltd had the following corporation tax computation:

	£
Schedule D Case I profit	6,000
Chargeable gains (as reduced by ⅖)	1,500
	7,500
Less charges on income (total £8,500) limited to	7,500
Taxable profits	£ nil
Unrelieved charges	£1,000

If all the charges had been laid out wholly and exclusively for Hee Ltd's trade then £1,000 can be carried forward as a loss under s 177(1). But if only £500 had been so expended, the remaining £500 is unrelieved.

b) *Relief for trading losses against current and previous profits* (TA 1970 s 177(2))

A company may set its trading loss against profits of the same accounting period. (The nearest equivalent for the individual is the relief afforded by TA 1970 s 168.) Notice that as the relief is to set the loss against other profits it follows that all current profits can be used, including capital gains.

EXAMPLE 7

Haw Ltd's accounts for the financial year show the following: a trading loss of £6,000; rental income of £5,000; chargeable gains (as reduced by ⅖) of £3,000; and charges on income of £1,000. The corporation tax computation would be:

	£
Schedule A	5,000
Chargeable gains	3,000
	8,000
Less trading loss	6,000
	2,000
Less charges on income	1,000
Profits for corporation tax	£1,000

Where a loss cannot be relieved, or cannot be fully relieved, against profits of the same accounting period a claim may be made to carry that loss back against an earlier accounting period of equal length to the accounting period in which the loss was incurred. The company must have been carrying on the same trade in that earlier period and the claim has to be made within two years of the end of the accounting period in which the loss was incurred (TA 1970 s 177(10), which applies to all claims under s 177(2)). Any claim for loss relief will take effect *before* any charges on income are deducted but *after* any loss made in that earlier year.

EXAMPLE 8

How Ltd incurred a trading loss of £8,000 in its 1984 accounts (it had no other profits in that year). For 1983 it had profits of £9,000 with charges on income of £1,000. Its corporation tax computation would be:

	£
Profits of 1984	nil
Profits of 1983	9,000
Less 1984 loss	8,000
	1,000
Deduct 1983 charges on income	1,000
Taxable profits	nil

Notes:
(1) Any corporation tax paid on the 1983 account will be recovered.
(2) In the event of the loss not being fully relieved against profits of 1983, it is not possible to re-open the 1982 period. The only relief for the balance of the 1984 loss is for the company to elect to carry it forward under TA 1970 s 177(1).
(3) In the event of the loss relief claim absorbing all the profits for 1983, the charges on income in 1983 would not obtain tax relief unless they could be carried forward as a trading loss under the provisions already discussed (p 387).

c) *Relief for terminal losses* (TA 1970 s 178)

A loss incurred in any accounting period ending within 12 months of the cessation of a company's trade may (on a claim being made within six years of that closure) be set against income from the trade in the three preceding years (cp for individuals TA 1970 s 174; p 118). This provision applies only if the loss cannot be relieved under some other provision, for instance under TA 1970 s 177(2). The relief is given against later periods in priority to earlier periods and is given after charges on income have been relieved. The provisions already discussed in connection with s 177(1), treating certain income as trading profits, apply for the purposes of a s 178 claim (see p 387). Unrelieved charges on income may be accorded terminal relief subject to the restrictions noted earlier (see p 387).

EXAMPLE 9

Zoco ceases trading on 30 September 1984. The accounts of the company for the final years are as follows:

	Trading income	Trade charges
	£	£
9 months to 30 September 1984	5,000 (loss)	1,200
Year to 31 December 1983	1,000 (loss)	1,200
Year to 31 December 1982	3,000	1,200
Year to 31 December 1981	5,000	1,200
Year to 31 December 1980	6,000	1,200

Loss relief would operate as follows:
(i) set the 1983 loss against profits of the preceding twelve months (TA 1970 s 177(2))
(ii) the loss of the last 12 months, therefore, becomes:
   £5,000 (trading loss January–September 1984)
   plus £1,200 (unrelieved charges January–September 1984)
   plus £ 300 (3/12 of unrelieved charges from 1983)
   £6,500

(iii) the claim for s 178 relief would result in the following:

Accounting period ended	Trading income	Charges on income	Available for loss relief	Relief claimed
31 December 1983 ($\frac{9}{12}$ths)	—	900	—	—
31 December 1982	2,000(1)	1,200	800	800
31 December 1981	5,000	1,200	3,800	3,800
31 December 1980 ($\frac{3}{12}$ths)	1,500	300	1,200	1,200
				5,800

Notes
(1) For the year ended 31 December 1982 the trading income has been reduced to £2,000 as a result of deducting the £1,000 loss from the year ended 31 December 1983.
(2) Total terminal loss relief amounts to £5,800 and the excess of £700 (£6,500–£5,800) obtains no tax relief.

d) *General restrictions on the availability of trading loss relief*

There are two principal restrictions on the availability of trading loss relief. First, the trade should be carried on commercially with a view to the realisation of a gain if s 177(2) relief is to be available. Carry-forward (s 177(1)) and terminal (s 178) relief will, however, always apply.

Secondly, TA 1970 s 483 restricts the availability of the carry-forward provisions (s 177(1)) in the case of companies where, after the loss has been incurred, there has been a substantial change in the ownership of the company's shares. The purpose of these provisions was to stop the practice of purchasing shares in companies in order to take advantage of their accumulated losses. Hence, two factors are relevant:
(1) whether there has been a substantial change of ownership; and
(2) what has happened to the business of the company.

TA 1970 s 484 contains detailed rules providing for what constitutes a substantial change in ownership; basically it amounts to a change in the beneficial ownership of more than 50% of the ordinary share capital. So far as the business of the company is concerned the rules in s 483 apply if either (a) there is a change in the ownership accompanied by a major change in the nature or conduct of the trade and both changes occur within a three year period (for the interpretation of 'major' see *Willis v Peeters Picture Frames Ltd* (1983)); or (b) a change in ownership follows a period when the trade carried on by the company has become small or negligible and only after that change has there been any considerable revival. In the latter case no time period is prescribed and the danger is that a new owner who merely improves the conduct and profitability of the company, as opposed to changing the nature of its trade, will find that accumulated losses are not available for relief.

Thirdly, when a company ceases to carry on a trade (eg when it is sold) that trade is generally treated as ceasing even though it may in fact continue by being carried on by another company (TA 1970 s 251(1)). So far as losses are concerned, the result will be that the carry-forward relief will cease to be available, although terminal loss relief may be claimed. Where a reconstruction has occurred as a result of which the trade passes from one company to another and both companies are under common control these consequences would be economic nonsense and penalise the parties concerned. Thus, TA 1970 s 252 contains provisions which operate in such circumstances to permit losses and capital allowances to be transferred from one company to another whilst terminal relief will not be available. For these provisions to operate the same person or persons must, at any time within the period of two years after the change, directly or indirectly, own the trade (or not less than a three-quarter share in it) and must have owned that trade or the same interest therein within the period of one year before the change. Ownership is normally determined by reference to the ordinary share capital which is, however, given by TA 1970 s 526 a wider definition than its normal meaning. The normal hiving-down operation satisfies these requirements. The successor company can amalgamate the predecessor's trade with another enterprise already carried on, although, in this situation, the carried-forward loss relief will only be available against future profits arising from the old trade.

EXAMPLE 10

The ordinary share capital of Zee Ltd and Pee Ltd is owned as follows:

	Zee Ltd	*Pee Ltd*
Alan	10	8
Ben	6	12
Claud	30	40
Dennis	29	20
Others	25	20

A transfer of a trade from Zee Ltd to Pee Ltd would fall within s 252 since the 75% common ownership test is satisfied albeit that the relevant shares in Pee Ltd are owned by the same persons in different proportions.

e) *Relief for income losses other than trading losses*

Schedule D Case VI losses may be set against Schedule D Case VI income for either the current year or first available future accounting period (TA 1970 s 179). In the case of losses under Schedule A the normal relieving provisions provided for in that Schedule apply (see Chapter 8).

f) *Relief for capital losses*

Losses which would be deductible in computing liability to capital gains tax can be set against the first available chargeable gains made by the company. Such losses cannot be offset against income profits. The loss is deducted before calculating the 2/5 fraction under FA 1972.

5 **Management expenses**

Investment companies can deduct sums paid out in management expenses (such as salaries and general office expenditure) from their total profits. If such expenditure is unrelieved, it can be carried forward and offset in future years, but not back to a previous accounting period. Unrelieved charges can likewise be carried forward and treated as management expenses in future years so long as such charges were incurred 'wholly and exclusively for the purpose of the company's business' (TA 1970 s 304(2)). The term 'investment company' is defined as including:

> 'any company whose business consists wholly or mainly in the making of investments and the principal part of whose income is derived therefrom ...' (TA 1970 s 304(5)).

Hence, authorised unit trusts and savings banks (with the specific exclusion of a trustee savings bank as defined under the Trustee Savings Bank Act 1981) are included. It follows that the relief will often be given by setting the expenses against the franked investment income of the company (see p 398). For companies whose business consists of managing land, expenses involved in administering that land will be deductible from the Schedule A profits, whereas the general running costs of the company will be management expenses. Trading companies do not, of course, require a provision dealing with management expenses since such sums will be deducted in arriving at the Schedule D profits.

IV DISTRIBUTIONS

Distributions made by a company are not deductible in arriving at that company's profits for corporation tax, but will be paid out of taxed profits.

1 Meaning of a distribution

Distribution is widely defined since the intention is to catch not just the most obvious methods of paying profits to shareholders (such as a dividend), but also all payments and transfers by a company to its members other than repayment of capital subscribed. The tax treatment of distributions depends upon whether they are 'qualifying' or 'non-qualifying'; this distinction will be considered later. The main instance of a distribution is a dividend (including a capital dividend); other examples are discussed below.

Any distribution out of assets which is made in respect of shares and which exceeds any new consideration received   Where sums are returned to shareholders on a reduction of capital, they will not be distributions so long as they do not exceed the original amount subscribed (including any premium paid on the allotment of the shares). Payments to members on a winding up are expressly excluded from the definition of a distribution (such sums will be liable to capital gains tax in the hands of the shareholders). The issue of bonus shares is not itself a distribution, but a repayment of share capital within the following ten years will be a distribution up to the amount paid up on the bonus issue.

EXAMPLE 11

U Ltd has a share capital of 100 ordinary £1 shares. It makes a 1:1 bonus issue by capitalising £100 of reserves. Later it repays the shareholders 50p per share on a reduction of capital. Each shareholder is treated as receiving a distribution on the reduction in capital.

Position of a shareholder: Originally, he owns one £1 share. After the bonus issue, he owns two £1 shares. After the reduction in capital, he owns two 50p shares and has £1 in cash. The shareholder is in the same position as if he had received a £1 dividend and is taxed as such.

A reduction of share capital followed by a bonus issue   Essentially, this is the same operation as above and has similar taxation consequences. These consequences will not follow if the gap between repayment and the bonus issue exceeds ten years, so long as the bonus issue is not of redeemable shares and so long as the company is not a closely controlled company within TA 1970 s 461D. In addition, the bonus issue cannot be regarded as a distribution if the repaid share capital consisted of fully paid preference shares.

EXAMPLE 12

As in *Example 11*, U Ltd has a share capital of 100 £1 shares. It makes a reduction of share capital by repaying 50p per share. It then issues 100 50p bonus shares (ie a 1:1 issue).

Position of a shareholder: Initially, he held one £1 share. After the repayment of capital, he owns one 50p share and has 50p in cash. After the bonus issue, he owns two 50p shares and has received 50p in cash. Hence, he has shares of identical aggregate par value to the one share held at the start and has received a 50p payment from the company which will be treated as a distribution.

The issue of bonus redeemable shares and bonus securities   A bonus issue of redeemable shares (ie shares which the company has express authority or an obligation to redeem in the future) and of securities is a distribution. Unlike the other examples of a distribution, however, this category is a 'non-qualifying' distribution. The taxation consequences of this will be considered later (p 400), but it should be noted that this category is unique in being the one distribution where the company is not at the time of the distribution paying out moneys to shareholders, but is entering into a commitment so to do in the future. Hence, the issue represents a potential rather than an immediate charge on profits. The value of the distribution will, in the case of shares, be the nominal value together with any premium payable on redemption. In the case of other securities, it will be the amount secured together with any premium payable on redemption. When redeemable shares and securities are redeemed, the redemption will normally be a qualifying distribution.

A transfer by a company to its members of assets or liabilities which are worth more than any new consideration furnished by the member   The excess of any assets or liabilities transferred by a company to its members over any new consideration furnished by the members will be a distribution.

The stock dividend option   F(No 2)A 1975 s 34 provides that where bonus shares are offered to shareholders instead of a cash dividend, the bonus shares will be treated as a distribution. The benefit for the issuing company is that no advance corporation tax is payable on the allotment of these shares.

Certain interest payments   Interest payments geared to the profits of the company (irrespective of the reasonableness of the rate) or excessive interest (which exceeds a reasonable commercial return) may be treated as distributions by TA 1970 s 233(2)(d)(iii). FA 1982 s 60 prevents these rules being used to achieve a tax advantage in the case of 'equity loans' and, accordingly, provides that when the lender is a UK company subject to corporation tax interest geared to profits is not a distribution, but is taxed in the normal way (see [1982] STI 107). Interest payments on bonus securities and on securities which are convertible whether directly or indirectly into shares in the company (unless listed on The Stock Exchange) are distributions.

EXAMPLE 13

Zec Ltd borrows £50,000 from Mr Con at a rate of interest of 20% pa. A reasonable commercial rate would be 12%. The company is paying £10,000 pa to

Con of which £6,000 is deductible from profits for corporation tax purposes. That sum is also interest for TA 1970 s 54 so that basic rate tax should be deducted at source. So far as the excess (£4,000 pa) is concerned it will be a distribution on which ACT is payable and Con will be assessed on the gross amount under Schedule F.

2   Distributions and the purchase by the company of its own shares

The Companies Act 1981 ss 45–62 allow companies (so long as authorised by their articles of association) to purchase their own shares. Generally, such purchases must be paid for out of distributable profits, but private companies may be able to use capital. However, but for FA 1982 s 53, any payment to a shareholder in excess of the sum paid for the shares would be treated as a distribution, unless the repayment occurs on a winding up of the company. Section 53 provides that, in certain circumstances, when shares are bought back moneys received by a shareholder will not be treated as a distribution so that any profit made will be charged, if at all, to CGT, so that shares sold to the company will be treated no differently from sales to any other person. However, the FA 1982 provisions are restrictive, so that in some cases there will still be a distribution. The requirements, if buy backs are not to involve a distribution, are complex and will be considered under three headings.

The purchasing company   The purchasing company must not be listed on The Stock Exchange but its shares may be dealt in on the Unlisted Securities Market. It must be either a trading company or the holding company of a trading group.

The vendor of the shares   The vendor may be an individual, a trustee, the PR of a deceased shareholder, or a company. He should be resident and, if an individual, ordinarily resident in the UK. Normally, the shares must have been owned for at least five years and it is not possible to aggregate different ownership periods (hence settlor/trustees and trustees/beneficiaries must each satisfy the five year period). In the exceptional cases of husband/wife and of the deceased/his PRs and legatees aggregation is permissible and in the latter case the aggregated ownership period need only be three years.

The vendor should either dispose of all his shares in the company or at least 'substantially reduce' his shareholding. The Revenue takes the view that a holding will only be substantially reduced if it falls by at least 25% and does not leave the vendor with a dominant (at least 30%) holding of the issued shares. In calculating these fractions, spouses and associates generally are treated as one person. As any transactions in the same shares within 12 months of the sale will form part of the same transaction, it follows that shares should not be repurchased within a period of one year.

The reason for the sale   There are two permissible reasons. First, the purchase by the company must benefit its trade (or that of a 75% subsidiary) and not be part of a scheme designed to enable the shareholders to participate in the company's profits without receiving a dividend or otherwise to avoid tax. The requirement that the purchase must be a 'benefit to the trade' is not an easy test to apply. For instance, the buying out of dissident shareholders is certainly for the benefit of the company but that, presumably, is not the same unless it can be shown that the continued dissention was harming the management and, therefore, the trade of the company. In practice the Revenue have stated (see

SP 2/82) that they will expect the requirement to be satisfied in such cases and indeed in cases where the vendor shareholder is 'genuinely' giving up his entire interest of all kinds in the company.

EXAMPLE 14

(1) It is proposed that WW Ltd (an unquoted trading company) purchases the shares of Mr Wam, one of the original founders of the company in 1970. He is willing to sell a 60% holding but wishes to keep a small (5%) holding for sentimental reasons. Mr Wam is retiring in favour of a new management team. The transaction will be for the benefit of the trade of WW Ltd and, the other conditions being satisfied, the payment for the shares will not be a distribution.

(2) Sal is the sole shareholder in Sal Ltd, an unlisted trading company. Profits amount to £100,000 for the present accounting period and Sal Ltd plans to use them to purchase 50% of Sal's shares. This scheme will not be within the provisions of FA 1982 s 53 because:

(a) It would appear to be a scheme designed to pass the profits to Sal without declaring a dividend;

(b) Sal is not substantially reducing her holding since, although she is selling in excess of 25% of the shares, she is retaining more than a 30% holding.

(c) The purchase is not for the benefit of Sal Ltd's trade.

The second permitted reason for the sale of the shares is where the whole, or substantially the whole, of the proceeds of sale is to be used by the recipient in discharging his CTT liability charged on a death. The money must be so used within two years of the death and it has to be shown that the CTT cannot be paid without undue hardship unless the shares are sold back to the company. In this case the above requirements as to the vendor of the shares do not apply. The CTT need not be owing in respect of the shares.

EXAMPLE 15

(1) Sam inherits the family residence on his father's death. Under the terms of the will it is to bear its own CTT which can be raised by the sale of Sam's shareholding in Sham Ltd (a trading company which is not listed). The only alternative would involve the sale of the family house. If the shares are sold to Sham Ltd the purchase moneys will not be treated as a distribution.

(2) Sue inherits 30% of the share capital of Carruthers Ltd. She does not want the shares and arranges for the company to buy them back. Although this arrangement falls outside the relief for hardship on a death, it would appear that there will be no distribution since such a payment will be for the benefit of the trade (see SP 2/82 and above).

Whenever the buy-back of shares is proposed, advance clearance can be obtained for the scheme and the same application (sent in duplicate) can be used for a clearance under TA 1970 s 460 (see Chapter 32).

3   The taxation of qualifying distributions

The taxation of distributions has been governed by the imputation system since 1973. The central feature is ACT which represents for the company making the payment a partial (or, for small companies, a total) discharge of its corporation tax bill. The shareholder will receive a credit for this ACT so that he will receive his dividend together with a credit for basic rate income tax. The rules to be considered in this section apply to all qualifying distributions. For convenience, however, examples will concentrate on the most common form of distribution, the cash dividend.

a) *The payment of a dividend*

A company is obliged to pay ACT to the Revenue when it makes dividend payments to its shareholders. For the purpose of collecting ACT the calendar year is divided into quarters and at the end of each quarter (ie on 31 March, 30 June, 30 September and 31 December) the company must make a return indicating what dividends have been paid in the three month period just ended. If dividends have been paid, the appropriate ACT should be paid within 14 days of the end of the quarter except where the company has franked investment income available to cover the distribution that it makes. In such a case ACT need not be paid (see p 398). Assuming that ACT is to be paid, the amount is currently 30/70 (or 3/7) of the dividend paid.

This fraction will be made up of: $\dfrac{\text{the basic rate of income tax}}{100 - \text{that rate}}$

This is the grossing-up formula at the basic rate.

EXAMPLE 16

On 1 February 1984 Zed Ltd pays total dividends of £70,000 to shareholders. This should appear in the quarterly return on 31 March 1984 and within 14 days thereof the sum of £30,000 (3/7ths of £70,000) should be paid as ACT to the Revenue.

b) *The use of ACT by the company*

The corporation tax that companies (other than pre-1966 companies) pay nine months after the end of the accounting period (see p 381) is known as mainstream corporation tax (MCT). In general, where dividends have been paid during the accounting period, the ACT paid can be deducted from the MCT bill on the *income* profits of that period (FA 1972 s 85(1)). Notice therefore, that although capital gains made by a company can be distributed as dividends, the ACT thereon can only be deducted from the subsequent corporation tax charged on income profits. Income profits for this purpose means the total profits of the company less chargeable gains, charges on income, losses, and management expenses.

EXAMPLE 17

In the above example Zed's accounts to 31 March 1984 show income profits of £500,000. The MCT bill is as follows:

	£
£500,000 at 50%	250,000
Less ACT paid during accounting year	30,000
Balance payable	£220,000

Zed's total corporation tax bill is £250,000 which will be paid in two instalments (the ACT portion and the MCT balance). Had no dividends been paid to shareholders during the accounting year there would have been no ACT payable and the MCT bill would have been £250,000 payable nine months after the end of the accounting period.

Thus, the payment of a dividend will not, unless full ACT set-off cannot be claimed (see below), increase the total corporation tax charged. It merely, as its name suggests, results in an advanced payment of that tax.

c) *The problems of surplus ACT*

One instance where surplus ACT occurs has been mentioned above.

EXAMPLE 18

The accounts of Eve Ltd for the period ended 31 December 1984 show no income profits, but chargeable gains (after the 2/5 deduction) of £200,000. During that year dividends of £70,000 were paid. The corporation tax position is:
(1) ACT of £30,000 (3/7 of £70,000) paid on the dividends.
(2) The MCT bill is 50% of £200,000, ie £100,000, and this cannot be reduced by the ACT paid.
(3) The company has surplus ACT of £30,000.

Surplus ACT also occurs where distributions exceed the 'permitted level' since there is a limit to the amount of MCT that can be cancelled by ACT, even where the MCT arises on income profits of the company. The maximum ACT set-off is the amount of ACT which would have been paid if the dividend declared together with ACT thereon equalled the income profits for the year. In practical terms this is equivalent to the basic rate of income tax on the income profits so that for small companies (taxed at 30%) the MCT bill can be reduced to zero.

EXAMPLE 19

Xerxes Ltd pays dividends of £700,000 in 1984. During the same accounting period it has income profits of £300,000. (This disparity between dividend and income can be explained by assuming that the company either distributed capital profits for the year or paid out past accumulated profits.) For corporation tax purposes:
(1) ACT of £300,000 (3/7 of £700,000) is paid on the dividend.
(2) MCT at 50% on the £300,000 income profits is £150,000. This cannot be wiped out by ACT. The maximum ACT available will be £90,000 (30% of £300,000) since:
Dividends of £210,000 plus ACT thereon of £90,000 equals the income profits (£300,000) for the year.
Hence, Xerxes Ltd will have surplus ACT of £210,000 (£300,000 – £90,000) and the total corporation tax bill will be:

	£	
ACT	300,000	
+ MCT	60,000	(£150,000 – £90,000)
	£360,000	

An alternative way of explaining how much ACT can be set off against MCT on income profits is to say that the rate of MCT can be reduced from 50% to 20% at the most, or, in the case of small companies, from 30% to 0%.

d) *The set-off of surplus ACT*

For accounting periods ending after 31 March 1984 a company can carry back surplus ACT and set it against MCT on income profits of the six accounting periods immediately preceding the period showing the surplus (FA 1984 s 52; previously the period was two years). A refund of corporation tax will only result if the permitted level of set-off has not been reached in those years. If a surplus still remains it can then be carried forward without time limit and set off against MCT on future income profits in the first year when the full quota of dividends has not been paid. (This extended carry-back period is particularly beneficial in view of the new order of set-off of foreign taxation credits (FA 1984 s 53; see p 408.)

EXAMPLE 20

The following represents the dividends paid and income profits made by a company during seven consecutive accounting periods (assuming a 50% rate of corporation tax throughout and ACT of 3/7).

	Dividend	Income profit	ACT	MCT	Maximum set-off	Amount unused in year
	£	£	£	£	£	£
Year 1	Nil	100,000	Nil	50,000	30,000	30,000
Year 2	70,000	100,000	30,000	50,000	30,000	—
Year 3	70,000	100,000	30,000	50,000	30,000	—
Year 4	35,000	100,000	15,000	50,000	30,000	15,000
Year 5	Nil	50,000	Nil	25,000	15,000	15,000
Year 6	14,000	40,000	6,000	20,000	12,000	6,000
Year 7	210,000	50,000	90,000	25,000	15,000	—
Year 8	35,000	60,000	15,000	30,000	18,000	3,000

In Year 7 the ACT is £90,000 which can only be partially offset against the MCT bill for the year. MCT at £25,000 (50% × £50,000) can be reduced by the maximum set-off of £15,000 to £10,000, but no further, leaving surplus ACT of £75,000.

Uses of surplus ACT
(1) Carry back to years 6, 5, 4 and 1 relieving £6,000, £15,000, £15,000 and £30,000 respectively and leaving surplus ACT of £9,000 (£75,000 − £66,000).
(2) Carry forward £9,000 to future years without time limit using the first available profits but subject to the permitted level of set-off in each year. In year 8 the surplus can be further reduced to £6,000.

e) *Franked investment income*

Dividends and other distributions received by one UK company from another are not generally subject to corporation tax in the recipient's hands. The sum paid, together with a tax credit for the ACT thereon, is known as franked investment income (FII: TA 1970 s 239). Generally, the recipient company will only be able to obtain a refund of the ACT paid on the distribution if either that distribution is expressly exempt from tax or if the recipient is wholly exempt from corporation tax or is exempt on all its income save for trading income (see FA 1972 s 86(3)—an instance of an exempt corporation would be a charitable company). For the majority of companies, therefore, there will be no question of a tax refund, and instead, the tax credit may be utilised in one of two ways. First, to 'frank' the receiving company's own distributions paid in the accounting period when the FII is received. Hence, ACT will not be payable on such distributions and, if already paid in an earlier quarter of the accounting period, will be refunded. If FII is not fully used in an accounting period, any surplus can be carried forward (without time limit) and used to frank future distributions.

EXAMPLE 21

During the 1984 accounting period Sellco Ltd has income profits of £200,000. It receives dividends of £70,000 from Buyco Ltd (another UK company) and itself pays out dividends of £140,000 during the year.
(1) Sellco has FII of £70,000 + £30,000 = £100,000.
(2) On paying the £140,000 dividend it can offset the credit on the FII to reduce its ACT liability:

	£
Dividend	140,000
ACT payable	60,000
FII set-off	30,000
Balance ACT owing	£30,000

(3) Income profits for the year are £200,000 (and do not include FII) so that the MCT liability will be:

	£
MCT at 50%	100,000
Less ACT	30,000
Balance owing	£70,000

(4) In effect Sellco passes its FII on to its own shareholders.

The second use to which an FII tax credit can be put is to obtain partial loss relief. If a company in any year has trading losses or charges on income or management expenses which exceed the profits of that year, any surplus FII received in that year is treated as if it were profits liable to corporation tax and the FII tax credit can be recovered directly from the Revenue. 'Surplus FII' excludes FII carried forward from an earlier year (TA 1970 s 254(8)).

EXAMPLE 22

Investaco Ltd has FII of £50,000 for the accounting year. It has unrelieved management expenses of £20,000. It may treat £20,000 of FII as profits subject to corporation tax. Hence:

	£
FII 'profits'	20,000
Less management expenses	20,000
Corporation tax payable	£NIL

The refund of tax paid is £6,000 (the ACT portion of £20,000 FII).
Notes
(1) Some loss relief (£6,000) has been obtained at once.
(2) The relief is only partial, however, since, had the expenses of £20,000 been set against profits subject to corporation tax at 50%, the tax saving would be not £6,000 but 50% × £20,000 = £10,000. To ensure that full relief is available compensating adjustments are made in later accounting periods where the distributions exceed FII to ensure that the balance of the loss relief is then given (TA 1970 s 254(5)).

f) *The position of individual shareholders who receive dividends*

Dividends are assessed to income tax under Schedule F on the gross sum, ie the dividend actually paid together with the ACT paid on it. The individual receives a tax credit equal to the ACT paid by the company (or treated as discharged by any FII used by the paying company). The credit is equal to the basic rate of income tax so that only if the recipient is subject to the higher rates will there be a further income tax charge.

EXAMPLE 23

Cam, Mem and Bert are three shareholders in Fromage Ltd and each receives a dividend of £70 in the income tax year 1984–85. Cam has no other income and unused personal allowances; Mem is a basic rate taxpayer; and Bert is subject to income tax at the highest rate (60%). Each has an income of £100 under Schedule F and each receives a tax credit for £30.

Cam, who has unused personal allowances, will be able to reclaim the £30 tax credit.

Mem has had the correct amount of tax deducted at source, having used all her personal allowances.

Bert will be subject to extra tax of £30 (60% of £100 = £60, less his tax credit of £30).

g) Conclusion on the taxation of dividends

As already noted, ACT is the pivot of the imputation system. For the company, it is an advance payment of corporation tax. For the shareholder, it represents basic rate income tax. For small companies the system results in the payment of a dividend being fully deductible for corporation tax purposes (since the ACT wipes out the MCT liability). For other companies, however, an element of double charge remains since the shareholder is not given a credit for all the corporation tax paid by the company. The residual MCT liability of 20% cannot be offset against his higher rate income tax liability so that the effective rate of tax on dividends may be as high as 72% (see *Example 24*). Dividends will, therefore, remain (at least until 1986 when the MCT rate will be 35%) an ineffective way of paying out profits. The advantages of raising money by debentures have been noted at p 386) and are further considered in Chapter 33).

EXAMPLE 24

	£
Company's profit	100
Corporation tax (at 50%)	50
Net profit	50
Distribute net profits	50
ACT (3/7 × £50)	21.42
Gross dividend	71.42
Income tax (at 60% on £71.42)	42.85
Less basic rate tax credit	21.42
Income tax bill	21.43
Net income after all the deductions is	£28.57
The total tax (MCT + ACT + income tax) payable is	£71.43

4   The taxation of non-qualifying distributions

An issue of bonus redeemable shares or securities is a non-qualifying distribution. The two main features of qualifying distributions (the payment of

ACT by the company and a tax credit for the shareholder) do not apply to non-qualifying distributions. The issue of the securities has no tax effect on the issuing company and, so far as the recipient is concerned, no assessment to basic rate income tax. It follows that the only tax consequence will be an assessment on the shareholder for any higher rate income tax calculated at higher rates less the basic rate. When the shares are redeemed the redemption will be a qualifying distribution with the normal taxation consequences (see p 395), save that, if the shareholder is then liable for income tax at the higher rates, a deduction is made for any higher rate tax paid on the non-qualifying distribution.

EXAMPLE 25

Shareholder Sam has a taxable income of £15,400. He receives bonus redeemable shares whose redemption value is £700. His income tax liability will be calculated by adding £700 to his other income and calculating tax on that £700 as the highest portion of that total. His taxable income is £16,100 (£15,400 + £700). The tax rate applicable on the top £700 is 40%. Therefore:

	£
Higher rate tax (40%) on £700	280
Less basic rate tax (30% × £700)	210
Income tax owing	£70

When the shares are redeemed and Sam is paid £700 his taxable income is still £15,600. The tax position is as follows:
(1) The company will pay ACT of £300 on the capital distribution.
(2) Sam's income under Schedule F will be £1,000 and he will have a tax credit for £300.
(3) Sam's income tax bill will be calculated thus:

	£
Tax on £1,000 at highest rate (40%)	400
Less tax credit	300
	100
Higher rate paid on non-qualifying distribution	70
Income tax owing	£30

V CLOSE COMPANIES

Companies controlled by one person or by a small group of individuals could be operated so as to secure tax advantages that would be unavailable to the individual taxpayer or to the larger corporate taxpayer. As a result there have been special rules since 1922 aimed at preventing such schemes. FA 1965 introduced a relatively fierce regime for the closely controlled company but since that date a gradual relaxation in the rules has occurred especially in FA 1972, FA 1978, FA 1980 and FA 1984.

1 What is a close company?

The definition of a close company is:

'one which is under the control of five or fewer participators, or of participators who are directors' (TA 1970 s 282(1)).

Hence, it may be either director-controlled (irrespective of the number of directors involved) or controlled by five or fewer participators.

a) *The meaning of 'control'*

A person (or two or more persons taken together) is deemed to have control of a company if:

(a) he can exercise control over the company's affairs, in particular by possessing or acquiring the greater part of the share capital or voting power; or

(b) he possesses or is entitled to acquire:

(i) such part of the issued share capital as would give him a right to the greater part of the income of the company if it were all to be distributed, or

(ii) the right to the greater part of the assets available for distribution among the participators on a winding up or in any other circumstances.

In deciding whether a person has control there must be attributed to him any rights vested in his nominees, his associates and companies controlled by him or his associates. For this purpose an 'associate' includes a person related to him as spouse, parent, or remoter forebear; a child or remoter issue; and a sibling or partner. A 'nominee' is a person holding assets for another and resembles a bare trustee.

b) *The meaning of 'participator' and 'director'*

'Participator' is defined as a person having a share or interest in the capital or income of the company and includes a person who is entitled to acquire share capital or voting rights and loan creditors (but not a bank lending in the ordinary course of its business).

'Director' is defined as a person who occupies that post; any person in accordance with whose instructions the directors act; and a manager paid by the company who, with his associates, owns or controls 20% of the company's ordinary share capital (TA 1970 s 303(5)).

c) *Companies which are not close*

The following companies which would otherwise fall within the above definition are treated as not being close companies:

(a) any non-resident company;

(b) companies which are registered industrial and provident societies;

(c) companies controlled by or on behalf of the Crown;

(d) companies which would be close companies save for the fact that they are controlled through the beneficial ownership of their shares by one or more companies which are not close companies (therefore, the subsidiary of a non-close company is normally not a close company);

(e) companies whose shares have been quoted and dealt in on a recognised stock exchange during the preceding 12 months, provided shares carrying at least 35% of the voting power are beneficially held by the public. Shares are not held by the public if (inter alia) they are held by a director of the company or his associates and the exception does not apply when the principal members (ie the five members who hold the greatest voting power in the company, but excluding any who hold less than 5% of the voting power) possess more than 85% of the total voting power.

d) *Illustrations of the definition*

Most small private companies will be close. Where there are fewer than ten shareholders the company must be close since five or fewer shareholders must control it. In other situations the matter may require some thought!

EXAMPLE 26

Aviary Ltd has an authorised and issued share capital of 60,000 ordinary shares of £1 each. Each share carries one vote. The shares are held as follows:

	Ordinary shares
Mr A Robin, Chairman	5,000
Mr B Raven, Managing Director	2,800
Mr C Crow, Director	2,400
Mr D Hawk, Director	4,400
Mr E Thrush, Director	2,200
Mr F Robin, son of A Robin	1,800
Mr G Magpie, Sales Manager	3,600
Mr H Magpie, father of G Magpie	3,000
Mrs J Eagle, sister of G Magpie	3,000
Mrs K Wren, sister of G Magpie	2,400
Sundry small shareholders	29,400
	60,000

Is Aviary Ltd a close company? It will be necessary to consider voting control and to discover whether it is either a company controlled by five or fewer participators or a company controlled by directors who are participators.

Participator/holding		5 largest shareholdings	Shareholdings of all 'directors'
G Magpie—Sales Manager	3,600		
Add associate holdings:			
H Magpie—father	3,000		
Mrs J Eagle—sister	3,000		
Mrs K Wren—sister	2,400		
	12,000	12,000	12,000
A Robin—Chairman	5,000		
Add associate holding:			
F Robin—son	1,800		
	6,800	6,800	6,800
D Hawk—Director		4,400	4,400
B Raven—Managing Director		2,800	2,800
C Crow—Director		2,400	2,400
E Thrush—Director		—	2,200
Total shares		28,400	30,600

Although not controlled by five or fewer participators, Aviary Ltd is a close company because it is controlled by its directors. Notice that for this purpose, Mr G Magpie, the sales manager, is treated as a director because with his associates he holds 20% of the company's shares (TA 1970 s 303(5)).

2   Special rules that apply to close companies

a) *Extended meaning of 'distribution'*

Close companies are additionally treated as making distributions when they incur expenses in providing living accommodation or other benefits in kind for a participator or his associates. This rule does not apply in cases where the benefit would be subject to taxation under the provisions of FA 1976 ss 60–72 (see Chapter 5), and is designed to catch benefits conferred upon shareholders and debentureholders who are neither directors nor higher-paid employees. The normal rules which govern the taxation of distributions apply.

EXAMPLE 27

DB Ltd, a close company, provides free holidays costing £1,400 each for Barry, a director, Barney, a shareholder and Betty, a debenture holder.

(1) *Barry's holiday*   The cost will be a deductible business expense of DB Ltd. Barry will be assessed under the Schedule E rules on the benefit of £1,400 which he has received.

(2) *Barney's and Betty's holiday*   In neither case would the expense be charged under Schedule E and, as both are participators, the expense will be treated as a distribution. Hence, DB Ltd will be required to pay ACT on the expense incurred (in each case this will amount to 3/7 of £1,400 = £600) and Barney and Betty will each have income under Schedule F of £2,000 with a credit for the £600 ACT paid.

b) *Loans to participators and their associates*

A close company which makes a loan to a participator or his associate is obliged to pay to the Revenue tax on that loan at the rate of ACT then in force. However, the loan itself is not a distribution. The sum received by the Revenue is not ACT and the borrower is not entitled to any tax credit. The payment to the Revenue may best be described as a 'forced' loan so that, if the participator repays the sum lent, the Revenue will repay the sum that it received. If, however, the loan is either released or written off, the sum held by the Revenue is likewise forfeited and, in addition, the participator will be assessed to income tax at higher rates (if applicable) on the amount of the loan grossed-up at the basic rate for the year of release. He will not be liable to the basic rate charge but cannot reclaim any basic rate tax. It follows that loans can be used to defer higher rate tax but not ACT (basic rate). The company will receive no credit against its corporation tax bill for the sum loaned to the Revenue. In practice, if the loan is repaid before an assessment to tax is made, no action is taken in respect of it.

EXAMPLE 28

In 1984 Simco Ltd lends £70,000 to Mr Needy, a shareholder. In 1987 it releases the debt of Needy.

(1) *Tax position in 1984*   Simco Ltd will have to pay the Revenue £30,000 (3/7 of £70,000). This sum is not ACT. Mr Needy suffers no tax consequences.

(2) *Tax position in 1987*   The Revenue will keep the £30,000. (The company will never get relief for the £30,000 that it has paid.) Needy will be subject to income tax at higher rates on the loan (£70,000) grossed-up by the basic rate of income tax for 1987 (say 30%). Hence, he will be taxed on £100,000; and if it is assumed that he is subject to a 60% rate of tax, he will be required to pay £60,000 − £30,000 = £30,000.

These loan provisions have been extended to catch debts owed to the company, save for the situation where goods or services have been supplied in the ordinary course of the business of the company and the period of credit is either normal or does not exceed six months. Debts assigned to the company are likewise treated as loans (for misappropriations see *Stephens v Pittas* (1983)). These rules do not apply to loans made in the ordinary course of a company's business of moneylending nor to loans not exceeding £15,000 to someone who works full-time for the company and who does not have a material interest in it (a material interest is normally 5% of the ordinary shares).

Two other points must be mentioned. If the loan is to a director or higher-paid employee, there may be income tax, under FA 1976 s 66, on the interest foregone; and secondly, loans to directors are severely restricted by legislation (see Companies Act 1980 ss 49–53).

c) *Statutory apportionment of income*

To prevent the hoarding of profits in a close company, apportionment provisions enable the Revenue to deem 'relevant income' to be distributed amongst those shareholders who would be entitled to such a distribution. Where the sum apportioned is at least £1,000 or 5% of the amount apportioned (whichever is the less), the normal results of a qualifying distribution ensue (FA 1972 Sch 16 para 5(4) as amended).

EXAMPLE 29

Sam leaves profits of £70,000 in his company Sam Ltd. His personal income tax rate is 60%, whereas Sam Ltd is a small company subject only to corporation tax at 30%. If an apportionment is made all the normal consequences of a qualifying distribution apply, viz:

	£
Company's profits	70,000
Less tax at 30%	21,000
Net profit	£49,000
Sam's deemed dividends	49,000
ACT credit	21,000
Gross income	£70,000
Income tax at 60%	42,000
Less ACT credit	21,000
Income tax payable	£21,000

The trading income of a trading company (or of members of a trading group) is not subject to apportionment. Further, the investment income of trading companies need not be distributed if the company can show that to distribute it would prejudice the requirements of the business.

Other companies must distribute all investment income and, unless they can justify its retention, up to one-half of their estate and trading income. A close company can apply for an apportionment clearance from its inspector of taxes who then has three months to decide whether or not to make an apportionment.

VI GROUPS OF COMPANIES

1 What is a group?

A group of companies comprises at least a parent company (a holding company) which controls another company known as a subsidiary. Groups may consist of any number of interlocking companies. Commercially, they may be regarded as a single entity; so far as the law is concerned, however, they are generally treated as separate legal entities. The tax legislation to some extent accords with commercial reality in conferring a number of useful reliefs upon companies in a group. These reliefs depend upon the structure of the group: some for instance are available to '51% groups'; some to '75% groups' and 'consortia'; and some to '100% consortia'.

A '51% group' exists where at least 51% of the ordinary share capital of one company is beneficially owned, directly or indirectly, by another company; and a '75% group' where at least 75% of the ordinary share capital of one company is so owned (TA 1970 s 526 and s 532).

Certain privileges may be available, even if the 75% or 51% group requirement is not satisfied, in cases where at least 75% of the shares of a trading company are owned by a consortium of UK corporate members.

2   Taxation privileges available to groups

a) *Group Relief* (TA 1970 s 258)

Group relief applies to 75% groups and, for accounting periods ending after 26.7.84, applies to consortia provided that at least 75% of its share capital is owned by UK corporate members who each own at least a 5% interest in the consortium company (FA 1984 s 46). Thus, individuals or non-resident companies can own up to a 25% interest although they will not qualify for group relief. The relief enables any of the items deductible from total profits (generally charges on income, losses, and management expenses) to be surrendered to another company in the group or consortium. Such items can, therefore, be used to reduce taxable profits by the 'claimant' company on being given up by the 'surrendering' company. It is not necessary to make a payment for group relief but if one is made it is ignored in computing profits and losses of both companies for tax purposes. The relief is more restrictive in the case of consortia since the claimant is only entitled to the fraction of the item available (eg a trading loss) which is proportionate to that member's share in the consortium.

The claimant company must use the relief in the year of surrender; it cannot be carried back or forward and is deducted from total profits after any charges on the income of the claimant company. It need not be surrendered in full (contrast loss relief under TA 1970 s 177(2) where the full loss must be relieved if there are sufficient profits).

EXAMPLE 30

Little Ltd is the wholly-owned subsidiary of Large Ltd. Both companies make up accounts to 31 March and for the year ended 31 March 1985 Little Ltd has trading losses of £20,000 and Large Ltd profits of £400,000. All the loss could be surrendered to Large Ltd resulting in the profits being reduced to £380,000. Alternatively, Little Ltd might carry back all or a part of the loss under TA 1970 s 177(2) and merely surrender the balance. If Large Ltd were to pay £5,000 for the surrender, that sum would be ignored for tax purposes.

FA 1984 s 47 contains provisions to prevent tax avoidance through the use of group relief in an accounting period when a company joins or leaves a group or consortium (eg the setting of losses of existing members against profits derived by an incoming member before entry). Generally, profits and losses of the company will continue to be time-apportioned between the two parts of that period, but if this works unreasonably or unjustly (eg where the profits are uneven) such other methods shall be used as may be just and reasonable.

b) *Surrender of ACT*

Within 51% groups a parent which has surplus ACT arising as a result of a dividend payment may surrender all or part of that surplus to a subsidiary (FA 1972 s 92). The recipient company may then use the surrendered ACT against its own corporation tax bill.

c) *Dividends and charges* (TA 1970 s 256)

Charges on income may be paid gross (without deducting basic rate income tax) between companies in a 51% group or 75% consortium (defined, for payments made after 31 December 1984, as for group relief). Similarly, dividends (but not other distributions) can be paid without ACT so long as both payer and recipient agree (the sum is called 'group income': see TA 1970 s 256(1)). So far as the recipient company is concerned, it will not be entitled to a tax credit and the sum it receives will not be franked investment income. There is, of course, nothing to stop ACT being paid and a credit given in the normal way; this may be advantageous when the recipient company wishes to make a dividend payment outside the group and so will wish to receive franked investment income.

d) *Capital reliefs—the transfer of assets and roll-over relief*

The transfer of an asset within a 75% group is treated as being for such consideration as ensures that neither gain nor loss results (similar principles apply for DLT; see DLTA 1976 s 20). The result is, therefore, to hold over any gain and any tax is postponed until the asset is disposed of outside the group or until the company owning the asset leaves the group (TA 1970 s 278). A potential purchaser of a company should, therefore, check whether the company will be subject to such 'exit' charges in the event of its leaving its existing group, or whether any company in a group he acquires has any member company with such a potential 'exit' charge. However, the charge will not arise on a company leaving a group more than six years after the intra-group transfer.

For roll-over or reinvestment relief trades carried on by companies in a 75% group are treated as a single trade. Hence, a chargeable gain made by one group member on a disposal of an asset outside the group can be rolled over into an asset acquired from outside the group by another group member (TA 1970 s 276).

EXAMPLE 31

R Ltd, S Ltd and Q Ltd are members of a 75% group. The following transactions occur:

(1) R Ltd disposes of an office block with a base cost of £100,000 to Q Ltd when its value is £150,000;

(2) Q Ltd sells that asset to T Ltd for £150,000; and

(3) S Ltd acquires a new office block for use in its business for £200,000.

The taxation consequences of these transactions are:

(1) *The intra-group transfer from R Ltd to Q Ltd* is treated as being for no gain/no loss so that tax on the gain (£50,000) is postponed. Q's base cost is, therefore, £100,000.

(2) *The sale by Q Ltd to T Ltd* The asset leaves the group so that a chargeable gain of £50,000 arises.

(3) *The replacement asset purchased by S Ltd* On a claim being made by both companies (Q Ltd and S Ltd) the gain of Q Ltd can be rolled over into the purchase by S Ltd. Hence, S Ltd's base cost of the new asset will be £150,000 (£200,000 – £50,000) and Q Ltd will not be assessed on a gain as a result of the disposal to T Ltd.

3 The advantages and disadvantages of forming a group

Commercially, groups of companies have obvious attractions; different enterprises can be segregated into different corporate units each with its limited liability and separate identity. Each trade will, to a greater or lesser extent, have a separate management and in the event of a decision to sell any branch of the enterprise, the appropriate company can be sold to the purchaser.

From a taxation point of view, however, and despite the various reliefs considered above, forming a group is often highly disadvantageous; this is particularly so for a group of companies managed by its owners. Generally, each company will be seen as a distinct entity; hence, a holding company with all its subsidiaries being trading companies suffers a number of problems: eg retirement relief will not be available when a holding company's shares are sold since the holding company will not be a family trading company (see Chapter 16: though note the Consultative Document proposals). Often, therefore, the decision whether to form a group or not must involve a balance between commercial advantages on the one hand and fiscal disadvantages on the other.

VII THE OVERSEAS DIMENSION

A company which is resident in the UK is liable to corporation tax on all its profits wherever arising (TA 1970 ss 238(2), 243(1)). A non-resident company will only be liable to corporation tax if it trades in the UK through a branch or agency and liability will then be restricted to the chargeable profits from that branch or agency (TA 1970 s 246).

1 The meaning of 'residence'

'A body corporate shall be deemed . . . to be resident or not to be resident according as the central management and control of its trade and business is or is not exercised in the UK' (TA 1970 s 482(7)).

Where the central management or control is exercised is a factual question of some difficulty. Generally, of course, such powers will be vested in the board of directors, so that the problem becomes one of identifying where the board exercises its powers. Two general points should be stressed. First, that the country where the company was incorporated is usually of small significance when it is a question of establishing residence. Secondly, it is possible under English law for a company to be resident in more than one country (for the Revenue's views on the meaning of residence see SP 6/83).

2 Taxing resident companies

All profits wherever made will be charged to corporation tax subject to any available double taxation reliefs. For accounting periods ending after 31 March 1984, any credit for foreign tax may be set against corporation tax on foreign income in priority to ACT (FA 1984 s 53). When a trade is to be carried out by a UK company in a foreign country there are three possible methods of operation available. First, the trade may be with that country so that there is no trading presence within the country and foreign tax is avoided. Secondly, a branch may be opened overseas which, from a UK tax point of view, results in any profits being subject to corporation tax. Perhaps more significantly, it also means that loss relief will be available and that problems of obtaining Treasury consent under TA 1970 s 482 are avoided. Thirdly, a subsidiary non-resident company may be formed; corporation tax is generally avoided on profits until they are distributed to the UK by way of dividend. The attractions are obviously considerable when the tax rates in the overseas country are very low in comparison with those in the UK and FA 1984 ss 82–91 and Schs 16–18 introduced provisions to prevent tax avoidance by the use of controlled foreign companies (CFC). The provisions enable the Board to apportion chargeable profits amongst all persons with an interest in the CFC and to assess a UK resident company holding such an interest, provided that at least 10% of the profits would be apportioned to it. These provisions only apply if the CFC is under UK control and is resident in a 'low tax' area, defined as one where the tax is less than one-half of what would have been charged in the UK (by FY 1986, therefore, at rates of less than $17\frac{1}{2}\%$), and which is not on the list of countries to which the provisions will not be applied (see [1984] STI 549). Even then, the CFC's chargeable profits must exceed £20,000. There are provisions to ensure that a charge will only arise where a CFC is used with the object of avoiding tax and to exclude CFCs which pursue an 'acceptable distribution policy', or carry on 'exempt activities'. The provisions do not catch chargeable gains which may be apportioned amongst UK shareholders under CGTA 1979 s 15 when the overseas company is 'close' (see Chapter 20).

3 Taxing non-UK resident companies

Companies not resident in the UK are charged on income arising from a trade carried on in the UK through a branch or agency. Other income arising from a UK source may be charged to income tax in the non-resident company's hands (TA 1970 s 238(2)). Hence, a property investment company with no branch or agency in the UK, but owning land in the UK, would be assessed to income tax on the profits arising from that land. Similarly, a trading company carrying out a UK contract without establishing any branch or agency would be subject to income tax and not corporation tax. Capital gains will be chargeable only if they arise from property associated with the trade carried on by the branch or agency (TA 1970 s 246(2); CGTA 1979 s 12). In the case, therefore, of a non-resident property company owning land in the UK, no chargeable gain will arise on a disposal of its capital assets.

4 Taxing non-resident shareholders of resident companies

The tax credit and franked investment income provisions only apply to a resident shareholder. Therefore, subject to any double taxation agreement, a non-resident is generally not entitled to any tax credit (FA 1972 s 86(1)) and neither is he liable to income tax at the basic rate. In the case of an individual, liability to income tax at the higher rates might arise, charged upon the amount of the distribution (not grossed-up) to the extent that those higher rates exceed the basic rate. The shareholder might be able to claim the benefit of double taxation relief.

29 The taxation of partnerships

   I   Income tax
  II   Capital gains tax
 III   Capital transfer tax

Unlike companies and unincorporated associations, a partnership, whether trading or professional, is not subject to any special rules of taxation. To some extent it is treated as a separate entity, but, generally, the ordinary principles of income tax, CGT and CTT have to be applied to each partner.

I INCOME TAX

For the purposes of assessing and collecting income tax a partnership is to a limited extent treated as a separate entity. A trading partnership will be taxed under the rules of Schedule D Case I, a professional partnership under Schedule D Case II. In either case, the precedent partner (which means the senior partner or the partner whose name appears first in the partnership deed) must make a return of partnership income (TMA 1970 s 9). Each individual partner should make his own separate tax return in which he claims his personal allowances (TA 1970 s 26). The Revenue will then make a joint assessment to tax in the partnership name (TA 1970 s 152). This tax bill, which is simply the aggregate tax for which each partner is liable, is based upon each partner's share of profits for the current tax year and takes into account his personal reliefs and charges on income. The Revenue will supply information to the senior partner as to how the bill was calculated so that on receipt of the tax bill individual accountability can be established between the partners. The tax will be due in two equal instalments, on 1 January in the appropriate tax year, and on 1 July following the tax year.

1 Liability for the tax

The tax can be paid either by each partner remitting his own share, or by the firm discharging the bill when arrangements will be made to charge individual partners with their proportion, normally by debiting their current account. Liability of the partners for the assessment is joint, but not several, so that if the bill is not paid the Revenue can proceed for the entire sum against any one of the partners who can join his fellow partners as co-defendants (RSC Ord 15 r 6). On the death of a partner his estate is released from liability for any unpaid tax, except where the deceased was the last surviving partner when his estate will be liable for all the tax, with the right of contribution from his former partners' estates (see *Harrison v Willis Bros* (1966)). Thus, if one partner is bankrupt, the Revenue will not be affected since they can proceed against the other (solvent) partners for the full amount of tax; it is they who will suffer because of that bankruptcy.

    The nature of the partnership tax bill was well illustrated in the case of *Stevens v Britten* (1954) where a retiring partner was to be indemnified by the continuing partners for all partnership liabilities outstanding at the date of his retirement since the partnership's liabilities included the income tax bill presented after his retirement, but in respect of a period before his retirement, the retiring partner was entitled to be indemnified against his share of that bill.

EXAMPLE 1

A and B have been in partnership for five years. Their net profits (for tax purposes) for the 12 month period ended 31 December 1983 are £30,000 assessable in 1984–85 (preceding year basis; see below).

In 1984–85 A and B share profits equally and A has charges on income and personal reliefs of £3,000; B has charges on income and personal reliefs of £4,000. The partnership income tax bill for 1984–85 is calculated as follows:

	A	B
	£	£
Share of profits	15,000	15,000
Less: charges and reliefs	3,000	4,000
Chargeable to income tax	£12,000	11,000
Tax payable	£x	£y

In 1984–85 an assessment for tax of £x + £y is made on the partnership; each partner is jointly liable for *whole* of tax bill (ie £x + £y).

2 How to calculate the profits of the partnership

The procedure for calculating the profits of a partnership under Schedule D Cases I and II is basically the same as for the sole trader or practitioner (see Chapter 6).

Generally, and the matter is essentially one of Revenue practice, trading partnerships will be assessed on the earnings basis. Professional partnerships will be required to render accounts on the earnings basis for the first three years, but thereafter may be permitted to change to either the bills delivered basis (so long as they give an undertaking to bill clients regularly) or even to the cash basis. The cash basis is particularly advantageous for an expanding business because the increase in debtors (unpaid bills) will be ignored.

The preceding year basis of assessment applies to partnerships (see p 87). Thus, the optimum accounting date in order to obtain the greatest delay in paying the tax bill is 6 April (this gives a 21 months delay before the first instalment is due with a further six month period before the second is payable). However, the firm should choose its accounting date carefully as the averaging procedure applied by the Revenue on a change of accounting date (see IR 26; p 93) may result in increased liability to tax.

Although tax will normally be charged on profits calculated on the preceding year basis, those profits will be allocated between the partners in accordance with the profit-sharing ratio in force for the tax year when the profits are assessed and not by reference to any arrangement in force for the accounting year when the profits were earned.

EXAMPLE 2

Zea and Co make up their accounts to 31 December. For the year ending 31 December 1983 profits were £60,000 divided equally between Z and E. On 6 April 1984 a new arrangement was entered into whereby Z agreed to take 60% and E 40% of the profit.

£60,000 will be the assessable profits for 1984–85 (preceding year basis). Tax will be assessed according to the profit-sharing ratio in force for that tax year (1984–85).

Hence:
Z.s share = 60% × £60,000 = £36,000
E's share = 40% × £60,000 = £24,000

Notice that Z is, therefore, taxed on £6,000 profits which E had received in 1983. If the changed sharing ratio comes into force on a day other than the first day of the tax year it is necessary to divide the profits on a time basis and then to apply the different sharing ratios to those divided profits. Say, for instance, that the change occurred on 5 October 1984:

Profits from 6 April to 5 October 1984 = £30,000 ($\frac{1}{2}$ × £60,000) divided between Z and E in the ratio 50:50. Therefore, Z's share is £15,000 and E's share is £15,000.
Profits from 6 October 1984 to 5 April 1985 = £30,000 ($\frac{1}{2}$ × £60,000) divided between Z and E in the ratio 60:40. Therefore, Z's share is £18,000 and E's share is £12,000.
Thus, of the total taxable profits for 1984–85 of £60,000 Z's share is £33,000 (£15,000 + £18,000) and E's share is £27,000 (£15,000 + £12,000).

Although standard accounting practice as amended by the appropriate tax statutes is applied in arriving at the taxable profit (see Chapter 6), a number of specific matters merit comment:

Salary paid to partners   How a partner's salary is taxed depends on whether he is a proper partner or merely an employee of the firm. The terms employed by the parties themselves are not decisive of the matter; it is the substance of the relationship between them, as determined from the partnership agreement that needs to be considered (see *Stekel v Ellice* (1973) discussed at p 47). Notice, however, that the Revenue's usual practice is to assess salaried partners under Schedule E with the result that changes involving them will not cause a cessation of the business.

If the individual is merely an employee the salary paid is a deductible partnership expense on which he should be assessed under Schedule E with tax deducted at source under the PAYE machinery. If the individual is held to be a partner, however, the salary is not an allowable expense of the firm but an agreed profit sharing method. Hence, the firm's accounts must show the profits as including salaries paid to partners which are then taken into account when apportioning those profits amongst the partners. Where salary entitlement changes between the accounting year and the tax year when those profits are assessed to income tax it follows that (i) any salary actually paid in the accounting year will be added back for the purpose of calculating the profits chargeable to tax but (ii) when the profits are allocated for the tax year it is the salaries then paid which are taken into account.

EXAMPLE 3

Balthazar, Mountolive and Justine are in partnership sharing profits in the ratio 3:2:1 after deducting salaries agreed at £1,000, £2,000 and £3,000 respectively. In the year ended 31 December 1983 the business profits (after deducting salaries) were £12,000.
For 1984–85 the assessment on the firm will be on £18,000 (the Revenue treating the salaries as a profit-sharing method) attributed to the partners as follows:

Balthazar: £1,000 (salary) plus £6,000 (3/6 × £12,000)   =   £7,000
Mountolive: £2,000 (salary) plus £4,000 (2/6 × £12,000)   =   £6,000
Justine: £3,000 (salary) plus £2,000 (1/6 × £12,000)   =   £5,000
               £6,000 (salaries) + £12,000 (balance of profits) = £18,000

If the partners are entitled to personal allowances and charges on income of £3,000, £2,500 and £2,000 respectively (£7,500 in total) for 1984–85, the tax liability of the firm and its division between the partners will be as follows (assuming that they have no other sources of income):

	Balthazar £	Mountolive £	Justine £
Total income	7,000	6,000	5,000
Less personal allowances	3,000	2,500	2,000
Taxable income	£4,000	£3,500	£3,000
Tax chargeable (at 30%)	£1,200	£1,050	£900

The total of the partners' liabilities is £3,150 (£1,200 + £1,050 + £900). Therefore, the firm is assessed on £18,000 *less* allowances of £7,500 ie £10,500 at 30% = £3,150.

The tax should be paid in two equal instalments on 1 January and 1 July 1985.

Interest paid to partners Partners may be paid interest on capital they contribute to the firm. As with salaries, the interest is not a deductible expense, but is treated a a profit-sharing method. Hence, the profits must be adjusted by adding back the interest and the share of each of the partners in the profit is then calculated.

Rent paid to a partner Where premises are owned by one partner and leased to the firm, any rent paid will be an allowable deduction from the firm's profits, unless it is exorbitant; the partner concerned will be taxed on that rent as unearned income under Schedule A. It may be more attractive for the premises to be let to the partnership at a nominal rent and for the partner to receive his payment in the form of·an increased share of the profits, with the benefit of assessment under Schedule D Cases I or II (rather than Schedule A) and of, potentially, CGT retirement relief on a disposal of the premises (see p 236). Notice, of course, that if the premises belong to *all* the partners they cannot let those premises to the firm since a person cannot let property to himself (see *Rye v Rye* (1962)).

Deposit interest on solicitor's clients' money (See LS Gaz 19 April 1978) Where client's money is held in an undesignated client bank account the interest earned belongs to the partnership, but will not form a part of the firm's profits assessed under Schedule D Case II. Instead the interest will be apportioned between the partners and taxed under Schedule D Case III as unearned income.

Where the firm pays a client interest on money held in that account the Revenue apply the following principles: first, the sums paid are not an allowable deduction in calculating the firm's profits; secondly, the sum is paid gross (ie basic rate tax is not deducted); thirdly, the partners will only be assessed under Schedule D Case III on any balance remaining after such payments.

Losses Losses incurred by the partnership will be apportioned between the partners in the same way as any profits, each partner dealing with his share of the loss under the normal relieving provisions (see Chapter 7). The operation of these provisions on a change in the constitution of the partnership is discussed at p 414. (On the calculation of losses for a limited partner see *Reed v Young* (1984).)

3   Interest relief on loans to acquire a share in a partnership

Tax relief is available for interest on money which is borrowed to acquire a share in a partnership, or to be used by the firm, or to acquire machinery or plant to be used by the firm. The relief operates by enabling the borrower to deduct the interest as a charge on his income (FA 1974 s 19(2), Sch 1 paras 11–12, 13–16; see Chapter 4). In contrast, where the firm borrows money, any interest paid can only be a deductible business expense (TA 1970 s 130; see Chapter 6).

4   Changes in the partnership

This section is concerned with a change in the personnel of the partnership not with an alteration in the profit-sharing ratios in cases where the members of the firm remain the same. The following examples all represent changes in the personnel of a firm:

old partnership	the change	new partnership
(1) AB	take in C	ABC
(2) ABC	C leaves	AB
(3) ABC	replace C with D	ABD
(4) ABC	death of C	AB
(5) A	creates partnership	AB
(6) AB	dissolution of partnership	A

Numbers (5) and (6) are not strictly examples of a change of partnership personnel, but as the income tax principles that apply in these two cases are similar to the position when partners change, they will be dealt with in this section.

a) *Basic income tax rule*

A change in personnel results in a deemed discontinuance of the partnership (TA 1970 s 154(1)). As the old partnership ceases to exist, the closing year rules will apply and the opening year rules will operate for the new firm (for a discussion of the opening and closing rules see Chapter 6). These deemed discontinuance rules do not, however, affect entitlement to loss relief. Instead, the loss provisions look to what actually happens to the individual partners. Hence:

(1) Relief under TA 1970 s 168 (carry-across) and TA 1970 s 171 (carry-forward) is available so long as the taxpayer remains engaged in the same business as a partner before and after the change. In (1), for instance, A and B will be able to utilise these loss provisions.

(2) Relief under TA 1970 s 174 (terminal relief) is only available to an outgoing partner. The continuing partners cannot take advantage of the deemed discontinuance to claim terminal relief. In (2), therefore, C can take advantage of s 174 (he will, of course, not be able to claim relief under either TA 1970 s 168 or s 171), but A and B will be unable to do so.

(3) Relief under FA 1978 s 30 (new businesses and professions) will be available only to new partners. Thus, in (1), C will be entitled to use s 30; and in (3), D.

b) *Electing for a continuance* (TA 1970 s 154(2))

The deemed discontinuance rules will not apply if all the partners (or their PRs) before and after the change make a written election (within two years of that change) that the firm shall continue to be taxed on the preceding year basis.

Whether a firm should make the election depends on the particular facts. As a general guide, if profits are rising the election will be advantageous. If profits are static or falling it may not be bearing in mind that after a cessation the profits of the first twelve months of business form the basis of taxation for the first three years of assessment. These profits can be kept low by advancing revenue expenditure and borrowing into that period. Notice, however, the potential disadvantages of a cessation: first, it may give rise to a profit on a deemed sale of stock or work-in-progress (TA 1970 ss 137, 138; p 80) although this may be avoided by a book entry sale to the new partnership at cost price; secondly, as there is a sale of all capital assets at market value, the old partners may suffer a balancing charge: unused capital allowances cannot be carried forward to the new partnership which is, however, entitled to a writing-down allowance on the market value of the relevant assets (Capital Allowances Act 1968 ss 48, 79; FA 1971 Sch 8 para 15(3)).

In any event, the continuing partners must ensure that all necessary consents for an election can be obtained. Hence, new partners will usually only be admitted to the partnership if they agree (often in a recital to the partnership deed) to join in making a TA 1970 s 154 election if required to do so by the other parties. Provision should also be made in the partnership deed to ensure that a partner who leaves can be required to join in any election and for the PRs of a deceased partner to be likewise under a duty to sign the notice of election if required to do so by the continuing partners.

Where an election is being made and the firm continues to be taxed on the preceding year basis, the new partnership will be assessed on profits earned by the old partnership.

EXAMPLE 4

For the year ended 31 December 1983 Zea and Co's adjusted profits were £100,000 divided equally between Z and E. On 6 April 1984 A became a partner receiving 20% of the profits and joined in a s 154(2) election.

£100,000 will be the taxable profits for 1984–85 (preceding year basis). Profits are allocated on a *current year* basis—ie in accordance with the profit-sharing agreement of the partners in 1984–85. As A is then a partner the allocation will be:

Total profits	= £100,000
A's 20%	= £20,000
Balance	= £80,000
Z and E (40% each)	= £40,000 each

Although Z and E will have each received £50,000 of the profits earned in 1983, they will be taxed only on £40,000 of those profits. A, on the other hand, will be taxed on £20,000 but received none of the 1983 profits!

It is common for an incoming partner, the personal representatives of a deceased partner and outgoing partners to be given an indemnity in the partnership deed for any extra tax occasioned by their joining in the s 154 election. The wording of such an indemnity is important; it will not provide for an indemnity for *all* the tax suffered by the elector, but only for any extra tax resulting from the election. Hence, if the tax paid, had the election not been made (calculated according to opening year principles), would have been less than the tax actually paid as a result of the election, that difference will be recoverable under the indemnity. Where profits are rising the indemnity will be valueless since tax on the opening rules would be *more* than tax calculated according to the preceding year rules. Even in cases where the profits are static, no advantage results and, in many cases a new partner will have been a former employee of the firm with the result that the profits are likely to rise to reflect the fact that his salary ceases to be payable and, therefore, to be a deductible expense. Only if profits are falling is there likely to be any payment made under the indemnity.

One alternative to an indemnity is to provide that each new partner shall pay tax on what he actually receives. This clause, however, is not easy to reconcile with the preceding year basis of assessment. In *Example 4*, for instance, should A only pay tax on 20% of the profits actually earned in 1984–85 when they are assessed in 1985–86 or (and preferably) should he pay tax on that sum in 1984–85 with the remaining tax apportioned between Z and E? Where profits are rising the incoming partner will pay more tax than on the preceding year basis: where they are falling he will pay less.

Where a partnership change occurs on a day other than the first day of the tax year, the tax assessment will be divided into two: one on the old partners, and one on the new with the profits being apportioned on a 'just' basis. In practice, time-apportionment is employed.

EXAMPLE 5

If in *Example 4* A had joined the firm on 5 October 1984, the income tax would be calculated thus:

Profits for tax year 1984–85 = £100,000 (preceding year basis)

Profits from 6 April–5 October = £50,000 (6 months)

    Z's share (50%) = £25,000
    E's share (50%) = £25,000

Profits from 6 October–5 April = £50,000 (6 months)

    A's share (20%) = £10,000
    Z's share (40%) = £20,000
    E's share (40%) = £20,000

The total profits for 1984–85 of £100,000 will, therefore, be allocated as to £45,000 to each of Z and E and £10,000 to A.

There is nothing to prevent a whole series of elections being made at short intervals. Indeed the operation of large professional partnerships makes such elections commonplace. Special provision is, however, made for the case where two changes occur within two years of each other and the election for a continuance is made on the first, but not the second of those changes (TA 1970 s 154(3)(b)). In this case, on the second change (the discontinuance), the closing rules will apply as if the first change had never occurred. Hence, although the earlier change is not treated as a discontinuance, the operation of the closing rules can increase the liability of a partner who left the firm at the time of the election for a continuance.

5   Income tax consequences of leaving the partnership

a) *Consultancies*

An outgoing partner may be retained as a consultant whereupon he will often be paid a substantial fee in return for relatively minor duties. For income tax purposes, the consultant is not a partner so that any such sum paid to him by the firm will be a deductible business expense under Schedule D Case II assuming that it can be justified according to the 'wholly and exclusively' test (see Chapter 6 and note *Copeman v Flood* (1942)). The consultant will normally be occupying a Schedule E office or employment so that PAYE should operate and he may benefit from joining the firm's pension scheme for a few years. In some cases he may establish that he is exercising a profession or vocation and should, therefore, be assessed under Schedule D Case II. This argument is more likely to succeed where the individual holds consultancies with several different bodies, or where he is not paid a 'salary' but an ad hoc fee each time advice is given.

b) *Payment of annuities by continuing partners*

Partnership agreements will often make provision for the payment of annuities to retiring partners in consideration for the outgoing partner surrendering his share of the firm's goodwill and of its capital assets (see p 423 ff). It is largely a matter of commercial expediency whether such annuities are to be payable and if so for how long and for what amount. The recipient would probably prefer an annuity linked to the profits of the business (eg 10% of the net profits) rather than a fixed sum, as this should offer 'inflation proofing'. The following income tax provisions should be noted:

Position of paying partners   It is usual for the cost of an annuity to be borne by the partners in the same proportion as they share the profits. They are treated as making fully effective annual payments which means that the payments are deductible from their income as a charge on income and should be paid net of basic rate income tax (see Chapter 10). Further, the annuity will not be caught by the anti-avoidance provision in TA 1970 s 457 and charged to higher rate tax in the paying partners' hands so long as it is payable under a partnership agreement to a former member of that partnership, or his widow or other dependents (where the partner is dead the annuity must not be payable for more than ten years) and is payable under a liability incurred for full consideration.

Alternatively, the annuity will be a fully effective annual payment if it is paid in connection with the acquisition of a share in the business of the outgoing partner (TA 1970 s 457(1)(a) and (2)).

The partnership agreement will often provide for any incoming partner to take over the cost of an appropriate share of the annuity and that should the firm cease to exist, the outstanding years of the annuity are to be valued and treated as a debt owed by the partnership at the date of it cessation.

Position of the recipient   The recipient will be taxed on the annuity under the rules of Schedule D Case III (see Chapter 10) with a credit for basic rate tax deducted at source. The annuity will be taxed in his hands as earned income to the extent that the amount payable does not exceed one-half of the average of that partner's best three years' profits out of the last seven; any excess is unearned income (FA 1974 s 16). Those profit figures are index-linked. Hence, where he is paid a fixed annuity the proportion treated as earned income may vary from year to year.

Notice that if the annuity is payable after the recipient's death to a widow(er) or dependants, they may have problems enforcing the payments should the continuing partners default (see *Beswick v Beswick* (1967)).

EXAMPLE 6

The partnership agreement of Falstaff and Co provides for retiring partners to be paid an annuity for ten years after retirement amounting to 10% of the annual net profits of the firm earned in the preceding accounting year.

Hal retires as a partner on 5 April 1984. His share of the profit (index-linked) in the last seven years before his retirement is as follows:

1983–84	£20,000*	1979–80	£11,000*
1982–83	£14,000*	1978–79	£ 8,000
1981–82	£ 8,000	1977–78	£ 9,000
1980–81	£ 7,000		

In the tax year 1984–85 Falstaff & Co's net profits (calculated on the preceding year basis) amount to £90,000. The continuing partners will pay Hal £6,300, ie 10% × £90,000 = £9,000 less basic rate income tax deducted at source under TA 1970 s 52. Hal must enter the gross amount of the payment (£9,000) in his income tax calculation for 1984–85 with a tax credit for £2,700 (basic rate tax deducted at source).

The £9,000 is treated as *earned* income in Hal's hands up to a limit of £7,500 (being half the average share of his taxable profits in the best three of the last seven years before retirement (ie 1983–84; 1982–83; 1979–80). The balance of £1,500 is treated as unearned income.

c) *Retirement annuities*

In addition to or instead of b) above, partners should provide for their retirement by taking out insurance in the form of a retirement annuity. So long as the policy is approved (see TA 1970 ss 226–227), the premiums paid will be allowable deductions for income tax purposes at his highest rates from the partner's share of profits. To be approved the scheme must generally provide for the annuity to be payable to the insured between the ages of 60 and 75 and must prohibit surrender, or assignment of the benefit of the annuity. The premiums must not exceed $17\frac{1}{2}$% of the partner's 'net relevant earnings' in the tax year. In the event of the $17\frac{1}{2}$% ceiling being exceeded the excess paid will not be an allowable deduction. 'Net relevant earnings' means the partner's earned income from the partnership less capital allowances and allowable expenses.

In addition to the above the Revenue may approve contracts which provide either for a lump sum to be payable to prescribed individuals on the death of the insured before the age of 75, or for an annuity to be paid in such circumstances to a surviving spouse. In the latter case, premiums on that annuity must not exceed 5% of net relevant earnings and total premiums paid must not exceed the $17\frac{1}{2}$% ceiling.

If a partner dies before retirement, the insurance company will return the premiums paid in a lump sum (interest may be paid as well) and it is possible for the partner to nominate the person(s) who are to receive these moneys. Failure to make such a nomination will result in the proceeds forming part of the deceased's estate and thereby suffering CTT. Where the partner survives to retirement and is paid the annuity, it is taxed as earned income and may be partially commuted for a tax-free capital sum.

Partners, especially in the early years, may be unable to afford the full $17\frac{1}{2}$% permitted premiums each year, in which case any shortfall in one year can be carried forward for six years and relieved in addition to the normal $17\frac{1}{2}$% relief in any of those tax years.

To a limited extent premiums paid in one tax year can, at the election of the taxpayer, be treated as paid in the previous tax year or, if he has no net relevant earnings in that year, in the tax year before that. The effect is to give tax relief as if the premium had been paid in that earlier year; such relief will, of course, only be available to the extent of the $17\frac{1}{2}\%$ ceiling. This provision is likely to prove of greatest benefit in the partner's final tax year when he may not earn sufficient income to cover his premiums for that tax year.

EXAMPLE 7

(1) Ray joins the firm of Wayne & Hank in May 1981. The following table indicates his net relevant earnings (NRE) and premium contributions in subsequent tax years:

Tax year	NRE	Premiums paid	Shortfall
	£	£	£
1981–82	10,000	1,000	750
1982–83	15,000	1,000	1,625
1983–84	15,000	2,625 (17½%)	—
1984–85	20,000	3,500 (17½%)	—

In 1985–86 his NRE amount to £25,000 and in addition to the full contribution for that year (£4,375) he can pay off the entire shortfall (£750 + £1,625 = £2,375) and will, therefore, obtain tax relief in 1985–86 on total premiums of £6,750 (£4,375 + £2,375). If he wishes to pay off only a part of the shortfall then the £750 from 1981–82 will be used first.

(2) Hank retires from partnership with Wayne and Ray in June 1985. The following table indicates his net relevant earnings (NRE) and premium contributions during his final years with the partnership.

Tax year	NRE	Premiums paid	Overpayment
	£	£	£
1985–86	5,000	1,750	875
1984–85	15,000	2,500	(125)
1983–84	15,000	2,000	(500)

The overpayment of £875 in 1985–86 can be partially offset by claiming additional tax relief in 1984–85 on £125 and in 1983–84 on £500. If tax has already been paid for those years, Hank will be entitled to a rebate. The remaining £250 overpayment will not attract relief. This example illustrates the dangers involved in any overpayment of premiums; underpayments can be made good in later years, but overpayments will often receive no tax relief.

II   CAPITAL GAINS TAX

1   General

The application of CGT principles to partnerships causes considerable difficulties which are exacerbated by the failure of the legislation to make express provision for the treatment of partnerships. It is, therefore, necessary to apply rules designed for individuals to firms and rely on the Revenue Statements of Practice SP D12 and SP 1/79 which do not have the force of law and are a poor substitute for proper legislation in this field.

In applying the CGT legislation to partnerships the general principle is that CGT is triggered by a disposal of a chargeable asset which is treated as made by the individual partners. Although the tax return is made by the firm, the assessment is made on the individual partners (CGTA 1979 s 60; TMA 1970 s 12(4)) in the proportions in which they own the chargeable assets. This is often referred to as entitlement to asset surpluses and is determined primarily by the partnership deed. In the absence of any specific agreement, such entitlement follows the profit-sharing arrangements. Often, however, the asset surplus entitlement will be different from the profit sharing ratios to reflect the partners' respective contributions to the capital of the business.

EXAMPLE 8

(1) Flip & Co, a trading partnership, has three partners, Flip, Flap and Flop, who share asset surpluses in the ratio 3:2:1. In 1981 the firm acquired a valuable Ming vase for a base cost of £60,000; they sell it subsequently for £180,000. The gain of the firm (ignoring any incidental costs of disposal and the indexation allowance) is £120,000. CGT will be calculated separately for each partner:

Flip owns 3/6 of the asset and, therefore, has a base cost of £30,000 and is entitled to 3/6 of the sale proceeds (£90,000); his gain is £60,000 (ie he is entitled to 3/6 of the partnership gain).

Flap's base cost is 2/6 of £60,000 (£20,000) and his share of the proceeds is 2/6 of £180,000 (£60,000) so that his gain is £40,000.

Flop's base cost is 1/6 of £60,000 (£10,000) and his share of the proceeds is 1/6 of £180,000 (£30,000) so that his gain is £20,000.

(2) Assume that the Ming vase is given to Flip in recognition of his 25 years service with the firm. It is worth £180,000 at the date of the gift. The position of Flap and Flop is basically unchanged and they have made gains of £40,000 and £20,000 respectively. Tax may be postponed by an election under FA 1980 s 79 if the donors and Flip agree. In that event Flap will dispose of his 2/6 share for £20,000 and Flop his 1/6 share for £10,000.

The position of Flip is that since he is given the asset he is not treated as making a disposal of his original 3/6 share in the asset (see SP D12 para 3).

Hence, the only difficulty is to discover Flip's base cost. Under general principles it will be:

	£	
	30,000	(cost of original 3/6 share)
plus	60,000	(market value of Flap's 2/6 share at date of gift)
plus	30,000	(market value of Flop's 1/6 share at date of gift)
	£120,000	

The result is that Flip's own gain (£60,000) is held over until such time as he disposes of the vase.

If an election is made under FA 1980 s 79 then Flip's base cost becomes:

	£	
	30,000	(as above)
plus	20,000	(balance after deducting held-over gain on Flap's share)
plus	10,000	(balance after deducting held-over gain on Flop's share)
	£60,000	

2   Changing the asset surplus sharing ratio

CGT may be triggered when the asset surplus sharing ratio is altered.

Old partners	New partners	Old asset surplus sharing ratio	New asset surplus sharing ratio
(1) AB	ABC	1:1	1:1:1
(2) AB	AB	1:1	2:1
(3) ABC	ABD	1:1:1	2:2:1

In all the above cases there has been a change in the entitlement to asset surpluses (and, in effect, to the beneficial ownership of the capital assets). No asset has been disposed of outside the firm, but there has been a disposal of a share of the assets between the partners. In (1) above A and B formerly owned the assets equally; C now joins the firm and is entitled to 1/3 of the asset surpluses. A and B have each made a disposal of 1/3 of their original share in the assets. A, for instance, is now entitled to 1/3 instead of 1/2 or, to put the matter another way, they have together made a disposal of 1/3 of the total assets to C. In (2), although the partners remain the same, the sharing ratio is altered so that B is making a disposal to A of 1/3 of his share of the assets. In (3), C is disposing of a 1/3 share in the assets amongst the continuing partners, A, B and D (A and B each acquire an extra 1/15 of the assets and D 3/15).

Such changes in the sharing ratio are likely to occur principally in three cases: (i) on the retirement or expulsion of a partner; (ii) on the introduction of a new partner; and (iii) on the amendment of the original agreement. It should be noted that the mere revaluation of an asset in the accounts of the firm has no CGT consequences since the revaluation is neither a disposal of an asset nor of a share in assets. (Compare the individual taxpayer who is not assessed to CGT merely because his Ming vase has risen in value from £50,000 to £75,000.)

Whether CGT will be assessed on the disponer depends upon whether he is paid for the share in the asset that he transfers, or whether an adjustment is made to his capital account in the firm by crediting it for that share so that no money is actually paid to him. The CGT position in the latter case will turn upon whether the asset of which a share is transferred has been revalued in the firm's balance sheet. In some cases, however, the relevant assets may not have been revalued in the accounts. Therefore, on the disposal, the disponer's capital account will not be credited with any gain. For CGT purposes, there has been neither gain nor loss so that no CGT will be payable. In effect, this is an example of the hold-over of a chargeable gain.

EXAMPLE 9

(1) Fleur and Camilla have been in partnership sharing profits and asset surpluses equally. The only substantial chargeable asset of the business is the freehold shop which cost £40,000 in 1981. Fleur now sells her share to Charlotte for £75,000.

Fleur has made a disposal of her half-share in the asset and her gain (ignoring any incidental costs of disposal and the indexation allowance) will be:

	£
Consideration received	75,000
Less base cost (50% of £40,000)	20,000
Gain	£55,000

(2) Slick and Slack are in partnership owning asset surpluses in the ratio 2:1. The main capital asset is the firm's premises which cost £30,000 in 1979 and have recently been revalued at £75,000. The two partners have the following interests in this capital asset:

	Slick	*Slack*
	£	£
Capital contributed	20,000	10,000
Share of increased value	30,000	15,000
	£50,000	£25,000

Sloth joins the firm and Slick disposes of one half of his share to Sloth with the result that the sharing ratio becomes 1:1:1. The capital account of Slick will be credited with the value of the share transferred and ultimately he will be paid that sum of money. Slick has thus disposed of 1/3 of the asset (or 1/2 of his share) which has a value of £25,000. That sum will be credited to his capital account with the result that he will have made a gain (ignoring the indexation allowance) for CGT purposes of £25,000 (consideration for the share disposed of) less £10,000 (base cost of the share disposed of) = £15,000.

Slick will be assessed to CGT on this gain despite the fact that he may not be entitled to receive the £25,000 until the firm is dissolved or until he leaves it. So far as the incoming partner Sloth is concerned he will acquire a 1/3 share of the capital asset, of a value of £25,000, and that figure will be his base cost (it will often be the capital sum that he will pay into the firm on becoming a partner).

(3) If in (2) above Slick and Slack had never revalued the premises (which appear in the accounts at their original cost price of £30,000) on the disposal to Sloth, Slick will be treated as transferring half of his share for its book value (£10,000) with the result that he will have made no gain. Correspondingly, Sloth's base cost will be £10,000 so that he is acquiring an asset pregnant with gain.

A failure to revalue an asset, with a subsequent transfer of it at cost, might be viewed as a gift to the incoming partner so that market value should be substituted for the share transferred. In *Example 9 (3)* this would produce a gain for Slick of £15,000 (£25,000–£10,000). However, although partners are generally connected persons, they are not so treated in respect of transfers of partnership assets. Hence, the presumption of gift will not apply unless the partners are connected in some other capacity, eg parent and child, and even in those circumstances the Revenue state that 'market value will not be substituted . . . if nothing would have been paid had the parties been at arm's length' (SP D12 para 7). In all cases, therefore, there will be no question of market value being substituted *so long as the transaction can be shown to be one entered into at arm's length*. Normally, the commercial nature of the arrangement will be assumed. Where there are connected persons, however, the onus is on the taxpayer to show that identical transactions would have been made with a stranger. This onus will usually be discharged by showing that the incoming partner was assuming a large share of responsibility for the running of the business and, thus, furnishing consideration for his share of the assets.

If the bounty element is so great that the transfer must be treated as a gift, the Revenue have stated that 'the deemed disposal proceeds will fall to be treated in the same way as a payment outside the accounts'. In such a case any CGT can be postponed by the parties electing to hold-over the gain under FA 1980 s 79.

EXAMPLE 10

Jake and Jules are brothers and are in business together sharing profits equally. The chargeable assets of the firm cost a total of £20,000 and are now worth £200,000 although they have not been revalued in the firm's books. Jake now transfers his 50% share to his two sons, Jason and Jasper. For CGT Jake's base cost is £10,000 ($\frac{1}{2}$ of £20,000). As those assets have not been revalued, they will be passed at that value to his sons. CGT will not be payable.

Should the Revenue successfully claim (as is likely) that the arrangement did not amount to an arm's length bargain, Jake, Jason, and Jasper could make an election under FA 1980 s 79 to hold over Jake's gain.

3 Goodwill

Goodwill is a chargeable asset for CGT purposes. Thus, the disposal of the whole or part of a firm's goodwill may be an occasion of charge to CGT. Problems have arisen in recent years (especially with regard to professional partnerships) when the existing partners decided not to charge future incoming partners for any share of the firm's goodwill and, therefore, to write off the goodwill in the partnership's balance sheet. On the question as to whether those partners who originally paid for a share of that goodwill (usually on becoming partners in the firm) can then claim immediate CGT loss relief, the following principles may be suggested.

First, on an actual disposal of the goodwill, whether on retirement or to an incoming partner, provided that its value has been written off in the partnership's balance sheet, an allowable loss for CGT purposes may be claimed by the disposing partner.

EXAMPLE 11

Alfie is a partner in Cockney Films & Co. When he joined the firm in 1979 he paid £10,000 for a share in the goodwill. The firm has decided to write off goodwill since incoming partners will no longer be expected to pay for a share of it. When he retires and a new partner, Slicker, joins there will be no payment for Alfie's share of goodwill and Alfie will have made a loss for CGT purposes of £10,000 (being the difference between what he originally paid for the asset and the consideration received on its disposal; for the CGT treatment of losses see p 210).

Secondly, at the time when the goodwill is written off in the balance sheet, the partners may wish to claim immediate loss relief based on CGTA 1979 s 22(2) which allows a claim for loss relief when 'the inspector is satisfied that the value of an asset has become negligible'. The Revenue do not agree that the mere writing off of goodwill has this result but appear to take the view that goodwill retains its value even though no longer paid for by incoming partners or shown in the firm's balance sheet, on the grounds that if the business were sold, the consideration would probably include a sum for goodwill. Whether this fact should influence the valuation of an individual partner's share in circumstances where he could not unilaterally receive consideration for it is most debatable. The law in this area is not settled with some inspectors apparently allowing loss claims and others refusing.

4 Payment of annuities

When a partner leaves the firm any annuity payments that he receives from the continuing partners will not only be subject to income tax (p 417) but also, their capitalised value may be treated as consideration for the disposal of a share of the partnership assets (CGTA 1979 s 31(3)) and CGT levied on any resultant gain. In SP D12 the Revenue have indicated when this will be the case:

'The capitalised value of the annuity will only be treated as consideration for the disposal of his share in the partnership assets, if it is more than can be regarded as a reasonable recognition of the past contribution of work and effort by the partner to the partnership. Provided that the former partner had been in the partnership for at least ten years an annuity will be regarded as reasonable for this purpose if it is no more than two-thirds of his average share of the profits in the best three of the last seven years in which he was required to devote substantially the whole of his time to acting as a partner.

For lesser periods the following fractions will be used instead of the two-thirds:

Complete years in partnership	Fraction
1–5	1/60 for each year
6	8/60 for each year
7	16/60 for each year
8	24/60 for each year
9	32/60 for each year'

Where the partner receives both an annuity and a lump sum, the Revenue's view is that:

'If the outgoing partner is paid a lump sum and an annuity, the Revenue will not charge CGT on the capitalised value of the annuity provided that the annuity and one-ninth of the lump sum together do not exceed the relevant fraction of the retired partner's average share of the profits' (SP 1/79).

The lump sum will, therefore, always be charged to CGT and it may cause the capitalised value of the annuity to be taxed.

EXAMPLE 12

(1) Charles and Claude agree to pay their partner, Clarence, who is retiring on 5 April 1984 after 18 years as a partner an annuity of £3,000 pa for the next 10 years. His share of the profits in the last 7 years of the partnership was as follows:

Tax year	Profits £	Tax year	Profits £
1983–84	5,000	1979–80	2,000
1982–83	10,000*	1978–79	4,000
1981–82	14,000*	1977–78	5,000
1980–81	12,000*		

The annuity does not exceed two-thirds of Clarence's average share of profits in the best 3 years (those asterisked) of the last 7 years before retirement, ie $\frac{2}{3} \times £36,000$ divided by $3 = £8,000$. Therefore, no CGT is paid on the capitalised value. (Note that for income tax purposes the annuity will be earned income in Clarence's hands up to £6,000; ie $\frac{1}{2} \times £36,000$ divided by 3).

Contrast the position if Clarence had been paid an annuity of £9,000 pa. As the permitted £8,000 figure is exceeded the entire capitalised value of that annuity will be subject to CGT.

(2) Assume that, in addition to the annuity (in (1)), it is agreed that Clarence is to receive a lump sum of £54,000. His CGT position is as follows:
  (i) the annuity will be subject to income tax;
  (ii) the lump sum (£54,000) will be subject to CGT in so far as it represents consideration for a disposal of chargeable assets; and
  (iii) the capitalised value of the annuity will also be included for CGT purposes since the annuity (£3,000) plus 1/9 of the lump sum (£6,000) exceeds the 2/3 limit of £8,000.

5 Reliefs

These reliefs have been considered in detail in Chapter 16. Those of particular relevance to partnerships are:

Hold-over relief under either FA 1980 s 79 (as amended) or CGTA 1979 s 126.

Roll-over (reinvestment) relief (CGTA 1979 s 115)   This relief is extended, by concession, to assets which are owned by an individual partner and used by the firm, so long as the entire proceeds of disposal are reinvested in another business asset used by the firm (see SP D11). Where a rent is charged for the asset it is doubtful whether this concession operates; the profits on any sale would probably be subject to CGT.

Retirement relief (CGTA 1979 s 124)   The relief will apply when a partner disposes of his share of the business. By concession (see SP D5) the relief is extended to cover

> 'a disposal of an asset used in the partnership if it is associated with the disposal of the business or part of the business and provided the individual satisfies the other conditions of relief. Where, however, the partnership has paid rent for it, the asset is treated as an investment—and excluded from relief—except for a fraction of it proportionate to the individual's share of the rent. A larger fraction of the asset may qualify for relief if the rent was clearly less than market rent'.

As the payment of rent may operate to deny relief a partner who wishes to keep an asset in his name, whilst allowing the firm to use it, should ensure that he is paid for its use by an increased share of the profits rather than by a payment of rent (see also p 413).

Hold-over relief (CGTA 1979 s 123)   This relief is available on the incorporation of a partnership.

III CAPITAL TRANSFER TAX

As with CGT, there are few specific references in the CTT legislation to partnerships. General principles, therefore, operate and gratuitous transfers of partnership assets or interests therein will be treated as transfers of value by the individual partners (see *Example 13*).

Normally, the share of a retiring partner in the firm will pass to the continuing partners. No CTT charge will arise where full consideration is paid, and, even where that is not so, CTT will be avoided if (as is usually the case) the transfer is a commercial transaction within FA 1975 s 20(4) (see p 278).

EXAMPLE 13

Big & Co has twenty partners all equally entitled to profits. The following changes are to occur:

(1) Partner Zack is retiring and is to receive an annuity for his share of the assets. His share of goodwill is to pass automatically under the partnership deed to the continuing partners.

(2) Partner Uriah is to devote less time to the business and will receive a reduced share of the profits (including capital profits). At the same time, partner Victor is to be paid an increased profit share to reflect his central position within the firm.

(3) Partner Yvonne is retiring and her place is to be taken by her daughter Brenda. No payment is to be made by Brenda.

The CTT consequences of these transactions are as follows:

(1) *Zack* No CTT is chargeable since consideration is given for his assets (there may not even be a fall in value in his estate). Regarding the automatic accrual of goodwill it is generally thought that the estate duty case of *A-G v Boden*

(1912) is still good law for CTT. Thus, mutual covenants by the partners that goodwill shall pass to the surviving partners on death or retirement without any cash payment will make the transfer of goodwill non-gratuitous within FA 1975 s 20(4). This principle should apply even where the other parties are, or include, connected persons since it should be possible to show that identical arrangements would have been made with partners who were not so connected.

(2) *Uriah*   The loss to Uriah's estate is the result of a commercial bargain since he is being allowed to devote less time to the business; CTT should not, therefore, be chargeable. Likewise, increasing the profit-sharing ratio of Victor is merely a recognition by the other partners of his commercial necessity to the firm.

(3) *Yvonne*   The new partner is a connected person and it will be hard to justify this arrangement on commercial grounds as it would not have been entered into with a stranger. On that basis, CTT will be assessed on the fall in value of Yvonne's estate.

The major CTT reliefs applicable to trading and professional partnerships will be business property relief, agricultural relief, and the instalment option (see Chapter 23). Two points of particular relevance to partnerships should be repeated: first, on a transfer of assets held outside the firm and consisting of land, buildings and machinery or plant, business relief at 30% may be available. If the asset is owned by the partnership the full 50% relief may apply. Secondly, the CTT business reliefs are not available where a partner's share is subject to a binding contract of sale at the time of transfer. Therefore, if it is desired to ensure that on the death or retirement of a partner his share shall pass to the survivors, the partnership deed should be drafted so as to give the survivors an option, but not an obligation, to purchase that share.

30 Development land tax

'the latest in a long line of attempts to find an efficient means of taxing land: starting with Lloyd George in 1909, the statute book is littered with planning Acts, betterment levies and development gains taxation, none of which ever achieved their ostensible aims.' (Sabine, *A Short History of Taxation*)

I INTRODUCTION

DLT was introduced in the Development Land Tax Act 1976 (DLTA 1976) with effect from 1 August 1976, and was originally part of the machinery of the Community Land Act 1975. This legislation was confiscatory; its espoused aim was to bring most development land into the ownership of local authorities through the Community Land Act and, in the meantime, to divert into local or central government purses (by means of DLT) virtually all profit realised from the development of land. To this end, DLT was originally levied at the penal rate of 80% with only a £10,000 annual exemption.

However, these draconian measures were never fully implemented. The Community Land Act was repealed in 1980 and the impact of DLT has been considerably reduced since 1976 so that it yielded only 0.09% of the total sum raised by direct taxes in 1982.

The aim of DLT is to tax the profit attributable to the development value of land. Thus, it is not a tax on all profits or gains and is quite distinct from CGT or income tax; it applies across the board whether land is held as an investment or as stock-in-trade. Broadly DLT is likely to be payable when either:

(a) land or a major interest in land is sold outright for a consideration which (on the application of a formula) is deemed to reflect the value arising from its development potential; or

(b) the existing owner begins to develop his land, so that the market value of that land (on applying a formula) is deemed to include an element of value arising from the development. It does not matter whether or not the land is subsequently sold.

DLT is not, therefore, chargeable on an increase in the market value of land reflecting only its current or existing use. For example, the farmer who sells agricultural land for a sum which represents its market value as agricultural land and thereby makes a profit is not liable to DLT (although he may be liable to CGT).

The concept of current use value, which is always deductible in arriving at the gain subject to DLT, ensures that the tax has a built-in mechanism to allow for the effects of inflation.

DLT operates on four basic principles: first, the tax is triggered either by a non-gratuitous disposal of land as a result of which development value is realised, or by a deemed disposal which occurs when land is developed.

Secondly, it is irrelevant whether or not the land disposed of is held as the personal property of a private owner, or as the stock-in-trade or fixed asset of a trader. When there is a chargeable disposal and the consideration is deemed to include development value, there is, prima facie, a DLT liability.

Thirdly, a disposal of land may trigger a liability to other taxes besides DLT; for example, to income tax under Schedule D Case I (where the disponer is a dealer in land); or to CGT where he is not; or to income tax under Schedule A where the transaction involves a lease. DLT overrides all other taxes and, although it is not a substitute for them, there is no overlap of tax liability. Complicated provisions, therefore, exist to ensure that a gain which is subject to DLT is free from other taxes.

Fourthly, a non-UK resident is liable to DLT on any development value that he realises from the disposal of an interest in land in the UK.

II   GENERAL PRINCIPLES

1   The occasion of charge

By DLTA 1976 s 1, a charge to DLT arises when a chargeable person disposes, or is deemed to dispose, of an interest in land in the UK on or after 1 August 1976 in circumstances where there is a realisation of development value. The tax is levied, at 60%, on the realised development value that accrues to that person in the financial year (which runs from 1 April to 31 March following).

2   Chargeable persons

Chargeable persons include individuals, partners, personal representatives, trustees, companies and pension funds. Husband and wife are treated as separate individuals. Local authorities and certain other bodies are excluded.

3   Meaning of disposal

For DLT, as for CGT, there are two types of disposal; actual disposals and deemed disposals.

a) *Actual disposals*

As in CGT, the term 'disposal' is not defined. Given its natural meaning, a disposal occurs whenever there is a change in the beneficial ownership of land; for example, through sale, exchange, gift or a distribution in specie by a company.

A disposal is chargeable only when it realises development value: so there must be consideration for the disposal. In certain circumstances there will be a deemed consideration; for example, on a distribution *in specie* by a company (see p 440). This is not the case with a purely gratuitous transfer, which although a disposal, is not chargeable. The donee, therefore, acquires the property at the donor's base value (DLTA 1976 s 10, see p 435). A transfer on death is not a disposal for DLT purposes and, therefore, attracts no liability (DLTA 1976 s 9; see p 435).

A disposal includes a part disposal (DLTA 1976 s 3) which occurs:

(a) on the grant of a lease;

(b) on a disposal of the disponer's entire interest in part of the land (eg a sale of one acre out of ten); or

(c) on receipt of a sum of money as compensation for damage to, or the forfeiture of, rights in or over land (eg for the release of a restrictive covenant), or as payment for the use or exploitation of the land (eg for the grant of an easement).

The grant of an option for consideration is treated as the disposal of a newly created interest and not as a part disposal. If the option is exercised, the grant of the option is treated as one transaction with its exercise to calculate any liability to DLT. The forfeiture by the vendor of a deposit paid by the purchaser on an abortive purchase is treated as the grant by the vendor of an option for a consideration equal to the deposit (DLTA 1976 s 8) and may, therefore, trigger a DLT liability.

The date when disposal occurs is important for calculating when any DLT is payable. It is usually the date of contract unless the contract is conditional when it is the date when the contract becomes unconditional. In the case of a compulsory purchase order it is the date of entry or of agreement of the compensation, if this is earlier.

b) *Deemed disposals*

Immediately before a 'project of material development' is begun on land in the UK every 'major interest' then existing in the land is deemed to be disposed of and immediately reacquired by its owner for a consideration equal to its then market value (DLTA 1976 s 2). That part of the notional profit arising on that deemed disposal which reflects the development value of the land is charged.

The idea behind s 2 is to charge the person who develops his own land, and who thereby increases its value and alters its then current use. Were it not for this provision the increase would escape DLT. A subsequent sale would not lead to a charge because it would be on the basis of the then current use of the land.

A *'project of material development'* This is basically any development for which planning permission is required other than minor development permitted by a general development order (DLTA 1976 s 7(7) and Sch 4 Pt II). Other developments excluded from the definition of material development include: the maintenance, improvement, or enlargement of a building provided that the cubic content of the original building is not increased by more than one-third (FA 1981 s 133); rebuilding work which does not increase the cubic content of the existing building by more than one-tenth; the use of land or buildings for agriculture or forestry or for advertising displays; and a change of use within certain broad classes.

A project is taken to commence at the date when any specified operation comprised in that project is begun (DLTA 1976 Sch 1 para 2(1)). 'Specified operations' include the start of building construction, trench digging, laying pipes, constructing roads and any actual change of use of existing buildings.

As it may be difficult to ascertain when the earliest specified operation occurred, the developer may select a 'specified starting date' and give notice of it to the Revenue. Provided that he selects and notifies his date within 60 days before and 30 days after the earliest of his specified operations the DLT liability is related to that date, unless the specified operation is a sham and is undertaken purely to avoid DLT (see *R v IRC ex parte Harrow BC* (1983) where this was the case).

A 'major interest in land'   An 'interest' is widely defined in DLTA 1976 s 46 to include any estate or interest in land (eg a lease) or over land so as to affect its use (eg a restrictive covenant). However, it does not include the interest of a mortgagee, so that the creation or redemption of a mortgage is not chargeable, nor the interest of a beneficiary under a trust, unless it is a bare trust (see p 440).

Further, a reversionary interest expectant upon a lease with at least 35 years unexpired and where the rent payable under the lease does not and cannot be made to reflect the value of the development, is excluded (eg a fixed ground rent or other fixed rent not subject to review). Finally, there is a de minimis exclusion for interests with a market value of less than £5,000 which confer no right to exclusive possession (eg an easement or restrictive covenant over another person's land).

It should be noted that the deemed disposal is of every major interest in the land and not only that of the developer. Thus, where the lessee under a building lease begins building work, there is a deemed disposal not only of his interest, but also of that of his landlord.

The market value of each major interest deemed to be disposed of is determined on the basis that the project is lawful. It includes the benefit of planning permission, but not the cost of the development nor the eventual profit that the developer hopes to make.

So as to give a developer some idea of the DLT liability resulting from the start of the project, he can serve a notice on the Revenue specifying the project and electing to be assessed and charged to DLT by reference to the circumstances existing at the date of the notice. Provided that he begins the project within two years of his notice he will be charged to DLT on the basis of the original assessment. This is known as the Advance Assessment Scheme (FA 1980 s 114). In certain circumstances a complete exemption may be available under DLTA 1976 s 18 (see p 438).

III   CALCULATION OF THE CHARGEABLE AMOUNT

1   General principles

DLT is charged on the 'realised development value' (RDV) arising from the disposal or deemed disposal of an interest in land. RDV is the amount by which the proceeds of the disposal (after deducting incidental costs) exceed the relevant base value of the interest disposed of.

The 'proceeds of the disposal' is the consideration actually received for the disposal (with no discount for any postponement of the right to receive it). Market value is, however, taken in three instances: first, on a deemed disposal at the start of development; secondly, when a company leaves a group within 6 years of receiving an intra-group transfer; and thirdly, on a distribution in specie by a company. On the grant of a lease, the consideration consists of the market value of the right to receive rent plus any other consideration (DLTA 1976 Sch 2 para 26). Contingent liabilities are ignored, although, if they subsequently become enforceable, adjustments are made to the DLT bill.

Deductible incidental costs consist of expenditure wholly and exclusively incurred for the purposes of the disposal (such as solicitors' fees), together with any valuation costs (DLTA 1976 Sch 2 para 32).

The 'relevant base value' of the interest disposed of is the highest of the results produced by three calculations, known as Bases A, B and C (ie it is whichever of the three which will result in the smallest chargeable amount).

Base A Under Base A the base value is calculated by deducting from the net proceeeds of disposal the aggregate of:
(1) the cost of acquisition (including incidental costs) of the land or the interest therein; *plus*
(2) the increase in the Current Use Value (CUV) of the interest since the date of acquisition or 6 April 1965, if later (CUV is the market value of the land on the assumption that planning permission will not be granted and that it is unlawful to carry out any material development not already begun. CUV is, therefore, the existing use value of the land); *plus*
(3) expenditure on relevant improvements which enhance the value of the land and are still reflected in its market value at the date of disposal (DLTA 1976 Sch 3), less any increase in CUV at the date of disposal which is attributable to that expenditure; *plus*
(4) a 'special addition' (DLTA 1976 s 6) which is available for interests in land acquired before 1 May 1977 (it is 10% of the original acquisition cost for each year of ownership up to a four year maximum of 40%; for acquisitions before 13 September 1974 the maximum is six years and 60%); *plus*
(5) a 'further addition' equal to the expenditure on relevant improvements multiplied by the fraction: $\dfrac{\text{special addition}}{\text{cost of acquisition}}$.

Base A was intended as a transitional provision for land acquired before 1 May 1977. It is unlikely to be the relevant base where land was acquired after that date because the owner will not have the benefit of the special and further additions.

Base B Under Base B the base value is calculated by deducting from the net proceeds of the disposal the following:
(1) 115% of CUV at the date of disposal; *plus*
(2) expenditure on relevant improvements.
The effect of Base B is that there will be no DLT liability where land is disposed of at not more than 15% above its CUV.

Base C Base C allows the deduction from the net proceeds of disposal of 115% of the cost of acquisition and expenditure on improvements. If the land is the taxpayer's stock-in-trade and the development is residential, a deduction of 150% is allowed instead (FA 1981 s 129). The effect of Base C is to allow a developer to make a 15% (or 50%) profit free from DLT.

EXAMPLE 1

Barry purchased land on 1 November 1975 for £200,000 (CUV £60,000). He spent £500,000 on improvements during his period of ownership. In December 1984, Barry sold the property to developers for £2,000,800 together with the benefit of planning permission for the construction of offices on the site. The CUV without the improvements was £760,000 and, with the improvements, £800,000. Legal fees on the sale were £800. His DLT calculation is as follows:

	£	£	£
Consideration received			2,000,800
Less: Incidental costs of disposal			800
			2,000,000

		£	£	£
Less: relevant base value	c/f			2,000,000
BASE A: Cost			200,000	
Expenditure on relevant improvements		500,000		
Less the difference between CUV:	£			
with improvements	800,000			
without improvements	760,000			
		40,000		
			460,000	
plus Increase in CUV			740,000	
plus Special addition:				
40% × £200,000			80,000	
plus Further addition:				
$£460,000 \times \dfrac{£80,000}{£200,000}$			184,000	
			£1,664,000	
BASE B: 115% × CUV (£800,000)			920,000	
plus Expenditure on relevant improvements			500,000	
			£1,420,000	
BASE C: 115% × cost (£200,000)			230,000	
115% × improvements (£500,000)			575,000	
			£805,000	
Highest = Base A				1,664,000
Therefore:				
Realised development value				336,000
Less: annual exemption				75,000
Chargeable realised development value				£261,000
DLT at 60% × £261,000				£156,600

As an anti-avoidance measure, when the acquisition is from a connected person (as defined in CGTA 1979 s 63) and occurs within 12 months of the disposal, Base A is calculated without the special or further addition and the deductible cost in Base C is limited to 100%.

2   Part disposals

RDV on a part disposal must be calculated in the same way as on a disposal of the whole. Items which cannot be separately identified (eg the acquisition cost of part), must be apportioned in accordance with the fraction that the value of the part disposed of bears to the value of the entire interest (DLTA 1976 Sch 2 Pt II; cp CGT). This reduction is achieved by the use of two formulae: one is for items other than CUV (such as the acquisition cost) and consists of multiplying the item by the fraction:

$$\frac{PD}{PD + MR}$$

where PD is the net proceeds of the part disposed of and MR is the market value of the interest retained. If the net proceeds of the part disposal are less than the market value of that part, market value is substituted for PD in the fraction.

The CUV of the part disposed of is calculated by deducting from the CUV of the entire interest before the disposal (CW) the CUV of the part retained (CR).

Base A requires the calculation of the CUV of the part disposed of at the date of its acquisition. This is found by multiplying the CUV of the whole at the date of acquisition by the formula:

$$\frac{CW - CR}{CW}$$

EXAMPLE 2

On 5 July 1973 Clod bought 50 acres of agricultural land for £100,000; the CUV was £80,000. On 6 September 1984, he sold 20 acres for £300,000. At that date the CUV as agricultural land of the whole 50 acres (CW) was £150,000 and the CUV of the 30 acres retained (CR) was £100,000. The market value of the 30 acres retained was £500,000.

The cost formula is: $\dfrac{PD}{PD + MR} = \dfrac{£300,000}{£300,000 + £500,000} = 0.375$

The CUV formula is: $\dfrac{CW - CR}{CW} = \dfrac{£150,000 - £100,000}{£150,000} = 0.333$

	£	£
BASE A:		
Cost of acquisition: £100,000 × 0.375		37,500
CUV on disposal: £150,000 − £100,000	50,000	
Less: CUV on acquisition: £80,000 × 0.333	26,640	
		23,360
Special addition (60% × £100,000):		
£60,000 × 0.375		22,500
		£83,360
BASE B:		
CUV on disposal (£150,000 − £100,000)		50,000
plus 15% × £50,000		7,500
		£57,500
BASE C:		
Cost of acquisition: £100,000 × 0.375		37,500
plus 15% × £37,500		5,625
		£43,125
RDV is calculated as:		
Net proceeds of disposal		300,000
Less: relevant base value (Base A)		83,360
		£216,640

DLTA 1976 Sch 2 para 1 contains special rules for calculating the RDV on disposals out of 'assembled land'; ie for cases where the various interests making up the whole were acquired at different times and where expenditure on improvements or relevant improvements is only referable to a particular part.

3 Leases and reversions

The grant of a lease or sub-lease is a part disposal. Special rules are necessary to ensure that on the various dealings with leases and/or reversions the same development value is not charged twice to DLT (see generally DLTA 1976 Sch 2 Pt III).

a) *The grant of a lease*

The owner of an interest in land with development value may realise that value by granting a lease. Accordingly, for DLT purposes the consideration for the part disposal is taken to be the capitalised value of the rent together with any other consideration payable (such as a premium). The value of the lessor's reversion, however, consists of the right to receive the rent under the lease plus the right to exclusive possession on the termination of the lease. Thus, applying the part disposal rules without any modification would result in both the PD figure (net proceeds of disposal) and the MR figure (market value of remainder —the reversion) including the capitalised value of the right to receive rent under the lease. This would yield an unsatisfactory fraction, resulting in too little tax. Accordingly, the part disposal rule is modified by omitting from the market value of the reversion the capitalised value of the rent.

EXAMPLE 3

Big grants a lease to Little and is treated as receiving £20,000 of which £6,000 is the capitalised value of the rent and £14,000 is paid as a premium.

The value of Big's reversion is £30,000 made up of £6,000 (capitalised rent) and £24,000 which is the value of the right to exclusive possession on the termination of the lease. If the capitalised value of rent were included in both limbs of the part disposal formula, the resulting fraction would be too small:

$$\frac{£20,000}{£20,000 + £30,000} = 0.40$$

Omitting the capitalised value of the rent from the market value, the fraction would become 0.45: $\dfrac{£20,000}{£20,000 + £24,000}.$

Similarly, in applying the CUV formula to the part disposal for Base A, the figure for CR (the CUV of the reversion retained) is reduced to the present value of the right to exclusive possession at the end of the lease.

b) *Grant of a sub-lease*

The grant of a sub-lease is a part disposal of the head lease and DLTA 1976 Sch 2 para 14(2) ensures that the sub-lessor is only charged on such development value as has accrued since the grant of the head lease.

c) *Special cases*

In an attempt to ensure that DLT is not over- or under-charged, adjustments have to be made to the RDV on the disposal of the reversion (DLTA 1976 Sch 6 para 15); on the disposal of the lease (DLTA 1976 Sch 2 para 16); on the material variation of the terms of an existing lease (DLTA 1976 Sch 2 para 17); and in cases where the lessor undertakes a contractual obligation to the lessee which is reflected in a higher rent (eg on the grant of a lease to a developer where the lessor agrees to bear some or all of the costs of development: DLTA 1976 Sch 2 para 13A).

4   Material development of part

A project of material development that is begun on part only of the land is not treated as a part disposal of the whole, but as a complete disposal of that part

(DLTA 1976 Sch 1 para 11). To calculate the relevant base value, the part disposal formula is not used and, instead, the items involved in the calculation are apportioned to the disposal on a just and reasonable basis (DLTA 1976 Sch 2 para 18). In order to calculate the base value on a subsequent disposal or part disposal of the whole land (including the part developed), its acquisition cost for DLT is taken to be the market value of the part that was the subject of the deemed disposal; *plus* the excess of Base A as calculated for the whole land before the development began over Base A calculated for the purposes of the development.

Base A is chosen for this calculation because it gives the balance of cost and expenditure on relevant improvements from the date that the whole interest was acquired (and the special and further addition) to the date of the disposal. Any expenditure on improvements and any increase in CUV after the date of the deemed disposal is calculated in the usual way.

IV GIFTS AND DEATH

1 Gifts

Liability to DLT can arise only where a disposal produces, or is deemed to produce, 'proceeds'. A gratuitous disposal of land neither yields, nor is deemed to yield, any 'proceeds' so that the donor is not liable to DLT. The donee acquires the land at the donor's base value, although he can add on his own incidental costs of acquistion. He is entitled to the special addition of the donor only at the date of the gift, but any further addition is calculated on the relevant improvements of both donor and donee.

For the transaction to be a gift, the donee must give no consideration. The payment by the donee of the donor's costs of disposal is not consideration, but, if, for example, the donee pays any CTT charged on the disposal, or if it is made pursuant to divorce or separation, he will have furnished consideration (DLTA 1976 s 10). Any consideration given (even a nominal sum) forms the purchaser's acquisition cost (unless the purchaser is a charity or heritage body within FA 1975 Sch 6).

EXAMPLE 4

Samson bought agricultural land in 1979 for £30,000 (including acquisition costs) with a CUV of £25,000. He improved the land at a cost of £20,000 and gave the land to his daughter Delilah in 1981. Delilah paid the solicitors' fees and the stamp duty on the transaction which amounted to £1,500 in all. Delilah made further improvements costing £10,000. For calculating the DLT liability on a future disposal of the land by Delilah, her acquisition cost is £31,500 (ie cost of acquisition of Samson (£30,000) plus Delilah's acquisition costs (£1,500)). Her expenditure on improvements amounts to £30,000 (£20,000 by Samson; £10,000 by Delilah).

2 Death

Death is not a disposal for DLT and, therefore, triggers no liability (DLTA 1976 s 9). Instead, the deceased's PRs step into his shoes so that they acquire the land at his base value. A sale by the PRs is treated as a sale by the deceased and the PRs are treated as a single body entitled to one annual exemption.

A distribution to a legatee under the will is a gift and the legatee acquires the land at the deceased's base value plus any incidental costs of disposal incurred by the PRs.

Variations and disclaimers which are read back into the will for both CTT and CGT may, as a matter of practice, also be read back for DLT purposes and treated as if made by the deceased with the result that they do not constitute a disposal for DLT.

The acquisition of land by a beneficiary from a PR, or under a deed of variation or disclaimer which has been read back into the will, is not treated as an acquisition from a connected person (see CGTA 1979 s 63). Hence, a subsequent disposal of the land within 12 months of its acquisition does not deprive him of the annual exemption (DLTA 1976 s 5(7)).

EXAMPLE 5

Larry buys land in 1970 for £50,000 and dies in 1982. Larry's death is not a disposal for DLT so that if his PRs sell the land, they do so at Larry's base value. If the PRs, instead, transfer the land to the legatee, Fred, he is treated as receiving a gift from the deceased, so that his base value is that of Larry (plus the cost of any improvements undertaken by the PRs) plus the value of any special addition available to Larry and, therefore, to the PRs at Larry's death.

V   EXEMPTIONS AND RELIEFS

The various exemptions and reliefs from DLT ensure that in many cases, development value accruing to an owner of an interest in land remains untaxed.

1   Transitional exemptions

a) *Exemption for certain dwelling-houses built for owner-occupation* (DLTA 1976 s 15)

Provided that the taxpayer owned the land on 12 September 1974 a subsequent deemed disposal occasioned by his building on the land a single dwelling-house will be exempt from DLT provided that the building is intended as the sole or main residence for that person, an adult member of his family, or a dependent relative (as defined in DLTA 1976 s 47). This exemption is available for a maximum of two houses, one of which must be built on land within the curtilage of a dwelling-house owned and occupied by that person on 12 September 1974.

b) *Exemption for land held as stock-in-trade* (DLTA 1976 s 16)

Where a person held land as stock-in-trade on 12 September 1974 and had at that date obtained full or outline planning permission for the development of all or part of the land, any development value realised on a subsequent development covered by that permission is exempt. The benefit of this exemption passes with the land on a transfer of it by gift or on death.

2   Exemption for certain bodies (DLTA 1976 ss 11, 26)

Bodies listed in s 11 (eg local authorities) are exempt from DLT on any sale or development of land. Development by approved co-operative housing associations is exempt from charge and this exemption is extended to

Housing Corporations and registered housing associations for development begun after 12 March 1984 (FA 1984 s 120).

Disposals by a charity after 25 March 1980 are exempt from DLT subject to a deferred liability restricted to the value of any land retained by the body should it cease to be a charity (DLTA 1976 s 24; FA 1980 s 111).

3 Non-commercial exemptions

a) *Annual exemption* (DLTA 1976 s 12)

For disposals after 31 March 1984, the first £75,000 of RDV that accrues to any person in the financial year is exempt from DLT (increased from £50,000).

Husband and wife are separate persons for DLT so that they together have an annual exemption of £150,000 in respect of land owned by them jointly or in common.

The exemption is not available on a disposal of land which was acquired from a connected person (see CGTA 1979 s 63) within the previous 12 months. Similarly, it is not available where the person making the disposal is not an individual (for instance, a company, a trustee of settled property, or a partnership) who acquired the interest on a part disposal (after 25 March 1980) from a connected person as a gift or at an under-value within the previous 6 years (DLTA 1976 s 12(5)). Thus, where companies have made intra-group disposals, a subsequent disposal to a stranger cannot benefit from the exemption unless it occurs more than 6 years after the earlier acquisition.

An unused exemption cannot be carried forward. Hence, there may be advantages in attempting to 'spread' the RDV over more than one financial year. This may be arranged by the use of 'cross' options, although such transactions may be attacked under the *Ramsay* principle (see Chapter 32).

b) *Exemption for the private residence* (DLTA 1976 s 14)

The disposal by an individual of a private residence with land of up to one acre (including the site), or such larger area as the commissioners consider reasonable for the enjoyment of the dwelling, is exempt from DLT subject to the following conditions:

(1) The property must be the individual's only residence, or his main residence if he has more than one. This is a question of fact and the test is the same as for the CGT exemption (see p 229), except that there is no right of election.
(2) The property must have been his only or main residence for at least twelve out of the 24 months ending with the disposal. If he owned it for a shorter period than 24 months it must have been his only or main residence for half that period, subject to a minimum period of occupation of six months. There are no reliefs for periods of interrupted occupation (contrast CGT).
(3) If any part of the property is used exclusively for business purposes an equivalent proportion of the RDV is chargeable. However, provided that no part is used exclusively for business purposes, the full exemption will be available (s 14(4)).
(4) The exemption is not available if the property was acquired wholly or partly for realising development value on a subsequent disposal.

The exemption is not limited to one house. It may also be claimed for one other house owned by the individual and occupied rent-free and for no consideration by a dependent relative (as defined in DLTA 1976 s 47).

The disposal by PRs of a house that was the only or main residence of the deceased is exempt from DLT provided that the disposal is made within two years of his death. So long as the deceased had qualified for the relief at his death, the PRs need not satisfy the six months minimum ownership and occupation requirement.

The exemption is also available to trustees who dispose of a dwelling occupied as the only or main residence of a beneficiary who is entitled to occupy it under the settlement or to receive the income from it when sold.

Notice that the exemption will not apply to land sold after the sale of the house because it is no longer part of the only or main residence (see *Varty v Lynes* (1976) and p 230).

4   Commercial exemptions

a) *Exemption for development within three years of acquisition* (DLTA 1976 s 18)

A person who acquires land in advance of development (eg a developer) may apply to the Revenue for a clearance on the basis that if he began development immediately no 'significant' RDV would accrue to him (ie that the price paid reflects the full development value of the land; 'significant' is not defined). If he obtains a clearance and begins the development within three years of the acquisition, he is not liable for DLT on the development (although he must inform the Revenue of its start). The exemption does not apply if land is actually disposed of (ie sold or leased) rather than developed.

If clearance is refused, and the developer wishes to allow for his potential DLT liability he can take advantage of the advance assessment scheme under FA 1980 s 114 (see p 430).

> **EXAMPLE 6**
>
> de Grand owns the unoccupied family mansion, 'Pyles'. He obtains planning permission to demolish the house and to erect 44 dwellings on the site. The DLT position is as follows:
> (1) If de Grand carries out the development, there will be a deemed disposal for DLT purposes when a project of material development begins.
> (2) If he sells the land to a developer, a portion of the gain realised on that actual disposal may be subject to DLT. The builder will be exempt from charge so long as he obtains clearance and begins development within three years of acquiring the land (see DLTA 1976 s 18).

b) *Enterprise zones* (FA 1980 s 110)

Any RDV occurring on a disposal of land within an enterprise zone is exempt from DLT provided that the disposal occurs within ten years of the land being included in the zone.

c) *Minerals* (DLTA 1976 s 17)

If the owner of land works minerals on or under his land he is exempt from DLT on any RDV attributable to the mineral operations.

On a sale of the land with planning permission to work the minerals, the consideration received is reduced by half of the excess over the market value of the land if sold without planning permission. Similar relief is given on the grant of a lease, the consideration being taken as the market value of the same lease, but without the right to work minerals. Any part of the consideration for a lease which represents mineral royalties is exempt from DLT if it is taxed under FA 1970 s 29.

5 Relief by a deferral of tax

To encourage certain types of development a developer may defer DLT until an actual disposal (eg sale or lease) whereupon the deferred tax becomes payable (together with any DLT thus arising) unless the actual disposal occurs more than 12 years after the deemed disposal in b) below, in which case the deferred liability is extinguished (FA 1984 s 119).

a) *Development for industrial use* (DLTA 1976 s 19)

DLT liability that arises on a deemed disposal as a result of a development for industrial use by a trader who carries out the work for the purposes of his trade, may be deferred.

Industrial purposes comprise manufacturing and processing, but not commercial activities, nor the provision of storage facilities unless incidental to manufacture. Development for employees' welfare (excluding the provision of dwelling-houses) qualifies for the relief.

The deferred liability is triggered if the owner actually disposes of the land or ceases to use it for his trade (or ceases to trade). It is not, however, triggered by a sale (or lease) and lease-back; nor by a transfer within a 75% group; nor by a disposal which is part of a group reconstruction; nor where further development is carried out.

b) *Development for own use* (DLTA 1976 s 19A; FA 1981 s 132)

DLT liability which arises on the development after 9 March 1981 of a non-industrial building for the owner's own use and occupation may be deferred provided that the development is of land or buildings used and occupied wholly or in part by the owner (and not, eg, by his family only) or, if he is a company, by another company in the same group; and that planning permission is obtained before the project is begun.

The liability is not triggered by a temporary letting (a lease for twelve months or less) nor by further development, nor by a disposal within a group of companies.

c) *Statutory undertakers* (DLTA 1976 s 23)

On development carried out by statutory undertakers (eg The British Steel Corporation) any DLT liability may be deferred as in (a) above.

VI SPECIAL KINDS OF TAXPAYER

1 Partnerships (DLTA 1976 s 31)

On disposal of land held as a partnership asset to an outsider, any DLT liability is assessed on the individual partners according to their share in the ownership of the assets. For disposals of partnership assets, the partners constitute a single person with only one annual exemption between them. For non-partnership assets each partner will also have an exemption available.

The Revenue practice for CGT will be followed wherever possible for DLT (see Chapter 29). Thus, a partner who reduces his asset-surplus sharing ratio (for instance on the introduction of a new partner) is treated as disposing of part or all of his share in each of the partnership assets which may include land and, hence, may result in a liability to DLT. However, on such a part disposal, the part disposal formula is not applied for calculating any RDV; instead, each item relevant to the calculation is determined on a fractional basis.

2 **Companies**

A company is liable to DLT in the normal way, except that the concept of disposal is extended in two circumstances. First, a distribution *in specie* by a company or by the liquidator, is deemed to be a disposal by the company at market value (DLTA 1976 Sch 2 para 31). Secondly, where a company disposes of land to another company in the same group which is resident in the UK and is not an exempt body, the transferee company acquires the land at the transferor company's base value so that there is no liability to DLT (DLTA 1976 s 20). However, if the transferee company leaves the group within 6 years from that acquisition it is treated as making a deemed disposal of the land at its current market value and is charged to DLT accordingly (DLTA 1976 s 21 cp TA 1970 s 278: p 407).

3 **Trusts**

Where property is held on trust for a person or persons who are absolutely entitled to the property as against the trustees (including co-owners under a trust for sale of land), or who would be so entitled, but for infancy or other disability, the property is not treated as settled property for DLT (DLTA 1976 s 28 and see Chapter 18). In *IRC v Matthew's Executors* (1984) it was held that, because of the terms of the will trust, a purported appropriation of the land to the beneficiaries was of no effect, so that immediately before the disposal the land was settled.

a) *Bare trusts* (DLTA 1976 ss 28, 29)

The creation of the trust is treated as a gift to the beneficiary who, therefore, acquires the property at the settlor's base value. Any actual disposals by the trustees are treated as those of the beneficiary, each of whom (should there be more than one) is entitled to a separate annual exemption. Transfers between the trustees and the beneficiary are ignored.

The interest of a beneficiary under a bare trust is not a major interest in land for DLT. Therefore, on a deemed disposal arising when the trust property is developed, the only interest disposed of is the legal estate held by the trustees (which is valued free from the interests of the beneficiaries). Any resulting DLT liability is chargeable to the beneficiary in the usual way and, where there is more than one, each should be entitled to utilise his annual exemption despite the Revenue allowing only the one exemption for the trustees.

Where a sole beneficiary disposes of his beneficial interest under the trust, this is treated as a disposal of the legal estate and his base value is calculated accordingly (DLTA 1976 s 29). If only part of the trust property consists of land, for the purpose of calculating the RDV, the consideration that he receives is reduced by the proportion that the value of the interest in land bears to the value of the rest of the trust property at the time of the disposal.

When there is more than one beneficiary, the base value of the beneficiary who disposes of his beneficial interest is calculated by reducing all the relevant items (eg cost) by the fraction that the market value of his interest bears to the market value of all the beneficial interests under the trust, including his own. However, where one beneficiary has acquired the interest of another beneficiary, on a subsequent disposal of it he can substitute the price he paid for it or (if nothing) the transferor's acquisition cost instead of using the above formula.

EXAMPLE 7

A, B and C are tenants in common who purchased land for £6,000. A buys C's interest for £10,000. On a subsequent sale of that one-third share, A's acquisition cost is taken as £10,000.

If A and B later sell the land for £30,000 so that A receives £20,000 and B £10,000, A's acquisition cost for the one-third share that he acquired from C is £10,000 and for the other one-third share is £2,000 (one-third of £6,000).

b) *Settled property* (DLTA 1976 s 30)

Settled property is defined as an interest in land held on a trust that is not a bare trust. The land may be held under either a trust for sale or under a strict settlement within the Settled Land Act 1925.

The creation of a settlement is treated as a gift and either the trustees of the settlement or, if the land is 'settled land', the life tenant or other estate owner who holds the legal estate, acquires the land at the settlor's base value. The trustees or life tenant are treated as one single continuing body with one annual exemption.

Any transfer by a trustee to a beneficiary is treated as a gift. A disposal by the beneficiary of his beneficial interest under the settlement creates no DLT liability, because the interest is not an interest in land.

Trustees only have one annual exemption between them which is not available for any disposal within one year of the creation of the settlement (because this is a gift from a connected person). Further, if the creation of the settlement involved a part disposal, there will be no annual exemption for six years (DLTA 1976 s 12(5)).

Trustees may discharge their DLT liability (excluding interest on overdue tax), out of the capital of the fund, or they may raise a mortgage on the property (DLTA 1976 s 43). If the trustees fail to pay the DLT within six months of the disposal any beneficiary who receives the sale proceeds can be assessed to any of the tax within two years after the date it became payable. If he received only a part of the sale proceeds, he is liable for a proportionate part of the tax (DLTA 1976 Sch 8 para 55 and notice that the same rule applies to PRs who distribute sale proceeds to legatees).

When a beneficiary becomes absolutely entitled to the property (so that a bare trust results) this is treated as a disposal and reacquisition by the trustees and the beneficiary takes over the trustees' base value (DLTA 1976 s 28(2)).

4 **Mortgages** (DLTA 1976 s 32)

A mortgagee does not have an interest in land for DLT purposes. Any action taken by him in relation to the land to enforce his security is taken as bare trustee for the legal owner so that if he sells the land, the owner is liable for any DLT. The aquisition of the legal estate in the land by foreclosure is treated as a disposal by the owner and an acquisition by the mortgagee for a consideration equal to the outstanding loan, interest and costs (DLTA 1976 s 32(3)).

VII INTERACTION OF DLT WITH OTHER TAXES

The disposal of an interest in land may create a liability not only to DLT but to other taxes. To CGT if the land is held as an investment; to income (or corporation) tax where it is held as trading stock; or to income tax under TA

1970 ss 80–82 or 488. Additionally, an earlier gift of the land may have resulted in a CTT and/or CGT liability.

The basic rule is that any profit chargeable to DLT should not be charged to any other tax. Thus, the complex provisions of DLTA 1976 Sch 6 aim to ensure that DLT takes priority over any other tax on the same disposal, and that the same development gain is never taxed twice.

Double taxation is prevented by three basic principles. First, where there is a contemporaneous liability to DLT and to either CGT, corporation tax or income tax, the amount charged to DLT is deducted from the amount charged to any of the other taxes. When the DLT liability arises within 12 years after a charge to CGT, corporation tax or income tax on the same interest in land (for instance on a gift or appropriation to or from stock-in-trade) credit is given for those taxes in calculating the DLT liability.

Secondly, if a liability to DLT arises within 12 years of a chargeable transfer for CTT, a deduction is made from the RDV equal to the CTT that was charged on the development value.

Thirdly, in applying the above reliefs, DLTA 1976 s 34(7) allows a person who is chargeable to DLT, but who acquired the land for no consideration (eg by gift) to claim relief for other taxes paid by the person from whom he acquired it.

EXAMPLE 8

Jack gives land to John who in turn gives it to Jim who finally sells it realising development value. Jim has a credit against his DLT liability for part of any CGT paid by Jack or John and can deduct a part of any CTT paid by either of them.

It is not intended to discuss these reliefs in detail. Notice, however, two further points: first, where the amount charged to DLT is deducted from a premium chargeable to income tax under TA 1970 ss 80, 82, this deduction is ignored when calculating both the amount of the gain chargeable to CGT and the relief for lessees under TA 1970 ss 83, 134. Secondly, DLTA 1976 Sch 6 does not deal with the case where the disposal attracts both DLT and income tax under TA 1970 s 488 as an artificial transaction in land. In practice, however, the amount chargeable to DLT is deductible from the chargeable gain under s 488.

VIII   ADMINISTRATION, NOTIFICATION AND PAYMENT

1   Administration

DLT is under the care and control of the Revenue and its administration is governed by the TMA 1970 as amended by DLTA 1976 Sch 8. Assessments are made by the Board, not by inspectors, and appeal lies to the Special Commissioners, except where the only point at issue concerns the exemption for private residences or dwelling-houses built for owner-occupation, when it lies to the General Commissioners.

2   Notification

The taxpayer has a duty in certain circumstances to notify the central DLT office in Middlesborough of the disposal of an interest in land to enable them to assess any DLT liability.

First, on an actual disposal or part-disposal of an interest in land where the consideration exceeds £75,000 and the taxpayer realises development value, he must inform the Revenue within one year of the disposal (DLTA 1976 Sch 8 para 35). If the disposal has resulted in a document requiring a 'Particulars Delivered' (PD) Stamp, notification is theoretically unnecessary. In practice, however, because of the date from which interest on unpaid DLT begins to run, the taxpayer should not rely on this procedure, but should inform the Revenue as soon as possible that a disposal has taken place.

Any person with a major interest in land who begins (or causes or allows someone to begin) a project of material development should ensure that the Revenue are notified within 60 days before and 30 days after the project is begun (DLTA 1976 Sch 8 para 36).

Apart from these specific circumstances, a taxpayer must give notice (within 12 months after it has occurred) of any disposal which has triggered a DLT liability (DLTA 1976 Sch 8 para 38).

For administrative reasons, this does not apply to a sale of a dwelling-house on land not exceeding one acre for a consideration not exceeding £25,000; nor to any disposal for a consideration not exceeding £75,000 which is the taxpayer's only disposal in the financial year.

Any event which triggers a deferred DLT liability must be notified within 12 months of its occurrence.

Finally, the Revenue have power to obtain information from any person whom they believe to hold or have held an interest in land on which development value has been realised.

3 **Payment**

a) *General*

DLT is payable by the later of either three months after the date of an actual disposal (date of contract), or a deemed disposal, or other event which triggers the deferred charge; or 30 days after the issue of a notice of assessment. Interest runs at 8% pa on any DLT unpaid after that date.

On the occasion of a deemed disposal; or the grant of a lease for a rent not exceeding a commercial rent; or where deferred DLT is triggered by an event other than an actual disposal, the taxpayer can elect to pay the tax in ten yearly instalments. In the case of a deemed disposal not covered by the advance assessment provisions, the first instalment is due within two years of the date of disposal; otherwise it is due 12 months after the date of the disposal or other triggering event (DLTA 1976 Sch 8 paras 44–51).

Interest runs at 8% pa on overdue instalments. If the consideration for the disposal is payable in instalments over a period of more than 18 months from the date of the event triggering the liability, DLT can be paid in instalments in cases of undue hardship. The period and the amount of the instalments are at the Revenue's discretion.

In all cases of payment by instalments, the balance of the tax can be paid off at any time and must be paid off on an actual disposal of the interest.

When a business is sold to a company wholly or partly in return for shares, and the assets include land, DLT may, in certain circumstances, be postponed. On a subsequent sale of the land or the shares, the postponed DLT will become payable (DLTA 1976 Sch 8 para 52).

When DLT which is charged on PRs or trustees is not paid within 6 months of the due date, a legatee or beneficiary who has received part of the estate or trust property, may be charged with an appropriate part of the unpaid tax (DLTA 1976 Sch 8 para 55).

Any DLT unpaid by a member of a company in a group may be recovered from another member in the group who, in turn, has a right of recovery against certain other members (DLTA 1976 Sch 8 para 56).

There is no clearance procedure for DLT except under the advance assessment scheme.

b) *Deduction at source: disposals by non-residents* (DLTA 1976 s 40)

To ensure that DLT due from a non-resident person on a disposal of land owned by him in the UK is paid, any person to whom the disposal is made may be required to deduct from the consideration paid a sum on account of the presumed DLT liability and account for it to the Revenue.

The amount of the deduction is 40% of the consideration on a disposal after 5 August 1984 by a non-resident vendor of any land (not just development land) in the UK. There is no such obligation in the following circumstances:

(1) Where for disposals after 31 March 1984 the consideration does not exceed £75,000 or the amount payable within seven years after the disposal does not exceed £75,000.
(2) From any payment of rent where basic rate income tax is deducted under TA 1970 s 89.
(3) From any instalment due more than eight years after the disposal.
(4) Where the purchase is of a dwelling-house and the consideration does not exceed £150,000.
(5) On payment of a deposit not exceeding 10% of the consideration.
(6) Where the Revenue have authorised the purchaser to make a smaller or no deduction.

A purchaser should be aware of these provisions because he will be liable to the Revenue for tax that he should have deducted unless he can show that after taking reasonable steps to establish the position, he failed to make the deduction in the belief that the vendor's usual place of abode was in the UK. To this extent, a purchaser may rely on the answer to a preliminary enquiry concerning the whereabouts of the vendor's home (see, for example, *Oyez Form of Enquiries Before Contract:* No 14), unless he knows differently; the vendor is a foreign company (apparent from its name); or subsequent information casts doubt on the original answer.

A mortgagee should note that the obligation to deduct applies even if the balance of the consideration is insufficient to redeem the mortgage, or if the mortgagee is selling under the exercise of a power of sale. Also, if the deduction proves to be an over-deduction, the mortgagee may still not recover his money because the Revenue will account for it to the mortgagor. Solicitors should be aware that under TMA 1970 s 85A, an agent can be assessed and charged to tax in the name of a non-resident. In practice this problem will not arise for domestic conveyances unless the purchase price exceeds £150,000.

An overseas vendor and a mortgagee exercising a power of sale may, however, apply to the Revenue for them to direct the purchaser either to make no DLT deduction or to make a deduction of more or less than 40% of the consideration. Full details of his base value and the name and address of agents acting for both parties must be supplied.

31 Stamp duty and capital duty

'The law upon the subject of stamps is altogether a matter *positivi juris*. It involves nothing of principle or reason but depends altogether upon the language of the legislature.' (Taunton J in *Morley v Hall* (1834)).

I   INTRODUCTION

The first stamp duties were introduced in 1694 during the reign of William and Mary and have since remained a permanent feature of the fiscal landscape. The present system of stamp duties depends primarily upon SA 1891 and Stamp Duties Management Act 1891 although later Finance Acts effected major changes. FA 1973 introduced capital duty as the first stage in the harmonisation of taxes on company capital in the EEC (see V below).

In 1983 the government issued a consultative document entitled 'The Scope for Reforming Stamp Duties'. Such reform is long overdue and there is much dead wood that could profitably be removed. One difficulty with stamp duty is that, although originally levied exclusively on documents and not transactions, the growth of charges to, and exemptions and reliefs from duty, have eroded its originally simple structure. Further, capital duty is now a charge on 'chargeable transactions', although the duty is collected on a statement of particulars.

Stamp duty is conceptually straightforward. It is levied upon any 'instrument' (the term includes 'every written document') which falls within one of the 'Heads of Charge' and is not covered by an exemption. Thus, if a transaction can be effected without a written instrument, duty will be avoided.

EXAMPLE 1

Alonzo executes a deed of gift by which he transfers his ancient grandfather clock to his son Bonzo. Stamp duty will be charged upon the deed. As chattels can be transferred by simple delivery, Alonzo would have avoided duty if he had merely handed the clock to Bonzo.

The amount of duty to be paid depends upon each individual head of charge but the sum will be either a fixed duty of 50p or an ad valorem duty which will be calculated (usually) by reference to the value of the transaction recorded in the instrument.

II   ENFORCEMENT AND ADMINISTRATION

The legislation does not directly state who is to be accountable for the duty. The main sanction for non-payment is that, unless properly stamped, no document executed in the UK or relating to any property that is situated in the UK, will be admissible in evidence in any civil proceedings (SA 1891 s 14(1) and see *Fengl v Fengl* (1914)). Unstamped documents are admissible in criminal proceedings; failure to stamp does not involve any criminal liability; and an agreement between the parties not to stamp the instrument does not amount to a criminal conspiracy. In some cases fines are imposed for offences in relation to stamp duty.

Technically an instrument should be stamped before execution. In practice, however, the Revenue permit stamping within 30 days after execution without imposing any penalty. Late stamping is permitted subject to the payment of a penalty of £10 and, where the duty exceeds £10, interest at 5% pa from the date of execution up to a maximum of the unpaid duty. In certain cases, the legislation names the person who is liable for the penalty—in the case of a conveyance or sale it is the transferee or purchaser (SA 1891 s 15(2)); in the case of voluntary dispositions it is the grantor or transferor (SA 1891 s 15(2); F (1909–10) A 1910 s 74(3)).

The administration of stamp duty is under the Commissioners of Inland Revenue but the day to day work of administration is carried out, in England and Wales, by the Controller of Stamps, and, in Scotland, by the Controller (Stamps) Scotland. In the event of a dispute there will normally be an adjudication followed by the stating of a case by the commissioners with a hearing in the Chancery Division of the High Court. There is a right of appeal to the Court of Appeal and, ultimately, to the House of Lords.

If required to do so the commissioners must state whether, in their opinion, any executed instrument is subject to a stamp duty charge and if so must state the amount of duty chargeable (SA 1891 s 12). Adjudication may be voluntary, in which case the individual will be asking the commissioners to confirm that no duty is payable on the instrument, or, alternatively, to ascertain the correct duty to be paid. In many cases, however, the Stamp Act makes adjudication compulsory to ensure that the correct amount of duty is paid (eg for voluntary dispositions: (F (1909–10)A 1910 s 74)). Such instruments are deemed not to have been properly stamped unless adjudicated and bear a stamp to that effect. The other cases where adjudication is compulsory generally concern instruments on which an exemption is claimed. Orders made by the court under the Variation of Trusts Act, 1958 also require adjudication (see Practice Note [1966] 1 All ER 672).

The process of adjudication is an essential step in the appeals procedure and it also provides the best means by which a third party can be satisfied as to the correctness of the stamp duty paid.

In three cases instruments must be produced to the commissioners. In general, production should be within 30 days of execution and the obligation lies upon the transferee or lessee. Such instruments will then be impressed with a produced stamp (a 'PD' stamp) which is quite independent of any stamp denoting duty or any adjudication stamp. Penalties for failure to produce are the same as those which apply on failure to stamp. Such instruments are:

(1) A transfer on sale of a fee simple of land.
(2) A lease (or agreement for a lease) of land for a term of seven years or more.
(3) A transfer on sale of a lease as in (2) (FA 1931 s 28 Sch 2).

These provisions furnish district valuers with information on land values. Originally the information was necessary for the assessment of the land tax imposed by FA 1931. With the abolition of that tax in 1934 the provisions were left unrepealed since they are useful to valuers in assessing compensation claims upon compulsory purchase.

III THE OCCASIONS OF CHARGE

For an instrument to be chargeable to stamp duty it must fall within one of the heads of charge. If it falls within more than one head, the Revenue, although only entitled to one of the duties, can choose the head that will produce the higher duty (*Speyer Bros v IRC* (1908)). Where several instruments are employed to carry out the same transaction, it is only the principal instrument of conveyance that is charged to ad valorem duty. The other instruments can only be charged with such other duty as is appropriate and which cannot exceed the ad valorem duty payable in respect of the principal instrument (SA 1891 s 58(3)).

EXAMPLE 2

Senson creates a strict settlement of land under the terms of the Settled Land Act, 1925. He, therefore, executes a vesting deed and a trust instrument. The trust instrument transferring the beneficial title is chargeable with ad valorem duty and the vesting deed which transfers the bare legal estate with a fixed duty of 50p only.

1 **Conveyance or transfer** (SA 1891 Sch 1)

This head of charge covers the conveyance or transfer on sale of any property and the duty charged is ad valorem at a rate for shares and securities of 50p per £50 or part thereof, or, if the consideration exceeds £500, £1 per £100 or part thereof (ie 1%). For other property the rate is 1% unless the consideration does not exceed £30,000 and the instrument contains a certificate of value, when the duty is nil. The certificate must state that the transaction effected by the instrument does not form part of a larger transaction or series of transactions in respect of which the amount or value or aggregate amount or value of the consideration exceeds £30,000. Little guidance is given as to the meaning of 'a series of transactions'. Take, for instance, the sale of four properties from A to B each for £30,000. Assuming that there are four separate transactions none would attract duty. Treated as one transaction, however, duty at 1% is charged. If the transactions are simultaneous they must amount to a single operation; even if not, such a series of conveyances has all the hallmarks of an associated operation (a similar inference will not be drawn for a series of gifts; see *AG v Cohen* (1937) but *quaere* the effect of the *Ramsay* principle: see further Appendix V).

The nil rate is not operated on the 'slice system' so that once the consideration exceeds £30,000, it is all taxed at 1%. The nil rate cannot be used on instruments which transfer shares and other marketable securities (FA 1963 s 55(2)), presumably because larger transactions could easily be split into £30,000 slices.

a) *Sales*

Although 'sale' is not defined, there will need to be a vendor, a purchaser, and normally a money consideration. Duty is charged on the amount or value of the consideration and where it is in sterling, there will be no problem. If the consideration is in foreign currencies, prescribed rates specify the sterling equivalent (FA 1899 s 12). Special provisions operate where the consideration is to be paid over a number of years (SA 1891 s 56). First, where the payments are for a definite period not exceeding 20 years the charge is on the total of all those payments (SA 1891 s 56(1)). Secondly, if the payments are to last in perpetuity; or for a period exceeding 20 years; or for a period of indefinite length which is not terminable on death, the charge is on the amount payable during 20 years starting with the date of the sale (SA 1891 s 56(2)). For a discussion of the meaning of 'a payment for a period' see *Blendett Ltd v IRC* (1983) and *Quietlece Ltd v IRC* (1984). Thirdly, if the payments are to last during a life or lives, duty is charged on the total amount payable during the 12 years from the date of the instrument. The payer's age is irrelevant (SA 1891 s 56(3)).

EXAMPLE 3

(1) If the consideration is £10,000 pa payable for eight years, duty will be charged on £80,000 (SA 1891 s 56(1)).
(2) If the consideration is £10,000 pa payable so long as the recipient lives in London, duty will be charged on £10,000 × 20 = £200,000 (SA 1891 s 56(2)).
(3) £10,000 pa is payable during the life of the payer. Duty is charged on £10,000 × 12 = £120,000 (SA 189 s 56(3)).

These rules for instalment payments apply only to periodic payments which are new requirements and part of the bargain for sale; they do not apply to payments which are naturally a part of the property sold (as, for instance, a payment of rent on the creation of a lease).

Although the consideration for a sale will normally be money, for stamp duty purposes stock or marketable securities and debts and other liabilities are treated as sale consideration (SA 1891 s 55, s 57).

EXAMPLE 4

(1) Julie sells her house to Samantha for £20,000. In addition Samantha agrees to repay Julie's overdraft of £10,000. The consideration furnished for stamp duty will be £20,000 + £10,000 = £30,000.
(2) Julie sells her lease to Jane in consideration for the transfer of 100 £1 shares in F Ltd. The consideration for stamp duty will be the shares. Generally, the shares will be valued in accordance with the procedure adopted for CGT (see CGTA 1979 s 150 and SP 18/80). Although the shares constitute the consideration for the conveyance of the house, the converse is not the case so that the transfer of the shares themselves will attract only 50p duty.

If consideration other than money, shares or the assumption of liabilities is furnished, the transaction will not be treated as a sale for stamp duty purposes. In *Littlewoods Mail Order Stores Ltd v IRC* (1962), for instance, the exchange of a freehold reversion for a leasehold interest in the same property was not treated as the sale of the freehold in exchange for the rent reserved by the lease.

Certain assents may be treated as sales: eg the satisfaction of a pecuniary legacy by the transfer of property with the consent of that legatee (see *Jopling v IRC* (1940)) and an assent to vest property agreed to be sold by the deceased (*GHR Co v IRC* (1943)). Wills commonly provide that PRs may appropriate assets without the consent of the beneficiary so that there is no sale and therefore no duty. Other assents will normally be liable to no duty or to 50p duty if under seal. Property specifically left to a beneficiary under a will is not subject to ad valorem duty when it is transferred to that person nor is property appropriated to a surviving spouse in accordance with the intestacy rules.

On the dissolution of a partnership, the division of the assets between the partners will not be treated as a sale (*MacLeod v IRC* (1885)) but, if an outgoing partner is 'bought out', the instrument effecting that arrangement will be a sale (*Garnett v IRC* (1899)).

EXAMPLE 5

Dave joins the partnership of Bob, Mick & Tom. He contributes capital of £10,000. This by itself will not amount to a sale. If, however, he pays the money to the other partners, the deed or instrument of partnership will be charged as a conveyance or transfer on sale.

It is important to distinguish sales and exchanges. There is a specific head of charge in the Stamp Act for exchanges which applies to exchanges of real or heritable property (SA 1891 s 73 Sch 1; see p 455).

EXAMPLE 6

(1) A exchanges 10 shares in Zee Ltd for B's 10 shares in Aah Ltd. This is a sale (*Chesterfield Brewery Co v IRC* (1899)).
(2) A exchanges Blackacre for Whiteacre which was owned by B. This is an exchange.

b) *Sub-sales*

A purchaser who resells land before it is transferred to him can avoid stamp duty by ensuring that it is transferred directly to a sub-purchaser. The duty is calculated on the sub-sale consideration (SA 1891 s 58(4)(5)).

EXAMPLE 7

Selina agrees to purchase Redmeadow from Angela for £40,000. She immediately agrees to resell Redmeadow to Anna for £50,000 and arranges for Angela to convey Redmeadow directly to Anna. Duty will be assessed on Anna on £50,000. No duty will be charged on Selina.

Instead of the sale of all of Redmeadow to Anna, assume that only one-quarter is resold to her for £12,500. The one-quarter sold to Anna is conveyed directly to her by Angela; the rest is conveyed to Selina. Duty would be charged:
(1) *On Anna* on £12,500 at nil rate.
(2) *On Selina* on three-quarters of her consideration (ie on £30,000). It forms part of a transaction for which the consideration exceeds £30,000 so that the nil rate does not apply.

Note that a partial resale to a connected person would not save any duty, as the operation would probably be treated as a series of transactions.

In order to counter a stamp duty avoidance scheme on the sale of land, s 58(4) and (5) do not apply in respect of sub-sale contracts made after 19 March 1984 where the sub-sale consideration is less than the value of the property immediately before the sub-sale (FA 1984 s 112). In such a case duty is calculated according to F (1909–10) A 1910 s 74 (below). Even before the introduction of this anti-avoidance legislation, the Revenue had begun to challenge the efficacy of this and similar schemes (see also p 454) under the *Ramsey* principle (Chapter 32 and Appendix V).

c) *'Leaving the matter in contract'*

Stamp duty is often avoided by agreeing to transfer the asset and then failing to execute the formal transfer. The contract itself will not normally be subject to duty but as the contract may be specifically enforceable (as in the case of land) the purchaser will become the equitable owner of the property by virtue of that agreement. The contract must contemplate that the transaction will be completed. Notice, however, that any attempt to transfer the full legal title (or to recite that the purchaser is the owner of the property) will be subject to duty at the full rate (see, eg, *Oughtred v IRC* (1960)).

d) *Conveyance or transfer not on sale*

In the case of conveyances or transfers not on sale the duty is fixed at 50p. This will include decrees or orders of the court or commissioners whereby property is transferred or vested in any person (SA 1891 s 62). It does not apply to voluntary dispositions. Typical instances of such conveyances are transfers where no beneficial interest passes (as for instance on the appointment of a new trustee); a distribution of assets by the liquidator to shareholders in satisfaction of their rights on a winding up; transfers to a beneficiary under a will; and a distribution of trust funds to beneficiaries.

2   Voluntary dispositions

A voluntary disposition was originally subject to fixed duty as a conveyance or transfer not on sale. F(1909–10)A 1910 s 74, however, provided for a charge to ad valorem duty on the value of the property transferred by a voluntary disposition 'as if' it was a conveyance or transfer on sale. This is, therefore, not strictly a separate head of charge and the rate of charge is as for a conveyance on sale. Accordingly, where the value of the property does not exceed £30,000 and the instrument contains a certificate of value, the nil rate applies. An adjudication stamp is required for all voluntary dispositions.

a) *Valuation*

No specific method of valuation is laid down in the stamp duty legislation. In practice, duty is calculated on the open market value of the property transferred (*Stanyforth v IRC* (1930)). It was possible to depress artificially the value of the property by including a power to revoke the transfer; this power could subsequently be released. FA 1965 s 90 prevented this scheme by providing that the value should not take into account such a revocable power. If such a power is exercised within two years, a claim may be made to the commissioners and duty will be refunded (FA 1965 s 90(5)).

Where property is conveyed subject to a mortgage the valuation of that conveyance will depend upon whether or not the purchaser has agreed to discharge the mortgage liability.

EXAMPLE 8

(1) Titan gives his house worth £100,000 to his son Titus. Titan is to discharge the outstanding mortgage on the property of £55,000 in favour of the Rookyu

Building Society. Ad valorem duty will be charged on the value of the property after deducting the mortgage debt. Hence, the assessment will be on £100,000 – £55,000 = £45,000 (ie the value of the equity of redemption).

(2) If Titus agrees to take over liability for the mortgage debt, stamp duty will be charged on the higher of a conveyance or transfer on sale in consideration of the mortgage debt (ie £55,000) and a voluntary disposition of the equity of redemption (ie £45,000).

b) *Meaning of 'voluntary disposition'*

In general a voluntary disposition is defined as a conveyance or transfer other than a disposition in favour of a purchaser or other person in good faith and for valuable consideration. Consideration will not be valuable if the commissioners are of the opinion that a substantial benefit has been conferred upon the transferee (see F(1909–10)A 1910 s 74(5); for a discussion of how this objective test is applied by the commissioners see the decisions of *Baker v IRC* (1923); *Lap Shun Textiles Industrial Co Ltd v Collector of Stamp Revenue* (1976); and *Thorn v IRC* (1976)). A 'bad bargain' can be subject to such treatment. The question for the commissioners is not whether a substantial benefit was intentionally conferred upon the transferee but is merely whether that was the consequence of the conveyance.

A disposition made in consideration of marriage is excluded from the charge on voluntary dispositions so long as the gift satisfies the requirements laid down for CTT relief for gifts on marriage (see FA 1975 Sch 6 para 6; Chapter 23). Unlike CTT, there is no financial limit for stamp duty relief.

EXAMPLE 9

(1) Junius conveys his house to his son Brutus for £20,000. There is evidence that the open market value of the property is £35,000. Ad valorem duty on a voluntary conveyance of £35,000 will be charged.

(2) In consideration of her daughter Amanda marrying Archibald, Clarissa executes a settlement of shares in Clarissa Launderwear Ltd worth £100,000. The beneficiaries under the settlement are to be Amanda, Archibald and any issue of the marriage.

For CTT purposes: there is a £5,000 marriage exemption available and Clarissa might have £6,000 annual exemption relief available. The remaining value transferred will be subject to CTT at the inter vivos rates.

For stamp duty: there will be no ad valorem duty although the deed will attract the fixed 50p charge.

A declaration of trust   Trusts may be created by self-declaration or by transferring the property to trustees to hold for the intended beneficiaries. In both cases there will have been a voluntary disposition so that any instrument in writing will be charged to ad valorem duty. If, however, the self-declaration is oral, no stamp duty is charged.

Orders under the Variation of Trusts Act 1958   A scheme whereby property is to be held on trusts for different beneficiaries will normally incur ad valorem duty.

Variations of dispositions of a deceased   Disclaimers and variations are discussed for CGT and CTT purposes in Chapters 15 and 22. A variation will be subject to stamp duty as a voluntary disposition (and the instrument of variation will, therefore, require adjudication) whereas a disclaimer, a refusal of property, will only be subject to the fixed 50p duty applicable to deeds (*Re Stratton's Disclaimer* (1958)).

A release of a life interest under a settlement   Ad valorem duty is charged on the release of a life interest valued on an actuarial basis (see *Platt's Trustees v IRC* (1953)). No duty is, however, chargeable on advancements of capital by the trustees of the settlement; under the Trustee Act 1925 s 32, they can advance up to half of the remainderman's prospective share and, in practice, they are often given an express power to advance his entire beneficial interest. In this way, the whole life interest could, in effect, be released without any charge to stamp duty.

3   Leases and agreements for leases

Duty is levied in accordance with SA 1891 Sch 1 on the grant of a lease or tack (tack is the Scottish equivalent of lease). To be dutiable the lease must be of land, tenements or heritable subjects; leases of personalty are not included. Likewise, duty is not charged on licences which do not confer exclusive possession of the property.

Stamp duty is charged on both the rent and the premium reserved in a lease. The premium is charged in the same way as if it were the consideration for a sale. Duty is, therefore, ad valorem unless the nil rate band applies which it does not if any associated rent payable under the lease averages more than £300 pa. Duty on the rent depends upon the average rent and the term of the lease. In the case of a lease for an uncertain rent or no rent or premium there is a fixed duty of £2. A lease may, however, operate as a voluntary disposition if granted on terms beneficial to the lessee; ad valorem duty would then be charged (*IRC v Littlewoods Mail Order Stores Ltd* (1962)). Leases to charities executed on or after 22 March 1982 are exempt from duty (FA 1982 s 129).

A lease or agreement for a lease for seven years or more must also be produced and stamped with a produced stamp (see p 446).

In general fixed duties are charged on short term leases at low rents and ad valorem duty on leases for more than a year and on periodic tenancies. The duty on rent is as follows:

Lease for a definite term of less than one year   In the case of a furnished letting for a definite term of less than one year there is no duty if the rent is below £500 pa; if it exceeds £500 pa, duty of £1 is payable. In other cases duty is charged as if the lease were a lease for one year at the actual rent reserved.

Leases for a definite term of at least one year or for an indefinite term

Term not exceeding 7 years or indefinite	
rent not exceeding £500 pa	nil
rent exceeding £500 pa	50p duty per £50 or part thereof (1%)
Term exceeding 7 years but not 35 years	£1 per £50 or part thereof (2%)
Term exceeding 35 years but not 100 years	£6 per £50 or part thereof (12%)
Term exceeding 100 years	£12 per £50 or part thereof (24%)

For leases exceeding seven years, duty on rent is charged at a sliding scale if the rent does not exceed £500 pa (for details see FA 1982 s 128(3)).

As mentioned above where all or a part of the consideration for a lease for a definite term in excess of one year, or for an indefinite term, is money or stock or security, duty is charged on the value of that consideration at the rates which apply to a conveyance or transfer on sale. Ad valorem duty will, therefore, be charged although the nil rate band will apply (if a certificate of value is included in the lease) unless the rent exceeds £300 pa.

EXAMPLE 10

Bos grants Big a ten year lease at a rent of £250 pa and a premium of £29,000. As the term exceeds seven years, the normal charge on the rent will be at 1%, but since the rent is below £300 pa a sliding scale will apply (currently duty will be £5). So long as the lease contains a certificate of value, duty will be charged at nil% on the premium of £29,000.

a) *Terminology*

There is no definition of 'rent'. It is in essence a payment reserved out of the land, paid by the tenant to recompense the landlord for loss of exclusive possession. Any service charge reserved in addition to rent is assessed as rent. If that charge is unascertained as where it is a proportion of the costs incurred from time to time, or is dependent upon services provided by the landlord, fixed duty of £2 is payable and the basic rent is subject to ad valorem duty.

If the amount of rent is unascertained but the lease stipulates for a maximum rent, that sum attracts duty. In the absence of a maximum figure, a specified minimum rent or a basic rent which is subject to adjustment could be charged (for this so-called 'contingency principle' see *Coventry City Council v IRC* (1978)). A progressive rent is averaged over the term of a lease.

EXAMPLE 11

Ju grants Dew a ten year lease. For the first five years the rent is £1,000 pa; thereafter £1,500 pa. The average rent (on which duty is assessed) is £1,250 pa. (Duty will be at £1 per £50—ie £25.) Had the lease merely provided for a rent review at the end of five years duty would be charged on the actual rent reserved (£1,000).

The term 'premium' does not appear in the Act which imposes duty on 'consideration, moving either to the lessor or to any other person, consisting of money, stock or security'. It should be noted, therefore, that the premium, if paid to a person other than the landlord, still attracts duty. Where the tenant is obliged under the terms of the lease to carry out improvements either to the property let, or to any other property of the landlord, the value of such works is not subject to stamp duty.

As duty on rent is determined primarily by the duration of the lease, its length must be identified at the date of execution. In general, any part of a term commencing before the date of execution of the lease is ignored (which can have unfortunate results). The following rules apply to ascertain the duration of a lease.

First, a lease for a term of years with an option to renew for a further specified period is subject to duty on the original term. Secondly, on a lease for a fixed term which can thereafter be determined by notice, the term is taken as the length of the fixed term plus the period that must elapse before determination

(FA 1963 s 56(3)). Thirdly, a lease for a specified period which may be terminable on an earlier event occurring is treated as a lease for the specified period and not as a lease for an indefinite period. Fourthly, leases for life or lives or for a term of years determinable on the marriage of the lessee are treated as leases for 90 years in accordance with the LPA 1925 s 149(6).

EXAMPLE 12

(1) A ten year term with an option to renew for a further five years is charged as a ten year lease.

(2) A seven year term is granted which may thereafter be determined on giving six months notice after the expiration of that term. Duty would be assessed on the basis of a lease for seven years six months.

(3) A lease granted for 99 years if A, B and C should live so long is treated as a lease exceeding 35 years and not exceeding 100 (*Earl Mount Edgcumbe v IRC* (1911)).

(4) A 99 year lease begins to run on 29 September 1983, but is only formally executed on 25 March 1984. If the rent charged is £50 pa for the first 33 years; £100 pa for the next 33 years, with £150 pa being charged for the final 33 years, duty will be charged on an average rent of £100.25 pa (ie the average rent taking the length of the lease to be $98\frac{1}{2}$ years). Duty is, therefore, £18 whereas on an average rent of £100 (ie if spread over the actual duration of the 99 year lease) it would have been only £12!

b) *Agreements for a lease*

An agreement for a lease for a term of less than 35 years or for an indefinite term has always been charged as a lease for the term and consideration specified in the agreement (SA 1891 s 75(1)). In order to counter a stamp duty avoidance scheme on the sale of land, FA 1984 s 111 provides that an agreement for a lease for a term exceeding 35 years, and made after 19 March 1984 (and prior thereto not chargeable) will be charged under s 75; the duty paid thereon must be denoted on any conveyance of a freehold or leasehold interest in land against which the agreement is directly enforceable (eg when the agreement is for a sub-lease it need not be denoted on a conveyance of the freehold reversion).

The penalty for not stamping any agreement for a lease made after 19 March 1984 falls on the 'lessee' (SA 1891 s 11). A lease later made to carry out (substantially) the terms of the agreement is chargeable on the difference between the duty paid on the agreement and any duty then payable (SA 1891 s 75(2)).

Notice also that even before FA 1984 the Revenue challenged the effectiveness of these schemes under the *Ramsay* principle (see Chapter 32 and Appendix V).

c) *Surrenders and variations*

When a lease is surrendered, the surrender is subject to duty as a conveyance or transfer on sale on any consideration paid by the landlord. If no consideration is paid, the fixed 50p duty is charged unless the surrender operates as a voluntary disposition inter vivos when ad valorem duty is charged. Where a lease is surrendered and a new lease granted the surrendered lease will attract 50p duty whilst the new lease will be assessed in the usual way.

4   The sale of a business

The practice of 'leaving matters in contract' has already been noted (see p 450). Duty may thereby be avoided on a conveyance of realty so long as the purchaser is prepared to take only an equitable title to the property transferred.

In practice this will often be unacceptable so that a formal transfer will be executed and duty paid. When goodwill and equitable interests are sold, however, the contract will be specifically enforceable and, for practical purposes, there would be no need to execute a formal conveyance or transfer. Duty would, therefore, not be paid on such sales (see *IRC v G Angus & Co* (1889)). To ensure that stamp duty is not so easily avoided SA 1891 s 59 provides that:

'Any contract or agreement for the sale of any equitable estate or interest in any property whatsoever, or for the sale of any estate or interest in any property except lands, tenements, hereditaments, or heritages, or property locally situate out of the United Kingdom, or goods, wares or merchandise, or stock, or marketable securities, or any ship or vessel, or part interest, share, or property of or in any ship or vessel, shall be charged with the same ad valorem duty, to be paid by the purchaser, as if it were an actual conveyance on sale of the estate, interest, or property contracted or agreed to be sold'.

The provision starts by imposing liability to ad valorem duty on all sales but then excludes from its ambit the most common categories of property (eg land and shares) leaving only a residue of assets subject to the duty, principally debts, goodwill, and the benefit of contracts. The asset must be situated in the UK. An agreement for a lease falls outside the section, but an option to purchase a legal interest in land is an equitable interest and, thus, within the charge (*George Wimpey & Co Ltd v IRC* (1975)). If duty is charged under s 59, a subsequent conveyance or transfer of the property is not subject to further ad valorem duty and should be stamped with a denoting stamp (see s 59(3)). In many cases assets of a different character are agreed to be sold for one consideration. For stamp duty purposes an apportionment of that consideration amongst the assets will need to be made on form Stamps 22. Perhaps the most important transaction caught by SA 1891 s 59 is the sale of a business (see further Chapter 34).

5 Exchange or partition (SA 1891 s 73 and Sch 1)

For exchanges or partitions of real or heritable property fixed duty of 50p is charged unless consideration in excess of £100 is given for equality. If so, ad valorem duty is charged on that equality money unless the nil rate applies (SA 1891 s 73 and Sch 1).

For exchanges or partitions of any other property, fixed duty of 50p is charged on a deed or, alternatively, on any document as a miscellaneous conveyance or transfer. If equality money is paid, the transaction may be seen as a sale and ad valorem duty will be payable on the equality money and other consideration within the meaning of SA 1891 ss 55–60 (see p 448).

It should be noted that an exchange of shares is two sales not an exchange (*Chesterfield Brewery Co v IRC* (1899)) and that two agreements for sale for cash effected by deed of exchange are treated as two separate sale contracts (*Portman (Viscount) v IRC* (1956)).

The severance and partition of an equitable joint tenancy in land can be carried out by a notice to sever (LPA 1925 ss 28(3), 36(2)) which must be in writing but will not be subject to duty unless effected by a deed.

EXAMPLE 13

Bee exchanges Readmeadow (worth £40,000) with Boo for Blackacre (worth £25,000) and £15,000 in cash. The equality money is subject to duty but so long as the appropriate certificate of value is included ('not exceeding £30,000') the £15,000 will be charged at the nil rate of duty.

6 Other documents subject to stamp duty

In addition to the occasions of charge already considered, stamp duty is charged on a variety of other documents. Contract notes issued in connection with sales and purchases of stocks and shares are subject to duty on a sliding scale with the maximum duty being 60p payable on values of over £1,500. Duty is generally payable on life insurance policies at the rate of 50p per £1,000 of the sum insured and a $\frac{1}{4}$% ad valorem duty is charged on the value of property put into a unit trust. Finally, there are still some 19 fixed duties, such as the residual 50p duty on deeds not chargeable under any other head.

IV   EXEMPTIONS AND RELIEFS FROM STAMP DUTY

1 General

Exemption from duty is conferred upon a number of documents, in particular:
(1) Wills.
(2) Contracts of employment.
(3) Transfers to a charitable body, charitable trust or to the trustees of the National Heritage Memorial Fund (FA 1982 s 129).
(4) Renounceable letters of allotment (see Chapter 34).
(5) Transfers of gilts and unconvertible loan stock (but including some convertible loan stock; see FA 1976, s 126(2) and SP 3/84).
(6) Mortgages.

It should be noted that no exemption is available for transfers between spouses.

2   Exemptions from stamp duty for companies

a) *Reconstructions or amalgamations* (FA 1927 s 55)

On a company takeover, where the target company's shares are to be acquired in exchange for shares in the purchaser, the transfer of shares in the target company would normally attract conveyance or transfer duty ad valorem on the higher of the value of the shares in the target and the value of the shares in the purchaser; capital duty would also be charged at 1% on (roughly) the same amount in respect of the consideration shares issued by the purchaser.

Relief is available from both duties; for stamp duty it is given by FA 1927 s 55 (as amended) and for capital duty by FA 1973 Sch 19 para 10 (see p 460). The two exemptions are similar but not identical. Detailed requirements have to be satisfied if the stamp duty exemption is to be claimed with the result that the 'pref-trick', or one of the variants thereon, has sometimes been used even where the takeover is effected by a consideration in shares, see further Appendix V.

Relief under s 55 may also be available in cases where the undertaking of an existing company is acquired in return for an issue of shares.

Many traps exist in the application of s 55) in particular: first, there must be a reconstruction or amalgamation. These terms are not defined. 'Reconstruction' appears to be limited to the transfer of the undertaking of one company to another which is to carry on substantially the same business as that transferred to it (see *Brooklands Selangor Holdings Ltd v IRC* (1970); *Baytrust Holdings Ltd v IRC* (1971) and (1972) BTR 226). Secondly, a sale of an undertaking is to be distinguished from a mere sale of assets. Thirdly, it must be a stated object of the increase in authorised share capital and issue of consideration shares that the purpose of that issue is to acquire the undertaking or shares (as the case may be) of the target. Fourthly, there must be actual registration of the target company's shareholders in the purchasing company's share register and these shareholders must receive the consideration shares pro rata to their holdings of shares in the target company. Fifthly, in a share exchange, at least 90% in nominal value of the issued shares in the target must be acquired by the purchaser. Lastly, the consideration must be as to at least 90% shares in the acquiring company; hence, if there is an element of cash or of loan stock in the consideration, relief may be denied and, in share exchanges, if the purchaser has already acquired more than 10% of these shares for cash, relief will be denied (*Lever Bros Ltd v IRC* (1938)). If those shares were first sold to an associate and then repurchased in exchange for shares in the purchaser, along with the rest (or at least 90% of) the target shares the relief should apply.

If all the requirements are satisfied relief is available from conveyance or transfer duty so long as the instrument is adjudicated and (broadly) so long as that instrument is executed within 12 months of the increase in capital or of the formation of the new company (as the case may be).

Relief which has been given will be lost in three cases with the result that the duty avoided will immediately become payable together with interest at 5% pa calculated from the date when the duty would have been paid:

Case 1 Before giving relief the commissioners will normally insist upon a statutory declaration made by a solicitor engaged in the scheme that the provisions of s 55 have been complied with. If any declaration or supporting evidence is untrue in any material particular the exemption is lost.

Case 2 Where the undertaking of the target was acquired and the target ceases within two years to be the beneficial owner of the consideration shares issued to it.

Case 3 Where the purchaser company acquired shares of the target and ceased within two years to be the beneficial owner of those shares.

EXAMPLE 14

(1) Boco Ltd acquires the undertaking of Daisy Ltd in consideration of an issue of shares. The stamp duty relief given to Boco Ltd will be lost if within two years of the resolution to increase capital (or of the formation of the company, if Boco Ltd was specifically formed for this purpose) Daisy Ltd disposes of any of the shares in Boco Ltd. Notice that even a conditional contract of sale entered into in the two year period will have this result (*IRC v Utifec Group Ltd* (1977)), and that all the shares must be retained (*A-G v London Stadiums* (1950)).

(2) Boco Ltd acquires all the shares of Hoco Ltd in consideration of the issue of its own shares to Hoco Ltd's shareholders. Relief on the share transfer is given to Boco Ltd under s 55 but will be lost if within the two year period it disposes of the shares in Hoco Ltd.

It should be noted that in *Cases 2* and *3* relief is not lost if a prescribed transfer of beneficial ownership within the two year period is attributable to a further amalgamation or reconstruction. A disposal by the shareholders in the target of the consideration shares that they receive does not prejudice stamp duty relief under s 55 on the transfer of the target company's shares.

b) *Transfers between associated companies* (FA 1930 s 42)

Conveyance or transfer duty is not charged on an instrument by which one company transfers property to an associated company. The detailed requirements are in FA 1930 s 42 which requires that one of the companies in question must beneficially own, directly or indirectly, at least 90% (by nominal value) of the issued share capital of the other, or a third company beneficially owns, directly or indirectly at least 90% of the issued share capital of each.

FA 1967 s 27(3) contains provisions to prevent abuse of the s 42 relief; of particular note is the requirement that the transaction in respect of which relief is sought must not form part of an arrangement whereby the transferor's interest in the transferee's share capital will be reduced below 90%.

c) *Demergers* (FA 1980 s 117 and Sch 18)

Under the demerger provisions of FA 1980, a document executed solely for the purpose of effecting an exempt distribution to carry out the demerger will not be subject to stamp duty as a conveyance or transfer on sale provided that it is submitted for adjudication and stamped with a denoting stamp. This relief from duty may not apply to transfers of assets within the group prior to the demerger.

V   CAPITAL DUTY

Capital duty was introduced by FA 1973 (with effect from 1 August 1973) to conform with UK obligations under an EEC directive. It is a duty on 'chargeable transactions' of 'capital companies'.

1   What is a capital company? (FA 1973 s 48)

For the purpose of UK capital duty the most important example of a capital company is a limited (as opposed to an unlimited) liability company incorporated in the UK. However the term 'capital company' also includes limited partnerships and companies incorporated elsewhere in the EEC. Duty is charged on capital companies which have either their effective management or their registered office in Great Britain. When it is only the registered office which is situated within Great Britain, however, the effective management must be sited outside one of the EEC member states for UK capital duty to be chargeable.

EXAMPLE 15

(1) Fromage Ltd was incorporated in the UK with limited liability and with its registered office in Cheese Street, Shrewsbury. The effective management of the company is at Nancy-sur-Yonne in France. Although Fromage Ltd is a capital company, capital duty is not chargeable in the UK, but will be in France.
(2) Brie Ltd is incorporated in France with limited liability. Its central management is located in Goole. It is a capital company and UK capital duty is chargeable.

2 **What is a chargeable transaction?** (FA 1973 Sch 19 para 1)

Generally a charge will arise whenever a capital company raises or increases its share capital. The duty is not charged on loans (debentures) to such companies. The following illustrations indicate when duty is charged:

(1) Sal forms Sal Ltd with a share capital of £100. Duty will be charged on the £100 on either form PUC1 or PUC2 or both according to whether the subscription shares were paid up on incorporation or whether the entire £100 was paid up on the allotment of the shares after formation.

(2) Sal Ltd resolves to increase its share capital to £1,000 and allots a further 900 shares for £900. Duty will be charged on the £900 share capital issued on form PUC2.

(3) Sal Ltd resolves to increase share capital by issuing a further 1,000 shares having a par value of £1 each. As to 500 of those shares the allottee is to pay £1.50p per share (hence, the issue is at a premium); as to the other 500 the allottee is to pay by a transfer of Blackacre (worth £750) to the company. Duty will be charged on the 500 shares issued for a cash premium on form PUC2 at the higher of the nominal value of the shares (£500) and the consideration received by the company (£750), ie on £750. Duty is charged on the 500 shares issued in return for Blackacre on form PUC3 which is appropriate whenever shares are allotted for a consideration which is not wholly cash and, again, is levied on the higher figure, ie £750.

(4) Sal Ltd resolves on a 1:1 bonus issue and accordingly applies £2,000 from its reserves in paying up at par 2000 shares. The company is obliged to file form PUC7 but no duty is charged since there is no increase in capital contributed from a source outside the company.

(5) Sal Ltd allots 1,000 £1 shares with 50p paid and 50p left outstanding. On an issue of such partly paid shares duty is levied in two stages: first, duty is charged on the issue on the partial consideration paid (50p per share) on form PUC2. Secondly, when the balance is paid to the company (on a 'call' being made) duty is charged on that sum, ie on a further 50p per share, on form PUC5.

Duty is also charged when a company is converted into a capital company (eg when an unlimited company becomes limited); when a limited partner increases his capital contribution to the partnership; and when the place of effective management or registered office of a company is transferred to Great Britain.

3 **Stamping and the rate of duty**

Prescribed details of any chargeable transaction must be recorded on the appropriate PUC (paid up capital) form and sent to either the Registrar of Companies or to the commissioners within one month of the transaction. The appropriate form bears the duty which is charged at a rate of £1 per £100 or part thereof on the share capital raised. Failure to comply with the requirements leads to a fine of 5% per month of the duty that should have been paid.

4 **Exemptions from duty**

There are two main exemptions from capital duty. First, an increase in capital which occurs within four years of a reduction in share capital is not subject to duty to the extent of that reduction. This relief is only available to the extent that the reduction was attributable to losses sustained by the business.

Secondly, exemption may be available for restructuring operations (ie reconstructions, take-overs, and amalgamations) under FA 1973 Sch 19 para 10. For the relief to apply the commissioners have to be satisfied that a capital company has beneficially acquired at least 75% of the issued share capital of a target company or acquired the whole or any part of its undertaking. The consideration paid by the acquiring company should consist of shares issued in that company. Cash can be paid in addition to a share issue so long as it does not exceed 10% of the nominal value of the shares issued as consideration. The assumption or discharge of liabilities of the target is not taken into account.

The relief will be withdrawn if during the period of five years following the transaction the acquiring company ceases to own (presumably beneficially) at least 75% of the issued shares of the target company or disposes of any of those shares which it held immediately after the transaction took place. The exemption will not be lost if those events are themselves an exempt transaction within the restructuring provisions or if the disposal occurs during the winding up of the purchasing company. If the duty is triggered it is payable within one month of the disposal of shares or failure to retain the 75% holding, as the case may be. Duty will be charged on the original chargeable transaction and interest will be charged at a rate of 5% pa from the date of that transaction.

5   Interrelation with stamp duty

The old stamp duty charge on the nominal authorised share capital of limited companies (known as companies capital duty) was repealed as from 1 August 1973. Stamp duty on loan capital and on the conveyance or transfer of debentures ('marketable securities') was likewise abolished as from 1 January 1973. Capital duty has, of course, superseded the old stamp duty charge as far as issued share capital is concerned but the raising of loan capital is now free from stamp duty. To accord with EEC policy the stamp duty system is, therefore, weighted against the raising of finance by share issues and favours loan capital.

Both capital and stamp duty cause problems on reconstructions and amalgamations. The relieving provisions afforded by FA 1973 Sch 19 para 10 (capital duty) and FA 1927 s 55 (stamp duty) should be carefully considered and contrasted. In general, the capital duty relief is more generous although note that there is a five year ownership period to be satisfied as compared with a two year period for stamp duty. Finally, it should be stressed that the incorporation of a business in return for shares will usually give rise to double duty: stamp duty will be charged (at 1%) on the conveyance or transfer of the business and capital duty (at 1%) on the value of the capital (ie the business) received by the company (see Chapter 34).

PART B PRACTICE AND PLANNING

32 The *Ramsay* principle', tax planning and anti-avoidance legislation

I   Introductory
II   Artificial schemes and the *'Ramsay* principle'
III Statutory provisions to counter tax avoidance

I INTRODUCTORY

The desire to avoid the payment of tax need scarcely occasion surprise. In the average case it will amount to no more than a sensible use of the available exemptions and reliefs which are provided in all tax legislation. In other cases, where the sums involved are greater, the methods adopted by the 'tax planning industry' to escape the fiscal net may take on a complexity that is beyond the comprehension of most individuals and may involve schemes which are divorced from reality. The potential tax avoided (or saved) by these schemes is considerable and to combat their effectiveness the Revenue have two main weapons at their disposal. The first is legislative and takes the form of enactments directed against specific avoidance schemes. The provisions designed to prevent artificial transactions in land have been considered in Chapter 8; those aimed at combating the transfer of assets overseas in Chapter 13; and the various provisions aimed at transactions in securities, bond washing and dividend stripping are considered in this chapter. The general characteristic of such legislation is that it is designed to deal with a specific problem, normally after it has arisen but does not purport to prevent new schemes in different areas. Given a sophisticated legal profession, loopholes in such provisions will be exploited and need constant plugging.

The second weapon in the Revenue's armoury is to challenge in the courts the legal efficacy of avoidance schemes. In the past they won few victories. In *IRC v Duke of Westminster* (1936) the object of the scheme was to make servants' wages deductible in arriving at the Duke's total income by paying them by deed of covenant. Hence, although there was no binding agreement to that effect, it was accepted that so long as payments were made under the covenant they would not claim their wages. The House of Lords upheld the scheme saying that, in deciding the consequence of a transaction, the courts will look at its legal nature and not take account of any supposed artificiality.

In recent years, however, the Revenue have achieved some successes especially in the House of Lords. The culmination of recent decisions are the House of Lords cases of *W T Ramsay Ltd v IRC; Eilbeck v Rawling* (1981), *IRC v Burmah Oil Co Ltd* (1982) and *Furniss v Dawson* (1984). These decisions have sounded the death knell to artificial avoidance schemes and coupled with the high level of hostility shown by the Revenue to such schemes (as evidenced by *IRC v Rossminster Ltd* (1980)) should deter potential customers from purchasing avoidance packages. The current status of *Westminster's* Case is left unclear by these judgments which do, however, show that present judicial attitudes to tax avoidance are very different from those prevailing in the 1930s. In *Furniss v Dawson*, Lord Roskill considered that 'the ghost of the Duke of Westminster has haunted the administration of this branch of the law for too long.'

II ARTIFICIAL SCHEMES AND THE '*RAMSAY*' PRINCIPLE

1 The decisions in *Ramsay* and *Burmah Oil*

In both *Ramsay* and *Burmah Oil* the taxpayers sought to obtain the benefits of capital gains tax loss relief in order to wipe out large profits. To achieve this result, both adopted schemes involving a series of steps to be carried out in rapid succession according to a prearranged timetable. Once started, it was intended that the schemes should be carried through to their conclusion which would be that a capital loss had been incurred. In reality, a comparison of the taxpayer's position at the start and finish showed that either no real loss was suffered, or, in *Ramsay's* case, that the only loss suffered was the professional fees paid for the implementation of the scheme! The House of Lords decided that such schemes should be viewed not as a series of separate transactions, none of which was a sham, but as a whole; the position of the taxpayer in real terms being compared at the start and at the finish. Thus, the scheme involved no real loss and was self-cancelling. In *Ramsay* Lord Wilberforce expounded this new approach to avoidance schemes and sought to explain the decision in *Westminster's* Case:

> 'While obliging the court to accept documents or transactions, found to be genuine, as such, it does not compel the court to look at a document or a transaction in blinkers, isolated from any context to which it properly belongs. If it can be seen that a document or transaction was intended to have effect as part of a nexus or series of transactions, or as an ingredient of a wider transaction intended as a whole, there is nothing in the doctrine to prevent it being so regarded; to do so is not to prefer form to substance, or substance to form. It is the task of the court to ascertain the legal nature of any transaction to which it is sought to attach a tax, or a tax consequence, and if that emerges from a series, or combination of transactions, intended to operate as such, it is that series or combination which may be regarded' [1981] STC at 180.

2 *Furniss v Dawson*

The *Ramsay* and *Burmah Oil* cases both involved circular schemes, the sole object of which was the avoidance of tax! *Furniss v Dawson* was concerned with the deferment of capital gains tax by channelling the sale of chargeable assets through an intermediary company. The facts of the case are simple. The Dawsons decided to sell shares to Wood Bastow Holdings Ltd ('Wood Bastow') for £152,000. To defer the CGT that would otherwise have been payable, the shares were first sold to a newly incorporated Manx company ('Greenjacket') for the sum of £152,000 which was satisfied by an issue of shares in that company. The purchased shares were then immediately resold by Greenjacket to Wood Bastow for £152,000. The attraction of the scheme was that at no stage did any CGT liability arise: the sale to Greenjacket was specifically exempted from charge under FA 1965 Sch 7 para 6(2), whilst the resale by Greenjacket did not yield any profit to that company (the shares were purchased and sold for £152,000). As the price paid by Wood Bastow was received and retained by Greenjacket the scheme was not circular or self-cancelling: it involved a separate legal entity (Greenjacket) which ended up with the sale proceeds of the shares.

Before the Special Commissioners, Vinelott J, and a unanimous Court of Appeal, CGT was held not to be payable. The sale proceeds had been paid to Greenjacket and, in the phrase of Slade LJ in the Court of Appeal, the existence of Greenjacket had 'enduring legal consequences'. Before the House of Lords it was accepted that for a *scintilla temporis* legal and beneficial title to the shares passed to Greenjacket. Lord Brightman, however, in the only fully argued speech (which was concurred in by the other Lords) viewed the series of transactions as a pre-planned scheme:

> 'The whole process was planned and executed with faultless precision. The meetings began at 12.45 pm on 20 December, at which time the shareholdings of the operating companies were still owned by the Dawsons unaffected by any contract of sale. They ended with the shareholdings in the ownership of Wood Bastow. The minutes do not disclose when the meeting ended but perhaps it was all over in time for lunch.'

As its purpose was to obtain a deferral of CGT, he concluded that the scheme should be viewed as a whole and 'the court must then look at the end result. Precisely how the end result will be taxed will depend on the terms of the taxing statute sought to be applied.' By applying the test 'there was a disposal of the shares by the Dawsons in favour of Wood Bastow in consideration of a sum of money paid with the concurrence of the Dawsons to Greenjacket'. The gain on this disposal was subject to CGT. Lord Brightman stressed that, so long as a pre-planned tax saving scheme existed no distinction should be drawn between the case where the steps were carried out in pursuance of a contract and one where, although the steps were pre-ordained, separate binding contracts only arose at each stage. Although Greenjacket was not contractually bound to resell the shares to Wood Bastow, it was pre-ordained (ie there was an informal arrangement) that this would occur. Hence, 'the day is not saved for the taxpayer because the arrangement is unsigned or contains the magic words "this is not a binding contract"'. In a similar vein, Lord Fraser of Tullybelton considered that 'the series of two transactions . . . were planned as a single scheme and . . . it should be viewed as a whole'.

The case is of fundamental significance and the following matters should be noted: first, the House of Lords restated the *'Ramsay* principle' on a broad base and laid down no precise guidelines for its future operation. Lord Scarman, in particular, stressed the uncertain extent of the new approach:

> 'I am aware, and the legal profession (and others) must understand, that the law in this area is in an early stage of development. Speeches in your Lordships' House and judgments in the appellate courts are concerned more to chart a way forward between principles accepted and not to be rejected than to attempt anything so ambitious as to determine finally the limit beyond which the safe channel of acceptable tax avoidance shelves into the dangerous shallows of unacceptable tax evasion. The law will develop from case to case. Lord Wilberforce in *Ramsay's* case referred to "the emerging principle" of the law. What has been established with certainty by the House in *Ramsay's* case is that the determination of what does, and what does not, constitute unacceptable tax evasion is a subject suited to development by judicial process. Difficult though the task may be for judges, it is one which is beyond the power of the blunt instrument of legislation. Whatever a statute may provide, it has to be interpreted and applied by the courts and ultimately it will prove to be in this area of judge-made law that our elusive journey's end will be found.'

A ready acceptance that new law is being created and that this is the proper function of the judiciary is apparent and Lord Scarman in the passage quoted above, appears to be giving a new meaning to the terms 'tax avoidance' and 'tax evasion'. Avoidance will apparently become evasion when it is 'unacceptable'.

Secondly, if it is proposed to enter into a scheme which may fall within the *Ramsay* principle it is not possible at present to obtain an advance clearance from the Revenue. The Chief Secretary to the Treasury has however, stated (see Appendix V) that no attempt will be made to re-open transactions already cleared and that the Revenue are considering giving clearance for groups of cases of particular importance or general guidance for the benefit of taxpayers. Thirdly, the width of the *Ramsay* principle calls into question the need for legislative anti-avoidance provisions. For example the CTT associated operations provisions (FA 1975 s 44) which, although couched in general terms, are not as wide as the statements in *Furniss v Dawson*.

3   The limits of the '*Ramsay* principle'

One of the features of the judgments in *Furniss v Dawson*, was a reluctance to lay down precise boundaries to the *Ramsay* principle. Lord Brightman did, however, suggest that there are two basic requirements. First, there must be a pre-ordained series of transactions (a 'scheme'); there need be no binding contract to carry the entire scheme through, and furthermore the scheme may include the attainment of a legitimate business end. In that case the scheme enabled shares to be sold from the Dawsons to Wood Bastow. Secondly, there must be steps in the scheme whose sole purpose is to avoid (or defer) a liability to tax. Such steps may have a 'business effect' but no 'business purpose'. The insertion of Greenjacket was such a step: in the words of Lord Brightman 'that inserted step had no business purpose apart from the deferment of tax, although it had a business effect. If the sale had taken place in 1964 before capital gains tax was introduced, there would have been no Greenjacket.' Both requirements involve a finding of facts (or inferences from such findings) and are matters for the commissioners.

The requirements are not, however, easy to apply. Two of their Lordships considered that *Westminster's* case could be distinguished as involving a single and not a composite transaction. Certainly the covenant was a single transaction, but its sole purpose was the avoidance of income tax and it was only entered into on the 'understanding' that the gardeners would not seek to claim their wages. Hence the making of the covenant was a step which had no commercial purpose save for the avoidance of tax. It is arguable, however, that unlike Greenjacket, which was an artificial person under the control of the Dawsons, the gardener's continuing right to sue for his wages serves to distinguish the case. Furthermore, as the covenant was to last for a period of seven years or the joint lives of the parties, it could have continued after the employment had terminated.

The following comments upon the possible application of the new approach may be made: first any pre-arranged scheme which involves either tax avoidance or tax deferral is potentially within the *Ramsay* principle. A single tax-efficient transaction is presumably not since the case does *not* state that persons must so organise their affairs that they pay the maximum amount of tax! Hence, the use of deeds of covenant in favour of children at college is not caught and indeed the Revenue issue a model form of covenant (see Appendix II). Secondly, the *Ramsay* principle is not limited to CGT as the approach of the courts was not concerned with any particular legislative provisions but was based upon principles of common application. In *Cairns v MacDiarmid* (1983) the taxpayer's claim for income tax relief for interest payments was dismissed by the Court of Appeal on the grounds, inter alia, that the scheme fell within the *Ramsay* principle. Sir John Donaldson MR concluded that:

> 'The whole transaction was "out of this world". Although no sham, it lacked all reality. It did not even have the reality of *Ramsay's* case in that [the taxpayer] neither paid a fee nor incurred any expenses. But, as in that case, at the end of a series of connected and intended transactions, his financial position was precisely as it was at the beginning!' [1983] STC at 182.

In the area of stamp duty, the Revenue consider that any scheme to avoid duty on the conveyance of an interest in land falls within the principle and is, therefore, liable to ad valorem duty (see p 454). Despite passing unremarked in *Furniss v Dawson*, the 'pref-trick' appears vulnerable (see Appendix V). Thirdly, despite *Furniss v Dawson* involving a 'channelling operation' the principle will not apply to intra-group transfers of corporate assets designed to avoid CGT (see the statement of the Chief Secretary in Appendix V); nor, presumably to arrangements designed to equalise spouses' estates for CTT purposes (see p 497); nor to inter-spouse schemes to maximise the use of retirement relief (p 238). Stamp Duty avoidance by the use of a series of gifts each worth less than £30,000 (see p 447) would, however, seem vulnerable since, once a series of transactions is shown to exist, the absence of a binding legal obligation is irrelevant.

Similarly, arrangements seeking CGT advantages by 'bed and breakfasting' appear to be caught.

The above conclusions are necessarily tentative: all that can be said with confidence is that it will be some time before the full implications of the new approach of the House of Lords are worked out; meanwhile uncertainty will persist as a steady flow of cases continues to come before the commissioners and the courts (see Appendix V for recent developments).

III   STATUTORY PROVISIONS TO COUNTER TAX AVOIDANCE

1   The legislation

The major provisions that have been enacted in attempts to deal with specific instances of tax avoidance are as follows:

Transactions in securities   TA 1970 ss 460–468 (originally enacted in FA 1960).

Bond washing and dividend stripping   Various provisions deal with these problems, the oldest dating back to FA 1927 (now TA 1970 s 30).

Transfer of assets overseas   Originally enacted in FA 1936 these provisions were amended in FA 1981 as a result of *Vestey v IRC (Nos 1 and 2)* (1980) (see Chapter 13).

The migration of companies TA 1970 s 482 (dating back to FA 1951) prevents companies from avoiding tax by transferring residence abroad.

Artificial transactions in land For TA 1970 s 488 see Chapter 8. Statutory provisions also regulate sale and leaseback transactions (TA 1970 ss 491–495; FA 1972 s 80); see Chapter 6.

Sale of income derived from personal activities TA 1970 s 487 (originally enacted in FA 1969) prevents the conversion of future taxable income into capital gains subject only to CGT. The avoidance typically involved entertainers who sold their services to a company formed for that purpose and then sold the shares in that company.

The use of tax losses and transfer pricing TA 1970 s 483 (originating in FA 1969) imposes restrictions upon the purchase of tax loss companies (see Chapter 28). Sales at under or overvalue may be subject to challenge under TA 1970 s 485, and under the *Sharkey v Wernher* principle (see Chapter 6).

2 Typical avoidance schemes involving securities

A company is a legal entity distinct from its shareholders and, therefore, provides fertile ground for such tax avoidance schemes as dividend stripping and bond washing.

Dividend stripping The simplest illustration of dividend stripping is where A owns A Ltd which has profits available for distribution. A sells the shares to B who is a dealer in securities. A receives a capital sum which reflects the undistributed profits in the company. B will take out the profits from A Ltd (as a dividend) which will be taxed as income but the shares will now be worth less (reflecting the fact that they have been stripped of their dividend). B will, therefore, make a trading loss when he sells the shares which can be set off against the dividend income that B has received (usually under the provisions of TA 1970 s 168: see p 112). The result is that corporate profits have been extracted free of tax.

The courts were often invited to hold that the purchase and sale of the shares was not a trading transaction. In some cases they decided that it was trading; in others, not (contrast, eg, *Griffiths v J P Harrison (Watford) Ltd* (1962) with *FA and AB Ltd v Lupton* (1971) and see *Coates v Arndale Properties Ltd* (1984)). The close company legislation sought to tackle one part of the problem by preventing the accumulation of profits in close companies (see p 405). In 1960 the general problem was attacked with legislation aimed at transactions in securities generally.

Bond washing Dividends only become a taxpayer's income when they are due and payable; when that happens the shareholder can claim the sum from the company as a debt. Usually there is a time gap between declaration and payment which provides an opportunity to wash the shares (or bonds) of their dividend. The washing process usually involves a taxpayer who is subject to no income tax or to lower rates only. Assume, for instance, that shares are owned by A who is subject to income tax on his income at 60%. When a dividend is declared on his shares he sells them to his cousin, a student with unused personal allowances. A is, therefore, receiving a capital sum for the shares and should be liable only to CGT at 30%. The dividends are paid to the cousin who suffers little if any income tax thereon. Finally, the shares may be repurchased by A after payment of the dividend. Legislative provisions (notably TA 1970 s 469) prevent the most blatant examples of bond washing.

3   **Transactions in securities** (TA 1970 ss 460–468)

These provisions are amongst the most obscure and complex in the tax legislation. Their object is to cancel (for taxation purposes) a tax advantage gained as the result of a transaction in securities. This cancellation will be effected either by an assessment to income tax under Schedule D Case VI at a maximum rate of 60%; or by such other adjustments as may be prescribed by the Revenue, such as the refusal of a tax repayment (TA 1970 s 460(3)). The three conditions which must be satisfied before the provisions of s 460 can be invoked are considered below.

There must be a transaction in securities   'Transaction' and 'securities' are given a wide meaning. A transaction apart from covering purchases, sales and exchanges can include the combined effects of a series of operations . Securities include stocks and shares (TA 1970 s 467(1)) and also a secured debt (see *IRC v Parker* (1966)).

As a result of the transaction the taxpayer either obtains, or is in a position to obtain, a tax advantage   'Tax advantage' is defined in TA 1970 s 466. One of the uncertainties raised by the definition is whether a capital gains tax advantage is included; the section was introduced before CGT and the widely held view is that CGT is not included. Where shares are sold, there is the possibility of both a CGT charge and an assessment under TA 1970 s 460. Revenue practice is to give a credit for CGT paid against a liability under s 460 (see *IRC v Garvin* (1981)).

There will be no liability under s 460 if the taxpayer can show that the transaction was carried out for bona fide commercial reasons and that obtaining a tax advantage was not one of its main objects (TA 1970 s 460(1)). This is a matter of intention and, as it is a question of fact, the findings of the Special Commissioners on such matters can only be overturned by the court in exceptional cases (*IRC v Brebner* (1967)). In *Clark v IRC* (1978), it was held that this commercial test had to be applied not just to the actual sale of the securities, but in the light of all the relevant circumstances. On the particular facts, the sole purpose of the sale was to enable the taxpayer to raise money for the purchase of a farm and there were sound commercial reasons for that purchase. Fox J decided, therefore, that there was a good defence to an assessment under s 460.

Any one of five circumstances specified in TA 1970 s 461 must be present   Paragraph A of TA 1970 s 461 is concerned with the distribution of an abnormal dividend to a person entitled to tax relief thereon and catches the classical dividend stripping operation.

Paragraph B prevents the use of trading losses that may arise for a share dealer on a sale of shares and applies where the value of shares has fallen after the stripping of a dividend.

Paragraph C is aimed at the party to a dividend stripping transaction who receives a capital sum whilst the other party receives an abnormal dividend and catches the original owner of the shares.

Paragraph D is limited to closely controlled companies whose shares are not dealt in on a UK stock exchange. It applies where, in connection with the distribution of the profits of a company, a person receives a consideration which represents the assets of the company available for distribution, or the value of its stock in trade, or is received in respect of future receipts of the company. Unlike Paragraph C, it does not require an abnormal dividend to be paid nor a resultant fall in value of the securities. The general purpose is to catch cases where the shareholders of a company obtain property which might have been used to pay dividends. It was considered by the House of Lords in *IRC v Parker* (1966); *Cleary v IRC* (1967); *Williams v IRC* (1980), and *IRC v Garvin* (1981).

Finally, Paragraph E overlaps to a large extent with the other paragraphs. It will be relevant when one Paragraph D company acquires another by means of a share exchange and in connection with that transfer a person receives non-taxable consideration in the form of share capital or other security. That consideration must either be, or represent, the value of assets available for distribution by a Paragraph D company.

Where there is a risk that a transaction falls within the scope of s 460, a clearance under TA 1970 s 464 may be obtained. The Revenue have 30 days from the date of the application, or receipt by them of any further information requested, to decide whether to serve a notice on the taxpayer stating that they believe the transaction(s) fall within s 460. If clearance is refused, although the Revenue are under no duty to give their reasons, they will do so in appropriate cases and occasionally grant the taxpayer an interview to clarify the position.

If a notice is served on the taxpayer to the effect that the Revenue believe that his transaction is caught by s 460 he is given by statutory declaration a right of reply within 30 days and if the Revenue decide to continue with the matter a Tribunal is set up under TA 1970 s 463 to determine whether there is a prima facie case for proceeding further (the taxpayer is not entitled to appear before this tribunal). If a case is found to exist, the Revenue will then serve a notice under s 460(3) indicating how they intend to counter the alleged tax advantage. The taxpayer has a right of appeal against their decision to the Special Commissioners.

4 Investment in 'roll-up' funds (FA 1984 ss 92–100 Schs 19, 20)

FA 1984 ss 92–100 and Schs 19, 20 seek to prevent UK residents from avoiding a charge to income or corporation tax on an investment in offshore 'roll-up' funds. Typically, the investment is in non-UK resident companies and unit trusts which do not distribute their income, so that the eventual return to the investor would only be charged to CGT at 30%.

FA 1984 s 96 now ensures that, subject to three conditions being satisfied, there will be a charge to income tax under Schedule D Case VI or to corporation tax on any such gain accruing after 31 December 1983 to a UK resident (including a trustee). The requirements are, first, that he must dispose of a material interest (i.e. one realiseable within seven years after investment; see FA 1984 s 94); secondly, in an 'offshore fund' (see FA 1984 s 94(1)); and, thirdly, after 1 January 1984, *except* where the fund has obtained Revenue clearance for each accounting period as a 'distributor' of its income (ie it distributes at least 85% of its income before permitted allowances: see FA 1984 Sch 19, para 1). Death is treated as disposal; there is no indexation allowance; and FA 1980 s 79 (hold-over) relief does not apply. The taxpayer should, therefore, dispose of his investment in his most advantageous tax year (the small company investor will only be charged the same rate as on its capital gains: ie 30%). Finally, s 94 ensures that normal trading ventures or consortia are not caught by any of the above provisions.

33 Choice of business medium

I Introductory—the available options
II Non-tax factors
III The taxation factors
IV General conclusions

I INTRODUCTORY—THE AVAILABLE OPTIONS

When commencing a business the participators will normally have an unrestricted choice between operating through the medium of a company or partnership. The only major restriction is that partnerships cannot, save in the case of certain professions, such as accountants and solicitors, be formed with more than 20 partners (Companies Act 1948 s 434; Companies Act 1967 s 120). Professions who because of professional regulations cannot operate through the medium of a limited company, may set up a company to service the running of their premises and notably to provide staff, furniture and equipment.

The typical company will be the limited private company and the typical partnership will consist of a number of partners with unlimited personal liability. There are, however, other possibilities such as:

The public company   Its attraction is the ability to raise funds from the public (contrast the restriction on private companies: Companies Act 1980 s 15). In practice, of course, it is unlikely that a new business would commence as a public company since the costs involved are considerable and only in very limited cases would a Stock Exchange listing or permission to deal in the company's shares on the Unlisted Securities Market be granted for a completely new enterprise.

The unlimited company   This suffers from the disadvantage that the liability of the shareholders is unlimited—hence, they are in the same position vis-à-vis creditors as partners (albeit with the convenience of corporate personality). However, the unlimited company need not file the statutory company accounts thus enabling it to preserve a greater degree of secrecy; and it can return share capital to members more easily than can a limited company. Nevertheless, the defect of unlimited liability will in most cases outweigh any advantages.

The limited partnership   In practice, these have been few in number. Their creation is regulated by formalities akin to those which have to be satisfied if a company is to be formed and although there can be partners whose liability for the debts of the firm is limited, there must also be at least one general (or unlimited) partner. Furthermore, if a limited partner takes any part in the management of the firm, he loses the protection of his limited liability and becomes a general partner. Thus, a limited partner who has put, say, £10,000 into the firm might have to let it be lost by inept management since any attempt to interfere would put at risk the whole of his personal fortune.

Partnerships with companies This hybrid business medium involves an individual joining in partnership with a limited company. If the individual is also a director of the company concerned, making him a limited partner offers attractions since he can participate in the management of the business qua director of the company. The particular advantages afforded by the arrangement lie in the regulation of profit-sharing ratios to take account of differential income and corporation tax rates and to maximise the use of business losses.

Any comparison between the practical alternatives of a partnership or a limited company involves a consideration of both non-tax and tax factors.

II NON-TAX FACTORS

1 Limited liability

A limited company is a separate legal entity and is solely liable for its debts and obligations. The shareholders' liability is restricted to the sum that they agreed to put into the business and this liability cannot be increased without their consent (Companies Act 1948 s 22). The limited company offers the ideal vehicle for the individual who wishes to set up in business, but who is not prepared to risk his entire personal fortune in the venture.

EXAMPLE 1

Sal is the sole shareholder of the private limited company Sal Ltd. The company is in liquidation with debts of £1m; it has total assets of £10,000. Sal is estimated to be worth £2m. The creditors of Sal Ltd can only look to the company for payment of their debts—only in exceptional circumstances will they be able to look to Sal personally for payment.

To this principle of limited liability, exceptions exist. The 'veil of incorporation' has, in certain circumstances been lifted by statute and the judiciary, but such instances are rare and the main reason for limited liability not affording total protection is the personal guarantee. If Sal starts a company with, say £10,000, and then attempts to obtain further finance for the company, it is likely that a lender will expect greater security than the assets of the company. Hence, they are likely to insist on a personal guarantee from Sal that, on default by the company, he will be accountable for any loss resulting. To the extent that personal guarantees are given, limited liability if illusory. However, who demands such guarantees? Major lenders, such as banks, and often landlords will, but rarely trade creditors and certainly not customers. Even then, it may be possible to avoid giving them; the Government, for instance, operates a scheme through the clearing banks and certain other institutions to provide loan guarantees for small businesses on loans of up to £75,000.

2 Corporate personality

A company will never die: it can only be liquidated. The death of a shareholder need not affect the business; the only result will be a transmission of some of the shares of the company. Sole traders and partners enjoy no such advantages, because the assets of the business will be vested in them so that death will disrupt the smooth running of the organisation. Further, from the point of view of simple estate planning, the company provides assets (shares) which are both easy to transfer and easy to divide into separate parcels. A large shareholding can be fragmented between different members of the shareholder's family whereas the ownership of an unincorporated business is not easily divisible.

The existence of a separate legal entity (the company) means that the shareholder/proprietor can enter into legally binding contracts with it (see *Lee v Lee's Air Farming Ltd* (1961)). Normally the shareholder in the small private company will be concerned in the management of the business as a director and will ensure that he enters into a lucrative long-term service contract with the company. Amongst a number of advantages that such contracts offer will be the protection of both statute and common law in the event of the employment being prematurely terminated and preferential treatment for arrears of wages in the event of the company's insolvency.

3   Obtaining finance

Companies have advantages when it comes to raising finance. Apart from issuing risk capital in the form of shares, money can also be raised by loans secured by fixed and floating charges. The fixed charge is common to both incorporated and unincorporated businesses (eg the land mortgage), but a floating charge is a unique advantage of companies. It operates as a charge over (usually) the entire undertaking and has the advantage of leaving the company free to deal with the assets of the business as it sees fit save to the extent that the terms of the charge provide otherwise. The floating charge will only crystallise on liquidation or when a default, as specified in the deed of charge, occurs.

How advantageous is the floating charge? This question can only be answered by considering whether creditors will be satisfied with the protection afforded by the floating charge and in many cases they will not be. Quite apart from the inherent defects of a non-crystallised charge, the steady addition by statute over the years to the list of preferential creditors on an insolvency has greatly weakened the attractions of such charges. Accordingly, the characteristic feature of company charging in recent years has been the practice of creditors to demand fixed security (see, eg *Siebe Gorman & Co Ltd v Barclays Bank Ltd* (1979) and the growth of *Romalpa* clauses).

4   Formality, rigidity and costs

By comparison with the unincorporated business, a company suffers from formality and rigidity and has greater operating costs. A partnership or sole trade can be established with an almost total lack of documentation and formality. A company can be bought 'off the peg' for as little as £100 but the costs of a tailor-made company are usually higher. The obligation to file forms is then a regular feature of a company's life, especially the obligation to file an annual return and to submit annual audited accounts to the Registrar of Companies. Such requirements, however, are probably a small price for the benefits of limited liability.

As an artificial entity, companies must be formed for specific purposes set out in the objects clause of its memorandum of association. Actions in excess of these prescribed objects are ultra vires and, at common law, were void. This difficulty should not be exaggerated, since objects clauses will generally be drafted in such wide terms that they will embrace all conceivable activities; even where the clause is restrictive it can be amended (Companies Act 1948 s 5); and third parties may be protected if they deal with a company which is exceeding its permitted objects (European Communities Act 1972 s 9).

III THE TAXATION FACTORS

The formation of a company always presents the danger that the company will be taxed as an entity distinct from its members so that double taxation will result. In certain areas specific provisions take away this problem, but elsewhere it remains a major argument against incorporation. Any comparison cannot be just between the taxation of individuals and the taxation of companies, since there is also the need to consider the individual as a director/employee of that company. The topic must, therefore, include some discussion of the pros and cons of being employed as opposed to self-employed.

1 Taxation of income profits

a) *Rates of tax*

Income tax on the profits of a partnership or sole trade will never exceed 60% and that level will only be reached when the individual's taxable income exceeds £38,100. Corporation tax will be charged on the income profits of the company at either 50% or 30% depending upon whether the company is a small company (see Chapter 28). Unlike income tax, corporation tax is levied at a flat rate so that in the case of a company taxed at 50% all its profits will be charged at this rate. For an individual whose taxable income exceeds £23,100, the marginal rate will be 50%, but this will, of course, only apply to the slice of income above £23,100. For small companies whose profits exceed £100,000 but fall below £500, 000 there is a system of tapering relief and the rate of tax on income profits which fall within that zone can be as high as 55% (see p 383).

EXAMPLE 2

Klone Ltd makes up its accounts to 31 December each year. For the 1984 period its income profits (there are no capital gains) are expected to be £108,000. The sole director/shareholder, Mr K, receives a salary of £20,000; he has no other income.
(1) *Corporation tax:* On profits of £108,000 tax will be charged at 30% on the first £100,000 (small company rate) and then at 55% on the remaining £8,000 (tapering relief).

$$£$$

		$£$
ie 30% × £100,000	=	30,000
55% × £ 8,000	=	4,400
Total tax		£34,400

(2) *Income tax:* if K is a single man with no charges on income, the income tax bill will be:

	$£$
Total income	20,000
Less personal relief	2,005
Taxable income	£17,995

Income tax:	$£$
£15,400 at 30%	4,620
£ 2,595 at 40%	1,038
Total income tax	£5,658

(3) *Total tax:*

	£
Corporation tax	34,400
Income tax	5,658
	£40,058

If, however, the company paid K a Christmas bonus of £8,000, thereby reducing the 1984 profits to £100,000, the tax position would be:

(1) *Corporation tax*
    30% × £100,000 = £30,000

(2) *Income tax:* K's income is £28,000. Taxable income is £25,995.

	£
£15,400 at 30%	4,620
£ 2,800 at 40%	1,120
£ 4,900 at 45%	2,205
£ 2,895 at 50%	1,447.50
Total income tax	£9,392.50

(3) *Total tax:*

	£
Corporation tax	30,000
Income tax	9,392.50
	£39,392.50

Total tax saving as a result of payment of £8,000 bonus to K:

£665.50 (£40,058 − £39,392.50)

EXAMPLE 3

Business profits are estimated to be £40,000 and the proprietor will take £15,000, but leave the remainder in the business to finance expansion.
(1) *If an unincorporated business:* total income tax on £40,000 (ignoring personal allowances etc) will be £16,960.
(2) *If a company* with £15,000 paid out as emoluments and the balance retained:

	£
Corporation tax on £25,000 at 30%	7,500
Income tax (Schedule E) on £15,000	4,500
Total tax	£12,000

The amount of profits that can be retained in a small company is 70%, ie after paying corporation tax at the rate of 30%. The tax saving in this example of £4,960 (£16,960 − £12,000) is extra profits retained for the business.

b) *The effect of paying all the profits out as remuneration*

Employees' remuneration is deductible as a business expense of the company (TA 1970 s 130), and will be subject to income tax under Schedule E. The amount paid to a full-time working director is unlikely to be challenged as excessive (contrast *Copeman v William J Flood & Sons Ltd* (1942)) so that the company will pay no corporation tax. The only tax charged on the profits will, therefore, be income tax so that the only difference between a shareholder/director who extracts all the profits as salary and the self-employed sole trader lies in the contrasts between Schedule E and Schedule D taxation. The main points of comparison are:
(1) Dates for paying the tax: this is discussed in more detail in (c) below.

(2) Pension entitlements: the pensions available for employees are considered in Chapter 5; for the self-employed in Chapter 29. Generally, the advantage lies with the employee.
(3) The (often relatively light) taxation of fringe benefits under Schedule E (see Chapter 5) favours the employee.
(4) Social security aspects: Contributions paid by employees and their employers are greater than the payments of the self-employed. The benefits enjoyed are correspondingly greater. The advantages enjoyed by employees in the event of their employment terminating (whether for redundancy, unfair dismissal, or because of the insolvency of the employer) should be noted.

c) *Dates for paying tax*

The sole trader can obtain a delay of up to 21 months in paying the first instalment of income tax with a further six months delay before the final instalment is due. Even with an accounting period which ends on 5 April (the most disadvantageous day for income tax purposes) there will be a delay of nine months before the first instalment (see Chapter 6).

For companies, there is a maximum delay of nine months from the ending of the accounting period to the payment of corporation tax (unless it was incorporated before 1965 when it retains the same delay in paying tax that it enjoyed under the income tax system). This is equivalent to the shortest possible delay before the first instalment of income tax is payable by a sole trader and a company does not have the advantage of paying in two instalments. Where company profits are all paid out in directors' fees the tax charge will be under the PAYE system. If a company pays a dividend it will have to pay ACT, an advance payment of its MCT. It should, therefore, delay paying the dividend until as late as possible in its accounting period.

d) *Trading losses*

The advantages afforded by relief for trading losses lie with the unincorporated business. Company losses are 'locked in' so that they cannot be used by the owners to set against their income and instead, relief will only be given when the company makes profits (see p 387). The unincorporated trader is subject to no such restrictions so that relief will be available against his other income under the provisions of TA 1970 s 168 and, so far as early losses are concerned, against previous income as a result of FA 1978 s 30 (see Chapter 7). It is often argued that when a new business is likely to show early losses, the ideal is to start that business as an unincorporated trade and then, when profitable, to incorporate. However, if early losses exceed the wildest expectations of the trader the advantage of income tax loss relief will not compensate for the disaster of bankruptcy. Had the loss been realised by a company of course, limited liability would have protected the proprietors from bankruptcy.

EXAMPLE 4

Having worked in the Civil Service for many years, Samantha has resigned to open a boutique. She anticipates trading losses in the early years. She has a substantial private income.
(1) If she forms a company to run the business, losses can only be relieved against future corporate profits.
(2) If she operates as a sole trader the losses can be set against her private income (TA 1970 s 168) or against her income from the Civil Service in previous years (FA 1978 s 30) or against both (*Butt v Haxby* (1983)).

e) *Interest relief*

Income tax relief is generally available on the interest paid on loans to acquire an interest in either a partnership or a close company. To qualify, the taxpayer no longer has to work for the greater part of his time in the business. Relief is also available on loans raised for the benefit of the close company or partnership. Interest paid by a sole trader on loans to finance the business will usually be a deductible business expense.

f) *Corporate investment reliefs*

Various reliefs have been introduced in recent years in an attempt to stimulate investment in trading companies.

Venture capital (FA 1980 s 37)   is designed to encourage the purchase of shares in unquoted trading companies, and allows a loss on disposal of the shares (including failure of the venture) to be relieved against income (see further Chapter 7). It is not available for moneys lost in an unincorporated enterprise.

Business expansion scheme (FA 1983 s 26 and Sch 5)   permits the sum invested in a company to be deducted from the investor's income at the highest rates (see further Chapter 4).

g) *Taking surplus profits out of a company*

One of the drawbacks of a company may occur when the proprietor desires to extract surplus profits for his own benefit. Legal theory—the company as a separate legal entity—means that the extraction will be charged to tax and, as the profits extracted may have already been subject to charge in the company's hands, there is a risk of double taxation. The major methods of 'bleeding off' profits are:

Paying dividends   In the case of small companies there is no element of double taxation since ACT paid on the dividend discharges the MCT bill of the company and surplus ACT may be carried back for up to six years. For other companies, an element of double charge occurs since the ACT will not discharge the full MCT bill and the shareholder obtains no credit for this extra corporation tax. By 1986, however, this extra tax will be reduced to only 5% (see Chapter 28).

Interest payments   Normally interest will be a deductible charge on income for the company but excessive interest payments, and any attempt to link the interest to the profits of the company results in an application of the rules that apply for dividends (see p 393). Interest payments have to be in respect of bona fide loans.

Lending the profits   Apart from restrictions on the making of loans in the Companies Act 1980, the company concerned will usually be close with the result that the provisions of TA 1970 s 286 will apply (see p 404), so that it is 'forced' to pay a sum of money to the Revenue which will only be refunded when the loan is repaid.

Extracting the profits by selling the shares   Profits made by the company will usually be reflected in the value of the shares. Hence, a sale of the shares should ensure that the profit is obtained by the shareholder. This method of extracting profits suffers from two defects. First, there will be double taxation since not only will the company's profit be subject to corporation tax, but also the share sale will be a taxable occasion.

Secondly, the sale of the shares might fall foul of TA 1970 s 460 (see Chapter 32) so that the gain made would be taxed as unearned income.

EXAMPLE 5

Hoco Ltd makes income profits of £100. Corporation tax at 30% is £30 so that £70 is retained by Hoco Ltd. If all the shares are owned by Mr Hoco they would be worth £70 more. Therefore, were he to sell his shares, he would make a gain of £70 subject to 30% CGT = £21. The total tax attributable to the company's £100 profit is therefore £51 (£30 paid by Hoco Ltd and £21 paid by Hoco.)

Extraction in the form of remuneration   As already discussed, this is an ideal method since the sum paid will be deductible for corporation tax and, therefore, subject only to income tax. In the typical small private company, where all the shareholders are also full-time working directors, profits are bled off in this fashion. (See *Ebrahimi v Westbourne Galleries Ltd* (1973) for a practical illustration of such a private company and for a salutary lesson in what can happen if things go wrong!)

2   Capital taxes

Gains will be taxed at a flat rate of 30%, although the £5,600 annual exemption only applies to sole traders and partners. For partnerships, the CGT rules are applied in accordance with SP D12 (see Chapter 29). For companies, the taxation of capital profits can lead to a double charge if the shareholder wishes to sell his shareholding.

EXAMPLE 6

Kafka Ltd makes capital profits of £100 thereby incurring corporation tax of £30 (3/5 × 100 × 50%). The profit of £70 is retained by the company. K is the sole shareholder; his shares are worth an extra £70 and if he realises this profit he will be subject to CGT of £21 (30% of £70). Hence, the total tax attributable to the company's £100 profit will be £51 (£30 corporation tax + £21 CGT).

Not surprisingly, the practice has grown up of keeping appreciating capital assets out of a company. The shareholder will allow the asset to be used by the company but will retain its ownership. On its disposal therefore, any gain will be subject to CGT only in the hands of the shareholder. Whether the indexation allowance for CGT will alter this practice remains to be seen. The difficulty is that although a double charge may be avoided, other problems can be created, for instance:

(1) *The availability of retirement relief*   This will depend upon the terms of Revenue concessions which can apply to assets used by both partnerships and companies so long as the owner is either a partner or a full-time working director (see p 235).

(2) *CTT business property relief*   Relief may be available if the asset is given away, but only at 30% and, in the case of an asset used by a company, only

if the owner is a controlling shareholder. For a partner the relief is available whatever the size of his share in the partnership (see p 329).

(3) *Payment for use of the asset*   Apart from such payments being subject to income tax, they will normally prevent retirement relief from applying. Hence, it will be better for the taxpayer to take, instead, an increased share of the profits or, in the case of a company, a greater salary.

(4) *Section 123 relief*   Hold-over relief for CGT will not be available if assets (except cash) are retained outside the company.

(5) *Paying CTT by instalments*   This is generally not available in the case of assets held outside a company except for land (when interest will be charged on the unpaid CTT).

Two comparisons should be noted. First, the facility to pay CTT by instalments, which is generally available on a transfer of a business or part of a business, is only available on a transfer of shares if that transfer satisfies detailed requirements (see p 307). Secondly, business property relief is only available at 30% for minority shareholdings (including, of course, a 50% holding which would not give the owner voting control). An individual with a small stake in a partnership would qualify for the maximum 50% relief. Land and buildings, plant and machinery used by a partnership attract 30% relief; if used by a controlled company, the relief is likewise 30% but if used by a company which the transferor does not control there is no relief.

3   Stamp duty and capital duty

Transfers of a business, a part of a business and of shares will normally lead to a stamp duty charge on the instrument of transfer. Share transfers are always subject to ad valorem duty. For businesses and shares in a partnership not only may the nil rate be available but also assets that can be transferred by delivery need not be subject to duty (see Chapter 34). Capital duty is levied (at £1 per £100 or part thereof) on share capital raised by companies. It is calculated on the value contributed to the company by the shareholder, not on the nominal value of the shares issued but does not apply to loan capital. It has no application to sole traders or to partnerships (other than limited partnerships) which can thus raise finance free from any revenue imposition.

IV   GENERAL CONCLUSIONS

It was often pointed out that, although the non-taxation factors tend to favour incorporation (notably the benefit of limited liability), tax considerations probably favoured the unincorporated trader. Recent changes, however, and especially changes in corporate tax rates, have arguably altered this conclusion and strengthened the arguments in favour of incorporation. Note in particular:

(1) The small company rate of 30%, which is equivalent to the basic rate of income tax and which encourages the retention of profits (up to £100,000 pa) in the company (see *Example 3* above). There is no statutory apportionment of trading income.

(2) The progressive reduction in the rate of tax for other companies, to 35% by FY 1986, which is only marginally higher than the present basic rate of income tax and which contrasts strikingly with the 60% top rate.

(3) The removal of discrimination against dividends which are (in effect) fully tax deductible by small companies and will be largely deductible in the case of other companies by 1986. Further, the extended set-off for surplus ACT means that MCT on past profits can be recovered.

(4) Loan capital is free of capital duty; the interest is deductible as a charge on companies' profits; and FA 1984 has encouraged the use of deep discount stock (see p 386) which possesses considerable attractions for the company and tax-saving opportunities for the investor.

(5) The consultative document on retirement relief (see p 238) envisages an improvement in the treatment of shares in a family trading company, notably by extending the relief to a holding company.

(6) Although reduced rates still do not apply, stamp duty has been halved (to 1%) for share transfers. The danger of an investor being 'locked-into' the private company has also been reduced by the 'buy back' provisions (see p 394).

(7) Taxpayers are given incentives to invest in corporate trades; notably through the business expansion scheme which for higher rate taxpayers offers an ideal 'tax shelter' (see p 36).

Two final points may be mentioned. First, that questions of commercial 'prestige' favour incorporation: perhaps the label 'company director' is more impressive than 'sole trader'! Secondly, and by way of a cautionary note, considerable tax reliefs are given to encourage firms to incorporate and new corporate businesses to commence, but the same is not true on dis-incorporation. It may well be the case that a company is easier to get into than to escape from and this is a factor to be remembered when the decision to incorporate is taken.

34 Takeovers and mergers

    I   Transfer of an unincorporated business to a company
   II Company takeovers
 III Demergers
 IV Management buy-outs

Some aspects of business takeovers will be considered in this chapter but in view of the complexities and technicality of the subject all that is attempted is a general introduction to the problems involved.

I TRANSFER OF AN UNINCORPORATED BUSINESS TO A COMPANY

This section is concerned with the problems when an existing unincorporated business is transferred to a limited company. There are obviously a variety of ways in which this might happen, for instance:
(1) The transfer could be to a company formed or purchased 'off the shelf' by the proprietor of the business to take over the running of that business. Normally the transfer will be in consideration of the issue of shares in that new company (see *Salomon v Salomon & Co* (1897)).
(2) The business might be taken over by an existing company in return for shares in the company, cash, or a combination of both. Where cash is received the recipient might then use the moneys to start a new business or he might retire on the proceeds of the sale.

1 Income tax

Unincorporated trades are subject to income tax under Schedule D Case I and the result of a company takeover is that the closing year rules will apply so that the proprietor will be assessable (at the election of the inspector of taxes) to income tax on his actual profits of the final three tax years. The sum payable will be due 30 days after the assessment so that the taxpayer should ensure that he has sufficient cash (from the sale of the business or elsewhere) to meet this bill. Where assets only are sold and the former proprietor continues trading, these results do not follow: he will continue to be taxed according to the preceding year rules.

    Termination of a business results in terminal loss relief (TA 1970 s 174). As an alternative, where the business is sold to a company wholly or mainly for shares, the taxpayer can elect for any year throughout which he retains beneficial ownership of the shares to set off unrelieved trading losses against income that he receives from the company. The set-off must first be used against salary if the proprietor is employed by the company but any balance can be used to reclaim tax on dividends paid by the company TA 1970 s 172: see Chapter 7). The loss cannot, of course, be transferred to the company.

    A discontinuance may result in a claw-back of capital allowances by a balancing charge. Where the transfer is to a company controlled by the transferor, however, an election can be made, in the case of machinery and plant, that the trade shall not be treated as discontinued so that the company will take over the tax position of that person (FA 1971 Sch 8 para 13).

2 Capital gains tax

Any takeover involves the transfer of chargeable assets to the company with a consequent risk of CGT. A number of reliefs may be available:

a) *Where the transfer is in return for shares*

Hold-over relief under CGTA 1979 s 123 is available and operates to roll any gain on the business assets into the replacement shares. Capital gains tax will, therefore, be postponed until the shares are sold. For the relief to apply, all the business assets (except cash) must be transferred to the company. It follows that retention of appreciating business assets prevents s 123 from applying. If the consideration is partly shares and partly cash an appropriate portion of the gain will be subject to charge and only the balance will be held over (see Chapter 16).

b) *A transfer for cash*

Roll-over reinvestment relief under CGTA 1979 s 115 may be available if the disponer reinvests the proceeds of sale of permitted assets within the prescribed period (see p 233).

Where the disponer is over 60, retirement relief may be available, since the disposal will be of a business and will exempt gains of up to £100,000 from charge. Retirement relief cannot be claimed where the transfer is in return for shares and CGTA 1979 s 123 relief is available, but it may be available on a subsequent disposal of those shares provided that the company is a 'family trading company'. For the purposes of the ten year ownership requirement aggregation of the ownership of business and shares is permitted (see Chapter 16).

c) *A gift to the company*

Under CGTA 1979 s 123 all the assets of the business must be transferred to the company. It is possible to avoid CGT when some assets are to be retained by using CGTA 1979 s 126 to hold over the gain on the assets transferred. Note that the general relief for gifts in FA 1980 s 79 (as amended) does not apply to gifts made to companies.

d) *The retention of appreciating assets outside the company*

The problems of a double charge when capital gains are realised by a company has been discussed in Chapter 33. Where a business is incorporated, therefore, there may be attractions in retaining outside the corporation assets which are likely to appreciate substantially in value and to allow the company to use or lease those assets. (With the introduction of the indexation allowance only assets likely to rise faster than the RPI need to be retained.) Difficulties arise if this is done. For instance, CGTA 1979 s 123 will not apply to the incorporation so that, unless retirement relief or hold-over relief is available, gains on the incorporation will be subject to charge. The owner of the asset may be entitled to retirement relief on the eventual disposal of the asset (subject to satisfying the terms of ESC D11). Were the vendor to sell the asset and reinvest the proceeds, roll-over relief may be available under CGTA 1979 s 120 whilst a gift of the asset should attract hold-over relief under either FA 1980 s 79 or CGTA 1979 s 126. Such gifts also attract business property relief for CTT at a rate of 30% so long as the transferor controls the company.

3   Stamp duty

The sale of a business to a company may involve a charge to stamp duty (see Chapter 31) |unless the nil rate applies. Duty will be charged on the land, goodwill, book debts, cash in a deposit account, patents, copyright and know-how. It need not be charged on goods, wares and merchandise which can be transferred by delivery. Items such as stock-in-trade and cash in hand or in a current account may be included in the contract for sale of the business but need not be included in the certificate of value so long as they are not transferred by the instrument of transfer. An apportionment of consideration between the chargeable and non-chargeable assets may be made on Stamps Form 22. Duty will, however, be charged on liabilities taken over by a purchaser.

EXAMPLE 1

Yol agrees to sell his business to M Ltd for £39,000. M Ltd further agrees to take over Yol's outstanding liabilities to secured and trade creditors. The state of Yol's business is:

Liabilities	£	Assets	£
Secured creditors	8,000	Freehold	23,000
Trade creditors	12,000	Goodwill	6,000
		Stock	9,000
Excess of assets		Book debts	12,000
over liabilities	39,000	Deposit a/c	9,000
	£59,000		£59,000

M Ltd will purchase the business for a consideration for stamp duty purposes of £59,000, ie £39,000 (purchase price) + £20,000 (liabilities taken over).

Stamp duty will be reduced if the following measures are adopted:

(1) Cash is put into current account before contract.
(2) Yol retains the book debts (£12,000) to pay off trade creditors.
(3) Yol could retain the freehold premises and grant M Ltd a lease or licence to use them. This may not prove satisfactory where the company is not owned by Yol.
(4) The title to the stock does not pass under the conveyance but by delivery.

As a result of taking steps (1), (2) and (4) the consideration for stamp duty is reduced by £30,000 (£9,000 (cash) + £9,000 (stock) + £12,000 (book debts)) from £59,000 to £29,000. As a result no duty is charged provided a certificate of value is inserted into the contract and the appropriate entries made on Form 22. Retention of the book debts means that CGTA 1979 s 123 relief will not be available on the disposal of the chargeable assets.

4   Capital duty

Where the business is transferred in return for shares in the purchasing company, capital duty will be levied on the value of share capital received by that company. Form PUC3 must be completed and duty will be charged at £1 per £100, or part thereof, on the higher of the nominal value of the shares and the consideration received by the company. Hence, in *Example 1* above, had the acquisition been for shares, capital duty would be charged on the value of the business acquired (ie £39,000). An element of double duty is, therefore, present in the sale of assets for shares. If the business is being incorporated capital duty may be saved by transferring the business for cash not shares.

EXAMPLE 2

Milo plans to incorporate his business which is worth some £50,000. Were he to issue 50,000 × £1 shares, capital duty would be charged at a rate of 1% (£500). He could avoid duty by the following procedure:

(1) Form the company with a paid up capital of £100 (duty is 1% of £100 = £1). All shares are owned by Milo.
(2) Sell the business to the company for £99. No capital duty is charged on sales to companies. A higher consideration could be fixed and left on loan account.

This type of scheme solves the capital duty problem; however, does it cause other difficulties?

For CGT Relief under CGTA 1979 s 123 is not available. As the sale is apparently not a bargain at arm's length any gain resulting may be held over under CGTA 1979 s 126.

For CTT Although the transfer to the company appears to be at a gross undervalue, as Milo owns the company, he owns the business. It follows that CTT will not be charged since his estate has not fallen in value.

5 Problems for a purchasing company

Where the business is not being incorporated by the existing owner but instead is being sold to an existing company other difficulties for that purchaser should be noted. For instance, if the business is acquired as a going concern it must be treated separately for corporation tax purposes from any existing trade already carried on. The price paid for items such as land, plant and machinery, and goodwill constitute the purchaser's base cost for the purpose of computing any future capital gains. So far as capital allowances are concerned, a conflict of interest is likely with the vendor being concerned to attribute as small a sum as possible to such assets in order to avoid a balancing charge whilst for the purchaser a high figure will give him a greater capital allowance. The agreed apportionment set out in Form 22 will normally be accepted by the Revenue but will probably only be reached after hard bargaining between the parties.

6 Other matters

A number of ancilliary matters should also be considered on incorporation or sale of a business. The following summarises the more important:
(1) If an existing trade is incorporated, contracts of employment automatically transfer with the business. Where assets alone are sold, however, claims for redundancy will occur if staff are reduced. (See especially the Employment Protection (Consolidation) Act 1978 and the Transfer of Undertakings (Protection of Employment) Regulations 1981.)
(2) If the vendor of the business is a director of the purchasing company (this will normally be the case when a business is being incorporated) under Companies Act 1980 s 48 a general meeting of the company will usually

have to approve the agreement. If new shares are to be issued it will be necessary to ensure that the company has available shares (if necessary, share capital should be increased: see Companies Act 1948 s 61); that the directors have the power to allot such shares (see Companies Act 1980 s 14); and that any pre-emption provisions in the articles of association have either been satisfied or do not apply to the particular company.

(3) So long as the company is registered for VAT before the transfer of the business as a going concern there will be no charge on the transfer of items which are subject to VAT on the sale of the business. VAT may be chargeable on a transfer of assets (see VAT (Special Provisions) Order 1981 (SI 1981/1471)).

(4) Ensure that all necessary consents are obtained and/or documents amended, eg a landlord's consent to the assignment of a lease.

(5) If the business is sold for cash, the vendor should remember that for CTT purposes, business property relief and the instalment option will not be available on any transfer of value of that cash. An asset which carries a partial exemption for CTT is, therefore, being exchanged for cash which has no such exemption.

II   COMPANY TAKEOVERS

A sale of a company may take one of two different forms. Either the assets of the target company may be purchased; or the shares of that company may be acquired. In the former, the shareholders of the target will be left with a company whose sole asset is cash; in the latter, the shareholders themselves will be left with cash. On a share acquisition, the purchaser will have acquired the entire enterprise as a going concern and, if a corporate purchaser, will have acquired a subsidiary company. In an assets takeover, the purchaser may simply amalgamate those assets with his existing business so that instead of acquiring a new enterprise he may simply be expanding the existing business.

1   Considerations on an assets sale

a) *The vendor*

If the vendor company intends to continue in business an asset sale has the advantage that the vendor company will not be subject to corporation tax on any capital gains realised on prescribed assets if these are rolled over into the purchase of new assets within the permitted time. It is possible to reinvest in a completely different trade (see SP 8/81 and Chapter 16). A disposal of stock results in a corporation tax charge and a disposal of machinery and plant may lead to balancing charges.

If the company plans to discontinue trading permanently, the consequences are far from satisfactory. The company will be assessed on the capital profits made on the sale. Terminal loss relief will be available; carry-forward relief will of course be lost and the receipt of cash coupled with the cessation of trade may lead to a statutory apportionment of income. Problems will arise if the shareholders wish to extract the cash from the company. The result will be either an income tax charge on a distribution, or a charge to capital gains tax on a liquidation in addition to the tax charge already borne by the company. Strictly, retirement relief will not be available on a liquidation although a measure of concessionary relief is provided by SP 5/79 and 6/79. Generally, however, if the vendors plan to discontinue their business they should not engage in a sale of assets; it is better for them to sell the shares.

b) *The purchaser*

An assets purchase has a number of attractions. The purchaser can select which he wants (he is not buying the entire enterprise) and he will be entitled to allowances, for instance, on the purchase of plant and machinery, and to roll-over relief on the purchase of the prescribed assets. So far as the employees of the target company are concerned, the purchaser will find himself taking them over if the transfer is of the business as a going concern.

2 Considerations on a share sale

a) *The vendor*

This will be the preferable solution if the vendors are intending to go out of business. The sale of shares will be a disposal for CGT purposes and, if applicable, retirement relief can be claimed. Because the company is sold, there is no change of owner of the business so that continuity of employment is automatically preserved and all debts and liabilities effectively pass to the purchaser. Needless to say the vendors will normally be required to give certain undertakings and warranties to the purchaser so that there will be some continuing personal liability.

If the purchase moneys are to be paid in instalments CGT will still be charged on the total sum at once unless the Revenue allow the tax to be paid by instalments (see CGTA 1979 s 40). Where the consideration is partly cash and partly a chose in action (*Marren v Ingles* (1980); see p 201) retirement relief will only be available against the cash received and the value of the chose (if any); it will not be available on the later disposal of the chose in action.

If the vendors intend to stay in business, a share sale is normally not recommended since, for CGT, gains on the sale of the shares cannot be rolled over into new business assets.

b) *The purchaser*

The company is bought in toto so that there will be continuity in the business. There will be no tax relief for the purchase of the shares themselves, but exceptionally, the company purchased will have the advantage of a pre-corporation tax accounting period. The ability to continue to use trading losses is difficult to achieve. The carry-forward relief of TA 1970 s 177 requires that company to make profits *in the same trade* in the future if relief is to be available and if the trade has ceased at any time carry-forward is not possible even if an identical trade is later restarted. Further, TA 1970 s 483 prevents relief in the event (inter alia) of a 'major change in the nature or conduct of the trade' within a period of three years (see *Willis v Peeters Picture Frames Ltd* (1983); p 390). The prudent purchaser should, therefore, tread warily for three years before attempting any major revitalisation of the target company.

One headache for the purchaser is to ascertain what skeletons are hidden in the target company's cupboards. To this end, warranties and indemnities will normally be sought. Typical questions that need to be investigated are whether PAYE and VAT payments are up to date; what bonus shares have been issued (important in view of the potential risk of a distribution when an issue of such shares has occurred; see p 393); and in cases where the target is leaving a group of companies, whether any exit charges will apply to that company's chargeable assets under TA 1970 s 278 (see p 407).

c) *Stamp duty problems*

The transfer of shares will normally be assessable to ad valorem stamp duty at

1%. In the interests of a purchaser, the sale is often effected by the 'pref-trick' which is designed to minimise duty. The scheme relies on a stamp duty exemption for renounceable letters of allotment. When a company proposes to issue shares it may send to the applicant a letter indicating that shares have been allotted to him. The allotment can either be of fully paid bonus shares or nil paid in a rights issue. Such 'letters of allotment' may be renounceable by the recipient and if the rights are renounced within six months after the issue of the letter, stamp duty will not be charged on that renunciation (FA 1963 s 65).

EXAMPLE 3

(1) Zico Ltd is the target company. It has an issued share capital of £100,000 and reserves of £900,000. The purchaser, Pek Ltd, is to pay £1m. Stamp duty will, therefore, be chargeable at 1% giving a bill of £10,000. The saving scheme operates as follows:

Stage 1: Zico Ltd increases its share capital to £1m by capitalising the reserves of £900,000. This sum funds a 9:1 bonus issue in favour of the existing shareholders who are issued renounceable letters of allotment.

Stage 2: On the completion of the sale the shareholders renounce the bonus issue in favour of Pek Ltd in return for £900,000 and transfer the remaining £100,000 of issued shares. Stamp duty will be charged only on this transfer and will amount to £1,000 (1% × £100,000). The total saving will be £9,000.

Notes:
(a) The scheme depends for its success on the target having available reserves.
(b) A careful search should be made to ensure that the issue of bonus shares will not be taxed as a distribution (ie check for reductions in capital in the previous decade).
(c) Saving is in direct proportion to the number of shares issued. The 'pref-trick', however, achieves savings unrelated to the number of shares issued and can overcome the problem that the target may not have substantial reserves.

(2) Zaza Ltd (the target) has an issued share capital of £100,000 divided into shares of £1 each. It has reserves of £100,000 so that the saving scheme in (1) above would halve the stamp duty. The purchaser, Vava Ltd, is to pay £1m for the company. Hence, potential stamp duty will be £10,000. The 'pref-trick' operates as follows:

Stage 1: Zaza resolves to capitalise the £100,000 reserves and convert the £100,000 issued shares into eg 4% non-voting preference shares. The result will be to reduce substantially the value of the existing shares to perhaps their nominal value of £100,000. The value of the company will largely have shifted to the bonus ordinary issue. (An alternative method often used in practice is to convert into deferred shares with rights such that a value of 1p is ascribed.)

Stage 2: On completion of the sale, stamp duty will be charged on the preference shares transferred (1% of £100,000—ie £1,000) but the renunciation of the bonus issue worth £900,000 will not attract duty. The saving, therefore, will be £9,000.

Notes:
(a) The 'pref-trick' should not normally have adverse tax consequences outside the field of stamp duty. For CGT, for instance, the value-shifting provisions are irrelevant since no gains tax is being avoided.
(b) The scheme is undoubtedly an artificial tax-saving device and in certain circumstances, the *Ramsay* principle will be invoked to prevent avoidance of duty (see Appendix V).

3 Takeover by means of a share issue

Shares or assets in the target may be acquired in exchange for an issue of shares in the acquiring company. In such an event:

(1) CGT should not apply to the vendors since a roll-over deferral is available provided that the arrangement is a bona fide commercial one and, generally, that more than 25% of the target's shares are owned or acquired by the purchaser (CGTA 1979 s 85). Deferral is also available if the exchange is as a result of a general offer made to the shareholders of the target which is conditional upon the purchaser acquiring control of the target and is for bona fide commercial purposes. A clearance can be obtained from the Revenue that these requirements are satisfied. For the vendors, there is a risk that although the old shares qualified for retirement relief the new shares do not.

(2) If assets of the target are transferred in return for shares by way of a bona fide commercial arrangement with the target going into liquidation, there will be no corporation tax on the transfer of assets by the target. Instead, the assets will be transferred at no gain/no loss, so that tax will be deferred until the purchaser sells (TA 1970 s 267). The shares in the purchaser company received by the vendor's shareholders are not subject to CGT until sold (CGTA 1979 s 86). Again a clearance is available.

(3) On a share-for-share exchange, the purchaser may be liable to capital duty on the shares that he issues. There is relief from this duty under FA 1973 Sch 19 para 10 if the issue is to the holders of shares in another company in return for assets or at least 75% of the shares in that company. Although liability to stamp duty may also arise, relief will often be available under FA 1927 s 55 or ESC dated 27 July 1984 (see Appendix V).

III DEMERGERS

Splitting up groups of companies or splitting a company into separate parts under separate ownership has not attracted, until recently, special taxation provisions. FA 1980 Sch 18, is designed to afford relief in cases of demerger, from the distribution rules, in particular, but also from other taxes such as CGT and stamp duty. The conditions to be satisfied are highly technical and limited (see generally SP 13/80). In general, three types of transaction constitute a demerger and qualify for advantageous tax treatment:

(1) A transfer to ordinary shareholders of shares in another company of which the transferor owns at least 75% of the ordinary share capital.

(2) A transfer of a trade by company 1 to company 2 which issues shares in return to company 1's ordinary shareholders.

(3) An amalgamation of (1) and (2): viz shares in company 1's 75% subsidiary are transferred to company 2 in return for shares in that company.

Even where a transaction would appear to fall within one of these transactions, further criteria have to be satisfied if relief is to be given. Only trading companies and groups are covered, and each entity resulting from any split must be a trading entity. Further, the reason for the split must be to benefit the resulting trading entities and not to avoid tax. A clearance procedure is available and the form of application is set out in SP 13/80.

EXAMPLE 4

Audivis Ltd carries on two separate trades as a result of a merger of two existing businesses. Its shareholders are family A and family B who are concerned in the running of the different trades. The merger has failed and so two new companies (Audi Ltd and Vis Ltd) are formed and the trades are split between these two companies. As a result, the A family receive shares in Audi Ltd and the B family shares in Vis Ltd. So long as the provisions in the demerger legislation are satisfied (eg the transfer must not occur on the liquidation of Audivis Ltd) the share allotments will be treated as 'exempt distributions'. Broadly, therefore, tax is postponed until the new shares are sold.

IV   MANAGEMENT BUY-OUTS

There has been a noticeable increase in management buy-outs (MBO's) in recent years and, in the majority of cases, they have been commercially successful (see Economist Intelligence Unit Special Report No 164). The distinction between an MBO and an employee buy-out is that in the latter the business is purchased by all or a part of the work force not just by the managers. There are three typical situations when a buy-out may occur; firstly, when a subsidiary (or division) is purchased from a group of companies; second, when the owners sell the family company or its business; and third when a receiver or liquidator sells all or a part of the failed undertaking often by means of a hive-down. As with any take-over the management may purchase either shares of the target company or the assets of the business and similar considerations to those discussed on p 484ff apply in deciding which is the most advantageous method for vendor and purchaser.

When the company is purchased (ie a share purchase) the normal indemnities and warranties should be sought by the management team although the vendors will often take the view that if there are 'skeletons in the cupboard' this is a matter of which the managers will have knowledge.

The major difficulties involved in buy-outs relate to the financing of the purchase since the management team will lack sufficient funds to purchase the business out of their own resources. Accordingly the bulk of the finance must be supplied by institutional investors and the target company or business is generally purchased by a newly formed company ('Newco') in which the managers have voting control but in which the majority of the finance has been provided by the institutions (this will normally be in the form of unsecured loan stock and convertible preference shares).

It may be possible to use the assets of the target company to assist in the purchase of its own shares (see the Companies Act 1981 and, especially when target is a private company, s 43). The target's assets may for instance be used as security for the institutions' loans after it has been purchased. Alternatively, dividends or loans may be paid to Newco to enable it to discharge interest payments to the institutions (care should be taken in such cases to ensure that the close company apportionment rules do not apply). Finally, the target could be liquidated after its purchase and its assets transferred up to Newco. This would have the attraction of ending the holding company/trading subsidiary structure but care should be taken to ensure that the transfer of assets does not trigger a CGT charge (see CGTA 1979 s 72). Accordingly, it might be more satisfactory to transfer the business of the target as a going concern at book value and to leave the consideration outstanding on an inter-company loan account. The target would then be left as a 'shell' company.

So far as the managers are concerned, apart from using their own personal wealth to purchase shares in Newco, it will often be necessary for them to raise additional funds by way of loans. Income tax relief may be available on the interest paid on such loans (see generally Chapter 4). Under FA 1974 Sch 1 para 9 relief is given if the taxpayer works for the greater part of his time in the actual management or conduct of the company. When the buy-out is arranged through Newco, it is essential to ensure that it satisfies the test for a close trading company if para 9 relief is to be available. In practice, this means ensuring that 75% or more of its income is derived from trading subsidiaries and the Revenue accept that, so long as it is in receipt of the appropriate amount of dividends or income from the target during its first accounting period, this requirement will be treated as satisfied at the time when the managers make their investment. Relief will be available under FA 1974 Sch 1 para 10(C) and (D). Newco must be employee-controlled (ie full-time employees should control more than 50% of the ordinary share capital and votes) and it must be an unquoted trading company or the holding company of a trading group and for the purpose of this requirement Newco may qualify even though it has only the one trading subsidiary. If the company ceases to be employee controlled, tax relief is withdrawn.

35 Taxation of the family unit

'The subject is topical and important, because there has been growing dissatisfaction with the present system, particularly over the last few years. Admittedly, the present system broadly reflects what is probably still the normal arrangement under which the husband is the principal breadwinner. But many would not accept this as the foundation upon which the tax laws should be built.' (Cmnd 8093)

I INTRODUCTION

The income tax system proceeds on the basis that 'a woman's income chargeable to tax shall ... be deemed for income tax purposes to be [her husband's] income and not to be her income' (see TA 1970 s 37—originally enacted in 1806). This system of aggregation has been subject to a growing body of criticism in recent times. In 1980 a Consultative Paper, *The Taxation of Husband and Wife* (Cmnd 8093) aired the problems but produced no obvious alternative to the present system. The problem had already been considered by two Royal Commissions in this century: the Royal Commission on Income Tax in 1920 and the Radcliffe Commission in 1954, both of which came down in favour of a continuation of the present system.

II INCOME TAX

1 The aggregation of income

The income of a wife is aggregated with that of her husband so long as it is income for a year of assessment, or for any part of a year of assessment, during which she is a married woman living with her husband (TA 1970 s 37; but see *IRC v Addison* (1984) at p 188). TA 1970 s 42 defines the phrase 'living with her husband' as follows:

'(1) A married woman shall be treated for income tax purposes as living with her husband unless—
(a) they are separated under an order of a court of competent jurisdiction, or by deed of separation, or
(b) they are in fact separated in such circumstances that the separation is likely to be permanent.
(2) Where a married woman is living with her husband and either—
(a) one of them is, and one of them is not, resident in the UK for a year of assessment, or
(b) both of them are resident in the UK for a year of assessment, but one of them is, and one of them is not, absent from the UK throughout that year,

the same consequences shall follow for income tax purposes as would have followed if, throughout that year of assessment, they had been in fact separated in such circumstances that the separation was likely to be permanent.'

For income tax purposes, therefore, marriage ends at the time of factual separation. Continuing to live in the same house will not amount to separation, but, if the building is divided into two flats which are self-contained, it is likely that the couple will be living apart for income tax purposes. In practice, the Revenue require proof that there are two different households; for instance, there must be separate sleeping arrangements and cooking facilities.

Under a tax system with progressive rates of tax this system of aggregation often produces an increase in a couple's tax liability compared with the liability of two single persons with the same incomes.

EXAMPLE 1

Hulk has income of £14,000; and his wife, Winifred, income of £14,000. Two single people with the same incomes would fall within the basic rate band (for 1984–85 it extends to taxable income of up to £15,400). As a result of aggregation, however, Hulk is taxed on a total income of £28,000 which means that some tax will be levied at higher rates.

The husband is liable for the entire tax bill, but TA 1970 s 40 enables the Revenue to recover a proportion of the tax from the wife in the event of his failing to pay.

2 Personal allowances

A husband is entitled to the married man's allowance for years of assessment when his wife is living with him (TA 1970 s 8(1)). For 1984–85 the amount is £3,155. This allowance is given instead of two single person allowances (for 1984–85 the single allowance is £2,005) but is less than two single persons' allowances (by £875 for 1984–85). If, however, the wife is working, a further relief is given (the working wife allowance) which, is equal to the single person's allowance. Hence, if the couple are both working, and the wife earns at least £2,005 to obtain the full working allowance, they will receive more personal reliefs than two single people as the combined total of the married man's and working wife's allowance exceeds two single allowances by £1,150.

For 1984–85 income tax is chargeable at 30% on taxable income up to £15,400. Thus, if the couple both work, the wife earns more than £2,005, and their combined incomes do not exceed £15,400, aggregation will result in less income tax being payable than by two single people, because of the higher aggregate personal allowances available to a married couple.

EXAMPLE 2

On the facts of *Example 1*, Hulk and Winifred will obtain the full married man's and working wife allowances. The tax bill will, therefore, be:

	£
Total income	28,000
Less: married man's and working wife allowance	
(£3,155 + £2,005)	5,160
Taxable income	£22,840

Income tax:

£15,400 at 30%	£4,620
£2,800 at 40%	£1,120
£4,640 at 45%	£2,088
Total income tax payable	£7,828

The wife's earned income allowance is given to a working wife who has her own PAYE coding. She is entitled to any repayments of tax deducted under PAYE from her earnings.

3   The option for separate assessment (TA 1970 s 38)

Either the husband or wife can elect for 'separate assessment' which does not affect the overall tax charge, but it makes both husband and wife liable for their respective share of the total tax bill. If they wish, they can complete separate tax returns. The tax bill of the couple is worked out in the normal way and the available reliefs and rate bands are divided between them in proportion to their respective incomes. If the wife has earned income, however, her share of the total allowances must be not less than her earned income allowance.

The advantage of separate assessment is not that the couple pay less tax; rather, it ensures that the wife can handle her own affairs and releases the husband from responsibility for the income tax attributable to his wife's income. Separate assessment cannot be used as a means of one spouse keeping his affairs confidential from the other. Even if separate returns are filled in, it remains possible for each spouse to work out the income of the other from the total tax that is being charged on the couple.

4   Wife's earnings election (FA 1971 s 23)

In contrast to separate assessment, the wife's earnings election alters the total tax that is payable. It is sometimes known as the 'separate taxation' election. A joint election by the couple is required and once made, it remains in force for subsequent tax years until revoked (FA 1971 s 23(3)). It is, therefore, crucial for couples to reconsider their tax position in each tax year and, if necessary, to make or revoke the election. The election, in respect of any tax year, may be made in the period starting 6 months prior to that year and ending one year after the end of that tax year.

If the election is made, the wife is taxed as a single woman on her earned income. For personal allowances, the couple will be treated as two single persons, so that each receives the single allowance of £2,005 for 1984–85. The married man's allowance and working wife's allowances are not, therefore, available and the couple cannot claim the extra single parent allowance for any children (TA 1970 s 14(4)).

Although the wife is taxed separately on her earned income, her unearned income continues to be aggregated with her husband's income. The election affects the availability of loss relief (see p 112) and life insurance relief (p 44) in cases where the policy was effected before 14 March 1984 on the life of one spouse and the premiums are paid by the other.

The fact that the wife's earned income is no longer aggregated with income of her husband can result in a saving of higher rate income tax. As the election means some overall loss of personal allowances, it is worthwhile only if the saving in higher rate income tax exceeds the extra tax charged because of the loss of allowances. For 1984–85, the election will only be worthwhile where the

*"And what are you going to give me to make up
for all those wasted years on a joint assessment?"*

combined taxable income of the couple is at least £23,795 and the spouse with the smaller earnings earns at least £6,388 during that year. Even when the election is in force, the husband remains responsible for completing the tax return showing his and his wife's total income, unless there is also an election for separate assessment in force.

5 Tax in year of marriage

In the tax year of marriage the income of the wife is not aggregated with that of her husband (FA 1976 s 36). She is, therefore, entitled to the single person's allowance for that year. The husband, however, is entitled to the married man's allowance for the year of marriage, reduced by 1/12th of £1,150 (the difference between the married and single person allowances) for each complete month that passes from 6 April to the date of marriage. To obtain maximum reliefs for the year, the marriage should, therefore, occur between 6 April and the following 5 May.

EXAMPLE 3

Alfred and Petula marry on 10 July 1984. Petula is entitled to a single person's allowance (£2,005) in respect of her income for 1984–85. Alfred receives an allowance of £3,155 – (3/12 × £1,150) = £2,867.50 in respect of his income for the tax year.

6 Death of either spouse

The income tax consequences of the death of a spouse depend upon which spouse dies first. If the wife dies first, the husband is entitled to the full married man's allowance for the tax year in which she dies. He has a right, within two months of a grant of probate being taken out, to disclaim liability for unpaid income tax in respect of his wife's income for any year when they were living together (TA 1970 s 41).

When the husband dies first, his PRs are entitled to the benefit of the married man's allowance to set against his income for the tax year up to the date of his death. His widow will, if she is working, be entitled to the working wife's allowance for the portion of the year during which he was alive, and thereafter to the full single person's allowance for the rest of the tax year. The wife will also be entitled to the widow's bereavement allowance for the year of the death and one following year provided she has not previously remarried (for 1984–85 it is £1,150. Thus, for the year of death and the following tax year a widow is given allowances equal to those of a married man (TA 1970 s 15A). The additional personal allowance (the single parent family allowance) will also be payable in appropriate circumstances when one spouse dies (see p 39; for 1984–85 it is £1,150). For the position if the husband dies first, see below.

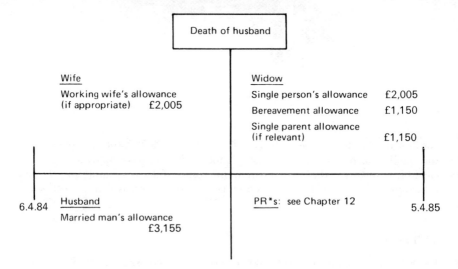

7   **Taxation of cohabitees**

When a couple are not legally married, they are taxed as two single persons even if they are living together. Each is, therefore, entitled to the single person's allowance, and, if they have a child, the single parent allowance will also be given. If they have two children it may be that they can each claim the allowance in respect of one of the children.

A married couple are entitled to mortgage interest relief for interest on a loan of up to £30,000 only; cohabitees are each entitled to that amount of relief.

8   **Taxation of children**

The income of infant children is not aggregated with that of their parents. They are, therefore, taxed as separate persons and will be entitled to the full single person allowance.

Covenants by parents in favour of their own infant unmarried children are ineffective for income tax purposes (see TA 1970 s 437 and Chapter 10); the amount covenanted is treated as the income of the parent. However, covenants to grandchildren by grandparents escape TA 1970 s 437 so that a child's personal allowance can be used to obtain a tax refund, if the child has no other income. For the use of a child's personal allowance on the breakdown of marriage see Chapter 36.

III CAPITAL GAINS TAX

1 Aggregation

The gains of a wife are charged on the husband in any tax year in which they are 'living together'; however, a wife can elect for separate assessment (CGTA s 45(1)). The definition of 'living together' is taken from income tax (TA 1970 s 42), but where spouses are deemed to be separated because one of them is absent from or not resident in the UK for the tax year, there will be no CGT charge on transfers between them (*Gubay v Kington* (1984) and TA 1970 s 42(2) proviso).

The couple share a single annual exemption (for 1984–85 £5,600) which is apportioned between them in accordance with their taxable amounts for that year. The 'taxable amount' is defined as the excess of chargeable gains for the year over allowable losses of that year and losses brought forward from a previous year (CGTA 1979 Sch 1 para 2(1)(a); see p 212). If the spouses' combined chargeable gains in any tax year do not exceed the annual exemption and either spouse has unused losses from earlier years an election can be made to divide the relief in the way most favourable to the utilisation of that loss (see p 213). For the year of marriage each spouse is entitled to the full £5,600 exemption (CGTA 1979 Sch 5 para 2(2)).

2 Losses

Generally losses of a spouse must be offset against the chargeable gains arising to that spouse in the tax year (CGTA 1979 s 4(1)). Surplus losses are offset against net chargeable gains of the other spouse in that year (s 4(2)). Any unused loss is then carried forward in the usual way against future gains of the spouse who made the loss; any loss still unrelieved is used against gains of the other spouse. Either spouse may elect, within 3 months from the end of the tax year in question, for the loss not to be offset against gains of the other spouse.

EXAMPLE 4

	Mr A	Mrs A
1984–85	£	£
Gains	5,500	1,300
Losses	(1,500)	(2,500)
Losses b/f	nil	nil
1985–86:		
Gains	4,000	2,800
Losses	nil	nil

In 1984–85 the net chargeable gains of Mr A (£5,500 – £1,500 = £4,000) will fall within the annual exemption and will not be taxed. He should elect not to have Mrs A's unused loss (£1,200) set against those gains.

In 1985–86 Mrs A will, if the above election is made, carry forward her loss of £1,200 and use it to reduce her gains in that year to £1,600. Therefore, the total gains of the couple will be £5,600 and will not be subject to CGT.

3 **Inter-spouse transfers** (CGTA 1979 s 44)

The disposal of an asset by one spouse to another is treated as being for such consideration as gives rise to neither gain nor loss. This rule operates whether or not any consideration is furnished for the transfer and in spite of the couple being connected persons. Effectively, therefore, gains are held over and the asset will be acquired at the base cost of the disponer spouse together with any incidental costs involved in the disposal. The rule in s 44 applies only as long as the spouses are 'living together'.

The indexation allowance will be included in the deemed consideration when a disposal occurs after 5 April 1982 and the disponer has owned the asset for 12 months. If the asset has not been owned for 12 months, there is no allowance; however, the transferee spouse will be able to claim the allowance by reference to the date when it was acquired by the transferor spouse. Accordingly if he has served the qualifying 12 month period of ownership the allowance is immediately available to the transferee spouse.

EXAMPLE 5

Jim gives his wife Judy two birthday presents on 1 January 1985, a Ming vase which he acquired from Christie's on 1 April 1984 and a painting by William Roberts acquired on 10 April 1983.
(1) *The vase* will not qualify for any indexation allowance when transferred to Judy, but she will be able to claim the allowance from 1 April 1985.
(2) *The picture* will qualify for the allowance from April 1984 to January 1985 so that Judy's base costs will be increased accordingly. Judy will enjoy the benefit of the allowance from 1 January 1985.

4 **Retirement relief**

Retirement relief is available to both spouses and may be used to ensure that gains of £200,000 in aggregate are exempt from charge (see Chapter 16).

5 **Cohabitees and children**

The general CGT principles operate for disposals between cohabitees and between parents and their children. In the case of disposals to children the connected person rules operate with the result that any disposal will be deemed to be made at market value. However, liability for CGT on gifts can be avoided by the hold-over election in FA 1980 s 79 (see Chapter 17).

IV CAPITAL TRANSFER TAX

1 **General principles**

There is no aggregation of spouses' chargeable transfers for CTT purposes so that they are treated as separate taxable entities and are each entitled to the full exemptions and reliefs. It is immaterial whether they are living together. If care is taken with the associated operations (p 285) and related property (p 283) rules, transfers between spouses offer an opportunity to mitigate CTT. A couple remain married for CTT until the decree absolute which terminates the marriage. During marriage transfers between spouses are exempt without limit (except where the donee spouse is domiciled abroad, when only £55,000 may be transferred free of CTT). The inter-spouse exemption means that full use may be taken of both spouses' exemptions and reliefs and benefits may be obtained by equalising their total chargeable transfers.

2 Equalisation between spouses

The standard tax planning advice given to spouses is that they should seek to make the same total of chargeable transfers; ie the chargeable transfers of a husband both during life and on death should be equal to those made by his wife. Both will then have taken full advantage of their lower rate bands of CTT.

EXAMPLE 6

H owns £1m (having made no chargeable lifetime transfers). W owns nothing.
If H leaves all to W:

	£	
CTT on H's death	nil	(spouse exemption)
CTT on W's death	528,250	(on £1m)
	£528,250	

Contrast:
If H leaves half to W and half to his children:

	£	
CTT on H's death	228,250	(on £500,000)
CTT on W's death	228,250	(on £500,000)
	£456,500	

Therefore, the CTT saving is £71,750 (£528,250 − £456,500).

If the first spouse to die makes chargeable transfers instead of leaving all to the survivor, CTT is paid earlier than it otherwise would have been unless only the nil rate band (for 1984–85, £64,000) is chargeable on the first death.

EXAMPLE 7

(1) H owns £150,000 (having made no chargeable lifetime transfers). W owns nothing.
If H leaves all his property to W:

	£	
CTT on H's death	nil	(spouse exemption)
CTT on W's death	30,850	(on £150,000)
	£30,850	

If H leaves £71,700 to the children tax-free (which grosses up to £75,000), to equalise chargeable transfers:

	£	
CTT on H's death	3,300	(on £71,700 grossed-up)
CTT on W's death	3,300	(on £75,000)
	£6,600	

By equalising chargeable transfers less CTT is payable, but CTT must be paid at the time of the first death.
(2) As in (1) but H leaves £60,000 to his children:

	£	
CTT on H's death	nil	(on £60,000)
CTT on W's death	8,050	(on £90,000)
	£8,050	

More CTT is payable overall than if chargeable transfers had been equalised, but no CTT is chargeable on the first death.

It may be desirable to ensure that the surviving spouse can obtain all the property should the need arise. At the same time, there are advantages of using up the nil rate band in favour of (say) children. One way of achieving both objectives is to set up a discretionary trust of £64,000 in the following terms:

(a) *duration of trust:* the full perpetuity period—for instance, 79 years;

(b) *beneficiaries:* surviving spouse, children and grandchildren;

(c) *the discretion:* a wide discretion in the trustees to appoint both income and capital during the trust period;

(d) *provision in default:* should there still be unappointed assets at the end of the trust period the amount should be divided in equal shares amongst the living beneficiaries; and

(e) *protection of surviving spouse:* provision that the surviving spouse is to be the beneficiary with the greatest claim upon the trustees (if desired, the spouse could be appointed a trustee).

Such a trust has the attractions that there will be no CTT payable on creation through the use of the testator's nil rate band; assuming that the rates of CTT remain linked to inflation, subsequent anniversary and exit charges are likely to be nil or very small; and the paramount wish of the testator for flexibility is achieved since, if need arises, the entire fund can be distributed to the surviving spouse; otherwise full use has been made of the testator's nil rate band.

Two other problems may be mentioned. First, due allowance for the continued ability of the surviving spouse to use the lifetime exemptions and lower lifetime rates of CTT must be taken into account in deciding how much to give to that spouse. Where the survivor is likely to live for at least a further three years, the lower life rates are obviously an attraction as compared to the testator spouse's death rates, particularly so, where the age difference between them is considerable. Hence, exact equalisation is often to be avoided.

The second problem is concerned with when a couple should divide their assets between themselves so that they can make equal chargeable transfers. In principle, the answer must be during their joint lives; if it is proposed to make the equalising transfer on death, the chance of equalisation will be lost if the poorer spouse dies first. Despite this argument, equalising transfers are often made on death. Whenever this is the case, the use of a survivorship clause in the will (see Chapter 22) should be avoided because if such a clause is used and the surviving spouse dies within six months of the first spouse, the property will pass in accordance with that clause so that the spouse exemption will not be used and, instead, the property will be taxed as part of the estate of the first to die.

3   Using the matrimonial home in tax planning

As this is often the only substantial asset of a couple its possible use in tax planning must be considered.

Both spouses have the annual CTT exemption which can be rolled forward for one year. Hence, at the end of two years the couple could have an exemption of £12,000. If they wish to utilise this by giving away a £12,000 stake in their home, they must give the donee an interest in the property; a mere charge in his favour is insufficient since, unless a liability is 'incurred in money or money's worth' it does not reduce the transferor's estate (FA 1975 Sch 10 para 1(3)).

EXAMPLE 8

H and W jointly own a house as tenants in common. The value of the house is £72,000. They have accumulated annual exemptions of £12,000.

To use the £12,000 exemption H and W give (say) their daughter a 1/6th share of the property. The result would be that the house is now owned by the three of them as tenants in common in the shares:

H: 5/12; W: 5/12; D: 1/6

At the end of a further two years the process could be repeated, and so on. Ultimately, the entire equitable ownership of the property may be vested in the daughter.

A scheme of the above kind creates its own problems. First, once the daughter becomes a co-owner of the property she has a right to occupy the premises and, as the house will be held under a trust for sale (see Law of Property Act 1925 ss 34–36), she might force a sale against her parents' wishes. Secondly, care must be taken in valuing the spouses' interest after each successive gift as the drop in value of their estates, because of the daughter's increasing share, may be greater than the amount of the exemption, thereby exposing them to a CTT charge.

The main residence may also be used to equalise the estates of husband and wife whilst ensuring that the surviving spouse can occupy it undisturbed (see the following examples).

An alternative arrangement involves the couple selling the house to their daughter, in return for a non-assignable long lease determinable on their death and a lump sum equal to the difference between the value of the lease and the freehold reversion. The lease confers exclusive possession, has no value for CTT on their death and is not a settlement for CTT purposes because it is created for valuable consideration. The capital sum can be left outstanding as an interest-free loan and written off against the couple's annual CTT exemption.

EXAMPLE 9

(1) H and W have a joint estate of £150,000 including the matrimonial home worth £100,000. H is the absolute owner of the house and settles it by his will which allows the surviving spouse to live in it.

If an interest in possession trust is created the surviving spouse is, for CTT purposes, treated as the owner of the property (see Chapter 25). CTT on H's death will be nil (spouse exemption) and on the death of W the full value of the house will be taxed.

If a discretionary (no interest in possession) trust is created, with the wife included among the class of beneficiaries, and, if the trustees permit W to reside there with the intention of providing her with a permanent home, the Revenue will argue that an interest in possession has been created (see SP 10/79 and p 343) with the results that:

(a) on H's death CTT is chargeable on the creation of the discretionary trust;

(b) on the trustees exercising their power to allow W to occupy the house there will be a CTT 'changeover' charge as property moves from one type of trust to another (see p 355). Although, if the power is exercised within two years of H's death, this charge will not arise and CTT paid on H's death can be recovered (FA 1975 s 47(1A): see p 320); and

(c) on the death of W, CTT will be charged on the value of the house since an interest in possession will terminate.

(2) As in (1), but assume that the house is beneficially owned in equal shares by the couple. The first spouse to die (say H) owns a half share valued at £50,000. He could settle that share on discretionary trusts for the children so that on his death CTT on the half share will be nil (nil rate band).

After H's death W will continue to occupy the house by virtue of her half share as a tenant in common. Presumably, when W dies CTT will be assessable only on that half share. The other share (in the discretionary trust) will not be charged since there will be no interest in possession therein.

If W was one of the beneficiaries under the discretionary trust, it could be said that the trustees were permitting her to live in the house giving rise to an interest in possession and a CTT charge on her death. Against that view, it could be argued that her occupation of the house was *qua* tenant in common not *qua* beneficiary of the trust. Obviously, the trustees should refrain from exercising a power in her favour within the terms of SP 10/79 (see p 343).

(3) As in (2), but H settles a half share in the house and allows the discretionary trustees to sell that interest to W for full value (£50,000). The sale contract should contain a provision that completion will occur only on W's death. Stamp duty will thereby be deferred until completion of the contract. Until completion interest at a commercial rate should accrue and should likewise be payable on W's death. The result is security for the surviving wife and, of course, her estate will be diminished on her death by the contractual debt and interest that will be payable on her purchase of the half share in the dwelling house.

4 Cohabitees and children

The general principles of CTT apply to transfers between cohabitees and between parents and children. In the latter case the connected person provisions apply.

IV STAMP DUTY

There is no exemption from duty on sales or gifts between spouses which will, therefore, be subject to duty in appropriate circumstances.

36 Matrimonial breakdown

I   Income tax
II Capital gains tax
III Capital transfer tax
IV The matrimonial home

Matrimonial breakdown often has major tax repercussions. It is also an occasion when there is considerable scope for tax planning.

I INCOME TAX

1 General principles

On the breakdown of a marriage, the parties revert to single status. For the year of separation, the man will receive the full married man's allowance; thereafter, normally the single person allowance only. The parties will be entitled to the working wife's allowance up to the date of separation; thereafter, the woman will receive a single person allowance. If there are children the single parent family allowance may be available to the parent who has custody of the children. For income tax purposes the marriage ends when the parties separate (see Chapter 35).

2 Maintenance payments to a former spouse

The income tax treatment of maintenance payments (to, eg, a former or estranged wife) varies according to how the payments are made.

a) *Voluntary maintenance*

Voluntary maintenance is paid by the husband under no legally binding obligation; there is neither a court order nor a deed of covenant. As a result, he will obtain no tax relief on the payments which will, therefore, be made out of taxed income. The recipient wife will not be treated as receiving income, so that she cannot obtain a refund of tax. Generally, therefore, voluntary payments should be avoided since they are tax inefficient, although, whilst the husband makes them he will remain entitled to the full married man's allowance up to the date of final divorce provided that the maintenance is at least equal to any other taxable income that the wife possesses (ie he must be substantially maintaining her).

b) *Maintenance payments by deed of covenant*

A maintenance payment by deed of covenant is taxed as an annual payment (see Chapter 10). However, certain points should be stressed. First, providing that the covenant is capable of lasting for more than 6 years (eg 'to my former wife for life or until remarriage') and is irrevocable it will be a fully effective annual payment for income tax purposes, since TA 1970 s 457 (which generally renders annual payments ineffective for the purposes of excess liability) does not apply to maintenance payments (TA 1970 s 457(1)(c)). Therefore, the payer will effectively alienate a slice of his income. Secondly, the covenanted maintenance payment is made after deduction of tax at source under TA 1970 s 52 or s 53 so that the wife will receive a net sum together with a certificate that basic rate tax has been deducted. Finally, the wife's income will include the gross amount of the maintenance payment, under Schedule D Case III, against which she can set any unrelieved allowances and charges in order to obtain a refund of the basic rate tax. Alternatively, she may be liable for tax on the payment at higher rates.

EXAMPLE 1

Jason has income of £23,000 pa. He covenants to pay his separated wife Julie £5,000 pa as maintenance for the rest of her life or until remarriage. She has income of £5,000 pa and has custody of the two children of the marriage.

(1) *The taxation of Jason*   The maintenance payment is a charge on Jason's income so that the gross sum is deductible from his income. He will pay basic rate tax on the payment (see TA 1970 s 3). His income tax bill is:

		£
Gross income		23,000
Less maintenance payment		5,000
Total income		18,000
Less single person allowance		2,005
Taxable income		£15,995
£15,400 taxed at 30%		4,620
£595 taxed at 40%		238
add tax at 30% on maintenance payment		1,500
Total income tax		£6,358

(2) *The payments of maintenance*   Under TA 1970 s 52 Jason will deduct and retain a sum equal to the basic rate tax (ie £1,500). He will, accordingly, give Julie £3,500.

(3) *The taxation of Julie*   Julie's income will include the gross amount of the maintenance payment (£5,000) and she will have a credit for the basic rate tax deducted at source. Her income tax bill is, therefore:

		£
Gross income		10,000
Less allowances:		
single person allowance	£2,005	
single parent family allowance	£1,150	
		3,155
Taxable income		£6,845
£6,845 taxed at 30%		2,053.50
Less tax credit		1,500
Total income tax payable		£553.50

It should be noted that similar tax consequences ensue if the maintenance agreement is oral or in writing (ie not by a deed) provided that the recipient furnishes valuable consideration. Giving up a claim to property or maintenance would be adequate for these purposes.

A formula can be used to ensure that the wife receives a net sum each year which does not vary with changes in the basic rate of income tax (see Chapter 10).

If the payer has the right to deduct basic rate tax at source but omits to do so, he may be entitled to concessional relief equivalent to the repayment of tax that the recipient would have received if tax had been deducted from the payment.

c) *Maintenance payments ordered by the court*

Maintenance payments ordered by the court in favour of a former or separated spouse are generally taxed in the same way as payments under a deed of covenant (see b) above). A small maintenance payment is, however, treated differently. This is defined in TA 1970 s 65 as a payment which:

(a) is ordered by a UK court (it may be by a consent order);
(b) must be made weekly or monthly (an order to make annual payments is, therefore, outside the definition); and
(c) must not exceed £33 per week, if payable weekly, or £143 per month, if payable monthly. (The total annual payment will not, therefore, exceed £1,716 which, for 1984–85, is less than the single person allowance of £2,005.)

Small maintenance payments differ from other maintenance payments in that they must be paid gross. The payer is not, therefore, subject to basic rate tax on the sum paid nor may he deduct an equivalent sum from the payment. Tax is collected by direct assessment on the payee, although small maintenance payments are designed for parties with lower incomes to avoid cash flow problems. These would arise if tax were deducted at source and subsequently reclaimed by the payee.

EXAMPLE 2

Julian, with income of £7,000 pa, is ordered to pay his former wife, Camilla, £140 per month. She has no other income.

(1) Julian will be taxed on £7,000–£1,680 (total maintenance payments for the year) ie £5,320 so that he will be taxed as follows:

	£
Total income	5,320
Less single person allowance	2,005
Taxable income	£3,315
Tax at 30%	£994.50

(2) Julian will pay Camilla £140 each month.

(3) Camilla's income is £1,680 per annum so that, with a single person allowance of £2,005, she will not be liable to income tax.

Tax relief is not available for voluntary payments made on separation. The courts, however, have a limited jurisdiction to make backdated maintenance orders (see, for instance, on initial applications, Matrimonial Causes Act 1973 ss 28(1), 29(2)) and the Revenue's attitude to such orders is set out in SP 6/81. For income tax purposes the backdated payments will be treated as effective annual payments so long as both parties agree; the payments do not relate to a period before the date of application for the order; and there has been no undue delay by the parties in proceeding with the application. Although backdated payments are so treated, it does not necessarily follow that the effect of a court order is to convert earlier voluntary payments into effective annual payments; however it is believed that this is done as a matter of Revenue practice.

Finally note that as the right to receive maintenance ceases upon the death of the payer, a divorced wife who has obtained a court order for maintenance for herself or her children may insure her ex-husband's life until he is 60 without his knowledge or consent provided that she can afford to pay the premiums, which, for policies made after 13 March 1984, attract no income tax relief.

3   Maintenance payments for the benefit of children

a) *The problems*

Securing adequate provision for children is a more complex topic from an income tax point of view than the provision of maintenance for a former or separated spouse. Any income that is set aside for their benefit may be charged to income tax in one of three ways: first, as the income of the payer, normally the father; secondly, as the income of the spouse who has custody of the child, normally the mother; or, finally, as the income of the child.

The ideal usually is to ensure that the income is taxed as the child's because he may have unused personal allowances which will result in an overall saving of income tax at basic and higher rates. If the income is taxed as that of either parent the sum will often be charged to income tax because there will be no unused allowances. The major difficulty to be surmounted if the income is to be taxed as that of the child are the anti-avoidance provisions of TA 1970 s 437 and s 457 (see below and Chapter 10). TA 1970 s 434 is avoided provided that the payments exceed or are capable of exceeding 6 years.

b) *Deeds of covenant in favour of children*

A deed of covenant in favour of a child of the settlor will usually be ineffective or partially ineffective for income tax purposes because of TA 1970 ss 437 and 457. First, if the covenant is in favour of an infant unmarried child of the settlor, TA 1970 s 487 treats the sum as income of the payer; as the child is, therefore, not taxed on covenanted income, her personal allowances are wasted.

Secondly, although a covenant in favour of an adult or married child of the settlor, escapes TA 1970 s 437, it falls within TA 1970 s 457 and is treated as the payer's income for higher rate tax. The payee is not, therefore, precluded from reclaiming basic rate income tax, if he has unused allowances (see p 151.)

EXAMPLE 3

On the breakdown of his marriage Toby, who has an income of £17,000, executed two deeds of covenant; one in favour of his two-year-old daughter, Sarah, to pay her £1,000 pa until she is 18; the other in favour of his 19 year old daughter Valerie to pay her £1,000 pa for the next 7 years. Sarah's covenant falls within TA 1970 s 437 so that the £1,000 is taxed as Toby's income and Sarah is deemed to have no income for income tax purposes. Valerie's covenant escapes s 437 but is caught by s 457 so that Toby is taxed on his income of £17,000 without distinguishing the payment; he deducts basic rate tax under TA 1970 s 52 from the payment so that she receives £700. However, the income is hers for basic rate tax purposes so that she has an income tax credit for the £300 deducted by Toby which she can reclaim if she has unused personal allowances.

c) *Deeds of covenant to a spouse for the benefit of a child*

Payments may be made to a former or separated spouse with the intention that they should be used for the benefit of a child. Where the payment is not directed to be held on trust for the child, it is taxed as the income (in effect, as extra maintenance) of the recipient spouse. It will be a charge on the income of the payer and taxed as income of the payee. From an income tax point of view, this method of payment may be better than having the payment taxed as income of the payer (which would be the case if the payment was direct to the child and not under a court order). However, it will be disadvantageous if the payee has no unused allowances so that basic rate tax cannot be reclaimed and the personal allowance of the child will be wasted.

If the payment is to be held on trust for the benefit of a child who is an unmarried minor, it is treated as a settlement for the child and taxed as the income of the payer under TA 1970 s 437.

d) *Court orders*

The difficulties that beset deeds of covenant do not apply to court orders providing for payments to children. The court order (including a consent order) should provide for payment to be made directly to the child because the sum paid will operate as a charge on the income of the payer and will be taxed as the income of the recipient child. It will not be caught by TA 1970 ss 437 or 457 (see *Stevens v Tirard* (1940) and *Yates v Starkey* (1951)) since those provisions only catch annual payments with an element of bounty, which a court order lacks. The order is, therefore, taxed as a fully effective annual payment and is normally the most satisfactory method of providing for a child.

EXAMPLE 4

Hugh, with income of £20,000, is ordered by the court to pay £1,500 pa to his daughter, Chlöe, aged 2, until she attains 18. (Chlöe has no other income).
(1) Hugh's income is reduced to £18,500. He will pay basic rate tax on the covenant (30% of £1,500 = £450).
(2) He makes the payment subject to deduction of tax under TA 1970 s 52, so will hand over to Chlöe £1,050 (£1,500 − £450).
(3) Chlöe's income is £1,500 and she will have a tax credit for £450. As her personal allowance of £2,005 exceeds her income she will be entitled to recover the £450 tax.

A payment into the mother's bank account for the benefit of the child does not affect the tax position. Nor is it affected if the court orders the payment in whole or in part to be made directly to a school for the benefit of the child, provided that the order directing payment contains the formula:

'that part of the order which reflects the school fees shall be paid to the [headmaster] [bursar] [school secretary] as agent for the said child and the receipt of that payee shall be a sufficient discharge.'

A form of contract between the child and the school which reflects this wording and which is acceptable to the Revenue is set out in Appendix IV. School fees are, therefore, tax deductible when paid by a separated parent, but not when paid by parents who are living together!

A court order may be for a small maintenance payment (defined in TA 1970 s 65) to a dependent child. As for payments to a spouse, the payments should be weekly or monthly and the same financial limits apply (ie £33 per week or £143 per month), with the additional requirement that the payment must be made 'to any person under 21 years of age for his own benefit, maintenance or education'. Additionally, a small maintenance payment may be ordered 'to any person for the benefit, maintenance or education of a person under 21 years of age'. However, the financial limits are reduced so that the payments must not exceed £18 per week or £78 per month and the payment will be taxed as the income of the recipient (normally the mother) and not as that of the child. Since payments directly to the child confer tax advantages and enjoy higher financial limits, it will be rare in practice for this type of small maintenance payment to be ordered by the court.

All small maintenance payments must be paid gross and any income tax owing is collected by direct assessment on the child.

In conclusion, a court order providing for payment direct to a child or to discharge school fees will normally be the most tax efficient method of providing for children on separation or divorce. In cases where the payment is ordered in favour of the Secretary of State for Social Services following a complaint from the Supplementary Benefits Commission, however, it cannot be a small maintenance payment despite being a weekly payment falling within the financial limits (*McBurnie v Tacey* (1984)). Accordingly, the payer is not entitled to deduct the payments in computing his total income. He can, however, ask the court to consider his tax position and substitute, for the order to the DHSS, a maintenance order in favour of his former spouse (see *Peacock v Peacock* (1984)). If the payee assigns the benefit of a court order to the DHSS in return for the payment of supplementary benefit, the payments continue to be taxed as annual payments for both payer and the original payee.

II   CAPITAL GAINS TAX

Disposals between spouses are not subject to CGT and are treated as made for a consideration which will produce neither gain nor loss (see CGTA 1979 s 44; Chapter 14). Once the spouses separate this provision ceases to apply and the ordinary rules of CGT operate (but note *Gubay v Kington* (1984) p 495). Hence, a transfer of chargeable assets between spouses after their separation may be subject to CGT (see, for instance, *Aspden v Hildesley* (1982)). Although the exemption for inter-spouse transfers is lost, the couple remain connected persons until final divorce so that disposals between separation and divorce are deemed not to be bargains at arm's length, but are treated as for a consideration equal to the market value of the property (CGTA 1979 s 62). The gain on such disposals may, however, be held over under FA 1980 s 79 if both parties agree.

EXAMPLE 5

Tom and Margot are separated and as part of the financial settlement on divorce, Tom conveys their holiday home in Cornwall to Margot with a chargeable gain of £35,000. If Tom and Margot jointly so elect, the gain can be held over under FA 1980 s 79. As a result Margot will acquire an asset pregnant with gain and with a lower figure of allowable expenditure for indexation purposes. (She will only qualify for the indexation allowance after she has owned the house for one year.)

After separation, the wife is entitled to the annual exemption from CGT (currently £5,600) which she can set against her chargeable gains in the remainder of the tax year of separation (CGTA 1979 Sch 1 para 2(2)).

III CAPITAL TRANSFER TAX

For CTT purposes marriage continues until the final divorce so that transfers between spouses after separation and before divorce continue to be exempt. After final divorce, the general rules operate, unless the dispositions are exempt under FA 1975 s 46 (see p 326). Maintenance payments fall within s 46 and are, therefore, exempt from CTT. However, s 46 is probably not wide enough to cover maintenance paid by way of a transfer of a capital sum or of a capital asset which may, therefore, be chargeable unless it does not reduce the transferor's estate (because it is in satisfaction of outstanding financial claims by the former spouse), or lacks gratuitous intent. In most cases the absence of gratuitous intent ensures no tax charge (see the statement of the Senior Registrar of the Family Division made with the agreement of the Revenue (1975) 119 SJ 396)).

IV THE MATRIMONIAL HOME

1 The difficulties

The matrimonial home will often be the only valuable asset owned by a couple so that its destination on divorce poses a number of tax problems. If the house is to be sold, or transferred in whole or in part from one (former) spouse to the other, problems of income tax, CGT, stamp duty, and (exceptionally) CTT may arise.

2 Income tax

Usually the property will be subject to a mortgage in favour of either a building society or a bank. It is important to remember that to qualify for tax relief on the mortgage the borrower must own an interest in the property, which he must occupy as his only or main residence or which is occupied by his former or separated spouse. Assume, for instance, that the husband has always paid the mortgage, but that on divorce the property is to be transferred into the wife's name. He will still be entitled to relief on payment of the interest so long as he retains some, even only a 1%, interest in the house. However, he is only entitled to interest relief on qualifying loans of up to £30,000 in total (not per house) so that if he continues to pay the mortgage on the former matrimonial home, he may be unable to obtain full relief on a loan to acquire a second house to live in himself.

One solution to this problem is for him to trransfer the mortgage into the name of the occupying spouse (usually the former wife). Building societies and banks will normally be willing to agree to this arrangement as long as they are satisfied that the wife will have sufficient funds to pay the mortgage. In practice, proof that the husband is obliged to make adequate maintenance payments, or that the wife has sufficient alternative funds of her own, will suffice. For the husband this arrangement will be attractive for two reasons. First, he will have the full relief on loans of up to £30,000 available to buy a house to live in; and, secondly, he can furnish the wife with extra funds to meet the mortgage repayments by means of (tax deductible) maintenance payments. However, this extra maintenance must be sufficient to cover the wife's mortgage repayments.

Assuming that the MIRAS scheme applies, the wife whose gross maintenance entitlement is sufficient to cover the gross mortgage, will not now be out of pocket through receiving a net sum of maintenance because she is entitled to pay a net sum to the building society. Despite MIRAS maintenance should still be ordered of an amount sufficient to cover the gross mortgage payments since, otherwise, the wife will not have funds with which to pay her basic rate tax bill.

EXAMPLE 6

Jim and Judy have separated. Jim's income is £25,000. Judy has no income. The matrimonial home is in Jim's name alone and is to be transferred to Judy. It is charged with an outstanding mortgage of £20,000. The alternatives open to Jim and Judy are:

(1) Jim could go on paying the mortgage and claiming tax relief from higher rate income tax, but he must keep an interest in the house. He could for instance arrange for Judy to own 95% of the property and retain a 5% share. Jim will then only obtain tax relief on a further loan of £10,000 if he wishes to buy himself a house.

(2) Alternatively, Jim could transfer the entire ownership of the house to Judy and arrange for the mortgage also to be transferred to her. She would then be entitled to the appropriate tax relief and Jim would pay her increased maintenance to cover the total cost of the payments. From Jim's point of view the extra maintenance will be a deductible charge on his income and will reduce his tax at the higher rates. Care should be taken to ensure that the correct sum is paid: for instance, if the net repayments are £210 per month Judy will require a gross payment of £300 per month to cover the repayments and the basic rate tax thereon. Jim will now have the full £30,000 loan relief available should he decide (and should he be able to afford) to buy a further house.

(3) If Jim deserts Judy, she may take over the mortgage payments even though the house is registered in Jim's name. Strictly, she should obtain no relief on those payments, since she does not own any interest in the property. By concession, however, relief is allowed (see the pamphlet '*Income Tax, Separation and Divorce*': IR 30).

3   Capital gains tax

Before separation any disposal of the matrimonial property will be exempt from CGT if it is the spouses' main residence. Once the parties separate, however, an absent spouse who has an interest in the property may incur a CGT liability on a disposal of it. Difficulties principally arise in two cases: assume in each case that the husband owns the house which he has left, and that the wife remains in occupation throughout.

Case 1   The house is to be transferred to the wife. This disposal by the husband will not fall within the no gain/no loss rules of CGTA 1979 s 44 since the parties have separated. Further, the husband has been absent from the house since the date of separation. So long as the disposal occurs within 2 years of that date, no charge will arise on any part of the gain (CGTA 1979 s 102(1)), but once that 2 year period expires, the proportion of the total gain that is deemed to have accrued from the end of that period may be chargeable (the appropriate calculation is described on p 232). The charge is avoided if concession D6 applies:

'Where a married couple separate or are divorced and one partner ceases to occupy the matrimonial home and subsequently as part of a financial settlement disposes of the home, or an interest in it, to the other partner the home may be regarded for the purpose of section 101 to 103 of the Capital Gains Tax Act 1979 as continuing to be a residence of the transferring partner from the date his or her occupation ceases until the date of transfer, provided that it has throughout this period been the other partner's only or main residence. Thus, where a husband leaves the matrimonial home while still owning it, the usual capital gains tax exemption or relief for a taxpayer's only or main residence would be given on the subsequent transfer to the wife, provided she has continued to live in the house and the husband has not elected that some other house should be treated for capital gains tax purposes as his main residence for this period.'

Provided that the wife has continuously occupied the house as her only or main residence and the husband has not elected for another house to be his main residence, the disposal of the house may occur many years after the separation. If the terms of the concession are not satisfied, payment of CGT may be postponed by a hold-over election under FA 1980 s 79.

Case 2 The house is to be sold. If the sale occurs more than 2 years after the separation, neither ESC D6 (because the disposal is not to the wife) nor s 79 hold-over relief (because it is a sale at arm's length) is available, so that there will be a charge on a proportion of the total gain. A similar result will apply if, on separation, the husband retains an interest in the house for the purpose of claiming interest relief (see p 507). When the house is eventually sold, a proportion of the gain attributable to that interest will be chargeable although if the interest is very small, the proportion should be covered by the annual exemption.

4 CTT and stamp duty

Transactions involving the matrimonial home will not usually involve CTT. Either the inter-spouse exemption still applies or, after divorce, there is no gratuitous intent (see p 507).

Dispositions between spouses and former spouses receive no privileged treatment for stamp duty. Thus ad valorem duty at 1% (unless reduced rates apply) may be charged on voluntary dispositions between the couple. A fixed duty of 50p is, however, charged under Stamp Act 1891 s 62 on a conveyance or transfer which is made under a court order; or as the result of a written maintenance agreement; or where the Revenue are satisfied that it results from matrimonial breakdown and that the parties have been separately advised. When the conveyance is made for consideration, ad valorem duty may be charged on that sum.

5 The taxation consequences of typical court orders

In order to consider the taxation implications of four typical court orders dealing with the matrimonial home on divorce, assume throughout that the spouse who has left (H) owns the matrimonial home.

a) *The outright transfer*

H is ordered to transfer the entire ownership of the house to W (see *Hanlon v Hanlon* (1978)). H may also be ordered to make maintenance payments covering, inter alia, any mortgage payments to be made by W.

Income tax   W will obtain relief on any mortgage interest payment if she makes them. H's maintenance payments will be a charge on his income.

CGT   The disposal to W attracts no charge if it occurs within 2 years of separation; if it occurs later, there is no charge if ESC D6 applies, or if FA 1980 s 79 hold-over relief is available.

CTT   No charge arises as a transfer pursuant to a court order lacks gratuitous intent.

Stamp duty   50p duty is payable on the transfer or conveyance of the property.

b) *H and W become joint owners of the house with sale postponed*

H is ordered to transfer an interest in the house to W. The couple will be tenants in common. W will be entitled to live in the house to the exclusion of H and the sale will be postponed until (for instance) the children reach 18 (see *Mesher v Mesher* (1980)).

Income tax   Both H and W have an interest in the house so that either is eligible for mortgage interest relief which is given to whoever makes the payments.

CTT and stamp duty   The position is as in a) above.

CGT   When the half interest in the house is transferred to W the result is as in a) above. On the eventual sale of the house, a proportion of the gain on H's share will be chargeable (corresponding to his period of absence), unless it can be argued that the effect of the order is to create a settlement. Normally, jointly owned land is not settled (see *Kidson v MacDonald* (1974) and Chapter 18). It may, however, be argued that because W has an exclusive right to occupy under the terms of the order the parties are not 'jointly absolutely entitled' since they do not have identical interests in the property. Accordingly, if the property is settled, no CGT will be charged upon its disposal, because it will have been occupied by W 'under the terms of the settlement' (see CGTA 1979 s 104).

c) *Settling the house*

W is given the right to live in the house for her life, or until remarriage, or until voluntary departure, whichever happens first. Thereafter, the house is to be sold and the proceeds divided equally between H and W (see *Martin v Martin* (1977)).

Income tax   Both spouses may have an interest in the property for the purpose of claiming tax relief on the mortgage payments. In the case of H who is entitled to a reversionary interest the matter is questionable.

CGT   The creation of the settlement will not be chargeable (as in a) above) and on the termination of the life interest although a deemed disposal under CGTA 1979 s 54(1) will occur (see p 251), no charge to CGT will arise because of either the main residence exemption (CGTA 1979 s 104) or because of the death exemption.

CTT   There will be no charge on the creation of the settlement (see a) above). W has an interest in possession and is, accordingly, deemed to own the house (FA 1975 Sch 5 para 3 and Chapter 25). On the ending of her life interest, a charge will not arise on the half share to which she or her estate then becomes entitled (para 4(3)). If H is still alive, the other half share is excluded from charge under the reverter to settlor provisions (p 349). If H dies before W, his reversionary interest in the proceeds of sale is not excluded property, however, and is, therefore, chargeable (FA 1975 s 24(3)(a); p 352) and a further charge will arise when the life interest ends in that half share.

d) *Outright transfer subject to a charge over the property in favour of the transferor*

H transfers the house to W, but is granted a charge over the property either for a specific sum (as in *Hector v Hector* (1973)), or for a proportion of the sale proceeds (as in *Browne v Pritchard* (1975)). Sale and payment may be postponed until the children attain 18 or until W dies or wishes to leave the house.

Income tax   To obtain mortgage interest relief W must make the mortgage payments, since H does not retain a sufficient interest in the property (FA 1972 Sch 9 para 6).

CTT   The property is not settled, but belongs to W—no charge.

CGT   The transfer to W should not be chargeable on the principles in a) above. On the eventual sale, the position is not entirely clear. If H's charge is for a specific sum, this must be a debt due to H. Therefore, when the house is finally sold and the debt repaid there will be no charge to CGT on the repayment (CGTA 1979 s 134; see p 228). If the charge is for a proportionate share of the proceeds of sale, however, H's right is not a debt, but a chose in action: ie the right to a future uncertain sum; see *Marren v Ingles* (1980). As a result, when the house is eventually sold and a sum of money paid to H, there will be a chargeable disposal of that chose in action.

e) *Conclusions*

It must be stressed that the taxation factors are not the most important considerations to be borne in mind when considering financial adjustments upon a matrimonial breakdown. The outright transfer may be the ideal for tax purposes, but it leaves the husband with no interest in the former matrimonial home and so deprives him of any capital appreciation. Further, the court has no power to adjust property orders once made, so they must be correct at the start. Finally, a transfer of the house or an interest therein is quite different from a declaration (normally under the Married Woman's Property Act 1882) that a woman owns, and has always owned, a share in the asset. No transfer is involved in such cases and all the taxation consequences of transfers discussed above are irrelevant.

37 Planning—gifts, wills and trusts

'. . . every man is entitled if he can to order his affairs so as that the tax attaching under the appropriate Acts is less than it otherwise would be (Lord Tomlin in *IRC v Duke of Westminster* (1936))

Even after the restatement of the *Ramsay* principle in *Furniss v Dawson* (1984) sensible financial planning, as opposed to tax avoidance on a large and artificial scale, remains possible; that the Revenue occasionally assist in this, is shown by their publication of a specimen covenant form (IR 47) which can be used to provide benefits for a child undergoing full-time education (see Appendix II).

Composite transactions containing an artificial step designed to avoid or defer tax are to be avoided, but a single transaction which achieves a tax advantage remains permissible, eg there is no reason why an individual paying income tax at the highest rate should not invest in assets which will show only capital appreciation. The following represents some of the basic tax saving methods that may be employed.

1 Use of exemptions and reliefs

Full use of the available exemptions and reliefs is probably the single most advantageous planning advice that can be given. Realising capital gains annually so as to utilise the annual exemption and ensuring that the CTT lifetime exemptions and reliefs are used whenever circumstances permit are obvious examples. The various reliefs require careful study because of the detailed conditions precedent to their application, eg CTT business property relief will not apply if a contract to sell the property has been concluded before the date of its transfer (the transfer is then considered to be not of business property, but of the proceeds of sale; see Chapter 23). Furthermore, an asset sale by a company will leave the proprietors with the problems inherent in a 'cash-shell' company and may be disastrous if they wish to retire from the business (see Chapter 34).

2 Planning opportunities for spouses

For income tax purposes spouses should consider whether the election for separate taxation of the wife's earnings is advantageous (see p 492; for the definition of earned income see p 25 and notice that income from furnished holiday lettings is now earned). So far as capital taxation is concerned, inter-spouse transfers are normally free of CGT and CTT, although they are not exempt from stamp duty. Equalisation of spouses' estates (preferably inter vivos) can greatly reduce their overall CTT bill (see p 497). The attractions of taking a spouse into business either as an employee or as a partner should be considered (in the case of a wife this may ensure that use is made of her earnings allowance). CGT retirement relief is available to both spouses so that, if they are in partnership, gains of up to £200,000 can be realised free of tax.

3 Provision for children

Although covenants in favour of the payer's own infant unmarried child are generally rendered ineffective for income tax purposes under TA 1970 s 437, grandparental covenants, or parental covenants to an adult child may result in an overall saving of basic rate tax (see TA 1970 s 457; Chapter 10 and Appendix II). On separation or divorce, financial provision for children should be by court order to ensure the most beneficial tax treatment of maintenance payments (see Chapter 36). Any trust set up for a minor should comply, for CTT purposes, with the requirements of FA 1982 s 114 ('accumulation and maintenance trusts'; see Chapter 26) and for income tax purposes if the minor is the settlor's infant unmarried child, should avoid TA 1970 s 437 (see Chapter 11). It may, however, be worthwhile considering a settlement of property upon a minor absolutely (ie his interest is not made contingent upon attaining a particular age).

EXAMPLE 1

Property is settled upon trust for Hubert, aged two, absolutely.

Income tax As Hubert owns the income, the 15% surcharge on trust income is not applicable. Hence, even if the income is accumulated (and it may have to be to avoid the deeming provisions of TA 1970 ss 437, 438), the trustees only pay tax at the basic rate of 30% and Hubert can set his personal allowances against the income.

CGT The property is not settled (CGTA 1979 s 46), but is treated as belonging to Hubert. Chargeable gains made by the trustees can, therefore, be reduced by his annual exemption.

CTT Hubert has an interest in possession (see p 340), so that were he to die the capital of the fund would form part of his estate.

4 Transfers of property inter vivos

In considering whether it is more tax advantageous to make gifts inter vivos or by will, it should be remembered that CTT rates on lifetime transfers are half those on death. Furthermore, the ten year cumulation rule means that the amount within the nil rate band can be given away at ten yearly intervals without any charge. For CTT purposes assets having a low value but which may be expected to increase (eg an option or a landlord's reversion) should be transferred before those with a high value which is expected to fall (eg a lease or life interest under a settlement). When a lifetime gift is contemplated, there may be advantages in placing the CTT burden upon the donee (see Chapter 21).

For CGT purposes, inter vivos gifts are chargeable disposals whereas on death there is no charge and the asset is acquired by the PRs for a consideration equal to its probate value. However the charge to CGT on lifetime gifts is, in a sense, optional as an election may be made under FA 1980 s 79 to hold over any gain (whereupon the donee acquires the asset pregnant with gain and with a low base cost for indexation; see Chapter 17). Further, on the gift of a business, retirement relief may be available to wipe out any gain.

Although DLT is not charged on gifts nor on death, the donee will be unable to use his £75,000 exemption for a further twelve months. A voluntary disposition effected by written instrument is subject to ad valorem stamp duty, except for gifts of under £30,000 in value to which the nil rate applies (splitting a gift into £30,000 slices would appear to fall within the *Ramsay* principle; see Chapter 32). If, however, the property is transferable by delivery no duty is payable.

Despite these general guidelines, the tax consequences of any gift largely depends on the particular facts, eg gifts of cash are exempt from CGT and not chargeable to stamp duty; reversionary interests avoid both CGT and CTT problems. The least tax efficient gift is one followed by the donor's death within three years, because as an inter vivos gift there is no CGT uplift and stamp duty may be payable, whereas the supplementary charge to CTT triggered by the death ensures that tax is charged at death rates.

In almost all cases tax is merely one item to be borne in mind; the personality of the would-be donor, his age, current life expectancy and willingness to part with anything before death are usually crucial.

5   Life and term assurance

In particular, the taxpayer should consider 'top-up' payments to pension schemes and insurance against CTT on death. A donee should insure the life of his donor, for instance, if there is a likelihood that the latter will die within three years after the gift thereby triggering a supplementary CTT charge. The normal life policy should be written in trust for another (eg children), so that it does not form part of the holder's estate on his death.

6   Flexible will drafting

In any medium or large sized estate advantages may be gained by the testator leaving all his property on a two year discretionary trust (see p 320). The 'reading-back' provisions of FA 1975 s 47(1A) will apply to all distributions by the trustees including those made to a surviving spouse and a charity (see FA 1984 s 103). Accordingly no extra tax can result from such an overriding trust. In other cases a post mortem rearrangement of the will or intestacy rules by a variation or disclaimer may effect a tax saving (p 320). Where an estate is relatively small (eg £100,000–£200,000) the will draftsman should consider the advantages of the mini (nil rate band) discretionary trust (p 498).

7   Foreign domiciliaries

Such persons should avoid a CTT charge on UK property. Take, for instance, the individual domiciled and resident in France who wishes to buy a house in Liverpool for his son. If he buys the property himself it will be subject to CTT on his death (no income tax or CGT problems arise). He can avoid such a charge by purchasing the house through an overseas (eg a Panamanian) company.

8   Business investment opportunities for the higher rate taxpayer

The attractions of the business expansion scheme have been discussed at p 36. Up to £40,000 can be invested in each tax year (from 1983–84 to 1987–88), either directly or in an approved fund. Investment in deep discount stock (p 386) enables the taxpayer to determine in which year his income profit is to arise. For those involved in the ownership of a company FA 1984 has so reduced the rates of corporation tax that small companies pay no more than the basic rate of income tax on profits of up to £100,000 whilst for other companies, by

1986, their rate will be 35% as opposed to the highest income tax rate of 60%. Further, dividends will suffer either no double charge (small companies) or only a small double charge (5% by 1986) so that the traditional problem of how to extract profits from the company should largely disappear.

9 Transferring the family business through a deferred ordinary share issue (see (1984) NLJ 399)

The following scheme may prove attractive, especially where the company is owned by a married couple who wish to transfer it to their children. In essence, new deferred ordinary shares carrying restricted rights are allotted (as a bonus issue) by the company to the couple who renounce them either in favour of the children, or on discretionary trust for them (this 'pref-trick' should avoid stamp duty). For CTT purposes, the limited rights attached to the shares should ensure that the transfer of value by the couple is relatively small and when the shares subsequently (eg 12–15 years later) come to rank pari passu with the ordinary shares (and, therefore, increase in value) no CTT should be chargeable, since these increased rights were automatically attached to the shares ab initio.

10 Use of trusts for tax efficiency

Discretionary trusts give the settlor great flexibility. He need not give the fund to any particular beneficiary, but can select a number of potential beneficiaries leaving his trustees to make the ultimate choice at a later date, after taking account of any changed circumstances. For a grandparent with five minor grandchildren, for instance, the attractions of such trusts are obvious. Hence, discretionary trusts may be advantageous in a will (the two year discretionary trust; see Chapter 22); in equalising estates (see Chapter 35); whilst a discretionary trust of the amount within the settlor's nil rate band can be created every 10 years. Accumulation and maintenance trusts can, of course, be drafted to give the trustees discretionary powers. Notice also that the insolvency of a beneficiary will not lead to the fund being available for the payment of creditors.

The main attractions of fixed trusts is to 'tie up' property. Income can be given to one person, capital to another. Hence, although lacking the flexibility of the discretionary trust, the settlor will have effectively restricted the use of the property settled for anything up to 100 years. Some flexibility can also be achieved by giving the trustees unrestricted powers of advancement (ie by extending Trustee Act 1925 s 32) and by including the life tenant as an object of the power.

In weighing up the merits of trusts as opposed to outright gifts, cost is obviously an important factor; the administration costs of a settlement may, of course, be considerable, except for a family trust which employs non-professional trustees.

Income tax and CGT do not, generally, discriminate against the use of the trust. The CTT position is, however, more complex. Fixed interest trusts are deemed to be gifts to the life tenant so that the decision to create such a trust or make an outright gift often depends on considerations other than tax. Discretionary trusts are more problematic because of the CTT charging system. A system of periodic charges with interim exit charges has to be compared with the position when a series of outright gifts are made. As the top lifetime rate of CTT is now only 30%, however, the maximum rate for an anniversary charge is 9%. For both outright gifts and interest in possession trusts the death of the beneficial owner may lead to a maximum 60% rate of charge; in contrast, the attractions of the discretionary trust are obvious.

11 Attractions of inheritance trusts

Published figures show that well over £1 bn has been invested in inheritance trusts in the last few years. The common features of the different schemes are, first, the settlor creates a trust in favour of the intended beneficiaries, but including himself and his spouse, by settling his nil rate CTT band and (possibly) making interest free loans to the trustees. Secondly, the trustees invest the fund in a single premium bond which allows them to encash 5% of the original investment each year and lend it, interest free, to the settlor (see p 44).

Basically, the settlor has given away a large slice of his estate which he can reclaim should the need arise, but from which, in the meantime, he receives an effective annual income of 5% net of tax.

One variation on the inheritance trust, involves the settlor taking out two policies, a single premium pure endowment policy and a single premium term assurance policy ('PETA Schemes'). Such a scheme results in an immediate discounted gift to the intended beneficiary but renders it harder for the settlor to recover his capital investment. Note, however, that the Revenue have begun to challenge the efficacy of some PETA Schemes under the *Ramsay* principle. (For a detailed analysis of both inheritance trusts and PETA Schemes, see B McCutcheon *Inheritance Trusts* (1983).)

12 Conclusion

Probably the best planning advice today is to avoid the wholly artificial pre-packaged scheme and to concentrate upon the opportunities specifically afforded in the legislation for tax saving. It should also be stressed that tax saving is not everything and that ultimately the personal whims and foibles of individuals will and should be paramount.

PART C APPENDICES

APPENDIX I: THE *GOURLEY* PRINCIPLE AND
GOLDEN HANDSHAKES

BTC v Gourley (1956) and subsequent cases are concerned with the assessment of
damages to be awarded by the courts in tort and breach of contract. The cases
are not concerned with the tax treatment of the sum once it has been awarded.
Damages in tort for personal injury are not taxed, but damages for breach of
contract, and, in tort, for financial loss, may be subject to charge if they
represent compensation for lost profits (see *London & Thames Haven Oil Wharves
Ltd v Attwooll* (1967)) and, especially, when they are payable on the termination
of an employment contract. The inter-relation between *Gourley* and the golden
handshake rules will briefly be considered below.

1   The assessment of damages by the court

Damages should compensate the innocent party in a breach of contract; they
should not normally penalise the contract breaker. Hence, if an employment
contract has been broken, the damages should reflect the fact that, had the
employee performed the contract, he would only have been left with the benefit
of a net sum after payment of tax. Therefore, the damages awarded should be
computed by reference to that net sum. Obviously this will adequately
compensate the plaintiff so long as the damages are not themselves taxed; if
they are the net sum will be insufficient.

2   The problem of TA 1970 s 187

Apart from the first £25,000 which is exempt, tax is imposed upon payments
made on a breach of an employment contract. It could be argued that once a
payment is subject to charge (as terminal payments are by virtue of TA 1970
s 187), there is no room for the application of the *Gourley* rule and a gross sum
should be paid. The courts, however, have distinguished between terminal
payments of less than £25,000 and those in excess of £25,000. A payment below
£25,000 is free of tax and, therefore, the amount awarded should be calculated
on *Gourley* principles (see *Parsons v BMN Laboratories* (1963)). *Lyndale Fashion
Manufacturers v Rich* (1973) shows that the calculation should proceed as if the
damages formed the highest slice of the recipient's income for the year (see LS
Gaz [1983] 346). If the net damages exceed £25,000 (after making the
appropriate *Gourley* deduction), those damages must be increased by a sum
equal to the estimated income tax that will be charged on the award under
TA 1970 s 187. This final net award will represent as realistically as possible the
actual loss suffered (*Shove v Downs Surgical plc* (1984) and see (1984) MLR 471,
where the conflicting decisions of the courts are discussed).

APPENDIX II: DEED OF COVENANT BY PARENT TO ADULT STUDENT

This form must not be altered or adapted in any way. The sum to be shown in the form is the gross amount payable, ie the amount from which basic rate income tax should be deducted when payment is made to the student. The date of the first payment under the deed must not be earlier than the date on which the deed is made. The witness should not be the student in whose favour the deed is made.

Forms IR 47

To be completed by a covenantor (parent) resident in England, Wales or Northern Ireland

Deed of Covenant

I...
      name of person making covenant

of...
      address of person making covenant

....

covenant to pay my son/daughter...
                          full name of child

of...
      address of child

the sum of £.................(gross) on

.... in each year
                        state date or dates

for the period of seven years, or for the period of our joint lives, or until he/she ceases to be receiving full-time education at any university, college, school or other educational establishment (whichever is the shortest period), the first payment to be made on

....   Dated..
Signed, sealed and delivered by

....
         signature of person making covenant

in the presence of...
         witness's signature and address

....

Person making the Covenant

Please state below the Tax District [and reference number] which deals with your tax affairs

District.............................. Reference..

To be completed by a covenantor (parent) resident in Scotland

Deed of Covenant

I...
   name of person making covenant
of...,
   address of person making covenant

....

hereby bind myself to pay to my son/daughter..
                                                    full name of child
of...
   address of child
the sum of £....................(gross) on

.... in each year
                                    state date or dates
for the period of seven years, or for the period of our joint lives, or until he/she
ceases to be receiving full-time education at any university, college, school or
other educational establishment (whichever is the shortest period), the first
payment to be made on

....

*

....

Signature............................... Date ....

*Please write here, in your own normal handwriting, the words 'Adopted as holograph' before signing.

Person making the Covenant

Please state below the Tax District [and reference number] which deals with
your tax affairs

District........................... Reference...

(Note: this form appears to be deficient in that it has no provision for a seal; see
[1983] BTR 122.)

APPENDIX III: COMPLETING THE CAP FORM 200

1   **General introduction**

CAP Form 200 is the appropriate form for PRs to use when applying for a grant of representation to the estate of a deceased person who dies domiciled in the UK where the estate is not an excepted estate and where CAP Form 202 is inapplicable.

For a description of how to complete the form see Form 213.

CAP Form 200 contains 12 pages. If tax is payable it must be accompanied by a form of warrant and, in appropriate circumstances, by Form 40 (schedule of shares and securities) and Form 37B (land owned by the deceased). It can be divided into the following parts:

(a) Pages 1 and 2 contain the personal details of the deceased and a declaration signed by the intended PRs that the form is correctly completed.

(b) Page 3 consists of questions designed to discover whether the deceased made chargeable lifetime transfers which would not otherwise be apparent from a list of his assets.

(c) Pages 4–9 comprise Sections 1, 2 and 3 of the form:

Section 1   lists all the property of the deceased in the UK which he owned solely and beneficially before his death and which now vests in his PRs (excluding property over which he had a general power of appointment exercisable by will). It is divided into two parts. Part A is for property on which tax cannot be paid by instalments (eg chattels) and on which PRs must pay CTT on delivery of the form. Part B is for property subject to the instalment option (eg land). In both parts the gross value of the property must be entered, any liabilities which reduce that value being shown separately.

Section 2   is for property beneficially owned by the deceased, which does not vest in his PRs on death, but for which they are liable to pay the CTT. It includes foreign and nominated property and jointly owned property which passes to a co-owner by right of survivorship. It is also divided into two parts; part A for property without the instalment option (less liabilities); part B for property with the instalment option (less liabilities).

Section 3   is for property in which the deceased had a limited interest under a trust (eg as a life tenant) including property over which he had a general power of appointment exercisable by will. The trustees of the settlement, not the PRs, are liable for CTT on this property but its value must be included to determine the deceased's estate rate. Provision is made in this section for the tax to be paid on the settled fund when the form is delivered, if the trustees so choose. (In practice, this will be unlikely.) The total values from Sections 1, 2 and 3 are carried separately to the assessment on page 11.

(d) On page 10 any CTT exemptions and reliefs (eg spouse exemption; business reliefs; charity exemptions) on property within Sections 1, 2 or 3 must be claimed. These are carried to page 11.

(e) Page 11 is the assessment page to which the totals from Sections 1, 2, 3 and page 10 are carried. It provides a format for calculating the total tax (if any) that is due (part A) and the tax (if any) that is payable on delivery of the form (part B).

(f) Page 12 is a summary of pages 1–11 for probate purposes. Unless no CTT is payable the warrant Form 35E must be sent, together with the CAP Form and any tax due to the appropriate probate registry. The warrant form is retained by the Revenue for information purposes; the CAP Form will be filed with the probate papers.

2 Completion of the form—case illustration

Siegfried George Lomax deceased

The following information is taken from the file of Mallet & Co (solicitors) of 11 Ducks Lane, Cooknam, Northamptonshire—solicitors for the PRs of the deceased.

Full name of the deceased	Siegfried George Lomax
Last residential address	Church View, Resurrection Lane, Cooknam, Northamptonshire
Occupation	Company director
Date of birth	5 November 1910
Date of death	4 July 1984
Surviving relatives	Two children and brother
Will	Dated 1 January 1982
Executors	(1) George Siegfried Lomax (son), 15 Sun Street, Hardwick, Yorkshire
	(2) Elspeth Georgina Pollax (daughter), The Range, Horseshoe Close, Barrowmouth, Devon
Terms of the will	Pecuniary legacy of £5,000 to the RSPCA
	Specific legacy of shares in Buttons Ltd to son, George Lomax
	Residue to children equally

Assets

	£
Cash	100
Midshire Bank, Cooknam:	
Current account	240
Deposit account	420
Interest to date of death	16
Personal chattels, household goods etc valued at	5,960
Director's fees to date of death	500
Policy of assurance payable to the estate by Moon Life Assurance Co	14,000
Thrifty Building Society account	17,900
Interest to date of death	64
Quoted shares as valued (all 'cum div')	20,765
Freehold property	
(1) Church View (above) owned solely and beneficially by deceased, but subject to a mortgage to the Halifax Building Society (below). House valued at	80,000
(2) Primrose Cottage, Rosetree Lane, Bangor, Wales owned by the deceased as a joint tenant with his brother Siegmund Ernest Lomax of the same address. The whole is valued at	40,000

Unquoted shares: 99% holding in Buttons Ltd, which manufactures
buttons. The holding comprises 10,000 unquoted shares,
the valuation of which has been agreed between the
Revenue and the deceased's accountants, Prigmore & Co
at £10 per share, ie   100,000

Liabilities

Electricity account outstanding	26
Housekeeper's wages (Annie Pringle)	40
British Telecom	32
Income tax (estimated)	1,225
Mark Cole & Sons (butchers)	12
Chins up (victuallers)	120
Funeral expenses (excluding tombstone)	560
Mortgage on Church View	10,125

Other relevant information
(1) On 25 December 1983 the deceased gave his daughter,
    Elspeth £20,000. He made no other gifts or settlements
    in the ten years prior to his death.
(2) The deceased was life tenant in the Lomax Will Trust
    established by the will of his father Tristan Lomax who
    died on 8 April 1960. The settled funds now pass to the
    deceased's son George. They consist of:

Investments valued at	48,640
Cash (uninvested)	400
Income accrued due	80
Income subsequently apportioned to deceased life tenant	60

Method of payment
The PRs will take out a loan to pay the CTT due on delivery of the form. They
will elect wherever possible to pay CTT by instalments so as to reduce the
amount that they have to borrow. Once probate has been obtained, they
propose to sell Church View to pay off the loan and the remaining CTT.

3   Page by page analysis

The CAP form will now be completed for this estate. Note that for the purpose
of this exercise, it is assumed that the valuations of all the deceased's assets have
been agreed with the Revenue. In practice, however, this is unlikely in the case
of certain assets (eg land and unquoted shareholdings) and PRs submit the
form on the basis of estimated valuations and complete a corrective account
when the valuations are agreed.

**Inland Revenue
Capital Transfer Tax**

Inland Revenue Account

- **For use where the deceased died on or after 27 March 1981 domiciled in the United Kingdom**
- **Please see Form No. 213 for instructions**

(1) Name and address Mallet & Co

  of Solicitors* 11 Ducks Lane

Reference L/H Cooknam

Telephone No. Cooknam 451

  County Northamptonshire Postcode NR2 4PQ

  *All communications concerning Capital Transfer Tax will be sent to the Solicitors unless the executors or administrators request otherwise.

In the High Court of Justice Family Division (Probate)

(2) The DISTRICT Registry CARLSHIRE

In the estate of (please use CAPITAL letters)

For Official Use

Date of Grant

(3)

Surname	LOMAX
Title and Forenames (*In full*)	SIEGFRIED GEORGE

Date of Birth	0	5	1	1	1	0	Date of Death	0	4	0	7	8	4	

Last usual address	CHURCH VIEW RESURRECTION LANE COOKNAM NORTHAMPTONSHIRE	Marital Status	tick "✓" as appropriate			
			married ☐		divorced ☐	
			single ☐		widowed ☑	
		Surviving Relatives	tick "✓" as appropriate			
			Husband ☐		Child(ren) ☑	
			Wife ☐		Parent(s) ☐	
	Postcode NR2 1PQ	Occupation	COMPANY DIRECTOR			

(4) Domicile (*Delete as appropriate*) England & Wales/~~Scotland/Northern Ireland~~

Names and addresses of executors or intending administrators:

(5)

GEORGE SIEGFRIED LOMAX 15 SUN STREET HARDWICK, YORKSHIRE Postcode YS3 1LP	ELSPETH GEORGINA POLLAX THE RANGE HORSESHOE CLOSE BARROWMOUTH, DEVON Postcode DL1 2BS
Postcode	Postcode

Cap Form 200

(1) Details of the PRs' solicitors with whom the Capital Taxes Office will communicate.

(2) Outside London, the CAP Form and other probate papers will usually be filed at the appropriate district probate registry.

(3) Personal details of the deceased.

(4) If the deceased had died domiciled outside the UK, CAP Form 201 would be the appropriate form to use.

(5) The deceased's executors complete the declaration on page 2.

Declaration

(6)   1. X/We desire to obtain a grant of   Probate of the will

of the aforenamed deceased.

(7)   2. To the best of my/our knowledge and belief all the statements and particulars furnished in this account and its accompanying schedules are true and complete.

(8)
*Delete
paragraph if
inappropriate*

3. I/We have made the fullest enquiries that are reasonably practicable in the circumstances but have not been able to ascertain the exact value of the property referred to in Exhibit   to section
So far as the value can now be estimated, it is stated in section   I/We undertake,
as soon as the value is ascertained, to deliver a further account thereof, and to pay both any additional tax payable thereon for which I/we may be liable, and any further tax payable by reason thereof, for which I/we may be liable on the other property mention in this account.

(9)
*Delete
what is
inappropriate*

4. So far as the tax on the property disclosed in sections 1B, 2B and 3 may be paid by instalments, I/we elect to pay/not to pay by instalments as indicated in these sections.

(10)   Signed by the above-named
                    GEORGE SIEGFRIED LOMAX
            date

            Signed by the above-named
                    ELSPETH GEORGINA POLLAX
            date

            Signed by the above-named
            date

            Signed by the above-named
            date

Warning

An executor or intending administrator who fails to make the fullest enquiries that are reasonably practicable in the circumstances may be liable to penalties. If he fails to disclose in sections 1A, 1B, 2A, 2B and 3 (as appropriate) and in his answers to the questions on page 3 all the property to the best of his knowledge and belief in respect of which tax may be payable on the death of the deceased (whether or not he is liable for the tax and whether or not the property is under his control) he may be liable to penalties or prosecution.

(6) The executors want a grant of probate as opposed to a grant of letters of administration with or without will annexed.

(7) The declaration made by the PRs requires them to take all practicable steps to ensure that the form is correct.

(8) There are no items in this estate that the PRs have been unable to value. (Notice that any valuations referred to should accompany the form).

(9) So far as possible the PRs elect to pay the tax by instalments.

(10) Declaration signed by the PRs. Before signing the declaration, the 'warning' at the bottom of page 2 should be brought to the PRs' attention to emphasise the seriousness of their task.

- If Capital Transfer Tax is payable on any property mentioned (or would be payable if that tax were payable on estates however small their value) such property **must** be included in sections 1A, 1B, 2A, 2B or 3 of this Account as appropriate.
  If it is claimed that the property is not subject to Capital Transfer Tax, reasons should be given.
- Even if a full report has been made or any other information relevant to the answers to any of the questions below has been given to an Inland Revenue Office, affirmative answers must nonetheless be given to the appropriate questions.
  Please also identify the office and quote any relevant official reference.
- Where necessary schedules may be attached.

For Official Use

tick "√" as appropriate

1. Gifts etc.

Did the deceased, after 26 March 1974, or within 10 years of his death (whichever is the shorter period)

Yes   No

    (a) make any gift, settlement or other transfer of value other than a transfer mentioned in footnote 1, or   ☑ ☐

    (b) make any disposition for the maintenance of a relative, or   ☐ ☑

    (c) pay any premium on a policy of life assurance not included in Section 1 of this form ?   ☐ ☑

(11)► If the reply to any question is "yes", please give full particulars including dates, details of any property affected and the names and addresses of the other parties concerned.

Gift of £20,000 to daughter ELSPETH GEORGINA POLLAX ON 25 December 198?

2. Settled property

(12)(a) Was the deceased, at the time of his death, entitled to a life interest, annuity or other interest in possession in settled property whether as beneficiary under the settlement or otherwise?   ☑ ☐

(b) Did the deceased cease to be entitled to any such interest in settled property after 26 March 1974 or within 10 years of his death (whichever is the shorter period) ?   ☐ ☑

- If the reply to either question is "yes", please give full particulars of the title (including, in the case of a Will/intestacy, the name and date of death of the testator/intestate and date and place of grant). Where the interest was under a settlement and no previous report has been made, kindly forward a copy of the settlement.

see Section 3

3. Nominations

Did the deceased in his lifetime nominate any Savings Bank Account, Savings Certificates or other assets in favour of any person ?   ☐ ☑

- If so, please give full particulars in Section 2 on page 8.

(13) ### 4. Joint property

Was the deceased joint owner of any property of any description or did he hold any money on a joint account (apart from property or money of which he was merely a trustee) ?   ☑ ☐

- If so, please give full particulars including
  - (a) the date when the joint ownership began (or the date of opening the joint account)
  - (b) the name(s) of the other joint owner(s)
  - (c) by whom and from what source the joint property was provided and, if it or its purchase price was contributed by one or more of the joint owners, the extent of the contribution made by each
  - (d) how the income (if any) was dealt with and enjoyed.

Freehold property: Primrose Cottage, Rosetree Lane, Bangor, Wales purchased in joint names of deceased and his brother SIEGMUND LOMAX on 28 June 1975 as holiday cottage see section 2B

---

1   Transfers of value which need not be reported are

    (a) gifts or other transfers of value made to the deceased's spouse unless at the time of transfer the deceased was domiciled in the United Kingdom and the spouse was not

    (b) gifts of money not exceeding £2,000 in any one year, where the executors or intending administrators are satisfied that they are wholly exempt as normal gifts out of income

    (c) outright gifts to one individual which are clearly exempt as not exceeding £250 in any one year (to 5 April) : (for gifts before 6 April 1980 the exemption is restricted to £100 in any one year)

    (d) other gifts of money, or of shares or securities quoted on the Stock Exchange, where these, together with any other gifts not within (b) or (c) above, do not in total exceed the exemption for gifts to the extent of £3,000 in any one year (to 5 April) :
        (for gifts before 6 April 1976 the exemption is restricted to £1,000 in any one year and from that date to 5 April 1981 inclusive to £2,000 in any one year).

(11) The gift to the deceased's daughter was made within ten years of the death. Accordingly, it must be cumulated for the purpose of calculating the rate at which the deceased's estate will be charged on death although it does not form part of the deceased's taxable estate on death (see page 11 of Form).

(12) (see also (29)) The deceased was a life tenant in the Lomax Will Trust. His death triggers a charge to CTT on the entire value of the settled fund. The tax is borne by the trustees not the estate. The value of the fund forms part of the deceased's estate for the purposes of calculating the estate rate at which both the deceased's free estate and the settled fund is charged.

(13) (see also (28)) Although the deceased's joint tenancy in Primrose Cottage passes by right of survivorship to his brother and does not vest in his PRs, the value of his interest immediately before death forms part of his estate.

Section 1

A schedule of all the property of the deceased within the United Kingdom to which the deceased was beneficially entitled and **in respect of which the grant is made,** excluding property over which the deceased had and exercised by will a general power of appointment. (The appointed property should be included in Section 3.)

Section 1A Property without the Instalment Option	Gross Value at Date of Death*	For Official Use
(14) Stocks, Shares, Debentures and other securities as set out in Form 40 :–	£	
• Quoted in the Stock Exchange daily official list except so far as included in Section 1B	20,765	
• Others, except so far as included in Section 1B		
Uncashed Dividends and Interest received, Dividends declared, and Interest accrued due, in respect of the above investments, to date of death, as statement annexed		
(15) Cash at the Bank :–		
• On Current Account and Interest (if any) thereon to date of death at MIDSHIRE BANK COOKNAM	240	
• On Deposit and Interest thereon to date of death at MIDSHIRE BANK COOKNAM	436	
Cash (other than Cash at Banks)	100	
Money at National or Trustee Savings Bank and Interest to date of death, as statement annexed		
Money out on Mortgage, and Interest thereon to date of death, as statement annexed		
Money with Building Society, Co-operative or Friendly Society, and Interest thereon to date of death, as statement annexed THRIFTY BUILDING–SOCIETY	17,964	
Money out on Promissory Notes, Bonds and other Securities, and Interest thereon to date of death, as statement annexed		
Other Debts due to the Deceased and Interest thereon to date of death, except Book Debts included in Section 1B, as statement annexed		
Unpaid Purchase Money of Real and Leasehold Property contracted in the lifetime of Deceased to be sold, as statement annexed		
Rents of the Deceased's own Real and Leasehold Property due prior to the death, but not received by the Deceased		
Apportionment of the rents of the Deceased's Real and Leasehold Property to the date of death		
(16) Income accrued due, but not received prior to the death, arising from Real and Personal Property, in which the Deceased had a life or other limited interest, viz :– LOMAX WILL TRUST	80	
Apportionment of Income from such source to date of death	60	
Any other income, apportioned where necessary, to which the Deceased was entitled at his death (e.g. pensions, annuities, directors' fees, etc.) as (17) statement annexed DIRECTOR'S FEES FROM BUTTONS LTD	500	
Policies of Insurance and Bonuses (if any) thereon, on the life of the Deceased, (18) as statement annexed MOON LIFE ASSURANCE CO. (without profits)	14,000	
Saleable value of Policies of Insurance and Bonuses (if any) not payable on the death of the Deceased, as statement annexed		
Carried forward	54,145	

*All claims for exemptions or reliefs should be made in the Summary on page 10

(14) The instalment option is not available for the deceased's quoted shares because none of the holding constitutes a controlling shareholding (see FA 1975 Sch 4 paras 13–15 and Chapter 22). The holdings must be listed (with values) on Form 40. If shares are quoted 'ex div' at the date of death the dividend must be added to this figure.

(15) Interest on the deposit account which has accrued to the date of death is included in the deceased's estate for CTT purposes.

(16) Any income which accrued to the trustees of the Lomax Will Trust before the deceased's death forms part of his estate for CTT purposes, even though the trustees have not paid it over (ie £80). Also, income paid to the trustees after the deceased's death and apportioned to him forms part of his estate (ie £60).

(17) The fees to which the deceased was entitled form part of his estate.

(18) The value of the policy forms part of the deceased's estate on death. Notice that if the policy had been written in trust for a third party it would not be included in the estate; details would, however, be given on page 3, question 1(c) because the payment of the premiums might have been chargeable transfers of value. If the deceased had paid money into an approved superannuation scheme giving the trustees an absolute discretion as to whom the benefits were payable on his death, those benefits would not form part of his estate and need not, therefore, be included in the form. If, however, certain beneficiaries are given benefits by the deceased's will or intestacy or if the deceased had a general power to nominate beneficiaries, the benefits are included and must be valued under 'other personal property' on page 5.

Section 1A	continued	Gross Value at Date of Death*	For Official Use
		£	
	Brought forward	54,145	

(19) Household Goods, Pictures, China, Linen, Apparel, Books, Plate, Jewels, Motor Cars, Boats, etc.   Sold, realised gross   £

Unsold,~~estimated~~ at   £ _5,960_ | 5,960

The Deceased's Interest expectant upon the death of

aged   years, under the will/intestacy of

who died on the
or under a settlement dated the
and made between

(setting out the parties to the deed), in the property set out in the statement annexed, of which fund the present trustees are

tick "√" as appropriate

Was the Interest at any time acquired for value,
whether by the deceased or a predecessor in title ?

Yes ☐   No ☐

Income Tax repayable

Other personal property not comprised under the foregoing heads, viz :–

| Gross Property not subject to the Instalment Option carried to page 6 and to Probate Summary, page 12 | 60,105 | |

All Claims for exemptions or reliefs should be made in the Summary on page 10

(19) Self-explanatory. In practice, the valuation would have to accompany the CAP form .(not shown here).

Section 1A   continued

Schedule of liabilities and funeral expenses. Particulars of the funeral expenses of the deceased and the liabilities due and owing from him at the time of his death to persons resident within the United Kingdom, or to persons resident out of the United Kingdom but contracted to be paid in the United Kingdom, or charged on property situated within the United Kingdom **(other than liabilities deducted in Section 1B or Section 2 under footnote (b) on page 8).**

Name and Address of Creditor	Description of Liability	Amount £	For Official Use
(20) Electricity Board	Electricity account	26	
British Telecom	Telephone account	32	
Annie Pringle	Housekeeper's wages	40	
Mark Cole & Sons	Butcher	12	
Chins Up	Wine	120	
Inland Revenue	Income tax (estimated)	1,225	
Funeral Expenses			
(21) S. Toomay & Bros., Cooknam		560	
Total – carried to Summary below and to Probate Summary, page 12		2,015	

Summary		
Gross Property (from page 5) not subject to the Instalment Option	60,105	
Deduct Total of liabilities and funeral expenses above	2,015	
(22) Net Property in the United Kingdom not subject to the Instalment Option carried to page 11, part A, 1a.	58,090	

(20) The deceased's debts which are not attributable to any particular property are included here.

(21) Funeral expenses are only deductible if reasonable. The cost of the tombstone is disallowed.

(22) The value of the deceased's Section 1A property less debts (ie £58,090) is taken to page 11.

Section 1B	Property with the Instalment Option		

	Important tick "✓" as appropriate		For Official Use
(23)	• Is the Tax on this Property to be paid on delivery of this Account? ☐ Yes ☑ No		
	• Is payment to be made by instalments? ☑ Yes, yearly ☐ Yes, half-yearly ☐ No (Deaths before 15.3.83 only)		

		Value at Date of Death* £	
(24)	**Land etc.** owned by the deceased in the United Kingdom (not being settled land) whether or not subject to a trust for sale as described on Form 37B annexed	80,000	
	Business Interests		
	• Net value of deceased's interest in business(es), as statement or Balance Sheet annexed		
	• Net value of deceased's interest as a partner in the firm of.................................... .... as statement or Balance Sheet annexed		
(25)	**Shares** (as set out on Form 40)		
	• Shares (or securities) within para 13(1)(b) Sch 4 FA 1975 which gave the deceased control of the company immediately before his death (see para 13(7) Sch 4 FA 1975) Shareholding in Buttons Ltd	100,000	
	• Other unquoted shares (or securities) within para 13(1)(c) or (d) Sch 4 FA 1975 (all other unquoted shares to be included in Section 1A)		
(27)	Value of Property with the Instalment Option, carried to Probate Summary, page 12	180,000	
	Deduct total of Liabilities listed below	10,125	
	Net Instalment Option Property in the United Kingdom carried to page 11, part A, 1c	169,875	

Liabilities charged at the date of the deceased's death on the property included above other than those already taken into account above

	Particulars of liability	Property on which charged	Amount £
(26)	Mortgage to Thrifty Building Society	Church View Resurrection Lane Cooknam Northamptonshire	10,125
		Total carried to Summary above and to Probate Summary, page 12	10,125

*All claims for exemptions and reliefs should be made in the Summary on page 10

(23) As far as possible the PRs elect to pay CTT by ten yearly instalments. (They hope to discharge the CTT liability before the first instalment falls due on 1 February 1985, by realising assets in the estate once they have obtained the grant of probate.) Instalment option property owned solely and beneficially by the deceased comprises Church View and his controlling shareholding in Buttons Ltd.

(24) The gross value of Church View is shown here. Full details of the property must be set out on Form 37B (not reproduced).

(25) The holding and its value must be detailed with the deceased's quoted shares on Form 40 (not reproduced). Valuation has been made by an accountant and agreed with the Revenue (not reproduced). Business property relief on the value of the holding is claimed elsewhere (see (31)).

(27) The deduction is given against the total value of the Section 1B property. As all the CTT is a testamentary expense this is irrelevant. If, however, Church View had been the subject of a specific tax-bearing devise, the devisee would only be liable for CTT on the value of Church View less the mortgage, ie on £69,875.

(26) The mortgage is a deductible liability.

Section 2

All other property on which the personal representatives are liable to pay the tax (or would be liable if any tax were payable) including :–
- all nominated property and property passing by survivorship
- all property situated outside the UK

Section 2A — Property without the Instalment Option

Particulars of the property, local situation and details of disposition if nominated or in joint names	Gross Value at Date of Death* £	For Official Use
Gross Value Deductions listed below		
Net value – carried to page 11, part A, 1a		

Liabilities ° in respect of the property above

Name and Address of Creditor	Description of liability	Amount £
	Total – carried to Summary above	

Section 2B — Property with the Instalment Option   tick "✓" as appropriate

- Is the Tax on this Property to be paid on delivery of this Account?   ☐ Yes   ☑ No
- Is payment to be made by instalment?   ☑ Yes, yearly   ☐ Yes, half-yearly   ☐ No
  (Deaths before 15.3.83 only)

Particulars of the property, local situation and details of disposition if nominated or in joint names	Gross Value at Date of Death* £
(28) Freehold property Primrose Cottage, Rosetree Lane, Bangor, Wales held by deceased and his brother SIEGMUND EARNEST LOMAX as beneficial joint tenants	18,000
Gross Value of deceased's share Deductions listed below	–
Net value – carried to page 11, part A, 1c	18,000

Liabilities ° in respect of the property above

Name and Address of Creditor	Description of liability	Amount £
	Total – carried to Summary above	

*All claims for exemptions or reliefs should be made in the Summary on page 10
° Liabilities (a) due from the deceased at the time of his death to persons resident outside the United Kingdom (other than liabilities contracted to be paid in the United Kingdom, or charged on property within the United Kingdom which have been deducted in Sections 1A and 1B) or
(b) (so far as not included in (a)) charged upon, incurred in connection with or otherwise affecting the property included in this Section.

(28) The deceased had no foreign or nominated property. The only property which he owned jointly (and which passes to his brother by right of survivorship) is Primrose Cottage. The instalment option is available for tax attributable to the value of the deceased's half share. Although the land is worth £40,000 the value of the deceased's half share (£20,000) will be discounted (usually by about 10%) to £18,000 to allow for the fact that it does not carry the right to exclusive occupation of any portion of the house.

Section 3

All other property in the UK and elsewhere in which the deceased had a beneficial interest in possession immediately before his death including :–
  • property over which the deceased had and exercised by will a general power of appointment.
  • property outside the UK comprised in a settlement made by a UK domiciled person.
    • Please see instruction booklet 213 as to how liabilities should be deducted.

Part 1 Property whereon tax is **elected to be paid** on delivery of this Account should be listed below and headed "Part 1".

tick "√" as appropriate

  • Is the tax on any property with the Instalment
    Option to be paid by instalments? ☐ Yes, yearly ☐ Yes, half-yearly ☐ No
                                                                (Deaths before
                                                                 15.3.83 only)

  • Separate net totals for Part 1 (non-instalment option property) and Part 1 (instalment option property) should be carried to page 11, Part A, 1a (non-instalment option property) and 1b (instalment option property)

Part 2 **Property whereon tax is not to be paid on delivery of this Account** should be listed below and headed "Part 2" and its net value carried to page 11, Part A, 1d.

Separate consecutive numbering for Part 1 and Part 2	Particulars of the property	Net Value at Date of Death*		For Official Use
		Property without the Instalment Option £	Property with the Instalment Option £	
Part 2 (29)	LOMAX WILL TRUST C.T.O. L4950. The deceased was the life tenant under the will of his father who died on 8 April 1960. No advances or property taken out of settlement. Quoted stocks and shares as per Form 40 (annexed)	48,640		
	Cash capital	400		
		£49,040		
	Sole surviving trustee: HENRY FEATHERSTONEHAUGH of the Paddocks, Field Lane, Furnham, Surrey			
	Solicitors: Messrs QUICKSHANK & CO., 5 The Hall, Furnham, Surrey.			

*All claims for exemptions or reliefs should be made in the Summary on page 10

(29) For the reasons stated at (12) the value of the whole settled fund at the date of the deceased's death must be included. Either (as here) the trustee(s) will account separately for the tax attributable to the settled property (Part 2 property); or, if the trustee(s) provide the deceased's PRs with the necessary funds to do so, the PRs can elect to pay this tax on the delivery of the Form together with the tax on the deceased's free estate (Part 1 property). As the settled property does not consist of instalment option property, the tax will be payable by the trustee(s) in one lump sum six months after the date of the deceased's death (ie by 1 February 1985).

Insofar as the settled fund comprises shares and securities, these must be set out on Form 40 (not reproduced). As there have been no advances or property taken out of settlement (which affect the calculation of the CTT bill) there must be a statement to this effect. The trustee and the trust's solicitors must be identified as the Revenue will need to communicate with them. The settlement has a CTO reference as a result of the admission of Tristan Lomax's will to probate.

Exemptions and Reliefs against Capital — Summary

- Please see instruction booklet 213 as to how this page should be completed.
- Schedules should be attached as necessary.

Property in respect of which exemption or relief is claimed. The description should not be more detailed than is necessary to identify the property	Nature of exemption or relief claimed	Net value of property £	Amount of exemption or relief claimed £	For Official Use
Property included in Section 1A				
(30) Pecuniary legacy (R.S.P.C.A.)	charity exemption	5,000	5,000	
Total of exemptions and reliefs Section 1A carried to page 11, part A, 1c			5,000	
Property included in Section 1B				
(31) Shares in Buttons Ltd	Business property relief (50%)	100,000	50,000	
Total of exemptions and reliefs Section 1B, carried to page 11, part A, 1c			50,000	

Property included in Other Sections — state which Section (Sections 2A and B and 3 (Part 1) and 3 (Part 2) separately.)
A separate total of exemptions and reliefs for each of these Sections to be carried to page 11, part A.

(30) The pecuniary legacy to charity is exempt from CTT. As the exemption does not relate to specific property it is claimed against Section 1A property.

(31) The value of the deceased's controlling shareholding in Buttons Ltd (£100,000) is eligible for 50% business property relief (ie £50,000). If the legacy were tax-bearing, the legatee, George Lomax, would be liable for tax at the estate rate on that reduced value.

(32)

Assessment of Tax

Part A — Summary for determining chargeable rates		Part B — Amount payable on this Account		

Part A — Summary for determining chargeable rates

Summary of chargeable transfers	Value of Property after reliefs £
1. **Capital Value now transferred**	
a. **Property without the Instalment Option**	
Section 1A net total 58,090 less total reliefs 5,000	
total after reliefs	
Section 2A net total less total reliefs	53,090
total after reliefs	
Section 3 Part 1 net total less total reliefs	
total after reliefs	
b. Total	53,090
c. **Property with the Instalment Option**	
Section 1B net total 169,875 less total reliefs 50,000	
total after reliefs	119,875
Section 2B net total 18,000 less total reliefs –	
total after reliefs	18,000
Section 3 Part 1 net total less total reliefs	
total after reliefs	
d. **Other property**	
on which tax is **not** being paid on this Account (From Section 3 Part 2) net total 49,040 less total reliefs –	
total after reliefs	49,040
e. Total after all reliefs	240,005

	Value of Property after reliefs £
2. **Cumulative total of chargeable transfers made prior to the deceased's death** (33)	20,000
3. **Aggregate Chargeable Transfers**	260,005

4. Tax thereon (34)		£	p
On first £ 232,000		70,100	00
On balance of £ 28,005 *a* 55%		15,402	75
5. **Total**		85,502	75
Less tax (at death rate) on 2 above (35)			
on first £ 20,000		NIL	
on balance of £ *a* %			
Less Relief for Successive Charges			
6. **Tax payable**		85,502	75

(36)	**Value on which tax is now being paid**	Value of Property	
		Non-instalment £	Instalment Option £
	7. Total Value at 1b	53,090	
	8. That part of 1c on which tax now to be paid		

Part B — Amount payable on this Account

	£	p
(37) **Non-instalment property**		
On £ 53,090 (7)		
$\dfrac{(7)}{(3)-(2)} \times (6) \quad \dfrac{53,090 \times 85,502.75}{240,005}$ Total	18,913 / 18,913	53 / 53
Deduct Reliefs against tax other than Relief for Successive Charges		
(38) Net Tax		
Add interest from 19		
to 19 (years days)		
Total Tax and interest on non-instalment property—carried to page 12		
(39) **Instalment Option property**		
On £ (8)	NIL	
$\dfrac{(8)}{(3)-(2)} \times (6)$ Total		
Deduct Reliefs against tax other than Relief for Successive Charges		
Net Tax		
Add interest from 19		
to 19 (years days)		
Instalments		
~~eighth(s)~~)		
tenth(s) · of net tax		
~~sixteenth(s)~~)		
Add interest on instalments now assessed		
from 19 (date last instalment due)		
to 19 (days)		
ø *Add* interest on whole of net tax on instalment option property from		
19 to 19		
(years days)		
Total tax and interest on instalment option property — carried to page 12	NIL	
Additional tax and interest due under S37 FA 1975 (as attached schedule) – carried to page 12	NONE	
(40)		

*NB Tax becomes due 6 months after the end of the month in which the death occurred. Unpaid tax carries interest from and including the day after the due date, irrespective of the reason for late payment.

ø   Only if the due date for the second or a subsequent instalment has now passed and interest relief (see form 213) is not in point, add here interest on the whole of the net tax on the instalment option property up to the due date of the last instalment

(32) Page 11 is the assessment page. The purpose of Part A is to calculate the rate of CTT at which the deceased's estate is chargeable and to calculate the tax payable. However, not all that tax is necessarily payable on delivery of the form or by the PRs. The purpose of Part B, therefore, is to calculate the amount of tax payable on delivery of the CAP Form.

(33) Part A1, 2 and 3, together, yield the value of the deceased's total gross cumulative transfers (£260,005) made up of the transfer on death (being the net value of property from Sections 1, 2 and 3 less any exemptions or reliefs), plus the value of any chargeable transfers made within ten years before death (ie £20,000 to daughter Elspeth).

(34) The tax on a chargeable transfer of £260,005 is calculated from the death table, ie £85,502.75.

(35) The £20,000 lifetime gift only forms part of the deceased's chargeable transfers for the purpose of calculating the rate at which tax is to be charged on death. Accordingly, a sum equal to the tax at death rates on a gift of £20,000 must be deducted from the tax bill. As the gift fell within the deceased's nil rate band, no tax is, or was, payable on this figure, so there is nothing to deduct. (Notice that the chargeable estate on death is £240,005, ie £260,005 − £20,000.)

(36) The total tax payable on this estate (£240,005) is £85,502.75. This tax is attributable to the three types of property comprised in the estate:
(1) the value of the non-instalment option property, ie £53,090 on which the PRs are to pay tax at once;
(2) the value of the instalment option property, ie £137,875 made up of Church View (£69,875); the holding in Buttons Ltd (£100,000 − £50,000 = £50,000); and Primrose Cottage (£18,000);
(3) the value of the settled fund (£49,040) on which the trustees are responsible for the tax.

The tax (£85,502.75) is allocated between these three groups of property pro rata.

(37) The tax attributable to the non-instalment option property is the proportion of the total tax (£85,502.75) that the value of that property (£53,090) bears to the total chargeable estate (£240,005). The tax payable on delivery of the form is £18,913.53. (Note that this property is charged at an effective estate rate of 36.625%, ie:

$$\frac{\text{Tax}}{\text{Chargeable estate}} = \frac{£85,502.75}{£240,005} \times 100).$$

(38) Interest at 6% is only charged on tax outstanding six months after the end of the month of the deceased's death. As he died on 4 July 1984 and this account is delivered on 18 September 1984, no interest is payable.

(39) The value of the instalment option property is £137,875. No tax is payable on the delivery of this account as the first instalment only becomes due six months after the end of the month of death. This sum is calculated as:

$$\frac{£137,875}{£240,005} \times £85,502.75 = \text{total tax of } £49,118.52.$$

The first instalment due on 1 February 1985 will be £4,911.85 (£49,118.52̂10). It carries interest from the date the first instalment is due (1 February 1985) to the date of payment.

Subsequent instalments insofar as the tax payable is attributable to the value of land (ie Church View and Primrose Cottage) carry interest on the whole of the unpaid CTT (and on the whole of the current instalment, if it is overdue). There will be no interest charged on the unpaid CTT attributable to the value of the holding in Buttons Ltd so long as each instalment is paid on time.

If any of the property is sold, the balance of the outstanding tax attributable to that property (with interest if applicable) becomes payable immediately. Remember that in this case, the PRs hope to sell Church View and discharge all the outstanding tax, ie £49,118.52 before the first instalment becomes due.

The total tax payable on the deceased's free estate is £18,913.53 + £49,118.52 = £68,032.05. The balance of the tax attributable to the settled fund and payable by the trustees is:

$$\frac{£49,040}{£240,005} \times £85,502.75 = £17,470.70.$$

(40) Any gift made within three years of the deceased's death must be re-assessed at death rates and any extra tax (ie the difference between the tax payable on that gift at the death rates at the date of death and the tax paid on the gift at lifetime rates) is due, not from the deceased's PRs, but from the donee (Elspeth Pollax). The gift of £20,000 fell within the deceased's nil rate band so that no CTT is payable.

Probate Summary

		£
Aggregate Gross Value which in law devolves on and vests in the personal representatives of the deceased, for and in respect of which the Grant is to be made	Section No. 1A	60,105
	Section No. 1B	180,000
	Section No. 3*	

(41) **Total (to be carried to the probate papers)** — 240,105

Deduct

Section No. 1A, Total of Liabilities and funeral expenses	2,015	
Section No. 1B, Total of Liabilities	10,125	12,140
(*absolute power property only*)		

For Official Use Only	(42) **Net Value for Probate purposes** 227,965

Total of Tax and Interest from page 11, Part B

	£	
Total Tax and Interest – Non-Instalment Property	18,913	53
Total Tax and Interest – Instalment Option Property	NIL	
Additional Tax and Interest due under S37 FA 1975	NIL	
Total tax and interest payable now on this Account	18,913	53

On the basis of this Account the tax (and interest) payable now is

£   18,913.53

MALLET & CO

Solicitor(s) for the applicant(s)

19.9.19 84

EDP

CAO's No.

Received on

the sum of

pounds

for Capital Transfer Tax and Interest.

for Commissioners of Inland Revenue

£

This receipt and stamp do not imply that the assessment is not subject to rectification: the account will be fully examined after the issue of the grant.

Prints of this form and of the instructions (Form No. 213) can be obtained from the Capital Taxes Office, Inland Revenue, Rockley Road, London, W14 0DF, and on personal application only at the Stamps Office, Room 2, South West Wing, Bush House, Strand, WC2B 4QN, the London Chief Post Office, King Edward Street, EC1A 1AA, the Branch Post Offices at Fleet Street, EC4Y 1BT, Chancery Lane, WC2A 1EA, East Strand, WC2R 1EL, High Holborn, WC1V 6RN, 11 Regent Street SW1, and Throgmorton Avenue, (57 London Wall, EC2), and Head Post Offices outside the Metropolitan Postal District.

Printed in the UK for HMSO 8393024 200M 11/83 JCM 65198/1

(41) This figure is entered in the executor's oath as the gross value of the estate which vests in the PRs and for which they are applying for a grant of probate. Section 2 and 3 property is excluded because it does not vest in the PRs; the fact that they may be liable for tax on it is irrelevant for probate purposes.

(42) Probate fees are calculated on this figure.

CAP FORM 35E

INLAND REVENUE   CAPITAL TRANSFER TAX

(43)   WARRANT FOR INLAND REVENUE ACCOUNT FORM 200 or 201

Except where *prima facie* no tax is payable, this Warrant should be completed and forwarded with the Form 200 or 201.

The tax must be paid before the grant of representation can issue. Payment may be made BY CHEQUE made payable to "Inland Revenue", and crossed. Payment may also be made by means of Certificates of Tax Deposit.

All remittances should be sent with the form 200 or 201 and this Warrant to:

CENTRAL ACCOUNTING OFFICE (CASHIER), INLAND REVENUE (A), BARRINGTON ROAD, WORTHING, WEST SUSSEX, BN12 4XH.

Name and full address of the person to whom the stamped Account is to be returned	M A L L E T & C O.,
	11 DUCKS LANE,
	COOKNAM, NORTHAMPTONSHIRE

N.B.   A note bearing this name and address should be attached to page 1 of the Form 200 or Form 201 if the name and address in the box on that page do not correspond.

Reference ....L/H............................Date ......18.........day of .September...19 .84..

Name of Deceased ..........SIEGFRIED..GEORGE.LOMAX...........................Died on ..4.July.1984........

late of ....Church View, Resurrection Lane, Cooknam, Northamptonshire...........

TOTAL NET PROPERTY DISCLOSED IN THIS ACCOUNT

(44)   It is essential that the Total shown at **3** on page II of the Account be restated here ⟶ **£** 260,005

(45)   Amounts in respect of which relief is claimed under S.29 Finance Act 1975   **£** 55,000

                                                                          TOTAL   **£** 205,005

TAX PAYABLE ON FORM 200 or 201
(From page 12 thereof)

	£	
Total tax and interest—property without the Instalment Option	19,632	44
Total tax and interest—Instalment Option Property		
Additional tax and interest—under S37 F.A. 1975		
Total tax and interest payable on the form 200 or 201	19,632	44

FOR OFFICAL USE ONLY

The details above have been compared with Account ....

Deposit No.	Date of receipt of remittance
£	
Date	Receipted £
	Repaid £
Deposit No.	Date
£	
Date	Receipt No.

(43) As tax is payable on delivery of the CAP Form 200, this form must be completed by the deceased's solicitors (Mallett & Co) and accompany the CAP form. The CAP form will ultimately be filed with the probate papers and this form is retained by the Revenue for information.

(44) The gross chargeable transfer on which the deceased's rate of CTT was calculated is re-stated here.

(45) The reliefs referred to consist of the business property relief, ie £50,000, and the charity exemption, ie £5,000, = £55,000 in total.

APPENDIX IV: PAYMENT OF SCHOOL FEES

Maintenance orders which contain an element in respect of school fees frequently have to be varied when the school fees increase. This requirement could be avoided if the relevant part of the maintenance order were to be automatically adjusted when the school fees go up. The Inland Revenue have agreed to this principle. A form of order which they would find acceptable is as follows:

'It is ordered that the [petitioner] [respondent] do pay or cause to be paid to the child AB as from the   day of   19   until [he] [she] shall attain the age of 17 years [or for so long as [he] [she] shall continue to receive full-time education] or further order periodical payments for [himself] [herself]
(a) of an amount equivalent to such sum as after deduction of income tax at the basic rate equals the school fees [but not the extras in the school bill] [including specified extras] at the school the said child attends for each financial year [by way of three payments on   and
and   ] [payable monthly]; together with
(b) the sum of £   per annum less tax payable monthly in respect of general maintenance of the said child.

'And it is further ordered that that part of the order which reflects the school fees shall be paid to the [Headmaster] [Bursar] [School Secretary] as agent for the said child and the receipt of that payee shall be sufficient discharge.'

A form of contract (between the school and the child) which is acceptable to the Inland Revenue is as follows:

'THIS AGREEMENT is made between THE GOVERNORS OF ....

....

by their duly authorised officer ....

.... (hereinafter called "the School") of the first part;
.... and the [Headmaster] [Bursar] [School Secretary]

of the second part, and ....
(hereinafter called "the Child") of the third part.

WHEREAS [it is proposed to ask the ....
Court to make an order] [the................... Court has made an order] in cause number............................. that the Father of the Child do make periodical payments to the child at the rate of £.......... per annum less tax until the Child completes full-time education (or as the case may be and that the part of the order which reflects the school fees shall be paid to the [Headmaster] [Bursar] [School Secretary] as agent for the Child and the receipt of that agent shall be a sufficient discharge.
1. The Child hereby constitutes the [Headmaster] [Bursar] [School Secretary] to be his agent for the purpose of receiving the said fees and the Child agrees to pay the said fees to the said School in consideration of being educated there.
2. In consideration of the said covenant the [Headmaster] [Bursar]

[School Secretary] agrees to accept the said payments by the Father as payments on behalf of the Child and the School agrees to educate the Child during such time as the said school fees are paid.

Dated the   day of   19   .'

(Practice Direction dated 16.6.1983—see [1983] 1 WLR 800).

APPENDIX V: SOME CONCLUSIONS AND *FURNISS v DAWSON*
UP TO DATE

Three topics are considered in this appendix. All may be seen both as illustrating the changing face of taxation in 1984–85 and as representing trends that may be expected to continue in the immediate future.

1   Statistics and The Constitution

The latest annual report of the Inland Revenue confirms that a number of the taxes considered in this book are relatively inefficient in terms of yield and of the costs involved in collecting them. DLT, for instance, raised only £13.51 for each £1 of cost in 1982–83, CGT £31.25, and CTT £41.67. At the opposite extreme, oil taxes yielded £10,000 of tax for each £1 spent and stamp duty £100 (rendering any suggestions that the latter's demise is imminent surely premature!). Income tax remains the greatest single revenue raiser (nearly 70% of the total in 1982–83; £31bn out of a total yield of £44bn from direct taxes). The enormous complexity of CGT, DLT, and CTT appears increasingly disproportionate to their yields. It must be questioned whether they are worth retaining. Particularly striking is the CTT legislation which has come to embrace many of the anomalies of its predecessor, estate duty, a tax which it was once said had:

> 'nominally fierce rates ... allied with substantial loopholes through which taxpayers would be shown with their proverbial coach and four, but with more than nominal pourboires for their guides.'

The constitutional difficulties created by extra statutory concessions have been mentioned (see p 5), whilst implications of judicial lawmaking in *Furniss v Dawson* (1984) (in an area where certainty was thought to be paramount), should provide ample ground for speculation (see, especially, the speech of Lord Scarman quoted at p 4). The passage of FA 1984 has been marked by major Government amendments at almost every stage; in a number of cases (eg controlled foreign companies and *Leedale v Lewis*), last minute amendments were made to legislation where draft clauses had been produced before the Finance Bill and numerous representations received, most of which were largely ignored in the Bill as originally published. These events can have only strengthened the case for a separate technical Finance Bill which could be considered without the parliamentary pressure to which the Finance Bill is always subject (see (1983) BTR 340).

A further trend is the continued stream of measures to be introduced in future Finance Bills: the FA 1984 incorporated some 48 sections promised in 1983 and the 1985 Bill already has a ghostly presence. Is this desirable, especially when it is announced that the measures are to be retrospective? Take, for instance, the change in the capital allowances legislation that will, effectively, reverse the decision in *Stokes v Costain Property Investments Ltd* (1984), but with effect from 12 July 1984 (the date of the Commons Statement by the Financial Secretary to the Treasury). In that statement Mr John Moore declared that, despite the Court of Appeal ruling in *Costain* that the Revenue practice in this area had 'no statutory foundation', he was authorising the Revenue 'to continue to apply those practices' (see 1984 STI p 529).

2   The 1984 Budget and business enterprise

Just how beneficial the 1984 Budget will prove to be for corporate enterprise is a matter of acute debate (see, for instance, IFS Report June 1984 on *Corporation*

Tax). The rapid withdrawal of the first year allowance on items of plant and machinery, apart from necessitating a reconsideration of investment policy, is likely to lead to a revival of interest in the distinction between items of capital and income expenditure (discussed on p 82). Before FA 1984, if the expense was income it was fully deductible in arriving at taxable profits; even if it were capital, the same result followed through the system of capital allowances so long as the expenditure was on plant or machinery. Today, there are obvious attractions in seeking to show that the expense is of an income rather than a capital nature and, in this context, two Court of Appeal decisions are instructive. First, in *Lang v Rice* (1984), the taxpayer ran two clubs in Belfast until they were destroyed by bombings. He did not resume trading thereafter and received compensation from the Northern Ireland Office for, inter alia, 'consequential loss'. The Revenue argued that the payment was a once and for all capital payment to compensate the taxpayer for the permanent loss of his business (in effect, therefore, a payment for goodwill). The Northern Ireland Court of Appeal held, however, that the payment was designed to compensate the taxpayer for loss of profit during the period that would elapse before business could be resumed. Accordingly, the fact that business did not recommence had no affect on the nature of the payment. An air of some unreality pervades this decision since, as the premises had been totally destroyed and the taxpayer held only a short lease, there was never any question of the business being resumed (compare *Glenboig Union Fireclay Co Ltd v IRC* (1922) and *London & Thames Haven Oil Wharves Ltd v Attwooll* (1967): p 77). Secondly, in *Whitehead v Tubbs* (1984) the payment of £20,000 to obtain a release from onerous restrictions contained in an agreement with a creditor was held to be a capital payment by the Court of Appeal, since it secured an enduring advantage for the payer (see also *British Insulated and Helsby Cables v Atherton* (1926) and *Van den Berghs v Clark* (1935): p 77).

3 Furniss v Dawson—an update

Probably the single most important conclusion to draw from the House of Lords speeches in *Furniss v Dawson* is that the *Ramsay* principle is still at a relatively early stage of development, so that it would be unwise to seek in the speeches precise limits beyond which the principle will not apply. Above all, the case has injected uncertainty into revenue law, although, given the level of sophistication and artificiality reached by the tax-avoidance industry, this is, perhaps, not necessarily undesirable.

a) *Parliamentary Statement by the Chief Secretary to the Treasury*

In commenting upon *Furniss v Dawson*, The Rt Hon Peter Rees QC, MP stated that:

> 'Taken with the decision in *Ramsay's* case, it is now clear that the widespread assumption based on the *Duke of Westminster's* case in the 1930s—that the courts will always look at the form rather than the substance of a transaction or various transactions is no longer valid.
> The House of Lords made it clear that this is an evolving area of law, but the emerging principles do not in any way call in question the tax treatment of covenants, leasing transactions and other straightforward commercial transactions. Nor is there any question of the Inland Revenue challenging, for example, the tax treatment of straightforward transfers of assets between members of the same group of companies. I also assure the House that, in accordance with normal practice, the Inland Revenue will not seek to reopen cases when assessments were properly settled in accordance with prevailing practice and became final before that decision.

The Board of Inland Revenue will also see whether clearance for types of case of special importance or general guidance for the benefit of taxpayers and their advisers can be given. The principle in *Furniss v Dawson* should lead, in future, to great simplicity in our tax system and will, I hope, enable us in time to prune out provisions which owe their existence to the complexities of a high rate—some might say a confiscatory rate—tax system with a multiplicity of special reliefs.' (HC Deb, Vol 58, col 254.)

A number of important matters are touched upon by this statement. First, that the new approach will not be applied retrospectively to cases where assessments have been finalised. It may, of course, be applied to identical cases which arise in the future or are 'in the pipeline', as is evident from the attitude of the Stamp Office to conveyancing schemes designed to avoid duty; they take the view that such schemes fall within the scope of *Ramsay* and assess the transaction accordingly, leaving it up to the taxpayer to challenge their assessment in the courts. Thus, only in a limited sense is *Ramsay* not to be applied retrospectively.

Secondly, as mentioned in Chapter 32, there is no intention to upset the treatment of covenants and 'straightforward commercial transactions'. On the question of covenants it is not entirely clear whether *Westminster* involved a scheme or a single transaction (a straightforward covenant), whilst the increasing use of capital covenants which are executed in favour of charities are surely not just simple covenants. The phrase 'other straightforward commercial transactions' is not particularly helpful: presumably in *Furniss v Dawson*, although the entire transaction was commercial (the sale of shares to Wood Bastow), it was infected by an artificial step (the insertion of Greenjacket) so that it ceased to be 'straightforward'. Lord Brightman, it should be remembered, considered that the *Ramsay* approach could apply only if steps were inserted 'which have *no* commercial (business) purpose apart from the avoidance of a liability of tax' ([1984] STC at p 166). Nevertheless, whether the insertion of some relatively insignificant business purpose will be sufficient to save a scheme, must be doubted: in all probability the law will develop to frustrate schemes where 'the main purpose, or one of the main purposes, is avoidance of liability to (tax) . . .'. (cp CGTA 1979 s 87(1).)

Thirdly, since the publication of this statement, there has been some clarification by the Revenue of the impact of *Furniss v Dawson* on stamp duty on company takeovers (see e) below). Interestingly, this first Revenue statement assumes that *Ramsay* applies generally to all taxes, but then introduces a limited exemption from its operation.

Fourthly, the statement envisages some simplification of tax legislation in the wake of the decision in *Furniss v Dawson*. Presumably, anti-avoidance legislation will be rendered unnecessary so long as the courts preserve the *Ramsay* principle on a broad basis. It will be surprising, however, if the existing provisions are removed from the statute book and one of the most puzzling problems left unanswered by *Furniss v Dawson* is how to marry the new approach with these statutory provisions (see b) below).

Fifthly, the Chief Secretary expressly exempts from *Ramsay* straightforward transfers of assets between members of the same group of companies. For some taxation purposes, groups are looked at as a whole (see, for instance, the group relief and the group income provisions). There is, however, no provision enabling the pooling of capital losses and it is, presumably, schemes designed to remedy this gap in the legislation that are to be permitted.

EXAMPLE 1

Subsidiary company Alpha intends to sell land to P, but will realise a capital gain of £80,000 on that sale. Assume that another subsidiary company (Beta) has unused capital losses of £100,000. The land could be sold to Beta for full value and then resold by Beta to P.

(i) *on the sale to Beta:* the disposal is on a no gain/no loss basis irrespective of the actual consideration paid (TA 1970 s 273: p 407). No gain is, therefore, realised by Alpha.

(ii) *on the sale to P:* the gain of £80,000 is realised by Beta, which can use its losses to avoid any corporation tax charge.

This operation is obviously a scheme; it contains an artificial step (the sale to and by Beta), and so would fall within the *Ramsay* principle. As a straightforward intra group transfer, however, it is presumably within the terms of the Chief Secretary's Statement. Would the position be different if the loss company (Beta) had been acquired for the express purpose of eradicating the gain on the land held by Alpha?

b)   Furniss v Dawson *and anti-avoidance legislation*

The contrasts between judicial and statutory anti-avoidance measures is striking. Legislation is reasonably precise, of a limited ambit and often contains advance clearance provisions. *Ramsay*, on the other hand, is potentially of enormous and, at present, uncertain ambit. The relationship between the two also may prompt speculation as to whether *Ramsay* can be invoked by the taxpayer against the Revenue.

EXAMPLE 2

Assume that H wishes to makes a gift of £50,000 to his daughter, but has exhausted his annual exemption and that his CTT rate is 30%. He decides to channel the gift through his wife who has her full nil rate band available (see *Example 14* on p 286). As he is not prepared to rely upon her to pass the gift to the daughter, he ensures that she is unable to keep the money herself by giving her a life interest in it for either her life, or 48 hours, whichever is the shorter period and providing thereafter for the fund to pass to the daughter. The object of the scheme is to ensure that (a) the transfer to his wife is exempt and that she is treated as owning the property for 48 hours (see p 344); and (b) when her interest ends and the fund passes to his daughter the transfer will be charged at his wife's CTT rates (ie 0%!). It seems clear that this arrangement falls within FA 1975 s 44(1), so that tax would be charged as set out in *Example 14* on p 286: viz on a chargeable transfer by H to his daughter of £100,000 (£50,000 to wife; £50,000 from wife to daughter). However, H has also entered into a scheme with an artificial step (the trust for his wife) and the *Ramsay* principle would also appear to apply. From H's point of view *Ramsay* would be preferable to s 44 since, viewed as a whole and excising the artificial steps, H is treated as making a chargeable transfer of £50,000 only to his daughter.

In principle, taxpayers should, in such cases, be able to avail themselves of the *Ramsay* decision, assuming the correct ratio of that case to be that schemes should be viewed as a whole and artificial stages omitted in arriving at their true legal import (arguably, therefore, it has a wider ambit than just taxation matters: see (1984) BTR 109). *Young v Phillips* (1984) affords some support for this view (see d) below).

c)   Furniss v Dawson *and third parties*

The lower courts in *Furniss v Dawson* rejected the Revenue's arguments, because, inter alia, the scheme in that case was not self-cancelling or circular, but resulted in the sale proceeds remaining outstanding in the hands of a third party (see p 463 for the facts of the case). The House of Lords, however, did not consider it important that the sale proceeds remained throughout in the Isle of Man company. Under the transaction as reconstructed (ie ignoring the artificial steps), the Dawsons were treated as selling the shares directly to Wood Bastow in return for a sum of money paid (with the vendors' agreement) to Greenjacket. The sale of shares to and by Greenjacket was, therefore, ignored although, in none of the speeches, do the House of Lords suggest that this involves lifting the corporate veil and viewing Greenjacket as merely the Dawson's alter ego; but this is undoubtedly the result of the judgments. Will this, however, be the case when the intermediate purchaser is not a closely controlled company but, for instance, a spouse? In *Example 2* above if W had been given a life interest which was terminable, not automatically, but by an independent trustee, would the scheme fall within the *Ramsay* principle? Would it depend upon whether the trustee exercised his power of termination within a short time of the creation of the settlement? Obviously, no definite answer can be given to these questions, but it should be stressed that nothing in the House of Lords speeches offers support for the view that the decision is limited to channeling through an artificial person.

d)   Young v Phillips *(1984) STI 511*

In this case the taxpayers, although UK resident, had retained a South African domicile. They owned UK companies ('RRC') and, with the aim of avoiding a CTT liability on those shares, were advised to export their interests to the Channel Islands (thereby turning the assets into excluded property; see p 371). A direct sale of the shares to Jersey companies would have triggered a CGT charge and, accordingly, a scheme involving a number of steps was adopted to avoid the CGT charge. Although not legally bound to continue with the steps one after another, once the scheme had started there was no doubt, in practice, that it would be completed.

Briefly, the scheme involved procuring the formation of Jersey companies ('Davian') which, at the relevant time, were wholly owned by the taxpayers; RRC capitalised its reserves and alloted bonus preference shares on renounceable letters of allotment to the taxpayers (leaving their original shareholdings worth less than 1% of the equity in those companies). The taxpayers then took the renounceable letters to Sark where they sold them to Davian. The cash transactions were effected through bank accounts in Sark which were opened and closed on the same day. As a result, some 99% of the shares in RRC were acquired by Davian which was wholly owned by the taxpayers.

The Revenue claimed CGT on two grounds: first, because the taxpayer had disposed of UK assets at a profit; and secondly, by an application of the *Ramsay* principle. On the first contention, Nicholls J decided that the renounceable letters of allotment were documents evincing rights against UK companies, ie choses in action which were enforceable in the UK. Accordingly, the assets were situated in the UK so that the taxpayers (although domiciled abroad) realised a chargeable gain on their disposal. It is arguable that, having found in favour of the Revenue on the first ground, the discussion by Nicholls J of *Ramsay* is obiter dicta. On this second contention, however, the judge concluded that the self-cancelling cash transactions carried out to effect the sale and purchase in Sark were artificial steps inserted for no business purpose, apart from the avoidance of tax. He, therefore, reconstructed the transaction as follows:

> 'Before the scheme was initiated the taxpayers owned all the shares in the United Kingdom companies. After the scheme had been carried through they still owned their original shareholdings, but by their direction new shares in the United Kingdom companies had been issued to the Davian companies in exchange for

shares in the Davian companies being issued to the taxpayers. That was the relevant transaction, or, using Lord Brightman's phrase, the end result.'

It should be noted that the separate legal entities (RRC and Davian) are ignored and that the entire scheme is said to be directed by the taxpayers. Nicholls J was, therefore, able to accept the Revenue's contention that the taxpayers exercised their control over RRC to pass value out of their shares into the bonus preference shares, so that a chargeable disposal occurred for CGT purposes (CGTA 1979 s 25(2)) and see p 267 above). As reconstructed by Nicholls J the transaction involved a share for share exchange (Davian acquiring RRC shares in exchange for its own), but the relieving provision ('roll over relief') in CGTA 1979 s 85 (claimed by the taxpayers) was not, however, available, because the main purpose or, one of the main purposes of the scheme was to avoid a liability to CGT (CGTA 1979 s 87). It should be noted that, despite rejecting this argument for the taxpayers, Nicholls J accepted that once the *Ramsay* principle has applied, so that the 'relevant transaction' has been ascertained, that result will bind both Revenue and taxpayer. Accordingly, he appears to accept that *Ramsay* may be invoked in appropriate cases against the Revenue.

The Revenue were unsuccessful on a second argument derived from *Ramsay*: viz that as the letters of allotment were originally situated in the UK, the result of treating all the steps as a composite transaction was that the disposal of those letters began in the UK. Nicholls J rejected this argument on the narrow ground that, in his reconstruction of the relevant transaction, the letters were never allotted to the taxpayers. More generally, it would seem surprising if the *Ramsay* principle could be used, not just to reconstruct the transaction, but also to deem the entire transaction to occur at the time when the first step was effected.

e)   Furniss v Dawson *and stamp duty*

To what extent the *Ramsay* principle can be applied to stamp duty is a matter of some uncertainty. An obvious difficulty derives from the fact that duty is levied only on instruments and not on transactions, so that the absence of a document should result in no duty being payable (see, further, on the difficulties of applying *Ramsay*, R S Nock in (1984) SJ 407).

EXAMPLE 3

On the death of his father, Silus effects a variation of the will, whereby bequests made to him, totalling £150,000, become payable to his daughter, Emma. If he had effected the variation by a single instrument in writing, ad valorem duty would have been charged at 1% (of £150,000), ie £1,500. Accordingly, in order to avoid duty, Silus executed five separate deeds of variation; dated on consecutive days and each for £30,000. A certificate of value was inserted into each instrument and the duty payable was, accordingly, nil (see p 447 above). Arguably, an application of the *Ramsay* approach would result in the five deeds being treated as a single variation, since the absence of a binding obligation to carry out the whole scheme is irrelevant. The required element of artificiality lies in splitting the transaction into five stages, so that a reconstruction of the transaction would result in Silus disposing of property worth £150,000 to his daughter.

The so-called 'pref-trick' is perhaps the best known and most widely used example of a scheme to avoid stamp duty (see p 486). The essence of the scheme is to pass the value of the target company out of its existing shares into new ordinary shares, which are issued to the existing shareholders on renounceable letters of allotment. The shareholders then renounce in favour of the purchaser and, so long as this occurs within six months of the share issue, there is no duty on the instrument of renunciation (see FA 1963 s 65).

The old shares are thereby rendered virtually valueless (often being converted into deferred or preference shares) and, accordingly, attract little duty on their transfer to the purchaser. The scheme has been employed for many years and, so long as the reorganisation of the share capital in the target company occurred *before* exchange of contracts with the purchaser, duty was successfully avoided.

This practice of avoiding stamp duty in takeovers was noted in the Consultative Document (*The Scope for Reforming Stamp Duties*: March 1983), which accepted that duty should not be levied on 'a paper for paper bid' (ie a share for share takeover), but concluded that in other cases the matter required further consideration and any legislation would need to take account of commercial practice (see para 6.22). *Furniss v Dawson* involved the use of the 'pref-trick', but the silence of their Lordships on this matter cannot be construed as a tacit acceptance of the trick, since the question of its efficacy was not argued before them.

Against this background, the Financial Secretary (Mr John Moore MP) announced on 27 July 1984 that the Board of Inland Revenue had been advised that the *Ramsay* decision applied to stamp duty schemes involving the 'pref-trick' and, accordingly, it would be applied to any scheme implemented after 17 July 1984, but he said nothing to suggest that a 'statutory *Ramsay* principle' would be introduced. Thus, the Revenue could be proved wrong in the courts. The effect of so applying *Ramsay* would, he concluded, be as follows:

> 'If on a takeover the offer for shares of the company being taken over is conditional on a reorganisation of its capital, so that the shares to be acquired are reduced in value by the creation of new shares for the purpose of achieving a stamp duty saving, the chargeable consideration for the transfer of the old shares will include the value of the shares issued in exchange for the newly created shares.'

The statement is restrictive in its terms. First, it suggests that *Ramsay* is to be applied only where the takeover is conditional on a reorganisation of the target's capital. Accordingly, if that reorganisation has already occurred *before* the contract is made so that the purchasers agree to buy the new shares, that purchase would appear to fall outside the Statement. Secondly, the recon-structed transaction seems to involve the excision of the newly created ordinary shares (which, presumably, is the artificial step). The old shares will be treated as sold for the entire consideration and will, therefore, be subject to ad valorem duty. If, however, those shares are retained by the vendors, it would appear that the takeover falls outside the terms of the statement and that duty would not be payable. Given that the old shares can be rendered valueless, their retention may not matter to the purchaser. If this is done, it would be difficult to see how *Ramsay* could be applied to the transaction. The contract is now for the sale of the new shares only (by means of a purchase of the renounceable letters of allotment) and it is difficult to see what step is artificial and can, therefore, be excluded. To treat the renounceable letters of allotment as stampable would be contrary to FA 1963 s 65.

In the same Statement the Financial Secretary announced that an exemption would be inserted into the 1985 Finance Bill to cover paper for paper takeovers (in effect, to widen FA 1927 s 55: see p 456). In the meantime, an extra statutory concession is to be applied to transfers of shares on or after 28

July 1984. This concession does not apply where the existing shareholders accept a cash offer for their shares. The concession is as follows:

> 'A transfer of shares in a company in exchange for shares or marketable securities of a second company resulting from a general offer made by the second company to the members of the first company or any class of them in consequence of which the second company has obtained control of the first company will be treated as exempt from stamp duties to the extent that the shares issued by the second company are pursuant to the offer registered in the name, or names, of the members of the first company. This treatment does not apply where the marketable securities consist of debt instruments maturing for payment in less than 3 years.'

The following conclusions on the application of *Ramsay* to company takeovers are tentatively suggested:

(1) If the reorganisation occurs as a result of the sale contract, the Revenue will seek to levy stamp duty under the *Ramsay* principle and are likely to succeed.

(2) If the reorganisation has already occurred before contracts are exchanged, it is not certain what the attitude of the Revenue will be. In practice, the taxpayer loses nothing by effecting a reorganisation either *before* a purchaser is found or *before* binding contracts are exchanged.

(3) If the original shares are retained by the vendors so that only the new shares are transferred, it would seem difficult for the Revenue to argue successfully that duty is chargeable under the *Ramsay* principle.

Index